D1417238

SECOND EDITION

W. B. SAUNDERS COMPANY

Philadelphia and London

1967

A MANUAL OF

Clinical Allergy

JOHN M. SHELDON, M.D.

Professor of Internal Medicine, The University
of Michigan Medical School; Chairman of the
Department of Postgraduate Medicine; Physician in Charge of the University of Michigan
Allergy Clinics

ROBERT G. LOVELL, M.D.

Associate Professor of Internal Medicine, The
University of Michigan Medical School

KENNETH P. MATHEWS, M.D.

Professor of Internal Medicine, The University
of Michigan Medical School

Illustrated

W. B. Saunders Company: West Washington Square
Philadelphia, Pa. 19105

12 Dyott Street
London, W. C. 1

A MANUAL OF CLINICAL ALLERGY

PREFACE
TO THE SECOND EDITION

In the first edition of this book, published in 1953, we wrote:

"The practice of allergy is a challenge to the physician's ingenuity and medical ability. Also it is a great deal of fun. An interest which brings great personal satisfaction and diversion, allergy presents a wide variety of cases. The relief which treatment provides for many patients may be complete and sometimes is quite dramatic. Not unlike a detective, the allergist must track down the offending agent which bothers his patient. Often the search is extended into such fields as otolaryngology, psychiatry, dermatology, neurology, chemistry, botany, and even into other realms which may have little direct relationship to medicine. The identification and elimination of the allergenic factor, or where this is impossible, building up of the patient's tolerance to this environmental allergen is the main activity which keeps an allergist at work.

"There is need for more physicians who practice a good quality of allergy based on a sound medical background. It is hoped that the following pages will stimulate some of the doctors and students who read them to afford their allergic patients the thorough etiologic management which they deserve."

Advances in the understanding of allergy during the thirteen years since the first edition of this book was printed have been sufficiently extensive to require a complete rewriting of most chapters. New developments have been especially prominent in the basic sciences relating to allergy, particularly immunology, pulmonary physiology and some areas of pharmacology. This newer fundamental knowledge already is affecting the practice of clinical allergy and has broadened enormously the scope of clinical immunology. An attempt has been made, by the addition of one chapter and major extension of two others, to indicate the possible importance of hypersensitivity in many non-atopic diseases, but the emphasis remains on the conditions most typically seen in the practice of allergy. A chapter on stinging insect hypersensitivity has been added because of the growing clinical interest in this subject.

As with the first edition, this manual is designed to serve a dual purpose: (1) to provide an introduction to the field which is sufficiently succinct to be useful to medical students and others not specializing in the area; (2) to provide more detailed information about certain aspects of allergy which is not so readily available to physicians elsewhere in the medical literature. In accordance with the first objective, illustrations are limited in number and the bibliographies given with each chapter are highly selective, but Appendix II provides sources of the innumerable additional references for readers who may be stimulated to delve more deeply into the subject. To implement the second objective, there is deliberate overemphasis on such subjects as pollen and mold identification. Innovations here include a short binomial key for the identification of the common airborne fungi and a new section on modern air sampling techniques. Detailed lists of the sources of various allergens and suggested materials for patch testing are retained, since some of this important practical information is becoming difficult to locate in the older literature. As stated in the previous edition, it is intended that the serious student of allergy would use this manual chiefly as a supplement to the more comprehensive textbooks in the field.

JOHN M. SHELDON
ROBERT G. LOVELL
KENNETH P. MATHEWS

Ann Arbor, Michigan

ACKNOWLEDGMENTS

Preparation of the Second Edition has involved the corporate efforts of a number of helpful individuals with special knowledge and possessed of the generosity one finds in the busiest people. Their willingness to interrupt their own active schedules to help in rewriting the manuscript, reviewing its content, and checking many details has been an inspiration to us.

To Drs. James A. McLean, William R. Solomon, Abba I. Terr, and Neal A. Vanselow, our colleagues on the allergy teaching staff at the University of Michigan Medical Center, go our special thanks and appreciation for their extensive help in preparing entire chapters of the book, and for their restraint as their hard-wrought pages were edited and modified by the authors to fit the general context of the entire book. Mr. Oren C. Durham and Mrs. Florence Ludwig McKay, again, as in the First Edition, have contributed importantly by bringing the section on pollen identification up to date. Likewise, Mr. George Phillips worked diligently to revise the chapter on manufacture of allergenic extracts. Drs. Harold Falls, Bruce Cohan, Bruce Fralick and Thomas Van Metre assisted us with the section on allergy of the eye. Drs. Richard Farr and Edward A. Carr, Jr., reviewed the chapter on drug allergy; Dr. Richard Cushing assisted with the pediatric portion of the chapter on useful drugs and Dr. Sheldon Siegel gave assistance with the section on corticosteroids. Drs. John Magielski and W. L. Draper made valuable suggestions regarding the section on serous otitis media. Drs. Martha Westerberg and Kenneth Magee helped with the chapter on headache. Drs. Arthur G. Johnson and Peter P. Barlow perused the section on immunology. Prof. Warren H. Wagner read the entire section on pollen; Prof. Willard Payne gave much basic information for the ragweed unit. Prof. Robert Shaffer advised on fungi; Prof. Gerald C. Gill on the air sampling section. Dr. Edmund D. Lowney reviewed the chapter on patch testing and advised us on the chapter on dermatological aspects of allergy. Dr. Gerald Abrams provided the photomicrographs in the chapter on asthma and hay fever and prepared the descriptions for them. Dr. James T. Cassidy reviewed much of the chapter on non-atopic immunologic conditions, as did Dr. Abrams. Drs. F. F. A. Rawling, Henry Beale and Carl Arbesman advised us on several aspects of the manuscript, including the May fly and caddis fly problem. Drs. David Shappirio, E. L. Foubert and R. A. Stier gave plates shown in the chapter on insect sensitivity; Dr. Frank Perlman also contributed to its preparation. Dr. James V. Neel assisted us with comment on heredity in allergy and Dr. Walter M. Whitehouse with radiological findings in allergy. Drs. Josef Smith, Richard DeSwarte, and Roy Patterson assisted in reviewing the section on pulmonary function. Dr. Alfred Y. Ching advised on the chapter on psychological aspects of allergy.

Drs. Paul Holinger and Richard Buckingham provided the plate of the tympanic membrane in Chapter 14. Dr. Dan Gordon gave us his photographs of the eyes in the same chapter. The National Geographic Society gave permission to use pictures of bee sting by Hashime Murayama. The United States Weather Service provided the picture of the cold front. Mr. Robert M. Borsky of the Los Angeles Air Pollution Control Office has allowed use of the smog picture.

Photography, always a difficult part of the preparation of a book, was made enjoyable through the extensive cooperation of Messrs. George E. Hess, Edgar L. Sherman, Wendell R. Rideout and Robert L. Bensinger. Mr. Gerald Hodge, and our medical illustration staff, assisted in arrangement of our charts.

Preparation, typing and revising of the manuscript was undertaken concurrently with all of the other demands made upon our secretarial staff. To Miss Sandra Buskirk, Mrs. Jane Johnston, Miss Mabel Kelley and her staff, Mrs. Darlene Long and Mrs. Alice Thomson goes our sincere appreciation for their cheerful completion of this arduous work. Dr. Lawrence Preuss gave the entire manuscript a final survey, though we retain in our own hands entire responsibility for any errors and shortcomings in the contents of the Second Edition.

We extend our appreciation and thanks to Mr. Robert Rowan, Medical Editor, and the staff at W. B. Saunders Company who have been so understanding of our efforts to write a book while simultaneously carrying on our obligations of teaching, patient care and research.

Finally, recognition is due our wives for their patience and support during the many hours of solitude while "the book" took precedence over all other activities.

J.M.S.
R.G.L.
K.P.M.

PREFACE
TO THE FIRST EDITION

This book is prepared primarily for the physician interested in devoting part of his time to the treatment of allergy patients, or in establishing an allergy practice. Since there is no field of medicine or surgery in which patients do not at times present themselves with allergic complaints, the book will perhaps be of interest to any physician or student of medicine.

There are a number of excellent textbooks and several journals on the subject of allergy. This manual does not attempt to replace or supplant such texts and periodicals but rather should be used in conjunction with them. An effort has been made to present the subject in a manner found practical at the allergy clinics of the University of Michigan Hospital and the University of Michigan Health Service. This work is an outgrowth of the training program provided for medical students and the post-graduate courses in allergy at the University Hospital.

In a manual of this type, it has been necessary to delete lengthy discussion of differential diagnosis, immunologic theory and controversial matters. Naturally these important points should not be ignored, and other texts and periodicals can be referred to for that information which is not covered here. On the other hand, undue emphasis purposely has been placed on certain aspects of allergy practice which often are not very thoroughly covered in the standard texts. This is exemplified by the sections on pollen and mold identification, the preparation of testing and treatment extracts, pulmonary function tests, allergy to plastics, and equipment for the allergist's office. In recent years, endocrine factors in allergic disease, drug allergy, collagen diseases, and vascular allergy have been recognized as being more important than was appreciated in the past, so relatively more space has been devoted to these matters than has been customary in standard texts.

By placing emphasis on the practical features of doing a sound allergy work-up and treating patients in a safe and medically acceptable fashion, this manual attempts to show how a physician can conduct the management of allergic patients in a way which will be of service not only to patients but also to medical colleagues in the community. As a larger number of doctors become interested in and capable of the proper handling of allergic diseases, a greater portion of the vast atopic population will receive the best type of medical care.

                                                                        J.M.S.
Ann Arbor, Michigan   R.G.L.
                                                                        K.P.M.

CONTENTS

Chapter One

IMMUNOLOGY
AND
IMMUNOCHEMISTRY
OF ALLERGY

ABBA I. TERR, M.D.

Clinical allergy is the branch of medicine which is most intimately concerned with diseases of altered immunologic responses. Because of the rapid advances in immunology in recent years and the application of immunologic principles and techniques to many problems in medical practice, the allergist today faces a difficult task in trying to assimilate and understand the vast literature in this field. Nevertheless, familiarity with the basic principles of immunology and immunochemistry is essential to an adequate understanding of allergic diseases.

ANTIGENS

An antigen is a substance which induces the formation of antibodies or of sensitized cells. Many naturally occurring substances from animal and plant sources are antigenic, including proteins, carbohydrates, lipids, and nucleic acids. Certain synthetic compounds, such as polyamino acids, may also function as antigens. Particulate antigens, including blood cells, tissue cells, bacteria, viruses, and pollen grains, are in fact made up of many different antigens which contribute to the structure of the cell. Ordinarily, antibodies are not produced to constituents of the host's own tissues; hence, antigens are "foreign" to the host.

Antigens are large molecules, seldom less than 5000 in molecular weight and often much more than this. The structural basis for antigenicity of a molecule is represented by one or more regions on its surface, known as antigenic sites or determinants. Simple organic chemical compounds, while in themselves nonantigenic, may act as antigenic determinants when coupled chemically with the surfaces of large molecules. These simple compounds are called haptens, and the large molecule, generally a protein or polypeptide, is known as the carrier.

1

Antigens responsible for clinical allergic manifestations are frequently referred to as allergens. These may be inhaled, ingested, injected, or absorbed through contact with unbroken skin. Inhaled allergens are usually encountered as particles, such as pollen grains, mold spores, dust particles, animal danders, or insect debris. Recently, a protein of molecular weight 37,800 has been isolated and purified from ragweed pollen, and it seems to be the major but not the sole allergenic component for most ragweed-sensitive patients.[1] Allergens may be ingested in foodstuffs or drugs. Protein drugs, such as liver extract, horse serum, or other biological products, may be antigenic per se, whereas low molecular weight drugs, such as penicillin, are haptens and become antigenic by a coupling of the drug itself or a drug metabolite with host protein.

ANTIBODIES AND IMMUNOGLOBULINS

Antibodies are substances synthesized by the host in response to an antigen and are capable of reacting specifically with that antigen. Chemically, antibodies are a class of proteins known as immunoglobulins and are found in serum, other body fluids, and certain tissues.

The immunoglobulins in serum are markedly heterogeneous but can be classified according to certain antigenic characteristics (Table 1–1). The three principal classes of human immunoglobulins, immunoglobulin G (IgG), immunoglobulin M (IgM), and immunoglobulin A (IgA), differ from each other not only antigenically but also in certain physicochemical and biological properties. Two additional classes of immunoglobulins have been described recently but have not yet been thoroughly studied. Immunoglobulin D (IgD) is present in very low concentration in normal serum,[2] and immunoglobulin E (IgE) is currently proposed as the carrier of human atopic reaginic activity[3] (see below).

Table 1–1.   *The Three Principal Classes of Human Immunoglobulins*

	Immunoglobulin G	*Immunoglobulin M*	*Immunoglobulin A*
Abbreviation	IgG or γG	IgM or γM	IgA or γA
Old terminology	γ_2-globulin	γ_{1M}-globulin	γ_{1A}-globulin
	7S γ-globulin	β_{2M}-globulin	β_{2A}-globulin
	6.6S γ-globulin	19S-macroglobulin	
	$\gamma_{s.s.}$-globulin		
Molecular weight	160,000	900,000	160,000 and higher
Sedimentation coefficient, $s_{20,w}$	6.6S	19S	7S to 15S
Electrophoretic mobility	γ-globulin	fast γ-globulin	fast γ- to β-globulin
Carbohydrate content	2.5%	12%	10%
Cross placenta	Yes	No	No
Heavy chain type	γ	μ	α
Light chain types	κ, λ	κ, λ	κ, λ
Average concentration in normal serum	1200 mg. per 100 ml.	120 mg. per 100 ml.	280mg. per 100 ml.

The basic structure of the immunoglobulin molecule has been most thoroughly studied in the case of IgG. This is a complex protein with a molecular weight (M.W.) of about 160,000, consisting of four polypeptide chains and a small amount of carbohydrate. The four polypeptide chains include two "heavy chains" of 55,000 molecular weight each and two "light chains" of 22,000 molecular weight each, covalently bound together by disulfide linkages, as shown schematically in Figure 1–1. Light chains are of two antigenically different types, known as κ-chains and λ-chains; approximately 70 per cent of the IgG molecules in serum have κ-type light chains and 30 per cent have λ-type. The heavy chains, called γ-chains, are also heterogeneous, and at least four subtypes have been identified. The two antigen-binding sites on the antibody molecule are each made up of a portion of one light chain and the adjacent heavy chain. The chains themselves are coiled in such a way that the intact molecule is roughly rod-shaped, with the two antigen-binding sites at opposite ends[4] (Figure 1–2).

IgM has a molecular weight of about 900,000 and is a polymer consisting of five monomeric subunits of 180,000 molecular weight each.[5] The IgM monomer has the same basic structure as the IgG molecule (Figure 1–1), but a larger carbohydrate moiety. There are two types of light chains, κ and λ, identical with those of IgG, but the heavy chains, called μ-chains, are antigenically unrelated to the γ-chains of IgG. The arrangement of the monomers in the intact IgM molecule and the number of effective binding sites is not currently known.

IgA also has a similar basic structure. The heavy chains are called α-chains and are unique to this class of immunoglobulins, and the two types of light chains, κ and λ, are indistinguishable from those found in IgG and IgM molecules. IgA in serum is heterogeneous in molecular weight, about 85 per cent of the molecules being monomers and 15 per cent being polymers made up of two to five monomers each. IgA is transported preferentially into certain tissue fluids, especially saliva, tears, and colostrum. In the case of salivary IgA this process is apparently

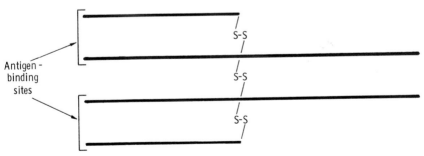

Figure 1–1. Schematic illustration of IgG molecule showing the relationships of the four polypeptide chains—two light chains and two heavy chains—and the two antigen-binding sites.

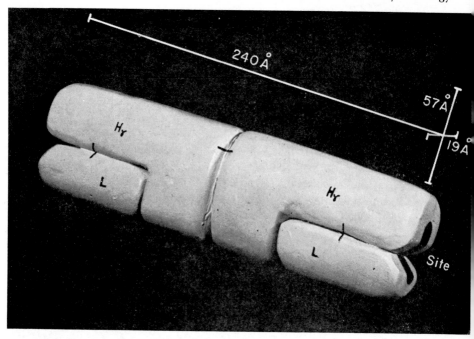

Figure 1–2. Three-dimensional model of proposed structure of IgG molecule. $H\gamma$ = heavy chain. L = light chain. The antigen-binding sites are represented by slots at each end of the molecule. (From Edelman, G. M., and Gally, J. A.: A model for the 7S antibody molecule. Proc. Nat. Acad. Sc. *51*:846, 1964.)

accomplished by coupling to a protein, called "transport piece," which facilitates its entry into the salivary secretions.[6]

IgD and IgE have not yet been isolated from normal serum so that no detailed information regarding their structure is currently available.

ANTIBODIES IN ATOPY

Atopy, a form of immediate hypersensitivity discussed more fully on page 13, is associated with certain antibodies of special interest because of their biological and immunochemical properties. Although such properties suggest that these antibodies have some importance in atopic disease manifestations, their ultimate role in pathogenesis has not yet been clearly defined.

The skin-sensitizing antibody, or reagin, is characterized by its ability to sensitize passively the skin of nonatopic subjects for subsequent challenge with antigen, i.e., the Prausnitz-Küstner (P-K) reaction. In this reaction, serum from an atopic patient is injected intradermally in a nonatopic recipient, and after a latent period required for fixation of the antibodies to the skin, usually 24 hours, the site is challenged by injection with antigen to which the donor is sensitive, resulting in a wheal and flare response in 15 to 20 minutes. Sensitization by this method first becomes manifest in a few hours and may persist for as long as six weeks (see page 71 for details of P-K testing technique). Generalized sensitization of skin and mucous membranes of the recipient can be achieved if large amounts of reaginic plasma or blood are transfused intravenously. Human reagins can sensitize human skin and the skin of most other primates, but not that of lower animals. The skin-sensitizing antibody in atopy is heat-labile, being inactivated after one to four hours at 56° C., and does not cross the placenta from maternal to fetal circulation. Many attempts to demonstrate a reaction between reagin and antigen by the usual in vitro techniques, such as precipitation, complement fixation, passive hemagglutination, or variants of these techniques, have so far been inconclusive. Whether skin-sensitizing antibody which is not fixed to cells is incapable of binding antigen or whether it is merely present in serum in a concentration too low to give readily detectable in vitro reactions with antigen is not known. The release of histamine from white cells upon the addition of allergen to allergic human blood in vitro may well be mediated by reagin, but this has yet to be demonstrated.

The class of immunoglobulin which carries the skin-sensitizing activity has been the subject of much research in recent years. Heremans[7] first suggested that IgA might be the carrier of reaginic activity, and later work strengthened this suggestion, since IgA and reagin have been found to be similar in electrophoretic mobility, molecular weight, chromatographic behavior, absence of placental transfer, and distribution in various body fluids.[8-10] Recently, however, detailed investigation of this problem by Ishizaka[3] now raises the possibility that skin-sensitizing antibody in the serum of atopic patients may be a unique immunoglobulin present in very low concentrations in serum but antigenically different from IgA. Skin-sensitizing antibodies in other diseases, however, such as serum sickness, have been found to be associated with the three major immunoglobulin classes.[11]

During hyposensitization therapy, a new antibody, called blocking antibody, appears in the patient's serum. When mixed with the antigen in vitro, this antibody combines with the antigen in such a way that subsequent reaction of the antigen with reagin in vivo is inhibited. Unlike reagin, blocking antibody is heat-stable, can cross the placenta, and is an IgG type of immunoglobulin. Since the quantity of blocking antibody produced during treatment does not seem to correlate with clinical improvement in symptoms, it is doubtful that beneficial results from hyposensitization can be attributed entirely to the presence of blocking antibody. There is some evidence that blocking antibody may increase the threshold level for symptoms from injected allergen. Blocking antibodies can be produced in normal individuals, as well as in atopic patients, by injections of allergenic extracts.

Antibodies have been detected in serum of atopic patients, both before and after hyposensitization injections, using the highly sensitive techniques of passive hemagglutination and the ammonium sulfate precipitation[12] and co-precipitation[13] methods for measuring primary antigen-antibody binding. It is clear that the antibodies detected by these methods are largely or perhaps entirely antibodies other than reagin and blocking antibodies, and their clinical significance is unknown.

Reaginic antibodies may be found in certain hypersensitive states other than atopy. Many patients with serum sickness develop transitory reagins, as well as precipitins, to the offending serum or drug. Drug reactions of the anaphylactic or urticarial variety may be associated with reagins. Anaphylactic hypersensitivity to stinging insects frequently, but not invariably, is accompanied by reagins in serum. Experimentally, skin-sensitizing antibodies have been produced by the injection of antigens such as Ascaris extracts, dextran, and ribonuclease. It is interesting to note that atopic individuals showed a more marked skin-sensitizing antibody production than nonatopics when ribonuclease was given by inhalation, whereas there was little difference between the two groups when the antigen was injected.[14]

ANTIBODY FORMATION

The characteristic pattern of antibody response to the first injection of an antigen consists of an initial latent period of several days, called the induction period, during which no antibody can be detected in the serum. This phase is followed by a rapid rise in antibody titer to a maximum level and then a gradual fall in titer to a very low level, which may persist for a long period of time or become undetectable. The duration of the induction period, the maximum quantity of antibody produced, and the persistence of detectable antibody in the primary response all vary with the particular antigen used, the route of administration, the animal species, and the method of assay for antibody. Furthermore, individual animals within a given species differ in immunologic reactivity depending in part on genetically determined factors. In most animals studied, both IgG and IgM antibodies are synthesized in the primary response, the IgM antibody usually appearing earlier and disappearing more rapidly from the circulation.

The secondary response to an antigen, even if the antigen is reintroduced many months or years after the first exposure, consists of a more rapid appearance of antibody which reaches a higher titer and persists longer than the primary response. In secondary and hyperimmune (repeated injections of antigen) responses, antibodies are principally of the IgG type, although some IgM antibody may also be present. Certain antibodies, such as the rheumatoid factor, the Wassermann antibody, and the complete Rh agglutinins in man, remain almost exclusively IgM in type.

Immunologic adjuvants are agents which enhance antibody responses nonspecifically. This enhancement is expressed as an increased peak titer of antibody and, in some instances, by prolongation of detectable antibody in the serum and shortening of the induction period. A wide variety of chemical, biological, and physical agents are capable of adjuvant activity. Examples of chemical adjuvants are aluminum, calcium, other metallic salts, bacterial endotoxin, and colchicine. Oils, such as mineral oil or paraffin oil, are also effective, especially if the antigen is dispersed in a water-in-oil emulsion. Certain bacterial organisms, such as Mycobacteria and *Bordetella pertussis,* enhance antibody responses when administered with the antigen. X-irradiation, though ordinarily thought of as an immunosuppressive agent, will increase antibody titers when given in certain dosage schedules.

The mechanisms by which these diverse substances stimulate antibody formation beyond that achieved with antigen alone are only poorly understood. Retention of the antigen in tissues and enhancement of phagocytosis have been suggested, especially for the chemical adjuvants. The water-in-oil emulsions have a definite depot effect whereby small amounts of antigen are released slowly over a prolonged period of time permitting continual antigenic stimulation, although this is probably not the sole explanation for the marked effectiveness of these adjuvants. Irradiation, endotoxin, and other adjuvants probably exert an influence, either directly or indirectly, on the number and availability of antibody-forming cells or their precursors.

Although the mechanism of action of adjuvants is not well understood, they have proved to be useful in clinical immunization as well as in the laboratory. Alum-precipitated vaccines are widely used at present, and water-in-oil emulsions have been employed in hyposensitization with allergenic extracts (see Chapter 6).

A large body of experimental evidence indicates that the site of antibody formation in the body is the reticulo-endothelial system of the spleen, lymph nodes, bone marrow, and other organs which contain lymphoid tissue, with the exception of the thymus. Although the thymus does not ordinarily synthesize antibody, recent investigations seem to point to an important central role of the thymus in the development of immunologic competence of the peripheral lymphoid tissue.[15] It has been suggested that the thymus functions by providing cells which populate the antibody-forming tissues where they divide into clones of cells capable of responding to antigen. Certain evidence also raises the possibility of a humoral factor produced in the thymus which influences the peripheral lymphoid apparatus in some, as yet undefined, way. In some species lymphoid tissue associated with the gastrointestinal tract also appears to play a regulatory role in the development of the immune apparatus.

Of the cell types which may be involved in the synthesis of antibody, the plasma cell has received the greatest attention. The earliest recognized precursor of the plasma cell, the primitive reticular cell, appears prominently in antibody-forming tissue during the early phase after antigenic stimulation. These cells then differentiate into immature and mature plasma cells which are present in large numbers during active antibody synthesis. Plasma cells have been shown by immunofluorescence and electron microscopy to contain antibody in their cytoplasm. Cells of the lymphocytic series, on the other hand, are clearly important in delayed hypersensitivity, but there is also evidence that these cells may have an equally important role in antibody formation, especially in the production of IgM antibody. It also has been suggested that the small lymphocytes may provide "immunologic memory" and that they are capable of transforming into plasma cells.

Antibody formation may require participation by more than one cell type. It has been proposed that antigen is first taken up by a phago-cytic cell, the macrophage, wherein it is processed in some fashion before being released to a different cell, perhaps a lymphocyte or primitive reticular cell. The latter then differentiates into the mature antibody-synthesizing plasma cell.[16]

There is abundant evidence that antibodies are synthesized by the same biochemical processes that are involved in the synthesis of other body proteins. In this case the information which determines the se-quence of amino acids in the antibody molecule is contained in the genetic material of the nucleus of the antibody-forming cell. Although many of the biochemical steps in the synthesis of the antibody molecule can be discussed in terms of a general model for protein synthesis, the fundamental question of how the antigen induces the formation of an immunoglobulin molecule with the appropriate specificity is presently unanswered. It is clear that specificity is imparted at some point during or before synthesis of the final structure. Furthermore, there is increas-ing evidence that specificity is determined by the primary structure (i.e., the sequence of amino acids) of the antigen-binding site on the antibody.

Current theories of antibody formation are conveniently classified into two main types called the instructive and the selective theories. Instructive theories maintain that all the immunologically competent cells of the body before contact with antigen have the potential for pro-ducing antibody of any required specificity. The antigen then instructs the cell in some way to produce antibody of the proper specificity. Vari-ous instructive theories differ from each other according to the presumed site of instruction by antigen, e.g., alteration of DNA in the nucleus, alteration of or interaction with messenger RNA serving as a template at the site of antibody synthesis, and so on. The selective theories, on the other hand, presume that a finite number of specificities is sufficient to provide antibodies to all possible antigens which an animal might en-counter. Furthermore, the animal possesses this number of antibody-forming cells, or clones of cells, each of which is capable of forming antibody of only one or perhaps a small number of specificities. Ac-cording to these theories the role of antigen is to select those cells of the proper specificity and to stimulate them for division, maturation, and antibody synthesis. Variations in the selective theories are based on differing views of the mechanism by which antigen selects the proper cell for stimulation. Immunologic tolerance (see below) is accounted for in the selective theories by assuming that contact by the cell with the antigen during the prenatal or neonatal periods or by excessive amounts of antigen during adult life results in cell destruction rather than stimulation. Much more information is needed before the mechanism of antibody formation is fully understood.

IMMUNOLOGIC UNRESPONSIVENESS

Immunologic unresponsiveness refers to the inability of an animal to respond to an antigenic stimulus with the production of antibodies and/or delayed hypersensitivity. Total body irradiation and alkylating agents produce immunologic unresponsiveness by destroying the lymphoid cells of the body. Those chemotherapeutic drugs which inhibit protein synthesis inhibit antibody synthesis as well. Some of these agents have clinical usefulness in certain diseases in which immunosuppression is beneficial, and this subject is presented in more detail in Chapter 7.

Suppression or inhibition of the usual immunologic response to a specific antigen is known as immunologic tolerance. There are two types of immunologic tolerance—natural and acquired. Natural tolerance refers to the absence of immunologic reactivity toward the body's own constituents. Acquired tolerance is the lack of immunologic response to foreign antigens induced artificially by some means. Acquired tolerance is most easily produced experimentally during the neonatal period before full development of immunologic reactivity. Injection into a prenatal or neonatal animal of relatively small amounts of antigen renders the animal subsequently incapable of a normal antibody response to that antigen. Such acquired tolerance is usually not permanent and probably requires the persistence of a minimum amount of antigen in the body, since the tolerant state can be prolonged by repeated injections of antigen. When the antigenic stimulus consists of viable cells capable of survival and multiplication in the host, tolerance may be permanent, resulting in a state of cellular chimerism. Tolerance to nonliving antigens may be induced in mature animals by injecting very large amounts of antigen ("immunologic paralysis"). This can be facilitated by exposure to the antigen at a time when the animal has been made nonspecifically unresponsive by irradiation or by chemical immunosuppression.

ANTIGEN-ANTIBODY REACTIONS

The specific reaction of antibody with antigen involves the interaction of the antigen-binding site on the antibody molecule with the specific determinant site on the antigen. This is known as the primary

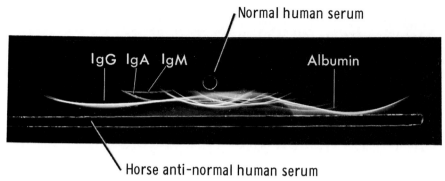

Figure 1–3. Immunoelectrophoresis of normal human serum. The serum sample was placed in a circular well in an agar-coated slide and subjected to electrophoresis. Horse antiserum to normal human serum was then placed in the longitudinal trough, resulting in a series of precipitin arcs, each one indicating an antigenically distinct protein in human serum.

reaction. Once this reaction has occurred, a variety of physicochemical or biological phenomena may occur, referred to as secondary reactions.

Only a few methods are available for the detection and quantitation of the primary antigen-antibody reaction in solution. For example, by using an antigen labeled with a radioactive isotope, the antigen-antibody complex can be precipitated from solution with ammonium sulfate (the Farr technique[17]) or with an anti-gamma globulin antiserum (co-precipitation).[18]

Most of the other commonly employed tests for antigen-antibody reactions utilize one or more of the secondary reactions. The precipitin reaction occurs when certain antigens and their antibodies react in solution in the proper proportions to permit the development of a large molecular lattice which precipitates out of solution. Since lattice formation requires a multivalent antigen, univalent haptens cannot precipitate with antibody but can inhibit precipitation by the corresponding antigen. Several modifications of the precipitin reaction have been devised in which the reactants are permitted to diffuse through clear agar gel so that the resulting precipitate forms a visible line or arc. These immunodiffusion methods, such as the Oudin or Ouchterlony techniques, are particularly useful for detecting impurities in antigens. Several quantitative immunodiffusion methods are available, and one of these methods,[18] employing antiserum incorporated in the agar, is available commercially for the quantitation of human immunoglobins in serum.* Immunoelectrophoresis (see Figure 1–3) is a valuable technique for qualitative analysis of serum proteins.[19]

Agglutination reactions occur when particles, such as bacteria or erythrocytes, bearing antigens on their surfaces, are suspended in the appropriate antiserum. A variety of antigens not normally present on red

---

* Hyland Laboratories, 4501 Colorado Blvd., Los Angeles, California 90039.

cell surfaces can be artificially coupled with erythrocytes, and the resulting reaction with antiserum to the coupled antigen is known as passive hemagglutination. Many polysaccharide antigens adhere directly to erythrocytes following simple incubation. Protein antigens couple with erythrocyte surfaces only after prior treatment of the cells with tannic acid or by covalent binding with a reagent such as bisdiazotized benzidine (BDB).

In the presence of complement (see below), erythrocytes or other tissue cells reacting with antibody may undergo cell lysis. Soluble, particulate, or cellular antigens may fix complement as a result of their union with antibody; that is, complement present in the system prior to the antigen-antibody reaction is taken up and the resultant loss of complement is then measured by failure of sensitized erythrocytes to undergo hemolysis when added to the system.

Antibodies to viruses may be detected by their ability to neutralize virus infectivity, and antibodies to enzymes or hormones sometimes may be detected by inhibition of enzymatic or hormonal activity.

A variety of hypersensitivity reactions may result directly from antigen-antibody combination in vivo, and these reactions may be used experimentally to detect the presence of either antigen or antibody. These are discussed below.

A number of factors are involved in the expression of each of these reactions. As already mentioned, the physical state, valence, and quantity of antigen are important. Furthermore, the quantity, quality, and type of antibody also determine whether a particular type of reaction can occur. Finally, the presence of accessory factors, such as complement or mediators of in vivo hypersensitivity, may be required. These multiple variables complicate the study of antigen-antibody reactions to the extent that a detailed review of this subject is not possible here. The reader is urged to consult appropriate immunology texts for further information if he is not familiar with standard immunologic techniques.[20, 21]

HYPERSENSITIVITY

Two major categories of in vivo immunologic reactions are hypersensitivity and auto-immunity. Hypersensitivity refers to a variety of local or systemic reactions which affect the host animal on exposure to antigens. These reactions in general are dependent upon the immunologic and physiologic state of the host and are largely independent of the nature of the offending antigen. Auto-immune reactions, on the other hand, occur when the antigen is native to the host or when a foreign antigen cannot be distinguished from some body constituent of the host. Auto-immunity, therefore, is dependent upon the nature of the antigenic challenge and, in some cases, its anatomic location within the host. This topic is discussed more fully in Chapter 19.

Hypersensitivity phenomena are classified into two types: immediate and delayed. In immediate hypersensitivity the antigen reacts with the antibody, either in the circulation or fixed to certain tissues, causing the release or formation of certain chemical mediator substances. Since immediate hypersensitivity is antibody-mediated, these reactions can be passively transferred to normal recipients with serum or purified antibody. Delayed hypersensitivity refers to those immunologic responses involving reaction of antigen with specifically sensitized cells. Hence, these responses are passively transferable with sensitized cells but not with serum or antibody.

Immediate Hypersensitivity

The most dramatic expression of immediate hypersensitivity is systemic anaphylaxis. Active systemic anaphylaxis can be induced in many animal species but has been most widely studied in the guinea pig. The initial sensitizing exposure to antigen can be given by any route which will permit formation of antibodies. Once antibodies have been produced, anaphylaxis will occur when the animal is challenged with the same antigen, usually introduced directly into the circulation. Within minutes severe bronchospasm, cyanosis, irritability, ruffling of the fur, itching, profuse respiratory secretions, and gastrointestinal and bladder muscle spasms occur. Death results from asphyxia because of the bronchospasm. Other species may react differently; e.g., anaphylaxis in the dog is characterized by profound shock from pooling of large amounts of blood in the liver and portal vascular bed as a result of hepatitic vein constriction. Human anaphylaxis may resemble the reaction in the guinea pig or may be dominated by shock.

Passive systemic anaphylaxis is produced by administering antiserum from an actively sensitized animal to a previously unsensitized recipient animal followed by challenge with antigen.

Certain models of systemic anaphylaxis have been devised to study the mechanism of the reaction in vitro; these involve reacting the antigen with certain tissues or cells removed from a sensitized animal or with similar tissues or cells from an unsensitized animal after exposure to the antibody in vitro. In the Schultz-Dale reaction, ileal or uterine smooth muscle is exposed to antigen in a bath, and the muscle contraction is then recorded by a kymograph. Contraction of a chain of isolated tracheal rings also has been used. Fragments of chopped guinea pig lung, isolated rat peritoneal mast cells, or rabbit platelets release histamine or other mediators in vitro on exposure to the appropriate antigen, and the released mediators are then detected by chemical or pharmacologic tests.

Although the manifestations of serum sickness appear some days after administration of antigen they are mediated by antibody, and hence this disease is a form of immediate hypersensitivity. The experimental disease in rabbits appears 7 to 14 days after first exposure of the animal to the antigen and is characterized by fever, arthritis, vasculitis, and an acute nephritis. The classic studies of Hawn and Janeway,[22] Germuth,[23] and Dixon[24] have established that the lesions of serum sickness result from tissue damage by antigen-antibody complexes formed in vivo as circulating antigen combines with antibodies as they first appear in the blood. The resultant soluble antigen-antibody complexes can be injurious to various tissues. The details of the experimental disease, as well as human serum sickness, are discussed in more detail in Chapter 18.

The Arthus reaction is a local hemorrhagic and inflammatory lesion produced by the injection of antigen into an animal previously immunized to produce a high titer of circulating precipitating antibody. Antigen diffusing through the tissues reacts with antibodies circulating within blood vessels resulting in damage to capillary endothelium with the production of stasis, thrombosis, and local hemorrhagic necrosis. The inflammatory reaction associated with the lesion is mediated in part by complement, which has been shown recently to be chemotactic for polymorphonuclear neutrophils[25] and in part by a coincidental state of delayed hypersensitivity.[26] The passive Arthus reaction is produced by intravenous administration of antiserum to an unsensitized recipient followed by challenge in the usual manner. In the reversed passive Arthus reaction the antigen is given intravenously followed by intradermal challenge with the antiserum.

Local anaphylactic reactions have been used widely as immunologic tools. In passive cutaneous anaphylaxis (PCA), the antiserum is injected intradermally, and after a latent period of several hours to permit fixation of the antibodies to receptor sites in the skin, the antigen is introduced directly into the circulation together with a blue dye. The reaction between skin-fixed antibody and antigen causes a local increase in capillary permeability which is detected as a blue spot produced by the indicator dye.[27] Skin fixation is a property of only certain immunoglobulin types of antibodies; for example, human IgG but not IgA or IgM will fix to guinea pig skin to produce passive cutaneous anaphylaxis reactions. In reversed passive cutaneous anaphylaxis (RPCA), antigen is given intradermally followed by intravenous challenge with antibody and dye; this is possible only in the case of antigens which are themselves immunoglobulins capable of skin-fixation.

Atopy. Coca[28] coined the term atopy, meaning strangeness, to refer to a group of human allergic diseases with certain features in common. The diseases included as atopic are hay fever, allergic bronchial asthma, certain cases of eczema, and occasional cases of urticaria. These diseases are characterized by a definite familial tendency, but different clinical manifestations may be expressed in various members of the same family. The tendency to develop sensitivities is apparently inherited, and not a specific sensitivity or a particular disease manifestation such as asthma or hay fever. A reaction to a particular allergen also depends upon the degree of exposure to that allergen, so that a severely atopic person will obviously not experience ragweed hay fever if he happens to live in a location where pollen is not present. There is currently no clear indication of the factors that determine which particular tissue will respond to antigens (e.g., nasal mucosa, bronchus, and skin). The distinctive immunologic feature of atopy is the skin-sensitizing antibody (atopic reagin), which has been described above. There is no evidence that the atopic individual has any other immunologic abnormality, such as impaired immune response to infections or immunizations, altered delayed hypersensitivity, or susceptibility to auto-immune diseases.

MEDIATORS IN IMMEDIATE HYPERSENSITIVITY

Immediate hypersensitivity reactions are characterized by the release or formation of certain chemical mediator substances during the antigen-antibody reaction. These mediators in turn act either locally or at distant sites by exerting certain pharmacologic properties which determine the nature of the hypersensitivity reaction. The relative contribution of each of these mediators to a particular reaction depends upon many factors, including the animal species, the cell type participating in the reaction, the immunoglobulin class of antibody, and others.

Histamine

Histamine is distributed widely throughout tissues of most mammals and is particularly abundant in tissue mast cells. Among the pharmacologic properties of histamine are smooth muscle contraction, capillary dilatation, and increased permeability of capillaries and venules. There is good evidence that histamine is an important, but not necessarily sole mediator in systemic anaphylaxis in many animals, including man. The fact that anaphylactic symptoms differ among species can be partially explained by the differences in histamine content and responsiveness of various organs. Histamine is also clearly important in the mediation of human atopic reactions, although a contribution by other mediators, particularly in bronchial asthma, must be considered.

Kinins

In recent years several pharmacologically active polypeptides have been found to appear in blood during the course of certain hypersensitivity reactions. Kinin formation results from enzymatic splitting of the active polypeptide from a plasma protein, kininogen, by one of several enzymes present in tissues, secretions, or plasma. Kinins are rapidly inactivated in vivo by a variety of kininases in plasma and tissues.

Bradykinin, or kallidin I, is a nonapeptide which produces an increase in capillary permeability and pain on injection, as well as smooth muscle contraction and vasodilation. It can be formed by the action of any of several enzymes on a plasma globulin, and there is evidence that this substance appears in the blood of guinea pigs, rats, rabbits, and dogs during anaphylaxis. Kallidin II, a decapeptide, has similar properties but is formed by different enzymes. Among the various plasma enzymes capable of kinin formation, kallikrein, which exists normally in plasma in an inactive form (kallikreinogen), may be involved in the pathogenesis of the disease, hereditary angioneurotic edema. Patients with this rare disease are lacking or deficient in a normal serum inhibitor of kallikrein, resulting in excessive formation of plasma kinin.[29] The same inhibitor also inhibits the activation of the first component of complement,[30] but whether the formation of kinin, the activation of the complement system, or both actually cause the attacks of angio-edema in this disease is unknown. There is no evidence at present that a similar mechanism is involved in nonherediatary forms of angio-edema or urticaria.

Slow-Reacting Substance

During the anaphylactic reaction of guinea pig lung in vitro, a substance, in addition to histamine, is released which differs from histamine in that it produces a more prolonged contraction of guinea pig ileum, is not inhibited by antihistamines, contracts only certain smooth muscle preparations, and does not produce vasodilatation. The chemical nature of this activity is currently unknown and has been given the name "slow-reacting substance" (SRS). This substance has been found to be released by several in vivo and in vitro types of antigen-antibody reactions. Of particular interest in the observation of Brocklehurst that slow-reacting substance is released from human allergic lung tissue upon exposure to allergen in vitro.[31] Slow-reacting substance cannot be extracted from lung tissue in the absence of antigen-antibody reaction, suggesting that it is formed in the tissue during the reaction.

Serotonin

Serotonin (5-hydroxytryptamine) is capable of contracting smooth muscle of certain species and has variable activity on blood vessels. It is released from rabbit platelets by antigen-antibody reactions in vitro and in vivo. However, it appears to be of little or no importance in primates. Human mast cells do not contain serotonin, and there is no evidence that serotonin is involved in any human allergic disease.

Complement

Complement is a term given to a group of serum proteins which react sequentially during certain antigen-antibody reactions. Currently, nine components of human complement have been described, some of which have been purified and partially characterized. Certain components are precursor forms of enzymes which are activated and in turn activate other components of complement during their participation in the antigen-antibody reaction. Furthermore, Ca^{++} and Mg^{++} are required for certain steps in the activation of complement. A detailed description of the complement system is beyond the scope of this book, but the interested reader can find many excellent reviews of this subject in the current literature.[32-33]

Complement is a mediator in certain types of antigen-antibody-induced injury to cells both in vitro and in vivo. In the absence of cells, complement may react with antigen-antibody precipitates or soluble complexes. The process by which complement is incorporated into the antigen-antibody aggregate is known as complement fixation and depends upon the type of antibody but not the antigen. Hence, the complement fixation reaction is often used as an indicator of an antigen-antibody reaction in vitro, especially in circumstances in which the nature of the antigen might preclude the use of other in vitro tests.

In the presence of complement, antibodies to cell constituents may cause destruction of the cell. The best known example of this is immune hemolysis, in which sheep erythrocytes sensitized by rabbit antibody are hemolyzed in the presence of complement. This system has been widely studied and is the indicator reaction used in complement fixation tests and in much of the research on the properties of the individual components of the complement system. Many other cytotoxic reactions involving complement have been demonstrated in vitro, such as the lysis of thyroid cells in tissue culture by auto-antibodies and of tumor cells by homologous or heterologous antibody. Lysis or neutralization of bacteria, viruses, and other microorganisms by antibody also requires complement.

The role of complement in various hypersensitivity reactions in vivo is uncertain because of difficulties in evaluating the participation of complement in the intact animal. Although total serum complement levels fall during systemic anaphylaxis, this in itself is not necessarily an indication that complement actually mediates the reaction. In experimental serum sickness at least one of the components of complement, C'3, has been found along with antigen and antibody localized specifically in the glomerular lesion by the immunofluorescent technique. However, changes in total serum complement levels have not been found to correlate with the severity of the tissue damage.

Anaphylatoxin

Exposure of guinea pig or rat serum in vitro to preformed antigen-antibody precipitates results in the formation in the serum of a substance called anaphylatoxin. This causes a syndrome indistinguishable from systemic anaphylaxis when injected into guinea pigs, but not rats. A similar substance can be produced by incubation of serum with certain nonimmunologic macromolecules, such as agar or inulin. Anaphylatoxin has not yet been characterized chemically, but it appears to be distinct from bradykinin. The formation of anaphylatoxin requires several components of complement, and the action of anaphylatoxin in vivo is mediated through the release of histamine. To date anaphylatoxin has not been shown to participate in anaphylaxis or other forms of immediate hypersensitivity.

DELAYED HYPERSENSITIVITY

Delayed hypersensitivity, or cellular immunity, is a form of immunologic reactivity in which exposure to the antigen results in an inflammatory reaction which does not become apparent during the first several hours but reaches maximal intensity in 24 to 48 hours. The prototype of delayed hypersensitivity is the tuberculin reaction. Intradermal injection of tuberculoprotein in a sensitized subject produces local inflammation characterized early by edema and leukocytic infiltration with neutrophils and later by the appearance of lymphocytes and plasma cells. Delayed hypersensitivity can be demonstrated to the appropriate antigen after infection with a variety of bacterial organisms, viruses, and fungi.

Passive transfer of delayed hypersensitivity can be achieved by using cells from the sensitized donor but not by serum, thus indicating that circulating antibody in the usual sense is not involved in this type of reactivity. Furthermore, those mediators which have been shown to be important in immediate hypersensitivity—histamine, kinins, complement—are not required for expression of delayed hypersensitivity. Lymphoid tissue, bone marrow, and peripheral blood leukocytes all are capable of passive transfer, and recent evidence indicates that the sensitized cell in these tissues is the small lymphocyte.

The actual mechanism of delayed hypersensitivity has not yet been established at a biochemical level. Although there has been speculation that the cells transferring delayed hypersensitivity are sensitized by small amounts of antibody of high affinity for the antigen, such antibody has never in fact been demonstrated in delayed hypersensitivity.[34] On the other hand, Lawrence has succeeded in transferring delayed hypersensitivity in humans by a substance extracted from lysed sensitized cells which he terms "transfer factor."[35] At the present time chemical studies suggest that transfer factor is a ribonucleotide of approximately 10,000 molecular weight. The transferred sensitivity persists in the recipient for months or even years, which raises the possibility that transfer factor may be capable of self-replication.

Delayed hypersensitivity can be induced experimentally with many antigens or with hapten-protein complexes in a variety of animal species. When antibody and delayed hypersensitivity are induced simultaneously to a hapten-protein complex, some antibodies have specificity for the hapten, whereas the specificity of delayed hypersensitivity is usually directed as well toward the protein carrier.[36]

Allergic contact dermatitis is mediated by delayed hypersensitivity. In this disease sensitivity is acquired by topical application to the skin of a chemically reactive compound, usually a low molecular weight organic or inorganic substance. The compound acts as a hapten combining irreversibly with dermal protein as it penetrates the skin. All the cardinal features of delayed hypersensitivity can be demonstrated in contact dermatitis: delayed cellular reaction in the skin to patch testing with the specific compound, passive transfer by lymphoid cells but not by serum, and passive transfer by "transfer factor" in humans. The clinical features of contact dermatitis and patch testing are described in detail in Chapters 11 and 12.

TRANSPLANTATION IMMUNITY

The grafting of an organ, tissue, or cells from one individual to a genetically different individual of the same species results in only temporary acceptance of the grafted tissue. This is followed by gradual tissue destruction, a process known as homograft rejection. Subsequent application of a second graft from the same donor to the same recipient results in a more rapid and intense rejection. The mechanism of homograft rejection has been extensively investigated and clearly involves an immunologic attack by the recipient on certain antigens in the grafted tissue. These antigens are known as "histocompatibility antigens." They are present in the cytoplasm of all nucleated cells of the body and possibly are a constituent of the cell membrane, or internal membranous components of various cell organelles. Histocompatibility antigens are genetically determined characteristics, so that genetically identical individuals (e.g., identical twins) do not reject tissues grafted from one to the other.

The process of homograft rejection has many characteristics of delayed hypersensitivity. The cellular reaction at the site of rejection closely resembles the tissue response in delayed hypersensitivity, and the rejection state can be specifically transferred to nonsensitized recipients by lymphoid cells but ordinarily not by serum. Circulating antibody, however, may contribute to at least some of the phenomena in homograft rejection, such as the white graft reaction and the response to grafts of cell suspensions. The homograft rejection phenomenon can be completely or partially abolished by immunosuppressive drugs, a fact of great clinical importance.

One particular variant of transplantation immunity of theoretical interest is the graft-versus-host reaction. Immunologically competent cells grafted into a recipient capable of accepting the graft, such as an irradiated animal or F_1-hybrid, can survive and function in the adopted host. The graft cells then proceed to react against the histocompatibility antigens of the host, producing widespread tissue damage characterized by generalized wasting, dermatitis, diarrhea, splenomegaly, auto-immune hemolytic anemia, and eventual death. In neonatal or immature hosts, the graft-versus-host reaction has been called "runt disease" because of failure of the animals to grow at a normal rate. Although several attempts have been made to explain certain human diseases as graft-versus-host reactions, no such naturally occurring human counterpart to this reaction has been proved.

REFERENCES

1. King, T. P., Norman, P. S., and Connell, J. T.: Isolation and characterization of allergens from ragweed pollen. II. Biochemistry *3:*458, 1964.
2. Rowe, D. S., and Fahey, J. L.: A new class of human immunoglobulins. II. Normal serum IgD. J. Exper. Med. *121:*185, 1965.
3. Ishizaka, K., and Ishizaka, T.: Physicochemical properties of reaginic antibody. I. Association of reaginic activity with an immunoglobulin other than γA- or γG-globulin. J. Allergy *37:*169, 1966.
4. Edelman, G. M., and Gally, J. A.: A model for the 7S antibody molecule. Proc. Nat. Acad. Sc. *51:*846, 1964.
5. Miller, F., and Metzger, H.: Characterization of a human macroglobulin. I. The molecular weight of its subunits. J. Biol. Chem. *240:*3325, 1965.
6. Tomasi, T. B., Tan, E. M., Solomon, A., and Prendergast, R. A.: Characteristics of an immune system common to certain external secretions. J. Exper. Med. *121:*101, 1965.
7. Heremans, J. F., and Vaerman, J. P.: β_{2A}-globulin as a possible carrier of allergic reaginic activity. Nature *193:*1091, 1962.
8. Fireman, P., Vannier, W. E., and Goodman, H. C.: The association of skin-sensitizing antibody with the β_{2A}-globulins in sera from ragweed-sensitive patients. J. Exper. Med. *117:*603, 1963.
9. Ishizaka, K., Ishizaka, T., and Hornbrook, M. M.: Blocking of Prausnitz-Küstner sensitization with reagin by normal human β_{2A}-globulin. J. Allergy *34:*395, 1963.
10. Terr, A. I., and Bentz, J. D.: Gel filtration of human skin-sensitizing antibody and β_{2A}-globulin. J. Allergy *35:*206, 1964.
11. Terr, A. I., and Bentz, J. D.: Skin-sensitizing antibodies in serum sickness. J. Allergy *36:*433, 1965.
12. Lidd, D., and Connell, J. T.: Specific binding of an I[131]-labeled ragweed pollen fraction by sera of untreated ragweed-sensitive humans. J. Allergy *35:*289, 1964.
13. Pruzansky, J. J., and Patterson, R.: Binding of I[131]-labeled ragweed antigen by sera of ragweed-sensitive individuals. J. Allergy *35:*1, 1965.
14. Salvaggio, J. E., Cavanaugh, J. J. A., Lowell, F. C., and Leskowitz, S.: A comparison of the immunologic responses of normal and atopic individuals to intranasally administered antigen. J. Allergy *35:*62, 1964.
15. Good, R. A., and Gabrielsen, A. B. (eds.): The Thymus in Immunobiology: Structure, Function, and Role in Disease. New York, Paul B. Hoeber, 1964.
16. Fishman, M.: Antibody formation *in vitro.* J. Exper. Med. *114:*837, 1961.
17. Farr, R. S.: A quantitative immunochemical measure of the primary interaction between I*—BSA and antibody. J. Infect. Dis. *103:*239, 1958.
18. Fahey, J. L., and McKelvey, E. M.: Quantitative determination of serum immunoglobulins in antibody-agar plates. J. Immunol. *94:*84, 1965.
19. Scheidegger, J. J.: Une micro-methode de l'immuno-electrophorese. Internat. Arch. Allergy *7:*103, 1955.
20. Kabat, E. A., and Mayer, M. M.: Experimental Immunochemistry. 2nd ed. Springfield, Illinois, Charles C Thomas, 1961.
21. Ackroyd, J. F. (ed.): Immunological Methods. Philadelphia, F. A. Davis Co., 1964.
22. Hawn, C. V., and Janeway, C. A.: Histological and serological sequences in experimental hypersensitivity. J. Exper. Med. *85:*571, 1947.

23. Germuth, F. G.: A comparative histologic and immunologic study in rabbits of induced hypersensitivity of the serum sickness type. J. Exper. Med. *97:*257, 1953.
24. Dixon, F. J., Vazquez, J. J., Weigle, W. O., and Cochrane, C. G.: Pathogenesis of serum sickness. Arch. Path. *65:*18, 1958.
25. Ward, P. A., Cochrane, C. G., and Müller-Eberhard, H. J.: The role of serum complement in chemotaxis of leukocytes *in vitro.* J. Exper. Med. *122:*327, 1965.
26. Gell, P. G. H., and Hinde, I. T.: Observations on the histology of the Arthus reaction and its relation to other known types of skin hypersensitivity. Internat. Arch. Allergy *5:*23, 1954.
27. Ovary, Z.: Immediate reactions in the skin of experimental animals provoked by antigen-antibody interaction. Progr. Allergy *5:*459, 1958.
28. Coca, A. F., and Cooke, R. A.: On the classification of the phenomena of hypersensitiveness. J. Immunol. *8:*163, 1923.
29. Landerman, N. S., Webster, M. E., Becker, E. L., and Ratcliffe, H. E.: Hereditary angioneurotic edema. II. Deficiency of inhibitor for serum globulin permeability factor and/or plasma kallikrein. J. Allergy *33:*330, 1962.
30. Donaldson, V. H., and Evans, R. R.: A biochemical abnormality in hereditary angioneurotic edema. Am. J. Med. *35:*37, 1963.
31. Brocklehurst, W. E.: The release of histamine and formation of a slow-reacting substance (SRS-A) during anaphylactic shock. J. Physiol. *151:*416, 1960.
32. Wolstenholme, G. E. W., and Knight, J.: Ciba Foundation Symposium: Complement. Boston, Little, Brown, 1965.
33. Osler, A. G.: Functions of the complement system. Advances Immunol. *1:*132, 1961.
34. Karush, F., and Eisen, H. N.: A theory of delayed hypersensitivity. Science *136:*1032, 1962.
35. Lawrence, H. S.: The transfer of hypersensitivity of the delayed type in man *in* Lawrence, H. S. (ed.): Cellular and Humoral Aspects of the Hypersensitive State. p. 279, New York, Paul B. Hoeber, 1959.
36. Gell, P. G. H., and Benacerraf, B.: Studies on hypersensitivity; IV. The relationship between contact and delayed sensitivity: a study of the specificity of cellular immune reactions. J. Exper. Med. *113:*571, 1961.

Chapter Two

NONIMMUNOLOGIC FACTORS IN ALLERGIC DISEASE

As indicated in the previous chapter, allergic reactions by definition are known or presumed to involve immunologic mechanisms. However, there are a number of additional factors which may significantly affect the course of clinical allergic diseases in man. These sometimes are referred to as nonspecific, precipitating or secondary factors in allergy. The interplay of these elements with specific immunologic factors determines when a patient will experience allergic symptoms. The concept of the *total allergic load* graphically expresses these interrelationships (Figure 2–1). This indicates that whether a patient has symptoms at a given instant in time depends on the equilibrium between his tolerance* and the various immunologic and nonimmunologic factors included in the total allergic load. Little is known about what may permit a host to tolerate allergic reactions, but presumably this reflects the sum of the physiologic and perhaps immunologic compensating factors which inhibit, ameliorate or terminate allergic reactions.

HEREDITARY FACTORS

Inheritance appears to play a role particularly in the atopic diseases, though in experimental animals it can be shown also to influence susceptibility to some forms of delayed hypersensitivity. In atopy the genetic factor pertains mainly to a heightened general capacity to become sensitized rather than a predilection to develop allergy to specific substances. The existence of a genetic factor in the atopic diseases seems very likely from the much higher prevalence of these conditions in certain families than in the populace at large. About 50 to 60 per cent of patients with these illnesses give a history of similar illness in their families. There is additional, suggestive evidence that bronchial asthma occurs more often in families of asthmatic persons than in families of persons with other allergic diseases.[2] Several extensive attempts have

---

* The term "tolerance" is not being used here in its immunologic sense.

21

been made to define the mode of inheritance of atopy, but unfortunately the results are contradictory.[2, 3] One possible explanation for these discrepancies is that, since environmental as well as genetic factors are necessary for the development of overt manifestations of the atopic diseases, environmental variables may obscure the underlying genetic mechanisms. Our observation that significantly fewer foreign university students afflicted with ragweed pollenosis give family histories of atopic disease than do native student patients supports this suggestion.[4] Likewise, there are many instances in which only one of a pair of identical twins exhibits atopic symptoms.

Another possibility, as pointed out by Neel, is that there are multiple points at which genetic control could be exercised regarding susceptibility to the development of an atopic disease such as ragweed pollenosis.[5] For instance, pollen allergens must cross the mucosal barrier of the respiratory tract, and there could be genetically controlled individual differences in these processes. Second, there might be individual differences in antibody production. There also might be other genetically controlled processes, such as the capacity of antibodies to enter into such relationships with the "target organ" that a local response takes place. If all these various steps were under genetic control, then, depending upon the frequency of the genes involved and the exposure to pollen, a variety of genetic patterns might be encountered. Further progress may depend upon focusing on the various steps involved. Recent observations by Salvaggio et al. that atopic persons produce skin-sensitizing antibodies following inhalation (but not injection) of crystalline ribonuclease more readily than a control group exemplify a type of approach which might be fruitful.[6] The data on hand indicate that all races of man may develop atopic diseases, and there appears to be no association with any of several blood groups.

STATE OF SENSITIZATION

The length of time since the last exposure to an allergen may importantly affect the reactivity to it. In many types of hypersensitivity, there is a brief refractory period following an allergic reaction after which there may be heightened reactivity. Atopic hypersensitivity to inhalants or foods which cause immediate symptoms tends to persist for many years or decades, whereas other allergies, e.g., to some drugs and contactants, may be more fleeting (but this is not always true).

CURRENT EXPOSURE TO ALLERGENS

This is the factor on which the allergist generally focuses his attention. Depending on the state of sensitivity, patients vary markedly in respect to the amount of allergens required to provoke symptoms.

Interpretation of the history may be complicated by exposure to multiple allergens simultaneously. The investigation of food allergy may be complicated by cooking, which can denature the protein in food allergens. Sequential, cumulative exposures to allergens also may affect patients' subsequent reactions. These complexities, together with the multiple nonimmunologic variables considered below, make it clear why, in some instances, the clinical evaluation of allergic patients can be very difficult.

INFECTION

As indicated by the overlapping brackets in Figure 2–1, infection may act either as a specific or as a nonspecific factor in precipitating allergic reactions. Antigens from infectious agents are among the most common sensitizers for delayed hypersensitivity. There also are some instances in which such antigens clearly induce immediate type hypersensitivity reactions in man, e.g., urticaria from Ascaris infestation. However, one of the most controversial points in the entire field of clinical allergy is whether the frequently observed exacerbations of bronchial asthma following respiratory tract infections reflect specific sensitization to the infectious agents ("bacterial allergy") or whether the infection is acting as a nonspecific precipitating factor, augmenting the inflammatory reaction in the respiratory tract. It should be emphasized that the argument is not *whether* asthmatic patients get worse with respiratory tract infections, since virtually all allergists would agree that this is a very common occurrence; the question at issue is the nature of the *mechanism* whereby the infection aggravates the disease.

The following are some of the arguments which have been used to support the contention that specfiic, immediate type hypersensitivity

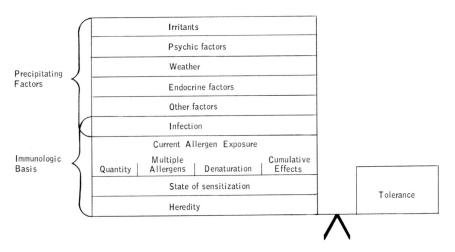

Figure 2–1. Concept of the total allergic load. (Modified from Feinberg.[1])

to antigens contained in the infectious agents is involved: (1) Many of these patients show positive immediate skin test reactions (with or without delayed reactions) to bacterial antigens. However, this observation is no longer emphasized even by the proponents of "bacterial allergy" since numerous positive skin test reactions to the same vaccines are also found in control groups. (2) Some patients experience systemic, allergic reactions from bacterial vaccines, just as these may occur after injecting pollen extracts or other allergens. In the relatively few patients in whom such reactions occur, this is relatively impressive evidence for immediate hypersensitivity to some component of the bacterial vaccine, but it should be noted that unequivocal, immediate reactions of this type are quite rare. (3) Provocative inhalation tests (page 68) employing bacterial vaccines should help to resolve this question. Hampton, Johnson and Galakatos succeeded in inducing prompt and severe bronchial constriction in patients with infectious type asthma by inhalation of an extract obtained from *Neisseria catarrhalis*.[7] Normal controls did not react. It is noteworthy, however, that their extract probably contained irritants, and thus it would be desirable to document that a larger number of patients with *recent** asthma not suspected of being caused by infection also would not react to this antigen. Further studies along these lines would be valuable, although in interpreting the results consideration must be given to the possibilities discussed in the next paragraph. (4) Results of the empiric use of bacterial vaccines in treating asthma associated with infection also are germane to the issue under discussion. As discussed in Chapter 6 (page 101), most double-blind studies with the types of bacterial vaccines in use today have shown no better effect than that from placebo treatment.

Alternative explanations for the aggravating effect of respiratory tract infection on bronchial asthma include the following: additive effects of the two types of inflammatory edema, possible adjuvant effects of bacterial products in enhancing sensitization, possible localization of allergic reactions in areas injured by infection, liberation of mediators by products of infectious organisms and the effect of endotoxins or exotoxins in altering the responsiveness of effector cells which are acted upon by mediators, as suggested by Szentivanyi and Fishel.[8] Oullette and Reed's observation that asthmatic subjects (and not normals) show increased responsiveness to aerosol methacholine after influenza vaccine lends some support to the last mentioned possibility.[9] Toxins might act by inhibiting the functional activity of the adrenergic beta receptor system (page 130), as is thought to occur in pertussis-induced hypersensitivity to histamine and serotonin in mice.[10]

---

* We have noted in unpublished observations that histamine and methacholine cause much more pronounced bronchial asthma in patients who have had recent asthma (e.g., within three weeks to three months) than in those whose last attack of asthma occurred one year or more before the tests.

IRRITANTS

Any substance which is chemically or mechanically slightly irritating to normal mucous membranes or skin may cause much more difficulty when it reaches a tissue which is already the site of allergic inflammation. In other instances, irritant reactions may simulate allergy, as, for example, in chemical conjunctivitis or abrasive dermatitis.

Innumerable substances are potential irritants. Only small numbers of persons are exposed to some of these, as in certain industrial processes, whereas agents like smog (Figure 2–2), cold air (even excessive cooling from air-conditioners), soap powder, road dust and automobile exhaust bother large numbers of people. In both man and animals the inhalation of chemically inert particles produces measurable increases in bronchial resistance.[11] These reactions appear to involve autonomic reflexes which are initiated by receptors throughout the respiratory tract below the glottis.[12]

Bronchial constriction as a reflex effect of nasal and pharyngeal stimulation has been found by some authors but not by others. Undetermined air pollutants appear to be the cause of "Yokohama asthma."[13] It has been noted that, in smoking, one voluntarily creates far greater air pollution for himself than he would ever be exposed to from outside sources. Prolonged increases in bronchial resistance have been observed to follow cigarette smoking by both normal subjects and patients with airway obstructive disease.[14] Because of their immunologic orientation, there is a tendency for some allergists to disregard irritants. From the patient's standpoint, however, irritants may be just as important as true allergens, and a number of allergists are becoming increasingly interested in the control of air pollution.

Figure 2–2. SMOG. The suspension of irritant gases and particles above some cities has become a major source of irritation to the mucous membranes of their inhabitants. (Los Angeles County Air Pollution Control District.)

ENDOCRINE FACTORS

Clinical observations that the course of allergic diseases may change at the time of puberty, with menstruation, during pregnancy or at the menopause suggest the possible importance of some endocrine factors, but these effects are variable. Some allergic children experience improvement or alleviation of their symptoms at the time of puberty, but this cannot be depended upon; in others, symptoms of allergy become manifest or exacerbated at this time. Relatively uncommonly, symptoms may fluctuate with different phases of the menstrual cycle. Perhaps this is seen most often in chronic urticaria and perennial allergic rhinitis. Although autosensitization to the patient's own sex hormones has been postulated, the evidence supporting this suggestion has not been confirmed.[15] The tendency toward premenstrual fluid retention and heightened nervous and vasomotor irritability at that time might account for some of the difficulty. Emotional factors also might be related to occasional exacerbations of allergic symptoms at the menopause. During pregnancy there may be a striking amelioration of allergic symptoms, with recurrence shortly after parturition.[16] However, other patients are distinctly worse or unchanged in pregnancy.[17] More systematic information is needed to clarify the frequency with which these different types of response occur. We, as well as others,[16] have noticed that in some multiparous women the severity of asthma during pregnancy seems to be related to fetal sex, but the direction of the change varies in different patients. In addition, it should be noted that pregnancy itself may be associated with a vasomotor rhinitis, which must be distinguished from allergic rhinitis (page 84). About one-fourth of tuberculin-positive patients show a diminution of their skin test reactions to tuberculin during pregnancy.[18] The clinical importance of the striking elevation of serum histaminase which normally occurs in pregnancy is largely unknown. Isoimmunization of the mother by fetal antigens during pregnancy is discussed briefly in Chapter 19 (page 497).

In experimental animals, anaphylaxis is enhanced by adrenalectomy. Atopic patients with Addison's disease may have exacerbations of their allergic illness relating to the degree of adrenal insufficiency.[19] In view of the striking therapeutic effect of corticosteroid drugs, many investigators have studied adrenal cortical function in atopic patients. Some severe, chronic asthmatic patients show evidence of a subnormal secretion of these hormones, but this could be a *result* of the disease. Normal adrenal and pituitary function appears to be the rule in early or intermittent atopic disease, indicating that insufficiency of their hormones in these people is not a primary cause for these disorders.[20] Atopic patients also maintain the normal diurnal pattern of corticosteroid excretion.[20]

Thyroxin enhances tuberculin hypersensitivity in experimental animals.[21] Clinically, atopic disease sometimes appears to be aggravated by hyperthyroidism, but this may be due simply to the nervous irritability and vasomotor instability associated with thyrotoxicosis. In myxedema, the nasal mucosa may become involved in the edematous process, with resultant nasal stuffiness which might aggravate or simulate allergic rhinitis.

WEATHER

As discussed in Chapter 16, meteorologic factors may indirectly affect allergic symptoms by importantly influencing the amount of pollen and mold spores in the air at a given time. Beyond this, some biometeorologists have long contended that weather factors per se influence allergic diseases, especially bronchial asthma.[22] The mechanism might involve either a direct effect on the allergic "shock organ" or the patient's state of sensitization might be influenced by these factors. Certainly, it is an everyday experience to hear asthmatic patients relate their symptoms to certain weather conditions, but it is hard to be certain of the significance of these observations in a situation in which there are so many variables. Temperature, relative humidity and barometric pressure have been shown to influence the incidence of inhalant sensitization and anaphylactic shock in guinea pigs under well controlled conditions.[23]

In humans, evidence for the possible importance of meteorologic factors has been obtained from retrospective observations, often based on hospital emergency room admissions, that substantial numbers of asthmatic patients in a locality may have simultaneous exacerbations of their symptoms under certain meteorologic conditions and in the absence of any increase of recognized aeroallergens. Especially remarkable was the finding of Nelson et al. that all seven asthmatic patients being carefully observed in an essentially pollen-free room simultaneously developed asthma during a rainstorm.[24] However, it also should be noted that the same effect did not occur during a rain eight days later when the meteorologic changes were less abrupt.

In general, most studies in this field have suggested that a combination of meteorologic changes may be most important; e.g., decreased temperature and changing relative humidity and barometric pressure, such as occur with the passage of a cold front, have been thought to adversely affect asthma (Figure 2–3). The rate of change may be important. In interpreting "epidemics" of asthma in a community, consideration also should be given to air pollution or respiratory infection as being the responsible agents.[25] In addition, it should be noted that careful records by other observers have failed to detect a clustering of asthmatic attacks relating to weather factors in other communities. It appears likely that additional information of importance will come from current work at several centers where asthmatic patients are being

Figure 2–3. A cold front forms when a mass of cold air forces its way beneath a warmer air mass, pushing the warm air aloft. A narrow zone of clouds forms at the front, and violent air turbulence and rainstorms often precede it. (U.S.W.B., Walter Henderson.)

studied in chambers in which meterologic parameters can be varied *individually*.

In addition to the usual meteorologic factors, many European investigators have claimed that positive air ionization worsens asthma, just as it is said to aggravate symptoms of many other diseases and even cause symptoms in normals (e.g., "Fohn disease"). Although there is good evidence that high concentrations of positive ions inhibit the ciliary activity of rabbit trachea, much further work would be required to confirm their adverse effect on asthma in humans.[26] Reported beneficial effects of negative air ionization in treating allergic diseases with commercially available equipment[27] have not been confirmed.

Along with meteorologic factors, *climate* also has received a good deal of attention. Many, but not all, patients with respiratory allergy and atopic dermatitis appear to be improved in warm, dry climates. To a substantial extent this may be due to less respiratory tract infection, fewer aeroallergens and little air pollution in most of such places. The relaxing effect of being removed from the stress of work and other problems also could be important. Beyond these factors, however, it is possible that the climate per se might be helpful. Considerations affecting suggested climatic changes as a form of therapy are discussed on pages 82, 99, and 237. For years Europeans have emphasized the salubrious effect of high altitude.[28] However, it is doubtful that the improvement which many patients report in the Swiss Alps is due to high altitude alone, since allergy is rife at some equally elevated places elsewhere in the world. Perhaps for this reason, treatment with high altitude chambers has not enjoyed the popularity elsewhere as it has in Europe.

PSYCHIC FACTORS

This subject is discussed in Chapter 20.

OTHER FACTORS

Allergic diseases may be aggravated by many other factors including fatigue, exertion and heat, and local trauma. Dysfunction of the autonomic nervous system was stressed in the older literature, and there is no doubt that interruption of the sympathetic nervous innervation to the nose produces physiologic disturbances which may simulate or aggravate allergic rhinitis. Bronchospasm resulting from vagal stimulation in experimental animals or methacholine inhalation in asthmatic humans is well known. Reflex bronchoconstriction was mentioned on page 25, and cholinergic urticaria is discussed on page 242. More recently it has been suggested that in bronchial asthma there may be partial adrenergic beta receptor blockade, which could prevent bronchial smooth muscle relaxation from adrenergic stimulation[29] (see pages 24 and 130). Increased airway resistance has been shown experimentally to follow forced breathing in asthmatic patients. These patients often seem to worsen with hyperventilation and with increased intrathoracic pressure associated with laughter, defecation and cough.

REFERENCES

1. Feinberg, S. M.: Allergy in Practice. Ed. 2, p. 85, Chicago, Year Book Medical Publishers, Inc., 1946.
2. Schwartz, M.: Heredity in bronchial asthma. Acta. Allergol. 5 Supp. II: 1, 1952.
3. Wiener, A. S., Zieve, I., and Fries, J. H.: The inheritance of allergic disease. Ann. Eugenics 7:141, 1936.
4. Maternowski, C. J., and Mathews, K. P.: The prevalence of ragweed pollinosis in foreign and native students at a midwestern university and its implications concerning methods for determining the inheritance of atopy. J. Allergy 33:130, 1962.
5. Neel, J. V.: Genetic criteria in dental research in Witkop, C. J. (ed.): Genetics and Health, p. 18, New York, McGraw-Hill Book Co., 1962.
6. Salvaggio, J. E., Cavanaugh, J. J. A., Lowell, F. C., and Leskowitz, S.: A comparison of the immunologic responses of normal and atopic individuals to intranasally administered antigen, J. Allergy 35:62, 1964.
7. Hampton, S. F., Johnson, M. C., and Galakatos, E.: Studies of bacterial hypersensitivity in asthma. I. The preparation of antigens of Neisseria catarrhalis, the induction of asthma by aerosols, the performance of skin and passive transfer tests. J. Allergy 34:63, 1963.

8. Szentivanyi, A., and Fishel, C. W.: Effect of bacterial products on responses to the allergic mediators *in* Samter, M. (ed..): Immunological Diseases. p. 226, Boston, Little, Brown and Co., 1965.

9. Oullette, J. J., and Reed, C. E.: Increased response of asthmatic subjects to methacholine after influenza vaccine. J. Allergy *36:*558, 1965.

10. Fishel, C. W., Szentivanyi, A., and Talmage, D. W.: Sensitization and desensitization of mice to histamine and serotonin by neurohumors. J. Immunol. *89:*8, 1962.

11. Dautrebande, L.: Microaerosols. New York and London, Academic Press, 1962.

12. Nadel, J. A., and Weddicomb, J. G.: Reflex effects of upper airway irritation on total lung resistance and blood pressure. J. Appl. Physiol. *17:*861, 1962.

13. Phelps, H. W., Sobel, G. W., and Fisher, N. E.: Air pollution asthma among military personnel in Japan. J.A.M.A. *175:*990, 1961.

14. Nadel, J. A., and Comroe, J. H.: Acute effects of inhalation of cigarette smoke on airway conductance. J. Appl. Physiol. *16:*713, 1961.

15. Zondek, B., and Bromberg, Y. M.: Endocrine allergy. I. Allergic sensitivity to endogenous hormones. J. Allergy *16:*1, 1945.

16. Derbes, V. J., and Sodeman, W. A.: Reciprocal influences of bronchial asthma and pregnancy. Am. J. Med. *1:*367, 1946.

17. Fein, B. T., and Kamin, P. B.: Management of allergy in pregnancy. Ann. Allergy *22:*341, 1964.

18. Lichtenstein, M. R.: Tuberculin reaction in tuberculosis during pregnancy. Am. Rev. Tuberc. *46:*89, 1942.

19. Carryer, H. M., Sherrick, D. W., and Gastineau, C. F.: The occurrence of allergic disease in patients with adrenal cortical hypofunction. J.A.M.A. *172:*1356, 1960.

20. Blumenthal, M. N., McLean, J. A., Mathews, K. P., and Sheldon, J. M.: Adrenal-pituitary function in bronchial asthma. Arch. Int. Med. *117:*34, 1966.

21. Long, D. A., and Miles, A. A.: Opposite actions of thyroid and adrenal hormones in allergic hypersensitivity. Lancet *1:*492, 1950.

22. Petersen, W. F.: The organic state in the problem of allergy. Ann. Allergy *3:*348, 1945.

23. Courtright, L. J., and Courtright, A. B.: Inhalant sensitization and shock in guinea pigs under controlled atmospheric conditions. J. Allergy *16:*146, 1945.

24. Nelson, T., Rappaport, B. Z., and Welker, W. H.: The effect of air filtration in hay fever and asthma. Further studies. J.A.M.A. *100:*1385, 1933.

25. Weill, H., Ziskind, M. M., Dickerson, R. C., and Derbes, V. J.: Epidemic asthma in New Orleans. J.A.M.A. *190:*811, 1964.

26. Krueger, A. P., and Smith, R. F.: Parameters of gaseous ion effects on the mammalian trachea. J. Gen. Physiol. *42:*959, 1959.

27. Kornblueh, J. H., Piersol, M. D., and Speicher, F.: Relief from pollenosis in negatively ionized rooms. Am. J. Phys. Med. *37:*18, 1958.

28. Williams, D. A.: Definition—prevalence—predisposing and contributory factors *in* Jamar, J. M. (ed.): International Textbook of Allergy. p. 109, Springfield, Ill., Charles C Thomas, 1959.

29. Cookson, D. U., and Reed, C. E.: A comparison of the effects of isoproterenol in the normal and asthmatic subjects. Am. Rev. Resp. Dis. *88:*636, 1963.

Chapter Three

MEDICAL
EVALUATION
OF THE
ALLERGY PATIENT

TAKING THE ALLERGY HISTORY

The point to keep uppermost in mind when taking an allergy history is that the patient as a whole must be thoroughly evaluated. It would be a grave mistake to assume that because a person comes to an allergist he has *allergic* disease. Every patient presents a challenge in differential diagnosis and the field of allergy is no exception. "All that wheezes is not allergy." The opportunity for diagnosing pulmonary tuberculosis, bronchogenic neoplasm, aspirated foreign bodies, and pulmonary infection, as well as functional and organic disease in the other systems of the body, exists wherever the treatment of allergy is practiced.

Since an allergy work-up involves a complete medical or pediatric evaluation, together with a good amount of additional, specialized history, a one hour appointment usually is needed for a new patient. The patient should be seated comfortably and reassured that the physician plans to devote serious attention to the chief complaint. This is especially important, because the idea has developed that there is something very humorous about hay fever, and asthma may be regarded as an insignificant curiosity by those who have never had it. The patient may seem almost apologetic for presenting himself with "nothing more than a stuffy nose." A good history will be obtained only if the doctor is genuinely interested. Furthermore, such interest is justified, because almost every case of intractable asthma in a respiratory cripple probably began with minor symptoms such as most patients present at their first visit. The objectives of the history are: (1) to determine whether the patient has an allergic disease and (2) to ascertain the factors which contribute to the occurrence of the symptoms.

Chief Complaint and Present Illness

One begins taking an allergy history in the same manner in which

31

an ordinary medical history is taken. After identifying data such as the patient's age, address, and occupation are obtained, he is asked to state his chief complaint in his own words. Then he is encouraged to describe his presenting symptoms. There are advantages in taking a *spontaneous* history, i.e., letting the patient outline his difficulty in his own words. Printed forms to be filled in by the patient or physician employing question-and-answer technique are used by some, but these should be only a supplement to and not a substitute for a narrative description of the history. The physician should not delegate this procedure to a nurse or technician.

Now at the very beginning of the history is an excellent time to make certain that some nonallergic condition is not the most probable cause of the patient's complaints. He should be questioned about symptoms such as hemoptysis, fever, ankle swelling, chest pain, "palpitation," purulent bronchial or nasal discharge, prominent sore throat, marked localized sinus pain or tenderness, and cervical adenopathy. Such complaints would suggest that the disease is not allergic or at least not entirely allergic in origin. It also is helpful to find out very soon whether the symptoms are continuous or intermittent. Although allergic symptoms occasionally may be continuous, most often they occur in paroxysms. Hence, one should consider other diagnoses or suspect some complication when the symptoms are continuous and progressive. Another clue is that allergic diseases are usually rather generalized. Unilateral chest or nasal symptoms or very localized skin lesions would suggest some nonallergic state or possibly a contact dermatitis.

It is desirable at this point to determine at what time of life the patient began to experience allergic symptoms. Inquiry is made about the patient's health during his early years. The presence of eczema or a "feeding problem" in infancy and childhood should be ascertained and recorded. Difficulty in getting a baby to drink milk or frequent bouts of colic or skin trouble when a new food is added may be significant points. In taking the history, this also is a good place to record the geographic location of the patient as he has gone through life. It is helpful later to correlate this information with the time and place of onset of allergic symptoms. The patient's health during his school years is recorded. Some persons can, when questioned, remember that in school they had frequent colds or "sinus trouble," which were minimized at the time. If much time was missed from school, the cause should be determined.

Employment should be traced in detail, particularly the job held by the patient when his symptoms started. Determining that the patient is, for example, an "inspector" is not sufficient. The physician should find out *what* he inspects and how he carries this out, with emphasis on environmental conditions at work. The relationship between symptoms and working conditions should be noted.

Details Relating to Course of Disease

Probably the most important part of the allergy history is a detailed account of the course of the disease. The physician should know whether the symptoms are continuous or intermittent and the date of onset of first manifestations of illness. He should inquire about the frequency and duration of the episodes.

Next, a very fruitful approach to obtaining clues about possible etiologic factors is to ascertain *when* the patient has symptoms (and also when he is free from symptoms), *where* he has difficulty (and where he is clear), and *what* agents in the environment cause trouble which he himself has noted. In regard to the first of these lines of inquiry, it is of interest to know the course of the allergic problems over the *decades*. Was there a change in symptoms at puberty, during pregnancy? Is the disease becoming progressively worse as the years pass, or is it spontaneously improving? Then *yearly seasonal* variations in symptomatology should be determined. This is important even if *perennial* symptoms are present, since a seasonal variation may also be superimposed. The patient should be strongly urged to be as exact as possible in regard to dates of the episodes; for example, it makes a significant difference in diagnosis and treatment whether "springtime" hay fever begins in early April or in late May. Thus, it is important to dwell on this point at some length, seeking to determine within a week or ten days the dates of onset and remission of seasonal symptoms. Sometimes, one can help the patient by having him recall whether he was having symptoms on holidays or other special occasions which are likely to be remembered. Even when the patient simply cannot recall dates, he is more likely to pay attention to these in the future if the physician emphasizes the importance of this information by energetic inquiry.

Next, one may ask about *monthly* fluctuations in symptoms. This usually is less important, but some women are worse premenstrually. Alterations in difficulty varying with time of *week* are more common. Workers or school children may be either better or worse on weekends than on weekdays—a point of considerable help in suggesting the importance of allergens either in the home, at work, or in the school environment. Then one determines the *time of day* or *night* at which symptoms are apt to appear and the hour at which they reach their maximal intensity. In evaluation of this information, it should be noted that nasal congestion increases with recumbency, and for reasons which are not entirely clear asthma tends to occur at night. Hence, nasal stuffiness on arising in the morning or nocturnal asthmatic bouts may not necessarily indicate allergy to something in the bedroom.

Consideration is next given regarding the locations at which the patient experiences or is free from trouble. Did his pattern of difficulty change when he moved from one place to another? Was improvement noted on vacation trips to distant places, such as the West Coast, Europe, or the far North? Is the patient any better at the homes of friends or relatives a few blocks away than he is in his own home? Does he improve rapidly in the hospital? Has he observed any places such as barns, damp basements, river banks, or certain fields, warehouses, or factories where he regularly gets worse? Is he better outdoors than indoors or vice versa?

The answers to the questions regarding when and where symptoms appear are of the utmost importance. Correlating this information with the known time and place of occurrence of various allergens often enables the doctor to be almost certain about the cause of the patient's symptoms, and further procedures will be used mainly to confirm his impression. Therefore, a careful history roughly defines the general types of allergens which could be causing the problem. Positive reactions to skin tests with the allergens can be considered clinically significant only if they are compatible with the possibilities suggested by the history.

At this point in the evaluation, it is well specifically to ask the patient whether he has observed any *environmental agents* which seem to precipitate or aggravate his symptoms. After allowing him to reply spontaneously without any element of suggestion, it is worthwhile to inquire in detail about some of the sources of major allergens such as house dust, animals, hay, foods, and medications. Then one should inquire about the relationship of symptoms to infection, emotional upsets, and endocrine factors such as pregnancy and menstruation. The influence of climatic factors, such as temperature and humidity, may be noted. In evaluating the replies to these questions, *the allergist should be sure that his patient is relating his or her own observations* and not simply repeating the opinions of friends, relatives, or previously consulted physicians, or reporting the results of earlier skin tests.

Particularly when an individual has not suspected an allergic cause for his symptoms, it may be impossible to obtain certain useful information from him at the time of his initial visit. However, by being asked questions of the type just discussed, the patient often will be stimulated to think along suitable lines and to make observations that can yield valuable clues at the time of later interviews. When details of the initial history are vague, it may be desirable for the patient to keep a written diary of the exact times when his symptoms occur in relation to his daily activities, such as food intake, work, recreation, and sleep. Occasionally it is helpful to "create history" by having the patient radically change his environment and activities for a short time. For example, he might spend a few days with relatives away from his own house, or perhaps he could travel to some distant geographic area while on vacation to observe the effect, if any, on his symptoms.

Detailed Environmental Survey

At times patients may be exposed to some relatively unusual allergen, or a common allergen may be exceptionally abundant in their particular environment. In other instances they may forget to mention known difficulty from certain substances unless they are reminded by direct questioning. The Environmental Survey Sheet provides a convenient guide for obtaining this type of specific information about the patient's environment and habits. Emphasis on minute detail will vary somewhat from one case to another depending on the type of symptoms under consideration. It also should be added that many of the questions on the allergy survey form are not pertinent to cases of contact dermatitis. A somewhat different approach is taken in such cases, as will be discussed in Chapter 11. In general, however, a detailed inquiry regarding possible environmental suspects along the lines suggested by the allergy survey sheet is indicated in patients with atopic disease. The reasons for the particular questions included on this form will become apparent in subsequent chapters dealing with the various allergens.

History of Previous Therapy

This inquiry has a five-fold purpose: (1) It is of interest to see whether the person studied has responded previously to drugs and other symptomatic measures usually effective in allergic disease. A good response tends to substantiate an allergic basis for the complaints, while failure to obtain relief would tend to make one reconsider other causes for the illness. However, not too much weight should be given to this point alone. (2) Previous therapy may have perpetrated the patient's disease. The excessive or prolonged use of nose drops, sensitivity to ointments that are being applied to the skin, and allergy to drugs are examples of this. (3) Knowledge concerning previous tests and treatment may save the needless repetition of procedures which have proved to be of no value. The physician should be certain that such previous measures really were properly carried out for an adequate length of time before considering them to have failed. (4) The patient may be taking medications such as antihistamines and sympathomimetic amines which alter the physical findings and the skin tests. It may be necessary to defer the latter until such medications have been discontinued. (5) It is important to know whether acutely ill patients have received corticosteroids within the past year (page 148).

Collateral Allergy

In addition to the presenting complaint, there may be elicited a history of urticaria, skin eruption, itching, sneezing, rhinitis, eye irritation, intermittent hearing loss, gastrointestinal upsets, wheezing, dyspnea, or cough. It is not uncommon to encounter several apparently allergic symptoms in one patient, although he has not recognized their common basic cause. If any of these collateral allergic symptoms still is

Environmental Survey Sheet*

Major symptom ....

Where employed ....

Doing what .... Past occupation(s) ....

Difference in symptoms between work and home ....

Change in symptoms on vacation .... Geographic location ....

Key:	0 = No symptoms	N.E. = No exposure	+ =	Present, describe symptoms produced

I. Inhalants
   A. Dust
      Symptoms induced by any dust ....   House dust ....
      Home   Suburbs .... Rural ....
         City ....   Tenanted for ....
         Age ....   Basement Dry .... Damp........
         Heating ....
      Bedroom
         Pillow type. .... Age ....   Quilts .... Comforters ....
         Mattress type .... Age ....
         Rug ....   Matting .... Furniture..........
      Living room
         Rug ....   Matting .... Furniture.........
      Anywhere in house where symptoms are worse ....
   B. Molds
      Symptoms around barns ....   Hay ....   Damp basement ....
         Old leaves ....   Lakeside ....   Lawnmowing ....
         Eating cheese, mushrooms, beer ....
   C. Danders
      Symptoms around animals ....
      Pets at home (how long)   Dog ....   Cat ....   Others ....
   D. Miscellaneous

Cosmetics	Chemicals	Newspapers
Perfumes	Paints	Wool
Hair spray	Dentifrice	Kapok
Wave set	Insecticides	Lint

II. Foods
   No suspects .... Suspects .... Previous allergy diets ....
   Wheat (incl. bread) .... $\times$/day   Oranges .... $\times$/wk.   Apricots .... $\times$/wk.
   Oats .... $\times$/wk.   Apples .... $\times$/wk.   Strawberries .... $\times$/wk.
   Rice .... $\times$/wk.   Melons .... $\times$/wk.   Bananas .... $\times$/wk.
   Rye .... $\times$/wk.   Peaches........ $\times$/wk.   Grapefruit .... $\times$/wk.
   Corn .... $\times$/wk.   Pears .... $\times$/wk.   Tomatoes .... $\times$/wk.
   Beans and peas .... $\times$/wk.

Beef .... X/wk.   Potatoes .... X/wk.   Chocolate .... X/wk.
Pork .... X/wk.   Nuts .... X/wk.   Milk .... X/day
Lamb .... X/wk.   Peanuts .... X/wk.   Oleo .... X/day
Fowl .... X/wk.   Coffee .... X/day   Eggs .... X/wk.
Fish .... X/wk.   Tea .... X/day   Soft drinks .... X/wk.

	Breakfast	Lunch	Supper	Bedtime
Typical Diet (list menu)				
Between meal Snacks:				

III. Drugs
Now on medication(s) .... Last dose ....
....
....
Suspects and symptoms: Is allergic to which drug(s) ....
Cross out drugs not used; indicate any suspects and symptoms:

Aspirin	Vitamins	Penicillin
Nose drops	Ointments	Other antibiotics
Nasal spray	Contraceptives	Antihistamines
Eye drops	oral	Tranquilizers
Sedatives	topical	Steroids
Tonics	Sulfa	Cathartics

Others: ....

IV. Immunization
Was patient in military service? ....
   Smallpox   Tetanus   Influenza
   Measles   Poliomyelitis   Pertussis
Other: ....

V. Hobbies
Symptoms from: ....

VI. Physical agents and habits
   Tobacco   Alcohol   Air-conditioning
     Cigarettes .... packs/day   Heat   Muggy weather
       for .... years   Cold   Weather change
     Cigars .... per day
     Pipe .... per day
     Never smoked ....
     Bothered by smoke ....

VII. Contactant reactions

VIII. Photosensitivity reactions

IX. Tension, worry: .... Fatigue: .... Working hours: ....

X. Insect sting reactions (describe in detail):

Survey taken by ....

* This sheet is used as a guide for supplementing the running narrated history. It should not replace the patient's spontaneous history.

causing difficulty, a detailed history should be taken regarding it in a manner similar to that just described for the main complaint.

Past Medical History

A compilation of the patient's past illnesses and general health should be noted, as in any medical evaluation. Hospitalizations and major injuries (especially nasal trauma) should be recorded. Operations are listed, particularly tonsillectomy and adenoidectomy, since some allergists feel that the history of a need for repeated surgical attacks on these tissues suggests an underlying allergic process. Information about previous pneumonitis, chronic bronchitis, and pertussis is germane in patients with chest complaints.

Family History

In addition to the usual questions pertaining to the family in a medical history, one should specifically ask about the occurrence of the atopic diseases in the parents, grandparents, siblings, aunts and uncles, cousins, and children of the patient.

Personal and Social History

The patient's marriage, family life, health of the spouse, and condition of the children should be investigated to a degree depending somewhat upon the earlier course of the interview. The patient's use of liquor, beer, cigarettes, and soft drinks should be ascertained. Nervous tension may have absolutely nothing to do with the allergic symptoms in some patients, whereas in others it may be an important precipitating factor. Very often it is the allergic symptoms that make the patient nervous, and not vice versa. These relationships are discussed at length in Chapter 20.

Systemic Review

A complete systemic history should be taken for every patient examined by the allergist. In this way, important symptoms which may point to other diseases will be uncovered. The following points should be covered:

General—well-being, weight (gain or loss), presence of fever
Head—eyes, ears, nose, throat
Cardiorespiratory system
Gastrointestinal system
Genitourinary system
Menstrual history
Neuromuscular system

Bones and joints
Endocrine glands
Skin

PHYSICAL EXAMINATION

It is necessary for every patient consulting an allergist to have a *complete* physical examination in order to receive good medical care. Many persons who consult a doctor for hay fever remain under his care to receive hyposensitization. Often such patients come to the allergist's office once or twice a week for treatment. That person will feel, correctly or not, that since he is under a doctor's care, he is receiving complete and proper medical attention. The physician must justify this confidence by making certain that he has not overlooked any disease accompanying the allergic problem. The only way to ensure this is to take a careful history and to make a complete physical examination.

The general appearance of the face, particularly in children, may be helpful. In addition to conjunctival redness in hay fever, periorbital swelling may be observed. Bluish coloration may be observed around the eyes, producing the "allergic shiner." Notation should be made regarding whether the patient is a mouth breather. There may be a long face with high cheek bones, pointed chin, narrow, highly arched

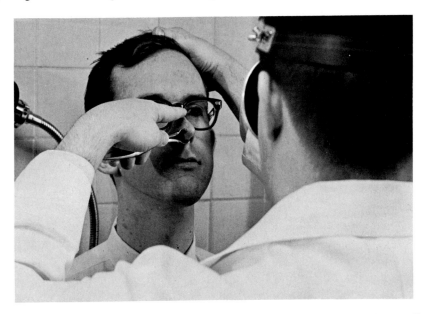

Figure 3–1. Satisfactory intranasal examination is accomplished with adequate illumination and a nasal speculum. The instrument is introduced so that the blades are in superior-inferior position, since touching the septum causes pain. The free hand on top of the head moves the patient in order to get complete visualization of the nasal passages. As the speculum is withdrawn, the blades are left partly open in order not to pull some of the vibrissae.

palate, and marked overbite—the "allergic facies"—denoting chronic upper respiratory tract obstruction. Of course, particular attention will be paid to the more common sites of allergic disease. The nose may be examined most satisfactorily by means of a nasal speculum and head mirror (Figure 3–1), but many of our colleagues prefer the otoscope for examination of the ears and tympanic membranes. It is important to have good exposure with adequate light. It is well to have equipment available to permit transillumination of the paranasal sinuses when indicated. Minimal asthmatic wheezing can often be detected by auscultation of the anterior chest as the patient forcibly exhales while sitting up and leaning slightly forward. The extent of the diaphragmatic excursion may be estimated by percussion on deep inspiration and expiration. Signs of pulmonary emphysema should be noted. Cyanosis, clubbing, or edema of the extremities merit particular attention. Testing for dermographia or hyperventilation may be indicated. Other important points in the physical examination will be stressed in later chapters in connection with the individual allergic diseases.

WORKING DIAGNOSIS

At this stage in the allergic work-up it is usually possible for the physician to record an impression, or working diagnosis. If he feels the disease is probably allergic in origin, it is also well to record an initial impression regarding the most likely causative factors based on history alone. It is of interest, after additional studies have been completed and a final diagnosis made, to look back and see how very often the initial impression based on the history alone will have been correct. The recording of the suspected allergens before skin testing is carried out will stimulate the physician to take a more accurate history, the most essential part of the allergic evaluation.

After a working diagnosis is made, the physician is in a position to decide what laboratory procedures or consultations are indicated. The skin tests and other specific diagnostic procedures are discussed in Chapter 4.

LABORATORY STUDIES

It is assumed that the reader is familiar with the more usual clinical laboratory tests. Therefore, the following discussion is devoted largely to less familiar techniques utilized in measuring pulmonary function. Additional special procedures are discussed in the chapters dealing with the individual diseases.

Urine

The urine of patients with allergic disease shows no unique characteristics. Because of the marked dehydration which may accompany severe asthmatic attacks, the urine may be greatly concentrated, giving it a high specific gravity. If the patient is receiving steroid therapy, glycosuria should be checked for specifically. Proteinuria may indicate the presence of a widespread "connective tissue" disorder such as polyarteritis nodosa which may have wheezing as the presenting symptom. The urine of all patients should be examined routinely in order to help rule out other nonallergic disease.

Stool

Examination of the freshly collected stool may be valuable in cases of unexplained urticaria, particularly if the patient also has a pronounced peripheral blood eosinophilia, because parasitic infestation of the gastrointestinal tract may produce this finding.

Blood Chemistry

There are no known alterations of the usual clinical blood chemistry values found consistently in atopic disease. The serum electrophoretic pattern is normal.

Blood Counts

The differential white blood count in the atopic patient usually is not altered except for the possible presence of eosinophilia. In extrinsic protein sensitivity (pollen or food allergy), one commonly observes 3 to 7 per cent eosinophils in the peripheral blood. If the count ranges from 12 to 20 per cent, an infectious factor is suggested, particularly in asthmatic patients. This elevation of eosinophils may occur in a patient with an otherwise normal white cell count. Eosinophilia much over 25 per cent is not ordinarily seen in the atopic diseases. A higher percentage than this suggests the possibility of an additional diagnosis or, in asthmatic patients, the presence of allergic granulomatous angiitis, or polyarteritis nodosa.*

---

* The allergist is expected to be thoroughly conversant with the various causes of eosinophilia since he is sometimes asked to see patients in whom only this abnormality is found. A relationship with hypersensitivity is obscure or unexplained in many of these conditions. One must consider parasitic infestation, Loeffler's syndrome, or eosinophilic leukemia when the eosinophilia is very high. In addition, one may observe an eosinophilia of varying degree in skin diseases of many types, especially pemphigus and dermatitis herpetiformis; in unrelated infections, such as scarlet fever; in some patients from many types of medications; in certain individuals with sarcoidosis, pernicious anemia, and Hodgkin's disease; in patients convalescing from an acute infection, accompanied by neutrophilia; following irradiation; as a family anomaly, and in "tropical eosinophilia."[20]

Sedimentation Rate

In allergic disease without complication, the sedimentation rate is normal. When the rate is elevated, the test should be repeated, and if it is still abnormal, the physician should re-examine his patient with the idea of looking for a complication.

Roentgenography

A chest roentgenogram should be obtained routinely in all patients with bronchial asthma. In uncomplicated asthma the film usually shows no abnormality. Occasionally one sees small, focal areas of plate-like atelectasis caused by obstruction of the smaller bronchi. The reason for obtaining a chest roentgenogram is to exclude other chest diseases which might not be detectable by physical examination alone. In protracted cases of asthma the chest roentgenogram is likely to show signs of hyper-inflation. This is reflected in an increased translucency of the lung (particularly in the retrosternal space as seen in the lateral projection), broadening of the intercostal spaces, and flattening of the diaphragm.[21] Occasionally there is bullous emphysema. It is important to recognize that the roentgenographic signs are helpful but may be out of proportion to the pulmonary disability as reflected clinically.

Children with allergic symptoms sometimes show symmetrical, thin, transverse lines of density in the long bones which are "growth-arrest lines." This is not specific for allergy but indicates a disturbance in normal growth and is associated with a previous episode of systemic disease.[1] With continued growth of the long bones these symmetrical growth-arrest lines may still be visible and tend to approach the center of the diaphysis of the bone. The density itself is composed of limesalt deposition occurring during a period of decreased growth.

In patients with gastrointestinal allergy, one may observe alterations in the appearance of the small intestine on examination by means of ingested barium. These alterations, when present, are usually quite mild and the appearance has been termed a "sprue-like pattern." This consists of slight thickening of the mucosal folds, and clumping and fragmentation of the barium column. This is believed to be related to the presence of large amounts of intestinal mucus. It is not at all specific and may be seen in a number of conditions (pancreatic disease, parasitic infestation, idiopathic sprue, Whipple's disease, and lymphoma). Intestinal allergy is one of the less common causes. It differs from idiopathic sprue in general in that the radiologic changes tend to be mild. If the offending allergen is added to the barium mixture, more definite alterations of the small bowel pattern can often be demonstrated. In addition, delayed emptying of the stomach, possibly due to pylorospasm, is said to occur under these conditions.[22]

It is important to obtain films of the skeleton in patients receiving steroid therapy since this medication is known to produce osteoporosis. Vertebral compression may occur as a consequence of such osteoporosis. In addition, a number of patients receiving corticosteroids, particularly in large doses and for prolonged periods, may develop aseptic necrosis.[23] This is particularly apt to involve the hips and shoulders, although it has been described in other joints. The development of this complication is not necessarily related to the disease for which the patient is receiving steroid therapy, and occasionally it may develop even after small dosages. It is essential to obtain roentgenograms in patients who suddenly develop joint symptoms while receiving ACTH or corticosteroids.

EVALUATION OF RESPIRATORY FUNCTION

Considerable information concerning respiratory function may be obtained by simple clinical methods. In severe chronic respiratory dysfunction, for example, clubbing of the digits, plethora associated with polycythemia, and cyanosis of the nail beds and mucous membranes may be apparent. Signs of right ventricular hypertrophy and pulmonary hypertension usually denote chronic respiratory insufficiency with hypoxia and hypercapnia, when they are observed in known cases of pulmonary parenchymal disease. In bronchial asthma, however, these signs are rare unless severe and prolonged pulmonary infection has also been present.

When there is significant diffuse bronchial obstruction, expiration is not completed during the normal expiratory interval, and the quantity of air remaining in the alveoli during the succeeding inspiratory effort (functional residual capacity) is increased. If the resulting hyperinflation of the lungs is chronic, the chest tends to remain in an inspiratory position, its anterior-posterior dimension is often enlarged, and cardiac dullness is diminished. In such patients, one can show by percussion that the normal 3 to 5 centimeter respiratory excursion of the diaphragms is decreased, and by use of a tape measure it is seen that the thoracic circumference does not increase normally with inspiration. By palpating the chest with the fingers widely spread, the expansion of corresponding portions of the two hemithoraces may be compared. Large areas of severely underventilated lung tissue may be suggested by this procedure. Auscultation of the chest during hyperpnea is also helpful in revealing localized (or generalized) alveolar hypoventilation. In true pulmonary emphysema, the breath sounds are usually decreased in intensity and do not become significantly louder following nebulization of a bronchodilator. In contrast, where reversible airway obstruction dominates the clinical picture, vesicular breath sounds are often heard well and these tend to become even louder after medication. Of course, in acute asthma the normal breath sounds are typically decreased in proportion to the severity of the airway obstruction, and when bronchial plugging is widespread, the chest may become relatively silent.

Expiratory wheezes are certainly the most familiar physical sign associated with bronchial obstruction. Between acute paroxysms of asthma, wheezes may still be heard in some patients; in others, they can be elicited at the end of a forced expiration, by expiration performed in recumbency, or by expiration while the examiner manually compresses the patient's chest. The presence of residual airway obstruction during symptom-free intervals in asthmatic patients has been confirmed by more formal and quantitative ventilatory tests.[2-3] Incidentally, it is this finding that has prompted us, as well as others, to favor the regular use of oral bronchodilators by asthmatic patients, rather than their use on an ad lib basis.

PULMONARY FUNCTION STUDIES

General Considerations

Quantitative tests of pulmonary function provide useful data which complement the physician's historical review and physical examination. Properly chosen and thoughtfully interpreted, such tests (1) yield insight into the type of functional defect which is associated with respiratory signs and symptoms, (2) indicate the relative severity of such defects, and (3) provide objective means for assessing changes in these abnormalities which may occur with time or be induced by treatment. None of the tests in use at present can indicate unequivocally the pathologic changes associated with a demonstrated functional abnormality, although the specific disease process may often be strongly inferred from comprehensive tests of function. Furthermore, single sets of test values describe conditions at designated points in time only and lack the synoptic quality that history alone provides. In conditions such as bronchial asthma, in which rapid pathophysiologic changes are the rule, this point requires special emphasis. In addition to observations made during episodes of asthma, it is desirable to test patients in their most symptom-free periods to document the best functional performance of which they are capable.

The normal exchange of respiratory gases requires that the alveolar-capillary membrane be permeable and that a requisite volume of pulmonary tissue receive *both* adequate alveolar ventilation and adequate pulmonary capillary blood flow. Thus, both the volume and the distribution patterns of inspired air as well as of perfusing blood are vital factors in determining the normality of lung function. This highly integrated process can be artificially divided into (1) ventilation (which includes the volume of respired air, the dynamics of its movement, and its pattern of intrapulmonary distribution or "mixing"), (2) the transfer of gases across the alveolar-capillary membrane, and (3) the volume and distribution of pulmonary capillary blood flow. Specific procedures have been developed to test each of these aspects of function. However, because these processes are so intimately related, the results of individual tests usually depend on several of the physiologic factors mentioned, although they may reflect one of them most clearly. A practical clinical division separates those studies which are readily performed with simple equipment in the physician's office from those requiring the equipment and facilities of a pulmonary function laboratory. This discussion will necessarily be confined to the first of these categories; several of the more complex laboratory studies are treated briefly on page 52 and details concerning the performance and interpretation of the results of other procedures will be found in references.[4–5] The relatively simple pulmonary function studies described below most readily provide information concerning the volumes of respired air and the dynamic characteristics of its motion. This is fortunate for the allergist since in bronchial asthma these factors, especially the latter, are usually most abnormal.

The Work of Breathing

The energy expended in pulmonary ventilation or "work of breathing" is frequently increased in pulmonary disease and seems to play an important role in the production of dyspnea. In both health and illness, three types of forces determine the magnitude of the work of breathing.[6] The most minor of these, termed "inertial" forces, must be overcome in changing the speed and direction of air movement. "Elastic" forces originating in the chest wall and in pulmonary tissue itself oppose the thoracic volume increase and distention of lungs which occur with inspiration. *Compliance,* expressed as the volume change occurring in response to a given transpulmonary pressure change, provides a measurement of the elasticity or stiffness of the lungs. The third class of forces is usually designated as "flow resistive" and arises from frictional interactions among moving molecules of respired air and between these molecules and the walls of the respiratory tract. The extent of these forces is most closely reflected by *airway resistance* at a given lung volume expressed as the pressure drop associated with a given rate of air flow. Airway resistance is increased by narrowing the air passages and, as expected, is found to be abnormally high in bronchial asthma as well as in pulmonary emphysema, chronic bronchitis, and other entities that involve airway obstruction.

Wells has shown that the work of breathing may be increased to a value that is from 5 to 25 times the normal in asthmatic patients at rest.[7] It is an important feature of uncomplicated asthma that the associated airway obstruction and indices of increased airway resistance are reversible and may be returned to normal by more or less intensive treatment with bronchodilator drugs. By documenting that airway obstruction is relatively fixed or that it is reversible by medication, pulmonary function studies can provide data that have value both in initial diagnosis and in evaluation of the prognosis of well documented asthma.

In addition to such factors as bronchial smooth muscle tone, mucosal vascular permeability, and the presence or absence of secretions in the lumina, bronchial patency varies normally during the respiratory cycle. The elastic pulmonary parenchyma normally exerts an outward pull on large and small air passages. Also, inspiratory pressure within the surrounding parenchyma is normally more negative than that within the bronchi, creating a gradient which tends to distend the air passages. Both of these related factors, which promote bronchial patency, are accentuated during the inspiratory phase as intrapleural (and intra-alveolar) pressure becomes more negative and the pulmonary elastic tissue undergoes greater stretch. Accordingly, airway resistance normally decreases during inspiration and is measurably increased during expiration, being maximal with forced expiration (which minimizes thoracic volume and elevates intrapleural pressure). The assumption of a thoracic position of inspiration, by patients with airway obstruction, may be thought of as providing at least partial compensation for intrinsic narrowing of the bronchi. For similar reasons, a full inspiration can be expected to minimize the physiologic flow-resistive forces opposing a succeeding expiration.

Specific Ventilatory Tests

Since the major defect in asthma is a ventilatory one marked by increased air flow resistance, the greatest impairment is encountered in moving large volumes of air quickly at high rates of flow. Several simple measurements that test this ability to perform with time may be made during maximal forced expiration. Of these, the "timed vital capacity" or "forced expiratory volume" determined in specified time periods (FEV_T) is probably simplest to measure. The vital capacity is that total volume of air which may be expired following a maximal inspiration. The vital capacity is depressed in many disease states marked by loss of functioning lung tissue or by impairment of thoracic motion. If the vital capacity is performed so that expiration is maximally rapid, as well as complete, it is referred to as the forced vital capacity (FVC). This quantity also reflects functioning lung volume and chest wall factors and, in addition, can provide an index of airway patency. Normally expected values for forced vital capacity vary with the height, age, and sex of the subject tested as well as with changes in position. Several published tables and formulae such as those shown in Figures 3–2 and 3–3 indicate normal values for forced vital capacity and timed vital capacity in accord with these variables in adults. Normal values for lung volumes and flow rates in children are also available.[8] To be considered within normal limits, the forced vital capacity should be at least 80 per cent of that predicted for a given subject. Exertional dyspnea is often

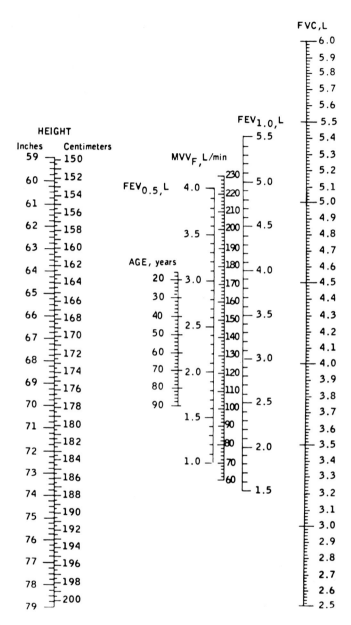

Figure 3–2. Nomogram for prediction of FVC, $FEV_{0.5}$, $FEV_{1.0}$, and MVV from age and height for male adults. A straight edge passing through the patient's height and age, on the appropriate scales, also passes through his predicted normal values for $FEV_{0.5}$, $FEV_{1.0}$, MMV, and FVC on the scales to the right. The predicted values are expressed at 37° C. and fully saturated with water vapor. To compare observed volumes of expired air (saturated with water vapor at approximately 25° C.) with these normal values, the former must be multiplied by the factor 1.075. (From Baum, G. L.: Textbook of Pulmonary Diseases. Little, Brown & Co., Inc. 1965.)

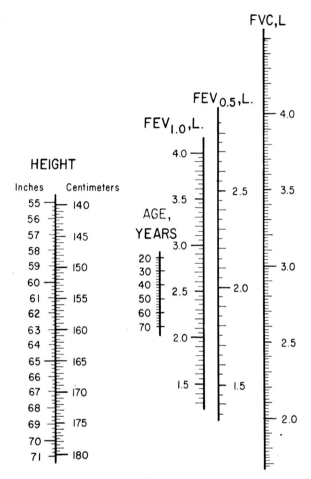

Figure 3–3. Nomogram for prediction of FVC, $FEV_{0.5}$, and $FEV_{1.0}$ in adult women based on studies of 450 normal women ranging in age from 20 to 70 years. To use this figure, lay a straight edge between the points representing the patient's age and height on the age and height scales. Predicted normal values can then be read directly from the points where the straight edge crosses the $FEV_{1.0}$, the $FEV_{0.5}$ and the FVC scales. As noted for Fig. 3–2, observed gas volumes should be multiplied by the factor 1.075 before comparing them with the values predicted by this nomogram. (From Baum, G. L.: Textbook of Pulmonary Diseases. Little, Brown and Company, 1965.)

present when the forced vital capacity has been reduced to 60 per cent of its predicted normal value.

Measurement of the vital capacity (and forced vital capacity) is done with a subject seated comfortably or standing. A cushioned nose clamp may be applied to prevent air leakage although its use is not essential. After as large an inspiration as possible, the patient exhales as rapidly and completely as possible into the recording apparatus. It is desirable to urge the patient to exert maximal effort during the test and to allow him to repeat the procedure two or three times, recording the highest value attained. Unfortunately, when airway obstruction is great, a single forced expiration may cause paroxysms of cough or severe

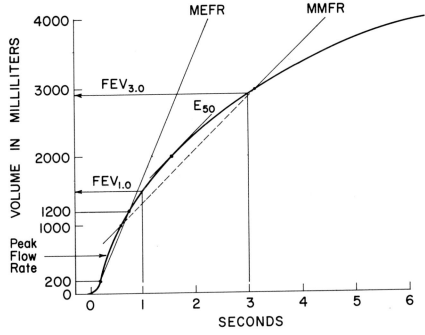

Figure 3–4. The forced expiratory spirogram in moderately severe airway obstruction. Although the total volume is in a normal range for many adults, six seconds are required for complete expiration. Accordingly, the $FEV_{1.0}$ of 1500 cc. and $FEV_{3.0}$ of 2910 cc. constitute, respectively, 38 per cent and 73 per cent of the total and are definitely below normal. In this example, approximate values for the MEFR and MMFR are 109 liters/minute and 47 liters/minute. The E_{50} is proportional to the slope of the curve just at the 2000 cc. volume point.

bronchospasm which preclude further testing. In severe asthma with bronchial plugging, the forced vital capacity may be low, and intrapulmonary gas mixing is commonly impaired. Frequently, however, the asthmatic has a relatively normal forced vital capacity; yet he requires not the normal two or three seconds for his complete expiration, but up to ten or more seconds. The timed vital capacity (see Figure 3–4) is usually determined for one second after the onset of expiration ($FEV_{1.0}$), for two seconds ($FEV_{2.0}$), and for three seconds ($FEV_{3.0}$); normally these volumes should be at least 84, 93, and 97 per cent, respectively, of the forced vital capacity. Less commonly, $FEV_{0.5}$ and $FEV_{0.75}$ are measured.

The timed vital capacity may be determined with a variety of instruments, of which one of the simplest is the Collins timed Vitalometer.* This is a water-sealed spirometer with a volume dial from which the total vital capacity and a timed vital capacity may be directly read. The time interval for the latter may be set at 0.5, 0.75, 1, 2, or 3 seconds. Other available devices provide a written record of the forced vital

* Further information and price quotations may be obtained from Warren E. Collins, Inc., 220 Wood Rd., Braintree, Massachusetts 02184.

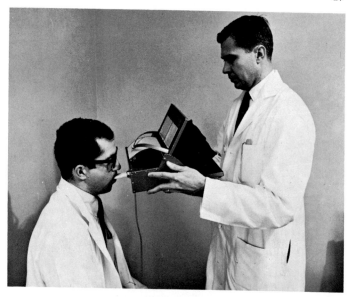

Figure 3–5. Use of the McKesson Vitalor to record the forced vital capacity. The written record permits calculation of timed vital capacity as well as of the MEFR and MMFR, which provide objective evidence of the severity of airway obstruction.

capacity from which the timed vital capacity for any chosen interval may be measured. The McKesson Vitalor,* which uses a bellows and writing point, has been widely used to follow the clinical progress of asthmatic patients (Figure 3–5).[9] It is light in weight and well suited to frequent interval measurements at the bedside, but its higher resistance and maximal capacity of 5 liters limit its value as a precise research instrument. The Jones Pulmonor,† a waterless spirometer, also has been satisfactory, but is decidedly less portable than the McKesson Vitalor. For many years, the 9 and 13.5 liter Collins recording respirometers have proved to be both satisfactory and versatile, allowing measurement not only of the forced expiratory volumes but also of maximal voluntary ventilation (MVV).‡ In addition, these spirometers permit the continuous recording of tidal breathing and the determination of inspiratory as well as expiratory flow rates.

The written record obtained with each of these devices can also be used to determine flow rates (volume/unit time) achieved at various points during forced expiration.§ Of the many flow rate determinations proposed, the maximal expiratory flow rate (MEFR) and maximal mid-

---

* This instrument is supplied by The McKesson Appliance Company, Toledo, Ohio.

† The Jones Pulmonor is manufactured by the Jones Medical Instrument Co., 3215 Honore Street, Chicago 12, Illinois, which may be contacted for additional details.

‡ Studies involving rapid movement of air require that the CO_2 absorbing cannister be removed from these instruments.

§ Several devices allow flow rates to be read directly from the tracings by the use of calibrated protractors.

expiratory flow rate (MMFR) have been studied most widely (Figure 3–4).

The maximal expiratory flow rate is calculated by measuring the time interval required to expire the liter of air between 200 and 1200 milliliters; the maximal midexpiratory flow rate, introduced by Leuallen and Fowler, is obtained by determining the time required to expire between 25 and 75 per cent of the forced vital capacity and dividing FVC/2 by this interval in minutes.[10] Normal values for men and women of different ages have been presented by these authors. The instantaneous air flow rate at the mid-volume point of the forced vital capacity is referred to as the E_{50}; although it is a useful variable, its accurate calculation requires that flow rate and volume be determined separately, necessitating a more complex apparatus than that described previously. One additional quantity, the peak flow rate, deserves mention. This is the flow rate at the steepest point of the expiratory spirogram and is measured by the Peak Flow Meter, a compact anemometer developed by Wright and McKerrow.[11] Measurements obtained by this method tend to show a greater variability than those of other single breath tests. Therefore, peak flow determinations are not generally regarded as a substitute for more conventional techniques reflecting airway obstruction. The peak flow meter was developed for survey work in the field, an application for which it is well suited by virtue of its small size and independence of external power sources. An even simpler but crude test of marked airway obstruction is the so-called Snider Match Test, in which a person's capacity to blow out a lighted match held 6 inches from his mouth, without pursing his lips, is assayed.[12] Failure to extinguish a match in this way has been correlated with a one second vital capacity usually less than 1200 milliliters in adults.

To document the presence of marked airway obstruction, any of the previously described single breath tests, in which performance is related to time, may be used satisfactorily. However, when more modest changes must be indicated, such as may occur in bronchial provocative testing (see page 68), the extent to which each of these methods reflects actual changes in airway resistance, as measured precisely by the body plethysmograph, merits consideration. Although available evidence has not established the superiority of any one single breath test, some pertinent generalizations can be made. It has been noted that bronchial patency is greatest at the end of inspiration and declines during expiration as lung volume decreases (page 46). In fact, during the latter half or two-thirds of forced expiration in a subject, the lung volume determines the maximal attainable air flow rate at any point. Conversely, in early expiration the attainable flow rate at a given lung volume is distinctly related to the effort of the subject. Since effort is difficult to standardize, tests related to the earlier portion of the forced vital capacity (e.g., $FEV_{0.5}$, peak flow rate, MEFR) may be expected to show greater variability than those which are based on less effort-dependent portions of expiration (MMFR, E_{50}, and FEV_{10}). Use of the maximal midexpiratory flow rate requires that expiration be especially complete; if it is not, the maximal midexpiratory flow rate will be calculated on an erroneously early and steep portion of the expiratory curve and will be falsely high. A requirement for marked effort and cooperation by subjects has also been a drawback in the use of the maximal voluntary ventilation (MVV) or maximal breathing capacity as an index of airway obstruction. To perform the test, the subject hyperventilates maximally for 15 seconds using his own individual breathing pattern, and the volume of air moved is measured and expressed in liters/minute. For repetitive measurements, this procedure can prove to be exhausting even to the most fit and cooperative of patients.

Critical studies comparing available methods for calculating changes in airway patency are definitely needed. In one such report in which airway obstruction was induced in trained subjects, results using the maximal midexpiratory flow rate, E_{50}, and maximal voluntary ventilation were most closely correlated with changes in airway resistance measured by the body plethysmograph.[13] At present, the $FEV_{1.0}$ and the maximal midexpiratory flow rate are simple measurements which we feel to be most useful.

When the previously described ventilatory tests are abnormal, it is often helpful to repeat them 10 to 20 minutes following subcutaneous injection of epinephrine or administration of a nebulized bronchodilator. The relative improvement induced by such medication is evidence of the extent to which the patient's airway obstruction was reversible, a matter of importance in differential diagnosis and in consideration of prognosis. In addition, the proper evaluation and management of certain patients will require more complex testing procedures available in the pulmonary function laboratory.[4-5] Bronchial obstruction is frequently associated with a marked nonuniformity in the filling and emptying of portions of the lungs, and such impairment of gas "mixing" has been shown to persist in localized areas of the lungs of some asthmatic patients for many months.[5] Early abnormalities in intrapulmonary gas distribution are often best revealed by a single breath oxygen test, which requires minimal effort on the part of the patient.[14] Especially when dyspnea is associated more with exertion than with spontaneous episodes of airway obstruction, a defect in gas diffusion should be suspected. Most procedures that evaluate this function use carbon monoxide as a test gas, and each one is more or less influenced by the abnormal relationship between alveolar ventilation and pulmonary capillary flow that exists in disease involving airway obstruction. When such nonuniformity in ventilation and perfusion exists, steady-state carbon monoxide methods or the rebreathing technique of Lewis and others[15] seem to offer advantages over determinations based upon a single breath.

In bronchial asthma, the diffusing capacity calculated by the former methods is usually normal, whereas in patients with pulmonary emphysema, low values are frequently recorded which increase only minimally with exercise and fail to improve following administration of bronchodilators. However, it is doubtful whether the diffusing capacity alone can be relied on in the majority of patients as a diagnostic test of the presence of emphysema.

The importance of determinations of arterial pO_2 and pCO_2 in the management of patients with respiratory failure is discussed in Chapter 8. Such measurements and the effects upon them of exercise and inhalation of 100 per cent oxygen are also valuable in defining vascular shunts and a number of pulmonary abnormalities including arterial emboli. In treating severely ill asthmatic patients, arterial blood pH determinations are of additional value, since metabolic as well as respiratory acidosis may occur in these patients. The measurement of pH and pCO_2 may be conveniently performed using the micro-Astrup apparatus.[16] Very small blood samples are required for determinations by this technique, and results based upon "arterialized capillary blood" can reasonably be substituted for those from arterial samples. Alternatively, the arterial pCO_2 may be determined using a carbon dioxide electrode[17] while a separate, accurate measurement of pH is made. Direct assessment of pO_2 in blood, using the electrode of Clark, has been described.[17] This information is distinctly more valuable in following severely ill patients than are determinations of blood oxygen saturation obtained by oximetry.

TESTS OF NASAL FUNCTION

Although means have been described for measuring changes in nasal patency, these techniques have not been adapted for widespread clinical use.[18-19] Furthermore, simple procedures, such as those involving the size of condensation patterns on cooled surfaces, have not lent themselves to sequential measurements although they provide an objective comparison of the right and left nasal airways at one point in time. All attempts to derive measurements related to nasal patency must take into account the high resistance and irregular contour of the upper airway as well as the remarkable effort dependency of all variables that involve forced nasal respiration. Furthermore, insertion of testing devices into the nose is likely to produce large experimental artifacts.

REFERENCES

1. Caffey, J.: Transverse Lines. *In* Section V, The Extremities. Pediatric X-Ray Diagnosis. 4th ed. Chicago, Year Book Publishers, Inc., 1961.
2. Beale, H. D., et al.: Pulmonary function studies in 20 asthmatic patients in the symptom-free interval. J. Allergy 23:1, 1952.

3. Kraepelien, S.: Respiratory studies in children. VII. A longitudinal study of the lung volumes in asthmatic children during symptom-free periods. Acta Pediat. *48*:355, 1959.

4. Comroe, J. H., et al.: The Lung: Clinical Physiology and Pulmonary Function Tests. 2nd ed. Chicago, Year Book Medical Publishers, Inc., 1962.

5. Bates, D. V., and Christie, R. V.: Respiratory Function in Disease. Philadelphia, W. B. Saunders Co., 1964.

6. Meade, J.: Mechanical properties of lungs. Physiol. Rev. *41*:315, 1961.

7. Wells, R. E.: Mechanics of respiration in bronchial asthma. Am. J. Med. *26*:384, 1959.

8. DeMuth, G. R., Howatt, W. F., and Hill, B. M.: The growth of lung function. Pediatrics (Suppl.) *35*:161, 1965.

9. McKerrow, C. B.: The McKesson Vitalor. J.A.M.A. *177*:865, 1961.

10. Leuallen, E. C., and Fowler, W. S.: Maximal mid-expiratory flow. Am. Rev. Tuberc. *72*:783, 1955.

11. Wright, B. M., and McKerrow, C. B.: Maximum forced expiratory flow rate as a measure of ventilatory capacity. Brit. M. J. *2*:104, 1959.

12. Barry, C. T.: The Snider Match Test. Lancet *2*:964, 1962.

13. Lloyd, J. C., and Wright, G. W.: Evaluation of methods used in detecting changes of airway resistance in man. Am. Rev. Resp. Dis. *87*:529, 1963.

14. Comroe, J. H., Jr., and Fowler, W. S.: Lung function studies. VI. Detection of uneven alveolar ventilation during a single breath of oxygen; a new test of pulmonary disease. Am. J. Med. *10*:408, 1951.

15. Lewis, B. M., et al.: Effect of uneven ventilation on pulmonary diffusing capacity. J. Appl. Physiol. *16*:679, 1961.

16. Astrup, P., et al.: Acid-base metabolism. A new approach. Lancet *1*:1035, 1960.

17. Severinghaus, J. W., and Bradley, A. F.: Electrodes for blood pO_2 and pCO_2 determination. J. Appl. Physiol. *13*:515, 1958.

18. Seebohm, P. M., and Hamilton, W. K.: A method for measuring nasal resistance without intranasal instrumentation. J. Allergy *29*:56, 1958.

19. Solomon, W. R., et al.: Measurement of nasal airway resistance. J. Allergy *36*:62, 1965.

20. Wintrobe, M. M.: Clinical Hematology. 5th ed. Philadelphia, Lea & Febiger, 1958, p. 257.

21. Lillington, G. A., and Jamplis, R. W.: Bilateral Hypertranslucency. Chapter 14. *In* A Diagnostic Approach to Chest Diseases. Baltimore, Williams and Wilkins Co., 1965.

22. Singleton, E. B.: Functional Disorders. *In* Chapter 12, Acquired Lesions of Small Intestine. X-Ray Diagnosis of the Alimentary Tract in Infants and Children. Chicago, Year Book Publishers, Inc., 1959.

23. Burrows, F. G. O.: Avascular necrosis of bone complicating steroid therapy. Brit. J. Radiol. *38*:309, 1965.

Chapter Four

SKIN TESTING
AND OTHER
DIAGNOSTIC
PROCEDURES

NEAL A. VANSELOW, M.D.

Special diagnostic procedures may be of great help in evaluation of the allergic patient. It may be safely said, however, that no single test procedure by itself is able to provide a final diagnosis. This pertains both to studies directed toward establishing whether or not allergy is present and to those designed to determine the cause of allergic reactions. The interpretation of these tests, including skin tests, without a thorough knowledge of the patient on whom they were performed may not only cause confusion but may actually be misleading. It is axiomatic in clinical allergy that skin tests and other special studies can be interpreted only in the light of the information obtained by a careful history and physical examination.

Several procedures of importance in clinical allergy will be discussed in this chapter: skin testing, ophthalmic testing, passive transfer techniques, inhalation (provocative) challenge, and examination of nasal secretions. Pulmonary function studies (Chapter 3) and patch testing (Chapter 12) are discussed elsewhere. A number of other laboratory procedures, such as the measurement of histamine release from white blood cells, tissue culture techniques, and the use of monkey ileum and primate skin for the demonstration of reagin, are experimental at present and, therefore, beyond the scope of this discussion.

SKIN TESTING

Scratch and intradermal tests are used to detect the presence of atopic reagin in skin. An aqueous solution of antigen is prepared by extracting the appropriate allergenic material (pollen, food, mold, house dust, and other materials) with buffered saline (page 510). When properly prepared and sterilized, this material is introduced into the patient's skin by one of a variety of methods. If skin-bound reaginic antibody capable of reacting specifically with the antigen is present, the ensuing antigen-antibody reaction results in the release of mediator substances, of which histamine is felt to be most important. The release of mediators in turn results in local vasodilatation and an increase in vascular permeability. Clinically, this reaction is manifest as a wheal and flare response at the site of the test. The reaction develops rapidly and is read in 20 minutes. It can be at least partially inhibited by the systemic or aerosol administration of sympathomimetic amines or by the systemic administration of antihistamines, theophylline derivatives, and hydroxyzine (Atarax). For this reason, these drugs must be omitted for at least eight hours prior to skin testing. Adrenal corticosteroids, or ACTH, when given systemically, do not affect immediate skin reactivity and need not be discontinued prior to skin testing.

Prick or Scratch Testing

Prick or scratch tests are performed by placing a drop of an aqueous solution of allergen on the patient's skin and pricking or scratching the skin through the drop. This procedure allows a small amount of allergen to penetrate the skin and react with reagin. These tests are usually done on the back of the patient while he is in the prone position. If extreme sensitivity to the allergen is expected, however, it is advisable to perform them on the volar surface of the forearm. The latter procedure allows a tourniquet to be placed proximal to the test site should a systemic reaction ensue, thus slowing further systemic absorption of the allergen.

Because of the comparative insensitivity to allergens applied in the prick or scratch test, relatively concentrated allergenic extracts are used. It is not uncommon to test with aqueous extracts of inhalant allergens as concentrated as 1:5 or aqueous food extracts as concentrated as 2:1. The aqueous test extracts, which contain equal parts of glycerine, are stored in small dropper bottles and kept refrigerated when not in use. It is most convenient to keep the dropper bottles in wooden or plastic racks, each row in the rack corresponding to a row of tests on the patient's back (Figure 4–1).

The patient should be placed in a comfortable position prior to testing. If tests are to be placed on the back, the patient strips to the waist and lies prone on a comfortable table. A sheet or towel is tucked in at the belt line to protect the clothing. The skin is cleansed with an alcohol-soaked cotton ball and air-dried. Small drops of test antigens and a drop of glycerosaline to serve as a control are then

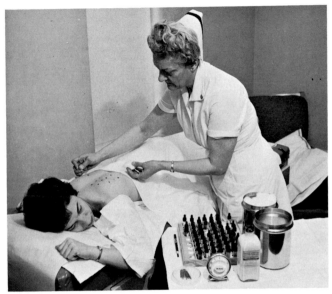

Figure 4–1. Prick test equipment. The patient lies prone on an examining table and the test extracts are placed on the back. Prick test equipment includes: rack with dropper bottles containing test extracts, sterile dry cotton balls and alcohol sponges in metal canisters, calamine lotion for application to the patient's back after tests are completed, photographic timer, sterile darning needles in sterile Petri dish, and skin-marking pencils.

placed on the back.* The drops are usually arranged in rows beginning in the upper dorsal area and running toward the lumbar region. It is not advisable to place more than seven to ten drops in a row, for if large reactions are encountered, the adjacent areas of erythema and whealing may coalesce, making interpretation of individual tests difficult. Similarly, the rows should be spaced at least 4 cm. apart. The use of a marking pencil to indicate the location of the drops is helpful. When all the tests are placed, the skin beneath each is punctured (prick test) or lightly scratched for two millimeters (scratch test). A sharp darning needle is used for prick testing and this or a scalpel blade is employed for scratch tests.† The procedure should be done gently so as to abrade the skin but not to draw blood (Figure 4–2). The needle or blade is wiped with an alcohol sponge after each prick or scratch. Either the scratch or the prick technique is satisfactory, but the latter

---

* In patients who have shown no positive skin test reactions in spite of a history suggesting extrinsic allergic factors, it is sometimes desirable to obtain a positive control test. This can be done by doing a prick test with histamine acid phosphate 1:1000 (with 50 per cent glycerine) or by performing intracutaneous tests with nonglycerinated histamine acid phosphate 1:10,000 and with a histamine-releaser such as morphine sulphate, 0.1 mg./ml.

† Other types of instruments may be used to puncture the skin when doing prick or scratch tests (e.g., circular scarifiers, Sterneedle apparatus, and others) depending upon the preference of the physician.

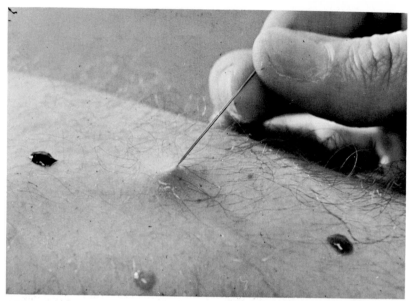

Figure 4–2. Prick test technique. A drop of each allergenic extract is placed on the test site (in this case, the forearm) after it has been cleansed with alcohol. The skin is then pricked through each drop of extract with a sterile darning needle. As illustrated, the needle is directed so that it raises the skin slightly as it punctures the epidermis.

has advantages of greater speed, less pain, and less risk of producing small scars.

Prick tests should be done only on the order of a physician, and a physician should be available while the testing is being done. The patient must be carefully observed following placement of the tests. Although the tests are usually read in 20 minutes, sensitive patients may develop large whealing reactions before that time. When this happens, the involved test sites should be wiped free of allergen with an alcohol sponge.

It is convenient to measure the 20 minute interval for reading the tests with a photographic timer. The reactions should be read through the drops of allergen and re-examined after gently wiping off the extract with a cotton sponge. The tests can be accurately interpreted only when the saline control site shows a negative reaction. If the control is positive, as in the case of dermatographism, the degree of reactivity at the control site should be noted. The other tests may be read and recorded, but interpretation of test results is difficult.

The criteria we use for the interpretation of prick or scratch tests are listed in Table 4–1. It should be noted that these are arbitrary and differ in some respects from those used by others. Pseudopods less than one millimeter in length are ignored when the tests are read. Since 4+ reactions can vary greatly in size, the wheals associated with them should be drawn as accurately as possible on the recording sheet. A similar procedure is followed for all 3+ reactions in which the wheal is larger than ten millimeters in diameter. This permits a more quantitative estimation of skin reactivity than does simple recording of the tests as 1+ to 4+.

When the prick tests have been read, the testing surface is wiped free of allergen with alcohol. Test results should be reviewed by a physician and a decision made regarding the need for intracutaneous (I.C.) tests. Although intracutaneous tests are often performed on the same day as prick tests, the presence of many large prick reactions may make this procedure inadvisable. Under these circumstances, the patient should be instructed to return on another day for completion of his tests.

The major disadvantage of the prick or scratch test method is its relative lack of sensitivity. Intracutaneous tests are much more sensitive and, not uncommonly, 3+ or 4+ reactions are encountered by the intracutaneous method when prick or scratch tests have been negative. For this reason, skin sensitivity to an allergen cannot be ruled out on the basis of a negative prick or scratch test alone. This disadvantage is balanced by a number of advantages which have made these tests widely used as the initial skin test of choice.

The first major advantage of this method is its safety. Because of minimal systemic absorption of allergen, constitutional reactions from prick or scratch tests are extremely rare. In addition, these tests can be performed rapidly with little discomfort to the patient. This is particularly important in the pediatric age group. It is also feasible to perform a relatively large number of tests simultaneously, an important advantage in evaluating patients who live at a distance. Finally, nonspecific inflammatory or "irritant" reactions seldom occur with prick or scratch tests, and erythema or whealing can usually be regarded as truly indicative of the presence of reagin in the patient's skin.

Intracutaneous Testing

Intracutaneous (I.C.) tests are performed by injecting a small amount of aqueous solution of allergen into the epidermis of the test subject. We use intracutaneous testing to supplement prick tests. Intra-

Table 4-1. Criteria Used to Read Prick or Scratch Tests

Reaction	Symbol	Criteria
Negative	—	No reaction or no different from control
One plus	+	Erythema smaller than a nickel in diameter (21 mm.)
Two plus	++	Erythema larger than a nickel in diameter with no wheal
Three plus	+++	Wheal with surrounding erythema
Four plus	++++	Wheal with pseudopods and surrounding erythema

cutaneous tests are both more sensitive and more dangerous than prick tests, and thus they are indicated only in those cases in which the prick test reaction to a suspected allergen is negative or weakly positive.* *Intracutaneous tests should not be performed with an allergen which has evoked a 2+ or greater prick reaction in the test subject, since* one can confidently assume that the intracutaneous test will be strongly positive and may result in a large local or systemic reaction.

Prior to intracutaneous testing, the subject omits all drugs which could influence the test result (see page 56). The tests may be done on the back of the subject while he is in the prone position but preferably are done on the arm or the volar surface of the forearm with the subject seated. The latter two sites are more desirable because it is feasible for a tourniquet to be placed proximal to the test site should a systemic allergic reaction ensue.

The allergenic extracts used for intracutaneous testing are similar to those used in prick testing but, because of the increased sensitivity of the intracutaneous method, are more dilute (e.g., 1:500 or 1:5000).† In addition, concentrations of glycerin beyond 5 per cent should be avoided or else false-positive reactions may result. Intracutaneous extracts are stored in sterile rubber-stoppered bottles which may be kept upright in wooden or plastic racks. Extracts should be refrigerated when not in use. Prior to testing, 0.02 to 0.07 ml. of each allergen to be used in testing is drawn into a separate 0.5 or 1.0 ml. glass tuberculin syringe. Care must be taken to ensure that the syringes are meticulously cleaned after each use to avoid contamination with previously used allergens. They should be autoclaved for adequate sterilization. It is best to mark the syringes in such a way that the same syringe is always used to inject the same allergen. Although adequate disposable syringes may become available in the future, those currently obtainable at reasonable cost are unsatisfactory because they do not deliver small volumes smoothly, are not marked off in 0.01 ml. gradations, and tend to trap small air bubbles, making it difficult or impossible to deliver 0.02 ml. accurately. On the other hand, disposable short 26 gauge needles are more desirable than the nondisposable type, since the latter becomes dull with repeated use.

The test sites are marked with a skin pencil and the area wiped with a cotton ball soaked in alcohol. Individual sites are placed at least 5 cm. apart. At each site 0.02 ml. of allergenic extract is injected, and a control site is injected with saline (Figure 4–3). It is important to make each wheal approximately equal in size. The patient should be

---

* Some allergists routinely use the intracutaneous test without prior scratch or prick testing. This procedure may be safe in experienced hands but only if relatively weak dilutions of extract are initially used.[1]

† The intracutaneous testing concentrations recommended in this manual are based on the assumption that preliminary scratch or prick tests have been done.

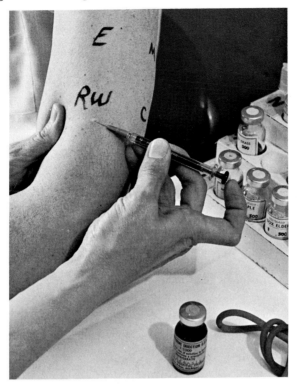

Figure 4–3. Intracutaneous test technique. A quantity of 0.02 ml. of each test extract is injected into the skin of the upper arm using a 0.5 ml. glass tuberculin syringe and a 26 gauge disposable needle. Aqueous epinephrine 1:1000 and a tourniquet are kept available in case a systemic allergic reaction should occur.

kept under observation and the tests read in 20 minutes. One set of criteria for interpretation of test results is listed in Table 4–2.*

The intracutaneous test is decidedly more sensitive than any other skin test available to the allergist. The advantage which its sensitivity offers must be balanced against a number of disadvantages. Intracutaneous tests are more difficult and tedious to perform than prick tests and cause more discomfort to the patient. In addition, they are more difficult to interpret accurately. Nonspecific inflammatory reactions produced by irritating test materials or poor testing technique are rarely encountered in prick testing but are not at all uncommon when the intracutaneous method is used. Such reactions are frequent when intracutaneous tests are performed with allergens such as house dust, feathers, and molds. These irritant reactions may mislead and confuse the physician, particularly if the history and physical findings are equivocal, and

---

* Physicians who perform only intracutaneous tests often employ more stringent criteria for grading these reactions. Having screened out the most sensitive patients by prick testing, we rarely see such large intracutaneous test reactions as are often required for a 3+ or 4+ reading by the criteria of others.

Table 4–2. *Criteria Used to Read Intracutaneous Tests*

Reaction	Symbol	Criteria
	1. When control wheal is 2 mm. or more in diameter	
Negative	−	No different from control
Plus-minus	±	Wheal 1½ to 2 times control wheal size without definite erythema; or erythema larger than control erythema but smaller than nickel (21 mm.) in size without wheal significantly larger than control
One-plus	+	Wheal 1½ to 2 times control wheal size with definite erythema; or erythema larger than nickel (21 mm.) in size without wheal significantly larger than control
Two-plus	++	Wheal 2 to 3 times control wheal size, disregarding erythema
Three-plus	+++	Wheal over 3 times control wheal size, disregarding erythema
Four-plus	++++	Wheal with pseudopods and erythema
	2. When control wheal is less than 2 mm. in diameter	
Negative	−	No different from control
Plus-minus	±	3 to 4 mm. wheal without erythema; or erythema definitely larger than control but smaller than a nickel in size (21 mm.) without significant wheal
One-plus	+	3 to 4 mm. wheal with erythema; or erythema larger than nickel in size (21 mm.) without significant wheal
Two-plus	++	4 to 8 mm. wheal without pseudopods, disregarding erythema
Three-plus	+++	Over 8 mm. wheal without pseudopods, disregarding erythema
Four-plus	++++	Wheal with pseudopods and erythema

may result in an unwarranted decision to institute specific hyposensitization. As previously discussed, intracutaneous tests may also be more hazardous than prick tests. Severe reactions to intracutaneous testing must be treated by placement of a tourniquet proximal to the test site and by systemic administration of drugs such as epinephrine and antihistamines (see page 118).

Selection of Skin Tests. Decisions regarding the advisability of skin testing and what skin tests to perform should always be made by a physician familiar with the clinical aspects of the case in question. In general, skin testing is indicated in patients having allergic rhinitis or bronchial asthma. Even in asthmatic patients whose attacks are brought on largely by infection, one set of skin tests is justified, since it is very common for both infection and extrinsic factors to cause difficulty in the same patient (page 95). The more limited usefulness of skin tests in urticaria and atopic dermatitis is discussed in Chapter 11.

On pages 74 and 75 a group of skin tests is listed, which we carry out whenever a fairly complete skin test survey is indicated. These tests include most common foods as well as the major inhalant allergens important in the midwestern and northeastern United States. Food and inhalant allergens of lesser importance and those encountered primarily in other sections of the United States are listed on a supplementary sheet (page 76). Prick test results are recorded in the left-hand column and intracutaneous test results in the right-hand column. It should be noted that no space is provided on the food test sheet for the recording of intracutaneous test results to groups F, G, and H. This is because most of these materials are extremely potent allergens, and intracutaneous testing with them is considered dangerous.

The number and variety of scratch tests ordered should be based upon the merits of the particular case in question. For patients with significant perennial symptoms or a confusing clinical picture, it is sometimes advisable to perform prick tests with the entire group of food and inhalant allergens listed on pages 74 and 75 (not including the supplementary group). Such a procedure may be helpful in pointing out potential sources of trouble which may then be re-evaluated by careful questioning or by observing the patient's clinical response following exposure to or withdrawal of the suspected allergen. When "complete" prick tests are indicated in small children, the tests should be apportioned over several visits.

In the majority of allergic children and adults, satisfactory information can be obtained by doing a smaller number of tests, often less than 30. This is referred to as "selective testing." The patient with seasonal allergic rhinitis between August 15 and September 30, for example, will seldom benefit from a complete series of tests. In such a circumstance all the necessary information can be obtained by scratch testing with ragweed and a few other representative allergens chosen for comparison or future reference.

The physician selects the desired intracutaneous tests from among those allergens giving negative or equivocal results on scratch testing. Because of the dangers inherent in the injection of large numbers of potential allergens and the relative discomfort to the patient produced by intracutaneous tests, it is customary to limit the number performed at any one visit to not more than 20 or 25. Intracutaneous tests with pollens and molds may be done with individual allergens or with test material which contains a mixture of allergens, such as mixed grasses, mixed weeds, mixed trees, and mixed fungi (page 531). Testing with mixtures of this type reduces the number of injections required, an advantage appreciated particularly by pediatric patients.

Attempting to reduce the number of injections by preliminary tests with mixtures of *unrelated* allergens is not recommended. Since each component of a mixture is diluted by the other ingredients, one may miss hypersensitivity to individual components when testing by this method. If the reaction to the mixture is positive, the individual specificity of the patient's allergy is obscured. Only very closely related allergens such as the common northern grass pollens or the ragweed family of weeds are entirely suitable for testing in mixtures. If the patient has a 2+ or greater scratch reaction to one or more of the allergens contained in the mixture, intracutaneous testing with the mixture is both unnecessary and potentially hazardous.

It is sometimes desirable to skin test the patient with allergens not included in the routine test battery. One occasionally encounters a patient with historical evidence of sensitivity to house dust in whom skin tests with stock house dust extracts are negative or only weakly positive. In such circumstances, the patient should be instructed to collect house dust samples from home, since the allergenicity of this material, to which he is frequently exposed, may differ significantly from that of the stock test material. "Autogenous" house dust samples may be collected from the vacuum cleaner bag or by inserting a small piece of cloth over the end of the pipe leading to the bag and vacuuming potential dust sources, such as mattresses and stuffed chairs, with vacuum cleaner attachments. Dust particles impinged on the cloth are then placed in an envelope. Autogenous extracts are prepared by placing each dust sample in a separate vial and adding enough phenolated buffered saline (page 51) to bring the mixture to a soupy consistency. Prick tests performed with this material are sometimes positive, thus providing a valuable clue in an otherwise puzzling situation. Scratch tests with extracts of animal danders, mold culture plates, or other unusual substances brought in by the patient may at times be of similar value. When testing with such materials, control tests should be performed on normal persons.

Interpretation of Skin Test Results. The interpretation of skin test results is not an easy task. The problems faced by the physician who uses this diagnostic procedure can be summed up as follows: A positive skin test to an allergen is not necessarily indicative of clinical sensitivity to that substance; and, conversely, a negative skin test to an allergen does not necessarily rule out clinical sensitivity to the material in question. In order to interpret skin test results correctly, the physician must be thoroughly familiar both with the patient on whom the skin tests were done and with the materials and procedures used in the skin testing.

False-negative skin test reactions can occur when improperly prepared or outdated extracts are used for testing. Some allergenic extracts rapidly lose their potency with storage, resulting in loss of ability to elicit skin test reactions. In our experience aqueous extracts of some fruits, for example, seldom elicit positive scratch test reactions in patients with unequivocal clinical evidence of urticaria or gastrointestinal allergy following their ingestion. If one tests the same patient with fresh juice, however, a positive reaction is often obtained.* False-positive skin test reactions can result when testing with extracts which contain nonspecific irritants. Poor technique, including the injection of an excessive volume of extract, can result in mechanical irritation of the

---

* When fresh foods are not available, fresh extracts of frozen foods have been found to be reactive in most cases.

skin and false-positive tests. Other factors which may influence skin test reactions probably include the mast cell content of the skin, old age in some patients, heavy melanin pigmentation, skin temperature, local blood flow at the test site, and the integrity of the autonomic innervation of cutaneous vessels. These in part account for the fact that some patients give more pronounced skin test reactions than others.

Aside from these local factors, there is no necessary correlation between the presence or absence of specific antibodies fixed to the patient's skin and his clinical reactivity to the corresponding allergen. This may be because antibodies are not always fixed in both the patient's skin and the allergic shock organ or because additional factors besides the presence of skin-sensitizing antibodies may be requisite for the development of clinical reactivity. Whatever the explanation for these discrepancies, a thorough knowledge of the history and physical findings is essential to the proper interpretation of skin test results. In the case of inhalant allergens, the combination of a positive skin test with clinical evidence of sensitivity obtained by history or physical examination is usually sufficient to incriminate an allergen as playing a significant etiologic role in the production of symptoms. Similarly, the combination of a negative skin test with a negative history strongly suggests that the allergen in question is not clinically significant. The major difficulty occurs when there is a discrepancy between skin test and clinical findings or when the history is vague. If the skin test is positive and the history is negative, the patient should be questioned again or re-examined during a period of maximal exposure to the inhalant agent. If there is still no clinical evidence of sensitivity, the positive skin test should be ignored. It may be regarded as a mere relic of past sensitivity which has disappeared, or perhaps as a herald of clinical sensitivity at some future date. If the skin test is negative in the face of a history which remains very suggestive after re-questioning the patient, provocative challenge with the allergen under consideration may be indicated to resolve the discrepancy (page 68).

The difficulties encountered in the interpretation of skin tests are illustrated by the results of a study done by Curran and Goldman on 182 subjects.[2] On the basis of their histories, these persons were divided into three groups: those with a personal history of allergy, those with a negative personal history but a positive family history of allergy, and those with no personal or family history of allergy. All 182 subjects were skin tested with a battery of nine common inhalant allergens by the scratch and, if necessary, the intracutaneous method. As expected, 90 per cent of 40 patients with a positive personal history of allergic disease had at least one positive skin test reaction. The most revealing results, however, were that 50 per cent of the patients with a negative personal history but a positive family history of allergy and 10 per cent of the patients with negative personal and family histories of allergy showed at least one positive test reaction.

Particular care must be exercised in the interpretation of skin test results to foods, since experience has shown that skin testing is less reliable in the case of food allergy than it is in allergy to inhalants. This may be because the antigens used for skin testing to inhalants more closely resemble those with which the patient's shock organ comes in contact than do those used in testing for food allergy. It has been estimated that only about 20 per cent of positive skin reactions to food can be correlated with actual clinical symptoms produced by the ingestion of the incriminated foods.[3] This correlation is greatest in the case of foods which cause allergic symptoms almost immediately following ingestion (e.g., sea food, nuts, berries and eggs); it is much less in the case of foods that produce allergic reactions whose onset is delayed for hours following ingestion (e.g., milk and wheat). Furthermore, as with inhalants, clinical symptoms characteristic of an allergic reaction are sometimes produced by foods that give a negative skin test. The discrepancy between clinical findings and skin tests in the case of food allergy may be due in part to the fact that ingestants are digested prior to systemic absorption. It is conceivable, therefore, that a patient could be allergic and skin test positive to an undigested foodstuff but nonallergic to its digestive breakdown products. Since it is primarily the latter which are systemically absorbed, no clinical allergic symptoms would result when the food is ingested. It is also possible for a patient to be nonallergic and skin test negative to an undigested food but allergic to one of the products produced during digestion. Such a food might cause clinical allergic symptoms in the face of a negative skin test. There is a small amount of experimental data which supports these possibilities.

The problems inherent in the interpretation of skin test results have led some allergists to discontinue skin testing with foods. Although it is true that the diagnosis of food allergy is made by careful diet manipulation and not by skin tests, the latter may be helpful in several respects. Skin tests to foods may give some idea of the patient's overall constitutional makeup, i.e., his ability to form reaginic antibody to commonly encountered environmental allergens. If all skin tests are negative to both foods and inhalants, the physician may be less inclined to search further for "extrinsic protein sensitivity" than if several tests are positive. Skin tests can also aid the physician in selection of the type of diet manipulation to recommend (page 202) and the order in which foods are added back to the diet.

OPHTHALMIC TESTING

The ophthalmic test may be used when it is desirable to test directly for the presence of reaginic antibody in mucous membranes. The patient is seated and instructed to look upward with his head tilted back. The lower eyelid is retracted, and in the patient whose skin test is negative, an amount of dried allergenic material about the size of a pinhead is tapped into the conjunctival sac from the flat side of a toothpick (Figure 4–4). In an alternative method an aqueous allergenic extract is used as the source of antigen. An initial concentration about the same as that used in intracutaneous testing is satisfactory, but if a more quantitative estimate of sensitivity is desired, titration techniques using serial dilutions of extract may be employed. The test is read in 20 minutes or sooner if convincing signs of a positive reaction occur. Definite reddening of the caruncle with or without injection of the conjunctiva constitutes a positive reaction. This may be accompanied by lacrimation, itching, and rhinitis. At the end of 20 minutes or as soon as a positive result is obtained, the eye is washed with normal saline. If dry pollen has been placed in the eye, much of it can be removed by wiping out with a cotton applicator the mucus in which it has

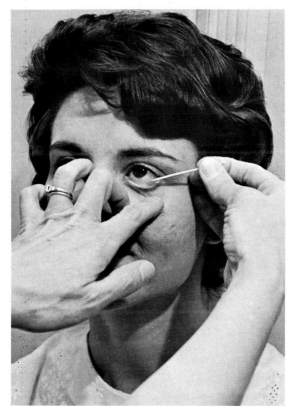

Figure 4–4. Ophthalmic testing technique. The subject is seated and looks upward. Dried allergenic material is introduced into the conjunctival sac from the flat side of a toothpick.

become entrapped. Epinephrine eye drops may be used when a positive reaction occurs. The patient should be instructed not to rub his eyes. If desired, one can perform control tests with inert pollen (e.g., pine) or the extract diluent in the opposite eye, but these will invariably be negative if the patient is not having conjunctivitis at the time of the test.

Ophthalmic tests are more sensitive than scratch tests but less sensitive than the intracutaneous method. Ophthalmic tests generally are not done until skin testing has been carried out. The major advantage of ophthalmic tests is that they are likely to correlate more closely with the clinical history than are skin tests. However, they are less reliable in this regard than the provocative tests described in the next section. The advantage offered by the ophthalmic method must be balanced against its major disadvantages—it is time consuming and, owing to the limited area available for testing, only one allergen can be tested at a time.

PROVOCATIVE TESTING

Provocative testing provides a method of determining the clinical significance of an allergen by placing it in direct contact with the respiratory mucosa. In the case of allergic rhinitis, allergists have traditionally performed such tests by placing a small amount of pollen or other inhalant allergens on the blunt end of a toothpick and instructing the patient to sniff it into one side of the nasal cavity. The presence or absence of subjective symptoms of allergic rhinitis is then noted, and the nasal mucosa observed for the development of pallor, edema, or excessive secretion. Although this procedure may be helpful in cases in which the history and skin tests are confusing, the rather gross endpoint involved has proven to be a distinct drawback, and the test has not been widely used. The recent development of techniques designed to provide an accurate and reproducible measure of nasal airway resistance offers promise as a more sensitive and quantitative method of determining the changes induced in the nose by inhalant allergens.[4] These techniques are still being used primarily as research tools, however.

Provocative testing has been more widely employed in the clinical evaluation of patients with bronchial asthma.[5, 6] In this situation, aqueous allergenic extracts are usually employed for challenge rather than particulate materials. The patient omits antihistamines, sympathomimetic amines and theophylline derivatives for 18 to 24 hours prior to testing. ACTH and corticosteroids are not routinely discontinued. It is advisable that smoking be discontinued for several days prior to testing and that the actual testing be done at a time when the patient is symptom-free or experiencing only minimal asthma.

The procedure is carried out by nebulizing an aqueous allergenic extract into the bronchial tree of the test subject and comparing its effect with that caused by prior nebulization of a control solution such as the extract diluent. The test solutions are aerosolized by a compressed air or oxygen driven nebulizer (e.g., DeVilbiss No. 40) at a flow rate of six liters per minute. A Y-tube is inserted between the pressure source and the nebulizer to permit the patient to coordinate nebulization of extract with inspiration by placing his thumb over the open end of the Y-tube. A volume of 0.5 to 1.0 ml. is usually administered over a period of five to ten minutes. Extracts as dilute as 1:5,000,000 have been used for initial testing, although many investigators routinely use materials as concentrated as 1:50 or 1:500. While undergoing provocative tests, the test subject must be under constant observation, and the procedure must be promptly stopped at the first subjective evidence of respiratory distress. A solution of 1:200 isoproterenol may be administered by nebulizer if symptoms of bronchospasm occur.

Three parameters are used to detect a positive response: subjective respiratory distress, demonstration of bronchospasm by careful auscultation of the chest, and abnormality in selected pulmonary function studies. Adequate evaluation of results requires that nebulization of the control solution produce no significant alterations in any of these parameters. A positive response to the aerosolized allergen usually develops during the nebulization or within 15 to 20 minutes thereafter. Because pulmonary function tests are sometimes altered when no subjective symptoms or auscultatory evidence of asthma are present, many allergists have relied heavily upon these in interpreting the results of testing. The total vital capacity (TVC), first second forced expiratory volume (FEV_1), and maximal mid-expiratory flow rate (MMF) have all been used to measure the bronchial response. Of the three, the maximal mid-expiratory flow rate is the most satisfactory since it is the least dependent upon patient effort and is a more accurate measurement of true airway resistance than the total vital capacity or the first second forced expiratory volume.[7] In actual practice it is feasible to follow all three parameters with tracings obtained from any simple recording spirometer.

More elaborate pulmonary function measurements also can be carried out, but one should avoid tests which cannot be repeated at frequent intervals due to fatigue or for other reasons. A suggested protocol would be to obtain three measurements before, immediately following, and 5, 10, 15, and 20 minutes following the inhalation of the control solution (extract diluent). Additional baseline determinations should be made if the first three do not show satisfactory reproducibility. The same procedure then is followed with each allergen to be tested. In general, testing is terminated for the day if a positive response is elicited. Further tests sometimes can be done if bronchoconstriction promptly subsides without the use of isoproterenol. In our experience, the maximal mid-expiratory flow rate must fall by more than 15 per cent of control values before a test can be called positive.

Some workers have performed provocative testing by injecting test antigens, particularly foods, into the patient's skin. If symptoms of sneezing, nasal congestion, itching, or asthma are elicited within 20 minutes, the response is considered significant regardless of the result of the skin test. More adequately controlled studies are required before the validity of this procedure can be accepted.

As already mentioned, provocative inhalation testing is of value in cases in which the history and skin tests are equivocal or contradictory. It is particularly useful in ascertaining the clinical significance of positive skin tests in patients whose histories are vague or unreliable. Indeed, some Scandanavian allergists will not institute hyposensitization in asthmatic patients unless they have reproduced the symptoms with provocative testing. Although more controversial, a number of observers, including ourselves, have obtained provocative test responses to allergens giving negative intracutaneous test responses when the history strongly suggested that the substance in question was a cause of clinical difficulty. The procedure may also help to establish the presence of sensitivity to unusual allergens.

The advantages of the method must be balanced against certain disadvantages. Provocative testing reproduces the asthmatic state itself and is, therefore, potentially dangerous if not used carefully. Delayed reactions have been reported eight to ten hours after provocative challenge, which present a potential hazard to the patient as well as a problem in interpretation of results. The time-consuming nature of the procedure makes its use impractical except with carefully selected patients and allergens. Furthermore, the usual test procedure is not at all quantitative, since the amount of allergen reaching the lower respiratory tract is not well controlled. This difficulty can be circumvented by special techniques in which an innocuous dye is incorporated with the allergen, acting as a tracer to facilitate measurement of the uptake of allergen by the patient.[6] In using very concentrated extracts for provocative testing, one also must guard against the possibility that resultant bronchospasm might represent an irritant rather than an allergic response. This can be controlled by administering the same extract to other persons with recent asthma (page 24). Finally, it must be remembered that the antigenic challenge given the patient by nebulizing relatively large amounts of allergenic extract over a short period of time is much different from that faced in nature, where smaller quantities of antigen in particulate form are inhaled over a much longer period of time. It is possible that a patient might develop asthma in the artificial circumstances of the provocative test but not in the course of natural exposure to the same allergen. Similarly, it is possible that the effect of factors such as temperature and humidity, when combined with the cumulative effect of prolonged exposure to an allergen, might cause wheezing which could not be reproduced in the usual provocative test. Provocative testing, therefore, should always be interpreted in light of the total clinical picture and not regarded as a procedure which can always be relied upon for final diagnosis.

PASSIVE TRANSFER (PRAUSNITZ-KÜSTNER) TEST

The passive transfer test is used to demonstrate the presence of skin-sensitizing antibody or atopic reagin in serum and to provide a semiquantitative estimate of the amount of such antibody present. Serum thought to contain reaginic antibody to a particular allergen or group of allergens is obtained from the donor and transferred to skin sites on a nonallergic recipient. If reagin is present in the transferred serum, it fixes to the skin of the recipient. The skin sites can subsequently be challenged with the appropriate allergen(s); an immediate wheal and flare response will result.

In performing the passive transfer test, sterile technique and equipment must be used to avoid bacterial contamination of the serum speciment. The donor must also be carefully questioned for a history of hepatitis or unexplained jaundice; if present, the serum cannot be used for passive transfer testing since infectious and serum hepatitis could be transmitted by this means. It has also been our policy to obtain a serologic test for syphilis on all donors. Serum is obtained by drawing 10 ml. of venous blood and allowing it to clot in a sterile glass tube. When the clot has retracted it is separated from the wall of the tube with a sterile applicator stick and the tube is centrifuged. The supernatant serum is withdrawn with a glass syringe and long lumbar puncture needle or with a sterile pipette and transferred to a rubber-stoppered vial for storage. Samples may be stored at $4°$ C. for several weeks or more or frozen at $-20°$ C. for an almost indefinite period prior to use. Before the serum is transferred to the recipient, it should be checked for sterility by culturing in thioglycolate medium and brain-heart infusion broth. If the serum is contaminated, it may be sterilized by passage through a Millipore or Seitz filter, the loss of material on the latter being greater than with the former. Swinney type titers are convenient for handling small volumes of serum, but they must be tightened very firmly to prevent leakage.

Recipients for the passive transfer test may be family members or unrelated volunteers. In either case, it is advisable to choose individuals who have no history of allergic disease. Since it is essential that the recipient give negative skin test reactions to the allergens being evaluated, it is desirable to confirm in advance that he is in fact skin test negative. Because 10 to 15 per cent of the general population are unsatisfactory recipients for passive transfer tests, persons who have previously been used successfully are ideal candidates.

The passive transfer test is performed by injection of 0.1 or 0.05 ml. aliquots of serum intradermally into the skin of the recipient's arm or back. If a more quantitative estimate of the amount of skin-sensitizing antibody in a given sample is desired, serial dilutions of the serum can be placed at separate sites and the titer obtained by determining the highest dilution which will give a positive test. Skin sites should be placed at 4 to 5 cm. intervals and marked with a skin pencil. The recipient should avoid ingestion of any foods which are to be tested subsequently. After an interval of 24 to 48 hours and when the erythema at the site of serum injection has subsided completely, 0.02 ml. of an aqueous extract of the test allergen is injected intradermally precisely at each skin site. The area is examined for wheal and erythema in 20 minutes, and reactions can be graded according to the criteria previously listed for reading intradermal tests (page 62). No meaningful interpretation of results is possible unless the following controls are performed with negative results: an intradermal skin test done with each test allergen at a site which did not receive the test serum, and an intradermal injection of saline both at a serum-planted site and in a remote area. In experimental work, an additional control is sometimes used. This involves challenge with the test allergens of sites previously planted with normal nonallergic serum.

Positive passive transfer tests have occasionally been obtained as long as four to six weeks after serum is planted. It is advisable, therefore, to wait two months or longer before a given skin area is used again.

Passive transfer tests are less sensitive than direct skin tests but produce fewer clinically false-positive reactions. The method is used primarily in experimental work. In clinical allergy, it is used in cases in which direct skin tests cannot be done or interpreted satisfactorily. Examples of situations in which passive transfer testing may be indicated include patients with dermatographism and patients with extensive atopic dermatitis. In the latter case, there may be a lack of normal skin surface on which to do direct skin testing, and there is the risk that extensive skin testing will cause the atopic dermatitis to flare. Passive transfer tests are sometimes done when evaluating infants and small children who lack testing surface and are often unable to cooperate with direct skin testing.

EXAMINATION OF NASAL SECRETIONS

The gross and microscopic examinations of nasal secretions may be of great value in differentiating allergic rhinitis from vasomotor rhinitis and infectious rhinosinusitis. In allergic rhinitis, the nasal secretion is typically copious, watery, and completely clear on gross examination. Occasionally, it is gelatinous and slightly colored, but yellow or green mucoid nasal discharge is more suggestive of infection in the nose and paranasal sinuses. In vasomotor rhinitis, the nasal secretions are usually clear and colorless. They may be copious or scanty in amount and vary in consistency from thin to mucoid.

Nasal secretion for microscopic examination is best collected by instructing the patient to blow his nose into an 8 by 8 inch square of heavy waxed paper. The secretions can be grossly examined and then transferred onto a glass microscope slide by placing the slide on the top of the mucus as it rests on the waxed paper. An applicator stick may be used to facilitate transfer and to spread the mucus more evenly on the slide. If the patient is unable to produce nasal secretion in the usual manner, a cotton-tipped applicator may be cautiously introduced into the anterior part of the nasal cavity to obtain a specimen. This procedure is less desirable, however, since it may result in discomfort to the patient, considerable disruption of the cellular elements present in the secretion and contamination of the specimen with cotton fibers. An alternative procedure for obtaining nasal secretion utilizes a cannula which is inserted into the mouth. Gentle suction is applied to the cannula and material aspirated from the sheet of mucus covering the posterior pharyngeal wall.

The slide containing the specimen of nasal mucus is air-dried and then stained. Wright's stain is satisfactory, but the Hansel staining method is particularly useful. The latter requires four reagents: 1:200 eosin stain (0.30 gm. eosin in 60 ml. methyl alcohol), 1:100 methylene blue stain (0.60 gm. methylene blue in 60 ml. methyl alcohol), distilled water, and 95 per cent ethanol. Stains should be kept in amber dropper bottles and freshly prepared every two months. The Hansel staining procedure is as follows: (1) The air-dried slide is flooded with eosin stain and allowed to stand for one minute; (2) an equal volume of distilled water is added for one minute; (3) the slide is drained and flooded with distilled water until all stain is removed; (4) the slide is flooded with 95 per cent ethanol and then drained; (5) it is then stained immediately with methylene blue for one minute; (6) an equal volume of distilled water is added and allowed to stand for two minutes; (7) the slide is

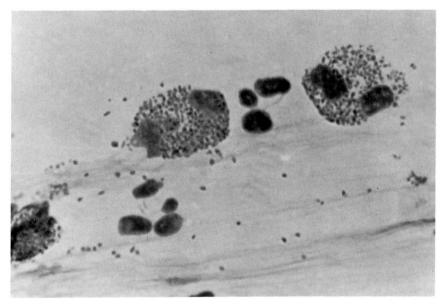

Figure 4–5. Nasal smear showing eosinophils. Photographed under oil immersion. Note larger dark-staining (red) granules and bilobed nuclei.

flooded with distilled water until all stain is removed; (8) it is flooded with 95 per cent ethanol and air-dried; and (9) it is examined under oil immersion.

With the Hansel procedure nasal mucus appears blue and homogenous. In addition to bacteria, which stain blue, three types of cells can be readily identified in nasal secretions. Nasal epithelial cells can be recognized by their unlobulated blue nuclei and abundant pale blue cytoplasm. Neutrophils have blue-staining lobed nuclei and pale pink cytoplasm. Eosinophils have blue-staining lobed nuclei but can be easily distinguished from neutrophils by their intensely eosinophilic cytoplasmic

*Allergy Food Test Sheet**

	Cut.	I. C.		Cut.	I. C.
A. 1 Beef			E. 1 Beet		
2 Lamb			2 Banana		
3 Pork			3 Cantaloupe		
4 Chicken			4 Squash		
5 Egg			5 Coffee		
6 Milk			6 Tea		
7 Barley			7 Cocoa		
8 Corn			8 Brewer's yeast		
B. 1 Oats			F. 1 Pecan		
2 Rice			2 Walnut		
3 Rye			3 Onion		
4 Wheat			4 Asparagus		
5 Grapefruit			5 Coconut		
6 Orange			6 Cabbage		
7 Lemon			7 Cauliflower		
8 Lettuce			8 Broccoli		
9 Pineapple					
			G. 1 Mustard		
C. 1 Navy bean			2 Cotton seed		
2 String bean			3 Flaxseed		
3 Pea			4 Castor seed		
4 Peanut			5 Chlorogenic acid		
5 Tomato			6 Ginger		
6 Potato			7 Buckwheat		
7 Sweet potato			8 Mushroom		
			9 Glue		
D. 1 Carrot					
2 Celery			H. 1 Tuna		
3 Almond			2 Clam		
4 Apple			3 Oyster		
5 Apricot			4 Lobster		
6 Peach			5 Shrimp		
7 Pear			6 Salmon		
8 Grape			7 Whitefish		
9 Vanilla			8 Smelt		
			9 Perch		

Cut. Tested by:_____

I. C. Tested by:_____

* From University of Michigan Medical Center.

granules (Figure 4–5). If the neutrophils do not stain well, steps 5 through 8 may be repeated. If the neutrophils or mucus are too intensely blue, a solution containing one drop of 1 per cent hydrochloric acid in 30 ml. of distilled water can be momentarily applied to the slide and then steps 7 and 8 repeated. The Hansel method can also be used to examine bronchial secretions or conjunctival mucus if such studies are deemed desirable.

Large numbers of eosinophils are commonly seen in the nasal secretions of patients with allergic rhinitis. Eosinophils usually constitute more than 30 per cent and may constitute as high as 80 to 90 per cent of all cellular elements. They may be distributed very unevenly on the slide, thus making it mandatory to scan many areas of the smear. Bac-

*Allergy Inhalants Test Sheet**

		Cut.	I.C.			Cut.	I.C.
I.	1 Cat				*Mixed Grass*		_____
	2 Cattle			M.	1 June grass		
	3 Dog				2 Orchard grass		
	4 Goat				3 Red top		
	5 Hog				4 Timothy		
	6 Horse				5 Plantain		
	7 Rabbit						
					Mixed Weeds		_____
J.	1 Feathers			N.	1 Dwarf ragweed		
	2 Kapok				2 Giant ragweed		
	3 Silk				3 Cocklebur		
	4 Endo house dust				4 Pyrethrum		
	5 House dust				5 Wormwood		
	6 Mattress dust				6 Lamb's quarters		
					7 Russian thistle		
K.	1 Indian gum (Karaya)				8 Pigweed		
	2 Acacia gum						
	3 Tragacanth gum				*Mixed Fungi*		
	4 Quince seed			O.	1 Alternaria		
	5 Orris root				2 Helminthosporium		
	6 Horse serum				3 Hormodendron		
	7 Wheat smut				4 Aspergillus		
	8 Corn smut				5 Penicillium		
	9 Oat smut				6 Mucor		
					7 Candida		
	Mixed Trees		_____		8 Fusarium		
L.	1 Maple						
	2 Box elder			P.	1 Caddis fly		
	3 Elm				2 May fly		
	4 Poplar				3 Control		
	5 Willow			Cut. Tested by:_____			
	6 Birch			I. C. Tested by:_____			
	7 Oak						
	8 Walnut						
	9 Hickory						
	10 Early trees						
	11 Late trees						

* From University of Michigan Medical Center.

Supplementary Allergy Test Sheet*

FOODS	Cut.	I. C.		Cut.	I. C.		Cut.
Fruit			*Vegetables*			*Sea Food*	
Grape	———	———	Bean, kidney	———	———	Bass	———
Grapefruit	———	———	Bean, lima	———	———	Codfish	———
Lemon	———	———	Bean, soy	———	———	Crab	———
Lime	———	———	Black-eyed pea	———	———	Haddock	———
Plum	———	———	Brussel sprout	———	———	Halibut	———
Watermelon	———	———	Cucumber	———	———	Herring	———
			Radish	———	———	Mackerel	———
Spice						Scallop	———
Hops	———	———	*Eggs*			Sturgeon	———
Vanilla	———	———	Lactoalbumin	———	———	Trout	———
			White	———	———		
Wheat			Yolk	———	———	*Meat*	
Glutenin	———	———				Rabbit	———
			Milk			Veal	———
Nuts			Casein	———	———		
Brazil	———		Goat	———	———		
Chestnut	———		Human	———	———		
Pistachio	———						

INHALANTS	Cut.	I. C.		Cut.	I. C.
Fur and Hair			*Weed Pollen*		
Goat-mohair	———	———	Chrysanthemum	———	———
Guinea pig	———	———	Dahlia	———	———
Monkey bf.	———	———	Privet	———	———
Wool sheep	———	———	Dandelion	———	———
Hamster	———	———			
			Grass Pollen		
Feathers			Bermuda	———	———
Canary	———	———	Johnson	———	———
Goose	———	———	Rye	———	———
Fowl			*Tree Pollen*		
Duck	———	———	Cottonwood	———	———
Guinea	———	———	Hickory	———	———
Squab	———	———	Mesquite	———	———
Turkey	———	———	Linden	———	———
Insect					
Mosquito	———	———	Cut. Tested by:———————		
House fly	———	———	I. C. Tested by:———————		
Deer fly	———	———			

* From University of Michigan Medical Center

teria and neutrophils are seldom present in large numbers in the nasal secretion of patients with allergic rhinitis. This can be contrasted with the findings in infectious rhinosinusitis where neutrophils and bacteria predominate. Eosinophils in moderate numbers are sometimes present in infectious rhinosinusitis, however, and their presence or absence alone cannot be used to distinguish the two disorders. The findings in vasomotor rhinitis can vary considerably, but the specimen is often relatively acellular with neither eosinophils nor neutrophils predominating.

REFERENCES

1. Sherman, W., and Kessler, W.: Allergy in Pediatric Practice. p. 283, St. Louis, C. V. Mosby Co., 1957.
2. Curran, W. S., and Goldman, G.: The incidence of immediately reacting allergy skin tests in a "normal" adult population. Ann. Int. Med. 55:777, 1961.
3. Hill, L. W.: Food sensitivity in 100 asthmatic children. New England J. Med. 238:657, 1948.
4. Solomon, W. R., McLean, J. A., Cookingham, C., Ahronheim, G., and DeMuth, G. R.: Measurement of nasal airway resistance. J. Allergy 36:62, 1965.
5. Bernstein, L., Kreindler, A., and Sugeman, D.: Direct bronchial testing in allergy. Ann. Allergy 22:49, 1964.
6. Itkin, I. H., Anand, S., Yau, M., and Middlebrook, G.: Quantitative inhalation challenge in allergic asthma. J. Allergy 34:97, 1963.
7. Lloyd, T. C., and Wright, C. W.: Evaluation of methods used in detecting changes of airway resistance in man. Am. Rev. Resp. Dis. 87:529, 1963.

Chapter Five

HAY FEVER
ALLERGIC RHINITIS
AND
BRONCHIAL ASTHMA

WILLIAM R. SOLOMON, M.D.

Detailed discussions of hay fever, allergic rhinitis and bronchial asthma may be found in reference texts cited on page 532. Only the main features of these conditions will be presented in this manual.

HAY FEVER

Taken literally, the term "hay fever" is a misnomer; the disease is not caused by hay nor is it generally associated with fever. The term properly denotes seasonal allergic rhinitis.

This condition is marked by sneezing, which is often repetitive, nasal obstruction and profuse watery nasal discharge. Ocular pruritus and lacrimation may be associated. Persistent itching of the nose, palate or pharynx is a frequent complaint and is especially suggestive of an allergic etiology for the rhinitis. The face and ears may itch as well. Dull frontal headache and a sensation of mild pharyngeal irritation are sometimes noted, but severe sore throat and cervical adenopathy are rare unless secondary infection has occurred. Some patients note malaise, fatigue and irritability; tendency to chilling is an occasional complaint. The symptoms and signs of hay fever may be readily correlated with local tissue pathology, which includes vascular dilatation and increased permeability leading to edema, hyperplasia of mucous glands and epithelium and proliferation of submucosal tissues with eosinophilic infiltration. (Figure 5–1).

Diagnosis. The aforementioned symptoms strongly suggest hay fever, and their occurrence yearly at the same season or following exposure to known allergens makes the diagnosis very probable. However, the absence of past symptoms should not exclude the disease from consideration, since the patient may be experiencing his initial onset of symptoms. There also may be a collateral history of atopic allergy in the patient. A family history of atopic (infantile) eczema, allergic rhinitis or bronchial asthma is obtained in over 50 per cent of cases. Some of the points which aid in distinguishing allergic rhinitis from other forms of rhinitis are summarized in Table 5–1.

The patient with active hay fever may appear quite well or he may present a picture of extreme discomfort. Many patients experience severe symptoms on arising which subside in the late morning or afternoon. Hence, the physician's impression of the severity of hay fever may depend on the time of day that the sufferer is seen. Frequently, however, such patients have almost continuous nasal blockage as well as reddened swollen conjunctivae, profuse lacrimation and swollen lids. Because of continual sneezing, pruritus and nasal obstruction, sleep is often severely disturbed and patients may appear exhausted. Such persons tend to be moody and listless, showing at times a peculiar resentment of the physician's efforts to help them.

Despite a profuse watery discharge, the allergic nose seldom shows a significant degree of the redness, crusting and excoriation about the nares which are usually so characteristic of viral and bacterial infections. Instead, the speculum examination reveals a remarkable pallor of the nasal mucous membranes, which may have a bluish cast. The mucosa

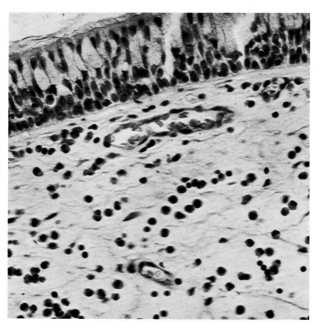

Figure 5–1. Allergic rhinitis. Edema of the nasal mucous membrane is prominent and there is marked spreading of connective tissue elements in the submucosa. Note the many eosinophils that have migrated into the submucosa. Their presence here and in nasal secretions is a frequent finding in nasal allergy. Mucin-producing cells are numerous and active in the surface epithelium.

Table 5–1.   *Characteristics of the Major Forms of Rhinitis*

	Hay Fever	Perennial Allergic Rhinitis	Infectious Rhinitis	Nonallergic Vasomotor Rhinitis
Seasonal incidence	Present	Largely absent	Absent or worse in winter	Absent or worse in changing seasons
Itching of nose, eyes, palate	Usual	Usual	Rare	Unusual
Sore throat	Rare	Rare	Common	Rare
Fever	Absent	Absent	Common	Absent
Collateral allergy	Common	Common	Occasional (coincidental)	Occasional (coincidental)
Family history of allergy	Common	Common	Occasional (coincidental)	Occasional (coincidental)
Conjunctival injection and edema	Common	Common	Occasional	Rare
Excoriation about the nares	Rare	Rare	Usual	Rare
Nasal pallor and edema	Usual	Usual	Absent or coincidental	Common
Polypoid changes in the nose	Occasional	Occasional	Uncommon	Occasional
Injection of the pharynx and nasal mucosa	Rare	Rare	Common	Rare
Cervical lymphadenopathy	Absent or coincidental	Absent or coincidental	Common	Absent or coincidental
Eosinophils in nasal mucus	Usual	Usual	Absent or coincidental	Occasional
Positive immediate skin reactions	Almost always	Almost always	Occasional (coincidental)	Occasional (coincidental)
Thick nasal secretions	Absent or coincidental	Absent or coincidental	Common	Rare
Headache and facial pain	Occasional	Occasional	Common	Occasional

is usually swollen or boggy, being easily indented by gentle pressure with a cotton-tipped applicator. The palate and posterior pharynx may appear normal or share in the general pallor. Occasionally, however, pallor is restricted to certain portions of the nose. Reddening of the pharynx and cervical lymphadenopathy are most unusual in uncomplicated hay fever. The nasal secretions are clear, thin and sticky. When smeared on a slide and appropriately stained (see page 72), large numbers of eosinophils are usually found.

Persons with typical hay fever usually show positive immediate skin test reactions to extracts of the responsible pollens and/or mold spores. However, such patients commonly give additional positive skin test reactions to substances which do not elicit clinical symptoms. As discussed in Chapter 4, it is imperative to regard as clinically significant only those test reactions which correlate with the clinical history. Rarely, the skin tests are negative despite typical signs and symptoms of hay fever. In this event, direct mucosal testing with particulate allergens or extracts may yield positive reactions in the conjunctival sac, nose or bronchi.

Complications. Of the conditions that may complicate hay fever, bronchial asthma has occasioned the greatest concern. In the past, retrospective studies by allergists have suggested that up to 30 or 40 per cent of their hay fever patients, untreated or treated only symptomatically, subsequently developed bronchial asthma. It is probable that these data are derived from groups especially prone to develop asthma, and are not necessarily typical of the populace at large. Indeed, in a total community survey, about 7 per cent of persons with hay fever of all degrees of severity, were found later to develop bronchial asthma.[1] This cumulative prevalence probably exceeds that for the general population but does not have the alarming prognostic connotations of the earlier reports. Asthma occurred prior to, simultaneously with or subsequent to the onset of hay fever in approximately 30 per cent of the population cited, and the clinical impression remains that those with more severe hay fever may be especially predisposed to develop asthma eventually. There is little published data concerning the occurrence of asthma de novo in patients receiving hyposensitization for hay fever, although this appears to be quite uncommon. Bacterial infection of the nose and paranasal sinuses is an additional important complication of hay fever. It can prolong the duration of nasal symptoms and, when several seasonal allergies are present, secondary infection can produce a state of perennial discomfort. Especially with lingering infection, nasal polyps (discussed on page 86) may develop, and in children, hearing may be impaired by chronic serous otitis media (page 311).

Treatment. Three principles which underlie the treatment of allergic disease in general are applicable to hay fever. These are: (1) avoidance of offending allergens, (2) increasing the patient's tolerance to the causative agents by hyposensitization and (3) decreasing the tissue response and resulting symptoms with various drugs.

Effective application of the first of these measures—avoidance—is difficult in hay fever, because the causative aeroallergens are so widely distributed. Furthermore, measures proposed to eradicate sources of allergenic pollen are either unfeasible or have proved to be ineffective. The dose of allergens inhaled can be reduced if patients can sleep with their bedroom windows closed, ride with their car windows shut and avoid trips through the country during known pollen seasons. Most patients show improvement in air-conditioned buildings, but some experience a paradoxical increase in their symptoms especially when such places are excessively cool.

Air conditioning in the home does permit the closure of windows without resultant discomfort. The filters on these units as well as simple window air filters intercept variable numbers of allergenic particles but may help reduce the inhalant exposure. Devices that precipitate suspended material using an electrostatic charge have high efficiencies even for submicronic particles, but with these, clinical benefit is still uncertain. A major limitation results from the inability of patients to remain continuously in the area supplied with filtered air. Similarly, placement of these devices so that they treat only a portion of the air reaching a patient will reduce their effectiveness considerably. These considerations and the evident variability among patients in the time spent in an aero-allergen-free atmosphere which is necessary for relief of hay fever, have dissuaded us from routinely suggesting the use of air-cleaning units. However, they should be considered when other forms of therapy have not given total relief. Persons who have noted rapid improvement in air-conditioned interiors might be considered especially good candidates for air-filtering devices, particularly if, like many housewives, they can remain at home for long periods. Air filters and precipitating units can be adapted to the windows of individual rooms or installed, at necessarily greater cost, in the duct work of central heating systems. Because of the high cost and unpredictable effect of these air purifiers, patients should be advised to use them for an extended trial period before deciding on their purchase.*

Some patients are able to escape offending pollens and spores by traveling to areas from which these allergens are absent. Such annual pilgrimages are apt to be expensive and inconvenient. Furthermore, if for some reason the trip cannot be made in a given year, the patient may be miserable. Every attempt should be made, therefore, to control the patient's symptoms in his own community. Only when an adequate trial of other forms of treatment has failed to give sufficient relief is the physician justified in suggesting a trial of change in geographic location. As discussed on page 28, circumstances rarely justify advising a patient to move permanently to a different area.

Hyposensitization therapy is discussed in Chapter 6.

Symptomatic treatment with drugs will produce additional benefit in patients who retain some symptoms despite optimal hyposensitization. Similar drug therapy alone may be effective and adequate for mild hay fever symptoms. However, increasing symptom severity and any suggestion of lower respiratory involvement are indications for the addition of more specific treatment. The antihistamines are certainly the most useful class of drugs for symptomatic relief, benefiting at least four out of five hay fever sufferers. However, in some patients, several of these agents may have to be tried before an effective one is found. Additional improvement may result from use of ephedrine-like drugs which are often marketed in combination with antihistamines. Such preparations, taken in long-acting form at night, are especially useful in reducing

---

* Most suppliers rent as well as sell these devices. If purchase without such trial is necessary, the patient should retain the option to return the device if not satisfied.

nasal congestion during recumbency and act to lessen severe early morning hay fever. Various vasoconstrictor nose drops and inhalers tend to produce temporary relief of symptoms. However, prolonged regular use should be avoided since it can lead to "rebound" nasal congestion which may be more severe and intractable than the original rhinitis. Patients with persistent hay fever are said to derive additional benefit from using aspirin regularly with their other medications, especially when nasal obstruction is the predominant symptom. Drugs employed for the treatment of hay fever, including intranasal steroids (page 152), are discussed in greater detail in Chapter 7.

ALLERGIC RHINITIS

Since hay fever is but a seasonal variety of allergic rhinitis, it would be expected that the signs and symptoms of both of these are qualitatively identical. In a strict sense, this is true. Frequently, however, "allergic rhinitis" is used to refer to *perennial* allergic rhinitis in which sensitivity to such factors as house dust, danders and foods promotes the occurrence of year-round symptoms. Such patients demonstrate sneezing, rhinorrhea and pruritus which are frequently less severe and acute than in hay fever. Often chronic nasal obstruction is the predominant or even the sole complaint. Occasionally, secondary pyogenic nasal infections or chronic serous otitis media brings the patient with perennial allergic rhinitis to seek medical care.

Because symptoms are often of low intensity and the clues provided by a clear-cut seasonal incidence are lacking, differentiation of allergic rhinitis from infectious or nonallergic vasomotor rhinitis may be difficult. Children and young adults with chronically stuffy and running noses often present the most unyielding problems. In searching for evidence of allergic factors, a history that symptoms are elicited or worsened by activities that involve exposure to known allergens assumes major importance. Attention to this point and to the diagnostic criteria previously discussed will usually lead one to the correct conclusion.

The same principles underlie the treatment of perennial allergic rhinitis as were cited in discussing hay fever. However, contact with perennial allergens such as dust and foods is much more subject to avoidance measures than is that with seasonal pollens. Skillful environmental manipulation, therefore, assumes a more dominant role in treating these perennial sensitivities.

VASOMOTOR RHINITIS

The term "vasomotor" or "hyperesthetic" rhinitis is used throughout much of the world to denote all forms of rhinitis in which transient changes in vascular tone and permeability, rather than infectious or neoplastic factors, determine the clinical picture. The symptoms are basically those described for allergic rhinitis. It is recognized, however, that this clinical picture may be seen without allergic causation as well as in frank allergic rhinitis. Many physicians prefer to employ the term "vasomotor rhinitis" to denote the former nonatopic group rather than use it in a more general sense. Such usage contrasts "allergic" with "vasomotor" rhinitis rather than considering one a subgroup of the other. This variation in the meaning of the term is confusing but remains unresolved. For clarity, "vasomotor rhinitis" should not be used in a restricted sense without qualification.

Persons with *nonallergic* vasomotor rhinitis experience nasal vascular changes in response to stimuli which call forth no obvious reaction in normals. Mild chilling, fatigue, anger, fright or even pleasant anticipation may induce symptoms in such persons. Their response to mild odors and to high atmospheric humidity may be tumultuous sneezing, rhinorrhea and nasal obstruction. In some patients with nasal septal deviation or spurring, diversion of normal air flow causes selective drying of portions of the mucosa, which may show squamous metaplasia. A bothersome vasomotor rhinitis often develops in this setting.

The complex nasal vascular bed is under autonomic control, permitting distant stimuli to cause reflex changes in the nose. Interruption of the cervical sympathetic nerves in man and animals. (Horner's syndrome) is followed by nasal obstruction and hypersecretion which is, clinically, a vasomotor rhinitis. Experimental ablation of the parasympathetic fibers produces, by contrast, a dry, crusted, atrophic mucosa.[2] These pathways may mediate the nasal changes observed during and after chilling of the extremities.[3] Nasal obstruction and rhinorrhea are sometimes observed in response to emotional stimuli. Overt signs and symptoms of rhinitis have been produced, for example, in emotionally labile subjects during psychiatric interviews.[4, 5] An interesting form of nonallergic vasomotor rhinitis often accompanies pregnancy. The reason for this association is unknown, but the condition usually disappears within days or weeks following parturition. Patients with frank myxedema may also develop nasal obstruction with rhinorrhea and mucosal pallor. These changes recede with restoration of a euthyroid state. There is no convincing evidence that thyroid hormone is beneficial in vasomotor rhinitis when administered to patients with normal thyroid function.

Abuse of local medication is another common cause of nasal obstruction. Nose drops and sprays are excellent for relieving the nasal stuffiness caused by an upper respiratory infection (in which the nasal obstruction is limited to a few days or a week). In the allergic person, however, the stuffiness usually persists for longer periods of time, and prolonged use of drops results in irritation of the nasal mucosa. When a topical vasoconstrictor is used in nose drops, the initial constriction may be followed by a "rebound" phase in which the mucous membrane becomes even more congested and swollen than before the application of the drug. Such patients must use the drops every few hours, since delay results in almost complete nasal blockage. This condition, produced by prolonged topical administration of a nasal medication, is termed "rhinitis medicamentosa." When it is suspected, the patient should discontinue using nose drops completely for a trial period to see if the condition improves. It will be necessary to encourage the individual to do this, and supportive aids such as antihistamines, oral decongestants, aspirin and sedatives may be needed for a few days. If the stuffiness is partly due to the topical medication, breathing should be easier in about four days, and relatively normal in one to two weeks. It has occasionally been found necessary to give the patient a brief course of oral steroids to shorten the period of discomfort following the withdrawal of the nose drops. Usually it has been possible to taper use of the steroid drug over a period of perhaps a week without a recurrence of nasal symptoms. Obstruction of longer duration after discontinuance of the nose drops, or a prompt return of trouble after steroids are stopped, suggests that other factors besides the medication are of major importance.

The differentiation between perennial allergic rhinitis and nonallergic vasomotor rhinitis may be simple. Frequently, however, it provides a maximum test of the allergist's diagnostic acumen. When doubt persists, a full allergic investigation is justified. Even if the results are negative, the allergist can render these patients an important service by assuring them that allergic factors are not involved. Lacking such a well-founded opinion, these persons tend to undergo endless inconclusive re-evaluations as they go from physician to physician in search of nonexistent allergies. The absence of symptoms on exposure to known common allergens is a helpful point suggestive of the nonallergic variety. This form is also strongly suggested when the history indicates hyperresponsiveness to emotion, high humidity, drafts and chilling, and so forth. It should be added, however, that during active allergic rhinitis, many persons also show a transient hyperresponsiveness to these nonspecific factors. Indeed, since their symptoms may be worsened most acutely with emotion, chilling or smoking, they may ascribe their discomfort to these factors alone. Because these patients may become asymptomatic with proper allergic management, the physician should not be led to abandon his search for allergic factors by such a history. The appearance of the nose may be identical in allergic and nonallergic vasomotor rhinitis. Prominent eosinophilia in nasal secretions is a point in favor of allergic factors. The adequacy of the specimen, the distribution of the cells and the presence of concurrent infection with neutrophilia must all be considered, however, in evaluating the stained smear. The elicitation of positive immediate skin test reactions also would favor an allergic etiology, but as discussed on page 64, these reactions do not prove that the symptoms in question are allergic.

Antihistamine and ephedrine-like drugs frequently afford benefit to patients with nonallergic vasomotor rhinitis. Aspirin, in regular doses, appears to be effective in relieving symptoms in certain patients. The advice of an otolaryngologist is often of value in ruling out significant structural nasal abnormality as a source of vasomotor changes. Avoidance of exposure to fumes including cigarette smoke, strong odors and rapid changes in environmental temperature should be stressed. Additional rest and assistance in solving prominent emotional problems can be of definite value to the patient. The patient's bedroom ventilation should be modified to prevent drafts and chilling during sleep.

NASAL POLYPS

The allergist frequently encounters patients who have nasal polyps (Figure 5-2). These often have developed in the course of allergic rhinitis, but any chronic irritation may cause their appearance. However, in many cases, no cause for the development of polyps is apparent. Polyps may be obvious on glancing at the nasal vestibule or may be visualized only on careful scrutiny of the nasal vault after application of vasoconstrictors. The appearance of a polyp may furnish a clue to its etiology. Those caused by extrinsic respiratory allergy are typically moist, smooth, glistening and bluish-white in color; polyps developing in the course of chronic infection may also have this appearance or they may be reddened with a wrinkled, granular surface. With chronic suppurative processes, pus may cover the polyp and the surrounding mucosa. In evaluating

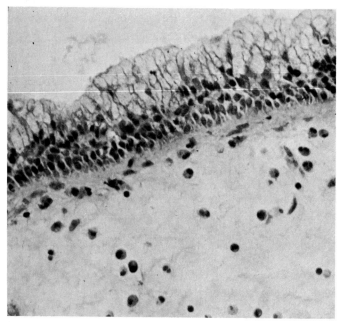

Figure 5-2. Nasal polyp. Epithelial hyperplasia and an increase in the proportion of goblet cells are apparent. There is widening of the epithelial basement membrane with striking edema and an infiltrate of eosinophils in the submucosa. The absence of other inflammatory cells is typical of polyps that arise in the course of allergic rhinitis without chronic bacterial infection.

polypoid growths of any description, the possibility of true neoplasm should be kept in mind. The unexplained association of polyps with aspirin allergy is discussed below.

Surgical removal of polyps requires careful consideration whenever a person is seen with significant nasal obstruction on this basis. Since they impair drainage of the nose and paranasal sinuses, polyps are conducive to persistent infection and further development of polyps. In part because of this vicious cycle, polyps rarely, if ever, show complete spontaneous regression. It is, therefore, generally agreed that surgical removal is the only way to eliminate the polyps. However, the incidence of recurrence after polypectomy is very high and thus surgery is generally limited to those cases in which there is a major degree of airway obstruction or in which the polyps are contributing to recurrent infection. When frank respiratory allergy is involved, it is wise to have the complete program of allergic management well under way before surgery is performed. This may be of value in preventing regrowth of polyps after their removal. An additional consideration is that surgery of this sort may provoke or worsen asthma in an occasional patient. The mechanism of such reactions is unknown and their possible occurrence should not preclude needed surgery in asthmatic patients. However, polypectomy should be deferred, if possible, until allergen avoidance measures and symptomatic medication have taken effect and, preferably, until indicated hyposensitization is being given in maintenance dosage. Such elective procedures also are best not done during a patient's major pollen seasons.

Paranasal sinus infection often accompanies nasal polyps and develops as well in their absence. Its occurrence, as signaled by headache, fever and pus in the middle meatus, should indicate intensive treatment with antibiotics, antihistamines and systemic and topical vasoconstrictor drugs. When sinus infection is recurrent or chronic (pus on antral irrigations, opacification of sinuses on x-ray examination), the question of surgery is bound to be raised. It should be emphasized that considerable improvement can often be obtained by symptomatic measures coupled with specific treatment of allergic factors. A gratifying regression of sinusitis, as well as a diminution in size of nasal polyps, may follow such a program. When improvement is suboptimal, and referral to a competent otolaryngologist has confirmed the need for sinus surgery, all necessary allergic management should again be well established prior to operation.

Regarding patients with nasal polyps and infection, especially when accompanied by bronchial asthma, the possibility of co-existent aspirin sensitivity must be kept in mind. Aspirin-sensitive patients develop grave paroxysms of asthma on ingesting the drug, although other salicylates are well tolerated. This group frequently shows a prominent nasal, blood and bronchial secretion eosinophilia and persistent wheezing. Seldom, however, can the usual ingestant and inhalant allergens be assigned an important role in causing either the polyps or the asthma. Patients who report such reactions should NEVER be test-dosed with aspirin since uncontrollable and fatal asthma may result. Even the first adverse reaction to aspirin in this group may be life-threatening. Skin tests with aspirin are always negative and may provoke serious bronchospasm. The frequency and danger of unsuspected aspirin sensitivity in the asthmatic patient with nasal polyps is sufficiently great that many physicians withhold aspirin, in any form, from these patients. This precaution is easy to observe if drugs such as Darvon and Tylenol are used.

BRONCHIAL ASTHMA

The onset of bronchial asthma should alert the physician to the urgent need for maximal use of specific and symptomatic treatment measures. If neglected or undertreated, this condition may progress to a chronic, disabling disease. In bronchial asthma, the symptoms and signs are referable to spasm of the bronchial walls coupled with hypersecretion of tenacious mucus (Figures 5–3 and 5–4). Pathological examination of patients dying with bronchial asthma typically shows persistent over-distention of the lungs and a bronchial tree filled with viscid mucus. Unless pneumonia is present, the lungs seldom exceed 400 gm. in weight (average normal weight: 350 gm.). Microscopically, there may be edema and eosinophilic infiltration of the mucosa, although edema is not readily

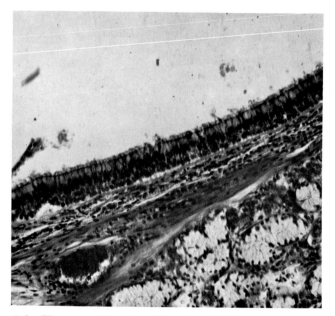

Figure 5–3. The normal bronchus. Note that the lumenal epithelium comprises mostly ciliated columnar cells; goblet cells are relatively few. The epithelial basement membrane is delicate and there is a thin layer of bronchial smooth muscle.

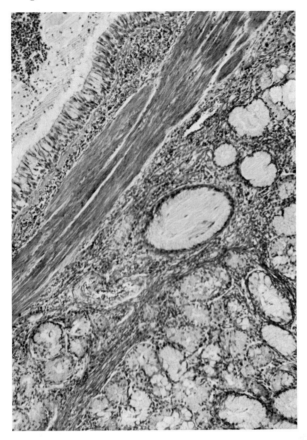

Figure 5–4. Bronchus of an asthmatic. There are many mucin-producing goblet cells and fewer ciliated cells in the surface epithelium. Mucus production by the submucosal glands appears to be increased and there is a mucus plug containing inflammatory cells in the bronchial lumen (upper left). The epithelial basement membrane is thickened and hyalinized. Widening of the layer of bronchial smooth muscle suggests spasm, hypertrophy or both. Edema of the bronchial wall is not at all apparent in this example.

demonstrated in many fresh postmortem specimens. The bronchial glands are hypertrophied and the bronchial smooth muscle thickened. One sees the bronchial basement membrane markedly thickened and hyalinized; the number of goblet cells lining the airway is much increased. Occlusion of many of the smaller air passages by mucus is striking. The plugs contain eosinophils and groups of mucosal epithelial cells. Evidence of patchy shedding of the bronchial mucosa is also seen in the sputum of living asthmatic patients as groups of adherent ciliated bronchial epithelial cells (Creola bodies).[6] (Figures 5–5 and 5–6). Loss of ciliated epithelium associated with goblet cell hyperplasia and, less commonly, squamous metaplasia may seriously impair the normal processes which cleanse the bronchi.

Asthma may be regarded as a symptom complex in which there

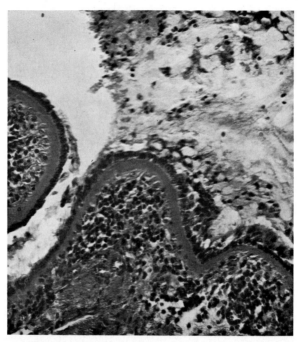

Figure 5–5. Bronchus of a severe asthmatic. The absence of ciliated epithelial cells is striking. Only the nuclei of some epithelial cells remain attached to the thickened basement membrane. Fragments of the detached epithelium are present in the lumenal secretions (upper right).

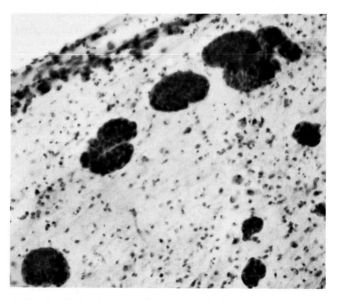

Figure 5–6. Creola bodies. Seen almost exclusively in the sputum of asthmatics, these rounded clumps of epithelial cells might be mistaken for malignant cells. Loss of the ciliated epithelium seriously impairs the normal mucus-clearing function of the bronchi.

are paroxysms of reversible airway obstruction manifested as wheezing and dyspnea. Unfortunately, there is no precise definition which is generally accepted. Likewise, there is no single clinical feature, physical sign or laboratory finding which is pathognomonic of bronchial asthma. Thus, the diagnosis must be based on evaluation of the entire clinical picture and relevant laboratory findings. Under these circumstances, it is inevitable that instances of legitimate disagreement about the diagnosis, at times, will arise; in the wheezing infant, for example, the differential diagnosis of asthma and bronchitis can present a particularly difficult problem.

The clinical history commonly indicates an onset in childhood or youth, but bronchial asthma can begin at any age. At least early in the disease wheezing dyspnea occurs in discrete attacks separated by variable periods without subjective symptoms. With chronicity or recurrent bronchial infection, however, wheezing may become constant. The onset of asthma often occurs at the height of severe seasonal hay fever or with bacterial infection following an intense bout of pollinosis. In other patients, it may accompany a pneumonitis or the inhalation of a gaseous irritant, or it may appear, dramatically, as an isolated event. With asthma, the patient notes a tightness in his chest, dyspnea, wheezing, which is often audible to others, and a cough which may produce thick mucoid sputum. The cough, at first, seems only to make the attack worse, but as the severity begins to abate, the cough becomes more effective in bringing up sputum and thus relieves the symptoms. The sputum tends to be clear, scanty and gelatinous but it can be copious and frothy at times.

In chronic asthma, especially following an attack, the sputum may contain mucus plugs, which are buffy-white casts bearing the shape of the bronchi from which they have been finally dislodged. Although the patient complains of tightness in his chest, there is no pain during the attack. Costal margin and intercostal aching, probably related to spasm of thoracic muscles, is occasionally reported at the end of a paroxysm, or the patient may note a sense of warmth or irritation substernally or at the suprasternal notch. The occurrence of significant acute chest pain during the attack of dyspnea suggests either a complication of asthma or another diagnosis. Complete symptomatic relief following injection of epinephrine or nebulization of isoproterenol is suggestive of bronchial asthma. However, other illnesses producing bronchospasm may respond similarly; furthermore, the advanced or infected asthmatic patient may not be at all improved by these drugs.

Physical Examination. During an attack of asthma, the patient may use his accessory muscles of respiration and the chest is held in a position of inspiration. The patient stands or sits up and leans slightly forward, complaining of increased dyspnea if forced into a position of recumbency. Except for malingerers, the only asthmatic patients who lie down during severe attacks are those who are so exhausted that they can no longer sit. Normal or increased resonance is noted on percussion, and the expiratory phase of respiration is variably prolonged. Musical wheezes, both sibilant and sonorous, are heard primarily on expiration throughout the chest.

Bronchial asthma does not affect one lung or a single lobe while sparing other pulmonary tissue. Indeed, signs of airway obstruction in uncomplicated allergic asthma tend to be present with great uniformity throughout both lung fields. Asymmetry in the auscultatory findings in asthmatic patients usually indicates the advent of bronchitis. Inspiratory rhonchi often make their appearance as an attack ends and tenacious secretions are mobilized. Many physicians regard persistent rhonchi as suggestive of an element of bronchial infection. Tachycardia may be marked during the attack and transient cyanosis may occur, although clubbing of the digits is absent in uncomplicated asthma. Unless infection is present, the rectal temperature is normal in adults and, at most, is minimally elevated in children. In severely ill patients, one occasionally observes disappearance of wheezing coupled with a decrease in audible breath sounds, the chest becoming almost silent despite continued respiratory effort. This grim picture denotes extreme bronchial plugging so that alveolar ventilation has been almost abolished. Needless to say, such a patient requires the most intensive treatment (discussed in Chapter 8) if a fatal termination is to be prevented.

Between attacks, the asthmatic patient may show no clinical abnormality. When asthma has been chronic, however, especially in childhood, the midinspiratory position of the chest is often retained. A few or many musical wheezes may be apparent on auscultation of the chest although the patient feels entirely well. When the chest is clear, one may still detect an increase in the duration of expiration. A pronounced wheeze may be heard when the asymptomatic asthmatic patient exhales forcefully, especially if the examiner compresses the patient's chest during expiration. The presence of mild degrees of airway obstruction between attacks is confirmed by pertinent studies of pulmonary function. Increases in the functional residual capacity and residual volume support the clinical impression of hyperinflation. Decreases in the timed vital capacity and in flow rates attained during maximal expiration may often be demonstrated. The restoration of these latter values to normal following a nebulized bronchodilator emphasizes the reversible nature of the airway obstruction in these patients.

Laboratory Studies. The chest x-ray examination of the stable asthmatic patient is usually normal or shows increased lucency of lung fields and diaphragmatic flattening consistent with hyperinflation.* Occasionally, discrete areas of density are noted on films of otherwise well

---

* Although these changes are frequently interpreted as showing "emphysema," the irreversibility and unfavorable prognosis implied by this term argue strongly against its usage in instances of potentially reversible hyperinflation.

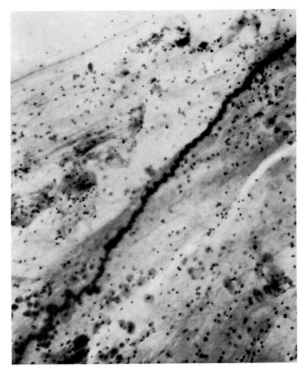

Figure 5–7. Curschmann's spirals. These may represent bronchiolar casts although their exact nature and origin are unknown. They are found almost exclusively in the sputum of asthmatics and only rarely appear in other pulmonary diseases.

patients. These remarkable findings, which apparently denote atelectasis from bronchial plugging, often disappear in hours or days. There may be a peripheral blood eosinophilia. This may appear in uncomplicated extrinsic asthma, but more than 10 per cent eosinophils usually suggests secondary infection when seen in members of this group. Sputum and blood eosinophilia are also noted in aspirin-sensitive asthmatic patients. The sputum also may reveal Curschmann's spirals or Charcot-Leyden crystals (Figures 5–7 and 5–8). The respiratory function studies mentioned above are abnormal during paroxysms of asthma and lesser degrees of airway obstruction may also be demonstrated between attacks. In addition, tests of intrapulmonary gas mixing show this process to be impaired. Asthmatic patients usually have a prompt and marked decrease in respiratory flow rates after the administration, by injection or aerosolization, of histamine or methacholine.[7] Persons with bronchitis and those with significant emphysema may also react to these compounds but usually not to such a marked degree as persons who have had recent asthma. (The use of pulmonary function studies in the evaluation of the asthmatic is discussed in Chapter 3).

Differential Diagnosis. In patients who present a complaint of wheezing dyspnea, one should always consider acute or chronic bron-

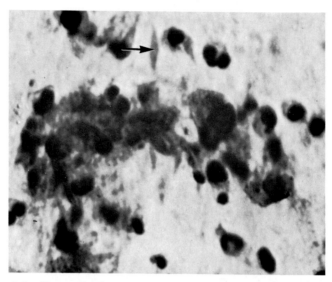

Figure 5-8. Charcot-Leyden crystals are found in sputum of asthmatic patients. They are associated with the presence of eosinophils. In Hodgkin's disease or other disease conditions associated with eosinophilia, Charcot-Leyden crystals can also be found in the sputum.

chitis, pulmonary emphysema, hyperventilation syndrome, bronchial adenoma or carcinoma, bronchiectasis and tracheobronchial foreign body. Typical discrete attacks of wheezing dyspnea occur also with pulmonary edema and congestion (cardiac asthma), metastatic carcinoid tumor, periarteritis nodosa and silo-filler's disease. In children, special attention is directed to foreign body, asthmatic bronchitis, chondromalacia, bronchiolitis, croup, compression of the trachea by aberrant vessels or an enlarged thymus, laryngeal malformations, middle lobe syndrome and mucoviscidosis. These conditions require consideration in approaching the difficult problem of diagnosis in the wheezing infant. At any age, obstructing lesions of the trachea and bronchi caused by tuberculosis, enlarged hilar and mediastinal nodes, aortic aneurysm, substernal thyroid and mediastinal cysts deserve additional consideration.

In the adult, the differentiation of chronic bronchitis and emphysema from bronchial asthma generally presents the most difficult problem. Usually the features of the disease are distinctive, either initially or during its evolution. Asthmatic subjects who are definitely worsened by specific allergens present little difficulty. A personal or family history of atopic disease lends support to a diagnosis of bronchial asthma; the family history is positive in over 50 per cent of such cases. Similarly, the onset of symptoms in infancy or childhood is suggestive of asthma, as is a history that, at least initially, attacks were separated by symptom-free periods. Patients with chronic bronchitis frequently experience years of cough and chronic sputum production before attacks of wheezing dyspnea appear and productive cough remains a prominent sign between attacks. Such patients have been noted to "cough themselves into an attack" unlike the asthmatic patients who typically "cough themselves out of an attack"[8] and who experience little cough between paroxysms.

Dyspnea occurring between attacks of wheezing is suggestive of emphysema or chronic bronchitis and such patients often have more or less continuous wheezing dyspnea without discrete paroxysms. Any patient with airway obstructive disease may experience wheezing on exertion and with emotional stress. In the asthmatic patient, whose attacks often begin during sleep, however, such obvious triggers may be absent. The emphysema patient's dyspnea, conversely, is usually related primarily to exertion and he may sleep without distress. Finally, it should be noted that, with extreme chronicity and recurrent infection, the asthmatic patient may develop secondary chronic bronchitis and emphysema with alveolar loss.

Clinical Types. Asthmatic patients traditionally are divided into two major groups: (1) those whose asthma is primarily caused by well-defined inhalant or food allergens (extrinsic) and (2) those in whom extrinsic factors cannot be demonstrated to cause the asthma (intrinsic). Many patients in this latter group have asthmatic attacks primarily associated with infection and nonspecific irritants. A definite subgroup in this second category is formed by aspirin-sensitive asthmatic patients. Although such a division is clinically valid, it is not exclusive. Patients worsened primarily by infection may also show underlying responses to environmental allergens that warrant specific treatment. Equally important is the frequency with which bacterial infection can trigger attacks of asthma in persons with primarily extrinsic sensitivities. Because of variable bronchial obstruction and impaired drainage of secretions, such persons are also more subject to secondary infection. Occasionally, symptoms are absent until an infection initiates the wheezing which then continues in response to specific atopic sensitivities. Whether the effects of infection in either group involve a bacterial allergy is still uncertain (see Chapter 2), but there is good agreement that control of infection is an important requisite for effective treatment in these cases.

Additional classifications of the asthma syndrome have been proposed. For example, Swineford has divided the known factors that can precipitate attacks into nine major types.[9] Unfortunately, many patients cannot be assigned to one of these etiological classes exclusively because several of the causes are observed to operate. Therefore, we restrict our formal classification to the broader headings of "extrinsic" and "intrinsic," recognizing the importance for comprehensive treatment of the plurality of potential inciting factors.

Prognosis. The above classification is of some prognostic value. In general, the outlook is most favorable for patients with symptoms due to inhalant and food allergies. Those who lack known allergic factors but worsen primarily with infection tend to experience recurrent asthma as infection waxes and wanes. In both groups, the development of chronic foci of respiratory infection or of destructive emphysema materially worsens the prognosis. Fortunately, the latter complication appears to be uncommon in the absence of repeated infection. Indeed, without a major component of pulmonary infection, respiratory function abnormalities continue to show a surprising degree of reversibility, even after prolonged and severe asthma in children.[10] The prognosis in childhood asthma is generally regarded as favorable, especially with specific treatment. Of 449 children evaluated prior to age 13 by Rackemann,[11] roughly three-fourths of these were free from symptoms of asthma when contacted by him 20 years later. Of this majority without asthma, slightly over one-fourth had subsequently developed allergic rhinitis; another one-fourth was still aware of allergenic exposures which could elicit wheezing but which they could successfully avoid.

Asthma, appearing first in middle adult life or later, is often primarily related to infection or to unknown causes and carries a less favorable prognosis than asthma with onset in childhood. In general, the aspirin-sensitive group of asthmatic patients do most poorly, their attacks being inexplicable in onset, prolonged and intractable. Persistent asthma with infection occasionally leads to bronchiectasis or to pulmonary hypertension and cor pulmonale. Additional complications of asthma include: pneumonitis, persistent segmental atelectasis, spontaneous pneumothorax and mediastinal or subcutaneous emphysema.

Death from uncomplicated extrinsic asthma is extremely rare. However, fatalities in all age groups, often associated with infection, cardiac complications and, in adults, aspirin sensitivity, are being increasingly recognized.[12] Suffocation due to mucus plugging of the air passages is probably a common immediate cause of death; oversedation may play a role in many fatal cases and theophylline toxicity has been emphasized in children.[13] Current mortality trends in bronchial asthma remain to be clarified.

Treatment. As with allergic rhinitis, treatment is predicated on careful identification of the factors which cause asthma. These are treated, when possible, by avoidance and when indicated, by specific hyposensitization. In addition, all asthmatic patients can derive benefit from regular use of medication designed to prevent symptoms and to mitigate those that do occur. The importance of infection and its prompt treatment with antibiotics cannot be overemphasized (page 156). Avoidance of irritants, particularly cigarette smoke and industrial fumes can, at times, significantly decrease the severity of asthmatic symptoms. Some treatment measures have been discussed in previous paragraphs dealing with allergic rhinitis; drugs useful for treating asthma are discussed in Chapter 7; the treatment of status asthmaticus and mechanical aids to respiration are discussed in Chapter 8 and avoidance measures and hyposensitization are detailed in Chapter 6.

In recent years, there has been interest in resection of the carotid body for treatment of bronchial asthma.[14] Cervical glomectomy has not realized early expectations that it would provide a means for controlling severe asthma.[15, 16] We do not advocate this procedure. We await further developments for the more effective management of bronchial asthma.

REFERENCES

1. Broder, I., Barlow, P. P., and Horton, R. J. M.: The epidemiology of asthma and hay fever in a total community, Tecumseh, Michigan. 2. The relationship between asthma and hay fever. J. Allergy 33:524, 1962.
2. Millonig, A. F., Harris, H. E., and Gardner, W. J.: Effect of Autonomic denervation on the nasal mucosa. Arch. Otolaryng. 52:359, 1950.
3. Ralston, H. J., and Kerr, W. J.: Vascular responses of the nasal mucosa to thermal stimuli with some observations on skin temperature. Am. J. Physiol. 144:305, 1945.
4. Wolf, S., Holmes, T. H., Treuting, T., Goodell, H., and Wolff, H. G.: An experimental approach to psychomatic phenomena in rhinitis and asthma. J. Allergy 21:1, 1950.
5. Holmes, T. H., et al.: The Nose—An Experimental Study of Reactions Within the Nose in Human Subjects During Varying Life Experiences. Springfield, Ill., Charles C Thomas, 1950.
6. Naylor, B.: Shedding of the mucosa of the bronchial tree in asthma. Thorax 17:69, 1962.
7. Townley, R. G., Dennis, M., and Itkin, I. H.: Comparative action of acetyl-beta-methylcholine, histamine and pollen antigens in subjects with hay fever and patients with bronchial asthma. J. Allergy 36:121, 1965.
8. Swineford, O., Jr.: Observations on infectious asthma. South. M. J. 51:637, 1958.
9. Swineford, O., Jr.: The asthma problem—a critical analysis. Ann. Int. Med. 57:144, 1962.
10. Tooley, W. H., DeMuth, G., and Nadel, J. A.: The reversibility of obstructive changes in severe childhood asthma. J. Pediat. 66:517, 1965.
11. Rackemann, F. M., and Edwards, M. C.: Asthma in children: a follow-up study of 688 patients after an interval of twenty years. New England J. Med. 26:815, 856, 1952.
12. Alexander, H. L.: A historical account of death from asthma. J. Allergy 34:305, 1963.
13. Richards, W., and Patrick, J. R.: Death from asthma in children. Am. J. Dis. Child. 110:4, 1965.
14. Overholt, R. H.: Resection of carotid body (cervical glomectomy) for asthma. J.A.M.A. 180:809, 1962.
15. Marschke, G., et al.: Carotid body removal in asthma. J.A.M.A. 191:125, 1965.
16. Swedlund, H. A., et al.: Glomectomy for chronic asthma. Mayo Clin. Proc. 40:895, 1965.

Chapter Six

SPECIFIC THERAPY: AVOIDANCE AND HYPOSENSITIZATION

By far the most satisfactory and effective treatment for allergic disease is to identify the causative allergen(s) and, when possible, to prevent further exposure to the offending substance(s).

SEPARATING THE ALLERGENS FROM THE PATIENT

In cases of allergy to foods, drugs, or contactants, avoidance usually is the sole form of specific therapy. It is important, however, to instruct the patient regarding any occult sources of the offending agent and possible cross-reacting substances (see Chapters 9 through 12). The same principle applies to treatment of patients sensitive to miscellaneous allergens such as orris root, cottonseed, flaxseed, castor bean, silk, kapok, and the vegetable gums. Sources of these materials are discussed in Chapter 17. Likewise, allergy to household pets generally is treated most satisfactorily and effectively by removing the pets from the home. Avoidance of house dust cannot be so complete, but nonetheless it is important for dust-sensitive patients to protect themselves from unnecessary exposures by utilizing dust avoidance measures such as are described on page 440. If there are local sources of mold spores, as in a damp basement, dehumidification and application of fungicides may be beneficial (see page 404). Reduction of ingestant sources of fungi by a "mold-free" diet also may be helpful in some cases (see page 403). The limiting of exposure to pollen, to fungus spores, and possibly to dust by air filtration (air conditioning, electrostatic precipitators) is discussed on page 82. Wearing a mask when exposure to allergens is unavoidable also may be helpful. The removal of ragweed from the patient's own yard by pulling or spraying with 2,4-D shortly before the pollen season is logical in view of available evidence that the bulk of pollen travels only a short distance through the air. However, community-wide ragweed eradication programs have yet to be proved efficacious in areas in which ragweed is abundant in the surrounding countryside.

SEPARATING THE PATIENT FROM THE ALLERGENS

Since some allergens are unusually prevalent in certain locales, it is advisable for sensitive persons to shun such places. For example, many patients could avoid significant exposure to May fly by staying away from involved lake shores at the time these insects are swarming. To a lesser extent, pollen-sensitive individuals can avoid unnecessarily heavy exposures to pollen by the common sense measures discussed on page 81. *It is important not to neglect this aspect of treatment:* massive allergen exposure is likely to result in symptoms in spite of other forms of therapy. Similarly, many mold-sensitive patients should be advised to avoid hay, barns, fallen leaves, and damp places. Beyond this, ragweed-sensitive patients can avoid exposure completely by traveling to areas free of this pollen. Circumstances relating to the advisability of this are discussed on page 82.

The ultimate form of avoidance therapy would be to have the patient move permanently to an area free of the pollen or mold to which he is sensitive. However, this is recommended only rarely. Such drastic measures seldom are necessary since the symptoms of a large majority of patients can be controlled by other forms of treatment, and a move to another area may create grave social or economic hardship (see page 28). Also, these atopic persons may acquire sensitivity to additional allergens in their new locale, resulting in a relapse after a temporary period of improvement. In any case, it is highly advisable for the patient to try out the new area before moving permanently. This type of "treatment" would be most logically considered in the case of the young adult who is completing his education and is in the process of deciding where to settle. If there are not strong family ties and there are equally attractive employment opportunities in an area free of his major allergen, severe allergic disease not responding well to other forms of treatment might logically influence his decision about where to move. In particular, patients with severe seasonal mold allergy living in the midwestern United States might consider leaving this area under these circumstances, since they often do not respond well to other forms of therapy (see below).

AQUEOUS HYPOSENSITIZATION THERAPY*

History and Rationale

Although there had been some earlier work, the first sustained use of hyposensitization therapy for pollenosis was initiated by Noon and Freeman in England in 1911.[1,2] Some of the early investigators

---

* This discussion excludes stinging insect hyposensitization, which is dealt with in Chapter 15.

regarded pollen extract injections as a means of immunization against toxins in pollen. When the existence of hypothetical toxins could not be demonstrated, however, the procedure was regarded as being analogous to desensitization of anaphylactically sensitive animals. Yet, more careful observations indicated that early in the course of pollen extract injections there might be substantial clinical improvement with unchanged or even increased skin test reactions or titers of skin-sensitizing antibodies in serum as measured by passive transfer tests.[3] In 1935, Cooke, Barnard, Hebald, and Stull presented evidence that this type of treatment resulted in the production of "blocking antibodies."[4] The evidence for this and the difficulties in interpreting the observation are discussed in Chapter 1. Recently, Sherman and Connell have presented *long-term* observations indicating that skin-sensitizing antibody titers are reduced by pollen extract injections.[5] It has been suggested that immunologic tolerance may be induced. Since the effects of this type of treatment are not completely understood and probably multiple, the more general term, *hyposensitization,* is used in preference to *desensitization,* a term which has immunologic connotations which may or may not be applicable here.

It is evident that clinical hyposensitization therapy has developed empirically. Because of this, variations in technique may be found among different allergists. The methods described below have evolved at our institution over the past 30 years, but alternative procedures, differing in certain details, would undoubtedly be equally satisfactory. An important consideration is that no rigid procedure can be suggested as suitable for all patients. Because of marked variability in the degree of sensitivity of different subjects, it is essential that hyposensitization treatment be individualized. Another factor leading to lack of precision and uniformity is the crude nature of the allergenic extracts used in therapy. Most often simple aqueous extracts are utilized without purification (but with sterilization by filtration). In some pollen extracts, it has been estimated that the allergenic material comprises less than 10 per cent of the nitrogenous substances in the extract. The allergen solutions also are very heterogeneous immunologically, as shown by the fact that rabbits immunized with some pollen extracts can produce antibodies to many antigens in the extract.[6] It is probable, however, that only a few of these antigens are relevant to human atopic disease.

Efficacy of Hyposensitization Treatment

Unfortunately, in the early part of this century it was not the custom of the times to require controlled double-blind studies before a new therapeutic modality was to be accepted. Thus, hyposensitization treatment gained wide usage without adequate documentation of its efficacy by present-day scientific standards; in fact, controlled evaluations of hyposensitization have been carried out only in relatively recent years. Undoubtedly, major reasons for this delay were special problems which make it unusually difficult to evaluate this form of therapy.[7] These include the following: availability of patient populations which can be given placebo injections at frequent intervals for months or years; need for placebos which give local swelling simulating allergy extract injections; necessity for modifying a standard dosage schedule to accommodate unusually sensitive patients; lack of reliable and simple objective measurements of the severity of hay fever; variability in pollen exposure as patients move about; variations in pollen counts from year to year; great variability in the sensitivity of different patients; and need for large numbers of patients with uncomplicated allergy, preferably to a single antigen, who have never had hyposensitization in the past. These requirements make it virtually impossible to carry out an ideal evaluation of hyposensitization therapy. However, enough problems have been solved to permit one to say that hyposensitization with ragweed pollen extract, grass pollen extract, and possibly house dust extract has been carried out under reasonably well controlled conditions, and in some of these studies a significant therapeutic effect was demonstrated.[8–13]

Adequate studies with tree pollen extracts and fungus extracts have not been reported. There is a widespread clinical impression that results of hyposensitization with fungus extracts are less favorable than with pollen extracts. Most controlled studies employing bacterial vaccines have failed to show a significant effect,[14–17] though in one recent experiment frequency of use of inhalers was significantly reduced even though other parameters of disease severity were not significantly changed.[18]

In most studies with pollen extracts, about 75 to 80 per cent of patients have reported beneficial results; the problem has been to determine whether these results indicate greater than chance variations in diseases whose natural course (i.e., without treatment) has not been very well described. The available data suggest that results are similar in children and adults and that asthma caused by pollen may be improved more than hay fever. However, in cases complicated by infection, results of pollen hyposensitization are likely to be obscured. In this sense, positive results of carefully controlled studies may be more meaningful than negative ones. However, the practical usefulness of hyposensitization requires that it have not only a demonstrable effect on symptoms of the patient but also advantages over less cumbersome forms of treatment. Many allergists believe that hyposensitization is superior to symptomatic treatment by drugs since, by altering the patient's immunologic status, one is more likely to prevent the possible progression in severity of the disease or to prevent the development of asthma complicating hay fever. More data carefully comparing untreated and treated (by hyposensitization) patients are needed before the validity of this belief can be fully evaluated. Studies of a whole community indicate

that in the absence of hyposensitization the occurrence of asthma complicating hay fever is much less frequent than stated in most allergy
texts (see page 81) .

Indications for Hyposensitization

This treatment should be prescribed only for sensitivities to allergens, generally inhalants, which cannot be avoided to an extent
sufficient to control the patient's symptoms. With only a few exceptions,
therefore, hyposensitization therapy is confined to treatment of pollen,
fungus, and dust allergies. Animal danders occasionally are administered to veterinarians or laboratory workers. Bacterial vaccines are used
by some allergists but not by others. Since hyposensitization often involves protracted therapy and may cause the patient considerable incon-
venience, the physician should be quite certain of the diagnosis and
need for such treatment before advising it. This generally requires a
clear history and confirmatory skin test reactions. When there is uncertainty, there is a trend toward increasing use of provocative inhalation tests, especially in asthmatic patients (see page 68). An all too
common error is to start hyposensitization with environmental allergens
in patients whose symptoms are caused by infection just because they
coincidentally have large positive skin test reactions. The great frequency of positive tests unrelated to patients' current symptoms was
pointed out on page 65. Lest the treatment seem worse than the disease,
hyposensitization reasonably may be deferred in patients experiencing
short periods of mild rhinitis easily controlled by symptomatic medication. Such patients should be followed periodically, however, so that
hyposensitization may be instituted if symptoms begin to progress or
any signs of asthma develop. Before injections are started, it is important to discuss the indications and general procedure with the patient,
since his cooperation is essential to carrying out the program properly.

Selection of Antigens for Treatment

The selection is made on the basis of the history with confirmatory
evidence from skin, ophthalmic, or inhalation tests. Hyposensitization
usually should be instituted only with substances incriminated by both
the history and the diagnostic tests. It generally is most practical to
include from the outset of treatment all antigens to which hyposensitization will be carried out. Although it is possible and sometimes desirable
to add more antigens to the injection program after treatment has been
started, such modifications require a temporary but inconvenient increase in the frequency of injections while the dosage of such added
material is raised to the maintenance level.

The use of excessive numbers of allergens in the injection program
should be avoided. Occasionally patients are seen who are receiving

injections of extracts actually containing a dozen or more different groups of allergens. This suggests that the physician is interpreting the skin tests entirely too literally without regard to the history or that he has not really isolated the cause of the patient's difficulty. Such a shotgun mixture is so nonspecific that it is likely to give poor results, partly because it leads to unnecessary dilution of the important allergens. Sometimes a small percentage of allergen is included to which the patient gives very large skin test reactions but has no corresponding incriminating history. This is done on the basis that it may prevent subsequent development of clinical symptoms to such material. Although some data support this procedure,[9] it should be used with restraint.

Mixtures of Antigens

Since multiple sensitization is commonplace, one frequently has occasion to treat patients with mixtures of antigens.

Mixtures of Related Allergens. It is well known that the pollens of plants which are closely related botanically seem in addition to be associated allergenically. Patients allergic to ragweed also are probably sensitive to cocklebur and burweed marsh elder. Allergies to grass and tree pollens likewise may be multiple. Even with the fungus group, an individual often reacts clinically to a number of different types. It is common practice for allergists to prepare mixtures of related antigens to use in treating the many patients who are sensitized to groups of immunologically similar allergens. Such preparations include mixed trees, early trees, late trees, mixed grasses, mixed weeds, and mixed fungi. The actual composition of these mixtures will depend upon the geographical location of the allergist and will represent plants which are troublesome in his particular area (see page 531 for the mixtures which we have found useful in the Great Lakes region, and Chapter 16 for information about other areas).

It is possible that the results of treatment with hyposensitization might be just as satisfactory through the use of only *one* constituent from each of these closely related mixtures. But until further information is available on their exact immunologic relationships, it seems advisable to use mixtures when multiple sensitivities are present and the patient actually is exposed to these allergens. Of course, exceptional cases occur which should be managed differently. For instance, the patient specifically sensitized only to certain trees, such as elm or oak, preferably should be hyposensitized with the specific pollen causing the symptoms; or one could supplement the mixed tree extract with added amounts of the pollen in question.

Mixtures of Unrelated Allergens. There are two general arrangements for carrying out hyposensitization. With the first, the physician has a set of serial dilutions of each of the main types of allergens commonly used in his practice. This includes the treatment mixtures mentioned above and house dust extracts. When materials from several different vials are being used, the most dilute allergen is drawn into the syringe first. Then, with caution, the other extracts are added to the syringe, mixed, and given as a single injection. If much more than 1.0 ml. of extract is to be given, it may be wise to divide the dosage and give part of it in each arm (see special instructions, page 111). Generally this is the preferred method of treatment, since it allows for considerable flexibility. If a patient begins to have significant local reactions, the various constituents may be injected at different sites to ascertain which is causing the trouble. The dosage of a single allergen thus may be reduced while other allergens can be progressively increased. When a certain pollen season arrives, the specific pollen extract dosage may be reduced, if indicated, while other allergens can be given as usual.

For physicians who treat only a few patients by hyposensitization, it may not be feasible economically to keep on hand a fairly complete stock of fresh allergens. In such a situation, allergenic extracts may be procured for each individual patient from suitable commercial sources (see page 531). If a person is to be treated with only one allergen, treatment is conducted in the same manner as if the physician were using stock bottles of extract. If the patient is to be hyposensitized to several allergens, however, it usually is most practical to have the pharmaceutical house mix the unrelated antigens together in one or two vials and then make serial dilutions of these materials. If the allergens are combined, they should be mixed in proportion to their relative clinical importance. For example, for a patient who has substantial ragweed hay fever together with slight wintertime symptoms on exposure to dust (and positive skin test reactions to both house dust and ragweed), one might prescribe a mixture containing 25 per cent house dust and 75 per cent ragweed extracts. Similarly, if an allergist is preparing a set of treatment extracts to be administered elsewhere by another physician, placing the various components in one or two vials will simplify treatment and reduce the likelihood of errors.

Usually, giving mixtures of immunologically unrelated allergens is feasible. However, there are certain instances in which it is advisable to keep the constituents separate. Included in this group are patients who are exquisitely sensitive to a certain allergen. In order to avoid reactions from the potent allergen, only very weak dilutions of the entire mixture may be administered, at least in the early phases of treatment. This means that the patient may receive only such minute amounts of the less potent allergens in the mixture that treatment may be entirely ineffectual in respect to these other materials. In addition, it should be remembered that mixture of several materials results in a proportionate reduction of each allergen in a given dose of the mixture. In part, this may be corrected by giving a larger volume of the extract, but there are limitations to the amount which may be injected.

In general, it is not advisable to mix together more than two or three unrelated allergens which are of major importance to the patient. If there are additional allergens of substantial import, it is recommended that they be provided in a separate vial.

Concentration of Allergy Extracts

Unfortunately, there are in use at present several different systems for labeling the concentrations of allergenic extracts. These include: the weight by volume method, pollen (or Noon) units, total nitrogen units, total nitrogen content, protein nitrogen units (P.N.U.), and protein nitrogen content. Because of differences in preparation techniques and variations in the antigens, there is no exact mathematical relationship between some of these units of measure. An approximate statement of the usual relationship between the various systems in indicating the concentration of ragweed extract is given in the table on page 516.

The labeling of extracts on the basis of their protein nitrogen content is recommended by some authorities, since the chemical assay involved provides some measure of standardization. However, it must be understood that this by no means is a direct measurement of the allergenic material in the extract, since the latter constitutes only a small part of the nitrogenous material being assayed. Furthermore, the term *"protein nitrogen unit"* is somewhat a misnomer, since the phosphotungstic acid generally used in separating the nitrogen-containing substances precipitates compounds of much lower molecular weight than proteins. The weight by volume and pollen unit methods are traditional ones and have been generally satisfactory for clinical use provided that the extracts are prepared by uniform techniques.* Physicians who purchase their testing and treatment extracts from commercial sources naturally must conform with the labeling system used by the supplier, but many of the latter are prepared to label extracts by whatever method the physician chooses. Adequate standardization of allergy extracts awaits purification and further knowledge of the immunochemistry of these materials. Clinical usage of highly purified ragweed allergens is under investigation.[19]

Ordering Allergenic Extracts

If the physician does not choose to manufacture his own allergy extracts (see Appendix I), he may procure them from commercial sources

---

* There is a tendency for allergists to adopt the protein nitrogen system, but some have hesitated to do so because of confusion which changing from an older system might entail. We have been able to circumvent this difficulty by assaying and standardizing our extracts on the basis of their nitrogen content while continuing to label them according to the weight by volume method.

(see page 531). If a mixture of several allergens is desired for an individual patient, it is customary to write a prescription for the most concentrated solution which is likely to be used. Serial dilutions then are made from the first mixture. It may be advantageous to order only the most concentrated allergenic extract from the pharmaceutical firm and make the serial dilutions in vials of sterile diluent (see page 530). This allows for increased flexibility in the treatment program and usually reduces the cost of the extracts. However, some commercial sources prepare the complete dilution series at very little extra cost.

Some illustrative prescriptions used for ordering allergenic extract mixtures are given below. Each modification of the first example contains approximately the same concentration of allergens, but they are expressed in different units. If the doctor wishes to include combinations such as "mixed grasses" or "mixed trees" in his prescriptions, he should designate what is desired in such a mixture. It is important to realize that the label on a vial containing a mixture of various allergens may not necessarily indicate the actual concentration of each component of the preparation. Certain of the individual antigens might purposely be added in higher dilution; for instance, prescription C (see list following) is labeled 1:50 but contains 1:400 Endo house dust. Furthermore, the dilution of one antigen with another lowers the final concentration of all the allergens in each of these mixtures.

A. a_1
   Rx
    50 per cent Ragweeds   1:50
    20 per cent Russian thistle 1:50   10.0 ml.
    30 per cent Bermuda grass 1:50
    Sig. label   1:50
    Dilute and label 1:500
                1:5000

a_2
Rx
    50 per cent Ragweeds
      (20,000 pollen units/ml.)
    20 per cent Russian thistle
      (20,000 pollen units/ml.)   10.0 ml.
    30 per cent Bermuda grass
      (20,000 pollen units/ml.)

    Sig. label 20,000 pollen units/ml.
    Dilute and label 2000 u/ml.
              200 u/ml.

a_3
Rx
    50 per cent Ragweeds
      (10,000 P.N.U./ml.)
    20 per cent Russian thistle
      (10,000 P.N.U./ml.)   10.0 ml.
    30 per cent Bermuda grass
      (10,000 P.N.U./ml.)

    Sig. label 10,000 P.N.U./ml.
    Dilute and label 1000 P.N.U./ml.
              100 P.N.U./ml.

a_4

Rx

    50 per cent Ragweeds
       (0.1 mg. protein nitrogen/ml.)
    20 per cent Russian thistle
       (0.1 mg. protein nitrogen/ml.)   10.0 ml.
    30 per cent Bermuda grass
       (0.1 mg. protein nitrogen/ml.)

    Sig. label 0.1 mg. protein nitrogen/ml.
    Dilute and label 0.01 mg. protein nitrogen/ml.
              0.001 mg. protein nitrogen/ml.

B. b_1

Rx

    25 per cent Box elder 1:30

    25 per cent Elm   1:30 10.0 ml.

    50 per cent Ragweeds 1:30

    Sig. label 1:30
    Dilute and label 1:100
              1:1000
              1:10,000

b_2

Rx

    25 per cent Box elder
       (15,000 P.N.U./ml.)
    25 per cent Elm   10.0 ml.
       (15,000 P.N.U./ml.)
    50 per cent Ragweeds
       (15,000 P.N.U./ml.)

    Sig. label 15,000 P.N.U./ml.
    Dilute and label 5000 P.N.U./ml.
              500 P.N.U./ml.
               50 P.N.U./ml.

C. c_1

Rx

    70 per cent Ragweeds   1:50
    30 per cent Endo house dust 1:400   10.0 ml.

    Sig. label 1:50
    Dilute and label 1:500
             1:5000

Initial Dosage

There is considerable variation in the recommended starting dose of an allergen, depending upon the degree of sensitivity which a patient exhibits. Ordinarily, hyposensitization begins with injections of an extract which is 100 times more dilute than the maximal concentration to be used. We most often treat patients with a series of three dilutions of allergen, starting with a concentration of 1:5000 and progressing through a 1:500 extract to reach the maintenance strength of 1:50.* In terms of approximately equivalent units of ragweed extract, this would mean starting with an extract containing 200 pollen units, 100 protein nitrogen units, or 0.001 mg. protein nitrogen per milliliter, and increasing the strength through serial injections up to

---

* The 1:50 label represents material in which 1 gm. of pollen has been extracted with 50 ml. of extracting fluid (see Appendix I).

a final concentration of 20,000 pollen units, 10,000 protein nitrogen units, or 0.1 mg. protein nitrogen per milliliter. Another popular system which is equally satisfactory involves use of successive allergen concentrations of 1:10,000, 1:1000, 1:100, and finally 1:33. The latter is roughly equivalent to 30,000 pollen units, 15,000 protein nitrogen units, or 0.15 mg. protein nitrogen per milliliter.*

Although the concentrations of allergens mentioned above are most often used to begin hyposensitization, much smaller initial doses should be used in the presence of the following circumstances: (1) unusually large skin test reactions; (2) history of a constitutional reaction from previous hyposensitization treatment; (3) atopic dermatitis; (4) pronounced symptoms in the patient, as in a pollen season; (5) administration of extracts of animal danders, insects, or orris root; and (6) treatment of pregnant patients. In these instances, one commonly uses initial allergen concentrations in the range of 1:50,000 to 1:1,000,000. If, following the initial injection of the extract, an excessive amount of local swelling occurs (page 117), the antigen should be diluted tenfold before continuing treatment. In the rare instances in which a constitutional reaction occurs after the first injection of an extract, the material should be diluted 100 to 1000 times before re-starting therapy. Such an occurrence should not suggest abandonment of hyposensitization; in fact it is excellent additional evidence that the patient is indeed allergic to the injected material, but of course the dosage should be greatly reduced.

There are instances in which treatment may be instituted with more concentrated extracts than usual. If the patient has had the same allergen in the past without reactions and has not received treatment for perhaps four or five months, usually therapy can be resumed safely with a 1:10 dilution of the material previously administered. If one decides to shift from treatment with one allergen to another which is immunologically closely related to the first, it generally is unnecessary to reduce dosage to the usual starting concentrations.

In addition to the clinical considerations just mentioned, certain "titration" procedures have been proposed to determine the proper initial dose of extract in any particular case. These procedures indicate in a roughly quantitative fashion the patient's threshold of sensitivity to a certain substance. Increasing concentrations of a particular allergen are applied by various techniques to the skin, conjunctiva, nasal mucosa, or bronchial tree. Some allergists believe that mucous membrane tests are most reliable, but the more common procedure involves intracutaneous injections of serial five-fold or ten-fold dilutions of allergen into an extremity until a definite reaction is elicited. Treatment then is begun with a dilution of allergen which produces a small intracutaneous test

---

* In treating with Endo house dust (manufacturer's label), it is customary to start with a dilution of 1:400,000 or 1:40,000 and increase serially to a maximal concentration of 1:400.

response or a concentration just below that giving a prominent skin test reaction.*

Although this procedure may give some clues regarding the proper beginning dose of allergen, the initial titration level is no indication of the final concentration of allergen which a patient may tolerate. Some very sensitive patients, who at first receive only extremely dilute allergen, ultimately can tolerate surprisingly concentrated extracts. Arbitrarily maintaining such individuals on dilute extracts after they progress through a fixed increment of allergen dosage may result in gross under-treatment, in our opinion. It is noteworthy that no controlled, double-blind studies have demonstrated the efficacy of low dosage hyposensitization, and indeed moderate dosage treatment appeared inferior to high dosage therapy in recent double-blind studies.[8-9, 20]

Hyposensitization Schedules

There are three methods of conducting hyposensitization: preseasonal, co-seasonal, and perennial techniques. The first or preseasonal approach is the traditional one in which treatment is started each year prior to the season during which the patient anticipates symptoms. The dosage is raised so that a maximal level is achieved just prior to the onset of the season. Injections are discontinued during or following the season only to be resumed at the same time the following year. Co-seasonal treatment pertains to hyposensitization initiated when the patient first presents himself *during* the season in which his symptoms already have started. This, for most patients, is the least satisfactory of the three types of treatment. Perennial treatment consists of year-round administration of allergens. Usually the frequency of the injections can be decreased considerably after a maximal dose of extract has been reached and the season of most pronounced symptoms has passed, but an interval of four weeks between injections should not be exceeded. Sometimes widely spaced dosages of seasonal allergens need to be reduced. The doses then can be increased again to maximal tolerance by more frequent injections just before the season.

In choosing between perennial and preseasonal treatment, there are several circumstances which favor the former as the method of choice. In the first place, a significant number of pollen- or fungus-sensitive persons are also allergic to house dust. Since exposure to dust is greatest during the fall and winter months—a time when preseasonal treatment ordinarily has been discontinued—a perennial program would seem preferable in this rather large group of individuals. Such treatment also

---

* Our experience with skin titration has been that it is a time-consuming procedure which seems unnecessary in the average case. However, it may be of some value in estimating the starting concentration of allergen in cases in which unusually great sensitivity is suspected.

would seem more practical for patients whose seasonal symptoms extend throughout a large part of the year. For example, preseasonal treatment in patients allergic to tree and weed pollens covers so many months that generally it is much simpler to convert to perennial injections. Another consideration is the fact that many patients who think their allergic disease is strictly seasonal actually have perennial manifestations. By treating the patient throughout the year, one is able to observe him more closely and associate symptoms with exposure to additional allergens. Also, with perennial treatment the total number of injections per year often is about the same or even less than that required by the preseasonal method. This is particularly so if the patient gets along well on a maintenance injection once monthly throughout the year except for a few extra injections just before and during the season. It is the clinical impression of many allergists that results are better with perennial than with preseasonal therapy, especially after several years of treatment, though this is not an irrefutable fact. On the other hand, there are certain persons who are unwilling to accept perennial treatment or who are careless about keeping up interval injections. In many such cases it would be better for the patient to follow a preseasonal program faithfully than to be treated haphazardly by the perennial method.

Initially, the procedure is essentially the same for both the preseasonal and perennial methods. The starting concentration of allergen is determined by the criteria discussed previously, and treatment usually begins with a dose of 0.05 ml. If a reaction does not occur, the dosage may be increased according to a schedule of the type given on page 111. Generally, the dose each time is increased by an increment of about 50 per cent of the previous dose. A geometric progression in dosage would be most logical, but in the early phases of treatment it often is permissible to increase the amount of each injection somewhat more rapidly than at a later stage when more concentrated extracts are being administered. This is especially true if therapy is instituted with unusually dilute allergens. With preseasonal treatment it usually is possible to increase the dose more rapidly than usual if the patient has received the same allergen in the past without reactions. On the other hand, certain very sensitive patients tolerate increases in the amount of the more concentrated extracts only at a more gradual rate than indicated in the tentative dosage schedule. In such cases, increases in dosage of 0.02 or 0.03 ml. are indicated. There is some tendency for very sensitive patients to have reactions as they start to receive material from a more concentrated bottle of extract, even though the amount of antigen injected is the same as in the previous dose of more dilute material.* Possibly, allergens may be absorbed more rapidly from concentrated solutions than from more dilute ones, and there also is evidence that after storage for a period of time, dilute extracts may lose potency more than concen-

---

* 0.5 ml. of 1:500 should be equivalent to 0.05 ml. of 1:50.

trated ones. In part this may be due to relatively greater absorption of allergen onto glass surfaces[21] or to inactivation at air-glass-fluid interfaces. Thus, in treating highly reactive patients it may be wise to overlap slightly on the dosage of allergen when passing from one concentration to the next; for example, one might increase the dose of a 1:500 extract to 0.7 ml. before starting in the 1:50 solution at a dose of 0.05 ml.

ALLERGY TREATMENT

TENTATIVE DOSAGE SCHEDULE

To Doctor_____Date_____

Address_____

Suggestions for hyposensitization to_____

In case of_____

In administering allergy extracts extreme care must be taken to prevent allergic reactions. Fresh aqueous epinephrine (Adrenalin) 1/1000 and a tourniquet should always be available for instant use. One cc. tuberculin Luer syringes and 26 or 27 gauge needles are best to give the extract. Doses are injected subcutaneously in an extremity. The needle should be wiped off on an alcohol sponge to remove retained antigen before injecting. Frequent retraction of the Luer plunger will reveal any evidence of blood. If this occurs, do not give dose at that location; try again at another site. DO NOT massage the area after injection. Place cotton firmly over site and have patient hold for one minute. All patients should be observed for a period of at least 20 minutes following each dose of extract. In the event of allergic reaction (such as syncope, generalized itching of the skin, nausea, tightness of the chest or hay fever), 0.3 cc. epinephrine 1/1000 is given in the opposite arm and 0.1 cc. epinephrine given at the site of the injection. In more severe reactions, also apply tourniquet above injection site and use an intravenous antihistamine and/or pressor agent as indicated. If there is an excessive local reaction, reduce dosage by at least 0.1 cc., and repeat twice before attempting to increase dose again. In the event of a systemic reaction, reduce dose by 50 to 90 per cent.

Treatment should be given_____until_____or maintenance dose

is reached; then once every_____, depending upon symptoms.

Date			Date			Date			Date		
	Extract			Extract			Extract			Extract	
_____	_____	conc.	_____	_____	conc.	_____	_____	conc.	_____	_____	conc.
_____	_____	0.05cc.	_____	_____	0.05cc.	_____	_____	0.05cc.	_____	_____	0.05cc.
_____	_____	0.1 cc.	_____	_____	0.07cc.	_____	_____	0.07cc.	_____	_____	0.07cc.
_____	_____	0.2 cc.	_____	_____	0.1 cc.	_____	_____	0.1 cc.	_____	_____	0.1 cc.
_____	_____	0.4 cc.	_____	_____	0.15 cc.	_____	_____	0.15 cc.	_____	_____	0.15 cc.
_____	_____		_____	_____	0.20cc.	_____	_____	0.2 cc.	_____	_____	0.2 cc.
_____	_____		_____	_____	0.3 cc.	_____	_____	0.25cc.	_____	_____	0.25cc.
_____	_____		_____	_____	0.4 cc.	_____	_____	0.3 cc.	_____	_____	0.3 cc.
_____	_____		_____	_____		_____	_____	0.4 cc.	_____	_____	0.4 cc.
_____	_____		_____	_____		_____	_____	0.5 cc.	_____	_____	0.5 cc.

_____, M.D.

Figure 6–1. Example of allergen dosage schedule.

It must be strongly emphasized that any dosage schedule, such as the one illustrated on page 111, is tentative and should be modified in individual cases, especially if there is a tendency for reactions to occur.

There is considerable variation in the frequency with which hyposensitization is given. Usually an allergen is administered twice weekly early in the course of treatment while the dose and concentration of extract are being increased. However, if the season of expected symptoms is almost at hand, injections occasionally are given as often as every other day. More material should not be injected while there is still local tissue swelling from a previous treatment. When it is inconvenient for a patient to receive more than one injection per week, treatment must be started further in advance of the season than when hyposensitization can be given twice weekly.

Generally, about 20 to 25 injections are required to reach the maximal dose of allergen. If the treatments are given twice weekly, about two and one-half to three months will be required to arrive at the final maintenance dosage. Therefore, hyposensitization preferably should be instituted at least three months prior to the anticipated season, and it is desirable to allow a little extra time in case the patient misses some injections or if a slower than average progression of dosage become necessary because of reactions. Hyposensitization for perennial symptoms may be instituted at any time.

After the maintenance dose of allergen is reached, the frequency of the injections depends upon the time of the year. When a patient's season is several weeks away, the allergenic extract usually is given once weekly until the beginning of the troublesome period. Weekly injections of allergen may be continued through the season if symptoms are mild or absent. However, if considerable allergic difficulty occurs, one may try giving treatments twice weekly or even more often if there is apparent temporary improvement following each injection.

Other changes in procedure may be required during the season. The dosage of allergen commonly is reduced by one-half if significant allergic symptoms are present or by a lesser amount if the discomfort is slight. The reason for this change is that when a patient is inhaling antigen from the air at the same time he is receiving it by injection, there is a chance that the combined exposure will cause a constitutional reaction. Some allergists also modify the usual procedure by giving the injections of extract intracutaneously rather than subcutaneously during the season. If more than 0.1 ml. is to be administered, the first 0.1 ml. can be placed intracutaneously, and then, without withdrawal, the needle can be pushed on through the skin into the subcutaneous tissue. However, published proof of the advantage of this procedure seems to be lacking.

If one wishes to continue with perennial treatment after the season is over, it usually is possible gradually to increase the interval between injections to ten days, two weeks, three weeks, and finally four weeks. There are a few individuals who tend to have reactions if the interval between injections is extended beyond seven to fourteen days. In such instances, a reduced dosage may be tried; if this fails, preseasonal treatment may be substituted. Starting about four weeks before the onset of the season, patients on monthly maintenance therapy are given injections every one or two weeks, and the dosage is increased if it had been cut back during the winter. During the season, the frequency of injection and dosages of extract are determined by the same principles outlined in connection with preseasonal treatment. As the years pass by, cases treated successfully on a perennial basis generally require less and less modification of their treatment program during the troublesome season.

Patients treated for significant sensitivity to house dust or to other perennially encountered allergens may not be able to increase the interval between injections during the winter months quite so much as those hyposensitized only to pollens. If the interval is extended beyond a certain point, there may be a recurrence or increase in allergic symptoms for a few days prior to the next treatment. In this event, the frequency of injections should be increased to a point at which maximal relief is maintained from one injection to the next. Dust-sensitive persons may require injections every few days, particularly early in therapy. Later, allergen administration every two or three weeks may be adequate, and as time passes most of these patients can be treated once monthly.

Before the advent of antihistamines and other relatively potent symptomatic medications for the relief of hay fever, the pioneer clinical allergists utilized co-seasonal hyposensitization quite extensively. Unfortunately, the immunologic basis for such treatment is not clear, and its efficacy was not well documented by the type of evidence required by modern standards. Nevertheless, co-seasonal treatment still is practiced by a number of allergists, but even most of its adherents would admit that it is more difficult and hazardous (since overdosage causes worsening of symptoms) to obtain good relief this way than by preseasonal or perennial hyposensitization. As discussed previously, low initial doses should be employed when injections are started during the season. The treatments are given frequently, even daily, and many doctors give intracutaneous injections. The objective in co-seasonal treatment is to increase the dose of extract to a point at which the patient appears to experience temporary relief from his symptoms for several days. Thereafter, this same dose is repeated as needed to tide him through the rest of the season in reasonable comfort. The crux of the problem is to find this optimal dose with reasonable speed and yet without precipitating a constitutional reaction. While many would not object to starting hyposensitization during a pollen season, a commonly employed alternative is to proceed by a usual type of schedule,* relying chiefly on symptomatic medications to produce temporary relief. After the season is over, one has made a good start toward perennial hyposensitization.

---

* A low initial dose and reduction of subsequent dosages if symptoms are aggravated are assumed.

Maintenance Dosage

Probably the ideal maintenance dose of an allergenic extract is the largest amount which a patient consistently can tolerate without reactions.* This may not be a very large quantity of allergen in certain patients who are unusually sensitive. On the other hand, one frequently is surprised to find that some extremely sensitive patients are able to tolerate large amounts of extract if the dosage is slowly increased over a long period of time.

When the patient's sensitivity is of average degree, it is customary to maintain him on certain arbitrary maximal doses of extract. It is assumed that these doses are near the limits of most patients' tolerance. A typical maintenance dose for such patients is 0.5 ml. of a 1:50 (or 1:33) extract. Larger amounts seem necessary occasionally, but there is apt to be an inordinate number of reactions if one *routinely* attempts to reach doses much greater than those just mentioned. We have the impression that *small* variations in dosage probably do not appreciably affect therapeutic results but do lead to reactions in some patients. Under no circumstances should reactions be induced in order to reach some arbitrary maintenance dose.

Persons treated with a mixture of allergens must be given a larger volume of extract in order to receive a comparable maintenance dose of any one of the constituent allergens. Thus, it is common practice to use a maintenance dose of 0.7 ml. or more of the most concentrated material when a mixture of allergens is used. The exact maintenance dose depends upon the number of ingredients in the mixture, their proportions, the patient's degree of sensitivity, and, of course, his clinical response to treatment. The tendency to employ smaller doses of *each* allergen is one of the disadvantages of treating with mixed extracts. Nevertheless, this usually can be worked out satisfactorily if one does not use excessively complex mixtures.

Technique of Hyposensitization and Prevention of Reactions

Injections of allergens should be carried out only in a physician's office or in some comparable place where professional personnel and drugs are available to treat any reactions which might occur. Because of this possibility, patients should not administer their own injections. Although some physicians prefer to give all the hyposensitization injections themselves, delegation of this function to professional nurses seems acceptable *provided* they are extensively instructed in the procedure and that the physician is present in the office or clinic when the allergens are being administered. At the time of injection, the physician or his nurse routinely should ask the patient if he had any reaction to

---

* See page 109 for comments about low dosage treatment.

the previous treatment. Reduced dosage in case of reactions is discussed on page 119, and procedure in case of a lapse in treatment is discussed on page 122. Hyposensitization generally is omitted if it is discovered that the patient has an intercurrent infection with fever over 100° F. Overheated patients are asked to wait until they "cool off" before being given their injection, and in general one should be conservative in the choice of extract dosage on hot humid days when cutaneous vasodilatation favors rapid absorption of allergen.

The proper allergenic extract should be selected and the label on the vial read three times (before, during, and after filling the syringe) before it is injected. We cannot overemphasize the need for correct identification of patient, chart, and extract, so that no error is made through mistaken use of the wrong chart or material. We have found that different-colored rubber stoppers (red for strong concentration of 1:50, yellow for middle concentration, 1:500, green for the 1:5000 usual starting doses, and white for 1:50,00 or weaker concentrations) are of help in correct identification of strength of solutions. The rubber-capped allergen vials should be wiped off with an alcohol sponge before the material is withdrawn. A 1.0 ml. or 0.5 ml. tuberculin syringe and No. 26 or No. 27 gauge needle are recommended. Removing adherent allergen from the outer surface of the needle by wiping it with an alcohol sponge just before injection reduces local swelling at the site of administration. Before injection, the first and last names on the patient's record and the *two* previously charted injections are noted. This prevents mistakes which occur from using the wrong chart or raising an improperly recorded previous dose.

The patient should be seated and should place his hand on his hip, thus exposing the arm for treatment. The injection area of the arm is wiped off with alcohol. While holding the skin taut with the thumb and forefinger of one hand, the needle is thrust into the patient's subcutaneous tissue at a site on the lateral side of the arm midway between the elbow and the shoulder (Fig. 6–2). To prevent temporary arthralgia, injections should not be made close to a joint. Alternate arms are used for the series of injections. Antigen should be given rather high in the midportion of the arm one time and low in the midportion the next time. Shifting the areas helps to prevent local hyposensitization which may occur if all injections are made at the same site.[22]

After the needle has been thrust into the skin and before any allergen is injected, one must always pull back on the plunger of the syringe. The appearance of blood in the syringe indicates that the needle should be withdrawn without injecting the allergen. If no blood is observed, the extract may be injected at a moderate rate. Occasionally pulling back again on the plunger is an extra measure of precaution. After the injection has been given, a cotton pledget soaked in alcohol is held over the needle and pressure is applied over the site. The needle then is withdrawn, and the patient shifts his finger to the pledget and holds it on his

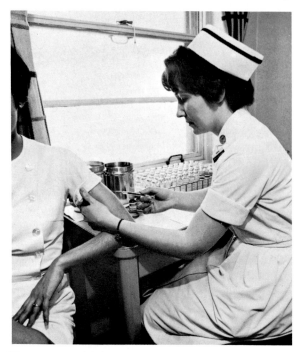

Figure 6–2. Injection administration technique (see text).

arm for at least one minute. This minimizes seepage of allergen into small vessels which may have been traumatized by the needle. The dosage given then is recorded.

The patient is required to wait in the doctor's office for at least 20 minutes after receiving treatment. This last precaution merits emphasis; severe reactions commonly begin within this period of time and respond readily to treatment, but it is essential that both patient and physician be present to institute therapy of the reaction promptly. Death is most likely to occur in the patient who leaves the doctor's office immediately and has a severe reaction on the street. Even after the 20 minute wait in the office, it is advisable that strenuous exertion be deferred for one hour or more. Probably because of an increased rate of allergen absorption associated with dilatation of cutaneous vessels, reactions are most likely to occur when, for example, a child rapidly bicycles home on a hot day.

Although the aforementioned precautions should avert potential constitutional reactions, a few may occur nonetheless. Sometimes these happen very unexpectedly in patients who have tolerated the same dose many times previously. Perhaps unavoidable, rapid seepage of allergen into blood vessels accounts for some of these untoward effects. In other patients a constitutional reaction may be the first indication that the dose of allergen has exceeded the patient's tolerance, though more commonly one is forewarned by increasing local reactions. It is important, therefore, that physicians administering these potent materials be familiar with the manifestations and treatment of reactions and that they have immediately available the drugs and equipment for managing these emergencies.

Local Reactions

It is common for a small amount of redness and swelling to appear at the site of allergen injections. In fact, this occurrence may be welcomed as additional evidence that the patient is sensitive to the material being given. However, excessively large local swellings should be avoided because they are uncomfortable and because they may presage development of more severe constitutional symptoms. There is considerable variability in the extent of local reactions that should be regarded as excessive. Some persons exhibit considerable redness and swelling of the arm at all dosage levels. In such individuals, one need be concerned only if the reactions seem to be increasing. In less sensitive individuals, even a small amount of swelling might be significant. For this reason, a conservative dosage schedule should be followed until the physician is familiar with the patient's pattern of response. Usually the local area of swelling should not exceed 6 cm. in diameter, and it should have subsided by the following day.

If a significant local reaction occurs, the subsequent dose must be reduced by about 0.1 ml. and held at this level for two or three treatments before increasing it. If the local reaction is slight or equivocal, it may be adequate simply to repeat the same dose once before increasing the amount given.

Constitutional Reactions

The mild type of constitutional reaction may be manifested by a repetition of the patient's symptoms for which he is receiving hyposensitization, e.g., rhinorrhea, nasal stuffiness, itching of the nose or eyes, sneezing, cough, wheezing, or conjunctival redness. Pruritus, particularly of the palms, may be noted with or without flushing or urticaria. In severe reactions, the patient may go on to demonstrate almost any or all manifestations of allergic disease. Usually the patient is frightened. In addition to progression of the previously mentioned symptoms, there may be shortness of breath, abdominal cramps, vomiting, and diarrhea. Hypotension and tachycardia are common. With shock, flushing may be replaced by pallor and sweating. Uterine cramps and vaginal bleeding have been observed. Pregnant women may abort, although this is an exceedingly rare occurrence which we have never seen. Angioedema commonly accompanies urticaria, and the glottis or tongue may become swollen. Convulsions occur rarely. Sometimes there is delayed fever, but initially hypothermia is more common. Death most likely results from respiratory tract obstruction at either the bronchiolar or laryngeal-tracheal level, or the patient expires from shock.

Treatment. Not only is it imperative for physicians administering allergenic extracts to be familiar with the method of treating constitutional reactions produced by these agents, but the following procedure should be useful for all physicians who might be required to treat an anaphylactic type of reaction from any cause (e.g., other drugs, insect stings, vaccines, or foreign serum). Immediately upon making the diagnosis, a tourniquet is applied on the arm above the site of injection. This may reduce the systemic absorption of the antigen. The tourniquet must be removed momentarily every 10 to 15 minutes. The patient should lie down, and the blood pressure and pulse rate are recorded and rechecked every few minutes. An emesis basin and bedpan should be available. As soon as possible, 0.3 ml. of 1:1000 epinephrine is injected subcutaneously in the arm opposite the tourniquet. If necessary, this can be massaged to facilitate absorption. It is often advisable to inject an additional 0.1 ml. epinephrine at the site of the allergen administration in order to produce vasoconstriction and thus slow down the rate of absorption. If the epinephrine seems to be effective, it is then wise to wait. Small doses can be repeated as often as every 5 to 15 minutes a few times. Several small doses are more effective and less dangerous than single large doses. Of course, this drug should be avoided, if possible, in patients with recent myocardial injury or histories of an arrhythmia.

If the patient does not respond rapidly to epinephrine, an intravenous antihistaminic should next be considered; for example, 60 to 80 mg. diphenhydramine (6 to 8 ml. Benadryl) could be given to an adult over a three minute period. This often gives dramatic relief of pruritus and, more importantly, may help prevent glottic edema. In treating very mild reactions, one may wish to defer giving intravenous antihistamines, since they are likely to make the patient so drowsy that he will need to be assisted home. Oral antihistamines lack the speed and potency needed in the acute therapy of a severe constitutional reaction, but they are of major value in preventing a relapse after the acute difficulty has been controlled.

If the reaction is characterized especially by severe asthma and shock is absent, intravenous aminophylline may be given to patients not responding to epinephrine. The usual adult dose is 0.5 gm. in 20 ml. of solution given over five to ten minutes. The injection is terminated if the patient develops nausea or other evidence of an adverse effect (see page 133).

If hypotension is observed, intravenous fluids are started to which may be added, if indicated, some pressor drug such as levarterenol or metaraminol. Moderate warmth should be maintained during shock and the blood pressure should be monitored frequently.

The patient must be carefully observed for signs of upper airway obstruction. A mechanical airway may be needed if he becomes unconscious. Oxygen should be administered for cyanosis. Tracheostomy may become necessary if severe laryngeal edema ensues.

The administration of corticosteroids has sometimes been overemphasized in the treatment of these emergencies: their effect often is too slow to be life-saving, and they are not potent in protecting animals against anaphylactic shock. However, there can be delayed deaths, and ,it does seem desirable to give at least 100 mg. hydrocortisone sodium succinate intravenously if the patient is not responding promptly to the previously described measures (see page 150).

Rarely is it necessary to utilize all these steps in the treatment of a constitutional reaction. In the vast majority of cases, the use of a tourniquet and epinephrine suffices to stop the reaction. Promptness in initiating treatment merits emphasis. Needless to say, the subsequent dose of allergenic extract should be markedly reduced after a constitutional reaction. Depending on its severity and other factors, 10 per cent to 50 per cent of the reactive dose might be administered the next time. No further attempt should be made to reach dosage levels which repeatedly have evoked even mild constitutional symptoms in very sensitive patients.

Duration of Hyposensitization Treatment

Unfortunately, there is a dearth of systematic long-term studies of patients which have been recorded during and after hyposensitization therapy. Consequently, advice about recommended duration of this treatment is based largely on clinical impression, and opinions about this may vary. Furthermore, it is difficult to make generalizations, since there is so much variability among individuals: some patients continue to do well indefinitely after stopping hyposensitization, while more relapse after a highly variable period of time. It would appear, however, that the longer hyposensitization is maintained, the longer patients continue to do well after the injections are discontinued. If the therapy is stopped after the first season, there is commonly an early relapse of symptoms. With more prolonged treatment, many individuals seem to feel well after discontinuing hyposensitization for a period at least as long as that during which apparently successful treatment was given. Therefore, in order to answer the question concerning how long treatment should be given, it seems best to familiarize the patient with the possibilities. These would suggest that in order to avoid a rapid relapse of symptoms, most patients should expect rather routinely to undergo at least three or more years of treatment. More prolonged hyposensitization is justified for patients who have had severe asthma rather than for those who suffer only from hay fever. Relief appears more likely to be sustained when the patient is essentially symptom-free on discontinuing hyposensitization than when improvement is only partial. If relapse does occur, hyposensitization may be resumed after re-evaluation of the patient's allergies. Although the prospect of three or more years of treatment may at first dismay certain patients, usually they are willing to maintain the hyposensitization program if they are getting along well, particularly if the injections are needed only at monthly intervals throughout much of the year.

Hyposensitization often is terminated when the patient has gone through three seasons with few symptoms. More prolonged treatment sometimes is requested by gratified patients who formerly had very severe difficulty. Before stopping the injections, one should remember that a lapse in therapy of more than a few months requires dropping the dose back to weaker dilutions of extract. Building up to the maintenance dose again often would require more injections than an entire year of monthly maintenance therapy. Since there is no known way to identify persons who are likely to have an early relapse, it may be wise to have *the patient* elect to discontinue hyposensitization, after giving him the available information. Finally, there are some persons who relapse every time treatment is discontinued, even after prolonged hyposensitization. For such people, particularly asthmatic patients, there seems to be little choice but to maintain therapy indefinitely. In general, because of the aforementioned lack of satisfactory long-term studies, these suggestions concerning duration of hyposensitization should be regarded as highly tentative. One recent report suggests that effects of hyposensitization therapy commonly may be lost within months after the injections are discontinued.[11]

Treatment Failures

Some treatment failures can be explained by incorrect diagnosis, the use of improper or impotent extracts, or inadequate dosage. Sometimes favorable results may have been obscured by complicating factors such as respiratory infections, emotional upsets, important food or animal allergies, or pregnancy. A few patients have such a broad base of sensitivities that adequate protection from all their allergens is virtually impossible.

Even though the results of treatment during the first season may have been somewhat disappointing, it is not uncommon for patients to do better during the second year of treatment than the first.[10] Sometimes a larger dose should be tried. However, before proceeding with further hyposensitization, a thorough review of the whole case should be made during and after a poor season. The physician should see whether the poor results can be attributed to any of the factors mentioned in the previous paragraph. Particular attention should be given to the completeness of the etiologic diagnosis; for example, many treatment failures in late summer hay fever are due to the fact that the person is allergic to fungi as well as ragweed, and he has been treated only for ragweed allergy. Sometimes patients have good relief of their symptoms for several seasons only to relapse while still under treatment. Newly developed sensitivities or undue exposure to the allergen should be suspected in such cases. In some instances, however, no explanation for treatment failures can be found, and hyposensitization should be abandoned after a reasonable trial.

Storage of Allergy Extracts

Solutions of allergenic extracts should be stored in the refrigerator at a temperature below 45° F. (but above freezing), since they deteriorate more rapidly at higher temperatures. However, exposure to ordinary room temperatures for a few days should not cause concern. In the course of mailing or travel, temporary warming of the material may be unavoidable, but even brief exposures to high temperatures should not occur. Bacterial contamination of the allergens also must be prevented. With proper aseptic technique, local infections from administration of contaminated extracts can be avoided.

Under proper conditions of storage, allergenic materials should not lose significant potency for a period of about 12 months. Unglycerinated extracts much older than this are unreliable. Therefore, it is advisable to order no more than one year's supply at a time. Since dilute allergen solutions deteriorate more rapidly than concentrated ones, it is wise to store them in undiluted form and prepare weaker solutions as needed. Glycerinated and lyophilized materials are much more stable,[23] but glycerine will cause stinging and irritant intracutaneous skin reactions if not diluted to low concentration before injection.

Special Problems

Pregnancy. Tolerance to allergenic extracts may change during pregnancy. Therefore, even when a woman has been accustomed to receiving a certain maintenance dose of allergen, it is advisable to reduce it (generally to about half) when she is pregnant. Following delivery there also may be alterations in tolerance to allergens, thus suggesting the advisability of a further temporary reduction in extract dosage at that time. *Initiation* of hyposensitization is permissible during pregnancy, but the added hazard makes it reasonable to defer this treatment unless the indications are strong. Besides, it is difficult to evaluate the results of hyposensitization during pregnancy (see page 26).

Children. In general, the procedure for hyposensitization in children is essentially the same as that in adults. They usually tolerate doses of extract which are relatively large in comparison with their size.

Large Local Reactions. A few patients have uncomfortable, inordinately large local reactions at all dosage levels without ever exhibiting signs of a systemic reaction. Giving the injection deeply subcutaneously may help relieve this problem. If this does not suffice, mixing the allergen with a small dose of epinephrine or an antihistamine solution is helpful. We do not favor this latter procedure as a routine, however, since it eliminates a valuable warning sign that one may be overdosing patients. Giving the dose in divided portions also may help.

Interrupted Treatment. If there is a lapse of substantially over one month in the hyposensitization program, the dose should be reduced. The exact decrement depends upon a number of factors. One should treat very conservatively patients who have experienced systemic reactions or who gave unusually large skin test responses, whereas in less sensitive cases there can be considerably more latitude in the procedure used. As a rough approximation, after two months without injections the dose usually would be reduced to 50 to 75 per cent, after three months to about 10 to 20 per cent, and after four or five months to about 1 to 5 per cent. Often the amount given can be built up again rapidly.

Starting A New Lot of Extract. If there is no interruption in hyposensitization, it is common practice to reduce the dose about one-third when starting with a fresh bottle of extract since the new extract may be more potent than the old. A larger decrease would be indicated if the previous extract were unusually old. A much greater reduction should be used if the source of supply is changed owing to the lack of precise standardization of these materials. After these temporary reductions in dosage, the amount given can generally be increased rapidly to the previous level. In patients who are receiving maintenance injections at relatively infrequent intervals, some temporary increase in the frequency of injections may be necessary during this period of readjustment to fresh extract. It generally is not advisable to increase the dose when injections are more than two weeks apart.

Oral Hyposensitization. Although it has been tried over a period of many years, the consensus is that the oral administration of inhalant allergens has failed to be a consistently effective form of therapy. Hyposensitization by inhalation also has been tried but has not received wide acceptance. Oral hyposensitization to plant oils for contact dermatitis is discussed on page 261, and this approach to food allergy is reviewed on page 218.

Administration of Bacterial Vaccines

The use of bacterial vaccines in the treatment of allergy is perhaps the most controversial subject in the field. This is discussed in Chapter 2. Some advocates of this treatment use autogenous vaccines made of organisms obtained from the patient, and others use "stock" vaccines. The former might seem more rational, but in view of the recovery of variable organisms in successive sputum cultures from the same patient, stock vaccines are most widely used. There are certain patients, however, from whom the same organism is repeatedly obtained from the sinuses or lower respiratory tract, and some physicians would favor the use of an autogenous vaccine in these cases. Unfortunately, skin testing has not been very helpful in clarifying this matter, since many vaccines give immediate and/or delayed reactions in a high portion of normal persons. This being the case, the most commonly used stock vaccines are mixtures containing a number of the organisms most commonly cultured from the respiratory tract. Preparations of this sort are commercially available (e.g., Bacterial Vaccine No. 615, Parke, Davis & Co.) and commonly contain about 10^9 killed organisms per milliliter. They can be administered according to a schedule similar to that employed for environmental allergens (page 111), commonly building up from a 1:100 dilution to the full strength extract. Usually the dose can be raised quite rapidly, since clear-cut immediate constitutional reactions are rare. In contrast with the pollen, mold, and dust extracts, it is necessary to shake these suspensions before withdrawing them into the syringe. This brief discussion of bacterial vaccines has been included for completeness and does not necessarily imply advocacy of their clinical use in atopic disease.

REPOSITORY HYPOSENSITIZATION
Neal A. Vanselow, M.D.

The rapid absorption of conventional allergenic extracts from the site of injection has given aqueous hyposensitization therapy several disadvantages. Frequent injections usually are required, making therapy difficult or impractical for the patient who, for occupational or other reasons, is unable to make numerous trips to the physician's office. Rapid absorption of aqueous extracts has also resulted in frequent allergic reactions in some patients extremely sensitive to the treatment antigen. These difficulties have made aqueous hyposensitization treatment impossible or dangerous for some patients who might otherwise be expected to benefit from it. In an attempt to decrease the number of yearly injections needed and to permit the injection of more highly sensitive patients, allergists long have been interested in developing methods of slowing absorption of antigen. A number of such methods have been used clinically in recent years and are collectively referred to as "repository" hyposensitization.

Water-in-Oil Emulsions

An emulsion may be defined as an intimate mixture of two immiscible liquids, one of which is dispersed in the other in the form of fine droplets. Oil and water are immiscible but are capable of forming two types of emulsions, depending upon the conditions under which they are combined and the type of emulsifying agent present. Water-in-oil emulsions can be visualized as mixtures in which each droplet of aqueous material is surrounded by minute droplets of oil. Oil-in-water emulsions

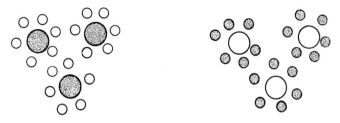

WATER IN OIL EMULSION   OIL IN WATER EMULSION

Figure 6–3. A water-in-oil emulsion can be pictured as a mixture in which each droplet of aqueous material is surrounded by multiple droplets of oil. The reverse situation is true in an oil-in-water emulsion, an example of which is milk.

—an example of which is milk—are mixtures in which the reverse is true (Figure 6–3).

It has been demonstrated by a number of investigators that if an antigen is injected in the form of a water-in-oil emulsion, the resulting antibody titer will be both higher and more persistent than that obtained when the same antigen is injected in the aqueous form.[24] The ability of a substance, such as the oil phase of an emulsion, to increase the antibody response to an antigen when injected with it has been termed an adjuvant effect. The mechanism by which water-in-oil emulsions exert an adjuvant effect is probably complex but is believed to depend in part upon prolonged retention of the emulsified antigen at the site of injection.[25]

Loveless[26] was the first to use water-in-oil emulsions in the treatment of allergic respiratory disease. Recognizing the potential advantages of delayed absorption of antigen, she treated ragweed-sensitive patients with a single yearly injection of emulsified ragweed extract. By 1957, she had administered more than 1200 injections of ragweed emulsion and concluded that a single yearly repository injection of emulsified extract produced the same clinical response as multiple aqueous treatments. Other investigators subsequently confirmed these observations, with resultant widespread use of emulsion therapy in the management of asthma and allergic rhinitis.

As presently used, allergenic emulsions are composed of three components: an aqueous extract of the desired allergen, a highly refined mineral oil (Drakeol 6 V R), and an emulsifying agent. The emulsifying agent most widely used is isomannide monooleate (Arlacel A), a substance with hydrophobic and hydrophilic terminal chemical groupings which promotes emulsification by its orienting action at the oil-aqueous interphase. Using any one of a number of mechanical devices, a shearing force is applied to a mixture of these materials. This causes dispersion of the aqueous extract into the oil, resulting in a water-in-oil emulsion which is homogeneous, opaque white in color, and the consistency of hand lotion. Allergenic emulsions are not commercially available and must be both prepared and tested by the physician prior to use. Adequate testing involves measures to ensure sterility, completeness of emulsification, and absence of tissue irritability.

Emulsion therapy has been used in the treatment of allergic rhinitis, extrinsic bronchial asthma, and, by a few clinicians, in the treatment of Hymenoptera sensitivity. Experience indicates that patients with isolated seasonal sensitivities are more apt to be good candidates for emulsion therapy than are patients with multiple sensitivities and perennial symptoms. Emulsions may offer a significant advantage over aqueous hyposensitization in the patient who is extremely sensitive to the allergen used in treatment, since a large dose of antigen can usually be injected with less probability of a systemic allergic reaction. Individuals unable to obtain regular aqueous injections because of occupation, physical disability, or other reasons may also be candidates for emulsion therapy. Negroes and children under six years usually are not treated with emulsions because of an apparently high incidence of cysts and sterile abscesses at the injection site. It is also felt that serious systemic disease in addition to asthma and allergic rhinitis is a contraindication to emulsion therapy.

The dose of allergen given in each injection of emulsion is dependent upon aqueous antigen tolerance. This can be determined in part by the patient's history and by skin tests with serial dilutions of aqueous extract, but it is best measured by giving each patient one or more injections of aqueous extract prior to emulsion therapy. Most allergic individuals can tolerate 10 to 25 times as much allergen in emulsion form as they can in a single aqueous injection. If the aqueous antigen tolerance is low, it can be increased by a series of "build up" aqueous injections prior to emulsion therapy. In practice, no more than 7500 to 10,000 pollen units of allergen generally are given in a single repository injection. Most allergists using emulsion therapy give one or two repository injections of each inhalant allergen to which the patient demonstrates significant clinical sensitivity. The timing of these injections in relation to the season of exposure has varied. We have given the initial injection 12 to 14 weeks before the season and a booster 10 weeks later. Just prior to each injection, a prick test is performed with the emulsion, and the dose reduced if the patient demonstrates a positive reaction.

The injections are given subcutaneously or, preferably, intramuscularly in the lower third of the triceps or in the deltoid area. Following each injection, the patient is observed for 20 minutes. He is also asked to avoid alcoholic beverages or strenuous physical activity for at least 24 hours, since these tend to speed absorption of allergen and increase the chance of an allergic reaction. For the same reason, local heat should not be applied to relieve discomfort at the injection site.

In emulsion therapy, as in aqueous hyposensitization, transient local or systemic allergic reactions may occur. Local allergic reactions consist of swelling, erythema, increased heat, and pruritus at the injection site.

Systemic reactions may range from mild rhinitis and urticaria to more serious anaphylactic reactions with asthma, hypotension, and syncope. In our experience, however, systemic reactions following emulsion therapy are usually mild to moderate in severity. As contrasted with aqueous hyposensitization, where most reactions appear within 30 minutes, allergic reactions from emulsion therapy are most apt to occur two hours after the injection and may be delayed as long as 24 hours.

In addition to immediate local allergic responses, delayed local reactions have been reported following emulsion therapy. These may appear weeks or months after the injection and may consist of nodules, cysts, and sterile abscesses at the injection site. These constitute a serious drawback to emulsion therapy since they are persistent and painful and may be associated with systemic symptoms such as fever. In certain cases these local reactions have required surgical drainage. The mechanism of production of these reactions is unknown. Some authors have postulated an immunologic reaction, but in other cases irritating substances in the emulsifying agent have been incriminated. It has been found that the incidence of these delayed local reactions can be greatly minimized by testing the emulsion and each of its components for tissue irritability in mice prior to use in humans.[27]

There are several other factors to be considered regarding the use of allergenic emulsions in humans. It has been demonstrated that the injection of an emulsified allergen into a nonatopic individual or into an atopic individual who is not already sensitive to it can result in the induction of delayed and/or immediate skin reactivity to the allergen.[28] Since the induced skin reactivity has not yet been associated with signs or symptoms of asthma or allergic rhinitis, the significance of this phenomenon is uncertain, but emulsion therapy should not be given unless there is unequivocal historical and skin test evidence to show that the patient is allergic to the antigen used in treatment. The ability of mineral oil to induce plasma cell tumors in mice and the possibility of production of immunological disease from chronic administration of adjuvant has also aroused concern in some circles. At the present time, however, there is little evidence to indicate that these potential side effects have actually occurred in humans.[29]

Attempts to evaluate the effectiveness of emulsion therapy have been hampered by the lack of objective parameters to measure the severity of allergic rhinitis and bronchial asthma. As with aqueous therapy, clinical results have not necessarily correlated with measurable changes in titers of reagin, blocking antibody, or hemagglutinating antibody. For this reason, there is little evidence to prove that the apparent therapeutic effect obtained in allergic patients is an adjuvant effect in the usual sense of the term. Many allergists have reported emulsion therapy to be effective, but in most cases these reports have been based on uncontrolled studies employing subjective methods of evaluation. Few double-blind studies with placebo controls have been attempted.

In the cases in which this has been accomplished, the groups studied were small and the results of emulsion therapy unimpressive.[30] Until better evidence of its efficacy is available and until present concern over possible long-term toxicity is resolved, emulsion therapy cannot be recommended without reservation. In the United States at present, it can be given only on an investigational basis with prior approval of the Food and Drug Administration.

Alum-Precipitated Extracts

Studies demonstrating that precipitation with alum can slow absorption of an antigen and result in an adjuvant effect have encouraged the use of alum-precipitated extracts in the treatment of persons with asthma and allergic rhinitis. Although early alum-precipitated materials were sticky and difficult to work with, recent work has resulted in the development of a preparation which is flocculent and easy to administer.* Nondefatted pollen is mixed with the organic solvent pyridine, resulting in extraction of some lipid as well as the water-soluble fraction. Alum is added, precipitating an antigenic complex. After excess pyridine and alum are removed by washing, the precipitate is suspended in buffered saline. The precipitate tends to settle with storage and must be resuspended prior to use by shaking the extract vial. Alum-precipitated allergenic extracts are administered subcutaneously in the same manner as aqueous extracts.

It has been claimed that therapy with alum-precipitated materials offers several advantages over conventional aqueous therapy. The delayed absorption of allergen is said to permit the administration of fewer yearly injections than required with aqueous hyposensitization. After a build-up series of eight or nine weekly injections of increasing dosage, it is recommended by the manufacturer that maintenance injections be given only every four weeks. It is also claimed that treatment with alum-precipitated extracts permits the administration of larger amounts of allergen to sensitive patients with a lesser possibility of systemic allergic reaction. Both local and systemic reactions have been reported, however. As with emulsion therapy, the onset of these reactions may be delayed several hours. Some authors believe that the inclusion of part of the lipid portion of ragweed pollen in the extract results in greater relief of nasal and ocular pruritus than does treatment with conventional extracts which contain only water-soluble fractions. This claim has not been clearly substantiated.

Although they must be administered more frequently than emulsified extracts, alum-precipitated extracts appear to offer some advantages over emulsion therapy. They are commercially available and relatively easy to administer. No cysts, nodules, or sterile abscesses have been re-

---

* Allpyral, Dome Chemicals, Inc., New York, N.Y.

ported following treatment, and there has been no evidence to suggest that alum-precipitated materials can induce skin sensitivity or malignancy in either man or experimental animals. The main uncertainty about alum-precipitated extracts is that of efficacy. Most of the studies carried out with these preparations have been poorly controlled. Until adequate double-blind studies are made, questions regarding the therapeutic efficacy of alum-precipitated allergenic extracts will remain unanswered.

Other Repository Methods

A number of other repository preparations have been advocated for the treatment of allergic respiratory disease. These include formalinized tannates of pollen extract, pollen allergens in gelatin, and alginates. None of these methods has gained widespread acceptance and none has proved superior to either conventional aqueous therapy or to repository techniques.

REFERENCES

1. Noon, L.: Prophylactic inoculation against hay fever. Lancet 1:1572, 1911.
2. Freeman, J.: Further observations on the treatment of hay fever by hypodermic inoculations of pollen vaccine. Lancet 2:814, 1911.
3. Levine, P., and Coca, A. F.: Studies in hypersensitiveness. XXII. On the nature of the alleviating effect of the specific treatment of atopic conditions. J. Immunol. 11:449, 1926.
4. Cooke, R. A., Barnard, J. H., Hebald, S., and Stull, A.: Serological evidence of immunity with co-existing sensitization in a type of human allergy (hay fever). J. Exper. Med. 62:733, 1935.
5. Connell, J. T., and Sherman, W. B.: Skin sensitizing antibody titer. III. Relationship of the skin-sensitizing antibody titer to the intracutaneous skin test, to the tolerance of injections of antigens, and to the effects of prolonged treatment with antigen. J. Allergy 35:169, 1964.
6. Augustin, R.: Grass pollen allergens. II. Antigen-antibody precipitation patterns in gel: their interpretation as a serological problem and in relation to skin reactivity. Immunology 2:148, 1959.
7. Conference on the evaluation of hay fever therapy, Asthma Research 1:355, 1964.
8. Johnstone, D. E.: Study of the role of antigen dosage in treatment of pollenosis and pollen asthma. A.M.A. J. Dis. Child. 94:1, 1957.
9. Johnstone, D. E., and Crump, L.: Value of hyposensitization therapy for perennial bronchial asthma in children. Pediatrics 27:39, 1961.
10. Lowell, F. C., Franklin, W., and Williams, M.: A "double blind" study of treatment with aqueous allergenic extracts in cases of allergic rhinitis. J. Allergy 34:165, 1963.
11. Lowell, F. C., and Franklin, W.: A double-blind study of the effectiveness and specificity of injection therapy in ragweed hay fever. New England J. Med. 273:675, 1965.
12. Frankland, A. W., and Augustin, R.: Prophylaxis of summer hay fever and asthma. A controlled trial comparing crude grass pollen extracts with the isolated main protein component. Lancet 1:1055, 1954.
13. Bruun, E.: Controlled examination of the specificity of specific desensitization in asthma. Acta allergol. 2:122, 1949.
14. Frankland, A. W., Hughes, W. H., and Gorrill, R. H.: Autogenous bacterial vaccines in treatment of asthma. Brit. M. J. 2:941, 1955.
15. Johnstone, D. E.: Study of the value of bacterial vaccines in the treatment of bronchial asthma associated with respiratory infections. Pediatrics 24:427, 1959.

16. Aas, K., Berdal, P., Henriksen, S., and Gardborg, O.: Bacterial allergy in childhood asthma and the effect of vaccine treatment. Acta paediat. 52:338, 1963.

17. Fontana, V. E., Salanitro, A. S., Wolfe, H. I., and Moreno, F.: Bacterial vaccine and infectious asthma. J.A.M.A. 193:895, 1965.

18. Barr, S. E., Brown, H., Fuchs, M., Orvis, H., Connor, A., Murray, F. J., and Seltzer, A : A double-blind study of the effects of bacterial vaccine on infective asthma. J. Allergy 36:47, 1965.

19. Norman, P. S., and Winkenwerder, W. L.: Treatment of ragweed hay fever by desensitization with antigen E. J. Allergy 37:103, 1966 (Abstract).

20. Lowell, F. C., Franklin, W., and Williams, M.: Comparison of two dosage levels of aqueous extract in the treatment of ragweed pollenosis. J. Allergy 36:214, 1965.

21. Hjorth, N.: Instability of pollen antigen solutions. Acta allergol. 11:249, 1957.

22. Lowell, F. C., and Williams, M.: The effect of subcutaneous injections of allergenic extract on the local reactivity to intracutaneously injected extract. J. Allergy 34:35, 1963.

23. Johnson, M. C., Schiele, A. W., and Hampton, S. F.: Studies on the optimum concentration of glycerine in the preparation and preservation of ragweed pollen extract. J. Allergy 26:429, 1955.

24. Davenport, F.: Applied immunology of mineral oil adjuvants. J. Allergy 32:177, 1961.

25. Barlow, P., and Bortz, A.: Studies on repository antigen preparations. I. Retention of antigen at the injection site in rats. Univ. Michigan M. Bull. 26:138, 1960.

26. Loveless, M.: Repository immunization in pollen allergy. J. Immunol. 79:68, 1957.

27. Vanselow, N., Barlow, P., McLean, J., and Sheldon, J.: Repository therapy in allergic respiratory disease. Postgrad. Med. 35:165, 1964.

28. Feinberg, S., Becker, R., Slavin, R., Feinberg, A., and Sparks, D. B.: The sensitizing effects of emulsified pollen antigens in atopic subjects naturally sensitive to an unrelated antigen. J. Allergy 33:285, 1962.

29. Beebe, G., Simon, A., Vivona, S.: Followup study on army personnel who received adjuvant virus vaccine. 1951–1953. Am. J. M. Sc. 247:385, 1964.

30. Dworetzky, M., and Isaacs, N. J.: Small-dose emulsion treatment of ragweed pollenosis. A double-blind study continued for three seasons. J. Allergy 35:438, 1964.

Chapter Seven

DRUGS
USEFUL
IN ALLERGIC
DISEASE

Each physician should have certain favored medications which he uses for particular problems. Working repeatedly with the same simple set of drugs to treat a single condition enables one to become familiar with the expected response to each drug. However, one should be aware of alternative possibilities in the event that the usual regimen does not prove satisfactory. In fact, this availability of a myriad of drugs for treating allergic conditions makes it absolutely necessary that the physician know the contents of each medication he uses; otherwise he may mistakenly administer two materials with completely unrelated proprietary names, not realizing that each contains the same chemical compound. The following groups of drugs have been helpful in the management of various allergic problems.

BRONCHIAL ANTISPASMODIC DRUGS

Sympathomimetic Drugs

There are two types of sympathetic receptors. The first are the so-called alpha receptors, stimulation of which constricts vascular smooth muscle of the skin, mucosae and major viscera. The beta receptors mediate relaxation of the bronchial musculature (bronchodilation), cardiac stimulation and muscular vascular dilation.[1] Thus, drugs producing primarily alpha receptor stimulation might be expected to reduce the edema in diseases such as allergic rhinitis and urticaria and to combat allergic shock, but beta receptor stimulators would be more valuable in bronchial asthma. Actually, all the sympathomimetic drugs have some effect on both alpha and beta receptors. However, norepinephrine primarily is an alpha receptor stimulator, isoproterenol acts mainly on beta receptors, and epinephrine affects both.

Epinephrine. Historically, epinephrine was the first potent drug used for treating allergic diseases, and it remains a standard with which newer agents are compared. Given subcutaneously in a dosage of 0.3 ml. (0.3 mg.) of a 1:1000 solution, epinephrine hydrochloride frequently relieves the clinical manifestations of bronchial asthma, urticaria, anaphylactic shock (see page 118) and other immediate type hypersensitivity reactions. This dose can be repeated several times, if necessary, at 5 to 20 minute intervals. Side effects are less marked than with single, large doses. Caution should be used in giving the drug to patients with cerebral atherosclerosis or with a tendency to cardiac arrhythmias. Like several other drugs, epinephrine has a much reduced bronchodilator effect in vivo and in vitro when the pH is below normal (see page 165).[2]

Aerosol epinephrine, in 1:100 concentration, also is an effective bronchodilator and also can augment the effect of the parenterally administered drug.[3] It is essential, however, that the aerosol be generated in a suitable nebulizer that delivers 0.5 to 3.0 micron droplets, which are carried down into the lower respiratory tract (e.g., a DeVilbiss No. 40 or No. 42 nebulizer or other similar glass or plastic nebulizers). It also is important to instruct the patient adequately in the use of the nebulizer. Generally, two to five inhalations are tried at a time as needed for relief. The effect usually is prompt and striking, and side reactions are not often encountered. Furthermore, in selected cases, the nebulizer provides the patient with a ready source of bronchodilator at home. However, since the pulmonary irritant effects of aerosol solutions have not been entirely overcome, even though aerosols have been widely used for many years, it is probably wise to reserve this treatment for patients who will not abuse it. Measured, therapeutic doses of aerosol epinephrine also can be delivered through metering valves from unbreakable, pressurized devices (Medihaler-Epi, Asthma Meter Mist). Vaponefrin is a 2.25 per cent solution of racemic epinephrine which also provides an effective aerosol when delivered by a hand nebulizer. In general, however, aerosol isoproterenol now is used more than nebulized epinephrine, since, as mentioned above, it acts primarily on the beta receptors.

Aqueous epinephrine has the disadvantage of being effective over a relatively short time. By suspending epinephrine in a preparation such as sodium thioglycolate it is possible to prolong the effect of the medication so that it lasts for as long as eight hours. This material is more convenient than epinephrine suspended in oil, since it is given subcutaneously. An example of this compound is Sus-phrine, which is given in a dosage range of 0.1 to 0.3 cc. of the 1:200 dilution. The use of this drug at regular six to eight hour intervals should reduce the need for prolonged intravenous aminophylline administration.

Isoproterenol (Isuprel, Aludrine, Isonorine, Isorenin or Norisodrine). When given sublingually in doses of 5 to 15 mg. (up to 60 mg. daily), definite relief from the dyspnea of asthma can be expected; syrups and elixirs also are available. Isoproterenol has a more rapid and intense effect than ephedrine. More commonly, isoproterenol in 1:200 concentration is given by aerosol, and this usually produces a prompt increase in vital capacity and excellent relief of symptoms. Five to fifteen inhalations may be taken from a hand bulb nebulizer of the same type used to aerosolize epinephrine (see above). Alternatively, special pressurized dispensers deliver a measured therapeutic dose in a single inhalation (e.g., Mistometer, Medihaler-Iso or Norisodrine Aerotrol). This drug also can be inhaled in powder form from a special dispenser (Norisodrine Aerohaler). An elegant way to give aerosol isoproterenol, primarily in hospitalized patients, is by intermittent positive-pressure breathing (IPPB) apparatus (page 168). Isoproterenol also is marketed in combination with other bronchodilator drugs for use as aerosol. Aerolone Compound also contains cyclopentamine (Clopane). The Medihaler-Duo combines phenylephrine with isoproterenol in a pressurized dispenser. The vasoconstrictor action of the former compound prolongs the bronchodilator effect.

The most common side effects of isoproterenol are palpitation, tachycardia, excitation and nausea. These can be avoided by diluting the drug, reducing the dose or both. This drug is not given by injection for allergic diseases because of the high incidence of side effects associated with this route of administration. Isoproterenol is contraindicated in anaphylactic shock, since it may accentuate hypotension.

Ethylnorepinephrine Hydrochloride. This sympathomimetic amine also appears to act mainly on beta receptors, and it can be administered parenterally or by mouth as well as by aerosol. The diastolic blood pressure is lowered without an elevation of systolic pressure, so that this drug may be given in the presence of hypertension. It is also said to influence the blood sugar less than epinephrine and thus may be preferred in diabetic patients who are difficult to control. An example of this form of drug is Bronkephrine HCl. Dosage by injection is 0.3 to 0.5 ml. of the 0.2 per cent solution (occasionally up to 2.5 ml.).

Phenylephrine. This sympathomimetic drug is predominantly an alpha receptor stimulator. Accordingly, it is used by allergists mainly as a decongestant agent in nose drops (Neo-synephrine or Isophrin) or eye drops. Precautions regarding the use of nose drops in allergic patients are discussed on page 157. Because of its constricting action on vascular smooth muscle, phenylephrine also is valuable in overcoming hypotension in allergic shock (page 118). It is a component of Medihaler-Duo (see above), Bronkometer and Bronkospray aerosols.

Ephedrine. Ephedrine sulfate is an old stand-by on the physician's list of sympathomimetic drugs and is still the most popular bronchodilator for long-term use. It also is employed in allergic rhinitis and urticaria, particularly in those cases not responding to antihistamines. Most often ephedrine is prescribed in combination with one of the theophylline drugs and a barbiturate (to diminish side effects; see page 134). The usual dose is 25 mg. given orally at three to four hour intervals. Ephedrine also is available as a syrup containing 16 mg. per 4 ml., as nose drops (0.5 to 3 per cent), as the hydrochloride salt and as a racemic mixture of the stereo isomers (racephedrine hydrochloride). The most common side effects are insomnia, nervousness, palpitation, dizziness, sweating and difficulty in voiding.

Other Sympathomimetic Drugs. A number of drugs have been marketed as substitutes for ephedrine. These include pseudoephedrine (Sudafed), phenylpropanolamine (Propadrine), methoxyphenamine (Orthoxine) and protokylol (Caytine). The latter drug may be given by injection or by inhalation as well as by aerosol. Pseudoephedrine is especially used (orally) for allergic rhinitis. It also can be used in combination with antihistamines. Undesirable side effects of ephedrine, such as those mentioned above, often can be relieved by substituting one of these other compounds, but sometimes they prove to be less efficacious.

Oxymetazoline (Afrin), mephentermine (Wyamine O), tetrahydrozoline (Tyzine), xylometazoline (Otrivin), methylhexaneamine (Forthane), phenylpropylmethylamine (Vonedrine) and naphazoline (Privine) are employed as nasal decongestants. In using nose drops, sprays or inhalers containing these drugs, an adverse "rebound" effect may occur, and frequent use of such medications may result in rhinitis medicamentosa (see page 85). Therefore, it is advisable to use oral medications for nasal decongestion, when possible, and certainly to avoid the prolonged use of intranasal drugs. Some of the newer preparations may be tolerated with fewer adverse effects. Indications for nose drops are discussed on page 157.

THEOPHYLLINE

Theophylline (1,3-dimethylxanthine) is a methyl purine found in tea. Other members of this group are caffeine (1,3,7-trimethylxanthine) and cocoa (3,7-dimethylxanthine). Since theophylline itself is relatively insoluble, in the practice of allergy it is most often employed in the forms of aminophylline (theophylline ethylenediamine) or choline theophyllinate (Choledyl), which are more soluble. Its most important pharmacologic effect in allergy is its capacity to relax bronchial smooth muscle. Other actions include diuresis, coronary artery dilatation, cardiac, central nervous system, respiratory and skeletal muscle stimulation and relaxation of smooth muscle in the biliary tract. Because of its favorable cardiovascular effects, it is the drug of choice in cases in which there is uncertainty whether the patient has cardiac asthma or bronchial asthma. It also merits special consideration in asthmatic patients who are not responding to epinephrine or in whom there is some relative contraindication to the latter drug. Toxic effects of theophylline include nausea, vomiting, dizziness, anxiety, palpitation, vascular collapse and cardiac arrest. One must be especially careful to *avoid overdosage in children and excessively rapid intravenous administration* of this drug. A cumulative effect from too frequent administration is a significant hazard. Full therapeutic doses probably should not be repeated sooner than every eight hours, a point which must be emphasized to mothers of asthmatic children. Remember that there are two sizes of aminophylline suppository—250 and 500 mg.

Oral administration of aminophylline in tablets gives low blood levels and poor therapeutic response. Alcoholic solutions of theophylline are much more effective. Preparations of this type include Elixophyllin, Lixaminol, Quibron and Theo-Organidin. (Quibron also contains glyceryl guaiacolate, and Theo-Organidin contains iodinated glycerol). Therapeutic blood levels are attained in 15 to 30 minutes, and the effect persists for 2 to 6 hours. Although suggested dosage ranges are provided by the manufacturers, the optimal dose for each patient is variable and must be established by trial. One must seek an amount of medication which is effective without producing nausea. The choline salt of theophylline (Choledyl) also gives therapeutic blood levels following oral administration in tablet form. Of course, in severe asthma the most potent and prompt effect can be obtained by giving aminophylline intravenously. The full adult dose is 0.5 gm. in 20 ml. of fluid given slowly into a vein over a period of at least 5 to 10 minutes. The injection should be terminated at once if the patient complains of any of the toxic symptoms mentioned above.

In the hospital an intravenous infusion containing aminophylline is less apt to cause toxic symptoms and may give more sustained relief (see page 165). In less urgent situations aminophylline can be administered effectively by the rectal route, usually with less likelihood of nausea than with oral preparations. Most commonly, 0.5 gm. rectal suppositories are prescribed for adults. Often these are used at bedtime. They can be prescribed every 8 to 12 hours, but local irritation may develop with frequent or prolonged use. A more rapid and potent effect can be obtained with a retention enema of 250 mg. theophylline monoethanolamine (Fleet Theophylline) or Rectalad-aminophylline. With all theophylline preparations, one should be careful not to exceed the manufacturer's dosage recommendations for children.

COMBINATION BRONCHIAL ANTISPASMODIC DRUGS

Combinations of ephedrine, theophylline and a barbiturate commonly used in the treatment of chronic asthma and emphysema are shown in Table 7–1. As indicated, racephedrine, phenyl propanolamine and benzylephedrine are substituted for ephedrine in other preparations; hydroxyzine replaces a barbiturate in Marax. Iodides are included in Quadrinal and Theo-Organidin, and glyceryl guaiacolate in Asbron, Verequad, Bronkotabs and Quibron (see page 135). The inclusion of aspirin in these combinations appears hazardous because of the severe reactions it would induce in some asthmatic patients. For patients intolerant of ephedrine or barbiturates, a different combination could be tried as indicated in Table 7–1, or the other sympathomimetic drugs

Table 7–1. Examples of Some Combination Drugs Used as Bronchial Antispasmodics in the U.S.A.

Combination	Ephedrine	Race-ephedrine	Phenylpro-panolamine	Benzyl-ephedrine	Theophylline	Barbiturate	Hydroxyzine	Iodide (Inorganic or Organic)	Glyceryl guaiacolate	Antihistamine	Aspirin
Amesec†	✓				✓	✓					
Asminyl*	✓				✓	✓					
Luasmin*†	✓				✓	✓					
Tedral*†	✓				✓	✓					
Zantrate	✓				✓	✓					
Amodrine*		✓			✓	✓					
Asbron*					✓				✓		
Franol				✓	✓	✓					
Marax*	✓				✓		✓				
Quadrinal*	✓				✓	✓		✓			
Verequad*	✓				✓	✓			✓		
Bronkotabs	✓				✓	✓			✓		
Arlcaps										✓	✓
Quibron*					✓				✓		
Theo-Organidin (elixir only)					✓			✓			

* Available also as suspensions or syrups.
† Available also in enteric-coated tablets.

listed on page 133 could be used alone. The latter, or syrups or elixirs of isoproterenol, also should be considered in patients who develop nausea from all medications containing theophylline. Table 7–1 also shows the combinations which are available in suspensions or syrups, especially for pediatric use, and those that are provided in enteric-coated preparations. Tedral enteric-coated half-strength tablets are suitable for children 6 to 12 years of age.

EXPECTORANTS

Compounds which would assist the patient in the removal of mucus from the trachea and the pulmonary tree are of major potential importance in treating bronchial asthma and in preventing death from asthma (see page 163). Expectorant drugs are designed to accomplish this objective by inducing the production of less viscous secretions, which can be coughed up more easily by the patient. It is very difficult to ascertain the efficacy of expectorants. There are large variations in sputum output by asthmatic patients without expectorants being used. The actual production of respiratory tract fluid is uncertain. Sputum viscosity is difficult to evaluate. Although several different instruments have been used to measure sputum viscosity, the lack of homogeneity of this material makes it difficult to assess the results. The instrument developed by Hirsch seems to have some advantages in this regard.[4]

Water

It seems almost superfluous to point out that water is one of the most useful agents in promoting the flow of bronchial secretions. Adequate hydration, parenterally, by inhalation or by mouth, appears to be essential in preventing inspissated bronchial secretions. Details are discussed in Chapter 8.

Iodides

Many allergists have believed from long clinical experience that iodides are effective expectorants and of major importance in treating asthma, particularly status asthmaticus. Skeptics have pointed out that although this clinical impression is very widely held, it is supported by little convincing data. Recently double-blind studies have supported the traditional viewpoint.[5] In addition to their use as expectorants, it has been observed that a prolonged remission in asthma occasionally follows the administration of iodides. Since this effect is observed in less than 5 per cent of patients, it is very difficult to be certain of a specific cause-and-effect relationship. Of the several available oral iodide preparations, probably the most popular is potassium iodide solution (the so-called "saturated solution") containing 1 gm. of KI per milliliter. The usual dose is ten drops four times daily (one drop per year of age in children) in milk or in other fluid. Because of unpleasant taste, children may prefer syrup of hydriodic acid in a dose of 5 to 10 ml. four times daily. It must be well diluted in order to prevent possible damage to the teeth. Iodinated glycerol (Organidin) is less apt to produce gastrointestinal irritation, but additional studies are needed in regard to its efficacy. Iodides are incorporated into mixtures of drugs for treating asthma (e.g., Quadrinal). Occasionally, in treatment of patients with status asthmaticus, sodium iodide, 0.5 to 1.0 gm., is added to the intravenous infusion. Since the iodide ion so rapidly is transmitted to the bronchial glands when given orally, the intravenous route might well be limited to patients who cannot ingest medications.

There are many possible adverse effects from iodides, some of which are discussed on page 182. A number of these untoward effects are potentially serious and even the common acneiform dermatitis can lead to permanent scarring if the process is allowed to progress too far. Allergists should be aware that rhinitis is one of the manifestations of iodism. Prolonged iodide administration may be followed rarely by hypothyroidism, occasionally with thyroid gland enlargement. Fetal thyroid abnormalities have been reported from use of iodide during pregnancy.[6]

Glyceryl Guaiacolate

Adverse effects from glyceryl guaiacolate are rare, but additional evidence for its efficacy appears desirable. It is available in a preparation containing 100 mg. per 5 ml. (Robitussin) or in combinations indicated in Table 7–1.

Ammonium Chloride

There are conflicting reports regarding the value of ammonium chloride as an expectorant. When used, it has been given in a dosage of 0.5 to 2.0 gm. three times daily with meals, but it appears unlikely to be very effective.

MUCOLYTIC AGENTS

These compounds are used in an attempt to diminish the viscosity of sputum by direct chemical or enzymatic attack rather than by dilution with thinner secretions. As mentioned in connection with expectorants, this therapeutic approach has great potential importance in asthma, but it is difficult to evaluate.

One of the most widely used mucolytic agents is N-acetylcysteine

(Mucomyst), which has the advantages of being nonsensitizing and of being capable of causing chemical lysis of both purulent and nonpurulent secretions. At times it appears to produce a rapid reduction in sputum viscosity, causing prompt clearing of the bronchial secretions.[7] In a 20 per cent solution it can be given by aerosol or by direct instillation through an endotracheal or tracheostomy tube. It may produce bronchospasm in asthmatic patients, but this can be averted by diluting it with an equal part of isoproterenol solution (for aerosol use).[8] A practical point involves using all plastic tubing and connections when delivering acetylcysteine. This drug attacks rubber with the liberation of hydrogen sulfide.

A second mucolytic preparation uses the detergent principle. Alevaire is a 0.125 per cent solution of tyloxapol in glycerin. By detergent action, it wets, thins and supposedly lowers the surface tension of sputum. It is administered by aerosol undiluted in a tent or face mask until an effect is observed. Alevaire is well tolerated and we have seen no adverse effects from its use.

It should be noted that in the more impressive reports on Alevaire large amounts of the preparation were nebulized into a tent; the efficacy of a small amount inhaled from a hand bulb nebulizer is less certain. Sodium 2-ethylhexyl sulfate (Tergemist) is another similar preparation, and it also contains 0.1 per cent potassium iodide.

Several enzymes have been utilized for thinning sputum. Because of the potential irritating and allergenic effects of many of these preparations, their administration by aerosol to patients with bronchial asthma is not to be undertaken hastily, and there is *no good evidence that most of these enzymes are effective in asthma* when used either by aerosol or by mouth.

SEDATIVES

Not only may the anxious and apprehensive asthmatic patient benefit dramatically from the judicious use of sedation, but these drugs also may be helpful in patients suffering from pruritic skin lesions.

Barbiturates

The barbiturates are useful in selected cases, but one should be certain there is not a history of sensitivity to barbiturates. Phenobarbital, 0.032 to 0.065 gm. four times daily (0.008 to 0.016 gm. for children), may be used in patients for whom sedation is indicated. Short-acting barbiturates, such as pentobarbital sodium, may also be used. Given in soporific doses, the barbiturates are only slightly depressant to the respiratory center. However, we do not use intravenous amobarbital sodium in asthma.

Paraldehyde and Chloral Hydrate

Paraldehyde, 5 to 15 ml., and chloral hydrate, 1.0 to 2.0 gm. (5 to 10 mg. per pound in children, 1 gm. maximum), given orally are almost ideal sedatives to use in asthmatic patients with the exception that confusion and disorientation occasionally result from their use. Chloral hydrate affects blood pressure and respiration little more than does ordinary sleep. In the hospitalized patient under close observation, it is perhaps the safest sedation to use in asthmatic patients, provided kidney and liver function are unimpaired. It may be given in water or milk. Capsules of 250 and 500 mg. (Noctec) also are available. Paraldehyde similarly may be used and is not contraindicated in asthmatic patients who have kidney disease. Of course, the odor of paraldehyde makes it mildly unpleasant for all except the patient. Paraldehyde may also be given in a retention enema in a dose of 8 to 16 ml. with equal parts of water. The deep intramuscular injection of 5 to 10 ml. paraldehyde affords prompt and effective sedation, but sometimes there is a local irritation. We have encountered no true allergy to paraldehyde.

Bromides

Sodium bromide is one of the oldest sedatives and is still used occasionally in doses of 0.3 to 1.0 gm. every four to eight hours. One must watch for bromism and bromoderma.

Narcotics

As discussed in Chapter 8 (page 163), morphine is contraindicted in bronchial asthma, and to a lesser extent other narcotics are ill advised in this disease and in urticaria pigmentosa. Only in specific cases in which suppression of a useless cough is desired is it wise to use codeine or a related compound for this effect.

TRANQUILIZERS

These drugs may be helpful either to the chronically anxious allergic patient or to the more acutely ill, apprehensive asthmatic patient. Especially in the latter situation, as an alternative to sedatives, one may elect to prescribe one of the *phenothiazine* drugs. The allergist should familiarize himself with a few representative compounds. We have particularly used promazine hydrochloride (Sparine) beginning with a dose of 25 mg. orally every four hours for adults. If this does not suffice, the dose may be increased and/or the medication may be given intravenously.

In chronically anxious or itching patients, one of the many "minor tranquilizers" may be helpful without producing sedation. Meprobamate

(Equanil, Miltown) and chlordiazepoxide (Librium) are among the more popular of these. Hydroxyzine (Atarax, Vistaril) has been particularly useful in urticaria, perhaps because it also is antihistaminic.[9] Our usual starting dose is 25 mg. four times daily in adults (10 mg. four times daily in children), and this is increased, if necessary. It should be noted, parenthetically, that it appears unwise to prescribe monoamine oxidase inhibitor type antidepressant drugs for allergic patients, e.g., isocarboxazid (Marplan), nialamide (Niamid), phenelzine (Nardil) or tranylcypromine (Parnate), since there is a major risk of a hypertensive crisis if the patient inadvertently is given a pressor amine for his allergic disease. Detailed descriptions of the pharmacology, recommended dosage and toxic effects of the large number of tranquilizer drugs now available can be found in standard references on drugs.[9]

ANTIHISTAMINES

This discussion of the antihistamines must be confined largely to their clinical applications, but a more comprehensive treatment of the subject may be found in the review by Feinberg et al.[10] The mechanism of action of these compounds in the allergic diseases does not involve interference with histamine release by antigen-antibody reactions; nor do the antihistamines react with or neutralize released histamine. Instead, the antihistamines appear to inhibit the action of histamine on tissues, such as smooth muscle and blood vessels. In addition to this capacity to inhibit the effects of histamine, it should be noted that many compounds in the group also have other important pharmacologic properties. These include local anesthetic effects, soporific action, atropine-like effect, anti-emetic property and antihyaluronidase activity. Thus, these drugs have been useful in a number of diseases outside the field of allergy (see page 143).

Clinically, antihistamines show remarkable variability in their efficacy and side reactions. For example, one patient may report that his hay fever is very well controlled by diphenhydramine without side effects, while the next patient may report no relief of a similar type of hay fever, and in addition he may experience severe drowsiness. This striking variation in relief afforded and in side effects produced justifies having several of these compounds available for clinical use. It also makes apparent the advisability of trying sample antihistamines before prescribing a large number of tablets. There are available "starter packets" for most of the antihistamines, and several of these may be tried in a series, each for two or three days, before prescribing a substantial number of pills.

Selection of the first antihistamine to be tried is based somewhat on the physician's personal preference. However, there is merit to picking one representative drug from each of the several groups having similar molecular structure. Members of each group are more likely to have similar effects on individual patients. The groups discussed below are based on variations in the following structural formula which is common to almost all antihistamine compounds:

$$R - CH_2\ CH_2N\diagup\diagdown\begin{matrix}CH_3\\CH_3\end{matrix}$$

where "R" represents any slightly basic, large radical which makes up about three-fourths of the molecular weight of the antihistaminic compound. It is the dimethylamino portion, $N(CH_3)_2$ which is primarily responsible for blocking the action of histamine. Substitutions on the carbon atoms of the ethylene group have not been very beneficial, and in many antihistamines the dimethylaminoethylene portion is maintained. By changing the linkage between the "R" portion of the molecule and the ethylene radical, however, it is possible to predict to some degree the properties of the resulting compound.

Compounds from Group I usually are very effective, but they tend to cause sedation. Those of Group II, while perhaps not so likely to induce sedation, are known in some patients to produce gastrointestinal upset. Members of Group III have a good record, with minimal side effects, but they, like the others, do not afford relief in all patients with allergic problems amenable to antihistamines. Group IV drugs may be metabolized in the tissues to form dimethylaminoethylene. Some agents in the miscellaneous group occasionally cause nervousness and insomnia while others may be soporific. These generalities, however, must be tempered by the widely variable clinical responsiveness of individual patients, as already mentioned.

From Group I, Benadryl (diphenhydramine) and Decapryn (doxylamine) are the most commonly used antihistamines. There may be an advantage to the sedation which many patients experience when receiving these drugs, especially if they are used at bedtime or when pruritus is present. Dramamine (dimenhydrinate), a modification of Benadryl, is used for motion sickness and in some cases of nausea accompanying

Table 7-2.   Effects of Altering Linkage of Antihistamine Drugs

Group	Formula	Example
I	$R-O-CH_2CH_2N\diagup\diagdown\begin{matrix}CH_3\\CH_3\end{matrix}$	Diphenhydramine (Benadryl)
II	$R-N-CH_2CH_2N\diagup\diagdown\begin{matrix}CH_3\\CH_3\end{matrix}$	Pyranisamine, Tripelennamine (Pyribenzamine)
III	$R-CH_2-CH_2CH_2N\diagup\diagdown\begin{matrix}CH_3\\CH_3\end{matrix}$	Chlorpheniramine (Chlor-Trimeton)
IV	Miscellaneous	Phenindamine (Thephorin)

pregnancy. Hydryllin is a combination of 25 mg. diphenhydramine with 100 mg. aminophylline. Ambodryl (bromodiphenhydramine) may cause less drowsiness in certain patients. Also chemically related are Clistin (carbinoxamine, racemic) and Twiston (carbinoxamine, d-form). Of the Group II compounds, there are more than 20 available preparations. A few examples are: Pyribenzamine (tripelennamine), Neo-Antergan and others (pyranisamine), Neohetramine (thonzylamine), Tagathen (chlorothen), Histadyl (methapyrilene) and Thenfadil (thenyldiamine). The members of Group III include Co-Pyronil (pyrobutamine), Chlor-Trimeton and Teldrin (chlorpheniramine), Polaramine (chlorpheniramine, d-form), Dimetane (brompheniramine, racemic) and Disomer (brompheniramine, d-form).

In Group IV are found three antihistamines causing low incidence of sedation: Forhistal (demethpyridene), Thephorin (phenindamine), and Perazil or Di-Paralene (chlorcyclizine). While causing more drowsiness than the others, Periactin (cyproheptadine) is especially useful in urticaria. Antistine (antazoline) is useful in ophthalmic drop form and for treatment of cardiac arrythmias. A number of compounds of the tranquilizer type have shown antihistamine activity. Of the cyclizines, Atarax (hydroxyzine) is valuable especially in management of urticaria, pruritus and nausea (see page 140). Others of this type are Bonine (meclizine) and Softran (buclizine). Chlorcyclizine has been associated in a few cases with abnormally developed fetuses, and therefore this compound should be avoided in pregnancy until this point is clarified.

The phenothiazine group of tranquilizers includes several preparations which have antihistamine activity. Temaril (trimeprazine) and Tacaryl (methdilazine) are examples. Phenergan (promethazine) is a potent antihistamine. Because of the sedation produced, Phenergan is especially valuable in relieving pruritus during the night.

It is worthwhile to check periodically to be sure that a patient is still deriving satisfactory relief from an antihistamine. After a few weeks or months, it may be beneficial to try, in series, several different ones and perhaps switch to another more effective kind.

Sometimes the therapeutic effect of antihistamines is enhanced by using them in combination with ephedrine or other sympathomimetic drugs. This also may serve to counteract sedation. Five examples of these very popular combinations are: Triaminic (phenylpropanolamine, pheniramine and pyrilamine), Ornade (chlorpheniramine and phenylpropanolamine), Co-Pyronil (containing methapyrilene, pyrrobutamine and cyclopentamine), Actifed (triprolidine and pseudoephedrine) and Dimetapp (brompheniramine, phenylephrine and phenylpropanolamine).

Clinical Response to the Antihistamines

In *allergic rhinitis,* seasonal and nonseasonal symptoms are relieved to some degree in the large majority of patients. Sneezing, itching and rhinorrhea are especially likely to respond, while stuffiness and eye discomfort are more refractory. *Asthma* usually is not very remarkably improved by the antihistamines, but for unknown reasons childhood asthma seems to be helped more often than is the disease in adults. Because of the drying effect of antihistamines on bronchial secretions, these drugs, if used at all, should be confined to those patients who have no trouble raising their secretions. Failure of antihistamines to be very helpful in asthma supports current hypotheses that mediators in addition to histamine are important in asthma. Temporary relief in *urticaria* can usually be obtained with antihistamines, but they are disappointing when used to treat the urticarial type of erythema multiforme. *Serum sickness* and serum-sickness-like disease caused by drugs may respond well, but large doses of the histamine antagonists may be required in severe cases. In *anaphylaxis*, intravenous injection of one of the parenteral forms may be very beneficial (page 118). In *dermographism* and in *physical allergy*, the antihistamines may be very helpful in reducing or in preventing the reaction. *Atopic dermatitis* and *contact dermatitis* are benefited by these drugs given systemically, since they exert an antipruritic effect which allows healing to occur. The patient with *allergic conjunctivitis* may report benefit from topical or systemic use of the antihistamines; in view of the local anesthetic effect of these drugs on the cornea, he should be warned not to rub his eyes. *Headaches* associated with nasal congestion may be relieved by antihistamines. Histamine headaches, unfortunately, are almost never influenced favorably by these drugs. In *serous otitis media,* they are used routinely as a part of the treatment program. A considerable number of patients who have *gastrointestinal allergy* are helped by antihistamines, perhaps partly because of their atropine-like action.

In diseases which have no allergic basis but are characterized by tissue injury, the histamine antagonists may be helpful. When Sir Thomas Lewis published his classic observations describing the triple response in injured skin and the H- or histamine-like substance produced, he indicated the possibility that histamine plays a part in the reaction following tissue injury of many types.[11] In more recent years, it has been thought that histamine liberation may occur in the *acute* phase of many inflammatory responses. Furthermore, as indicated on page 140, antihistamine drugs have many important pharmacologic properties in addition to their capacity to antagonize histamine. These compounds have thus been used with varying success for a wide variety of indications: for relief of cough due to a multitude of causes; as an antipruritic agent for many skin diseases including measles, chickenpox and dermatitis herpetiformis; as an anti-emetic for motion sickness, nausea and vomiting of pregnancy, postoperative symptoms, irradiation sickness and overdigitalization; for prompt control of phenothiazine drug toxicity manifested by extrapyramidal disturbances; for parkinsonism and for narcotic withdrawal symptoms. Their value in treating the common cold is much in doubt.

In some patients, certain of the antihistamine drugs are effective, short-acting sedatives and can be used to promote sleep.

Dosage

The adult dosage of antihistaminic drugs is usually one tablet or one teaspoonful of liquid given three or four times daily as needed. Dose ranges from 2 mg. to 100 mg. depending on the compound being used, but must be established by trial and observation.

When required for relief in severely ill patients, double the usual dosage of antihistamine drugs can be given under close supervision for short periods. Children's doses must be reduced proportionally. Many antihistamines are dispensed in elixirs, syrups or suspensions for pediatric use. Some compounds also are available in long-acting formulations. Intravenous administration may be indicated for anaphylactic type reactions or severe serum sickness—a dose of 30 to 80 mg. diphenhydramine being commonly employed.

A concentration of 0.25 to 0.5 per cent usually is used in ophthalmic drops (Antistine).

Side Reactions and Toxicity of the Antihistaminic Compounds

Although some of the side reactions to antihistaminic compounds have already been mentioned, the following summarizes these: Drowsiness certainly is the most common reaction. This may be mild and temporary, disappearing after one to five doses of the medication, or it may be severe and persistent as long as the drug is given. Coffee, caffeine or amphetamine may be used to counteract this. Gastrointestinal upset also is fairly common. Nausea, vomiting, diarrhea, abdominal cramping or constipation may occur. Dryness of the mouth, vertigo, visual blurring and personality changes (irritability) may be observed, especially in children.

The reactions so far mentioned account for at least 90 per cent of all side effects. Fatigue, insomnia, nervousness, perspiration, early menses, headache, paresthesias, extrasystoles, urinary frequency, impotence and chilly sensation have been reported. Allergic reactions resulting from both the filler in the tablet as well as the antihistaminic compound itself have been observed on rare occasions. A few cases of agranulocytosis also are known to have occurred. Serious toxic reactions with coma and, at times, convulsions have been observed primarily in infants receiving a large overdose of one of these drugs. In general, however, the safety record of the antihistamines actually is better than that of aspirin. The only source of relatively frequent difficulty from these drugs was allergic contact dermatitis from their use in ointments. Accordingly, this dosage form has largely been abandoned.

Precautions for Use of the Antihistamines

Because the antihistamines are detoxified by the liver, a patient with possible liver disease should be evaluated carefully before he is given drugs of this group. Thousands of pregnant women have taken antihistamines without apparent harm to the fetus. However, this matter currently is being re-evaluated, since there has been some suggestion that certain compounds (page 142) may possibly be associated with fetal anomalies. Nursing mothers taking antihistamines will pass the medication on to the infant through the breast milk. This is not dangerous, but the mother should be alerted to watch for excessive sleepiness of the baby. There is no known habituation to antihistamines. Withdrawal after five years of constant use caused only some restlessness and temporary anorexia in a patient we observed.

Adult patients should be advised to try new antihistamines in the evening or on a weekend before they drive a car or work near machinery. The sedation and reduction of depth perception by the drugs makes them potentially dangerous until tolerance of them is observed. For this reason pilots should not fly airplanes while using antihistamines, since depth perception is so important in the final stages of landing. When side effects occur, they usually are evident after the first or second dose and tend to decrease if the administration of the drug is continued.

ACTH AND ADRENAL CORTICOSTEROIDS

Since Hench, in 1948, showed that cortisone has a beneficial effect on rheumatoid arthritis, apparently suppressing inflammatory manifestations, an enormous amount of data regarding the metabolic, physiologic and therapeutic effects of adrenocorticotrophic hormone (ACTH) and the corticosteroids has accumulated. This discussion will be limited perforce to a consideration of the effects of those hormones on immune mechanisms and hypersensitivity states. ACTH is a peptide which has as its function stimulation of the adrenal cortex with ultimate release of corticosteroids. It is therefore apparent that ACTH depends for its metabolic action on an adequate adrenal cortical response. Thus, if the adrenal cortices are not functioning normally, corticosteroids will be effective if given to such a patient, but ACTH will not. Cortisone and hydrocortisone are the prototypes of the group of steroids which has anti-allergic properties.[12]

Possible Mechanisms of Action in Hypersensitivity

Theories of the mechanism of action of these drugs in allergy must take into account the following facts:

1. ACTH and corticosteroids do not prevent anaphylactic shock in highly sensitized animals, nor do they prevent histamine shock. In

clinical practice we have seen a horse serum-sensitive patient who promptly developed an allergic reaction from tetanus antitoxin in spite of prior administration of ACTH.

2. ACTH and corticosteroids do not change the immediate type of wheal and erythema skin reaction to allergens in man significantly.

3. ACTH and corticosteroids do not inhibit the release by pollen extracts of histamine from the leukocytes of allergic subjects.

4. ACTH and corticosteroids have not been found by most observers to alter significantly the titer of circulating reagins as shown by quantitative passive transfer tests.

5. ACTH and the corticosteroids substantially inhibit the development of vascular lesions of serum sickness in animals injected with foreign proteins, such as horse serum.

6. ACTH and the corticosteroids fail to inhibit the development of experimental nephritis produced by "nephrotoxic" sera. There is good evidence that such sera contain specific antibodies to kidney tissue. Other data, too, indicate that these compounds do not inhibit antigen-antibody reactions in vivo or in vitro.

7. In general, the effect of ACTH and the corticosteroids on antibody production in man is not appreciable at clinically used dosage levels of these drugs. The hormones do not interfere with adequate development of blocking antibody if one administers steroids simultaneously with hyposensitization injections. Much larger amounts of corticosteroids do suppress antibody production in experimental animals.

8. ACTH and corticosteroids may attenuate or suppress tuberculin or other delayed skin test reactions. They have a similar effect on patch tests.

Although much work has been done, it is still not possible to explain the marked and rapid effect of ACTH and corticosteroids on hypersensitivity states. The evidence accumulated suggests that steroids act directly upon the cells of sensitized tissues to prevent an inflammatory reaction of the allergic type. It has also been suggested that these hormones may affect certain enzyme systems, such as that involved in the conversion of histidine to histamine. Another possibility is that the eosinopenic action of ACTH and the steroids may in some way be related to the therapeutic effects of these drugs in hypersensitivity states. So little is known regarding the normal function of eosinophils that this possibility is difficult to evaluate. The effect of corticosteroids on the transport mechanisms of cell membranes, lysosome stability, vascular tone and fibroblasts also might be relevant.

Indications for Treatment with ACTH and Steroids in Hypersensitivity States

These drugs have been used with benefit in practically all allergic diseases: bronchial asthma, status asthmaticus, hay fever, perennial al-

lergic rhinitis, nasal polyps, urticaria, angioneurotic edema, atopic dermatitis, contact dermatitis (especially poison ivy dermatitis), exfoliative
dermatitis, drug eruptions and serum sickness. They also are of value
in some of the connective tissue diseases, although the part which hypersensitivity plays in these latter diseases is unclear (see Chapter 18).

The use of ACTH and the glucocorticoids is not advocated in the
routine management of patients with allergic disease because of the high
rate of relapse after treatment is discontinued, the potential hazards
involved and the fact that very satisfactory results can be obtained in
most patients by the use of treatment with well established methods.
The physician always must keep in mind, especially when using these
drugs to cope with a chronic condition, that he may be committing the
patient to permanent reliance on them. Many times the initial short
burst of steroids may need to be repeated at shorter and shorter intervals
until the patient cannot seem to get along without continuous use of
the drug. This may not necessarily be a medical disadvantage, since adequate control of the disease may be achieved in no other way. Nevertheless, the potential of possible permanent need for ACTH or steroids
should influence the physician's decision to start the drugs in every
instance.

Special circumstances which usually merit favorable consideration
for the use of these hormones are as follows:

1. In desperate situations, such as some cases of status asthmaticus,
when other methods of treatment have failed or seem inadequate. In
allergic emergencies, such as severe angioedema, bee or wasp sting, allergic drug reaction, the hormones may be used, if necessary, as a supplement to other emergency medications (see page 118).

2. For maintaining the patient through certain self-limited allergic
diseases; for example, in patients with severe serum sickness, glottic
edema, drug reactions or those with severe seasonal hay fever or asthma
who cannot be maintained in comfort by the usual methods of treatment.
In cases of severe rhinitis medicamentosa, where an attempt is being
made to remove the patient from the overuse of medication, nasal congestion usually can be ameliorated promptly by a short course of the
hormones. The discomfort from poison ivy dermatitis (Rhus) and other
dermatitis venenata of extensive degree often can be shortened greatly
with these drugs.

3. In selected patients in whom a very thorough and prolonged attempt at etiologic treatment short of using hormones has been unsuccessful. Elderly emphysematous asthmatic patients are especially apt to fall
into this group. An extended course of treatment with ACTH or the
steroids usually must be anticipated if one initiates their use in order
to provide more than transient benefit. It is unwise to initiate treatment
with one of these drugs in such patients unless a prolonged course of
therapy will be possible, with good patient follow-up and cooperation.
Even then the end results are often disappointing and there is danger of

severe relapse when treatment is discontinued. The physician must compare the beneficial effects that he hopes to provide with these potent medications with the complications and problems· which frequently arise eventually with prolonged use. If, without them, the patient is incapacitated, then a trial of ACTH or the steroids should be considered.

4. In the acute phases of severe exfoliative dermatitis, regardless of whether it is allergic in origin.

5. In certain patients with atopic dermatitis, neurodermatitis or other severely pruritic skin diseases. The relief of itching afforded by ACTH or the corticosteroids may break the scratch reflex pattern and permit the patient's skin to heal. However, relapse after the drug is discontinued is very likely unless the cause of the problem has been identified and removed.

6. Prior to surgery. Because of the possible failure of the hypothalamic-pituitary axis or of the pituitary-adrenal axis to respond adequately in the patient treated with hormones, special consideration should be given to such persons prior to surgery. Anyone subjected to more than the most minor procedure, who has received steroids for more than about three days within the past year, should be considered for such precautions.

The day prior to surgery, 50 mg. hydrocortisone is given intramuscularly; 100 mg. is administered intramuscularly the morning of surgery and 100 mg. in two doses (100 mg. each time) later in the day, with subsequent injections over the next two or three days as the patient recovers from his surgery. It is important to tape intravenous hydrocortisone to the chart sent to the operating room with the patient, in case it is needed.

Contraindications for Treatment with ACTH and the Corticosteroids

These are more relative than absolute, for they depend on such factors as the severity of the patient's illness, his availability and cooperation with the physician, the therapist's experience with these drugs and laboratory facilities. In critically ill patients added risks may be accepted when the hormones may help; for example, a patient with pulmonary tuberculosis and concurrently active disseminated lupus erythematosus may be treated successfully with a combination of antimicrobial medication and steroids. Live viral vaccines should not be given to patients on steroids.

Among the group of patients usually seen in the practice of clinical allergy, two conditions generally constitute absolute contraindications to the use of ACTH or steroids: chicken pox and herpes simplex ophthalmicus (see page 238). Relative contraindications, in which the physician must weigh anticipated clinical improvement against the possibility of undesirable results, include: pregnancy—especially the first trimester—active or past tuberculosis or peptic ulcer, history of active gastrointestinal bleeding, agitated psychotic states, congestive heart failure, significant hypertension, renal insufficiency, diabetes mellitus, osteoporosis, emotional instability and an unreliable patient.

Selection of Corticosteroids

Table 7–3 shows nine currently available analogues of the corticosteroids. For treating a condition in which the duration of steroid administration will be brief (perhaps two or three weeks), selection of a steroid is a matter of personal preference of the physician. The cost of the particular drug should be considered. In general, the analogues of cortisone and of hydrocortisone listed in Table 7–3 have an advantage over the parent compounds because they have less mineralocorticoid effect; this would be particularly advantageous in edematous or hypertensive patients in whom sodium retention would be especially undesirable. Unfortunately, it has not been possible substantially to dissociate the desired anti-allergic and anti-inflammatory actions of the steroids from their undesirable effects on protein and carbohydrate metabolism.

With prolonged corticosteroid therapy, there may be merit in trying the short-acting types (e.g., prednisone or prednisolone) in the hope of being able to use the drugs intermittently and at a low dosage. Harter points out that alternate-day single morning doses of prednisone produce less adrenal-pituitary suppression and fewer Cushingoid side effects than when this or other analogues are given in regular daily doses.[13] Thus, a patient receiving 2.5 mg. four times daily would be given 20 mg. in the morning every other day. Harter also advocates a monthly "booster" dose of ACTH—a controversial point. Steroids with a longer half-life may not be suitable for the alternate day regimen, since there might not be sufficient time for metabolic recovery during the day the steroid is withheld if a drug exerted marked suppression. For example, dexamethasone and betamethasone suppress 17-ketogenic steroid production roughly three times as long as comparable doses of prednisone, prednisolone, hydrocortisone or methylprednisolone, and the latter all have a suppressive effect for not more than one and one-half days. The dura-

Table 7–3. *Analogues of the Corticosteroids in Strength Equivalent to 25 mg. Cortisone*

A. SHORT-ACTING:
    Prednisone....................... 5 mg.
    Prednisolone..................... 5 mg.
    Hydrocortisone.................. 20 mg.
    Methylprednisolone.............. 4 mg.
B. INTERMEDIATE-ACTING:
    Paramethasone................... 2 mg.
    Triamcinolone................... 4 mg.
    Fluprednisolone................. 1.5 mg.
C. LONG-ACTING:
    Betamethasone.................. 0.6 mg.
    Dexamethasone................. 0.75 mg.

tion of this period following paramethasone and triamcinolone administration is of intermediate length. However, not all asthmatic patients can be kept reasonably well controlled with intermittent treatment. In these cases any of the corticosteroids may have to be used on a continuous basis.

Initiation of Steroid Therapy and Dosage Schedules

When used in proper dosage for a patient whose adrenal glands are functioning, both ACTH and the steroids usually yield satisfactory therapeutic results in allergy problems. When a very rapid effect is desired, an intravenous corticosteroid such as hydrocortisone (Solu-Cortef) is the therapy of choice. We would give 100 mg. directly intravenously, injecting it in 10 to 15 seconds, followed by an additional 100 to 200 mg. in a continuous intravenous drip using 5 per cent glucose in distilled water. As much as 600 mg. may be given in 24 hours to control severe status asthmaticus. Methyl prednisolone (Solu-Medrol) 40 mg. also may be given intravenously, as may prednisolone (Hydeltrasol) and dexamethasone (Decadron). Improvement may occur in a number of hours but can be delayed for as long as several days in severe asthma. ACTH also can be given intravenously at a rate of about 4 units per hour. The patient may improve in as short a time as 4 to 8 hours, but the effect generally will be less rapid than following intravenous corticosteroids.

When prolonged administration of hormones is likely to be necessary, oral steroids have an obvious advantage, and usually have a sufficiently prompt effect if one is not dealing with an emergency problem. Benefit in symptoms often will be observed in 12 to 24 hours, although several days may be required in severe asthma. These preparations generally are given every four to six hours at first. Careful attention to the circular accompanying the particular form of steroid used will enable the physician to use it properly.

Adequate dosage of either ACTH or corticosteroid is the smallest amount which will produce the desired therapeutic effect. This, of course, will vary considerably from one patient to another. During the first few days of a severe allergic problem, most physicians give 200 to 400 mg. hydrocortisone, 80 units of ACTH (often as the gel twice daily), 40 to 60 mg. prednisone or equivalent amounts of the various other steroids (Table 7–3) per day. It is likely that dosage amounts of only 50 per cent of these cited would suffice in many cases, particularly when the symptoms are mild. On the other hand, if improvement is not observed in two to four days (the longer period applies mainly to bronchial asthma), the dosage should be increased by increments of about 25 to 50 per cent at intervals of two or three days until a therapeutic effect is achieved. The best guide to adequacy of dosage is the patient's symptomatic clinical response.

When definite improvement has been noted after the first several days of treatment, the dosage is gradually tapered off, and an effort is made either to stop the drug or to find the lowest dose, perhaps intermittently given, which will control symptoms. For self-limited allergic reactions, a short course of about five to ten days of steroid treatment generally suffices. If a sustained remission of chronic symptoms is the therapeutic goal, a course of several weeks or months of hormone treatment may be necessary. In these circumstances, the full therapeutic doses mentioned are given until there is good relief of symptoms. The dose then is tapered rapidly at first and subsequently more slowly. At the later stages, the amount given often is decreased by one-half tablet every few days.

With prolonged steroid administration, changes in dosage usually should not be made more often than about every three to five days to allow time to determine whether signs or symptoms of relapse will appear before further changes are made. Alteration in the schedule should be made even more slowly as the lowest dosage levels are reached. If the patient is getting along satisfactorily, the drug may be withdrawn carefully after a variable period of time. Often, however, signs and symptoms of relapse begin to appear when the dosage is reduced below a certain level. If this occurs, the dose may be increased again, or more supplementary therapy with other drugs can be tried, until the symptoms are again under control. Later, one can again cautiously determine whether a reduced dose could be tolerated. It should be emphasized that full doses of the ordinary bronchodilator drugs and expectorants should be employed in asthmatic patients receiving steroids in order to allow the greatest possibility for being able to taper off the hormones or to achieve the lowest maintenance dosage.

Since ACTH must be given by injection, the use of this preparation when a "burst" of steroids is used has the psychological advantage that it is impractical to continue it for prolonged periods. Thus, the "burst" is less likely to evolve into chronic steroid administration. However, possible allergy to ACTH, although quite rare, is known to occur.

Other Dosage Forms of Corticosteroids

Aerosols. The solubility of dexamethasone phosphate makes it suitable for administration by inhalation. For asthma the Respihaler Decadron provides a metered dose of aerosol drug delivered under pressure. Each puff yields approximately 0.1 mg. dexamethasone 21-phosphate. A frequent starting dose is three puffs four times daily for adults (two puffs four times daily for children) until the symptoms are under control. Then dosage is reduced to the minimal amount required to keep the patient fairly comfortable. Although there is some systemic absorption of corticosteroids administered by aerosol, a much larger amount usually must be given by mouth or by injection to achieve an equivalent therapeutic effect. Sometimes patients on long-term oral steroid administration can be switched over to the aerosol; more frequently the nebulized steroid permits a reduction in the oral maintenance dose.[14] We do not recommend the combination of dexamethasone and isoproterenol in the same aerosol unit. Patients soon discover that they get prompt relief from the isoproterenol and use the sprayer at frequent intervals, just as they would rely on a unit containing only the isoproterenol.

Corticosteroids in nasal sprays are useful for carefully selected cases of severe nasal congestion associated with allergic rhinitis not responding to other forms of treatment. The Turbinaire Decadron phosphate is similar to the Respihaler Decadron and provides the same metered amount of medication with each spray. The recommended full dosage for adults is two sprays in each nostril two or three times daily (one or two sprays in each nostril twice daily for children, depending on age). Again, there may be a small amount of steroid absorbed, but the therapeutic effects exceed those caused by systemic absorption.[15] There are other commercially available nasal sprays containing corticosteroids, but the dosage cannot be regulated as satisfactorily from squeeze-bottle dispensers.

A large number of ointments, creams and lotions are available containing the newer synthetic corticosteroids. Examples are Medrol in Veriderm (methylprednisolone acetate) 0.25 and 1.0 per cent, Cordran (flurandrenolone) 0.025 and 0.05 per cent, Synalar (fluocinolone acetonide) 0.025 and 0.01 per cent, Kenalog (triamcinolone acetonide) 0.1 and .025 per cent, Cort-Dome 0.125 to 2.0 per cent (hydrocortisone alcohol), Celestone (betamethasone) 0.02 per cent and others. Various mixtures are supplied with tar and with neomycin.

Most of the corticosteroid analogues listed in Table 7–3 also are available in the form of ophthalmic solutions or ointments, the prednisolone preparations being among the most commonly used. Many of these are available with and without antibiotics or vasoconstrictor drugs. All steroid preparations used in the eye are potentially hazardous (page 306).

Long-acting injectable corticosteroids, such as suspension Aristocort (triamcinolone diacetate) and Depo-Medrol (methylprednisolone acetate) have been used to reduce the frequency of injections and to sustain the corticosteroid effect. The former may cause local subcutaneous atrophy.

Adverse Effects of ACTH and Corticosteroids

Since these hormones are remarkably potent in their metabolic effects, carelessness in their use may result in serious consequences. The most important precaution is for the physician to be aware of the more common undesirable effects of these drugs. If treatment is discontinued promptly or the dose adequately reduced, most of these untoward reactions are rapidly reversible. The following are some commonly seen adverse effects:

1. Osteoporosis is one of the commonest complications seen with chronic use of these drugs, especially in older patients. Spontaneous fractures may occur.

2. Gastrointestinal bleeding is seen, particularly in patients with a history of peptic ulcer, but it may occur in those with no previous history of gastrointestinal trouble.

3. Because of the tendency of infection to disseminate in patients while on these drugs, special care must be exerted to check for presence of tuberculosis and other unsuspected infection. There is particular danger with herpes.

In persons already on steroids who inadvertently develop chicken pox, it has been shown that those receiving large doses of hormones for a *hematologic* disorder are likely to demonstrate a high mortality rate (44 per cent) in contrast with much less or no mortality among those receiving smaller doses for an *allergic* condition.[16] Abrupt withdrawal of steroids may prove to be unwise in allergic patients.

4. Psychic disturbances, particularly manic or hypomanic states, may develop very promptly after hormone therapy is begun and can create a major problem.

5. Failure to grow may be observed in children receiving large daily doses of these drugs. Intermittent doses may help those patients who must be given the hormones continuously.

6. Prolonged topical or systemic use of steroids can lead to glaucoma or to posterior subcapsular cataracts.

7. Hirsutism, "moon facies" and "buffalo hump," abdominal striae, ease of bruising and acne (signs of Cushing's syndrome) can be distressing.

8. Fluid and sodium retention and potassium depletion can occur. ACTH, cortisone and hydrocortisone promote these effects, but they are rarely seen with the newer steroid analogues which have almost no effect on sodium and potassium balance.

9. A temporary state of diabetes mellitus with glycosuria, hyperglycemia and a diabetic type of glucose tolerance curve may be seen. This probably occurs only in genetically predisposed patients.

10. Triamcinolone, though very effective for short courses, has been observed to produce muscle wasting with prolonged use. Weakness, anorexia or mental depression are common complaints of patients to whom it is given.

Clinical Follow-Up

In order to detect early signs of untoward effects and thus avoid serious difficulty, the following is the minimal recommended follow-up program for patients receiving full therapeutic doses of these hormones:

1. Periodic clinical observation of the patient—daily, weekly or less frequently depending upon the duration of treatment. Visits should

be frequent enough that any complications can be observed promptly. Patients taking steroids must be seen by a physician at least once a month.

2. In asthmatic patients, regularly timed vital capacity determinations and expiratory flow rates are helpful in following progress. Spectacular improvements often are noted even in chronic cases. The serially recorded values also are helpful in following the progress as the patient is tapered off corticosteroids.

3. Chest roentgenograms and skin tests with tuberculin and the appropriate pathogenic fungal antigens should be performed before starting therapy, the roentgenograms being repeated at 6 to 12 month intervals.

4. Roentgenograms of the skeleton should be taken if there are any symptoms to suggest the development of osteoporosis. Such films should be taken routinely in elderly patients before and during the course of therapy. Particularly those on prolonged treatment may develop vertebral compression or aseptic necrosis, especially of the hips and shoulders, regardless of the disease for which the steroid is being given. Ischemic necrosis of the head of the femur is being reported with increasing frequency in such patients.[17]

5. Urinalysis for reducing substance is done every week or two while giving large doses and every few months after the drug has been decreased. Two hour postprandial blood sugar determinations should be obtained if large doses are continued for long periods.

6. Blood pressure is determined at each visit. Serum potassium measurements are made if ACTH or a corticosteroid having significant effects on electrolytes is being used.

7. Ocular tension and slit-lamp examinations are indicated when protracted corticosteroid treatment becomes unavoidable.

Preventive Measures

1. Antacids should be used if the patient develops gastrointestinal symptoms while taking steroids. Patients with previous history of peptic ulcer are better protected from bleeding by the prophylactic use of antacids from the beginning of steroid therapy, and some physicians use this precaution routinely in all patients who are likely to remain on the hormones for a long time.

2. Since ACTH and steroids will mask the signs and symptoms of infection without combating the causative agents, supplementary antibiotics or chemotherapy should be used liberally whenever there is indication of an infectious factor. Many prescribe isoniazid for all tuberculin-positive patients being given steroids.

3. Additional measures should be instituted if there is evidence that osteoporosis is developing. In such cases steroid or ACTH should be discontinued if this is at all possible; the alternate day regimen should

be attempted if steroids are essential. The patient also should be put on a high protein diet and instructed to drink one quart of milk daily. If the latter is impossible, supplementary calcium and vitamin D should be prescribed. In addition to these measures, sex hormones may be given for their anabolic effect. In adult males, 25 mg. testosterone propionate is used intramuscularly daily, or every other day at first. Following this, longer-acting anabolic steroids (e.g., nandrolone decanoate (Deca-Durabolin) or testosterone cypionate (Depo-Testosterone Cypionate)) may be injected every three to four weeks. Alternatively, daily buccal administration of testosterone propionate or methyl testosterone is carried out, although one must be alert for possible development of cholestatic jaundice from the latter drug.

In addition, 0.5 mg. stilbestrol may be given by mouth, though one must be on guard against adverse side effects from this medication in young men. Estrogens are administered in cycles of 20 days with treatment and 10 days without treatment. In women the dose usually is 1 to 2 mg. stilbestrol daily by mouth and 10 to 20 mg. daily of testosterone propionate or methyl testosterone given buccally. This treatment also is given in cycles of 20 days with 10 days of no treatment. Of course, one always should perform a pelvic examination before prescribing estrogens for a woman to be sure that pregnancy or neoplasm is not present.

4. It has been advocated that ACTH be given perhaps at monthly intervals to a patient on continuous steroids to stimulate his own adrenal glands (page 149). This method of treatment is still a controversial subject and many authorities feel that it accomplishes little.

5. In the circumstances in which an allergic patient is on prolonged administration of ACTH or a corticosteroid which has a substantial effect on electrolyte balance (e.g., cortisone or hydrocortisone), some restriction on sodium intake and potassium supplementation may become necessary.

Results of Treatment

When used in adequate dosages, ACTH and corticosteroids temporarily afford definite to spectacular symptomatic relief in most patients suffering from allergic disease. The big problem is that after a short course of treatment is discontinued, relapse is the rule if the causative agents are still present. However, relapse does not appear to be quite so inevitable or rapid as is apparently the case in rheumatoid arthritis. Some patients get along quite well for several months after a five to ten day course of hormone therapy, but in many others relapse occurs in a few weeks or even days. Experience has shown that relapse is apt to occur more quickly in patients with asthma of the type associated with infection than in those with definite sensitivity to environmental agents. It is apparent that the final results of this type of treatment in chronically ill allergic patients frequently are unsatisfactory. But the hormones are an important means for keeping the patient with serious illness under control, and they are most useful in severe acute allergic diseases. It should be emphasized that steroid and ACTH therapy should be used as a supplement to, and not a substitute for, well established methods of allergic management.

MISCELLANEOUS DRUGS AND AGENTS

The physician should not overlook some of the drugs which have wide usage in other fields of medicine and which are also of value in allergy.

Acetylsalicylic Acid (Aspirin)

Aspirin may be helpful in treating arthralgia and fever associated with serum sickness. There also is a clinical impression (J.M.S. and R.G.L.) that regular doses of aspirin reduce nasal congestion in allergic rhinitis.

Aspirin sensitivity is discussed on pages 87 and 182. When aspirin-sensitive patients require an analgesic drug, acetaminophen (Tylenol) or propoxyphene (Darvon) can be used. If the latter drug is prescribed, specify *"plain* Darvon" to make certain that the patient does not get Darvon Compound, which contains aspirin. Perhaps surprisingly, these patients also appear uniformly to tolerate sodium salicylate.

Antibiotic Drugs and Sulfonamides

The use of antibiotic drugs in respiratory allergy has become widespread. It is logical and necessary to use the antibiotic drugs when there is superimposed infection in the respiratory tract; control of the respiratory infection is essential for management of wheezing. Sputum cultures should be obtained before initiating treatment, but since these frequently show no specific pathogenic organism, it is permissible and, indeed, desirable to initiate treatment at once with a broad spectrum antibiotic drug. The preponderance of reports in the literature would advise starting with tetracycline in doses of at least 1 gm. daily in adults and 10 mg. per pound per day for children, in divided doses. The antibiotic drug can be changed if indicated by the outcome of the culture. Ampicillin (Polycillin), 250 or 500 mg. four times daily for adults (50 to 100 mg./kg. per day in divided doses for children), may also be very effective. This choice sometimes is favored for small children and pregnant women, since there may be possible staining of developing teeth by the tetracyclines. Ampicillin, however, may produce diarrhea. Other antibiotic drugs and chemotherapeutic agents may be used as indicated by the sputum cultures or by failure to respond to the aforementioned drugs. When the asthmatic patient observes a recurrence of his infection, often characterized by an increased amount of thick, colored sputum, prompt resumption of the antibiotic drug is indicated. In patients who relapse in spite of this, sustained use of the drug may be justified in a prophylactic dosage over a period of months, throughout the winter or throughout the year.

Oxygen

This is discussed in Chapter 8, page 166.

Calcium

The intravenous or oral administration of calcium has long been used to combat pruritus. This practice should now be largely abandoned, since more effective agents are available.

Sodium Lactate or Sodium Bicarbonate

These agents are discussed in Chapter 8, page 165.[2]

Nicotinic Acid

Some allergists have the clinical impression that in certain cases of urticaria, which are refractory to other forms of therapy, the daily intravenous or oral administration of nicotinic acid may be of value. Ten milliliters of a sterile solution containing 10 mg. nicotinic acid per milliliter is the usual amount given (slowly) intravenously. An intense flush is to be expected.

Histamine

The use of parenteral injections of histamine in the diagnosis and treatment of histamine cephalgia is discussed in Chapter 13 (page 300).

Nose Drops and Sprays

The problems created by using topical nasal medications in a chronic condition such as allergic rhinitis are noted in Chapter 5. Occasionally, when allergic symptoms are poorly controlled, nose drops administered for two or three days may help break up a cycle which is perpetuated by the stuffy nose. They also may be prescribed for limited periods when allergic rhinitis is complicated by sinusitis or otitis media. A number of available preparations are listed on page 133.

Immunosuppressive Drugs

As physicians have searched for more effective means of controlling allergic disease, attention has been directed toward attempts to suppress the formation of antibody in atopic persons. This has been tried in laboratory animals with some success, using irradiation, which is obviously an impractical method for man. Also, antibody suppression has been achieved with certain immunosuppressive drugs in human subjects. In view of this, these compounds are being used in an attempt to ameliorate a variety of diseases in which immunologic phenomena appear to play a part. Among these are allergic diseases, such as bronchial asthma and atopic dermatitis. The significant toxicity of these compounds, however, should make one very reluctant to use them in diseases that are not life-threatening, and 6-mercaptopurine has been found to be ineffective in suppressing pre-existing antibody titers, including reagin.[18-19] One must watch with interest efforts to develop chemical agents which can safely suppress antibody formation.

Atropine

Atropine and pharmacologically related drugs often relieve rhinorrhea and even bronchial asthma. However, because of their tendency to cause thickening of the respiratory tract secretions, some of the previously mentioned antispasmodic drugs are to be preferred in most cases.

THE PASSING PARADE OF MEDICATION

Some older drugs still are prescribed for allergic diseases in spite of the present-day availability of more efficacious compounds. Others are used without adequate documentation of their effectiveness.

Ipecac

Ipecac, prepared as syrup of ipecac, is given in the dosage of 15 drops for adults and five drops for children in their first year of life and one drop for each additional year of age. In children it is used for relief of croupous bronchitis, since it supposedly produces a bronchorrhea. Its usefulness in promoting bronchorrhea in asthma does not appear to have been well studied.

Stramonium and Nitrates

A treatment, now largely obsolete, involved burning stramonium leaf combined with equal parts of potassium nitrate to increase combustibility. Sometimes it was beneficial in relieving mild asthmatic attacks, especially in children. The leaf may be dispensed as a powder and burned in a dish, with the patient inhaling the fumes from a distance of about a foot, or it may be smoked in an "asthmatic cigarette." One disadvantage is the unpleasant odor which permeates the entire house in which it is used.

Histamine-Azoprotein

This conjugate of histamine and despeciated horse serum globulin (Hapamine) was widely used a generation ago, but because results have been disappointing, it has almost been abandoned as a means for non-specific therapy in allergic problems.

Others

A poison oak extract, Anergex, has been advocated for the treatment of the entire gamut of allergic conditions. There is double-blind information in the medical literature to support the contention that this material has no therapeutic effect.[20]

Clinically available histaminase proved ineffective. Typhoid vaccine and other foreign proteins probably stimulated the pituitary-adrenal axis and have been largely supplanted by treatment with the corticosteroids themselves. Innumerable other "therapeutic" agents, including various vitamins, lobeline, hydrochloric acid and snake venoms, have almost passed out of usage.

REFERENCES

1. Goodman, L. S., and Gilman, A.: The Pharmacological Basis of Therapeutics. 3rd ed. New York, Macmillan, 1965.
2. Blumenthal, J. S., Blumenthal, N. M., Brown, E. B., Campbell, G. S., and Prasas, A.: Effect of changes in arterial pH on the action of Adrenalin in acute Adrenalin-fast asthmatics. Dis. Chest 39:516, 1961.
3. Mosko, M. M., Arkin, M. C., Miller, B. H., and Snider, G. L.: Studies on the effects of sympathicoamines in asthma. Dis. Chest 38:264, 1960.
4. Hirsch, S. R., Kory, R. C., and Hamilton, L. H.: Effect of Saline, Alevaire and Mucomyst on sputum volume and consistency. (Abstr.) J. Allergy 36:211, 1965, and Am. Rev. Resp. Dis., Nov. 1966.
5. Falliers, C. J.: Iodotherapy appears effective in children who have asthma. Report. J.A.M.A. 191:28, 1965.
6. Galina, M. P., Avnet, N. L., and Einhorn, A.: Iodides during pregnancy: an apparent cause of neonatal death. New England J. Med. 267:1124, 1962.
7. Sheffner, A. L., Medler, E. M., Jacobs, L. W., and Sarrett, H. P.: The in-vitro reduction in viscosity of human tracheobronchial secretions by acetylcysteine. Am. Rev. Resp. Dis. 90:721, 1964.
8. Bernstein, I., and Ausdenmoore, R.: Iatrogenic bronchospasm occurring during clinical trials of a new mucolytic agent, acetylcysteine (Mucomyst). Dis. Chest 46:469, 1964.
9. New Drugs, p. 121, Chicago, The American Medical Association, 1965.
10. Feinberg, S. M., Malkiel, S., and Feinberg, A. R.: The Antihistamines. Chicago, Year Book Medical Publishing Co., 1950.
11. Lewis, T.: The Blood Vessels of the Human Skin and Their Responses. London, Shaw & Sons, 1927.
12. Siegel, S.: ACTH and corticosteroids in allergic disorders. J. Pediat. 66:927, 1965.

13. Harter, J. G., Reddy, W. J., and Thorn, G. W.: Studies on an intermittent cortico-steroid dosage regimen. New England J. Med. *269*:591, 1963.
14. Arbesman, C. E., Bonstein, H. S., and Reisman, R. E.: Dexamethasone aerosol ther-apy for bronchial asthma, J. Allergy *34*:354, 1963.
15. Norman, P. S., Winkenwerder, W. L., Murgatroyd, G. W., and Parsons, J. W.: The demonstration that intranasal dexamethasone aerosol suppresses hay fever by local action. J. Allergy *36*:202, 1965.
16. Falliers, C. J., Ellis, E. F., and Bukantz, S. C.: The course and management of vari-cella in children receiving steroids for intractable asthma. South. M. J. *57*:1054, 1964.
17. Burrows, F. G. O.: Avascular necrosis of bone complicating steroid therapy. Brit. J. Radiol. *38*:309, 1965.
18. Vanselow, N. A., Kelly, J. R., Meyers, M. C., and Johnson, A. G.: The effect of 6-mercaptopurine on antibody production in atopic individuals. J. Allergy *37*:145, 1966.
19. Arkins, J. A., and Hirsch, S. R.: Clinical effectiveness of 6-mercaptopurine in bron-chial asthma. J. Allergy *37*:90, 1966.
20. Brown, E. G., Ipsen, J., and Popovits, C.: Use of poison oak extract in ragweed hay-fever: a double-blind study. New York J. Med. *64*:2050, 1964.

Chapter Eight

STATUS ASTHMATICUS AND AIDS IN TREATMENT FOR RESPIRATORY ALLERGY

Asthma may at times progress so that the patient becomes critically ill. When the attacks are no longer intermittent and a person experiences continuous asthma over 24 hours and fails to respond to injections of epinephrine (1:1000), he is said to be in "status asthmaticus." This is one of the most difficult conditions in medicine to treat, and because the patient is so severely uncomfortable and alarmed, it takes a well trained and soundly competent physician to handle the treatment properly. This is truly a medical emergency. There is always the pressure exerted by relatives of the person affected and indeed by the natural reaction of the physician himself to do something to relieve the patient's dyspnea. For this reason, it is well to remember the first rule of treating status asthmaticus; namely, *do not overtreat.* It is best to have one person writing all orders for the patient, as there is less likelihood that some medication will be omitted, duplicated or inappropriate. A second rule is to *start proper treatment soon enough.*

There were 4896 deaths associated with asthma recorded in the United States in 1962, and 216 of these occurred in persons under age 19.[1] Death in status asthmaticus may be caused by: overmedication—especially with aminophylline[2]—infection, failure of the respiratory center, cardiac failure[3] and suffocation by accumulation of bronchial mucous plugs. The latter is the most common immediate cause of death, a point to be remembered in treating these patients (Figure 8–1). The other pathological findings in asthma also should be borne in mind in connection with treatment (page 88).

Like the patient in diabetic acidosis or in adrenal crisis, the patient in status asthmaticus must be hospitalized. It will be helpful to have available means for obtaining a chest roentgenogram, blood count and urine examination, in addition to serum electrolytes and, if possible,

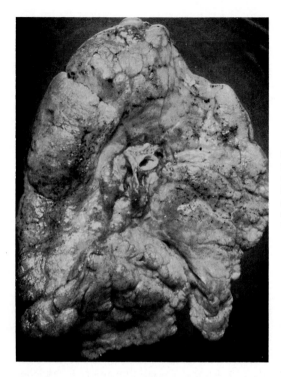

Figure 8-1. Gross appearance of lung of a 37 year old male who died in acute status asthmaticus. The lung remains inflated after sectioning, a characteristic finding in death from asthma, because mucous plugs in the bronchi prevent collapse.

blood gases and pH. When arterial bloods cannot be obtained, one can convert approximately from venous carbon dioxide pressure (pCO_2), by noting that venous carbon dioxide pressure is approximately 6 to 7 mm. Hg higher than arterial blood carbon dioxide pressure. Careful monitoring of the patient, with recording of vital signs and, when indicated, electrocardiographic recording can be obtained.

PRINCIPLES OF TREATMENT FOR STATUS ASTHMATICUS

There are *seven* principles of treatment which help to bring the patient out of his status asthmaticus and break up the vicious cycle of factors which are keeping the asthma going.

1. Rest. Every patient in status asthmaticus is fatigued and requires rest. The effort of breathing is considerable, and the subject turns his entire attention to that effort when having a severe episode. The patient should be in a hospital where he can receive superior care under trained personnel and be spared much of the exertion which home care cannot eliminate. Furthermore, by hospitalization the patient often is removed from one or several of the environmental factors which contribute to his asthmatic attack. The head of the bed should be elevated to a comfortable position. A sympathetic but strongly reassuring attitude on the part of the physician and nursing staff is of major importance in helping the patient to relax. Mild sedation may help to give the patient greater comfort. Sedation should not be excessive or continuous, since the patient's life depends upon his coughing up his secretions. Increased sedation at night with little or none during the day is recommended. Sedation may be accomplished by giving moderate doses of barbiturates if one is certain that the patient is not sensitive to that group of drugs. Alternatively, we have found that promazine hydrochloride (Sparine) 25 mg. four times daily provides good relief from anxiety and enables the patient to rest (see page 139). Chloral hydrate or paraldehyde are especially good choices. Morphine should never be administered. It is harmful because it depresses respiration, may lead to addiction and has a drying effect on the bronchial secretions. To a lesser extent the same criticisms may be made of meperidine (Demerol), and therefore we also do not use this drug in treating status asthmaticus.

2. Fluids and Nutrition. These comprise the second important factor in the control of status asthmaticus. Patients soon learn that eating and drinking will increase the severity of their dyspnea, and so their intake is sharply curtailed. Furthermore, asthmatic patients lose an exceptionally large amount of water in sweat and exhaled water vapor. This starts a vicious cycle which, if unattended, will result in a severe upset of fluid balance. It is almost certain that a patient in status asthmaticus brought into the emergency room of a hospital will be dehydrated. It is wise to start these patients on intravenous fluids, using 5 per cent glucose in distilled water by slow drip. It has been shown that during an acute attack an asthmatic patient may lose 2500 ml. of water in 24 hours in urine, sweat and water vapor, and this is certainly the very minimal fluid requirement for replacement in the adult patient.[4] It will add to the patient's comfort if he is given small sips of coffee, soup or water by mouth, but he will be too dyspneic to take significant amounts orally. Oral fluids should be warm or at room temperature, *not* iced. Cold fluids may cause a reflex bronchospasm which may increase the severity of the attack. The diet should be liquid or semisolid, and feedings must be spaced so that no great quantity is given at one time. Large quantities of food increase the asthmatic patient's dyspnea. Of course, known food allergens should be avoided, but the emphasis should be placed on adequate hydration during severe status asthmaticus. If the total fluid intake is by the intravenous route over one or two days, supplemental electrolyte replacement will be necessary.

3. Expectorants. One of the basic considerations in treating patients with severe asthma is that as long as they are able to bring up their sputum, they seldom have severe respiratory decompensation; and if treated symptomatically, they often recover satisfactorily. But just as soon as these patients stop bringing up their secretions, a series of events occurs which leads to serious complications.

The sputum is composed of mucus which has poured out of the bronchial glands in response to the allergic reaction and perhaps also as part of a reaction to infection of the respiratory tract. The mucus is

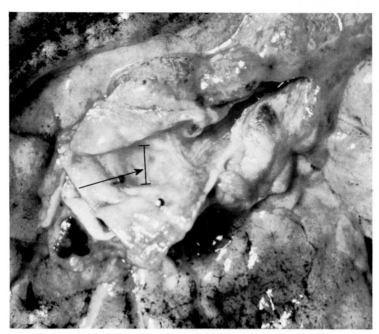

Figure 8–2. Mucous plug occluding the entire lumen of the secondary bronchus. There is no plug in the main bronchus. This plug could extend continuously into successively finer bronchial rami peripherally. Could bronchoscopy dislodge a plug as firmly fixed as this?

often thick like glue (Figure 8–2). It takes very little additional physiologic disturbance to make raising this mucus impossible. As stated previously, dehydration, fatigue, improper medication and excessive sedation each may make it difficult to raise sputum. This leads to the formation of mucous plugs, which in turn cause distal atelectasis and pneumonitis. Although judicious use of bronchoscopy and antibiotic drugs may help this complication, it is easier to prevent it than to treat it.

Problems in evaluating the efficiency of expectorants or mucolytic drugs are discussed on page 136. As indicated, recent evidence furnishes firmer support for the long-standing clinical impression that iodides do exert an expectorant effect. Potassium iodide and syrup of hydriodic acid are the most commonly used preparations given orally (page 136). Sodium iodide may be given intravenously in 0.5 to 1.0 gm. doses. One should be sure that the patient is not iodide-sensitive before the material is administered. Glycerol guaiacolate also is claimed to have an expectorant effect. Preparations such as Robitussin, Quibron, Verequad and Asbron may be used if the patient can retain oral medications (page 137). Patients often find that coughing, in an attempt to raise thick sputum, prolongs the attack of asthma. When the secretions of the bronchi are thinned out, raising is accomplished merely by clearing the throat. Discussion of aerosolized mucolytic medications and of warm saline aerosol appears below. Again, *adequate hydration* to help expectoration cannot be overemphasized.

4. Specific Bronchodilator Medications. The group of epinephrine-like sympathomimetic drugs plays an important part in the treatment of severe asthma. By definition, status asthmaticus patients fail to respond to epinephrine.

Aminophylline, given by vein or by retention enema, may be extremely helpful in reducing the severity of the asthma (page 133). It is most important to ascertain how much aminophylline the patient has received in the past 24 hours and when he received it, since a common cause of fatalities in patients, especially children, is the disastrous infusion of aminophylline into a patient who already has been given more than a maximal dose by an anxious parent.[2] By including 0.5 gm. in adults or 4 mg. per kilogram per six hours in children of aminophylline in the intravenous drip, considerable benefit may be expected, as the fluid and medication run in over a one half to two hour interval. It is convenient to have a continuous intravenous infusion running and then to add the aminophylline and other medications by a "piggyback" Y-tube arrangement whenever needed. Oral aminophylline and aerosol isoproterenol rarely are helpful in status asthmaticus. However, a trial of aerosol isoproterneol or epinephrine is warranted.[5] Aminophylline retention enemas often are effective in less severe asthma, but in status asthmaticus it generally is preferable to give this drug intravenously.

Special attention should be given to the possibility of using sodium bicarbonate or sodium lactate in status asthmaticus. Recent investigation indicates that the bronchial musculature of animals becomes less responsive to epinephrine in an acid medium. When the pH is made more alkaline, epinephrine again exerts its relaxing effect on bronchial smooth muscle. It has been proposed that the production of acidosis (respiratory or metabolic) in human asthma may be a possible metabolic explanation for "epinephrine refractoriness" which occurs in status asthmaticus.[6] Consequently, the use of alkalinizing agents may be considered in this condition. If at all possible, arterial pH, pCO_2 and PO_2 should be obtained to select patients for this treatment. When this is not possible, sodium bicarbonate sometimes is tried empirically while the patient is carefully observed, but the results will be disappointing if the patient was not initially acidotic. Two to three hundred milliequivalents of sodium bicarbonate or 150 to 300 ml. of 1 M sodium lactate can be given intravenously in approximately 30 to 45 minutes. It has been shown to be most effective when this material is administered *early* in the course of status asthmaticus before the patient has become dehydrated and the sputum has become thickened and tenacious. The physician should realize that considerable sodium is being given intravenously with this procedure; thus, it may be relatively contraindicated in the patient who already has edema secondary to steroid therapy or concurrent congestive heart failure. Response, when the patient is indeed acidotic, is dramatic and prompt, and frequently there is no need for additional epinephrine. Results appear within 30 to 60 minutes when the procedure is successful.

5. Control of Infection. A remarkably high percentage of asthma patients who develop status asthmaticus have an accompanying infection of the respiratory tract. In fact, the infection usually appears to be the triggering element which precipitated the status asthmaticus. Sputum specimens should be obtained early, and cultures started. Meanwhile an antibiotic drug should be prescribed. In adults, we prefer tetracycline, 250 to 500 mg., four times daily. In children under eight years of age and in pregnant women, ampicillin or erythromycin in the proper dosage for weight (10 mg. per pound in 24 hours in divided doses) are good drugs with which to start, since tetracycline may cause permanent staining of developing teeth. When indicated, the antibiotic drug can be changed when the sputum culture report becomes available.

6. ACTH and Corticosteroids. In the treatment of status asthmaticus these drugs can be life-saving. Although a physician would not resort at once to use of these compounds in a young patient who appeared uncomfortable but not severely ill, he might start intravenous hydrocortisone immediately in a critically dyspneic or moribund patient. Patients who have *previously* been on steroids do no fare well in status asthmaticus, and withholding these drugs may be a fatal miscalculation. Thus, each patient must be carefully assessed. The severity of the attack, previous treatment with steroids, the initial response to the standard regimen and the clinical course over the first few hours of therapy all need to be evaluated. Although authorities differ in their opinion regarding treatment of the patient who has not received steroids previously, it is certainly worthwhile to treat by all the previously mentioned modalities before these hormones are added. In any event the use of ACTH and corticosteroids should not give the physician a false sense of security so that he overlooks the other well established principles of therapy. Some patients in status asthmaticus *do* still respond without the use of steroids when followed carefully and treated intelligently. However, it is important not to wait too long. Details of initiation of steroid therapy are given on page 150. After the patient has experienced marked relief, the dosage should be reduced and (hopefully) discontinued when no longer needed.

7. Supportive Therapy. The patient is indeed fortunate if he can be hospitalized in an intensive care unit, with air filtration, temperature and humidity control and constant attention by well trained personnel. *Oxygen* may be used especially when the patient is cyanotic, extremely dyspneic (even without cyanosis), or when it is not possible to provide a humidity-controlled and air-conditioned room. It is important for oxygen to be given at room temperature, since cold oxygen may cause bronchospasm and make the patient worse. Helium is of little additional benefit over oxygen. Now it is possible for the oxygen therapist to add water vapor to the environment of the oxygen tent to provide any humidity desired, as well as to control the temperature, and to deliver clean air which is almost free from pollen, dust and other contamination. Plastic face masks or nasal catheters may be used when a tent is not desired, and such equipment delivers a higher concentration of oxygen. Patients also may be less apprehensive with a face mask, since an oxygen tent may be thought to imply an ominous prognosis. Because oxygen has a drying action on the respiratory mucous membrane, it is important to give oxygen always with adequate humidification.

The effects of high concentrations of oxygen are not always beneficial, especially in patients with pulmonary emphysema.[7-8]

a. Respiration may be depressed by administration of high concentrations of oxygen. The alveolar hypoventilation of these patients may result in a persistent hypercapnia. In time the medullary respiratory centers become unresponsive to this excess of carbon dioxide and the respiratory drive is taken over by anoxic stimulation of the chemoreceptors. If one then gives oxygen to such a patient, the stimulus to breathing is removed and respiration slows or may cease.

b. Lethargy, confusion and coma may ensue. Although the reasons for this may be complex, narcosis, resulting from increasing carbon dioxide retention associated with the progressive hypoventilation, may play an important role.

c. Removal of nitrogen from the body may result from high concentration of oxygen. The nitrogen content of the paranasal sinuses and the middle ear may be reduced, causing a vacuum type of pain. It may be corrected by removal of the patient to atmospheric air.

In spite of possible complications, carefully controlled continuous oxygen administration appears to be better than its intermittent use in relieving hypoxemia, particulary in patients with respiratory acidosis. An oxygen concentration of less than 30 per cent seems to produce adequate saturation without further aggravation of hypercapnia. A mechanical respiratory aid may be used to ensure continued alveolar ventilation.[9-10]

Mention should be made of a time-honored procedure, namely, ether in oil, given to adults in a dose of equal quantities of 60 to 90 ml. of each (ether and corn or olive oil), as a retention enema. This is a safe form of treatment, it may furnish the patient with some sedation and rest, and the ether as it is volatilized from the lungs may initiate some bronchorrhea and help break up the cycle of the presistent asthma. This treatment may be repeated twice at about two hour intervals. However, since this form of therapy is rather cumbersome, it is being used less and less frequently as other measures are found which can accomplish the same therapeutic goals more conveniently.

AEROSOL THERAPY

In treatment of the patient who has bronchial asthma, a very help-ful implement to therapy is the administration of medications by aerosol. Whether the asthma is due primarily to bronchial constriction, bronchial edema (page 89) or the presence of pulmonary infection, aerosolization of medication for its topical application to the bronchial mucosa may be beneficial.

The only disadvantage of such therapy is the tendency of anxious patients to use the aerosol too frequently. A definite understanding should be reached concerning the frequency and dosage, and periodic check-ups are needed by the physician to see that his directions regard-ing use of the aerosol are being followed. Suitable aerosols may be de-livered from nebulizers which produce droplets of a size (0.5 to 3 mi-crons) which are carried down into the lower respiratory tract (page 131). Pressure to operate the simplest nebulizer is provided by having the patient squeeze a rubber hand bulb attached to the nebulizer. More recently bronchodilators have been dispensed in pressurized, plastic con-tainers (page 131). By simply pressing the valve, the patient receives a metered amount of the drug. When larger quantities of an aerosol are required, a pump or an oxygen or compressed air tank may be used as the source of pressure. Usually a Y-tube is inserted between the pressure source and the nebulizer, thereby permitting the patient to deliver the aerosol as needed by placing his thumb over the open end at the Y-tube during inspiration. With this type of apparatus and a flow rate of about 6 liters per minute, 1 milliliter of solution can be administered to the patient in aerosol form in about 12 to 15 minutes. This simple type of arrangement can provide for very effective treatment and may be the only feasible method in a number of situations (e.g., in the home or small hospital). In order to operate a nebulizer there must be enough liquid in the bottom to reach up to the lower end of the side-arm capil-lary tube. The nebulizer should be held vertically and placed well back in the patient's mouth, pointing directly toward the posterior oro-pharynx. If the mouthpiece of the nebulizer is pointed upward or down-ward, most of the aerosolized medication will be wasted by its precipita-tion on the mucous membranes of the mouth. The patient must be taught to activate the nebulizer early in inspiration. Another suitable and inexpensive unit for home inhalation therapy has been reported.[11]

Intermittent Positive Pressure Breathing (IPPB)

With the commercially available Bennett or Bird intermittent posi-tive pressure breathing machines, intermittent positive pressure breathing may also be used to nebulize bronchodilator solutions for therapeutic purposes. There is some difference of opinion regarding its effective-ness in comparison with the hand nebulizer, but there is no doubt about the beneficial effect of this device in hospitalized patients, particularly when certain physiologic principles are followed.[12] The positive pressure machine actually is a reliable means for delivery of appropriate-sized particles of medication at proper velocity over a prolonged period of time, since it is doubtful that positive pressure per se is beneficial in asthma. Although occasional patients experiencing severe asthma are not able to cooperate with this therapy and will "fight the machine," most asthmatic patients obtain substantial temporary relief.

Positive pressure forces the bronchodilator aerosol into the mouth, and inspiration draws it into the bronchial tree. Positive pressure greater than 12 to 14 cm. of water pressure has been shown to produce turbulence with decreased air flow, and thus pressure greater than this is not commonly used. Inspiratory flow should be smooth and regular; therefore, the machine needs to be adjusted so that there is no sudden sharp increase in pressure delivered at the end of inspiration. This, of coure, tends to cause hyperinflation of the lungs. At the end of inspiration the machine automatically shuts off, interrupting the positive pressure aerosol. The patient should be instructed to hold his breath for a second or two, if possible, before exhaling, allowing for more adequate mixture of the aerosolized medication in the lung itself. Expiration should not be forced since this tends to cause premature collapse of the bronchioles and trapping of air in these areas distal to the collapsed airways. At the end of expiration the patient may rest his arms against his chest wall and lean forward to help force out the last remaining air from the expiratory reserve volume. This particularly helps in the emphysematous asthmatic patients. It is very important for the physician to supervise the patient in the proper use of the intermittent positive pressure breathing machine and to check the machine's adjustment and function frequently on his rounds. When available, the assistance of an oxygen therapist is invaluable. The correct application of intermittent positive pressure breathing is a helpful adjunct to therapy, while its improper use or a poorly functioning machine adds nothing to the program.

Isoproterenol usually is the drug of choice for administration by intermittent positive pressure breathing. Approximately 1 milliliter of solution is administered at each treatment. The usual 1:200 concentration of isoproterenol is diluted, often about two- to four-fold, with warm saline or other agents (see below). This treatment may be indicated in the asthmatic patient who is responding slowly to routine hospital care and who continues to have wheezing. Improvement may occur despite previous failure to respond well to continuous oral bronchodilators, aerosolization by hand nebulizer, sympathomimetic amines by injection and the other forms of treatment mentioned previously. Sputum which is thick and tenacious often will begin to loosen sufficiently so that it can be raised. The warm saline in which the medication is delivered also is beneficial to the bronchial mucosa. Saline is preferred to water as a diluent, since the latter is irritating to the bronchial mucosa. If

1:100 epinephrine or Aerolone Compound is used as the bronchodilator instead of isoproterenol, these also should be diluted with at least an equal amount of warm saline. All these compounds may be absorbed in significant quantity when given by intermittent positive pressure breathing, with consequent tachycardia and jitteriness; further dilution of the medication is indicated if this occurs. Intermittent positive pressure breathing treatment is given regularly three times a day before meals, since the patient can breathe more deeply on an empty stomach, and one more time in the late evening. If indicated, additional intermittent positive pressure breathing treatments can be added to the above schedule. Postural drainage can be carried out immediately after the intermittent positive pressure breathing and is more effective at this time, each mode of treatment complementing the other. In the chronic asthmatic patient, daily outpatient or office use of intermittent positive pressure breathing treatment has been advocated to supplement, but not replace, a complete program of therapy for asthma. Besides its effectiveness in delivering aerosol bronchodilators, intermittent positive pressure breathing may be used for administering mucolytic agents such as N-acetylcysteine (Mucomyst). Other mucolytic agents are discussed on page 137. Antibiotic drugs are now administered systemically rather than by aerosol. Sensitization of patients and nurses was not uncommon when antibiotic drugs, especially penicillin, were used in aerosol form.

Complications from Intermittent Positive Pressure Breathing. The most common difficulty encountered with intermittent positive pressure breathing aerosol is irritation of the bronchopulmonary tree either from too strong or too prolonged administration of the medication. This is easily identified, often after four to seven days of therapy. The patient's throat begins to feel irritated. His cough, which previously was productive and helpful, becomes dry, uncomfortable and aggravated by the treatments. This finding should warn the physician to discontine the aerosol until he can observe the effect of withdrawal.

A second problem may arise from the use of N-acetyl-cysteine (Mucomyst). It is said that this medication may produce such a copious flow of sputum in some patients that the physician may have to call for bronchoscopy and aspiration to assist in mechanical removal of sputum. More commonly, N-acetyl-cysteine may cause initial bronchospasm in asthmatic patients. This is usually relieved by a short course of aerosolized isoproterenol.

Finally, severe pulmonary infection may be a temporary contraindication to the use of intermittent positive pressure breathing, since employing it too soon may tend to aggregate thick, purulent secretions and cause a temporary decrease in ventilation. This results in less wheezing but an increase in body temperature and respiratory insufficiency. The use of an appropriate antibiotic drug and other forms of therapy for a few days prior to the addition of intermittent positive pressure breathing will tend to prevent this problem. It has been shown in animals that intermittent positive pressure breathing may reduce venous return to the left auricle during the inspiratory cycle, but a significant drop in cardiac output does not occur unless the circulating blood volume is also depleted. It is not felt that the intermittent positive pressure breathing therapy seriously compromises the cardiac output in an asthmatic patient with or without associated myocardial insufficiency.

BRONCHIAL LAVAGE

In recent years, beneficial effects of aerosolized superheated normal saline on irritated bronchial mucosa have been reported.[13] Furthermore, incorporation of 40 per cent propylene glycol into an aerosol will promote the flow of mucus from the bronchial glands and "create" sputum in a dry respiratory tract.[14] An ultrasonic aerosol generator (DeVilbis Co., Toledo, Ohio) may also be used to reduce the viscosity of bronchial secretions. These measures should be carried out under close supervision by the physician. Since some asthmatic patients are made much worse by this aerosol treatment, it should not be forced into the program. When the aerosol fails to dislodge inspissated sputum, direct lavage of the bronchial tree, using 10 to 15 ml. of warm saline, has been advocated. Instillation of the saline by means of a catheter will dislodge and assist in removal of plugs of mucus which otherwise are retained for long periods of time. This procedure should only be carried out by adequately experienced personnel.

BRONCHOSCOPY

The question concerning whether to perform a bronchoscopy frequently arises. There usually is no reason why bronchoscopy should not be carried out on a patient with asthma, particularly when the diagnosis is not clearly established or when there are retained secretions which are causing respiratory embarrassment. Physicians have for a long time advocated bronchoscopy as a life-saving measure in severe bronchial asthma, since, following removal of the retained secretions and bronchial plugs, the patient frequently responds with dramatic improvement. The bronchorrhea induced by bronchoscopy also may be of considerable benefit. On the other hand, asthmatic patients sometimes develop severe bronchospasm when the bronchoscope is inserted, and it is impossible for the bronchoscopist to aspirate the smaller bronchi where obstruction by mucus is apt to be most pronounced. Thus, the presence of asthma is not a contraindication to bronchoscopy, but before it is undertaken the entire case should be evaluated from the standpoint of the cardiac condition, the emotional status of the patient and what one hopes to accomplish.

Special indication for bronchoscopy exists when the asthmatic patient, who is not doing well, clinically develops a "silent chest." On auscultation, the wheezing appears to have subsided, and breath sounds are almost absent. This finding should be cause for alarm and should alert the physician to consider calling for therapeutic bronchoscopy. Removal of retained secretions may restore the patient's ability to exchange air.

In addition to its therapeutic value in asthma, bronchoscopy also is a valuable diagnostic aid, particularly in cases in which an obstructing bronchogenic neoplasm, tuberculous bronchitis or a foreign body is suspected to be the cause of the patient's "asthma." Also, it is prudent, after it has been decided to perform a bronchoscopy, to arrange for collection of some of the aspirated bronchial secretions in sterile containers. Cultures can be made of this material for pyogenic organisms, tubercle bacilli and fungi. Smears are stained for acid-fast bacteria and eosinophils, and a search for neoplastic cells can be carried out when indicated.

BRONCHOGRAPHY

Whereas bronchoscopy usually can be undertaken in almost anyone with safety, this is not so with bronchography. The patient with a low vital capacity may have such a limited respiratory reserve that the addition of the opaque medium into the bronchial tree may be sufficient to cause death through asphyxiation. Therefore, even assuming that the patient will not be allergic to the iodized oil, bronchography should be avoided or postponed in certain patients. Prior to the test the vital capacity values always should be obtained according to the method described previously (see page 48). If the patient's vital capacity is much below expected normal values, there is potential danger in undertaking bronchography.

Bronchography should not be performed while an individual is having an asthmatic attack. In such instances, the bronchogram is not accurate because of incomplete filling of the bronchi with the contrast medium. Also, the procedure cannot be carried out satisfactorily from the technical standpoint, and the patient's vital capacity may be dangerously impaired by adding contrast medium during the attack.

Sometimes a patient in whom bronchography is contemplated is referred to an allergist because of a history of iodide sensitivity. There is no test which can be performed ahead of time to determine definitely whether the patient is allergic to iodized oil. Although severe reactions to the newer preparations are unusual, there is no reason why they cannot take place in sensitized individuals. A number of workers have advocated using a very dilute mixture of barium sufate as the bronchographic contrast medium in these patients and report excellent results.[15]

THE MORIBUND ASTHMATIC PATIENT

Advances have been made in the management of the asthmatic patient who appears to be on the verge of death in spite of optimal treatment with bronchodilators, fluids, antibiotics, steroids, expectorants, aerosols, and perhaps bronchial lavage and aspiration (page 162). However, if he is to receive the full benefit of available therapy, the patient should be cared for in a facility in which essentially constant observation is possible and in which blood gas analysis as well as the skills of the surgeon, anesthesiologist and inhalation therapist are available. Many factors, including exhaustion, hypoxia, hypercapnia, heart failure and circulatory collapse, may contribute to a moribund appearance. In such cases, the possibility of severe respiratory or metabolic acidosis or of drug intoxication from overtreatment must be considered. Especially in asthmatic patients who are comatose when first seen, a reaction to aspirin must be ruled out.

With any of these contributing factors, the condition of the patient is subject to rapid changes necessitating prompt modifications of treatment. Because life-threatening hypoxia and hypercapnia may develop without apparent clinical signs, frequent determinations of arterial pO_2 and pCO_2 are extremely helpful (page 53). Monitoring of end-expiratory pCO_2 with the aid of a rapid-response carbon dioxide analyzer is also of value. However, decisions involving carbon dioxide tensions cannot be based on the carbon dioxide combining power of venous blood, although this determination is widely available. Since, in gravely ill asthmatic patients, hypoxia and hypercapnia usually develop relatively rapidly, they are less well tolerated than are comparable pO_2 and pCO_2 states which are reached over longer periods in chronic bronchitis and emphysema patients. Therefore, when blood gas values are even modestly abnormal, in the asthmatic patient they provide a definite indication for more intensive treatment.

In the exhausted patient, a period of mechanical assistance to ventilation may be adequate to correct hypoxia and hypercapnia. A recent study on the pathophysiology of ventilatory failure has emphasized that the degree of hypoxemia may be out of proportion to the degree of carbon dioxide retention, indicating the need for adequate ventilation with moisturized oxygen.[16]

Pressure or flow-limited devices such as the Bird, Monaghan and Bennett machines provide oxygen or air-oxygen mixtures to assist inspiration. Automatic ventilation control is also possible when apnea is present or when the patient's inspiratory efforts are too weak to cycle the machine. It is essential to moisturize the gas mixture to prevent drying of the airway mucosa and crusting of secretions; the nebulizer should never be allowed to run dry. An essentially closed system, usually obtained with endotracheal intubation or a cuffed tracheotomy tube, is required when these devices alone are used to accomplish ventilation in the moribund asthmatic patient. When ventilation by pressure and flow limited devices does not correct the blood gas abnormalities, use of a volume-cycled ventilator such as the Mörch or Engström respirator will usually succeed. In addition, for short periods of time, the anesthesiologist may be needed to "bag breathe" the patient.

Tank type respirators that alter the pressure around the body rather than at the mouth can also be used to assist and initiate ventilation. Their use in the confused patient may be beneficial and does not require intubation or tracheostomy. As with the powerful Mörch respirator, management of these machines is difficult and hyperventilation with respiratory alkalosis can easily occur with their use, unless the arterial pH and pCO_2 are frequently determined, at least initially. In treating such induced alkalosis, the frequent need for supplementary potassium should not be overlooked. Respiratory stimulants such as ethamivan or nikethamide usually are not indicated in severely ill asthmatics.

Tracheostomy should be considered in the moribund asthmatic patient since the respiratory failure is often largely reversible. Indications for tracheostomy include the failure of less vigorous types of therapy to correct hypoxia and hypercapnia and the inability to remove secretions adequately by more conventional means. Coma or an arterial pCO_2 value in the 60 mm. Hg range is generally an indication for this procedure. Tracheostomy causes a reduction of respiratory dead space, although this is not its most outstanding effect. Airway resistance also may be minimally decreased; however, the relative simplicity of removing secretions via the tracheal stoma is a major advantage. Suctioning should be frequent as long as secretions are copious and must be carried out with careful sterile technique. This procedure must also be maintained because the patient is no longer able to cough effectively. The inner cannula must be cleansed regularly to prevent its occlusion by viscous secretions. If the patient is ill enough to require a tracheostomy, assistance to respiration will probably already have been initiated. As the patient improves, mechanical means of ventilation may be gradually discontinued. An inflated cuff on the tracheostomy tube is a necessity when assisted ventilation is employed.

The use of controlled ventilation following muscle paralysis with curare-like drugs has been advocated in the moribund patient to gain time for medical therapy to become effective.[17] Recently, a terminal patient was successfully treated when oxygen was administered by the anesthesiologist while voluntary respiration was interrupted by an intravenous drip of 0.2 per cent succinylcholine chloride. In order to remove bronchial secretions, bronchial lavage was also carried out several times at ten minute intervals, with 15 ml. portions of warm physiologic saline each containing 1 ml. of 1:100 isoproterenol. The intense bronchospasm abated after direct instillation into the bronchial tree of a solution containing 1.5 ml. of 4 per cent Xylocaine in 15 ml. of physiologic saline. The possibilities exist that there was a direct relaxant effect exerted on the bronchial smooth muscle and that the irritative processes that were triggering the bronchospasm were relieved by the topical anesthesia.[18-19]

SURGICAL TREATMENT OF ASTHMA

Vagotomy, pulmonary plexus resection and other surgical treatment for chronic bronchial asthma generally have not been beneficial. In recent years, there has been interest in resection of the carotid body as a form of therapy. As reviewed in a recent editorial, controlled studies indicate that this procedure should be abandoned.[20]

REFERENCES

1. Lanoff, G., and Crawford, O.: Fatalities from bronchial asthma in children. Ann. Allergy *22*:349, 1964.
2. Richards, W., and Patrick, T. R.: Deaths from asthma in children. Am. J. Dis. Child. *110*:4, 1965.
3. Quintero, J. M.: Studies on the pulmonary circulation and the mechanics of breathing in chronic bronchial asthma and considerations of the causes of death. Ann. Allergy *22*:60, 1964.
4. Sheldon, J. M., Howes, H., and Stuart, G.: Observations on total water and sodium exchanges in asthmatic patients. J. Allergy *11*:1, 1939.
5. Mosko, M. M., Arkin, N. G., Miller, B. H., and Snider, G. L.: Studies on the effects of sympathomimetics in asthma. Dis. Chest *38*:264, 1960.
6. Blumenthal, J. S., Blumenthal, M. N., Brown, E. B., Campbell, G. S., and Prasad, A.: Effects of changes in arterial pH on action of adrenalin in acute adrenalin-fast asthmatics. Dis. Chest *39*:516, 1961.
7. Comroe, J. H., Jr.: Mental changes occurring in chronically anoxemic patients during oxygen therapy. J.A.M.A. *143*:1044, 1950.
8. Callaway, J. J., and McKisick, V. A.: CO_2 intoxication in emphysema. New England J. Med. *245*:9, 1951.
9. Campbell, E. J. M.: A method of controlled oxygen administration which reduces the risk of carbon dioxide retention. Lancet *2*:12, 1960.
10. Massard, D. J., Katz, S., and Luchsinger, P. C.: Effect of various modes of oxygen administration on the arterial gas values in patients with respiratory acidosis. Brit. M. J. *2*:627, 1962.
11. Petty, T. L., and Nett, L. M.: Home inhalation equipment for less than $10. Letters to the Editor. J.A.M.A. *196*:1027, 1966.
12. Sheldon, G. P.: Pressure breathing in chronic obstructive lung disease. Medicine *42*:197, 1963.
13. Beck, G. J., and Nanca, K.: Use of superheated saline aerosols as a diagnostic measure in pulmonary tuberculosis. Dis. Chest *42*:74, 1962.
14. Johnson, J. R., Cohen, B. M., Crandall, C., and Sonio, O.: Aerosol induced sputum: an effective, inexpensive method for nebulization of super-heated mixture of 40 per cent propylene glycol in isotonic saline. Dis. Chest *42*:251, 1962.
15. Nelson, S. W., Christoforidis, A. J., and Pratt, P. C.: Further experience with barium sulfate as a bronchographic contrast medium. Am. J. Roentgenol.*92*:595, 1964.
16. Sukumplchantra, Y., and Williams, M. H., Jr.: Pathophysiology of ventilatory failure. Am. Rev. Resp. Dis. *92*:428, 1965.
17. Beam, L. R., Marcy, J. H., and Mansmann, H. C.: Medically irreversible status asthmaticus in children. J.A.M.A. *194*:120, 1965.
18. Sinha, Y. K.: Studies on local anesthetic drugs. J. Pharm. & Pharmacol. *5*:620, 1953.
19. Wiedling, S.: Xylocaine, the Pharmacological Basis of its Clinical Use. Stockholm, Almqvist & Wiksell, 1959.
20. The rise and fall of glomectomy for asthma (Editorial). New England J. Med. *274*:971, 1966.

Chapter Nine

DRUG ALLERGY

Adverse reactions to drugs are receiving increasing attention not only from physicians but also from the public, governmental agencies, and medicolegal experts. Clinicians in all phases of medical practice encounter these reactions, and there is reason to believe that these will continue to grow in importance as more and more therapeutic agents are brought into clinical usage. The problem commands attention particularly since, as iatrogenic diseases, these reactions should be at least partly preventable. Recent surveys show an astounding incidence of drug reactions; for example, at one well-known teaching hospital 15 per cent of patients were observed to experience an adverse effect from some drug, though many of these "reactions" were very minor.[1] Practicing physicians can provide helpful information by reporting important drug reactions to manufacturers of the drugs and agencies such as the Bureau of Medicine of the United States Food and Drug Administration or the Council on Drugs of the American Medical Association.

There are several types of drug reactions. Adverse effects as would occur in anyone upon first exposure at sufficiently high dosage levels generally are toxic reactions. Occasionally toxicity appears at unusually low doses (e.g., tinnitus after 0.30 gm. aspirin). Sometimes this can be explained by delayed drug metabolism or excretion, as in patients with liver or kidney disease. Adverse reactions also occur which differ qualitatively from the usual pharmacologic or toxic effects of a drug. Some may be caused by an enzymatic abnormality, such as the hemolytic anemia produced by primaquine type drugs in persons with glucose-6-phosphate dehydrogenase deficiency. Other types of adverse drug reactions include side effects, secondary reactions, and Herxheimer type reactions. A detailed classification of additional kinds of drug reactions has been presented by Carr.[2]

To keep the term *drug allergy* meaningful, it seems advisable to limit its use to instances of patient injury known or presumed to be consequent to the interaction of drugs with antibodies or to delayed hypersensitivity. If relevant antibodies or delayed hypersensitivity cannot be demonstrated because of technical limitations, the immunologic basis of the reaction is inferred at times from the cardinal features of such reactions, i.e., an induction period or sensitization by previous exposure, relatively marked specificity, and manifestations known to be produced by allergic reactions. The latter usually differ from the pharmacologic

176

or toxic effects of the drugs. In actual practice, however, it is extremely difficult at times to decide whether certain types of drug reactions have an immunologic basis (e.g., some hepatic reactions). The allergic reactions do not constitute the majority of drug reactions, but they do comprise a substantial portion of them; for example, in one survey of 1560 drug reactions, about 25 per cent were considered to be related to sensitization.[3] This was the largest individual category except for a group which included reactions caused by unknown mechanisms. Although many of the more serious reactions are toxic, the subsequent discussion will be limited to allergic reactions.

A few biological drugs may serve as complete antigens, but the large majority of drugs, or their metabolites, presumably act as haptens in inducing and eliciting hypersensitivity reactions. Allergy to drugs may be of either the immediate or delayed type. The mechanism of both types of reactions follows the principles of hapten immunochemistry discussed in Chapter 1.

FACTORS INFLUENCING THE INCIDENCE OF DRUG ALLERGY

Type of Drug

The incidence of hypersensitivity reactions to various drugs ranges from nil to higher than 80 per cent (from phenylethyl-hydantoin). Probably to a major extent this variability depends on differing capacities of drugs, and especially their metabolites, to form covalent bonds with proteins and thus function as haptens. In estimating the sensitizing potentials of a drug, it is important to consider its frequency of administration as well as the number of reactions reported.[1]

Route of Administration

Under many circumstances, drugs are most apt to sensitize when applied to the skin or mucous membranes. Oral administration produces the least sensitization, and the parenteral route is associated with an intermediate degree of difficulty.

Type of Patient

Allergic reactions to either systemic or topical administration of most drugs are less common in children than in adults. This surprising occurrence has not been satisfactorily explained. Though one would expect that less previous exposure to drugs would lead to less sensitization in children, allergy to drugs appears infrequently even in children who are known to have received the same compound repeatedly. Certain types of drug reactions occur with increased frequency in persons with a personal or familial history of atopy; for example, asthmatic patients are more likely to manifest aspirin allergy or *anaphylactic* penicillin reactions. However, there is no convincing evidence that most types of drug allergy occur more often in atopic persons. Even in regard to penicillin allergy, our data show that the usual types of reactions are as common in nonatopic individuals as in atopic individuals.[4] Thus, the absence of a familial or personal history of atopy is no assurance that a patient will not react to a drug. It is probable that patients with systemic lupus erythematosus show an increased incidence of drug allergy.

There also is an impression that patients who have reacted to one drug are more likely to react to others; striking instances of this are encountered in treating patients with tuberculosis and allergic contact dermatitis from ointments. It is likely that genetically determined enzymatic pathways for metabolizing drugs also may influence the occurrence of reactions to their biotransformation products.

Degree of Exposure

Clinically, dosage and duration of treatment do not appear to be closely related to the development of hypersensitivity, though there is evidence for increased penicillin allergy in patients receiving extremely large doses of that drug. As in experimental animals, intermittent courses of a drug may predispose to sensitization. Once allergy has developed, very minute amounts of the drug may precipitate a reaction in highly sensitive individuals, but this is not an all-or-none type of reaction. From work with experimental animals, one would expect to find increasingly severe reactions with larger challenging doses of antigen, but when marked allergy is present, this relationship may be discernible only in a very low range of drug doses.

Effect of Adjuvants

Experimentally, the use of immunologic adjuvants increases sensitization to antigens incorporated in them. Although such adjuvants are not ordinarily used clinically with drugs, sensitization to pollen extract emulsions may be regarded as an example (see Chapter 6).

MANIFESTATIONS OF DRUG ALLERGY

The protean manifestations of a drug allergy contribute to the difficulty in making this diagnosis. See page 179 for a list of some of these manifestations. This list could be extended considerably but at the risk of including types of reactions which are not immunologically mediated. Indeed, the allergic character of some of the listed reactions is assumed from circumstantial evidence rather than from actual demonstration of relevant antibodies or delayed hypersensitivity. Some of these reactions, such as urticaria and anaphylaxis, clearly fall in the category of immediate or humoral hypersensitivity; others, such as allergic contact dermatitis from ointments, represent delayed or cellular hypersensitivity. However, the classification of still other reactions is uncertain. It is to be emphasized that there is no clinical syndrome which is diagnostic of drug allergy; all these manifestations can be produced by other allergens and many can be caused by nonimmunologic mechanisms. Some can be produced by drugs either on a nonallergic basis or because of hypersensitivity; for example, thrombocytopenia, agranulocytosis, and anemia from drugs most often represent toxic effects but occasionally are due to allergy.

Some Manifestations of Drug Allergy

Cutaneous
    Urticaria and angioedema
    Allergic contact dermatitis
    Erythema multiforme (including bullous type)
    Stevens-Johnson syndrome
    Morbilliform or scarlatiniform eruptions
    Pruritus
    Fixed drug eruption
    Purpura
    Exfoliative dermatitis
    Photoallergic reactions

Respiratory
    Bronchial asthma
    Rhinitis
    Loeffler's syndrome
    Pulmonary infiltrative disease with eosinophilia

Hematologic
    Thrombocytopenia
    Agranulocytosis
    Hemolytic anemia

Hypersensitivity vasculitis
    Periarteritis type
    Hypersensitivity angiitis type

Serum sickness
Lupus erythematosus-like disease
Drug fever
Anaphylactic shock
Allergic conjunctivitis
Abdominal cramps
Jaundice(?)

Most of the listed manifestations of drug allergy are discussed elsewhere. *Fever*[5] commonly is associated with other signs of an allergic reaction, such as serum sickness or dermatitis medicamentosa, but occasionally drug fever is the only evidence of an untoward effect. The mechanism often is not certain, but experimentally fever can be shown to accompany delayed hypersensitivity reactions or result from release of leukocytic pyrogen by antigen-antibody complexes. *Fixed drug erup-*

tions[6] most closely approach a syndrome unique to drug allergy, though rarely similar eruptions may have other causes. The lesions vary in morphology and may be single or multiple. Most typically they consist of erythematous or violacious plaques; vesiculation may occur. The lesion or lesions may be located anywhere, though the hands, face, and genitalia are sites of predilection. The unique feature of these lesions is that they recur repeatedly in the same location or locations each time that the offending drug is administered; other areas are not affected. Particularly after repeated exacerbations, there tends to be residual pigmentation at the affected sites. Several drugs are particularly prone to produce *photosensitivity reactions;* prominent among these are demethylchlortetracycline, thiazides, phenothiazines, griseofulvin, coal tar derivatives, and sulfonamides. Some photosensitivity reactions are photoallergic, and some are phototoxic (see page 263). A number of drugs produce effects on the *liver,* with or without jaundice; multiple mechanisms are probably involved, and at the present time the possible role of allergy in many of these reactions has not been adequately evaluated. Likewise, the adverse effects of a number of drugs on the nervous system, cardiovascular apparatus, and kidney have not been well studied from the immunologic standpoint.

COMMON DRUG ALLERGENS

Various publications periodically review some of the thousands of reports of adverse reactions,[7] and Alexander's valuable monograph summarizes much of the older literature.[8] Only the most salient information can be presented here.

Penicillins

During the past decade, penicillin reactions have commanded the greatest attention among the drug allergies because of their relative frequency and the substantial number of fatal reactions. Depending upon factors discussed previously, the incidence of these reactions ranges from almost zero in children given oral penicillin to over 10 to 20 per cent in adults from use of penicillin ointment; the most commonly reported reaction rates from parenteral administration in adults is about 1 to 2.5 per cent. Patients with atopic *Penicillium* hypersensitivity usually tolerate penicillin satisfactorily. For clinical purposes, persons known to be allergic to any of the penicillins should be considered sensitive to the entire group, since the side chain on the penicillin molecule seems to contribute to its antigenicity only to a limited extent. Allergy to penicillin often is spontaneously lost over a period of six months or more, but this cannot be depended upon. However, this fact and the low incidence of penicillin reactions in children may account for the apparent success of some "hypoallergenic" forms of penicillin. Patients allergic to penicillin generally tolerate cephalothin, but patients have been reported to react to both drugs, and cephalothin itself is capable of causing allergic reactions.

There are numerous types of possible reactions to penicillin; in fact, most of the general manifestations of drug allergy can be caused by penicillin. Of these, serum sickness-like disease, urticaria, "id-like" eruptions, and other dermal reactions are particularly common. Though rare, anaphylactic shock has received much attention because of its potentially fatal outcome. Another unfortunate feature of penicillin reactions is their occasional persistence for weeks or even months.. Repeated occult exposures to trace amounts of penicillin (e.g., in dairy products) have been suggested as a possible explanation for this. The firm adherence of penicillin to erythrocytes might be another factor. As discussed in the last section of this chapter, extensive studies of penicillin allergy have led to diagnostic tests which not only are of some value in themselves but also provide a model for further investigation of other drug allergies.

Sulfonamides

Reactions from these drugs were seen with great frequency in the pre-antibiotic era, and they still are not uncommon. Topical application resulted in such an extremely high incidence of allergic contact hypersensitivity that this route of administration largely had to be abandoned. Numerous manifestations of sulfonamide allergy have been observed, erythematous skin rashes and drug fever being among the more common of these. Sulfonamides still are a leading cause of hypersensitivity vasculitis. There is a variable pattern of cross-reactivity among the sulfonamides; some patients appear to react only to certain of these compounds, whereas others react to several of the group. Still other patients may react also to additional compounds containing the p-aminophenyl group*: many local anesthetics of the procaine type, paraphenylene diamine type dyes, azo dyes, and paraminobenzoic acid. The sulfonylurea oral hypoglycemic agents, thiazide diuretics, and carbonic anhydrase inhibitors also have related structures. Among the sulfonamide drugs themselves, some of the long-lasting types (sulfamethoxypyradizine, sulfadimethoxine) seem particularly prone to produce allergic reactions including the Stevens-Johnson syndrome. Considerable data, particularly Mayer's, indicate that many of these compounds probably are converted in vivo to highly reactive compounds of quinone structure which would be likely to act as haptens.[9]

---

* This is sometimes referred to as "para group" sensitivity and has been studied particularly well in respect to allergic contact dermatitis.

Aspirin

Bronchial asthma and urticaria are the most common manifestations of aspirin allergy. As discussed elsewhere, many of these aspirin-sensitive asthmatic patients have nasal polyps and a very refractory form of asthma. Asthma usually begins 20 to 40 minutes after the patient takes aspirin, it is commonly very severe and prolonged, and there have been a number of reported deaths from this cause. These patients generally can tolerate other salicylates. The mechanism of these reactions still is a controversial matter.

Local Anesthetics

Some of the apparent reactions to local anesthetics probably are psychogenic responses to the associated operative procedure, and many, including the severe collapse responses, probably result most commonly from toxic effects of these drugs on the central nervous system or heart. Immediate hypersensitivity is relatively infrequent, but urticarial reactions would be considered examples of this. Delayed hypersensitivity is more common. Allergic contact dermatitis from these agents in ointments is seen frequently, and they are an important cause of occupational contact dermatitis, as in dentists. A rarer form of delayed hypersensitivity is manifested by pronounced, delayed swelling at the site of injection of these drugs. Often this edema is mistakenly thought to be due to operative trauma.

As mentioned previously, procaine and a number of other local anesthetics contain the p-aminophenyl group (some with substitutions on the amino group). Other anesthetics of this type include Tautocaine, Larocaine, Monocaine, Butyn, Pontocaine, Borocaine, Benzocaine and Butesin. Careful study of patients showing allergic contact dermatitis indicates that cross-sensitization among members of this group of local anesthetics is frequent, though not invariable. On the other hand, a number of local anesthetics lack the p-aminophenyl group. These include Alypin, Metycaine, Stovaine, Nupercaine, Diothane, phenacaine (Holocaine), Apothesine, Intracaine, cocaine, Xylocaine (lidocaine) and Carbocaine (mepivacaine). These generally do not cause reactions in persons having contact sensitivity to the procaine group of local anesthetics. The extent to which this information applies to the injection of local anesthetics is less certain, but it is likely that it has some relevance. This classification, of course, does not pertain to toxic reactions. Although not ordinarily used for anesthesia, procaine amide should be noted as having caused a number of allergic reactions.

Iodides and Bromides

Acneform skin eruptions and salivary gland enlargements are common, but there is no good evidence that they are produced by immunologic mechanisms. On the other hand, erythema nodosum, iododerma with necrotizing skin lesions, urticaria, bullous eruptions, fever, and hypersensitivity angiitis from these drugs may well represent a true allergic response. Sometimes these lesions resemble periarteritis nodosa, and marked eosinophilia often accompanies reactions of this type. In Weber-Christian's disease associated with halogen administration the mechanism is unclear.

Reactions to iodinated x-ray contrast media merit special attention. Of these, many cases of urticaria and rare instances of shock occurring immediately after injection are often suspected of representing allergic reactions. However, the following facts are contrary to this assumption[10]: these reactions often occur immediately following the *first* administration of these agents; the patients may tolerate subsequent injections of the same material without difficulty (though this practice is not recommended); and attempts to demonstrate antibodies generally have been unrewarding. It is difficult to interpret this information, but it is tempting to speculate that a release of mediators by a nonimmunologic mechanism could explain many of these observations.

Antituberculous Drugs

Although otologic effects of the *streptomycins* are toxic in type, the relatively common drug fevers and erythematous and maculopapular rashes probably indicate allergy. Sometimes the skin lesions progress to a severe exfoliative erythroderma, which can be fatal. Allergic contact dermatitis among professional personnel handling these drugs also is relatively frequent if care is not exercised to prevent spillage onto the skin. In addition to causing frequent gastrointestinal irritation, *para-aminosalicylic acid* may produce rashes and drug fever. Some of these reactions are accompanied by lymphadenopathy, lymphocytosis, eosinophilia, hepatomegaly, jaundice, and splenomegaly. *Isoniazid* less frequently causes untoward effects, mainly rashes with or without fever; the peripheral neuropathy associated with the administration of this drug quite clearly is not allergic in etiology.

Anticonvulsant Drugs and Barbiturates

Adverse effects from *hydantoin* drugs are relatively common, especially in patients taking Mesantoin and trimethadione. Some of these, such as aplastic anemia, very probably are toxic, while the mechanism in many reactions, such as nephrosis, hyperplasia of the gums, and hepatitis, is obscure. Megaloblastic anemia from these agents appears to be related to disturbed folic acid metabolism. Allergy is more likely to be the basis of many skin eruptions produced by these drugs including morbilliform lesions, erythema multiforme, urticaria, bullous lesions, exfoliative dermatitis, and Stevens-Johnson syndrome. Some reactions simulate lupus erythematosus and may be accompanied by the finding of some lupus erythematosus cells. A serum sickness-like syndrome occurred in over 80 per cent of patients taking phenylethylhydantoin (Nirvanol), a drug used primarily in Europe for chorea several decades ago. Numbers of patients with convulsive disorders appear to be intolerant of several of the hydantoin drugs.

Barbiturates cause reactions in a much smaller portion of patients, but rashes (most often morbilliform), sometimes also accompanied by fever, are seen fairly often in view of the wide usage of these medications. Barbiturates are a leading cause of fixed drug eruptions. Careful studies have shown that Sedormid can produce thrombocytopenic purpura on an immunologic basis.

Hormones

Immediate hypersensitivity reactions from the injection of foreign protein or peptide hormones might be expected. Urticaria is the most common manifestation and shock the most serious. Contaminants or species-specific proteins may cause some reactions, but many appear to be caused by the hormone itself. Insulin, corticotropin (ACTH), crude preparations of pituitrin (for either antidiuretic or oxytocic activity), and parahormone have all caused allergic reactions. Some of the most alarming have followed intravenous ACTH. Marked insulin resistance may be due to insulin antibodies, but these appear to differ from those causing insulin allergy. Skin-sensitizing antibodies also may be produced by glucagon injections. The administration of crude pituitrin snuff seems especially to promote sensitization. In contrast, allergic reactions to thyroid preparations, gonadal or adrenal steroid hormones, or catacholamines, such as epinephrine, are rare.

Vaccines

Urticaria or shock also can occur when vaccines containing egg antigens are injected into extremely egg-sensitive individuals. Though there has been a trend away from preparing some of these vaccines with egg embryos, one should consider the possible presence of egg antigens in most virus or rickettsial vaccines, such as influenza, yellow fever, typhus, Rocky Mountain spotted fever, and Q fever vaccines. The rare severe or fatal reactions occur mainly in exquisitely egg-sensitive patients who cannot eat the slightest amount of egg. When virus vaccines are prepared in tissue culture, the possibility of reactions to the minute amount of antibiotics (usually streptomycin and/or penicillin) contained in the culture medium must be considered, as with the Salk poliomyelitis vaccine. The quantity of antibiotics in the vaccine is so small that severe reactions would be unlikely except in rare patients, such as those with anaphylactic penicillin hypersensitivity. About one in every 3000 persons receiving the nervous tissue type rabies vaccine develops encephalomyelitis in the spinal cord or brain. This is generally thought to represent an allergic response evoked by the rabbit central nervous system tissue contained in the vaccine. Authentic allergic reactions to bacterial toxoids or vaccines of killed pathogenic bacteria are extremely uncommon. A few such apparent occurrences were due to silk allergy from vaccines which had been passed through silk bacteriologic filters.

Miscellaneous Drug Allergens

Among the innumerable other drug allergens, mention should be made of *quinine* and *quinidine*. Cutaneous reactions, especially urticaria, are seen more commonly with the former of these isomers, while thrombocytopenic purpura is more common with the latter. An immunologic basis for the thrombocytopenia has been firmly established by extensive immunologic studies. Shulman's data[11] suggest that the thrombocytopenia arises from the adherence of drug-antibody complexes to the surface of platelets rather than as a result of action of antibodies directed toward a drug-platelet complex, as previously postulated by others.[12] *Aminopyrine* once was the most common cause of immunologically mediated agranulocytosis due to drugs. As stated previously, the *thiazide* diuretics are related to the sulfonamides, thus allowing for the possibility of immunologic cross-reactions. Photosensitivity reactions and other rashes caused by these drugs may be allergic, but probably most of the blood dyscrasias and other adverse effects of the thiazides are not immunologically mediated.

Tranquilizers, particularly those of the phenothiazine group, have caused many drug reactions: extrapyramidal symptoms, blood dyscrasias, cholestatic jaundice, photosensitivity reactions, and skin pigmentation. The mechanism of most of these reactions is uncertain at present. The *nitrofurantoin* group of drugs has produced many adverse reactions, some of which are probably allergic. Of the latter, dermatologic manifestations, particularly urticaria, are most common. Allergic contact dermatitis from nitrofurazone is relatively frequent when ointments containing this drug are used in adults. *Hydralazine* produces a syndrome simulating lupus erythematosus in a substantial portion of patients, particularly those receiving a relatively large amount of this drug. Lupus erythematosus cells and antinuclear factors commonly are found. Although rather extensively studied, the mechanism of this reaction still is not well understood. Heavy metals, such as *arsenic* and *gold,* caused much difficulty in the past, probably largely on a toxic basis. Exfoliative dermatitis from gold therapy is still seen and possibly represents an allergic reaction. *Phenolphthalein* caused numerous allergic reactions in the past and still is a significant drug allergen, being dispensed primarily in proprietary laxatives. Fixed drug eruptions and urticaria are the most common manifestations of this hypersensitivity.

ESTABLISHING A DIAGNOSIS OF DRUG ALLERGY

The prime requirement for recognition of allergic reactions to drugs is to consider this diagnostic possibility when presented with one of its numerous manifestations. The clinical history is the most important aid in the further evaluation of such patients. Obviously, one should inquire whether any drugs have been taken and concerning the temporal relationships of these to the onset of the apparent reaction. Particularly if the presenting complaints are known commonly to occur as features of reactions to a drug the patient has been taking, one generally assumes that the patient is, in fact, experiencing a drug reaction until proved otherwise by discontinuing the drug and observing whether the process subsides. In case of early reaction to drugs, one theoretically should be able also to obtain the history that the patient took the drug previously (the sensitizing exposure). However, negative responses should not dissuade one from the diagnosis, since memory may be fallible, the patient may not know the names of the medications he has received previously or he may have been sensitized by a cross-reacting substance. Inquiry should also be made about previous reactions to drugs, including excessive local swelling at injection sites.[4] If the patient is known to be sensitive to a certain compound, an energetic attempt to discover a recent re-exposure to some perhaps occult source of this same substance or a related material is indicated.

A patient's denial that he has taken any drugs should not be glibly accepted: some may misinterpret a physician's inquiries along these lines as referring to the use of narcotics, and others may take certain medications so habitually that they forget to count them as "drugs." Compounds that are employed other than by the oral or parenteral route are especially apt to be overlooked. It is advisable, therefore, routinely to review with the patient the list of drugs shown on the allergy survey form (page 37), elaborating upon each item in the list. It is important to ascertain *all* the medications which have been used, since the one which the patient mentions first may not necessarily be the offender. Finding a peripheral blood eosinophilia would lend some support to a tentative diagnosis of drug allergy, but this is neither a diagnostic nor consistent finding. Occasionally biopsy of a skin lesion might be helpful, particularly in cases of purpura or suspected hypersensitivity vasculitis. One may discover the minute blood vessels to be surrounded by inflammatory cells, a finding not observed in many nonimmunologic types of purpura. Immunofluorescent staining might show gamma globulin in the vessel walls in some of the angiitic lesions of a hypersensitivity type.

Further evaluation commonly involves stopping all drugs. Prompt subsidence of signs and symptoms provides enough evidence for a presumptive diagnosis of a drug allergy to suffice for many practical purposes. However, one is always left with uncertainty about whether the improvement might not have been spontaneous or due to factors other than the withholding of the drugs. Furthermore, there still may remain the question as to which of several drugs is the offender. Thus, additional objective and safe methods for confirming a diagnosis of drug allergy are much to be desired, particularly if the drug in question is of major importance to the patient or if the type of reaction is of academic interest.

Patch tests, as indicated in the following outline, commonly are of value for patients with allergic contact hypersensitivity to medicaments in ointments. Outside of this large and important group, however, patch tests have limited value. The appearance of purpura under patches has been reported in some cases of thrombocytopenic purpura caused by drugs, but this is not a constant finding. In patients with negative tests, it has been suggested that the physician, using a Rumpel-Leeds test, look for increased capillary fragility at the patch site (in comparison with a control site). Positive patch test reactions sometimes can be elicited in patients exhibiting dermatitis medicamentosa caused by drugs, but a negative reaction does not exclude allergy. Scratch-patch tests have been advocated especially by European investigators, but others have been dissatisfied with this procedure (see page 258).

Skin Testing for Drug Allergy

Patch tests
    Allergic contact dermatitis
    Dermatitis medicamentosa
    Purpura
    Scratch-patch tests(?)

Scratch or intracutaneous tests
    Occasionally dangerous
    Often reliable with high molecular weight biologicals
    Usually unreliable with low molecular weight drugs, with exceptions
    False-positive reactions with histamine liberators
    Serum containing drug apt to give false-positive reactions
    Multivalent conjugates of drugs or drug metabolites with suitable carriers
    Delayed (tuberculin type) skin tests

When drugs are given systemically, one would think it more rational to use *scratch* or *intracutaneous tests.* Such tests, however, may be dangerous. The prime example of this is intracutaneous testing of asthmatic patients for aspirin sensitivity. This test is contraindicated since the skin reaction invariably is negative, but the test procedure may provoke severe asthma. Though it is not contraindicated, testing of patients suspected of having anaphylactic penicillin hypersensitivity must be carried out with considerable care.

As would be expected from theoretical considerations, patients showing immediate hypersensitivity reactions to high molecular weight biologicals commonly show wheal and erythema reactions to scratch or intracutaneous tests. Hence, these tests often are useful in cases of suspected allergy to such agents as ACTH, insulin, posterior pituitary extracts, foreign antisera, liver extract, or egg-containing vaccines. In these instances, the test material presumably contains the complete, multivalent antigen. Conversely, drugs of low molecular weight generally would not be expected to elicit skin test reactions, since they usually would possess only one antigenic determinant per molecule and thus, like univalent haptens, would be more likely to inhibit than to elicit biological reactions. Experience shows that this is usually the case, but as with all generalizations, there are occasional exceptions. A few patients do give wheal and erythema reactions to simple chemical compounds such as quinine, sulfonamides, tannic acid, chlorogenic acid, chloramine-T, halazone, and others.

There is also a problem of "false-positive" skin test reactions to drugs. It is well known that a large number of compounds chemically liberate histamine from its bound form in mast cell granules. Consequently, these substances produce immediate skin test reactions in everyone. Numerous drugs fall into this category, including morphine, codeine, meperidine, stilbamidine, thiamin, d-tubocurarine, and polymyxin B. Skin test reactions of questionable significance also have been evoked by serum containing drugs. With the hope that there might be conjugation between drugs and serum proteins in vivo, Leftwich many years ago proposed using serum containing a measurable level of the drug in question as a skin testing reagent for drug allergy. However, the original work with sulfonamides could not be confirmed, and subsequent knowledge emphasizes the possibility that these skin test reactions may be due to serum components other than the hypothetical drug-protein complexes. Since normal human serum may produce larger skin reactions in certain individuals than in others, providing adequate controls for drug-in-serum tests is difficult. However, in vitro conjugation of drug haptens with more suitable carrier substances offers promise of better materials for skin testing for drug allergy, as discussed on page 193.

Observations on delayed, tuberculin type skin test reactions in drug allergy have been relatively scanty. There is evidence that some uncommon, delayed reactions to procaine are associated with delayed skin test responses, and this form of hypersensitivity has reportedly been transferred by means of leukocytes. As in cases of allergy to metals, intracutaneous testing for suspected allergic contact dermatitis caused by drugs may be employed more commonly in the future (page 257).

Hematologic reactions afford unique opportunities to test affected tissues in vitro. Of course, these reactions more often result from drug toxicity than from hypersensitivity, but when the latter mechanism is suspected, some of the more commonly used methods of evaluation are summarized below. Details of these tests are described by Ackroyd.[12] The most extensively studied reactions have been thrombocytopenic purpura due to Sedormid and quinidine. The capacity of the suspected drug to inhibit clot reaction provides a simple but crude screening test. Platelet agglutination tests require careful controls to exclude nonspecific ag-

Some Tests for Hematologic Drug Allergy

Thrombocytopenia
   Inhibition of clot retraction
   Platelet agglutination
   Platelet lysis
   Complement fixation
   Indirect antiglobulin consumption test

Agranulocytosis
   Leukocyte agglutination

Hemolytic anemia
   Hemagglutination
   Antiglobulin tests
   Hemolysis

---

glutination in the absence of the drug. A source of complement is required for platelet lysis. Complement fixation tests are said to have ten times or more the sensitivity of the aforementioned methods. It has been recommended that tests for leukocyte agglutinins be carried out at both 37° and 4° C. with serum obtained shortly after the patient has taken the drug. Hemagglutination tests, like the other agglutination reactions, require the simultaneous presence of drug, the patient's serum, and either the patient's cells or compatible cells. Antiglobulin reactions may be of the gamma type or may result from complement components on the cell. Hemolysins due to drugs are rarely detected, but the use of trypsinized cells or erythrocytes from paroxysmal nocturnal hemoglobinuric subjects may facilitate their demonstration. Drug-induced hemolytic anemias in general are much less often demonstrated to have an immunologic basis than they are shown to result from enzyme deficiencies, particularly a lack of glucose-6-phosphate dehydrogenase. Phenacetin and PAS (p-aminosalicylic acid), like the fava bean, have been found to produce hemolytic anemia either on an immunologic or an enzyme deficiency basis. It also should be noted that agglutinins for drug-treated blood cells have been found in the absence of any overt hematologic abnormality. More convincing evidence for the pathogenetic role of such antibodies is obtained by elution of drug-specific antibodies from the cells. Hemagglutination tests for penicillin allergy are discussed on page 194.

Apart from hematologic reactions, Shelley has proposed that the degranulation of basophils in the presence of a drug and the patient's serum is a reliable indication of hypersensitivity to that medication.[13] Both human and rabbit basophils have been employed. It is surprising that these tests have been reported to give positive results with serum from patients exhibiting types of hypersensitivity reactions in which histamine release is not known to occur. Conversely, inconsistent results have been obtained in tests with pollen extracts and blood of atopic patients—conditions in which histamine release is known to occur. Since some observers also have been unable to obtain positive results with sera of patients known to be drug-sensitive, it appears that wider experience will be needed before this can be accepted as a routine clinical test for drug allergy. Likewise, direct measurements of histamine release from leukocytes by drugs cannot at present be regarded as a reliable means for assaying drug hypersensitivity, particularly when negative results are obtained. Many other in vitro tests for drug allergy have been proposed but are of uncertain reliability. However, there are encouraging prospects for the future, as discussed at the end of this chapter.

Reproduction of a reaction by readministration of the drug would strongly support the provisional diagnosis of drug allergy but could be hazardous. This procedure is justified in some circumstances, such as when the drug is especially important for the patient or when firmly establishing and reporting the reaction would be a significant scientific contribution; but sufficiently small doses should be employed initially to avert a major reaction.

PREVENTION OF DRUG REACTIONS

Some, but not all, drug reactions are predictable. By far the most important preventive measure is to make it a routine practice, before prescribing any medications, to ask patients whether they have had the same drug previously and whether they have ever had any drug reaction. Even if the patient's description of an alleged reaction seems somewhat dubious, it is generally prudent to prescribe a different compound for legal as well as for medical reasons. Another precaution is to make it routine to have patients wait in the office for 15 minutes following the first injection of any drug and, if possible, to give the injection in an extremity. After consideration of the previously discussed factors favoring sensitization to drugs, it is advisable to avoid the indiscriminate use, intermittent courses, and topical application of potent sensitizers, especially antibiotics. If there are strong indications for using a specific drug in spite of a history of possible sensitivity, one or more of the previously discussed tests for drug allergy should be carried out whenever applicable. In this era of multiple drugs available for most purposes, it is rarely necessary to prescribe a compound when sensitivity is known to be present. In this very exceptional circumstance, "desensitization" should be considered. At times one attempts to achieve this quite rapidly by administering the compound every 20 to 30 minutes, as in penicillin or insulin allergy. One commonly starts with 1/100 or 1/1000 the usual dose and doubles the amount given every 20 to 30 minutes until the therapeutic range is reached or a reaction occurs. Much smaller initial doses should be used if there are indications of anaphylactic penicillin hypersensitivity. On the other hand, "desensitization" to the antituberculous drugs is generally carried out according to a similar dosage schedule but with administration of the drug only once or twice daily. Desensitization to equine tetanus antitoxin has been largely superseded by the use of human antitoxin. The concomitant administration of antihistamines cannot be relied on to prevent severe or delayed reactions to drugs.[4] Univalent haptens of the offending drug metabolite theoretically might desensitize patients without eliciting an allergic reaction, but this is a purely hypothetical form of preventive treatment at the present time.

TREATMENT OF DRUG REACTIONS

Obviously, the most important therapeutic measure for drug reactions is to discontinue the offending drug. Often no other treatment is required, particularly when the drug in question is metabolized or excreted rapidly. It is important to inform the patient of the probable diagnosis so that further difficulty from the same compound can be avoided. In addition, information should be provided about unexpected or hidden sources of the offending substance or materials which are likely to cross-react with it. This advice is especially relevant in cases of allergic contact dermatitis. If the sensitivity is life-threatening and especially if the drug is apt to be given while the patient is unconscious (e.g., penicillin or horse serum), the patient should be encouraged to carry this information on his person. A card, signed by a physician and carried in the purse or wallet, may serve this purpose, but metal tags or bracelets (e.g., Medic Alert Emblems, Turlock, Calif.) are advantageous.

When reactions are prolonged, the physician may try to rid the patient of the remaining drug. Dimercaprol (BAL) is used for this purpose in heavy metal reactions, such as exfoliative dermatitis from gold or arsenic. Enzymatic degradation of residual drug has also been proposed. It should be noted, however, that enzyme preparations are likely to be quite antigenic themselves; for example, severe reactions have occurred on readministration of penicillinase. Furthermore, this preparation causes considerable local pain, its use in very prolonged penicillin reactions has yielded disappointing results, and it is not recommended now for the treatment of anaphylactic reactions to penicillin. With prolonged penicillin reactions, it is advisable for patients temporarily to discontinue the ingestion of dairy products, since these may be contaminated with penicillin.

Symptomatic treatment is unnecessary for mild drug reactions, but in the case of severe or prolonged difficulty, the patient can be kept more comfortable by suitable measures. The precise mode of symptomatic treatment will depend, of course, upon the manifestations of drug hypersensitivity. Such treatment is discussed elsewhere in connection with the various allergic syndromes (e.g., urticaria and angioedema, page 249, serum sickness, page 464; anaphylaxis, page 143). In general, antihistamines, sympathomimetic drugs, and salicylates are among the commonly used medications. Corticosteroids of ACTH are indicated for some of the more severe reactions, especially those involving the skin and blood vessels. The fact that drug reactions are limited in duration is favorable to the use of corticosteroids, but it should be remembered that many of these patients need treatment only with "tincture of time." Transfusions are required for a few of the more severe hematologic reactions. Topical applications of lotions and ointments have little place in the treatment of cutaneous drug reactions.

RECENT ADVANCES RELATING TO PENICILLIN HYPERSENSITIVITY

Largely from extensive studies of the mechanism of penicillin hypersensitivity in recent years (particularly the work of Levine, Parker, De-Weck, and Eisen), the importance of the following three immunologic principles to the problem of drug allergy has been emphasized:

1. Only reactive compounds capable of forming covalent bonds with suitable carriers are likely to serve as drug haptens. Since many drugs themselves do not have this property, much more attention will be paid to drug metabolites as possible offenders. In penicillin, for example, the drug itself is unlikely to conjugate with proteins, but it is converted in vivo as well as in vitro to penicillenic acid. This metabolite is capable of forming covalent bonds with proteins either (1) by way of mixed disulfide linkages to give penicillenates or (2) by reaction with free amino groups on proteins, such as the epsilon amino group of lysine, to give penicilloyl conjugates. In addition, other penicillin biotransformation products (e.g., penamaldoyl, penicillamine) also may conjugate with proteins and become antigenic. The validity of this hypothesis has been confirmed by finding that penicilloyl-bovine gamma globulin complexes or conjugates of penicillenate and thiolated bovine gamma globulin are very antigenic in rabbits.[14] Moreover, penicilloyl-human gamma globulin conjugates have been found to elicit immediate skin test reactions in some penicillin-sensitive humans. However, since there would be danger of sensitizing patients with such antigenic test material, conjugates of penicilloyl hapten with relatively low molecular weight polylysines were evaluated. Penicilloyl polylysine conjugates, especially the D isomers, were found to be essentially nonantigenic for animals, but they were very active in eliciting hypersensitivity reactions using sera from rabbits sensitized with other penicilloyl conjugates.[15]

Subsequent field trials in humans have shown that about one-third to three-fourths of penicillin-sensitive subjects give positive wheal and erythema skin test reactions to penicilloyl polylysine.[16] A much higher percentage of positive reactions is obtained in patients who have reacted to penicillin within three years.[17] Unquestionably, however, there are persons with current penicillin allergy who fail to give skin test reactions to penicilloyl polylysine. Some of these may be allergic to other penicillin metabolites. An important consideration is that persons with anaphylactic type penicillin hypersensitivity commonly are negative on skin testing with penicilloyl polylysine, but these rare individuals frequently exhibit positive skin test reactions to penicillin itself. Thus, if skin testing is to be done at all (generally in patients with life-threatening infections and history of possible penicillin allergy), testing both with penicillin and penicilloyl polylysine is advisable. Because some of these patients are extremely sensitive, it is well to begin by testing with dilute solutions on an extremity; for example, successive prick tests with solutions containing 1, 100, and 10,000 units of aqueous penicillin G per ml. may be followed, if negative, by an intracutaneous test with 0.02 ml. of 10,000 units penicillin per ml. However, if severe anaphylactic sensitivity is suspected, direct testing, if done at all, may have to be initiated with even more dilute penicillin solutions, or one may resort to passive transfer. The usual test concentration of penicilloyl polylysine is $6 \times 10^{-5}M$, and again it is advisable to perform a prick test on an extremity before injecting the material intracutaneously. A positive reaction to this material suggests ordinary type penicillin allergy, while reactions to penicillin itself suggest anaphylactic sensitivity.

2. In order to elicit several forms of immediate type hypersensitivity reactions, including skin tests, it appears essential to have two or more drug haptens per molecule of test material. Univalent haptens not only generally fail to produce test responses but often are inhibitory. The penicillin system again illustrates this principle: the univalent hapten, penicilloyl epsilon aminocaproate, generally inhibits skin test responses to penicilloyl polylysine.[16, 17] Multiple haptens per test molecule may elicit more prominent reactions than divalent agents unless one is dealing with antibodies of high avidity.[18] Antigens are less effective elicitors if haptenic groups are too far apart on the surface of the molecule. The reason for the requirement of multiple drug haptens per test molecule is that more than one molecule of antibody must react with the same molecule of antigen in order to elicit several types of biological reactions. One possible explanation for this is that the aggregation of antibody molecules about the test antigen may somehow activate enzymes involved in immediate type of hypersensitivity. This hypothesis is discussed further in the chapter on serum sickness (page 458). There are other possibilities; e.g., when the antibody molecules are fixed to a cell membrane, their aggregation by antigen might affect the cell membrane or its enzymes. Regardless of the precise explanation, however, it seems clear that in the development of biological tests for allergy to additional drugs, it will be advantageous to prepare test materials containing multiple haptens of the suitable drug metabolite conjugated to carrier molecules.

3. The presence of antibodies to drugs or their metabolites is not necessarily associated with clinical allergy to these drugs. With extremely sensitive immunologic tests, such as passive hemagglutination, the Farr technique, "double antibody" tests or radioimmunoelectrophoresis, it is possible to show the presence of antibodies to a variety of antigens in many humans regardless of associated clinical allergy.

This generalization also applies to drugs, and the experience with passive hemagglutination tests for penicillin allergy is illustrative. Penicillin, or some of its biotransformation products, is firmly bound to red cell membranes, thus providing the opportunity for homologous antibodies to agglutinate washed, penicillinized erythrocytes. Although under some conditions penicillin hemagglutinins have been found more commonly in persons who have exhibited penicillin allergy, it has been evident from the beginning of work with this test that many persons had hemagglutinating antibodies for penicillinized red cells without having manifested any evidence of penicillin allergy previously or subsequently. More recently, the sensitivity of the test has been enhanced to the extent that hemagglutinating antibodies can be detected in 100 per cent of persons who have received penicillin,[19] though sera from patients who have exhibited allergic reactions tend to show high titers of 7S antibodies. Also, as with pollen antigens, the hemagglutinating activity can be separated from skin-sensitizing activity by absorption of sera with suitable numbers of penicillinized cells.[20] Antibodies apparently unrelated to clinical allergy also have been found to other drugs (e.g., to insulin).

FUTURE PROSPECTS FOR EVALUATING DRUG ALLERGY

With attention to these principles, it should be possible to exploit current immunologic techniques to develop more satisfactory tests for drug allergy in some of the many instances in which there are presently no suitable objective tests for hypersensitivity to low molecular weight drugs. As the work with penicillin illustrates, however, the problem is complex when a large number of metabolites needs to be considered. There also is a dearth of techniques suitable for evaluating delayed hypersensitivity. Some current immunologic methods for detecting circulating antibodies offer advantages of marked sensitivity and would not necessarily require conjugation of the drug metabolite hapten with a carrier molecule. However, antibodies detected by such means might not necessarily be related to clinical allergy, and thus there may be some tendency to resort to biological tests. Some success has been reported already in achieving stimulation of lymphocytes from sensitive subjects in short-term tissue culture in the presence of the offending drug.[21-22] When suitable antisera are prepared in animals, the double layer leukocyte agglutination technique of Ridges and Augustin may perhaps become applicable.[24] Other techniques, including skin tests and skin windows, may be fruitful if suitable drug metabolites can be selected for the production of conjugated, polyhaptenic test antigens.

Finally, further consideration must be given to the possibility that some drug reactions are not immunologically mediated even though the manifestations of the adverse effect are suggestive of allergy. Mention already has been made of drugs which act as chemical histamine liberators, and there is an additional possibility that drugs might activate or liberate other immunologic mediators without reacting with antibodies. There is some evidence in experimental animals that such effects can be genetically determined.[23] Further developments in pharmacogenetics may shed additional light on many types of drug reactions, particularly those in which enzyme deficiencies may play a role. It is also possible that some drugs might produce nonspecific gamma globulin aggregation or anaphylatoxin formation.

REFERENCES

1. Cluff, L. E., Thornton, L. F., and Seidl, L. G.: Studies on the epidemiology of adverse drug reactions. J.A.M.A. *188*:976, 1964.
2. Carr, E. A., Jr.: Drug allergy. Pharmacol. Rev. *6*:365, 1954.
3. Zbinden, G.: Experimental and clinical aspects of drug toxicity. Advances in Pharmacology *2*:1, 1963.
4. Mathews, K. P., Hemphill, F. M., Lovell, R. G., Forsythe, W. E., and Sheldon, J. M.: A controlled study on the use of parenteral and oral antihistamines in preventing penicillin reactions. J. Allergy *27*:1, 1956.
5. Cluff, L. E., and Johnson, J. E., III: Drug fever. Progr. Allergy *8*:149, 1964.
6. Welsh, A. L.: The Fixed Eruption. Springfield, Ill., Charles C Thomas, 1961.
7. Samter, M., and Berryman, G. H.: Drug allergy. Ann Rev. Pharmacol. *4*:265, 1964.
8. Alexander, H. I.: Reactions With Drug Therapy. Philadelphia, W. B. Saunders Co., 1955.
9. Mayer, R. L.: Group-sensitization to compounds of quinone structure and its biochemical basis; role of these substances in cancer. Progr. Allergy *4*:79, 1955.
10. Coleman, W. P., Ochsner, S. F., and Watson, B. E.: Allergic reactions in 10,000 consecutive intravenous urographies. South. M. J. *57*:1401, 1964.
11. Shulman, N. R.: A mechanism of cell destruction in individuals sensitized to foreign antigens and its implication in autoimmunity. Ann Int. Med. *60*:506, 1964.
12. Ackroyd, J. F.: Immunological Methods. Philadelphia, F. A. Davis Co., 1964, p. 453.
13. Shelley, W. B.: Further experience with the indirect basophil test. Arch. Derm. *91*:65, 1965.
14. DeWeck, A. L., and Eisen, H. N.: Some immunochemical properties of penicillenic acid. An antigenic department derived from penicillin. J. Exper. Med. *112*:1227, 1960.
15. Parker, C. W., DeWeck, A. L., Kern, M., and Eisen, H. N.: The preparation and some properties of penicillenic acid derivatives relevant to penicillin hypersensitivity. J. Exper. Med. *115*:803, 1962.
16. Parker, C. W., Shapiro, J., Kern, M., and Eisen, H. N.: Hypersensitivity to penicillenic acid derivatives in human beings with penicillin allergy. J. Exper. Med. *115*:821, 1962.
17. Finke, S. R., Grieco, M. H., Connell, J. T., Smith, E. C., and Sherman, W. B.: Results of comparative skin tests with penicilloyl polylysine and penicillin in patients with penicillin allergy. Am. J. Med. *38*:71, 1965.
18. Levine, B. B., and Fellner, M. J.: The nature of immune complexes initiating allergic wheal and flare reactions. J. Allergy *36*:342, 1965.
19. Levine, B. B., and Fellner, M. J.: Immune responses of human beings to penicillin. Studies in penicillin-allergic and nonallergenic patients. J. Allergy *36*:198, 1965.
20. Mathews, K. P., and Pan, P.: Unpublished data.
21. Holland, P., and Mauer, A. M.: Drug-induced in vitro stimulation of peripheral lymphocytes. Lancet *1*:1368, 1964.
22. Girard, J. P., Kunz, M. L., Rose, N. R., and Arbesman, L. E.: Humoral and cellular factors in immediate hypersensitivity of humans. Fed. Proc. *24*:632, 1965.
23. West, G. B., and Harris, J. M.: Pharmacogenetics—a fresh approach to the problem of allergy. Ann. New York Acad. Sc. *118*:441, 1964.
24. Ridges, A. P., and Augustin, R.: An in vitro test for atopic reagins by double-layer leukocyte agglutination. Nature *202*:667, 1964.

Chapter Ten

FOOD ALLERGY
AND
GASTROINTESTINAL
ALLERGY

FOOD ALLERGY

Food allergy appears to be relatively common in the community at large. In taking the past histories of atopic patients, substantial numbers mention acute episodes of urticaria, angioedema, itching, or gastrointestinal symptoms following the ingestion of certain foods such as strawberries, seafood, fish, or nuts. These manifestations of hypersensitivity to foods are well known and the reactions are transient. Many of these patients do not even consult a physician for such complaints, and still fewer come to the attention of the specialist. However, the frequency with which *persistent* allergic symptoms are due to foods is a highly controversial subject. It is important not to overlook food allergy, since it is so readily and satisfactorily treated merely by elimination. Thus, we feel that one should be thorough in his evaluation for the possibility of food allergy in all appropriate cases. However, our experience has been that it has infrequently been possible to document sensitivity to foods as a cause of persistent allergic disease. Nevertheless, for the reasons mentioned, we shall continue to search for food allergy particularly in cases of urticaria, angioedema, suspected gastrointestinal allergy, unexplained or sporadic respiratory allergy, and atopic dermatitis. In comparison with inhalant sensitivity, it appears that food allergy occurs more frequently in infants and children, but it is also a cause of disease in some adults. Although perennial symptoms are ordinarily expected, a seasonal pattern may be observed with seasonal food allergens (e.g., fresh tomatoes, peaches, or berries). In accord with the total allergic load concept (Chapter 2), some pollen-sensitive patients may experience allergic symptoms from foods only during their pollen season.

There are two distinct types of allergic reactions to foods. One is characterized by the *rapid* appearance of symptoms, often within a few minutes after the offending food is eaten. Some patients begin to react even before the food is swallowed. On the other hand, some foods tend to cause a *delayed* type of allergic response. In such cases, a number of hours or even a day or more (rarely) may elapse between the ingestion of the allergenic food and the appearance of symptoms.[1] It has been suggested that the actual allergen in the case of the immediate type of reaction to foods is the whole protein. With delayed reactions, however, the allergen may be some protein breakdown product such as proteose or polypeptide formed during the process of digestion of the protein. Since skin tests usually are done with extracts of the whole food protein, the above hypothesis is in agreement with the fact that reactions to skin tests usually are positive in persons having immediate symptoms from foods, while the results of tests often are unreliable in cases of delayed food allergy.

It is known that incompletely digested foods tend to pass into the circulatory system of infants and young children more readily than in

*Biologic Classification of Foods**

Animal Foods

MOLLUSKS	Trout	Sunfish	Butter
Abalone	Salmon	Bass	Cheese
—†	Whitefish	Perch	Gelatin
Mussel	Chub	Snapper	Pork
Oyster	Shad	Croaker	Ham
Scallop	—	Weakfish	Bacon
Clam	Eel	Drum	Goat
—	—	Scup	Goat's milk
CRUSTACEANS	Carp	Porgy	Cheese
Crab	Sucker	—	Mutton
Crayfish	Buffalo	Flounder	Lamb
—	—	Sole	Venison
Lobster	Catfish	Halibut	Horse meat
—	Bullhead	—	Rabbit
Shrimp	—	Rosefish	Squirrel
—	Pike	—	—
Squid	Pickerel	Codfish	BIRDS
	Muskellunge	Scrod	
AMPHIBIANS	—	Haddock	Chicken
Frog	Mullet	Hake	Chicken eggs
	Barracuda	Pollack	Duck
FISH	—	Cusk	Duck eggs
	Mackerel		Goose
Sturgeon	Tuna	REPTILES	Goose eggs
Caviar	Pompano	Turtle	Turkey
—	Bluefish		Guinea hen
Anchovy	Butterfish	MAMMALS	Squab
Sardine	Harvestfish	Beef	Pheasant
Herring	Swordfish	Veal	Partridge
Smelt	—	Cow's milk	Grouse

* Compiled by Dr. Theron G. Randolph. This is based on Vaughn's original classification as modified slightly by Ellis and confirmed by the Shedd Aquarium, Chicago, in respect to the fish and seafood, and by the Field Museum in regard to plants.

† Dashes between various groups of fish represent subdivisions, as there is some doubt as to the grouping of these fish. Authorities are not in complete agreement regarding the relationship of one group to another.

Biologic Classification of Foods (Continued)

Plants

GRAINS	BUCKWHEAT FAMILY	Peanut	LILY FAMILY
Wheat	Buckwheat	Peanut oil	Asparagus
Graham flour	Rhubarb	Licorice	Onion
Gluten flour		Acacia	Garlic
Bran	POTATO FAMILY	Senna	Leek
Wheat germ	Potato		Chive
Rye	Tomato		Aloes
Barley	Eggplant	MUSTARD FAMILY	
Malt	Red pepper	Mustard	GOOSEFOOT FAMILY
Corn	Cayenne	Cabbage	Beet
Corn starch	Green pepper	Cauliflower	Beet sugar
Corn oil	Chili	Broccoli	Spinach
Corn sugar		Brussels sprouts	Swiss chard
Corn syrup	COMPOSITE FAMILY	Turnip	
Cerulose	Leaf lettuce	Rutabaga	PARSLEY FAMILY
Dextrose	Head lettuce	Kale	Parsley
Glucose	Endive	Collard	Parsnip
Oats	Escarole	Celery cabbage	Carrot
Rice	Artichoke	Kohlrabi	Celery
Wild rice	Dandelion	Radish	Celeriac
Sorghum	Oyster plant	Horseradish	Caraway
Cane	Chicory	Watercress	Anise
Cane sugar			Dill
Molasses	LEGUMES	GOURD FAMILY	Coriander
	Navy bean	Pumpkin	Fennel
SPURGE FAMILY	Kidney bean	Squash	
Tapioca	Lima bean	Cucumber	MORNING GLORY
	String bean	Cantaloupe	FAMILY
ARROWROOT FAMILY	Soy bean	Muskmelon	Sweet potato
Arrowroot	Soy bean oil	Honey dew	Yam
	Lentil	Persian melon	
ARUM FAMILY	Black-eyed peas	Casaba	SUNFLOWER FAMILY
Taro	Pea	Watermelon	Jerusalem artichoke
Poi			Sunflower seed oil

adults, and some believe that this explains the more frequent occurrence of food allergy in children. However, there still is much to be learned regarding the fundamental mechanisms of food allergy.

Almost any food may be responsible for allergic symptoms. Fish and seafoods, berries (especially strawberries), nuts, and sometimes egg whites are the most common causes of the immediate type of allergic reaction to food. The most frequently seen sources of delayed food reactions are the cereals (especially wheat and corn), milk, eggs, beef, white potato, orange, pork, chocolate, and the legumes. Although cross-reactions from foods derived from closely related biologic sources are not as common as cross-reactivity within the groups of pollen-producing plants, this phenomenon is observed to a limited extent. For example, an individual allergic to wheat may react to corn, rye, or rice. The biologic classification of foods given below is an aid in estimating what cross-sensitivities might be present when food allergies are known to exist. We have encountered rather frequently patients who are clinically ragweed-sensitive and also have allergic symptoms when they eat cantaloupe or watermelon. Such patients usually have positive skin test reactions both to ragweed and to the melons.

Biologic Classification of Foods (Continued)
Plants (Continued)

POMEGRANATE FAMILY
Pomegranate

EBONY FAMILY
Persimmon

ROSE FAMILY
Raspberry
Blackberry
Loganberry
Youngberry
Dewberry
Strawberry

BANANA FAMILY
Banana

APPLE FAMILY
Apple
Cider
Vinegar
Apple pectin
Pear
Quince
Quince seed

PLUM FAMILY
Plum
Prune
Cherry
Peach
Apricot
Nectarine
Almond

LAUREL FAMILY
Avocado
Cinnamon
Bay Leaves

OLIVE FAMILY
Green olive
Ripe olive
Olive oil

HEATH FAMILY
Cranberry
Blueberry

GOOSEBERRY FAMILY
Gooseberry
Currant

HONEYSUCKLE FAMILY
Elderberry

CITRUS FAMILY
Orange
Grapefruit
Lemon
Lime
Tangerine
Kumquat

PINEAPPLE FAMILY
Pineapple

PAPAW FAMILY
Papaya

GRAPE FAMILY
Grape
Raisin
Cream of tartar

MRYTLE FAMILY
Allspice
Cloves
Pimento
Paprika
Guava

MINT FAMILY
Mint
Peppermint
Spearmint
Thyme

Sage
Marjoram
Savory

PEPPER FAMILY
Black pepper

NUTMEG FAMILY
Nutmeg

GINGER FAMILY
Ginger
Tumeric
Cardamon

PINE FAMILY
Juniper

ORCHID FAMILY
Vanilla

MADDER FAMILY
Coffee

TEA FAMILY
Tea

PEDALIUM FAMILY
Sesame oil

MALLOW FAMILY
Okra (Gumbo)
Cottonseed

STERCULA FAMILY
Cocoa
Chocolate

BIRCH FAMILY
Filbert
Hazelnut
Oil of birch
(wintergreen)

MULBERRY FAMILY
Mulberry
Fig
Hop
Breadfruit

MAPLE FAMILY
Maple Syrup
Maple sugar

PALM FAMILY
Cocoanut
Date
Sago

LECYTHIS FAMILY
Brazil nut

POPPY FAMILY
Poppy seed

WALNUT FAMILY
English walnut
Black walnut
Butternut
Hickory nut
Pecan

CASHEW FAMILY
Cashew
Pistachio
Mango

BEECH FAMILY
Chestnut

FUNGI
Mushroom
Yeast

MISCELLANEOUS
Honey

Diagnosis of Food Allergy

It may be surprising to find that it is difficult to recognize the existence of food allergy in a patient. However, there are a number of factors which confuse even the most observant patients. Easy diagnosis is prevented by a delayed reaction in some cases, the great frequency with which the offending food may be eaten, and the fact that a certain food may cause allergic symptoms only at certain times.

There are several reasons for this variability in clinical response. First, there is a *quantitative* factor which, when sensitivity to a food is not extreme, allows small amounts to be tolerated without difficulty. Larger quantities will precipitate symptoms. Second, the degree of *cook-*

ing will affect the allergic response. Usually foods in their raw condition are more allergenic than those which are thoroughly cooked. Some persons, for example, who have no difficulty from hard-boiled eggs cannot tolerate eggnog. The *cumulative* factor also is important. Patients who have no symptoms following occasional ingestion of a food may react if it is eaten on successive days. There may be a cyclic nature of the state of food hypersensitivity.[2] Immediately after an allergic reaction from a food there may be a brief *refractory period* during which further ingestion of the allergen will not provoke symptoms. After about four days a phase of heightened sensitivity may occur, which gradually is replaced over a long period of time by a state of waning or subclinical sensitivity. Therefore, the time which has elapsed since a previous allergic reaction to a food is another factor which determines the response of a patient to that food.

Still another confusing point is that food allergies frequently are *multiple*. The difficulty in working out such problems is further enhanced if the several food sensitivities are relatively mild in degree. A patient thus might not experience clinical symptoms after eating individually small amounts of two or three foods to which he is mildly sensitive. However, if he should happen to eat all three foods at the same meal, symptoms might result. It is apparent that more than superficial study may be necessary to work out problems of food allergy in many cases. The considerations mentioned above account for the puzzling fact that patients sometimes experience allergic symptoms after the ingestion of certain foods but fail to have symptoms on other occasions after eating the same foods.

Although the allergist should have a keen awareness of the possibility of food sensitivity, he must use sound medical judgment in order to avoid the pitfall of overdiagnosing food allergy. Many people would rather attribute their complaints to food allergy than to a less acceptable but correct diagnosis of psychoneurosis. For the doctor to make a poorly substantiated diagnosis of food allergy in such cases is a grave error. Ultimately, the allergy program fails to give relief, and such a fixation to being sensitive to foods is developed that subsequent psychotherapy is most difficult. Particularly in patients presenting gastrointestinal complaints, one should be very circumspect before settling upon a diagnosis of food allergy (see page 221).

One also must be on guard against mistakenly interpreting the observed change which occurs in the patient's condition when a food is added or withheld as food allergy.[3] Antibiotic drugs in foods might be the cause; for example, gastrointestinal and even systemic allergic reactions may occur from ingestion of milk containing penicillin in a highly sensitive patient. Other food additives also might be responsible. For example, we have recently encountered three patients who had gastrointestinal symptoms from the saccharine contained in artificially sweetened diet food and low-calorie soft drinks. Symptoms could be reproduced by giving amounts of saccharine too small to induce diarrhea in normal persons. Some foods may cause gastrointestinal symptoms on a toxic basis. Mushrooms, shellfish, and certain poisonous fish are examples. Food poisoning from bacteria or bacterial toxins also could be confused with food allergy. Metabolic disorders, such as galactosemia and other inherited disaccharidase enzyme deficiencies, will lead to milk intolerance manifested by vomiting, diarrhea, anorexia, and abdominal swelling. These symptoms are relieved when milk sugar lactose (which is a disaccharide made up of glucose and galactose) is deleted from the diet, but no immunologic mechanism is involved. Likewise there is no evidence that wheat allergy is involved in sprue patients' intolerance for gluten. The physical or chemical properties of some other foods may cause irritation of the gastrointestinal tract.

History. The first step in the diagnosis of food allergy is a thorough initial history. The patient should be asked whether he suspects that any specific food causes symptoms. Any food he names should be considered carefully. One also may inquire about the food likes and dislikes. Children occasionally refuse to eat something to which they are allergic, although it has been shown that this is not a reliable index of food allergy. People are apt to eat large amounts of foods which they enjoy, and the chances of allergy to these foods may be increased. Finally, an account of the patient's food intake should be a routine part of the initial allergy history (page 36). Special note should be made of foods taken in unusually large amounts and of those whose ingestion is associated with onset of allergic symptoms.

Skin Testing for Food Allergy. A great amount of confusion has arisen regarding how to evaluate reactions to the skin tests for food allergy, and many physicians have become so discouraged with these tests that they no longer perform them. Certainly, this course is better than placing a patient on a diet for an indefinite period, based entirely on reactions to skin tests. The correlation between clinical food sensitivities and the skin test reaction may depend to some extent on the food being considered, the age of the patient, and the type of allergic condition affecting the patient. For example, in testing for fish, nuts, or peanuts the correlation is very high, but with foods which produce more delayed reactions the correlation is very poor. Thus, the skin tests are most accurate when they are least useful.

Should skin tests for foods be carried out? Since relatively few of the positive reactions are correlated with clinical sensitivity, it would seem that one might do as well or even better simply by guesswork. Nevertheless, there are several reasons for going ahead with some tests for food sensitivity. One is that testing gives an evaluation of the patient's over-all constitutional make-up. If reactions to all the skin tests are negative and the patient has not had antihistamine drugs, aminophylline, ephedrine, or epinephrine, the physician is justified at least in questioning whether he is dealing with "extrinsic protein sensitivity."

It should be possible in most patients with environmental allergy of at least several weeks' duration to demonstrate antibodies by positive reactions to skin tests. Another reason for performing the skin tests for food sensitivity is that they are of practical aid in the determination of the type of elimination diet to be used. For example, one of the most useful basic elimination diets prohibits the patient's ingestion of all milk, eggs, and cereals but does allow him to eat white potato. If a person gave a strongly positive reaction to a skin test for white potato, it would be sensible to use a type of elimination diet which temporarily withholds this vegetable. A strongly positive reaction to one of the cereals, such as corn, might lead the investigator to eliminate for a time all cereals from the diet, since sensitivity to one cereal may indicate allergy to others. This relationship also is seen among the legumes (peas, peanuts, beans) and between mustard and flaxseed.

The skin tests also are of use at times in deciding in what order foods should be added again to an elimination diet. For example, if the symptoms of a hospitalized patient with urticaria clear up while he is on an elimination diet, it often is of interest to add rather early some of the foods which previously gave positive skin reactions. This is done to see whether clinical symptoms can be reproduced while the patient is in a relatively well-controlled hospital environment. On the other hand, sometimes when the symptoms of an individual with severe allergic disease clear up while he is on an elimination diet, it may be well not to add too early to the diet the foods that have given marked positive reactions to skin tests. The patient thereby obtains a rest from his symptoms. However, one sooner or later must reproduce clinical symptoms by the addition of a food in order to demonstrate that a state of clinical allergy to the particular food exists at that time. The old adage, "the proof of the pudding is in the eating," is literally true when one is dealing with the evaluation of food allergies.

In conducting the skin tests for sensitivity to foods, no special problems arise except in those groups of foods which are particularly potent antigens. As discussed on page 55, we always perform prick or scratch tests before injecting antigens intracutaneously and omit entirely intracutaneous tests with the very potent allergens in groups F, G, and H on page 74.

Testing with Natural Foods. Certain food allergens, particularly some of those from fresh fruits and berries, are notoriously labile, and extracts of these foods rapidly become inactive. Referring to the way skin tests originally were carried out, several investigators have shown that patients allergic to these foods often will react to skin tests with juice expressed from the fresh fruit or berry just before testing, whereas reactions to standard extracts were negative.[4] If fresh fruit is not in season, it has been shown that frozen food may provide active skin testing material at times. More recently it has been suggested that seeds provide a source of potent allergens for skin testing.[5]

In summary, then, the point to be most strongly emphasized is that positive skin reactions to foods should not be interpreted literally as indicating clinical sensitivity to the reacting foods at the time of the tests. The only proof of the existence of allergy to a food is the repeated precipitation and relief of clinical symptoms as the suspected food is added or withdrawn from the diet under controlled conditions. The outmoded practice of handing patients long lists of positive skin test reacting foods for indefinite elimination from the diet is to be deplored. A hardship is imposed upon such patients in that many foods are needlessly eliminated for prolonged periods. We have seen instances of frank vitamin deficiencies and malnutrition in patients who, in spite of little or no relief, have followed such diets for years. Any type of allergy elimination diet should be prescribed for a definite period, usually not exceeding two or three weeks. If there is no improvement in that length of time, the diet should be modified or abandoned. If the patient is relieved, previously eliminated foods should be added one at a time to see which ones actually will cause symptoms.

Diet Diary. If a patient has only occasional allergic manifestations occurring less often than about every two weeks, the best initial approach in evaluating the possibility of food allergy is simply to have him keep a diary of all foods which he eats. In this he indicates the exact times at which symptoms occur. A convenient form for carrying out such a procedure is shown on page 212. Environmental changes and tensional situations also should be recorded in the diary. If symptoms are caused only by a single food or even several items which are taken infrequently, this soon becomes apparent to both patient and physician after several reactions have been recorded in the diary. Occasional hives resulting from eating watermelon and cantaloupe might be diagnosed in this way. If the patient has allergic symptoms only very rarely (e.g., once or twice a year), it may be helpful simply to have him write down, in retrospect, all foods eaten and other activities for 48 hours before his symptoms appeared.

Elimination Diets. When a patient is having allergic symptoms continuously or with considerable frequency, some form of elimination dietary procedure is usually the method of choice for evaluating possible food allergy. It is unwise, however, to begin a diagnostic elimination diet if there are other factors in the situation which are known to be causing symptoms. For example, if it is known that the patient is dust-sensitive and one wishes to find out if there are also food allergies present, institution of an elimination diet while the dust factor is entirely uncontrolled is apt to be of no value. The continuing allergic response to dust might well mask any beneficial effect from the diet. In such a case, it would be well to defer the diet until the dust factor is moderately well under control by means of an anti-dust program with or without dust hyposensitization. Likewise it is advisable in most cases not to try elimination diets during the pollen or fungus seasons in patients who are allergic to these inhalants. Elimination diets also cannot be evaluated satisfactorily in the presence of infection. Furthermore, immediately following severe infections there may be a refractory period during which the patient may be much improved. Investigational diets also should not be started soon after severe trauma or surgery. It is almost impossible to evaluate extrinsic allergens properly at these times. It now is suspected that these well-known refractory periods may represent an alarm reaction to the stress of the acute situation.

Elimination diets should not be started at the same time that other forms of treatment are instituted. Eager resident staffs may place the hospitalized asthmatic patient at once on an elimination diet, anti-dust program, and numerous medications. It is impossible to tell which of these measures, including hospitalization itself, could account for any improvement observed. If possible, symptomatic medications should be stopped before and during the trial of an elimination diet. To control as many of the variable factors as possible, it is generally wise to make only one change at a time in the management program of allergic patients unless they are desperately ill.

After it has been decided that an elimination diet is indicated and that the time is propitious for its initiation, the next step is to choose the type which will be most satisfactory for the particular patient being studied. Diets eliminating one or two foods at a time are not recommended for general use. Since food allergies frequently are multiple, one could spend months eliminating one food at a time without obtaining any improvement. The limitations of diets based solely on skin tests have been discussed previously (page 203). Although there is no objection to a trial of such diets for a *limited period* of time, we have been inclined to use rather rigid arbitrary diets containing foods which statistically are relatively uncommon causes of allergy. However, one should make liberal modifications or substitutions depending upon information obtained from the diet history. It would be unwise to retain in the initial diet a food which there is reason to suspect from the history. If skin tests have been performed and have shown some strongly positive reactions, the initial diet usually is modified so as to delete any of these foods. It should be emphasized that most of the diets described in the following pages are inadequate nutritionally. Therefore, it must be made very clear to the patient that his diet should be followed no longer than the prescribed period, which usually does not exceed two or three weeks. If improvement has not occurred within this period of observation, the diet should be abandoned or modified. If relief occurs, previously eliminated foods should be added to the diet one at a time and in large amounts to see which ones actually cause the symptoms.

Initial Allergy Diet No. 1.   Our initial allergy diet No. 1 is a modification of one of the Rowe elimination diets. Its main items consist of rice, lamb, sweet potatoes, carrots, peaches, and pears. Very few patients have allergic trouble from these foods and most seem able to exist for

Allergy Diet No. 1

FOODS ALLOWED:

Rice wafers*	Beets
	Carrots
Puffed Rice	Chard
Rice	Lettuce
Rice Flakes	Okra
Rice Krispies	Sweet potato

Apricots ⎫
Cranberries ⎪ also the
Peaches ⎬ juice of these
Pears ⎭ fruits

Lamb

Acetic acid vinegar (white vinegar)
Olive oil, Crisco, Spry, or any vegetable oil except oleo-
   margarine which may contain milk solids†
Sugar, cane
Salt
Tapioca
Vanilla extract (synthetic)
Water

Eat and drink only the foods listed.

SUGGESTED MENU:

Breakfast	*Dinner*	*Supper*	*Avoid:*
Rice Krispies	Lamb chop	Lamb pattie	Coffee
Rice	Sweet potato	Boiled rice	Tea
Peaches	Beets	Carrots	Coca Cola
Apricot juice	Rice wafers	Lettuce with	Soft drinks
Peach jam	Cranberry juice	acetic acid	Chewing gum
Water	Pears	Apricot juice	All medications except
		Peaches	those ordered by
			doctor

INSTRUCTIONS:

Stay on basic diet for ____ days.   (Amount)
Then, on _____, add _____ all by itself, first thing in A.M. _____.
Next, on _____, add _____ all by itself, first thing in A.M. _____.
Next, on _____, add _____ all by itself, first thing in A.M. _____.
Next, on _____, add _____ all by itself, first thing in A.M. _____.
    etc. . . .

Keep a diet diary as instructed.

---

* Rice wafers can be ordered from Cellu Co., Chicago, Illinois.
† Kosher oleomargarine Mar-par, or Mazola Margarine contains no milk.

about a week on this diet without too much complaint. If there is a pronounced distaste for any of these items, however, it is possible to substitute a few foods which the patient rarely eats, as these are unlikely to be the cause of his symptoms and may make the diet more acceptable. Since the most common food allergens are excluded from this diet, it frequently is chosen for use both in children and in adult patients. Small children accept it well, since the constituents are familiar and almost all items can be obtained in cans or jars of baby food at the grocery store. For some patients, such as those who must eat in restaurants or carry their lunch, diet No. 2 may be more practical. Furthermore, because diet No. 1 contains rice, it is unwise to use it when cereal sensitivity is suspected. Occasionally the patient's symptoms actually become *more pronounced* while the initial allergy diet No. 1 is being followed. This may be highly significant and suggests allergy to one of the allowed foods, particularly to rice.

In this diet, as in any elimination diet prescribed, it is essential that the patient be instructed properly. If he merely is handed a diet list and sent on his way, the procedure almost never is carried out correctly and must be repeated again at a later date. The patient is instructed to take only the foods on the diet list. It must be specifically pointed out that such things as chewing gum, beer, coffee, vitamin pills, and antihistamines should be discontinued while the test period is in force. Many patients do not consider coffee to be a food, or vitamin pills and laxatives "medicine." That it is not sufficient to tell the patient to discontinue all other foods and drugs or medicines except those listed must be emphasized. We have seen a case in which a prescribed diet failed to give results because the doctor forgot to tell the patient not to chew gum. The physician also can give helpful suggestions which will make it easier for the patient to carry out his diet. At the same time that he admonishes the patient not to put milk on his rice cereal, he may suggest that pouring peaches or apricots over the cereal will make it palatable. It also is of considerable help to tell the patient at which stores he can get acceptable rice wafers. It is important to see that some grocer in town keeps this item in stock. The patient next is told how to keep the food diary described on page 212. Usually these instructions can be given by the physician, but he may refer this task to a dietician. Consultation with a dietician is especially helpful when unusual problems arise, such as preparing a diet for diabetic patients who simultaneously require instructions for allergy.

Opinions differ concerning the length of time the initial diet should be adhered to, and this also depends to some extent on the disease being evaluated. Some advocate relatively long periods on the initial diet, but it should be pointed out that the longer the time before the patient shows improvement, the greater is the possibility that the observed clearing of symptoms was spontaneous or due to factors other than the diet. It also seems improbable that the improvement from food elimination would be delayed for an extended period of time. Thus, we have felt that relatively brief trials of elimination diets—a matter of days or weeks—are adequate. For example, if a patient has evanescent urticarial lesions, five days might be adequate. In cases of chronic atopic dermatitis, however, improvement of the skin, if it occurs, is apt to be more gradual on an elimination dietary program. Therefore, one might wish to leave such patients on the basic diet for ten to fourteen days or longer. In patients with respiratory symptoms, generally a seven to ten day trial period is used. It is hoped, of course, that significant or complete clearing of symptoms will result from the initial diet. Even if there is no improvement, however, some information of value may be salvaged. Adding singly a few important foods that were eliminated is justified to see whether the symptoms are made even more pronounced. Failure to improve on any one elimination diet does not rule out the possibility of food allergy. Sensitivity to some food in the initial diet or the previously discussed effects of other allergens, infections, and environmental forces might account for such failures.

After the patient has been on the basic diet for the indicated period, addition of foods should be started in an attempt to aggravate the symptoms. For this reason foods are reinstituted one at a time, in large servings, especially on an empty stomach. Breakfast is the best meal during which to start a new food. Particular attention should be paid to any change in symptoms during the three or four hours following ingestion of the new item. If it is a prime factor in causing the patient's difficulty, usually an increase in symptoms results within three to six hours after eating, but reactions occasionally may be delayed for 24 hours or rarely even longer.[1] The test food, upon addition, should be eaten not only for breakfast but also at intervals throughout the day. If no reaction is observed, the food is left in the diet and may be eaten as desired in addition to the items on the basic diet.

The rate at which previously eliminated foods are added to the diet is determined by circumstances in each individual case. As previously stated, allergenic foods usually produce symptoms within a few hours after ingestion. Thus, it is possible to add one new food each day. This is most feasible when it is necessary to carry out the dietary manipulation within a very limited period of time (e.g., in the case of students at home for relatively brief vacations). On the other hand, since the allergic reaction from a food may be delayed, confusion might arise if a new food were added every day, and the wrong food might be suspected. In order to minimize this type of error, it is advisable to add new foods only every two or three days. In patients with chronic and persistent allergic manifestations, the three day interval is usual. When the condition is more acute, a two day period between additions is satisfactory. However, if there is any doubt regarding a possible increase in symptoms toward the end of the second day of testing a food, an additional day of observation should be employed before further additions are made. Some authorities advise a much slower rate of food additions. It should be pointed out, however, that the longer the interval between the introduction of a food and the precipitation of symptoms, the greater the possibility that the symptoms are not actually caused by the food.

If a flare-up in the patient's symptoms occurs during the process of food additions, he should discontinue eating the food most recently added. After his symptoms have quieted down again, the next food should be started, usually a day or two after the reaction has cleared or after a "base line" of existing symptoms has been re-established.

To illustrate the procedure of food additions, the patient adding milk is instructed to drink a glass of milk upon arising without taking any other food. If no reaction is encountered, another glass of milk should be taken 30 minutes later. Breakfast, selected from the basic list, is eaten an hour later. More milk is taken each meal. When adding eggs, usually two soft-boiled eggs are eaten, with salt permitted. If no reaction is observed in 30 minutes, another egg is eaten. When wheat is returned to the diet, a bowlful of Cream of Wheat is eaten with sugar and warm water. Fresh orange juice is a satisfactory form in which to test orange. Corn may be challenged as corn flakes, but fresh corn also should be tested individually. Tomato may be given as tomato juice but, if possible, fresh tomato should be tried first.

There are some foods which cannot easily be added "by themselves" in the morning on an empty stomach. Such foods should be eaten with a light accompanying meal at noon and in the evening for three days in succession. The diet becomes progressively easier to follow as additional foods are added.

Foods should be replaced in the diet in as pure and unaltered a form as possible. Commercially made bread is very likely to contain milk. Thus, bread should not be included in the diet until milk and wheat have been added separately. The yeast in bread also may cause trouble. If suspected, yeast should be tested by a separate ingestion trial. In general, mixed food preparations such as hot dogs, pizza, hash, gravy, and most soups should be avoided until the food allergy problem has been worked out.

It is best to add first to the diet staple foods which are the major components of the patient's normal diet. In this way his intake is nutritionally adequate more rapidly and is more enjoyable. It is usual practice to add milk, wheat, eggs, beef, white potato, and orange as the first six additions to the initial diet. Thereafter, the patient is advised to decide for himself which foods he wishes to add, and these are tested one at a time. Many patients miss coffee very much, and in such cases it may be added early. Variations in the order of re-institution may be made in individual cases, in which suspects were elicited from the history or skin testing (page 201).

While instructing a patient on these dietary procedures, it is necessary to point out that if one food is discovered which causes difficulty, he should still continue to look for other offenders. Otherwise, he may abandon the diet after discovering one troublesome food. Although it is common for patients to be allergic to two or three different items, we are inclined to regard with skepticism patients' claims of being allergic to 30 or 40 foods. Usually such statements are based largely on positive reactions to skin tests only, and rarely, if ever, does one obtain clear-cut clinical evidence for clinical allergy to so many ingestants.

Another very important point concerns having the patient *re-check* what seems to be an allergic reaction to a food added. The appearance of asthma on the day that eggs are returned to the diet might well be coincidental, rather than indicative of allergy to egg. One therefore should delete egg from the diet a second time, wait for the symptoms to subside, and then proceed with the additions of other foods. After three or four other foods have been added, eggs again should be tested. Probably a third trial of eggs should be made at still a later date. If symptoms can be induced on two or three occasions by the addition of a substance and the patient is comfortable in the interim, a coincidental relationship between the administration of the food and the appearance of symptoms is slight, and one can assume that the food is responsible for the allergic manifestations. A very rare exception to this general procedure is encountered in the patient in whom exceptionally violent symptoms follow the ingestion of a food. Under such circumstances it would be prudent not to repeat the addition.

Although one should not be concerned about throwing a well nourished patient into a state of significant malnutrition during the three or four week period in which allergic dietary manipulation takes place, it is not wise, on the other hand, to impose a rigid diet on an already severely undernourished patient. Particularly in the case of malnourished, underweight, growing children, nutritional deficiencies should be corrected before allergic dietary maneuvers are attempted. It should be pointed out again that food allergies are quantitative in degree. After proving that large amounts of milk will provoke symptoms, the physician should test his patient's tolerance to smaller amounts. Although he may not be able to remain free of symptoms with significant amounts of milk as such, perhaps small quantities of milk in commercial breads and baked goods or moderate portions used in cooking will not produce symptoms. This makes it much easier for an individual to remain on his diet for a prolonged period.

A perplexing sequence of events sometimes occurs, especially in children, when an elimination diet is carried out. The symptoms may promptly subside as the patient starts the basic diet, but when all foods have been added, he may continue to remain free from the previous symptoms. Does this mean he was not allergic to the foods withheld, or could it indicate that interrupting the challenge by the antigen has altered the allergic equilibrium so that the child no longer is reacting as he previously did? One can only guess; the successful elimination of the symptoms is authentic. The mechanism, perhaps even a nonallergic one, is obscure.

Initial Allergy Diet No. 2. The initial allergy diet No. 2 (modified from Rowe's cereal-free 1, 2, 3 diet) is prepared for the physician who wants to place his patient on a program which is completely devoid of all cereals as well as milk, eggs, and certain other items. Since persons sensitive to one cereal may be allergic to many of them, this diet is of value when the physician suspects allergy to one of the grains. Elimination of milk and egg (and foods containing them) further enhances the possibility of finding the food at fault. This diet is more liberal than the initial allergy diet No. 1, for it allows the patient to have bacon, chicken, beef, white potato, and vegetables of the legume group. Hence,

Allergy Diet No. 2 (Cereal-, Milk-, Egg-Free Diet)*

FOODS ALLOWED:

Tapioca	Squash	Water
White potato, potato chips	Asparagus	
Sweet potato or yam	Peas	Prunes
	String beans	Peaches
Lamb	Lima beans	Pears
Beef		Pineapple
Chicken	Cane or beet sugar	Cranberries
Bacon	Salt	Apricots
	Gelatine, plain	
Soybeans, soybean sprouts	Maple syrup or syrup	
Lettuce	made wtih cane sugar	
Spinach	flavored with maple	
Chard	White vinegar, olive oil	
Carrots	(equal parts make	
Beets	French dressing)	
Artichoke	Vanilla extract	

Prunes, Peaches, Pears, Pineapple, Cranberries, Apricots — and the juices of these fruits

Crisco or Spry, any
    vegetable shortening
    except oleomargarine. †

Eat and drink only foods listed.   AVOID: Coffee, tea, Coca Cola, soft drinks, chewing
                            gum, all medications except what is ordered by
                            the doctor.

SUGGESTED MENU:

Breakfast	*Dinner*	*Supper*
Bacon	Lamb or beef pattie	Cube steak (beef)
Fried potato	Baked potato	Mashed potato
Tapioca and peaches	Lettuce and carrot salad	Peas
Prune juice	Apricot juice	Lettuce and pineapple salad
Water	Baked pears	Canned peaches
	Water	Water

INSTRUCTIONS:

Stay on basic diet for _____ days.   (Amount)

Then, on _____, add _____ all by itself, first thing in A.M. _____

Next, on _____, add _____ all by itself, first thing in A.M. _____

Next, on _____, add _____ all by itself, first thing in A.M. _____

Next, on _____, add _____ all by itself, first thing in A.M. _____

    etc. . . .

Keep a diet diary as instructed.

---

* Modified from Rowe's Cereal-Free 1-2-3 Diet.
† Kosher margarine contains no milk solids.

diet No. 2 is easier to follow and is useful for persons who travel and must eat in restaurants. Other factors bearing on the choice of using the initial allergy diet No. 1, diet No. 2, or other diets have been discussed on page 204.

Study of the initial allergy diet No. 2 shows that bacon is allowed but pork is not. Few patients have trouble from bacon, but this is not true of pork. In both diets No. 1 and No. 2, vegetable shortenings such as Crisco or Spry are allowed. Hypersensitivity to these refined products is most unusual, if it exists at all. Kosher margarine (which contains no milk solids) may be used. If butter is permitted, it should be washed carefully before use. A pound of butter may be put into a wooden bowl and covered with warm water. It then is kneaded by hand or with a spoon in the water and rinsed. The procedure is repeated five or six times, using progressively colder water and rinsing frequently with fresh water. This procedure removes nearly all traces of lactalbumin and preservatives from the butter. Tapioca may be used as a cereal substitute. Whole tapioca (pearl) should be boiled with water into a gruel. It may be eaten with fruit or sugar syrup.

The patient is instructed regarding the initial allergy diet No. 2 as for diet No. 1. He stays on the basic diet for a period varying from five to twelve days and then begins additions as described on page 207. Also, as indicated previously, the physician should feel free to make modifications in the initial diet if any suspected foods can be elicited by history or skin testing.

Food Diaries for Use with Elimination Diets. A particularly helpful tool in the evaluation of the patient's response to diet manipulation is the food diary. This is a chart kept by the patient on which he records not only all foods which he eats during the trial period, but also keeps a running account of his symptoms and notes any unusual environmental, tensional, or physiologic occurrences which might influence the experiment. The patient is given a form (see example on page 212) upon which he lists at the end of each day the foods eaten that day. Each food is listed only once, and if ingested on following days, it is checked off in the same horizontal space as was used to record it the first time. Only one check need be made for a single food on any given day, no matter how many times it is eaten on that day. At the bottom of the page the patient records the severity of his symptoms each day. He also indicates any medications taken according to the physician's orders. He should at this time be limited only to those drugs needed to relieve flare-ups which might occur as a food is added.

If the patient has more than one allergic manifestation, a separate notation should be made daily for each type of symptom. As a definite flare-up occurs, a further note should be written indicating the exact food intake for the day, the temporal relationship between the foods eaten and the appearance of symptoms, and any other information which might possibly pertain to the onset of difficulty. The diet diary should be brought in by the patient on each return visit, and through its careful study allergenic foods may be identified. For example, it is apparent from the sample chart (page 212) that the patient is allergic to milk and chocolate.

In addition to its important function as an adjunct to elimination diets, a diet diary alone is of considerable value in identifying food allergy in patients who have experienced only very occasional symptoms. This has been discussed on page 203. Furthermore, a diet dairy also gives the physician an excellent idea of his patient's dietary habits and

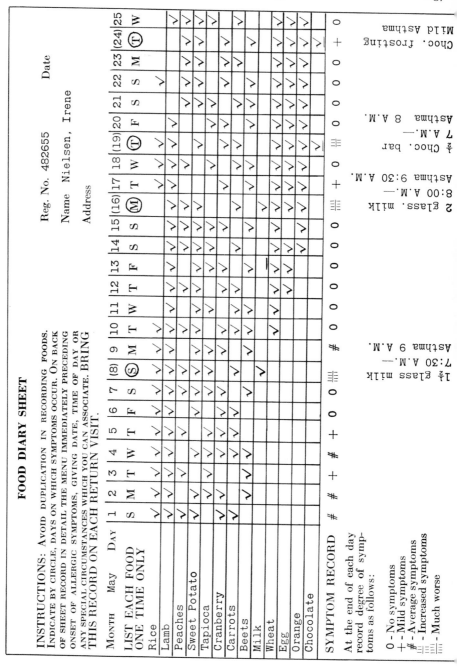

Figure 10–1.

may bring out some unusual eating customs which were not revealed at the time the history was taken. This is especially true when a language barrier makes taking the history difficult.

Provocative Diet. There are instances in which elimination diets have not made it clear whether a patient is food-sensitive. His report of observations, since it is subjective, may be equivocal, and the doctor wonders whether to search further. For this situation, the provocative diet (below) may be helpful. The foods therein are administered in hope of definitely aggravating the patient's symptoms while he is on the diet. The foods it contains are common sources of allergic trouble and are eaten in large amounts. The patient is instructed to take generous portions, for a period of five to seven days, of only the foods listed. The diet itself is rather pleasant, and the patient finds it easy to take large quantities of milk, wheat, eggs, beef, white potato, orange, sugar, and salt. If allergic symptoms are more pronounced while he is on this diet, the doctor is justified in pursuing his search for a causative food, perhaps by imposing a synthetic diet if other types of elimination diets have failed to give relief. Occasionally patients may *improve* while on the provocative diet. This suggests sensitivity to foods other than those included, and items should be added one at a time as is done in the usual elimination diets. On the other hand, if the patient's symptoms are unchanged while on this diet, it may indicate that foods are not a major factor in evoking symptoms. However, failure of a patient's condition to become aggravated while he is on the provocative diet by no means completely excludes the possibility of food allergy, since this diet, though restrictive, may not differ very much from a patient's usual food intake. If his chief food allergy is to some item or items not included in the provocative diet, his symptoms, of course, will not get worse on the diet.

The Provocative Diet

This diet consists of wheat, milk, egg, beef, potato, orange, sugar, salt, and water.

FOODS PERMITTED

Wheat cereal (bran, Cream of Wheat, Grape Nuts, Puffed Wheat, Ralston, Shredded Wheat, or Wheaties)
White bread—plain or toasted. Whole wheat bread, French bread
Biscuit
Rolls
Crackers—plain or graham
Waffles or griddle cakes
Plain angel food cake, plain pound cake, or vanilla wafers
Sweet milk, buttermilk, cream, malted milk, butter, cottage cheese, American cheese, Swiss cheese
Macaroni or spaghetti with cheese
Postum
Eggs
Vanilla ice cream
Beef steak, roast beef, veal, veal or beef liver, tongue, brains, gravy
Potato—creamed, boiled, baked, fried, or au gratin
Orange, orange juice, orange marmalade, orange-flavored custard or pudding, orange sherbet

No food is to be used
unless it is shown above.

If there is any food listed above which you do not like, it is not necessary that you eat it. You may use any food shown above as often and in as large quantity as may be desired.

Synthetic Diet. Either because of multiple food sensitivities or poor cooperation on the part of the patient, food allergy at times is not clearly delineated by the measures already described. No matter what foods are allowed on an initial elimination diet, occasional sensitivities to them are seen. Pioneers in the field of allergy sometimes circumvented this difficulty by simply placing their patients on a "diet" of nothing by mouth except sucrose and water ad lib. for a period of four days. Thereafter, foods were added one at a time. When other conditions are well controlled, this serves as an effective method for ruling out food allergy. Needless to say, however, such a procedure is rather drastic for general use and is not popular with patients. More recently, synthetic diets composed of protein hydrolysates have been used to provide nonallergenic diets. Usually these are prepared from casein by means of hydrolysis with acid or with enzymes. These protein hydrolysates consist mainly of amino acids and small peptides. In spite of the casein source, such compounds do seem to be nonallergenic. Even the symptoms of very milk-sensitive patients clear up entirely while taking casein hydrolysates. Although most synthetic diets are far from adequate nutritionally, they do provide an excellent source of protein nitrogen and are a distinct improvement over the sugar and water diet. Their chief disadvantage is an undesirable taste, which probably results largely from their glutamic acid content. It is largely for this reason that synthetic diets are not used more extensively. Usually one of the previously described elimination diets is tried first, but if it does not solve the problem and food allergy is suspected, then the physician can try a synthetic diet.

Protein hydrolysates commercially available at present are Amigen,* the Stuart Amino Acids,† and Nutramigen.‡ Their compositions are given below.

AMIGEN
(Baxter Laboratories)

Composition	*Per cent*	
Amigen (casein hydrolysate)	5.0	⎫
		⎬ in sterile solution
Dextrose	5.0	⎭

There are several Amigen preparations, including Levugen.

We recommend trial of the 5 per cent solution. Although prepared for intravenous use, Amigen can be taken orally, 250 ml. (1 glassful) as needed four to six times daily to allay hunger.

STUART AMINO ACIDS
(The Stuart Company)

Composition

Amino acids as derived from the total acid hydrolysis of casein, fortified with 1 per cent tryptophan. No flavoring or carbohydrate is added. Up to 3 tablespoonfuls six times daily can be dissolved in hot or cold liquids.

---

* Supplied by Baxter Laboratories, Inc., Morton Grove, Illinois 60053.

† Supplied by the Stuart Co., 3360 E. Foothill Blvd., Pasadena, California 91109.

‡ Supplied by Mead Johnson Laboratories, 2404 W. Pennsylvania St., Evansville, Indiana 47721.

NUTRAMIGEN
(Mead Johnson Laboratories)

Composition

Nutramigen contains hydrolyzed casein, sucrose, arrowroot starch, corn oil, and vitamins and minerals. The preparation is free from intact protein. It provides 20 cal./fl. oz. For infant feeding, 1 measure of powder in 2 oz. water. For adults add 8 ounces of powder to 1 quart water. Sweeten to taste with sucrose as desired. Serve iced.

It will be noted that Nutramigen contains arrowroot, corn oil and crystalline vitamins in addition to the sucrose and protein hydrolysate. Thus, it is more adequate nutritionally but, on the other hand, one might wonder about possible allergy to one of the added constituents. Such a development is in reality rather remote, but some physicians feel that resorting to the synthetic diet justifies use of the most completely nonallergenic material. The palatability of these preparations can be increased by allowing ginger ale or white soda water. These may be either mixed with the synthetic formula or used as a "chaser." Allergy to ginger ale is exceedingly rare, but the same theoretical objections could be raised to its use as mentioned above in connection with the added components of Nutramigen.

Hospitalization of the patient may be advisable while carrying out a synthetic diet, since it places him in a controlled environment in which he is less likely to despair of the synthetic diet in favor of some more enjoyable food. After the procedure is explained to the patient, the diet is started and he receives nothing by mouth except the formula and water or ice. He may vary the amount of water added to the formula; some prefer to dilute the hydrolysate to a volume greater than one liter, thus diminishing the bad taste. This provides more formula to drink, however, and most patients prefer to take the material in concentrated form. More than the prescribed amount of sucrose could be added to the diet if desired. Since it is easier to drink these formulas when cold, they should be iced before serving. Almost half the infants placed on a synthetic diet demonstrate diarrhea, but this usually is quite mild. It is desirable from the nutritional standpoint for the patient to take all his formula each day, but if he is unable to do so owing to the taste or to anorexia, no serious harm will be done as long as hydration is maintained.

The synthetic diet is served for three to seven days, depending on the patient's response, though it is difficult for many to stay on the formula for longer than three or four days. As soon as clearing of symptoms occurs or a satisfactory baseline of symptoms is established, additions can be started. It is advisable to continue, when possible, smaller amounts of the synthetic formula while the patient is receiving only a few foods. Debilitated or critically ill persons should not be subjected to the rigors of a synthetic diet until a diet is devised that is completely palatable.

Ingestion Tests. The allergenicity of individual foods may be evaluated by ingestion tests carried out under controlled conditions. The patient is advised to eat, in addition to his regular diet, average amounts of the particular food in question up until four days before the test is to be performed. The significance of a four day avoidance interval has been stated elsewhere (page 200). The patient, in a fasting state, reports to the physician's office in the morning and is served a moderate portion of the food to be studied. If no reaction occurs within 30 minutes, another helping is given. Notice is taken of any allergic signs or symptoms before the test is started and for several hours afterward. Further records should be kept by the patient for 24 to 48 hours following his return home. Some individuals have definite preformed opinions regarding their allergy to certain foods, and this may influence the results of the test. Thus, sometimes it is helpful to give the food in a disguised form; for example, if it is known that a person can tolerate white potato, the test food may be incorporated in mashed potato and fed to the patient without his knowledge. Flavor can be disguised by adding spices or flavoring (e.g., peppermint). It also is of value to carry out control tests and "placebo feedings" which are similar in appearance to food preparations which seem to cause allergic symptoms.[6] In rare instances, largely for academic reasons, the test food could be given by gavage. Since it is not practical to carry out ingestion tests with every item in a diet or every patient, they commonly are reserved for cases where it is especially desirable to verify the patient's observations. We do not use them routinely.

Other Diagnostic Procedures. A different type of *provocative food testing* has been suggested relatively recently. This involved attempting to induce allergic symptoms soon after the intradermal injection of relatively concentrated food extracts. If a reaction occurs, it is claimed that it can be relieved promptly by a further intradermal injection of the same extract in higher dilution. The validity of these observations awaits confirmation by blind tests. A much older technique, the *leukopenic index,* was used to evaluate possible food allergy on the basis of the decrease in peripheral blood leukocytes after ingestion of the food in question. Although there is no doubt that the white cell count sometimes changes after eating, the consensus is that this response is not a reliable index of immunologic food hypersensitivity. The same statement applies to changes in the *pulse rate* after food ingestion.

It is obvious that better means of evaluating food allergy are needed. Current methods are largely subjective and cumbersome. Modern, objective, in vitro immunologic techniques have been applied to the milk allergy problem. The sera of many children contain antibodies to various milk proteins as shown by precipitin, complement fixation, and passive hemagglutination techniques. However, the clinical significance of these antibodies is obscure, since the majority of these patients have no symptoms after drinking milk,[7] and these antibodies occur in normal as well as atopic persons. It is of interest, however, that significantly more allergic adults have circulating antibodies to bovine serum albumin, as measured by the Farr Test, than do nonallergic subjects, even though the antibodies being detected are not skin-sensitizing antibodies and the allergic subjects were not clinically sensitive to milk.[8]

Treatment of Food Allergy

The treatment of food allergy consists of partial or complete elimination from the diet of those foods to which the patient has been found to be clinically sensitive. There is a quantitative factor in the tolerance of a patient for each food to which he is sensitized. Some items may have to be removed absolutely, while others will be harmless if taken in moderate amounts. Complete avoidance of an allergenic food substance is easy to achieve only when it is relatively uncommon in the diet. The duration of this abstinence varies considerably. In contrast with inhalant allergies, which usually are relatively permanent, food sensitivities sometimes are transient and may be lost after an avoidance period of weeks or months. Thus, when an important substance is involved, the patient should be advised to re-check his sensitivity to that food allergen perhaps every three months. After a few ingestion trials he may find that he can tolerate at least moderate amounts of the food in question. Only by such trial can it be determined which foods must remain completely out of the diet and which can be taken in small amounts. However, after an item is returned to the diet, clinical sensitivity to it may return. Also, as some food allergies are lost, new ones may develop. For this reason, if a patient's symptoms return after a period of relief, it may be necessary to re-evaluate his entire diet.

Hidden Food Sources. Although the elimination of allergenic foods per se usually is easy, difficulty may arise in a patient highly sensitive to one or more major foods such as milk, wheat, or eggs. These items are incorporated in so many diverse food products that without special instruction the patient is likely to eat them unintentionally. Lists of sources of major foods may be obtained by physicians from the Ralston Purina Company.* These diet sheets are very helpful to patients who must avoid milk, wheat, or eggs, and they also provide a guide to adequate nutrition in spite of this restriction.†

General Nutrition and Food Substitutes. The effect of a food's complete removal always should be weighed against the severity of the patient's symptoms before it is taken from the diet. Sometimes it is better to allow a baby to have mild eczema or nasal stuffiness than to deprive him of such necessary foods as milk or cereals. The total effect

---

* St. Louis 2, Missouri.

† A group of parents of food allergic patients have formed a nonprofit organization whose purpose it is to disseminate information regarding the exact composition of foods, recipes, and cooking substitutes. Address: Allergy Information, 5 Moford Cres., Weston, Ontario, Canada.

on the child's over-all health should be the determining factor in making such decisions. When the degree of sensitivity is sufficient to warrant complete elimination of whole cow's milk, substitutes should be tried. One of the modified forms of milk may be tolerated in some cases. Considerable evidence has accumulated to show that of the protein fractions of milk—casein, lactalbumin, and lactoglobulin—all are antigenic in animals and man, though many patients are clinically sensitive only to one.[9] While casein is relatively heat-stable, lactalbumin and the globulins are considerably heat-labile.[10] Patients sensitive to the latter two fractions might tolerate heated milk formulations better (e.g., evaporated or boiled milk).[1] The caseins of various mammalian milks are quite similar, if not identical, but there is a difference in the whey proteins. Thus, patients sensitive to the latter may not have difficulty from goat's milk,* for example.

If milk allergy is pronounced, however, it may be necessary to have the patient omit all forms of mammalian milk. In these cases, soybean milks (Mull-Soy,† So-Bee,‡ or Soyalac§) or homogenized meat milks,|| made up of individual types of meats, are preferred. Nutramigen could be substituted in infant feeding. Evaporated milk always should be tried first in such cases, however, since it may be quite well tolerated. If this fails, boiled cow's milk or goat's milk might be tried. If milk or other essential foods are withdrawn from the diet, calcium and vitamin supplements (especially riboflavin) should be prescribed as indicated. Adequate protein intake should be assured. A dietician can be of great help in recommending substitutes and in checking for the nutritional acceptability of the final diet which is advised for the patient.

Rotating Diets. In unusual cases in which sensitivities to so many major foods exist that their elimination is next to impossible, a rotating diet may be tried. If the patient is only moderately clinically allergic to these foods, such a procedure may enable him to tolerate occasional exposure to the allergens with less severe reactions.

Hyposensitization to Foods and Other Methods of Treatment for Food Allergy. There is general agreement that parenteral injection of extracts is unsuccessful in treating food allergy. Oral "hyposensitization" occasionally is employed. There is no harm in trying this, but its effectiveness is open to question. It is done simply by starting with a minute amount of the food in question and doubling the amount given daily. However, simple avoidance for an equal period of time might well provide a similar increase in ability to ingest the food without allergic symptoms.

---

* Goat's milk and literature on its use may be obtained from Jackson-Mitchell Pharmaceuticals, Inc., Los Angeles 64, California.
  † Obtained from the Borden Company, 350 Madison Ave., New York 17, New York.
  ‡ Made by Mead, Johnson & Company, Evansville 21, Indiana.
  § From Loma Linda Food Company, Mt. Vernon, Ohio.
  || Armour and Company, Chicago, and several baby food manufacturers make meat milks of beef, lamb, and other animal meat.

An inhalant allergy to food protein is seen in so-called "bakers' asthma," which usually is manifested as attacks of wheezing and dyspnea associated with wheat flour (although other cereal flours have been observed to cause trouble). The sensitivity is rather obvious to the patient, and he usually improves when he avoids this exposure. Such persons almost always show good positive skin test reactions to the cereals. It is sometimes impossible for bakers, cooks, and others who prepare food to stay away from flour. Here is the one instance in which hyposensitization to a food is justified.

Dietary Supplements and Instructions

When it is found that a patient is sensitive to eggs, milk, wheat, or some other food, it may be necessary for him to avoid that food for a period of time. One can help by suggesting recipes or sources of foods which are permitted.

Where to Buy Dietetic Food. The physician can, by writing to National Dietary Foods Association,* obtain the names of grocers in his vicinity who handle dietetic foods. If there are no nearby suppliers of such foods, the following sources are available:

Chicago Dietetic Supply House, Inc.
1750 W. VanBuren St.
Chicago 12, Illinois
Ralston Purina
Checkerboard Square
St. Louis, Missouri

General Instructions to Patients. When foods are purchased, all labels on canned goods should be read carefully to be sure that the ingredients are permitted in the diet. Particular attention must be paid to types of flour and shortenings used and whether eggs and milk are present. When recipes are being used, the ingredients should be reviewed.

It should be explained to the patient that it is almost impossible to make *bread* without wheat. Biscuits, cookies, and muffins, however, may be made from substitute flours.

Special Foods Available. The following special foods are available:
1. Evaporated goat's milk. This is suitable as a milk substitute only when it is definitely shown that sensitivity to milk does not also include sensitivity to goat's milk.
2. Canned rye bread. It's a good bread substitute for wheat-sensitive patients. (A source is Chicago Dietetic Supply House.)
3. Rye flour. This is the only flour other than wheat which contains enough gluten to make a yeast-raised bread.
4. Rice biscuits. These can be used as bread substitutes for wheat-sensitive patients. They can also be eaten while on initial allergy

---

* Cincinnati, Ohio 45224.

diet No 1. (They can be obtained from Chicago Dietetic Supply House.)

5. Rice flour. This is best when used combined with milk or eggs. It is unsatisfactory when used alone in baking.

6. Soybean flour. By itself, it is a poor flour for baking. It should be mixed with potato starch flour, in order to make baked goods lighter. (Use one-third soy and two-thirds potato starch flour.)

7. Potato starch flour. This makes fair biscuits when mixed with soybean flour.

8. Barley flour. This flour has a mild flavor, is light in color, and yields smooth-textured products.

9. Oat flour. It is agreeable to taste and makes fair cookies and muffins.

10. Tapioca, arrowroot, and corn flour. These make such solid baked food that they are not recommended.

Baking Instructions and Recipes. Only the type of shortening allowed should be used.* Cereal-free and egg-free baking powder ought to be used when indicated. When milk is not allowed, a milk substitute, such as water or fruit juice, should be employed for liquid in the recipe. When eggs are allowed it is well to use them in muffins, cakes, and cookies for best results. Brown sugar, maple sugar, molasses, spices, and grated orange or lemon peel add a variety of flavor.

Baked products made from flours other than wheat have different physical characteristics and require longer and lower baking temperature, particularly when made without eggs and milk. The outside crust will be harder and the product tends to dry out more quickly. Only small quantities should be made and stored carefully for use.

All flours other than wheat and rye need to be made into "quick breads" using baking powder as a leavening agent. When eggs are not allowed, most of the baked goods need to be on the order of baking powder biscuits or pie-crust type of dough. If corn starch is permitted, it is possible to substitute rye flour for wheat flour if one includes 3 teaspoonfuls corn starch in each cup of sifted rye flour, as called for in the recipe for cakes. In cookies and biscuits, 2 teaspoonfuls corn starch in each cup of rye flour may be used. A particularly successful recipe for bread made without wheat, milk, or egg, is as follows:

RYE BREAD (2 Loaves)

Follow recipe closely, and be sure to bake it long enough.

3 pkg. active dry yeast	1 cup boiling water
¼ cup lukewarm water	¾ cup cold water
½ cup brown sugar, packed	5¼ cups sifted rye flour
3 tbs. Melted Shortening	5¼ tsp. corn starch
1 tbs. salt	6 tsp. baking powder (2 tbs.)
½ tsp. nutmeg	

Soften yeast in warm water.

---

* Hydrogenated baking shortenings are allergen-free, but margarines may contain milk (except Kosher oleomargarine).

In large bowl, combine brown sugar, shortening, salt, and boiling water. Stir to dissolve sugar. Add cold water. Cool to lukewarm. Stir in yeast. Beat with electric beaters to blend well. Beat in ½ of sifted dry ingredients. Then, stir in remainder of ingredients by hand.* Smooth surface as well as you can. Cover with towel and put in warm place for an hour or until doubled in bulk.

With heavy spoon stir 25 times. Then, divide dough into 2 well-greased bread pans. Place in warm spot, again covered with towel for another hour or until again doubled in bulk Bake at 350° F. for 50 to 60 minutes.

RYE YEAST BREAD (If milk and egg are permitted)

1 cup scalded milk	2 tsp. salt
1 cup boiling water	½ cake yeast dissolved in ¼ cup lukewarm water
2 tbs. shortening	
2 tbs. sugar	6 cups Cellu Rye Flour†

To milk and water add shortening, sugar, and salt; when lukewarm add dissolved yeast cake and enough flour to make a soft dough, beat thoroughly, cover, and place in warm place to rise. Add the flour until the dough is stiff enough to knead; more flour may be necessary to handle dough well. Knead well, shape in loaves, let rise until double its size, and bake in a 375° oven for about 50 minutes.

Menus and Special Recipes for Specific Diets. Rather than printing lists of diets and recipes on these pages, we refer the reader to the professional service departments of the Chicago Dietetic Supply House or the Ralston Purina Company (addresses on page 219). These companies will send pamphlets of diets and suggested receipes which permit preparation of foods without using milk, eggs, wheat, or combinations of these. They are very helpful in instructing the patient how to live on a restricted diet.

GASTROINTESTINAL ALLERGY

Gastrointestinal allergy includes those disorders of the gastrointestinal tract which are caused by antigen-antibody reactions. The offending allergen most often is a food, but there are instances in which drugs, inhalants, and injectants have produced gastrointestinal symptoms on an allergic basis. All food intolerances are not indicative of a state of gastrointestinal allergy. Certain persons may develop nonallergic symptoms from ingestion of various foods. Intolerance to cabbage, raw onions, or greasy foods is a common example of this. Estimates of the incidence of true gastrointestinal allergy vary widely among different authorities. It is logical that the gastrointestinal tract should be involved in allergic reactions, since it includes both a large epithelial surface (like the skin and respiratory tree) and much smooth muscle. Gray, Harten, and Walzer showed many years ago that passive transfer sites on the gastrointestinal mucosa will react to administration of antigen in the same manner as does the skin.[11]

---

* Put into large greased bowl and turn to grease sides.

† Use 1 cup potato flour, 5 cups rye flour, 1 egg, 3 tbs. butter, and 1 cake of yeast if potato is also tolerated.

Gastrointestinal allergy manifests itself in two different types of syndromes. One is the immediate reaction which occurs within minutes or even seconds after exposure to the offending substance. Certain foods such as nuts, seafoods, and berries are especially apt to produce this type of reaction. The gastrointestinal symptoms frequently are accompanied by urticaria in this type of case. The other type of reaction is a delayed one in which the symptoms come on less abruptly a number of hours after the antigen is taken. Milk and cereals are apt to produce this kind of difficulty.

Symptoms

The symptoms of gastrointestinal allergy are protean and indeed include practically every imaginable gastrointestinal complaint. It is to be emphasized, however, that not one of these symptoms is specific for gastrointestinal allergy, thus creating a difficult problem in differential diagnosis. Some of the possible manifestations of this disease are as follows: cheilitis due to contact hypersensitivity; angioneurotic edema of the lips, palate, or other parts of the gastrointestinal tract; and contact stomatitis to such things as dentures. There also may be an allergic factor in some cases of recurrent canker sores or aphthous stomatitis. The oral mucous membranes may be involved in eruptions from drugs, particularly of the erythema multiforme type. There may be itching and edema of the soft palate and uvula so often seen in association with hay fever; edema and spasm of the esophagus; upper abdominal symptoms, such as nausea, dyspepsia, vomiting, cramping epigastric pain, gaseous eructations, and the like—many of these symptoms probably being due to pylorospasm; right upper-quadrant pain and associated symptoms suggestive of biliary tract disease; lower abdominal complaints, such as cramping pain, diarrhea, constipation, and excess mucus in the stool (possibly some instances of infantile colic); rare cases of acute abdominal pain suggestive of a "surgical abdomen"; and some cases of pruritus ani.

Diagnosis

1. The *history,* as previously mentioned, reveals nothing characteristic for gastrointestinal allergy. However, this possibility should receive consideration in patients complaining of chronic, recurrent gastrointestinal symptoms not explainable by other means, particularly if the patient suspects certain foods, if the symptoms are worse after meals, or if there is a history of collateral or familial allergy. The type and number of foods suspected also give a helpful clue.

2. The *physical examination* often is not helpful except in patients with oral lesions, but evidence of collateral allergy, such as a boggy nasal mucosa, may give a valuable lead.

3. The *routine laboratory studies* usually show no abnormality, a

normal stool being especially important in excluding other diseases. A very high peripheral blood eosinophilia would be more suggestive of a parasitic infection than of allergy to food.

4. Reactions to *skin tests* are usually positive for the offending allergen in cases of the immediate, acute type of gastrointestinal allergy, but they often are negative in the chronic, delayed types. Skin tests also would be of value in those rare cases in which inhalant factors seem to be responsible for gastrointestinal allergy.

5. *Sigmoidoscopy* presents no picture diagnostic of gastrointestinal allergy.

6. *Gastroscopy* may show definite changes after the administration of a food allergen.[12] These changes consist of hyperemia, edema, and thickening of the rugal folds together with diminished peristalsis and grayish mucus clinging to the mucosa. Submucosal hemorrhages may also occur. The changes are most prominent in the lower third of the stomach. A control gastroscopy should be performed before administering the suspected food.

7. Routine *gastrointestinal roentgenograms* usually show no abnormality. However, if the studies are repeated with the suspected food admixed with the barium, definite abnormalities often may be demonstrated (page 42).

8. The *effect of antihistamine drugs* on the patient's symptoms has some diagnostic value if interpreted properly. It is thought that almost 50 per cent of patients with gastrointestinal allergy are benefited by antihistamines. However, some of the therapeutic effects of these drugs may be due to their atropine-like properties or sedative effects rather than to their antihistaminic activity. Hence, for diagnostic significance the patient must be helped by the antihistamines but not by belladonna and its related compounds or by sedatives. Failure to respond to a placebo antihistamine would give added weight to a response to the antihistamine drug itself.

9. Various types of *dietary manipulation* form the backbone of the diagnostic studies in most cases of gastrointestinal allergy, since most of the above-mentioned procedures are too expensive and time-consuming to be performed repeatedly in order to test every item in the patient's diet. Depending on various factors discussed in the first section of this chapter, a diet diary, elimination diet, or ingestion tests could be used.

It is apparent from the foregoing that there is a great need for additional objective but practical means of identifying the causative agents in cases of gastrointestinal allergy.

Differential Diagnosis

Because of its extremely varied manifestations, gastrointestinal allergy must be differentiated from virtually all other diseases of the gastrointestinal tract. It is a grave error to make haphazard diagnoses of gastrointestinal allergy without first having carefully excluded other organic gastrointestinal pathologic states. Particularly in relatively acute cases in which the possibility of some urgent surgical condition exists, sound over-all medical judgment is most important. When in doubt, it probably is best to err on the side of discarding rather than accepting the diagnosis of gastrointestinal allergy. It is also an unfortunate mistake to attribute functional gastrointestinal symptoms to allergy. Victims of such an error are apt to develop a fixation on food allergies, follow freakish diets, and become very difficult patients later on when the allergy program fails to give relief.

There has been particular interest in the possible role of allergy in causing chronic ulcerative colitis. Various types of inflammatory reactions can be induced by antigens in the colonic mucosa of sensitized animals, and acute allergic reactions have been elicited in human colonic mucosa by the injection of allergens. Nevertheless, there is a strong consensus that chronic ulcerative colitis rarely, if ever, is primarily due to extrinsic allergy. There also are doubts about the pathogenetic significance of the anticolon antibodies which can be demonstrated in the serum of many patients. Currently, there is major interest in the possibility that a delayed type of autosensitivity to colonic antigens might be significant.[13] Possible autosensitivity is also being evaluated in aphthous stomatitis,[14] gastritis, chronic pancreatitis, and in some types of cirrhosis (see Chapter 19).

Treatment

The treatment for gastrointestinal allergy usually is simple and consists of elimination of the offending substance or substances from the patient's diet or environment. When multiple or major food allergies are present, the use of rotating diets or food substitutes may be helpful (see first section of this chapter). Appropriate vitamin or mineral supplements are indicated when their major sources are eliminated from the diet. Since food allergy may be lost after a period of avoidance of the offending items, the patient's tolerance to the interdicted foods should be re-checked periodically. Antispasmodics, antihistamines, and sympathomimetic amines may be used as required for symptomatic relief.

REFERENCES

1. Goldman, A. S., Anderson, D. W., Sellers, W. A., Saperstein, S., Kniker, W. T., Halpern, S. R., and collaborators: Milk allergy, 1. Oral challenge with milk and isolated milk proteins in allergic children. Pediatrics 32:425, 1963.
2. Rinkel, H. J., Randolph, T. G., and Zeller, M.: Food Allergy. p. 6, Springfield, Ill., Charles C Thomas, 1951.
3. Fries, J. H.: Factors influencing clinical evaluation of food allergy. Pediat. Clin. North America 6:873, 1959.

4. Ancona, C. R., and Schumacher, T. C.: The use of raw foods as skin testing material in allergic disorders. Calif. Med. *73:*476, 1950.

5. Hale, R.: Seeds as a source of food testing material, Ann. Allergy *18:*270, 1960.

6. Loveless, M. H.: Allergy for corn and its derivatives: experiments with a masked ingestion test for its diagnosis. J. Allergy *21:*500, 1950.

7. Peterson, R. D. A., and Good, R. A.: Antibodies to cow's milk proteins—their presence and significance. Pediatrics *31:*209, 1963.

8. Barrick, R. H., and Farr, R. S.: The increased incidence of circulating anti-beef albumin in the sera of allergic persons and some comments regarding the possible significance of this occurrence. J. Allergy *36:*374, 1965.

9. Dees, S. C.: Allergy to cow's milk. Pediat. Clin. North America *6:*890, 1959.

10. Hill, L. W.: Immunologic relationship between cow's milk and goat's milk. J. Pediatrics *15:*157, 1939.

11. Gray, I., Harten, M., and Walzer, M.: Studies in mucous membrane hypersensitiveness. IV. The allergic reaction in the passively sensitized mucous membranes of the ileum and colon in humans. Ann. Int. Med. *13:*2050, 1940.

12. Pollard, H. M., and Stuart, G. J.: Experimental reproduction of gastric allergy in human beings with controlled observations on the mucosa. J. Allergy *13:*467, 1942.

13. Perlmann, P., and Broberger, O.: Cytotoxic actions of white blood cells from patients on human fetal colon cells. J. Exper. Med. *117:*717, 1963.

14. Lehner, T.: Recurrent aphthous ulceration and autoimmunity. Lancet *2:*1154, 1964.

Chapter Eleven

DERMATOLOGIC ASPECTS OF ALLERGY PRACTICE

The three conditions of the skin which confront the allergist most frequently are atopic dermatitis (including infantile and juvenile eczema), urticaria (together with angioneurotic edema), and allergic contact dermatitis. In addition, hypersensitivity probably is involved in many cutaneous drug eruptions, erythema multiforme, erythema nodosum, photoallergic reactions, allergic granulomas, allergic purpuras, "id" reactions, and several of the cutaneous manifestations of infectious diseases and connective tissue disorders. No attempt is made here to discuss fully these numerous diseases. Complete descriptions of them may be found in the standard texts on dermatology and allergy. In the following brief summary, emphasis is placed on the allergic aspects of these skin conditions. Some of the main contrasting features of the most common cutaneous diseases seen by the allergist are shown in Table 11–1.

ATOPIC DERMATITIS

Atopic dermatitis (atopic eczema) is a chronic eczematoid skin eruption involving principally the flexural surfaces and occurring chiefly in the earlier years of life. Inflammatory changes are present in the dermis, and the epidermis shows cellular and intercellular edema (spongiosis). In more chronic stages the epidermis shows hyperkeratosis, parakeratosis, and acanthosis. The inflammatory reaction, together with secondary changes due to scratching, may lead to a variety of skin abnormalities: erythema, whealing, papules, weeping, lichenification, scaling, and pigmentation.

There are three forms of atopic dermatitis: infantile eczema,* juvenile eczema, and the adult type of eczema. Although infantile atopic eczema differs from the others in certain respects (see page 229), there are good reasons for believing that these three conditions are simply phases of

---

* The term atopic dermatitis is preferable to "eczema," since the latter simply is a descriptive term which could be applicable to a variety of skin diseases. However, "eczema" is so commonly used to refer to the particular type of dermatitis being discussed that this term will be retained here in this context.

Table 11–1. Some Cutaneous Diseases Seen in Allergy Practice

	Atopic Dermatitis	Urticaria	Contact Dermatitis
Lesion: early	Erythema, papule	Wheal, with surrounding flare	Erythema, vesicle
late	Lichenification	None	Eczematization
Reaction times	Variable	Rapid—minutes to a few hours	Usually 18 hours or more
Site of predilection	Face, neck, antecubital and popliteal spaces, upper thorax, and wrists	Generalized or pressure areas	Anywhere—more often on exposed areas
Causative substances	(See discussion.)	Foods, drugs, etc. (See discussion.)	Simple chemicals
Age at onset	Infancy to 25 years; occasionally later	Any age, but more often 3rd and 4th decades	Any age, but usually in adults
Prognosis	Variable; excellent in infants, less hopeful in adults	Good	Excellent

the same disease process. Though it is still a relatively common disease, it is noteworthy that at Boston Children's Hospital there has been a decrease in the number of patients seen yearly with infantile eczema from an average of 435 in the period from 1930 to 1935 to only 52 in 1959.[1] Eczema commonly begins in infancy when the child is three to six months of age but infrequently starts before two or three months. Most of these babies experience complete clearing of their skin by the time they are two or three years old even without any vigorous treatment. However, in some cases the lesions persist until the child is four or five years of age. An even smaller group of patients continues to have eczema throughout childhood. At about the time of puberty eczema may flare up or go into remission. Or, the condition may develop at this age for the first time. During adolescence, eczema often is more persistent than during infancy, but it may disappear in a few years. Flare-ups may occur in the 18 to 21 year period, and the disease may persist in a form very refractory to treatment for decades during the middle years of life. Although most adults with eczema also had the condition in infancy or adolescence, sometimes the disease may make its first appearance in individuals 18 to 20 years of age but rarely over 30 years of age. When it appears in adults, the diagnosis is usually less definite and the pattern atypical.

Diagnosis

The diagnosis of atopic dermatitis is based on the history and physical examination. The history usually reveals a chronic skin disease having its onset or exacerbations in infancy or adolescence as discussed in the foregoing paragraph. Pruritus almost always is present and may be intense. In more than 50 per cent of the older patients one can elicit symptoms suggestive of other allergic diseases. Often the family history reveals the presence of allergic disease.

Examination in the early or acute phases of the condition reveals edema, papules, and diffuse erythema of the skin. Weeping occurs when the disease process becomes more severe. Linear excoriations may be present as a result of scratching. Lichenification of the skin usually develops later, and there also may be residual pigmentation. Scaling is prominent in the more inactive, dry stages of the lesions. Perhaps because of persistent rubbing and scratching, patients with eczema often have rather sparse eyebrows; in some, the lateral portions are entirely rubbed off. The lower eyelid may show a fold of skin extending laterally and downward from the inner canthus. The fingernails usually have a

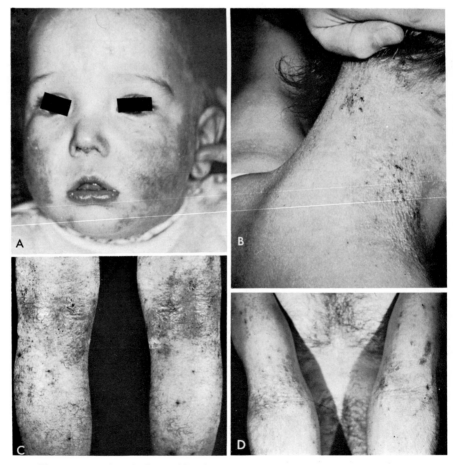

Figure 11–1. Atopic dermatitis. *A,* Erythematous maculopapular lesions often appear first on the cheeks of infants. *B,* In young adults, there is often a scaling collar-like involvement of the neck. *C,* Characteristic erythematous patches appear in popliteal and, *D,* antecubital fossae.

glossy sheen caused by the buffing action which accompanies frequent rubbing. In adults and children the sites of predilection of the skin lesions are the flexural surfaces of the elbows and knees as well as the dorsal surface of the wrist (over the styloid process of the radius) and the ankles (Figure 11–1). The neck, forehead, and face also are frequently involved, and often the dermatitis extends down over the upper part of the chest and back. The lesions, which usually are symmetrically distributed, seldom occur on the abdomen and lower back. In infants, the picture often is somewhat different from that just described. The cheeks frequently are involved first. Later the dermatitis may become quite extensive, but the face, neck, and extensor surfaces of the extremities are affected more often than the trunk or abdomen. In children the lymph nodes often are enlarged.

There are no specific laboratory tests for atopic dermatitis. Peripheral blood eosinophilia is usual. Leukocytosis is present if there is secondary infection. In this case, cultures of the skin should be obtained. Most often these yield *Staphylococcus aureus*. Serum protein electrophoresis and immunoelectrophoresis usually give normal results.

Differential Diagnosis

Usually the diagnosis of atopic dermatitis is relatively easy to make, but there are certain other skin conditions which at times may be mistaken for it. Even more confusing is the fact that atopic dermatitis may co-exist with some of these other skin diseases (especially seborrheic and contact dermatitis). *Seborrheic dermatitis* is especially apt to be confused with infantile eczema. However, the scales from seborrheic skin usually are greasy rather than dry. The lesions are most prominent in the scalp, at the hairline, and about the ears, but they may extend to the eyelids, axillae, upper chest, and pubic area. In rare cases the whole body may be involved. Severe seborrheic dermatitis in infants can be accompanied by constitutional symptoms. The "cradle cap" of infancy is a manifestation of seborrheic dermatitis, and some pediatric allergists feel that infants with this condition are predisposed to atopic dermatitis. In young children it also is important to make certain that the eczema is not a manifestation of agammaglobulinemia, phenylketonuria, or Aldrich's syndrome. Nummular eczema consists of sharply demarcated areas of scaling dermatitis occurring especially in the vicinity of the wrists.

Contact dermatitis is discussed at length in a later part of this chapter, and some of the contrasting features of atopic and contact dermatitis are presented in Table 11–1. The distribution of the lesions is an especially helpful point of distinction. However, persons with atopic dermatitis may develop secondary contact sensitivities, especially to various ointments which they have applied topically. Patients with contact dermatitis also may have an "absorption spread" to the flexural surfaces which somewhat resembles atopic dermatitis. The absorption phenomenon also occurs in nonallergic skin conditions and clears with treatment of the primary disease.

Although the character and distribution of the lesions of _disseminated neurodermatitis_ resemble atopic dermatitis, the skin areas involved in the former condition often are more extensive and may include the extensor surfaces. Neurodermatitis is most severe in those areas easily accessible to scratching. Patients with this disease often are meticulous, tense, and agitated, and it is believed that these factors contribute importantly to the condition. It commonly occurs in an older age group than does atopic dermatitis. Some of the _cutaneous lymphoblastomas_ may present a picture resembling that of atopic dermatitis in certain stages of their development. The "premycotic" lesions of mycosis fungoides and some cases of leukemia cutis are especially apt to fall into this category. The pruritus associated with these conditions may lead to secondary skin changes similar to those seen in atopic dermatitis. Cutaneous lymphoblastoma usually occurs in older persons than does atopic dermatitis, and sooner or later other physical signs and laboratory evidences of the malignant process will appear. One should not hesitate to obtain a skin biopsy whenever there is any question of this disease being present.

Pathogenesis of Atopic Dermatitis

The etiology and pathogenesis of atopic dermatitis are so unclear at present that discussion focused on this topic was not even attempted at a recent national conference on infantile atopic eczema.[2] In accordance with its name, there are cogent reasons for believing there is some type of relationship between this disease and atopic hypersensitivity: (1) There unquestionably is a strong correlation between the occurrence of atopic dermatitis and a personal or family history of asthma or hay fever. Several studies have shown that half the children who have had atopic dermatitis will develop respiratory allergy even before they reach ten years of age. (2) These patients usually give many strongly positive reactions on skin testing. (3) In at least some patients, infantile eczema, in particular, flares up after eating certain foods, especially egg (but see text following). Exacerbations of atopic dermatitis also have been noted after experimental challenge by inhalants. (4) It is well known that eczema is readily exacerbated following hyposensitization injections with allergenic extracts unless one is careful to start with relatively low doses.

In spite of the evidence cited for some type of connection between atopic dermatitis and hypersensitivity to various allergens, there are strong arguments which indicate that a simple, direct, causal relationship does not pertain here: (1) On a priori grounds, one would not expect atopic dermatitis to represent an immediate type hypersensitivity lesion in view of its microscopic pathology. Urticaria is the cutaneous expression of immediate type hypersensitivity. Some have suggested that delayed hypersensitivity is involved, but this is not generally accepted and would not explain the relationship to atopy. (2) When one gives a food producing a strongly positive skin test reaction to a child with eczema, urticaria is more likely to be observed than eczema.[3] It also is stated that one cannot induce new areas of atopic dermatitis by this procedure, though pre-existing lesions may flare up.[4] (3) In some experiments on reproducing eczema by foods, it was observed that bandaged areas did not flare up, while lesions accessible to scratching became worse.[4] In general, atopic dermatitis improves when scratching can be prevented. (4) Lesions rather similar to atopic dermatitis occur with unusual frequency in children with agammaglobulinemia. Yet, in these cases, immediate type skin test reactions are negative, and one cannot induce skin-sensitizing antibodies to Ascaris antigen (as can be done in normal individuals). (5) Empirically, most would agree that results in treating patients with atopic dermatitis primarily by an immunologic approach are less satisfactory than, for example, those obtained in treating patients with hay fever.

Many years ago, Hill referred to an X-factor in the relationship between atopic hypersensitivity and the skin lesions of atopic dermatitis, and it is evident from the preceding paragraphs that this factor remains an enigma.[5] Some of the available information suggests that allergens may produce pruritus in these patients with or without urticaria. The resultant scratching then may produce the eczematous response in the skin. Thus, the atopic allergy would be an indirect cause of the eczematous lesions. Of course, there may be other, unknown interrelationships of either direct or indirect type. In any case, any other factors causing pruritus and scratching also would precipitate or aggravate the disease. Undoubtedly this is an oversimplified explanation for what may be some complex interrelationships. Nevertheless, this may be an operationally useful concept for approaching these patients until a more adequate basic understanding of atopic dermatitis is achieved.

Regardless of what the exact role of allergy may be, undoubtedly a number of other factors are very important in producing, aggravating, or perpetuating the lesions of atopic eczema, though it is noteworthy that different authorities give varying emphasis to the relative importance of these several factors.[6] Eczema patients have been shown to have a low threshold of tolerance for itching.[7] As previously mentioned, the consequent tendency to scratch and rub the skin is very important. Often the skin is dry, sometimes ichthyotic, and this predisposes to itching. There also appears to be a tendency to lichenification. Disturbances in sweating may be present. Skin *irritants* such as wool clothing aggravate atopic dermatitis. The skin often gets worse during periods of emotional stress, perhaps because of increased scratching. Superimposed *infection* of the skin lesions is a major cause of exacerbations of the disease.

There also is evidence of a cutaneous *vascular abnormality* in these patients. It has long been known that stroking their skins produces a white line at the site of pressure (white dermographism) rather than the usual red line. This is due to an abnormal vasoconstriction at the site of trauma. Likewise, these patients show an abnormal "delayed blanch" surrounding the sites of intracutaneous methacholine injections (0.1 ml. of 1:1000 solution) after three to ten minutes. Acetylcholine, nicotinic acid esters and nicotinamide produce similar responses. These abnormalities are not specific for atopic dermatitis, but they are most commonly observed in this disease. Atopic persons without dermatitis and relatives of atopic persons also may demonstrate this phenomenon, but observations along these lines have given somewhat variable results.[8] Environmental temperature change also causes an exaggerated cutaneous temperature response in patients with atopic dermatitis. They also may have abnormal cold pressor responses, a pale face, and a decreased flare surrounding intracutaneous histamine injections.

It has been reported that the norepinephrine content of uninvolved skin of patients with atopic dermatitis is abnormally elevated, while blood levels of this amine are below normal.[9] These observations require confirmation, however, and it is possible that the cutaneous vasoconstrictive tendency shown by these patients simply may represent compensatory vascular reflexes in a patient with dermatitis. Atopic skin also has been reported to have an increased content of acetycholine and histamine, the latter associated with increased numbers of mast cells.[10] The possibility of a *metabolic* factor in this disease is raised by the production of eczematous lesions in young infants on histadine-free diets[11] and the presence of eczema in patients with phenylketonuria. Current investigations also involve exploration of possible autoimmune mechanisms. As in a few other diseases, patients with atopic dermatitis give skin test reactions with autologous leukocytes. It is also reported that tissue cultures of lymphocytes taken from these patients are stimulated by extracts of human epithelium.[12] This requires confirmation because, utilizing some other techniques, this approach was abandoned after receiving some attention in the past. Explanation of the frequent occurrence of eczema in agammaglobulinemia and its coincidence with increased susceptibility to infections, thrombocytopenia, and increased levels of I_gA in Aldrich's syndrome constitute a major challenge to the immunologically oriented investigator.[13]

Allergy Study of Patients With Atopic Dermatitis

In view of the foregoing discussion, it is obviously impossible in the present state of knowledge to make dogmatic·recommendations on this subject. Whereas it is clear that factors other than allergy are important in these cases, it also appears to be incorrect to ignore allergy altogether as a possible direct or indirect precipitating factor in this disease. At the least, an allergy history (Chapter 3) appears to be indicated. In interpreting the history, it should be noted that worsening of the disease during the winter may be due to excessive dryness of the skin at that time rather than to some household allergen, such as house dust; likewise, aggravation in the summer may be due to warmth and sweating rather than seasonal pollen or mold allergy. In infants, particular attention should be paid to the relationship of the eczema and the addition of new foods to the diet. How much additional allergy evaluation is warranted depends on the results of the history, the patient's age, the severity and persistence of the disease, the response to topical therapy, and whether studies for allergy have been done previously. One is most inclined to investigate infants having moderate or severe disease, especially when the history suggests a possible relationship to some food or foods. The probability is very slight that an allergy evaluation will yield information useful to the college student with mild, chronic eczema flaring mainly with emotional stress and well controlled with topical steroids. Often the severity of the disease is a major consideration. Extensive atopic eczema, especially in cases controlled only by systemic steroids, is a medical problem of major magnitude. Such patients merit attempts at control of all factors which may influence the disease.

If skin tested, patients with atopic dermatitis usually show multiple positive reactions, only a few or none of which may have any direct or indirect relationship to the patient's eczema. We mainly perform prick tests on babies, though a few intradermal tests may be done if the prick tests are negative (page 59). When the skin is extensively involved, one may resort to passive transfer tests (page 71). The main prospect for helping infants by allergy studies lies in dietary manipulation with or without antecedent skin tests (Chapter 10). If no success is achieved with a carefully carried out elimination diet in a reasonable period of time, the procedure should be terminated (page 206; unnecessarily prolonged or repeated trials of nutritionally inadequate diets are not justified. In older children or adolescents, the possibility of inhalant allergy also needs to be considered. Skin tests may help in evaluating this, but the importance of correlating the reactions with the patient's history cannot be overemphasized, especially in atopic dermatitis. Many positive reactions may correlate with the patient's concomitant respiratory allergy but not with his atopic dermatitis; other reactions may have no clinical significance whatever at the time of testing. Patch testing has been suggested by some allergists on the assumption that it produces skin lesions more closely simulating eczema, but it is unusual to obtain positive reactions by this technique. After patients are about age 21, we have found it generally impossible to correlate allergic factors with atopic dermatitis, even in patients in whom there seemed to be such a relationship in infancy. This opinion is not shared by some allergists, whereas others, particularly some dermatologists, would dismiss the entire allergy evaluation.

Treatment

In many cases, all the numerous factors which may be contributing to the eczema must be controlled before the patient's skin will clear, and the management of the patient with atopic dermatitis may indeed be very difficult. When a patient is doing very poorly at home, hospitalization should be encouraged. Not only does this facilitate trial of various types of local and symptomatic treatment under close observation and controlled conditions, but the patient also may benefit by removal from specific allergens and tensional situations in his home environment. Methods of treatment may be divided into local, symptomatic, allergic, and psychiatric.

Local Treatment. Local therapy in atopic dermatitis is carried out according to the principles governing dermatologic treatment in general.

1. Wet dressings are indicated during the acute phases of the dermatitis when weeping is present. Many solutions can be used for this purpose. Often boiled water or saline is adequate. However, there may be some advantage in using a slightly antiseptic solution such as Burow's solution (aluminum acetate) in a dilution of 1:16 to 1:40. The patient, using a rubber bulb, can add more solution as needed. Wet dressings should be removed periodically to prevent maceration of the skin, but they may be left on for eight to twelve hours at a time, if necessary. Care should be taken to keep the wet dressings warm when they are applied to large areas on infants.

2. Topical corticosteroids constitute the local therapy of choice for most cases of atopic dermatitis. Lotions are preferred on moist lesions, ointments on relatively dry skin, and creams for intermediate stages. Generally, application is two or three times a day, and this therapy is especially suitable for localized areas of eczema. The effectiveness of the applications can be increased by the intermittent use of occlusive plastic dressings. However, the skin lesions of children with atopic dermatitis usually respond rapidly to topical corticosteroids without occlusive dressings. This procedure also enhances the systemic absorption of steroid and is not recommended in the presence of infection. Commonly used preparations are: 0.5 and 0.025 per cent flurandrenalone acetonide (Cordran); 0.025 and 0.01 per cent fluocinolone acetonide (Synalar); 0.1, 0.025, and 0.01 per cent triamcinolone acetonide (Aristocort, Kenalog); 0.2 per cent betamethasone (Celestone); and numerous others. Particularly when there are fairly large areas of relatively mild dermatitis, it is more economical to prescribe the weaker strength preparations. In the presence of infection, systemic or topical antibiotic therapy should be used concomitantly (see below).

3. Of the innumerable topical applications used for acute atopic dermatitis before the advent of the corticosteroids, tar ointments are about the only ones effective enough to warrant continued consideration. Unfortunately, the crude tars seemed to be most valuable, but they are

messy to use because of their propensity to stain clothing and bed linens. Three to 5 per cent crude coal tar (e.g., Guy's or White's crude coal tar) may be applied every 12 hours. No attempt is made to remove the tar for several days. The patient or his mother should be warned that these materials will stain clothing and bed linens, and the lesions should be covered with appropriate dressings of gauze and stockinet or old sheets. When one finally wishes to remove the coal tar, it may be dabbed off with cotton pledgets soaked in olive oil, corn oil, or mineral oil. Water-soluble, nonstaining light tar preparations (e.g., 3 per cent liquor carbonis detergens) also are commercially available at relatively low cost but usually do not give as good results as crude coal tar. There also are topical preparations containing both tar and corticosteroids. Another way to apply coal tar and at the same time to relieve pruritus is to use daily baths containing liquor carbonis detergens; 30 ml. of the liquor carbonis detergens are added to a bathtub filled with water.

4. When the dermatitis is less active, an important objective of topical therapy is to keep the skin adequately lubricated, since excessive dryness is common in these patients. One very satisfactory way of accomplishing this is to take daily baths containing mineral oil with triton (contained in Alpha-Keri), 15 to 30 ml. in a tub filled with tepid water, or mineral oil with isopropyl sebacate (Domol); or cottonseed oil with a wetting agent (Lubath). These cover the skin with a thin film of the emulsified oil. Incidentally, patients should be warned that it also makes the bathtub very slippery. In addition, when the skin is very dry, a bland lubricant may be applied liberally over most of the skin surface. Simple hydrophilic ointment or a number of other preparations are used for this purpose. If the skin is very thick and scaly, 1 to 3 per cent salicylic acid in yellow petrolatum usually is an effective keratolytic agent for removing excessive scales from thickened skin.

Regardless of which local applications are used, it is best when prescribing a new type of medication to apply it only to a limited skin area at first to make certain that it is not irritating. One also should avoid overtreating with local applications. It is not uncommon for patients with atopic dermatitis to develop secondary contact sensitivities to various topical medications. This unfortunate occurrence usually can be averted by keeping the treatment simple and avoiding the local use of compounds containing mercury, sulfonamides, most antibiotic drugs, anesthetics, nitrofurans, and other substances known to be potent sensitizers.

Symptomatic Treatment

1. The patient's skin should be protected from all types of irritants. Wool should not be worn next to the skin, nor should starched collars and cuffs. Ordinary soaps should not be used. During the more acute or active stages of the disease the skin may be gently cleansed with

olive oil. Later "hypoallergic" soaps* may be used on uninvolved areas provided they are well tolerated. Prolonged wearing of sneakers or rubbers is likely to aggravate dermatitis of the feet. Participation in sports which provoke much sweating is likely to be troublesome; swimming is better tolerated. However, excessive bathing should be avoided, as it tends to dry out the skin. Means for protecting the hands from irritants are described on page 259.

2. The skin must be protected from the damaging effects of scratching. Fingernails should be trimmed very short. It may help the patient to wear mittens or stockings over his hands during the night if he scratches while asleep. The legs can be protected by wearing pajamas with feet in them. It may be necessary to restrain infants and children too young to cooperate. Ten minutes of vigorous scratching can undo the results of a week's intensive therapy. Simple elbow splints will prevent the child from scratching his face. Very restless children who rub against the sheets or the sides of the crib may be restrained by pinning the sleeves of their night clothes to the mattress cover. Although this may seem cruel, with proper attention and sedation of the child, it results in less psychic trauma than allowing him to continue to be tortured by intense pruritus from the self-perpetuated skin disease.

3. Relief of pruritus is another important objective of treatment. Not only is this necessary for the patient's comfort, but it is an essential prerequisite for the prevention of scratching.

The *antihistamines* may be very helpful in relieving pruritus. It may be wise to select one of those which generally has some sedative effect (e.g., Phenergan, Benadryl, or Decapryn), particularly for use at bedtime. Enteric-coated tablets or the longer-acting Phenergan also have an advantage for bedtime use. Antihistamines generally should not be applied topically in the form of ointments or creams, because of the not infrequent development of sensitivity to these preparations. Ordinary sedatives are of value in many cases, particularly when sleep is difficult or when there is a prominent tensional factor. Tranquilizers are often used (page 139).

Colloidal baths may afford a variable period of relief from itching. One cup of cornstarch and one cup of soda (sodium bicarbonate) are added to a tub of tepid water, or one may use a commercial preparation such as Aveeno. The patient is allowed to soak for 15 minutes twice daily. The liquor carbonis detergens or mineral oil baths mentioned above also may help to relieve itching. One should be certain that the water is not too hot or the dermatitis will be aggravated. Also, the patient should pat himself dry rather than rub vigorously with a towel. Many of the local applications discussed in the previous section also have some antipruritic effect.

4. ACTH or corticosteroids in sufficient dosage almost always pro-

---

* For example, Dermolate, Basis Soap, Lowila, Phisoderm, or Aveeno bar.

duce marked amelioration of atopic dermatitis (see Chapter 7 for details of their administration). However, a recurrence of the condition almost always takes place within a few days or weeks after discontinuing these compounds, and the dermatitis may flare up badly if the hormone is withdrawn abruptly. Thus, there seems to be little or no justification for the use of ACTH or corticosteroids in treating the average case of atopic dermatitis. In certain exceptional cases, however, a short "burst" of such treatment may be of great value in bringing severe, extensive eczema under control. Following this the skin usually can be maintained in satisfactory condition with topical corticosteroids. There are rare patients whose atopic dermatitis is so severe that it is incapacitating unless they are maintained on low doses of oral corticosteroids. Such individuals are at risk of developing any of the complications of prolonged steroid administration discussed in Chapter 7, including growth suppression in children, but at times very low, intermittent doses will suffice to control the disease.

5. Complications of atopic dermatitis should be treated as they arise. Most often these are infectious in nature, and treatment consists primarily of wet dressings and appropriate antibiotic drugs or chemotherapeutic agents.

6. Climatic change often is tried by atopic eczema patients. Frequently a sojourn in a pleasant, warm location such as Arizona or Florida results in a marked remission of the disease, particularly in patients who tend to improve in the summer. As discussed on page 28, there are many possible explanations for such a change. Specifically in atopic dermatitis, the abnormal response of the patients to temperature change might be a factor (page 232). Precautions in advising a change in climate are discussed on page 99.

Management of Allergy

When the diagnostic studies have shown that certain allergens are contributing to the difficulty, they should be eliminated from the patient's environment, if possible. With rare exceptions this can be accomplished satisfactorily in cases of sensitivity to foods, danders, vegetable gums, orris root, silk, and other miscellaneous allergens. When allergy to house dust seems relevant to the patient's eczema, an antidust program should be instituted (page 442). Many of these patients have concomitant respiratory allergy for which hyposensitization may be indicated. If this is carried out, care must be exercised to avoid a flare-up of the eczema through overdosage (page 108). Hyposensitization for atopic dermatitis per se is rarely indicated, since it is infrequently possible to be certain that the skin disease is directly or indirectly related to inhalant allergens.

Immunosuppressive drugs have been suggested for use in treating atopic dermatitis. Aside from theoretical reasons for questioning the validity of this therapeutic approach (page 158), the potential toxicity of these compounds makes their use generally unwarranted in a benign disease such as atopic dermatitis; the danger of complicating infection seems very real.

Psychiatric Treatment. Emotional and tensional factors often are prominent in patients with atopic dermatitis, particularly adolescents and adults. It is difficult to be certain whether these are causes or results of the disease. In many instances superficial, supportive therapy on the part of the allergist, dermatologist, or the patient's family physician is adequate (Chapter 20). However, some of the adult patients in particular require long-range therapy by a competent psychiatrist.

Complications

Secondary Infection of the Skin. Patients with infantile and juvenile eczema are very apt to develop secondary bacterial infections of their skin lesions, and adult patients are by no means free from the threat of this complication. The skin is inoculated with organisms in the process of scratching. In the acute phases, local wet dressings and a suitable antibiotic or chemotherapeutic agent are indicated. Many use antibiotic lotions, such as Neosporin, which rarely cause sensitization. However, the possibility of developing a superimposed allergic contact dermatitis to neomycin must be kept in mind, particularly in patients who are not doing well. Because of this slight risk, some physicians prefer to give antibiotic drugs and chemotherapeutic agents orally or by injection. Later creams with some bacteriostatic powers may be used (e.g., 3 per cent Vioform cream). The lesions of atopic dermatitis more rarely may develop secondary mycotic infections. These are difficult to treat. Cultures of the skin lesions for bacteria and fungi should be carried out in the more resistant cases.

Eczema Vaccinatum. If a child or adult with atopic dermatitis is vaccinated, he may develop a generalized infection of the skin with the cowpox virus. This condition, called eczema vaccinatum, is serious, especially if the cornea should become involved. Encephalitis and death may occur. Hence, vaccination should not be performed on patients with atopic dermatitis or on any member of the family. In fact, eczema patients should not be allowed to associate with others who recently have been vaccinated, for the virus is readily transmitted to the skin. Figure 11–2 shows an adult eczema patient who contracted eczema vaccinatum following vaccination of her child. Human vaccinia immune globulin has improved the outlook for such patients. The therapeutic dose is 0.6 ml./kg. intramuscularly. This material may be obtained from one of the regional blood centers of the American Red Cross after obtaining approval of the consultant designated by the regional center. Methisazone may prove to be of value in arresting progress of this disease.

Eczema Herpeticum. This also is a widespread vesicular eruption superimposed on atopic dermatitis and is caused by the herpes simplex

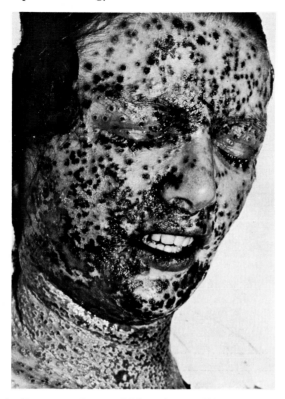

Figure 11–2. Eczema vaccinatum. This patient's child was vaccinated for smallpox and transmitted the cowpox to the eczematous skin of his mother. The entire body was involved. She recovered following treatment with vaccinia immune globulin (human).

virus. It is clinically indistinguishable from eczema vaccinatum, and the two conditions sometimes are referred to as Kaposi's varicelliform eruption. Eczema herpeticum often is associated with marked constitutional symptoms and may be fatal. Hence, patients with atopic dermatitis also should avoid exposure to persons with herpes.

Cataracts. Cataracts having distinctive morphologic features may develop in eczema patients at an early age. Fortunately this complication is not common. Possibly the fact that both the skin and the lens are ectodermal structures embryologically may have some bearing on the development of this complication.

Allergic Contact Dermatitis. As stated previously, this may occur particularly from topical medications used in treating the eczema.

Possible Prevention of Infantile Eczema and Other Allergies

Although a majority of cases of infantile eczema clear up spontaneously by the time the child reaches the age of two or three years, as stated previously, more than 50 per cent of these children will have exhibited other allergic manifestations by the time they reach the age of ten years. Such a strong possibility of further allergic difficulty later in life raises the question whether anything could be done to prevent this sequence of events. Thinking along similar lines, one might also wonder what could have been done to prevent the development of eczema in the first place. Allergists frequently are asked by allergic parents if any measures can be taken to prevent their children from having clinical allergies. The question is particularly pertinent if there is atopy in the families of both husband and wife, but unfortunately there are no controlled studies which permit one to answer this question with assurance. However, the observation that foreign university students frequently remained free from allergic symptoms until they became exposed to ragweed in this country, together with the usual absence of atopic disease among their relatives remaining in other lands (page 22), provides hope that genetically predisposed people at times can avoid the development of overt clinical atopic disease if exposure to potent environmental allergens is minimized. Thus, based simply on logic rather than established fact, the following measures might be suggested in an attempt to decrease the probability of the development of allergic disease among infants and children of atopic families. At least this program entails little trouble for the parents and cannot harm the child.

1. Breast feeding or feeding evaporated milk is preferable to whole cow's milk during infancy.

2. When cereals are added to the baby's diet, single cereals (e.g., barley, oatmeal, or rice) should be used. If the baby develops symptoms following ingestion of a single cereal, he can be changed to another. This cannot be done if he is started on a mixture of cereals.

3. No egg or chocolate should be fed until the child is at least one year of age.

4. Orange and orange juice should be withheld until after the child is one year of age. Vitamin drops actually are a less expensive source of ascorbic acid.

5. Wool should not be allowed to contact the infant's skin.

6. Heavy or frequent use of oils or lotions after bathing the baby should be avoided.

7. No soap should be used on the baby's face.

8. All new clothing must be washed before putting it on the baby. This removes sizing and dye which might be irritating.

9. No pets, such as cats and dogs, should be introduced into the household of a potentially allergic child.

10. The use of wet-proof (and hence dust-proof) covers on the mattress should be continued as the child gets older. Pillows should be covered with dust-proof encasings. Only washable throw rugs and curtains should be in the child's room.

11. Fuzzy, stuffed toys (e.g., teddy bears), except those stuffed with foam rubber or similar material, should be avoided.

12. The child should be protected from massive exposure to dust.

URTICARIA AND ANGIONEUROTIC EDEMA

Although a few occasional hives are of such little concern to most persons that they scarcely merit much attention, severe, acute urticaria and angioneurotic edema can be fatal and chronic urticaria may be most distressing. *Angioedema* may be a better term than angioneurotic edema, since there is little evidence for the involvement of neural or psychic factors in many cases. However, the latter designation appears to be firmly entrenched in the literature. Urticaria and angioneurotic edema are considered together, since they are believed to have a common pathogenesis. In urticaria, small blood vessels in the upper part of the corium are the site of the main pathophysiologic change, while more deeply situated vessels are affected in angioneurotic edema. This explains why the swelling is more diffuse in the latter condition and also why there generally is more pruritus associated with hives, as the cutaneous nerve endings are most abundant in the more superficial portions of the skin. Microscopically, the main finding in both disturbances is evidence of edema. The minute cutaneous blood vessels are dilated and engorged, and they are surrounded by a meager cellular infiltrate which may include some eosinophils. The lymphatic vessels also are dilated.

Probably more than 20 per cent of persons in the United States experience at least one episode of urticaria and/or angioneurotic edema during their lifetimes. Chronic urticaria* is more common in adults, especially women, than in children. Some statistics indicate that urticaria occurs with significantly greater frequency in those with a personal or familial history of atopic disease, but hives also are commonly encountered in patients without such a background. Very possibly some forms of urticaria are related to atopy and others are not.

Pathogenesis

Many cases of *acute* urticaria appear to represent immediate type hypersensitivity reactions, but in *chronic* urticaria no causative allergen can be found in the large majority of instances. In an attempt to understand better the pathogenesis of the disease in this large group of patients, re-examination of the mechanism of urtication is in order. Sir Thomas Lewis' experiments many years ago showed that a triple response is involved in dermographic wheal formation: first, there is a red line where the skin was stroked; this is followed by an enlarging linear wheal; and around this area there appears an erythematous flare.[14] Underlying these gross phenomena are dilatation of capillaries and venules, increased permeability of the involved vessels, and dilatation of surrounding arterioles caused by an axon reflex. In the ensuing years, the essential

---

* Arbitrarily, urticaria is considered to be chronic when it occurs frequently or persistently for a period exceeding three weeks to three months, according to different authors.

correctness of Lewis' deductions have been confirmed by others using more sophisticated techniques, such as cutaneous capillary microscopy and experimental injection of dyes or fluorescent compounds into urticating patients. Sir Thomas also recognized that the triple response could be elicited by a wide variety of physical and chemical means, among them the intracutaneous injection of histamine. Since it was known that histamine is liberated during certain immediate type hypersensitivity reactions, the deduction was made that hives result from allergy. This concept completely dominated clinical evaluation of urticaria until about the time of World War II.[15]

In recent years, evidence has continued to accumulate indicating that histamine is released in urticaria. Skin biopsies at sites of recent hives show a diminished quanitity of histamine, which is consistent with the hypothesis that histamine was released from the cutaneous mast cells during urtication and then carried away. Likewise, whole blood histamine and basophil counts are decreased during urticaria.[16, 17] One might expect that plasma histamine would be elevated, but this is not the case except in rare instances of cold urticaria.[17] The explanation is that released histamine is very rapidly removed from plasma, probably largely by being taken up into certain tissues.

The traditional explanation that hives result from histamine release by antigen-antibody reactions may well be correct for many cases of acute urticaria, but, as mentioned previously, usually no causative allergens can be found in chronic urticaria. Although this may simply reflect gaps in the present state of knowledge concerning allergens causing human disease, consideration should be given to possible alternative mechanisms of urtication. Major possibilities are that histamine might be liberated by nonimmunologic means, or that other mediators of small vessel permeability are operative. In regard to the former of these possibilities, it is know that a large number of chemical compounds are capable of liberating histamine from mast cell granules without the intervention of an antigen-antibody reaction. Among these histamine liberators are numerous drugs, some of which are listed on page 188. These compounds, like mechanical trauma, are known to cause histamine release and urticaria in patients with urticaria pigmentosa. Conditions under which they might cause hives in others have not been carefully evaluated.

Another example of nonimmunologic hives is *cholinergic urticaria* following heat, emotion, or exercise. This condition can be reproduced by immersing the patient's feet in hot water or by injecting cholinergic drugs. After studying the inhibitory effects of tourniquets, nerve blocks, and various drugs, Grant, Pearson, and Comeau concluded that in such patients the central nervous system was stimulated by heated blood to send out impulses via cholinergic nerve fibers of the autonomic nervous system to the skin, where acethylcholine is released.[18] *Dermographism* is another variant of urticaria which may not involve an allergic mechanism (page 251). Finally, much has been learned recently about nonimmunologic mechanisms responsible for *hereditary angioneurotic edema* (page 251).

Diagnosis

Almost everyone is familiar with the appearance of these papular lesions surrounded by an erythematous flare (Figure 11–3). Their size varies from a few millimeters to huge, coalescent lesions actually the size of a serving platter. If there is any question about the diagnosis, the

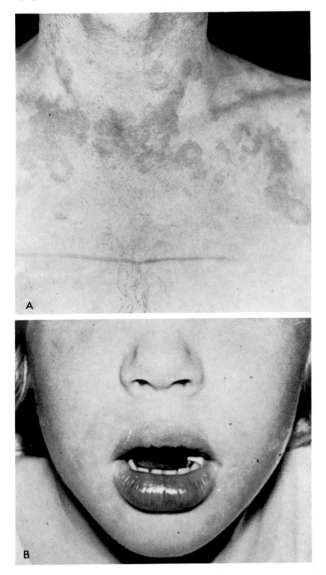

Figure 11–3. *A,* Acute urticaria due to aspirin. *B,* Angioneurotic edema (angioedema).

evanescent nature of the individual hive is very helpful, since there are few other skin conditions which last only minutes or hours. New hives may crop out in other areas as the old ones subside. *Pruritus* is almost invariably present, though some patients complain more of a burning, prickling, or tingling sensation.

Angioneurotic edema is most apt to occur or to be most apparent in areas such as the eyelids, lips, genitalia, hands, and feet where the skin is loosely bound down by the subcutaneous tissue. It is a transient disturbance, but a large area of angioedema may take as long as several days to subside completely. In this instance, pruritus is absent or mild. Helpful points in differentiating this from other forms of edema are that the swelling usually is asymmetrically distributed, it is generally not dependent, it is transient and recurs in different areas, and it often is associated with urticaria. The external lesions may be accompanied by swelling of the larynx, tongue, or mucous membranes lower in the gastrointestinal tract, with accompanying retrosternal and abdominal complaints. The laryngeal swelling is important, since it may cause death by asphyxiation. In some cases urticaria and angioneurotic edema will be accompanied by other features of serum sickness (page 463).

Cases of angioneurotic edema involving the lips and nose need to be differentiated from *elephantiasis nostras,* a lymphedema of these parts due to low-grade, recurrent lymphangitis usually caused by streptococcal infection. In these cases, the swelling usually lasts for weeks at a time, and on inspection one may find a crack or fissure which serves as a portal of entry for infectious agents. Patients with *Melkersson's syndrome* have episodic swelling of the face and lips, the attacks lasting from a few hours to several weeks. They also have lingua plicata, and facial paresis is present in 20 per cent of these individuals. Some cases are familial. Swelling of the face associated with the *superior vena cava syndrome* has been confused with angioneurotic edema. The periorbital edema seen in some cases of *trichinosis* should be considered among the several causes for facial swelling. Ordinary urticaria also must be differentiated from *urticaria pigmentosa.* These patients, usually children, have persistent pigmented macules or papules which do not at all resemble hives. However, if one rubs these lesions, urtication occurs at the site (Darier's sign). The macules are actually benign mast cell tumors from which histamine is liberated by mechanical trauma. The lesions also occur in organs other than the skin. Systemic manifestations in response to liberated histamine are sometimes observed, including wheezing on occasion.

Special Forms of Urticaria

Cholinergic urticaria has been discussed above. It is characterized by tiny 1 to 3 mm. wheals surrounded by a large area of relatively intense erythema in which, at times, satellite wheals may be located. *Aquagenic urticaria* has been suggested as a term to describe those cases in whom

1 to 3 mm. perifollicular urticarial lesions occur not only when the patient is sweating, but also if he merely applies water at any temperature to the skin.[19] An interaction of water or perspiration with sebum or some portion of the sebaceous glands to produce a histamine liberator has been suggested as a possible mechanism. *Papular urticaria,* or lichen urticatus, is characterized by more persistent urticarial lesions. These are most often seen on the lower extremities of children and are usually thought to be caused by insect bites (flea, mite, bedbug). *Dermographism* and *hereditary angioneurotic edema* are discussed on page 251.

Agents Thought to Precipitate Clinical Urticaria

1. *Drugs* and foreign *serum.* These are the first items to be considered, since urticaria and angioedema are common manifestations of reactions to these materials. The procedure for evaluating possible drug allergy is described in Chapter 9. *Serum sickness* is discussed in Chapter 18.

2. *Foods.* Foods commonly precipitate acute urticaria. It has been suggested that this possibility be given special consideration in atopic patients and when gastrointestinal symptoms accompany the urticaria or angioneurotic edema. The evaluation of possible food allergy is discussed in detail in Chapter 10.

3. *Infection.* This was stressed as a causative factor in the older literature. There appears to be little doubt that urticaria may be associated with parasitic infestation, particularly with Ascariasis. Hookworms, strongyloides, schistosomes, echinococcus, Giardia, amoebae, malaria, and others also have been implicated. Substantial esosinophilia is likely to be present in these cases, but this is not invariably found. Urticaria also occurs rather frequently in association with acute infecttions, such as viral upper respiratory tract diseases. In these instances, one must first exclude allergy to a medication given to the patient for the infection. There is no evidence that the urticaria is due to hypersensitivity to the infectious agent. Possibly cutaneous vasodilation associated with fever might be a factor.

The possible role of chronic focal infection was stressed in past years and still is a controversial subject (see page 23). Since urticaria may be associated with a great number of systemic diseases, a complete history and physical examination are manditory, and if these reveal evidence for an infection, further diagnostic studies and treatment are indicated in any case. However, even when infection is found, there commonly is no improvement of chronic urticaria in spite of adequate treatment; for example, Rorsman found dental problems in 63 of 96 patients hospitalized for urticaria, but in only two was there improvement in hives following appropriate dental treatment.[16] It appears that an elaborate search for inapparent infection is unwarranted.

4. *Psychic* factors. Clinical experience suggests that it is common for urticaria to worsen with emotional stress. The most impressive docu-

mentation of this clinical impression is found in the studies carried out by Graham and Wolf a number of years ago.[20] Skin temperature, histamine and pilocarpine iontophoresis effects, cutaneous response to mechanical stimulation, and reactive hyperemia threshold after removing a weight from the skin all showed objectively measurable changes when stressful emotional material was brought up during psychiatric interviews. Some of the patients at this time also broke out in hives, but this could have been due to concomitant dermographism and scratching. Several psychiatrists have tried to delineate a personality or behavior pattern typical for urticaria, but the results have been conflicting. Although it is easy to accept the concept that psychic factors can precipitate or aggravate hives in some patients (particularly those with cholinergic urticaria), the question of whether such factors *alone* are sufficient to be the sole cause is not yet answered. (See also Chapter 20.)

5. *Inhalant allergens.* Occasionally urticaria occurs seasonally along with hay fever and asthma, and rare seasonal cases due to pollen have been reported in the absence of respiratory symptoms. Animal danders, various cosmetics, flour (in bakers), castor bean dust, house dust, fish odors, and other inhalant allergens produce hives at times. This is most likely to occur in atopic persons.

6. *Physical allergy.* The production of cholinergic urticaria by heat has been mentioned. Solar urticaria is one of the less common cutaneous reactions to *light,* but these intriguing patients have attracted considerable attention. They constitute a heterogeneous group in that different patients react maximally to varying wave lengths of light. An allergic mechanism is most strongly implicated in the type I cases according to the classification by Harber et al.[21] These patients react to light in the 2850 to 3200 Å range, and both passive transfer and reverse passive transfer tests can be achieved with their sera. In evaluating patients with solar urticaria, it is important to exclude a defect in protoporphyrin IX metabolism by suitable examination of the red cells and stools.

Cold urticaria, on the other hand, is relatively common. Change in temperature is more important than absolute temperature, and these cases are seen even in tropical climates. Although sometimes only a trivial annoyance, the more severe form of the disease can be incapacitating; drowning can occur subsequent to massive histamine release and syncope when an affected person swims in cold water. In contrast with patients with most other forms of urticaria, these patients have normal levels of whole blood histamine and circulating basophils while they are experiencing urticaria. However, if one arm is submerged in cold water for five minutes, following rewarming there is a pronounced increase in the *plasma* histamine in blood returning from the chilled arm (but not on the opposite arm).[17] This is essentially the only circumstance under which elevated plasma histamine has been observed in humans, and the data suggest it is coming from mast cells in the chilled tissues rather than from the circulating basophils. The histamine content of whole blood in the general circulation is normal, because excess plasma histamine is rapidly taken up by various tissues. Passive transfer of cold allergy can frequently be achieved, but success is facilitated by using fresh serum and challenging the passive transfer site in three hours.[21] In rare cases cold urticaria is associated with paroxysmal cold hemaglobinuria (usually luetic) or with cryoglobulinemia, but the latter condition much more commonly produces purpura than urticaria. Cases have been reported in which the patient developed cold urticaria only when ingesting a simple chemical substance, such as menthol or griseofulvin. There are rare families in which cold allergy is frequent. In these families the lesions are unusual in that they do not itch.

7. *Connective tissue disease.* Urticaria may be associated with systemic lupus erythematosis and others of the connective tissue diseases discussed in Chapters 18 and 19.

8. *Insect bites* and *stings.* Hives and angioedema usually are prominent features of systemic reactions from Hymenoptera and other insect stings (Chapter 15). This possibility should be considered when one encounters an unconscious patient with urticaria. The production of papular urticaria by insect bites is mentioned on page 245.

9. *Contactants.* Although one does not ordinarily expect immediate type hypersensitivity reactions to occur simply on contact with various allergens, this is possible if the allergy is marked or the skin is penetrated during contact. Some of these substances also may contain histamine liberators or, in the case of nettles, histamine itself. One or another of these mechanisms is presumably involved in urticaria following contact with various mammals, caterpillars, beetles, moth and butterfly scales, Portuguese Men-of-War,* and other aquatic forms.

10. *Neoplasms.* Urticaria has been observed in some patients harboring neoplasms, particularly large carcinomas with central necrosis. Relief of the urticaria following resection of the neoplasms provides suggestive but not conclusive evidence of an etiologic relationship. Hives and angioedema have also been reported in association with Hodgkin's disease.

11. *Familial* types. As mentioned previously, there are rare families wherein cold urticaria is frequent. Hereditary angioneurotic edema is discussed on page 251.

13. *Other possible factors.* Many patients with urticaria tend to develop new lesions after drinking alcoholic beverages. Possibly this is due simply to cutaneous vasodilation, as with fever or exercise. Endocrine factors are frequently mentioned, but reported autosensitization to sex hormones has not been confirmed. More general aspects of this subject are discussed on page 26.

---

* This is a fact of utmost importance in Sir Arthur Conan Doyle's Sherlock Holmes story, *The Adventure of the Lion's Mane.*

Diagnostic Procedures in Urticaria

In view of the multiple diseases with which urticaria may be associated, it is obvious that these patients merit a *complete* history and physical examination. The latter should include testing for dermographism. The appearance of the skin lesions may suggest cholinergic or papular urticaria. Solar or cold urticaria or dermographism may be suggested by the distribution of the lesions. From routine laboratory testing a pronounced eosinophilia would direct attention toward possible parasitic infestation.

Additional diagnostic tests are selected on the basis of what is suspected from the foregoing procedures, especially the meticulous history. Details of methods used for evaluating possible drug, food, or insect allergy are given in other chapters. At least three *fresh* stool examinations for ova and parasites should be done when parasitic infestation is suspected. A screening test for cholinergic urticaria consists in an attempt to reproduce the lesions by immersing both lower legs for 40 minutes in water maintained at about 44° C. One also should inject 0.01 mg. methacholine in 0.05 ml. saline (i.e., a 1:5000 solution) intracutaneously, looking especially for satellite wheal formation and comparing results with normal individuals. A similar test with one-tenth this concentration of nicotine picrate (i.e., 1:50,000) also is informative. A common screening test for cold allergy is done by application of an ice cube on the forearm for five minutes. A positive test is demonstrated by the development of lesions within a few minutes after the arm is rewarmed. A serologic test for syphilis and testing for cryoglobulins also should be routine in these patients. Confirming a diagnosis of solar urticaria is more difficult without special equipment,[21] but a reasonable screening procedure is to observe whether urticaria develops in a circumscribed area within 20 minutes after a two minute exposure to noontime sunlight. In all these tests for physical allergy it is important not to challenge the patient during the refractory period which is present immediately after naturally occurring symptoms.

Scratch or intracutaneous tests are indicated in the occasional patients in whom inhalants are suspected of causing urticaria. They are very unlikely to be of much help in other cases except for slight screening value in respect to food allergy (page 201).

When a thorough history and physical examination provide no clues as to etiology, the physician finds himself in a very difficult position. Sometimes it is desirable to create more history by, for example, asking the patient to take a short trip out of town or to a motel where he can change his environment significantly. Even in the absence of leads from the history, one may wish more definitely to rule out certain possibilities. Stool examinations for ova and parasites probably should be done routinely in such cases, but in our community almost no useful information has come from this. Usually occult food allergy should be excluded by a brief trial on a strict elimination diet (Chapter 10). This may be undertaken fairly hopefully in acute urticaria, but in the chronic form of the disease it very rarely solves the problem. It should be recognized that since there is no evidence that allergy causes the large majority of cases of chronic urticaria, prolonging diagnostic studies for allergy beyond a certain reasonable point is likely to result only in increasing frustration on the part of both the patient and the physician.

Opinions differ so widely about the relative frequency with which various factors apparently cause urticaria that it is impossible to generalize about the usual results of diagnostic evaluations. Especially noteworthy is the fact that there seems to be an inverse relationship between the frequency of diagnosing a psychogenic cause and unknown etiology in different reported series of cases. These two categories certainly predominate in *chronic* urticaria. In more acute urticaria, drugs, foods, psychic stress, infection, and physical allergy are frequently diagnosed as precipitating factors.

Treatment

This is outlined in Table 11–2. Obviously, the most satisfactory therapy consists in the elimination of any causative factor or factors which have been identified. With the exception of a few drug reactions, urticaria usually disappears within a few days after this is accomplished. Instruction regarding occult sources of drugs and the limitations of penicillinase are discussed in Chapter 9. When emotional factors seem important, supportive psychotherapy may suffice, but occasionally re-

Table 11–2. *Management of Urticaria and Angioneurotic Edema*

I. Elimination and avoidance of causative factor(s)
   A. "Tincture of time"
   B. Instruction regarding possible occult sources
   C. (?) Enzymatic destruction of persisting allergen
   D. Control of emotional factors and exposure to physical agents

II. Symptomatic
   A. Antihistamines
   B. Epinephrine (aqueous and long-acting)
   C. Ephedrine-containing drugs
   D. Sedatives or tranquilizers
   E. Hydroxyzine
   F. Cyproheptadine
   G. (?) Intravenous nicotinic acid
   H. Corticosteroids or ACTH
   I. (?) Topical applications

III. Hyposensitization (rarely)
   A. Inhalants
   B. Insect hyposensitization (Hymenoptera)
   C. (?) Physical allergy
   D. (?) Drugs (very rarely)

IV. Reassurance—indicated in all forms

ferral to a psychiatrist may be indicated (Chapter 20). When physical allergy to cold or to light is present, ingenuity can be exercised to minimize exposure. In addition, various sun screen preparations (e.g., Uval) may afford the light-sensitive patient additional protection, which is especially needed in the spring and early summer. Instructions for avoiding various inhalant allergens and environmental factors, including stinging insects, are given in other chapters.

No symptomatic treatment is required in cases of mild urticaria of known cause. However, if the etiology is unknown or if the patient is acutely uncomfortable while awaiting relief following withdrawal of a known causative factor, the drugs in table 11–2 represent the agents most widely used among a host of medications suggested for relief of urticaria.[23] These compounds are discussed in some detail in Chapter 7. As noted, in severe acute urticaria double the usual doses of antihistamines can be given, if necessary, for a short period with the patient under close observation. Intravenous antihistamines may be effective in severe cases, but the effect may be short-lived, and the patient is apt to become very drowsy. Epinephrine may provide great relief in acute urticaria and is the drug of choice when laryngeal edema threatens. Tracheotomy may be required if this fails. It should be recalled that ephedrine commonly was used for urticaria before the advent of the antihistamines, and some patients still prefer the former drug. Hydroxyzine has been useful in many patients. Hydroxyzine and cyproheptadine should be considered in cases in which the antihistamines are not effective; some physicians try them initially. The corticosteroids generally are neither necessary or desirable in chronic urticaria, but they may be a valuable adjunct to treatment of severe, acute urticaria (usually caused by a drug or foreign serum) not responding to other treatment. The management of urticaria and angioneurotic edema associated with anaphylactic type reactions is discussed on page 118. Topical therapy is unimportant in urticaria, but, if desired, bland, antipruritic topical medications, such as calamine liniment, may be used. Topical corticosteroids are not used for this disease.

Hyposensitization with pollen extracts is justified in patients experiencing seasonal urticaria along with asthma or hay fever (Chapter 6). It is probably even more strongly indicated for persons who have experienced generalized urticaria or angioedema following insect stings (Chapter 15). Hyposensitization to cold has been attempted by such measures as bathing once or twice daily in water maintained at a designated temperature, which is decreased by 1° F. daily. Our experience with this has not been encouraging. Tolerance to light has been increased by successive exposures which produce sun tanning, but this is not widely employed. Hyposensitization to drugs is discussed in Chapter 9.

Reassurance is very important, especially in chronic urticaria of unknown cause. Hives and angioneurotic edema give the appearance of being medically more serious than they actually are. Although it is important to alert the patient to seek immediate medical attention if swelling in the throat develops, in general strong reassurance can be given that the disease is reversible and will eventually disappear. Many patients with chronic urticaria will have to learn to live with the disease for a prolonged period, and the sooner they can accept this, the better off they will be. Meanwhile, the physician can provide such medications as are needed to keep the symptoms under control and should extend sympathetic support.

Dermographism (Urticaria Factitia)

About 5 per cent of the populace will develop urticarial whealing following mild trauma to the skin. This increases to about 20 per cent if the pressure applied in stroking the skin is increased fivefold. This phenomenon occurs as frequently in nonatopic as in atopic individuals. Ordinary acute or chronic urticaria is not associated with dermographism,[24] though some clinicians have noted that dermographism may follow in the wake of urticarial penicillin reactions.[25] The skin wheal in this condition appears to be identical with that produced by injecting histamine into normal skin; it is at least partly suppressed by antihistamines, and local exhaustion can be observed after repeated trauma to the skin. It has been known for many years that dermographism can be passively transferred at times by the Prausnitz-Küstner technique. As with the other physical allergies, this observation is most easily explained by an allergic reaction to some substance formed in the skin by mechanical trauma. However, other explanations are possible, and some students of the subject feel that dermographism results from a direct effect of trauma on blood vessels.[26]

Clinically, dermographism may result in itching welts under rough or tight articles of clothing, such as shoulder straps, buckles, brassières, girdles, and waist bands. Scratching also produces welts. The diagnosis can be confirmed by stroking the skin. Treatment is by familiarizing the patient with the nature of the disease. The drugs used for treating urticaria can be used prophylactically or therapeutically.

Pressure urticaria is a more delayed response to mechanical trauma. It consists of swelling and urticaria developing a number of hours after pressure is applied to the skin. Consequently, the soles of the feet, palms of the hands, and buttocks are the usual sites of involvement.

Hereditary Angioneurotic Edema

This is a rare disease which is inherited in an autosomal dominant pattern. Symptoms begin in childhood or young adulthood and consist of irregularly occurring episodes of angioneurotic edema. Typical urticaria is absent, but abdominal pain is common. No allergic cause for the disease is discernible, the only apparent precipitating factor being trauma. Laryngeal edema is common and has been responsible for death in 26 per cent of the reported cases.[27] Methyltestosterone has been reported to reduce the number of episodes of edema, though further data confirming this report are needed.[28]

Of major importance is recent work which indicates that a non-immunologic mechanism is responsible for this form of angioneurotic edema. Most of these patients lack an alpha-2 globulin which acts as an inhibitor both of the activated first component of complement (C'1) and of plasma kallikrein. This deficiency can be demonstrated at a research level by failure of these patients' sera to react immunochemically with a specific antiserum prepared against the alpha-2 globulin inhibitor,[29] failure to inhibit the esterase activity of C'1, and failure to inhibit enzymatic and physiologic effects of kallikrein to a normal degree. These patients also tend to have low serum levels of C'4 and C'2, presumably since the enzymatic activity of C'1 is not inhibited to the normal extent. A convenient clinical test for the disorder, therefore, is to measure serum C'2 levels, which are subnormal most of the time and are extremely low during attacks.[30] It still is not clear whether the kallikrein or the complement enzyme systems are actually responsible for the disease. Also, in certain families the alpha-2 globulin inhibitor is present, as measured by immunologic techniques, but it appears to be functionally inactive.[29] In still rarer families, the inhibitor is present and active, and the mechanism of the disease is obscure.

ALLERGIC CONTACT DERMATITIS

This disease may occur at any age but is most common during the middle and later years of life. It is about as common in the population at large as it is in individuals with collateral allergy or with a family history of allergy. Thus, although some cases of contact dermatitis are considered to be allergic, they do not fall within the group of atopic diseases. The first reaction following exposure to the offending agent is erythema. Raised lesions develop next, and finally vesicles may form owing to fluid accumulation within the epidermis. If the disease becomes chronic, thickening, scaling, and lichenification supervene. Microscopically, nonspecific inflammatory changes are seen in the dermis, and the epidermis shows spongiosis followed by intra-epidermal vesicles in the acute stage of the disease.

A distinction between dermal and epidermal sensitivity has been suggested,[31] but it is difficult to demonstrate two clear-cut histologic reaction patterns. Contactants differ in such factors as rate of absorption and the distribution of proteins with which they conjugate, so that slightly different patterns of localization of the inflammatory reaction may be seen with different sensitizers. In all cases, however, there is a dermal component, as the inflammatory cells must come from blood vessels in the dermis. Frequently a mild contact reaction shows primarily a dermal change, while a more severe reaction shows epidermal destruction, also.

The lesion of contact dermatitis results from a delayed type of immunologic reaction rather than from the immediate type of whealing response seen in atopic conditions. Simple chemical substances produce contact hypersensitivity by acting as haptens firmly conjugated to skin proteins. That the hapten mechanism actually applies to allergic contact dermatitis is supported by observations that the capacity of a series of simple compounds to induce or elicit this type of cutaneous hypersensitivity closely parallels their capacity to conjugate with proteins in vivo or in vitro.[32] Although contact allergy ordinarily is produced by topical application in experimental animals, it also may be induced by injection of the sensitizer in suitable immunologic adjuvants. Immunologic aspects of allergic contact dermatitis and delayed type hypersensitivity in general are discussed in Chapter 1.

The initial sensitization of the skin may develop over a period of many years, but patients may become allergic after a few weeks of close contact with a new environmental agent capable of acting as a potent sensitizer. Once sensitized, re-exposure typically is followed by the first appearance of lesions about 18 or more hours later, though a considerably more rapid onset is observed in some cases. Allergic contact dermatitis can be elicited by exposure to the offending agent in minute quantities which are incapable of causing any reaction in a nonsensitized skin. Therefore, this reaction differs from the dermatitis produced by certain chemical or physical primary irritants to the skin of many or all normal, nonsensitized individuals. Furthermore, no previous sensitizing exposure is needed to elicit a skin reaction to primary irritants. In many patient populations, contact dermatitis actually is more often due to irritation than to allergy, but both are common. Sometimes it is difficult to decide whether a substance is acting as an irritant or as an allergen. Uncertainty may arise especially by virtue of the fact that irritants usually are chemically reactive, and thus these very materials may be more likely to conjugate with proteins in skin and become antigenic. The crucial point of differentiation is whether the material will elicit a reaction in the patient's skin at a concentration outside the range of irritant levels in normal individuals. Severe irritant reactions may show necrosis and subepidermal bullae, as in a chemical burn, but less severe reactions may be indistinguishable from allergic contact dermatitis. Microscopically, too, differences between mild, chronic irritant and allergic reactions are subtle.

Diagnosis

The diagnosis of allergic contact dermatitis may be suspected not only from the morphologic appearance of the lesions but also from their distribution. Although any part of the skin surface may be involved,

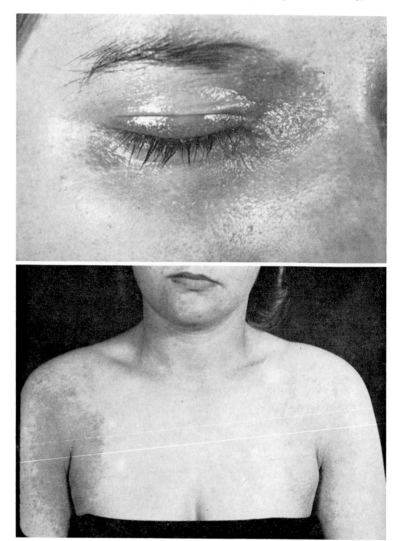

Figure 11–4. *Top,* Contact dermatitis of eyelid. *Bottom,* Contact dermatitis of axillary area due to dress shields.

contact dermatitis very often is found on exposed surfaces such as the face, neck, and dorsal surface of the hands and feet and on the lateral aspects of the forearms and legs. The eyelids, sides of the neck, and genitalia also are familiar sites for this condition, possibly because of the thinness of the skin in these areas (Figure 11–4). Sometimes, however, the distribution of the lesions is very bizarre, especially if the contact agent is within the patient's clothing. The palms, soles, and areas well covered by hair usually are spared. The dermatitis may be associated with some local edema, which may be rather pronounced when the eyelids, fingers, or genitalia are involved. Contact dermatitis almost always is accompanied by pruritus. This is such a constant symptom that its absence should lead the physician to reconsider the diagnosis.

Some of the conditions to be differentiated from contact dermatitis were discussed earlier in this chapter as well as in the standard texts on dermatology and allergy. Unfortunately, it is not rare for contact dermatitis to co-exist with some other skin disease, such as fungus infection, stasis dermatitis, atopic dermatitis, and many others. For example, patients who have had proved fungus infection of the feet may develop a contact eruption from a dye in their shoes or from proprietary ointments used to treat the infection. It would seem that almost anything which breaks the continuity of the skin enhances the ease of development of a contact dermatitis. Dermatologic consultation often is valuable in these complex cases.

Determination of Specific Cause

When a diagnosis of allergic contact dermatitis has been made, the allergist's work has just begun. The main problem in allergic management of such persons is to discover one or more agents in the patient's environment which produce the skin lesions. Sometimes this is very easy, but other cases constitute a supreme challenge to the physician's diagnostic acumen and detective powers. No allergist claims to be able to solve all the cases of allergic contact dermatitis which he sees, but the percentage of success achieved is more than enough to compensate for the persistent effort and patience which some of the more difficult investigations require. Although contact dermatitis almost never is fatal, many patients with this disease experience prolonged periods of disability, repeated hospitalizations, and inability to maintain gainful employment until the cause of their condition is found. Consequently these people are extremely grateful to the physician who finds the answer to their problem. Furthermore, from the physician's point of view the solving of a difficult case of contact dermatitis is one of the most satisfying experiences in medical practice.

The etiologic diagnosis of contact dermatitis usually is established by means of patch testing with the suspected contactants. The delayed type of skin reaction which is evoked by a patch test is a good reproduction in miniature of the disease itself. The technique of patch testing is very simple and is described in detail in the following chapter. The most difficult problem is, of course, deciding which substances to use for the patch tests. There are literally thousands of materials in everyone's environment which might possibly cause contact dermatitis. Thus, a sagacious selection of items for patch testing is essential. The following three methods of approach should be fully exploited in deciding which items should be suspected and thus used for patch testing:

1. The distribution of the lesions provides a very obvious clue in certain cases (e.g., dermatitis from jewelry, wrist watch bands, shoes, and other materials). In other instances the distribution is compatible with a

broader group of possible offenders. Further discussion of this subject and lists of contactants which are suggested by various types of contact patterns are presented in the following chapter.

2. The history of the time and place of occurrence of symptoms often provides valuable clues for determining the cause of contact dermatitis. Inquiry should be made regarding changes in the skin condition on vacations, over weekends, and during seasonal variations. The effect of changing jobs or of moving from one place to another also is important. From questions of this type the allergist tries to determine in which of the following broad categories the offending contactant probably falls: something in the patient's *work situation,* objects in his *house, plants* growing outdoors or indoors, articles of *clothing* or *cosmetics,* materials used in his *hobbies,* or *ointments* and other local applications which have been applied to his skin. After broadly surveying these various possibilities, the patient should be questioned intensively about contactants within the general categories suggested by the history. The physician should make a list of possible agents as he goes along, for this list later can be used in reference to patch testing. Serious attention should be paid to any materials which the patient himself may suspect. It also may be helpful for the physician to refer to the lists of common household and occupational contactants given in the following chapter. Items from the lists which the patient uses should be considered as possible suspects. Although contact dermatitis not infrequently is caused by solid objects, one should be especially suspicious of liquids and aerosolized materials, for these often remain in more intimate and prolonged contact with the skin than do solid articles.

Sometimes the initial interview is not very helpful in determining the cause of the dermatitis, particularly if the patient had not realized that his skin eruption was of the contact type. The physician's time and effort in closely questioning this type of patient generally has not been wasted, however. Such an approach usually causes the patient to become observant of the effect of environmental factors on his skin condition. He then may provide the physician with some valuable clues at the time of subsequent visits. It is well to have the patient write down at once a detailed account of his exact activities for the preceding 48 hours if an exacerbation occurs. Sometimes the offending contactant is a substance whose presence in the patient's environment the physician could not suspect. Such cases will be solved only if the patient's power of observing and recording are cultivated by the physician. In certain obscure cases in which more superficial study has failed to solve the problem, it may be profitable for the physician to inspect the patient's home or place of work. When the history is of no help because both the patient's environment and his dermatitis have been quite constant, it may be advisable to create history by altering the environment. The effect of a vacation from work, a temporary visit with nearby friends or relatives, or a trip to a distant place may give a good indication of the locus of the offending contactant. In chronic and obscure cases, a prolonged period of observation with patch testing to many substances may be necessary before success is achieved. When it appears from the outset that a case will be difficult, in order to prevent the patient from becoming discouraged and giving up the investigation prematurely it is always a good plan to forewarn him that a considerable period of study may be necessary. Sometimes it is impossible to establish the exact nature of the contactant by means of a positive reaction to a patch test, but from the history and experience it is obvious that the dermatitis is associated with certain places or definite activities. By avoiding these situations patients may be relieved even though the exact cause of their dermatitis remains unknown.

3. One should look for contact with substances which are known to be potent sensitizers. A list of 25 items which are recognized as being among the most common causes of allergic contact dermatitis is given on page 284. The physician caring for these patients should be familiar with the numerous everyday articles which contain these chemical compounds (page 278). Certain other substances are common offenders in special occupational groups. Lists of these contactants also may be found in the following chapter. In difficult cases the physician may be inclined, in desperation, simply to patch test the patient with some of the more common contactants, hoping that if a positive reaction is elicited it can be determined retrospectively how the patient is being exposed to the material in question. However, this type of "shot gun" procedure is not recommended as the best *initial* approach in patch testing patients, as it is less likely to be successful than selective testing. It also should be noted that although a positive patch test reaction usually indicates that a patient would be likely to develop allergic contact dermatitis if sufficiently exposed to the item in question, his actual disease might be due to some additional contact hypersensitivity. Thus, it is essential to correlate positive reactions with the patient's history.

Other Diagnostic Procedures

It has been known for many years that delayed, tuberculin-like reactions can be elicited by intracutaneously injecting contact allergens, such as certain metals and drugs. Several investigators have confirmed that intracutaneous testing quite regularly produces delayed reactions in sensitized patients with concentrations of allergen substantially below those used in patch testing.[33] Some instances have been reported in which the intracutaneous test was positive but the patch tests were negative. However, simply patch testing with higher (but nonirritant) concentrations of the contactant suffices to increase the number of positive patch tests in some instances,[34] and further experience will be required to be certain that intracutaneous testing is not more likely to *sensitize* the patient. Sometimes the reactions, though positive, are so small that they are not easily read.[34]

As an alternative to intracutaneous testing, European investigators in particular have tried to increase the sensitivity of the patch testing procedure by scratching the skin at the time the patch test is applied (scratch-patch test). Others have used epidermal stripping with tape or have abraded the skin in some other manner.[33] At present, however, these procedures are not widely accepted, and some have found such tests difficult to read.[34] The use of dimethylsulfoxide to increase the penetration of test materials has not passed the investigational stage.

Treatment

The treatment for allergic contact dermatitis may be divided into two phases, the symptomatic and the etiologic.

Symptomatic Treatment. Symptomatic treatment is necessary during the acute phases of contact dermatitis to promote healing of the skin and to relieve the itching and discomfort, which may be severe. The use of local applications is guided by the general principles of dermatologic practice. Wet dressings are employed while the lesions are weeping. Burow's solution (aluminum acetate) in a dilution of 1:20 to 1:40, saline, or boiled water may be used. In cases in which the eruption is moderate in extent and severity, corticosteroid lotions or creams may be used to good advantage in a manner similar to their application in atopic dermatitis (see pages 152 and 234). However, in acute, severe disease (e.g., severe poison ivy dermatitis), topical corticosteroids often fail to arrest the dermatitis, and one must resort to the systemic administration of these agents (see below). With milder disease, older, bland remedies, such as calamine or Wise's shake lotions, are still used. Overtreatment must be assiduously avoided, for these patients may develop secondary contact sensitivities to whatever ointments are applied. Generally, local therapy is neither necessary nor advisable when the dermatitis is very mild. If the skin is secondarily infected, wet dressings are used together with topical or systemic antibiotic drugs or chemotherapeutic agents. The precautions mentioned on page 238 should be observed when considering topical application of these medications.

Relief of pruritus is another objective in treatment. Aside from control of the dermatitis by agents such as wet dressings or corticosteroids, the oral administration of adequate doses of an antihistamine drug also may be helpful. Often it is advisable in such cases to select an antihistamine that has a slight sedative effect, especially for use at bedtime (see page 236). Tranquilizers or sedatives sometimes are used. Colloidal baths also may provide some temporary relief from itching (see page 236).

Systemic administration of a corticosteroid or ACTH may be necessary in severe cases of allergic contact dermatitis not responding well to other forms of treatment (page 145). Usually a five to ten day "burst" of therapy suffices, especially when the contactant is known and further exposure can be prevented. Prolonged oral corticosteroid administration is almost never justified in this disease.

Persons with contact dermatitis also should protect their skin from all types of irritating substances. Sometimes this presents a rather difficult problem when the rash is on the hands. Furthermore, there is a large group of patients who have a contact type of eruption on the hands because of exposure to nonspecific primary irritants over a long period of time. The familiar "housewife's hands" is an example of this. A brief attempt may be made to discover possible specific allergic contactants in this type of case, but the reactions to patch tests usually are entirely negative. Regardless of whether the rash on the hands is a true allergic reaction or a nonspecific irritation, it is advisable for all these patients to wear white cotton gloves underneath loose rubber gloves every time they place their hands in dish water or otherwise expose them to irritant materials. An alternative but somewhat less desirable method of protection is to wear loose cotton-lined rubber gloves. Use of long-handled brushes for household tasks also will avert exposure to some irritants. Women with dermatitis of their hands should wear finger rings as infrequently as possible, for irritating substances are likely to collect under rings. Certain ointments have been used in industry to protect workers' hands. Although these substances may be of some value in protecting the skin against certain primary irritants, they generally should not be relied upon to furnish adequate protection against proved specific contact allergens. Industrial workers whose dermatitis is due either to irritating chemicals or to contact allergens may have a spontaneous subsidence of their skin condition as a result of a "hardening process." In the allergic patients this may result from desensitization by natural exposure.

Etiologic Treatment. This therapy of contact dermatitis consists of removal of the offending substance from contact with the patient's skin. Usually this is very simple; for example, if the patient is allergic to nail polish, complete relief may be expected if she stops using nail polish. The problem is more difficult, however, when the contactant is some more ubiquitous substance (e.g., mercury, paraphenylenediamine, or chromates). It is totally inadequate to tell a patient to "avoid mercury." In such cases one should familiarize the patient with possible hidden sources of the contactant. Reference to specialized treatises in the allergy,[35] chemical or industrial literature may be helpful in certain cases, and the patient should be given a written list of articles which contain the offending agent. He also should be taught to read the labels on everything he handles.

In contrast with inhalant allergies, deliberate hyposensitization to the relatively simple chemical substances which cause allergic contact dermatitis is not generally attempted. In the case of plant oil dermatitis, however, such therapy can be carried out but usually is unnecessary, since avoidance generally suffices. Furthermore, the procedure not infrequently

Figure 11–5. *Left,* Poison ivy. This plant is found in nearly all parts of the United States and southern Canada. It may grow as a bush, shrub, or vine. Note the characteristic three leaflets, alternately branching from the vine. Root tendrils hold the stem to the tree it is climbing. In the fall, it may have white berries.

Many people become sensitized to the oleoresin by casual contact. Even burning of the branches or leaves may, through oil droplets in the smoke, cause sufficient exposure to sensitize.

Right, Poison sumac is located in swampy land from New England to Minnesota and south through Texas. The white berries hang in drooping clumps in contrast with the red, erect clusters of berries of the harmless sumacs which are so commonly seen on hillsides and along highways. The oleoresin of poison sumac is closely related to that of poison ivy.

is attended by undesirable side effects, such as dermatitis or pruritus ani. Thus, hyposensitization to plant oils generally is reserved for exceptionally sensitive patients who continue to have difficulty in spite of sincere efforts at avoidance. It also is considered when a change of occupation would be necessary to accomplish avoidance of the offending plant or pollen oil.

By far the largest experience has been with Rhus desensitization for patients markedly allergic to poison ivy (Figure 11–5, left), poison oak or poison sumac (Figure 11–5, right). These plants all contain urushiols (pentadecylcatechols) as the sensitizers.[36] The patients, incidentally, also react to cashew nut oil and Japanese lac. There is general agreement that Rhus extracts should not be given to persons already suffering from dermatitis caused by one of these agents, since the extracts are likely to increase the difficulty. Many parenteral and oral preparations have been used prophylactically over the years—in fact, dating back to ivy leaf chewing by the American Indians. Proof of the efficacy of many preparations which have been used is lacking. Because of variable exposure to the Rhus plants, double-blind studies or objective changes by quantitative patch testing are needed to be certain of a therapeutic effect, but controlled evaluations of this type have been conspicuously meager. Unfortunately, too, in some of the most convincing studies experimental preparations have been employed which are not available to the medical profession, such as crystalline 3-n-pentadecyl catechol.[37] However, the crude oleoresin also is effective. This material is obtained by extracting cut-up parts of the plant with a lipoidal solvent. Generally, it is dissolved in alcohol or oil (corn, sesame, peanut, olive), but one commonly used pyridine extract is precipitated with alum and suspended in an aqueous medium.

Although it is possible to produce a change in the quantitative patch test reaction by parenteral injections of Rhus oleoresin, Kligman's data show that a total of approximately 600 to 800 mg. oleoresin are required for a discernible effect, and 2000 to 2500 mg. are needed for a maximal effect in the average patient.[37] It should be noted that these quantities are more than 100 times greater than the amounts called for by the usual dosage schedules for most commercial extracts. To give these large amounts of oleoresin without an excessive number of reactions, weekly injections are needed for about six months. In view of this and the fact that oral hyposensitization also is effective and requires only slightly larger doses, many experts in this area feel that intramuscular administration of these materials should be abandoned.

The oral administration of Rhus oleoresins also usually produces no change in quantitative patch tests if the dosage schedules recommended by commercial suppliers are followed,[38] but a significant effect was obtained in certain patients when larger amounts of some of these same materials* were given over a longer period of time (e.g., six months). Kligman's data suggest that a total dose of 2500 to 3000 mg. of the oleoresin given orally produces a maximal effect. On the average there is about a hundredfold decrease in reactivity to quantitative patch testing under these circumstances. It should be emphasized that only partial protection is afforded to very sensitive individuals by these procedures. Thus, patients should be urged still to avoid contact with Rhus plants as carefully as possible. In addition to a diminished reactivity, as shown by quantitative patch testing, treated patients may have less prolonged dermatitis with less tendency to spread, even when they are incompletely protected. However, the therapeutic effect is only temporary, requiring retreatment each year. With consideration also of the substantial

---

* Poison Ivy Oleoresin Desensitization Kit, Graham Products, c/o Hollister-Stier Laboratories (see address on page 530).

incidence of adverse side effects (page 260), it is evident that this is quite a cumbersome form of therapy which would be justified only in exceptional cases, as has been noted. Recent data indicate that it may be possible, in some instances, to administer a substantial enough dose of Rhus oleoresin by mouth in two to three weeks to decrease the patch test reactions significantly, but it is noteworthy that four of seven patients so treated developed a rash or itching after one or more doses.[39]

Sensitive patients treated experimentally with large doses of Rhus oleoresin have provided an opportunity to make some interesting immunologic observations. Stomatitis may occur with oral administration, and fever, wheezing, and urticaria may be observed after parenteral injections. Loeffler's syndrome occurred in seven of Kligman's cases.[37] Substantial eosinophilia, leukocytosis, and degranulation of the circulating basophils also are observed.[39] There is no evidence of blocking antibody production, and leukocytes from hyposensitized subjects still are able to transfer Rhus hypersensitivity to normal individuals. Conversely, the hyposensitized patients show heightened patch test reactivity when given leukocytes from highly sensitive donors.[37]

Oral hyposensitization also is employed in patients with allergic contact dermatitis of severe degree to other plant oils, especially rag-

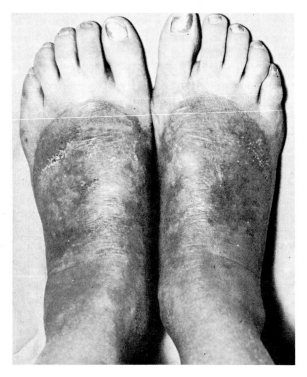

Figure 11–6. Photosensitivity reaction. Patient had been given demethylchlortetracycline. Note that shoes protected skin from the reaction.

weed (page 279). Preparation of the plant oil is described on page 510. We have used quantitative patch testing to estimate our starting dose, which is one drop of the most dilute concentration of plant oil giving a positive patch test reaction.[40] The material is dropped onto a cube of sugar, a cracker, or a slice of bread. It is preferable for the patient not to handle the extract bottle. The dose is increased by one drop each day until 15 drops are given at one dose. Then serial tenfold more concentrated solutions are used until the patient's tolerance is reached or the most concentrated extract is being given (e.g., 1:25). As with Rhus desensitization, treatment is prolonged, side effects (itching, flare of dermatitis) are relatively frequent, and the impression that this treatment helps the patient has not been substantiated by well controlled studies. However, it is likely that this therapy is analogous to Rhus desensitization, suggesting that sufficiently large doses of these plant oils may be beneficial. A number of different plant oils are commercially available (see preceding footnote). The supplier's recommendations should be followed for administering these plant oils, but more prolonged therapy may be advisable, especially if improvement is at first disappointing.

Oral hyposensitization also has been used for allergic contact dermatitis from drugs.[41] Experience with this type of procedure is limited, and patients usually can avoid exposure to this type of contactant.

OTHER SKIN DISEASES OF POSSIBLE CONCERN TO THE ALLERGIST

Photosensitivity

Some patients develop erythematous, cutaneous lesions in light-exposed areas when certain drugs or naturally occurring substances are present in the skin (Figure 11–6). The photosensitizer either may be administered systemically or applied topically on the skin. Reactions of this type may be *phototoxic* or *photoallergic*. The differing mechanisms thought to be operative in these two types of reactions are outlined in Figure 11–7. This explains why phototoxic reactions occur on first exposure to light in a significant portion of persons receiving the photosensitizer, while an induction period is required before photoallergic reactions develop, and the latter then may occur in the presence of only very small amounts of the photosensitizer in the small group of persons reacting immunologically to its oxidation product. This latter concept is supported by the experiments of Schwarz and Speck in which it was shown that guinea pigs sensitized to oxidation products of sulfanilamide reacted on exposure to sulfanilamide and light.[43]

Photoallergic reactions are diagnosed by photopatch testing, as described on page 272. Sometimes plain patch tests are positive in these cases, but this may be due to exposure to light through the patch or after

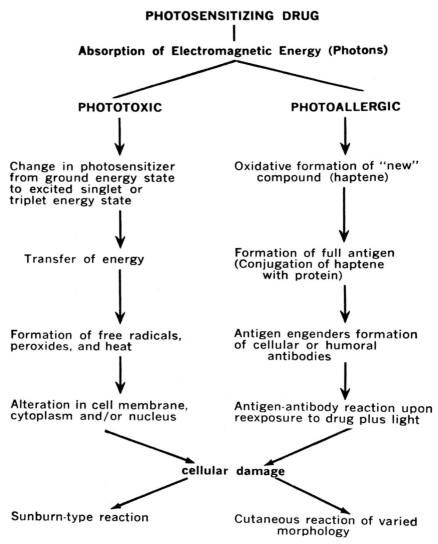

PHOTOSENSITIZING DRUG

|

Absorption of Electromagnetic Energy (Photons)

PHOTOTOXIC	**PHOTOALLERGIC**
Change in photosensitizer from ground energy state to excited singlet or triplet energy state	Oxidative formation of "new" compound (haptene)
Transfer of energy	Formation of full antigen (Conjugation of haptene with protein)
Formation of free radicals, peroxides, and heat	Antigen engenders formation of cellular or humoral antibodies
Alteration in cell membrane, cytoplasm and/or nucleus	Antigen-antibody reaction upon reexposure to drug plus light

cellular damage

Sunburn-type reaction   Cutaneous reaction of varied morphology

Figure 11–7. Mechanisms of photosensitization. (From Baer, R., and Harber, L. C.: J.A.M.A., *192*:990, 1965.)

the patch is removed ("masked photopatch tests").[44] The very large number of drugs which may act as photosensitizers have been enumerated in recent reviews.[42, 45, 46] Some most often produce phototoxic reactions and others photoallergic phenomena.[42] Among the major groups are the sulfonamides and their derivatives, the phenothiazines, the tetracyclines (especially demethylchlortetracycline), thiazides, griseofulvin and naturally occurring substances like the porphyrins and furocoumarins (plant substances, such as the oils responsible for the classic berlock dermatitis).

Granulomas

As discussed in Chapter 18, granuloma formation is a pathologic feature of a number of diseases in which hypersensitivity appears to play a role, but the place of allergy in the production of granulomas is not at all clear. Thus, results of studies on experimental cutaneous zirconium granuloma formation in human volunteers are of particular interest. Transient inflammatory papules quite uniformly follow the injection of sufficient quantities of insoluble zirconium salts, which localize in macrophages. In the small number of sensitized subjects, however, Epstein et al. found focal clusters of lymphocytes appearing in skin biopsies taken after three to four weeks, and these seemed to evolve gradually into granulomas of epithelioid cells.[47] However, the Zr^{95} was not located in the epithelioid cells but, surprisingly, was concentrated outside the granuloma. This last finding is not in accord with assumptions usually made about the pathogenesis of granulomas in infectious diseases, such as tuberculosis, and emphasizes the current lack of knowledge in this area. Epstein et al. speculate that a unique type of delayed hypersensitivity may be involved.[48]

Erythema Nodosum

These lesions usually are thought of as representing an allergic response to an infectious agent or drug. Often they are associated with a state of delayed hypersensitivity, which, particularly in patients with coccidioidomycosis, may be quite pronounced. The predominating etiology has varied at different times and places: tuberculosis in Scandinavian and other European countries in past years, streptococcal infection in the northern United States, and coccidioidomycosis in the southwestern United States. Sarcoidosis also is a major cause, and in many cases no etiologic factor can be uncovered. More infrequently it may be associated with many other diseases including, in particular, histoplasmosis, chronic ulcerative colitis, lymphogranuloma venereum, psittacosis, cat scratch disease, leprosy, and many others. Iodides, bromides, and sulfonamides are the drugs most frequently implicated.

Other Skin Diseases

Several other types of cutaneous *drug reactions* are mentioned in Chapter 9. *Thrombocytopenic purpura* and *anaphylactoid purpura* are discussed on pages 188 and 468 respectively. The etiology of *erythema multiforme* is not clear, but many believe that at least in some cases it represents a hypersensitivity reaction involving small subcutaneous blood vessels. Infection and drugs are the most commonly suspected factors, though there is no apparent cause in many instances. Drugs quite clearly precipitate some cases of the *Stevens-Johnson syndrome.* Much more rarely, *Weber-Christian* disease is exacerbated by drugs, especially halogens, but it is unknown whether an immunologic mechanism is involved. *"Id" reactions* appear to represent a hypersensitivity phenomenon. Fungal, bacterial, or viral infections are the usual causes of these reactions, but they also can result from insect bites. The possible role of allergy in the cutaneous manifestations of many *infectious* and *connective tissue diseases* is beyond the scope of this discussion, but more general aspects of their immunology are presented in Chapters 18 and 19.

REFERENCES

1. Sedlis, E.: Natural history of infantile eczema: its incidence and course. J. Pediat. *66:*161, 1965.
2. Conference on Infantile Eczema. J. Pediat. *66:*153–274, 1965.
3. Sedlis, E.: Some challenge studies with foods. J. Pediat. *66:*236, 1965.
4. Rostenberg, A., and Bogdonoff, D. R.: Atopic dermatitis and infantile eczema *in* Samter, M. (ed.): Immunological Diseases. p. 635, Boston, Little, Brown and Co., 1965.
5. Hill, L. W.: The pathogenesis of infantile eczema. J. Allergy *18:*60, 1947.
6. Baer, R. L.: Atopic Dermatitis. New York, New York University Press, 1955.
7. Kepecs, J. G., Robin, H., and Munro, C.: Tickle in atopic dermatitis. Arch. Gen. Psychiat. *3:*243, 1960.
8. Johnson, L. A., and Winkelmann, R. K.: Cutaneous vascular reactivity in atopic children. Arch. Derm. *92:*621, 1965.
9. Solomon, L. M., Wentzel, H. E., and Tulsky, E.: The physiological disposition of C 14-Norepinephrine in patients with atopic dermatitis and other dermatoses. J. Invest. Dermat. *43:*193, 1964.
10. Winkelmann, R. K.: Nonallergic factors in atopic dermatitis. J. Allergy *37:*29, 1966.
11. Snyderman, S. E.: An eczematoid dermatitis in histadine deficiency. J. Pediat. *66:* 212, 1965.
12. Hashem, N., Hirschhorn, K., Sedlis, E., and Holt, L. E., Jr.: Infantile eczema. Evidence of autoimmunity to human skin. Lancet *2:*269, 1963.
13. Krivit, W., and Good, R. A.: Aldrich's syndrome (thrombocytopenia, eczema and infection in infants). J. Dis. Child. *97:*137, 1959.
14. Lewis, T.: The Blood Vessels of the Human Skin and Their Responses. London, Shaw and Sons, Ltd., 1927.
15. Calnan, C. D.: Urticarial reactions. Brit. M. J. *2:*649, 1964.
16. Rorsman, H.: Basophilic leucopenia in different forms of urticaria. Acta Allergol. *17:*168, 1962.
17. Beall, G. N.: Plasma histamine concentrations in allergic diseases. J. Allergy *34:*8, 1963.
18. Grant, R. T., Pearson, R. S. B., and Comeau, W. J.: Observations on urticaria provoked by emotion, by exercise, and by warming the body. Clin. Sci. *2:*253, 1936.
19. Shelley, W. B., and Rawnsley, H. M.: Aquagenic urticaria, contact sensitivity reaction to water. J.A.M.A. *189:*895, 1964.
20. Graham, D. T., and Wolf, S.: Pathogenesis of urticaria. Experimental study of life situations, emotions and cutaneous vascular reactions. J.A.M.A. *143:*1936, 1950.
21. Harber, L. C., Holloway, R. M., Wheatley, V. R., and Baer, R. L.: Immunologic and biophysical studies in solar urticaria. J. Invest. Dermat. *41:*439, 1963.
22. Rose, B.: The cryopathies *in* Samter, M. (ed.): Immunological Diseases. p. 713, Boston, Little, Brown and Co., 1965.
23. Sheldon, J. M., Mathews, K. P., and Lovell, R. G.: The vexing urticaria problem: present concepts of etiology and management. J. Allergy *25:*525, 1954.
24. Lorincz, A. L.: Hypersensitivity to trauma *in* Baer, R. L. (ed.): Allergic Dermatoses. p. 11, Philadelphia, J. B. Lippincott Co., 1956.
25. Beall, G. N.: Urticaria: a review of laboratory and clinical observations. Medicine *43:*131, 1964.

26. Winkelmann, R. K., Wilhelmj, C. M., and Horner, F. A.: Experimental studies on dermographism. Arch. Derm. *92:*436, 1965.
27. Landerman, N. S.: Hereditary angioneurotic edema. I. Case reports and review of the literature. J. Allergy *33:*316, 1962.
28. Spaulding, W. B.: Methyl testosterone therapy for hereditary episodic edema (hereditary angioneurotic edema). Ann. Int. Med. *53:*739, 1960.
29. Rosen, F. S., Charache, P., Pensky, J., and Donaldson, V.: Hereditary angioneurotic edema: two genetic variants. Science *148:*957, 1965.
30. Austen, K. F., and Sheffer, A. L.: Detection of hereditary angioneurotic edema by demonstration of a reduction in the second component of human complement. New England J. Med. *272:*649, 1965.
31. Epstein, S.: Contact dermatitis due to nickel and chromate. Observations on dermal delayed (tuberculin-type) sensitivity. Arch. Derm. *73:*236, 1956.
32. Eisen, H. N., Orris, L., and Belman, S.: Elicitation of delayed allergic skin reactions with haptens: the dependence of elicitation on hapten combination with protein. J. Exper. Med. *95:*473, 1952.
33. Marcussen, P. V.: Eczematous allergy to metals. Acta Allergol. *17:*311, 1962.
34. Epstein, E.: Detection of neomycin sensitivity. Arch. Derm. *91:*50, 1965.
35. Schwartz, L., Tulipan, L., and Birmingham, D. J.: Occupational Diseases of the Skin. Philadelphia, Lea and Febiger, 1957.
36. Kligman, A. M.: Poison ivy (Rhus) dermatitis. Arch. Derm. *77:*149, 1958.
37. Kligman, A. M.: Hyposensitization against Rhus dermatitis. Arch. Derm. *78:*47, 1958.
38. Kanof, N. B., and Baer, R. L.: Attempts to hyposensitize with poison ivy extracts. Ann. Allergy *22:*161, 1964.
39. Shelley, W. B., and Resnik, S. S.: Basophil degranulation produced by oral poison ivy antigen. Arch. Derm. *92:*147, 1965.
40. Sheldon, J. M., and Blumenthal, F.: Observations on the oral administration of ragweed oil in patients hypersensitive to ragweed oil. Am. J. Med. Sci. *202:*98, 1941.
41. Morris-Owen, R. M.: "Cover-dose" management of contact sensitivity to Chlorpromazine. Brit. J. Dermat. *75:*167, 1963.
42. Baer, R. L., and Harber, L. C.: Photosensitivity induced by drugs. J.A.M.A. *192:*990, 1965.
43. Schwarz, K., and Speck, M.: Experimentelle Untersuchungen zur Frage der Photoallergie der Sulfonamide. Dermatologica *114:*232, 1957.
44. Epstein, S.: The photopatch test. Its technique, manifestations and significance. Ann. Allergy *22:*1, 1964.
45. Kirshbaum, B. A., and Beerman, H.: Photosensitization due to drugs. A review of some of the recent literature. Am. J. Med. Sci. *248:*445, 1964.
46. Fitzpatrick, T. B., Pathak, M. A., Magnus, I. A., and Carwin, W. L.: Abnormal reactions to light. Ann. Rev. Med. *14:*195, 1963.
47. Epstein, W. L., Skahen, J. R., and Krasnobrod, H.: Granulomatous hypersensitivity to zirconium: localization of allergen in tissue and its role in formation of epithelioid cells. J. Invest. Dermat. *38:*223, 1962.
48. Epstein, W. L., Skahen, J. R., and Krasnobrod, H.: The organized epithelioid cell granuloma: differentiation of allergic (zirconium) from colloidal (silica) types. Am. J. Path. *43:*391, 1963.

Chapter Twelve

PATCH TESTING

ABBA I. TERR, M.D.

The patch test is the specific diagnostic procedure for establishing the etiologic agent or agents responsible for allergic contact dermatitis.[1] In principle, patch testing is simply a "reproduction in miniature" of a small area of contact dermatitis performed by applying the suspected agent to unbroken skin. A positive test is indicated by a delayed skin response which is maximal in 24 to 48 hours and resembles the primary lesion in gross appearance. Since delayed hypersensitivity is the mechanism by which allergic contact dermatitis is mediated, scratch and intradermal testing for immediate wheal-and-flare reactions are not indicated in this disease, although delayed reactions to intradermal testing have occasionally been used.[2] Conversely, patch tests are generally useless in other allergic diseases, with certain exceptions as mentioned in Chapter 9.

PRECAUTIONS IN PATCH TESTING

Patch testing is easy to perform, requiring a minimum of materials and time. However, the physician who undertakes patch testing must be aware of the serious complications which occasionally may result from this procedure. The following precautions should always be kept in mind.

1. The proper concentration of test material must be used. As indicated in the preceding chapter, many of the substances which cause allergic contact dermatitis are potent primary skin irritants in themselves; in fact the ability of a particular compound to combine chemically with dermal protein is an important factor in its ability to induce true allergic contact sensitivity. Therefore, it is essential that these materials be diluted adequately before being used for patch testing. There are two reasons for this: first, a serious chemical burn can be produced by many of these substances in high concentration; and, second, a positive patch reaction may be interpreted erroneously as indicating true allergic

sensitivity. The latter is not demonstrated unless it can be elicited with a concentration of the material which will not cause a skin reaction in a large number of normal controls. The proper diluent depends upon the solubility of the test material and should not be irritating in itself. Water, liquid petrolatum (mineral oil), olive oil, ethyl alcohol, and acetone are the usual diluting agents. Others may be used when appropriate, but a control patch test with diluent alone should also be applied. Recommended concentrations for patch testing to various groups of substances are listed on pages 282 to 284 at the end of this chapter. If there is any doubt about the proper dilution of a certain material, control tests should be made on normal individuals.

2. Patch tests should not be applied in the presence of a severe contact eruption. One should certainly wait at least until the patient has recovered from the weeping phase. There are two reasons for this precaution: first, generalized hyperreactivity of the skin at this time may result in false-positive reactions; and, second, patch testing with the correct materials may cause a flare-up of the primary skin lesions.

3. Highly sensitive patients may develop a severe dermatitis or even sloughing of the skin at the site of the patch test if the contactant is allowed to remain for the full 48 hour period. In order to avoid this occurrence, the patient should be advised routinely that if any patch begins to itch or burn, he should lift up one corner and look at the skin. If redness is present, the patch should be removed at once and the skin area washed off with soap and water.

4. Patch testing should not be performed while the patient is receiving ACTH or corticosteroids, since these drugs tend to suppress delayed hypersensitivity reactions. On the other hand, antihistamines and sympathomimetics, which inhibit immediate skin tests of the wheal-and-flare variety, do not suppress patch reactions.

5. Materials for patch testing should be selected on the basis of the history and the distribution of lesions. Unlike scratch and intradermal testing for immediate hypersensitivity, patch testing may actually induce sensitization, especially to potent sensitizers, and if unnecessarily high concentrations of test materials are applied.[3] "Routine" testing often is not an effective initial approach to diagnosis, though sometimes this is resorted to subsequently if the problem is a difficult one.

TECHNIQUE OF PATCH TESTING

Patch tests may be placed on the broad area of the back when a large number of tests are applied at one time.[4] The skin of the upper arms is also often used and is a satisfactory site if the number of tests is small enough. Theoretically, sensitization involves the entire skin so that any area could be used for patch testing; actually, however, it has been observed in many patients with small localized areas of dermatitis,

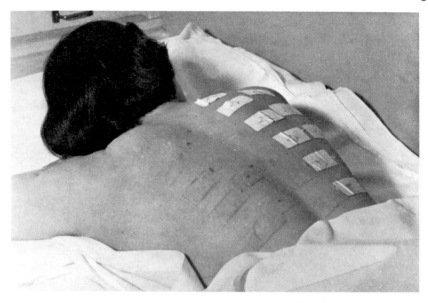

Figure 12–1. Patch testing technique. Patient has had patches on for 48 hours. First three vertical rows removed show reactions of first row to be negative. Second row shows four positive reactions.

especially on the hands, feet, or face, that patch tests may give negative responses when applied to a distant site such as the back. In these cases it would be preferable to perform the tests as close as possible to the site of the skin lesion. If the dermatitis has healed, patch testing directly on the previously involved skin area provides the best chance of all to obtain a positive response. However, this procedure should not be done on the face.

When a patient presents himself for patch testing, the back or other area to be used is washed with alcohol and allowed to dry. The tests are placed in rows on the skin, the distance between patches being at least 2 or 3 inches, as shown in Figure 12–1. In this way as many as 25 tests can be applied at one time to the back, provided that this many tests are truly indicated. Liquid contactants in the proper dilution are applied directly to the skin with a dropper. Solid materials which are inert or water-soluble should cover an area of skin no larger than a few millimeters in diameter and then are moistened with a drop of saline or "synthetic sweat."* Oil-soluble articles should be touched with a drop of mineral oil or olive oil; acetone may also be used as a solvent in appropriate cases together with a control test with plain acetone. A square of clean white linen sheet or gauze approximately 1 by 1 cm. in size is placed on each drop of test material to help prevent the liquid from running off. A 2 by 2 cm. square of plain typewriter bond paper is placed over this to protect the test area of skin from the adhesive cover-

---

* A formula for a "saline mixture" similar to perspiration is given on page 284.

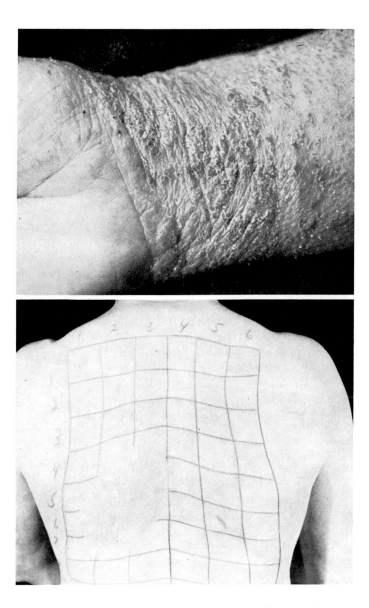

Figure 12–2. (*Top*) Dermatitis due to ragweed plant oil. The lesions appeared on the exposed areas of the skin of this farmer during the summer months. Patch testing with weed and plant oils is indicated. Oral hyposensitization may be helpful later. (*Bottom*) Positive reaction to skin test for ragweed oil. A drop of the ether-soluble portion of ragweed plant oil was placed in the second row, sixth space. In 24 hours edema, erythema, and itching were observed, indicating a strongly positive reaction.

ing. Finally a strip of adhesive tape* is applied to hold the patch in place. Alternatively, prepared patches may be purchased commercially at low cost.† Each patch should be numbered with a colored pencil and a record made of the materials applied and their respective numbers. The patient then is sent on his way with instructions to remove any patch which causes definite itching, burning, or redness and to wash that area thoroughly with soap and water.

A slight variation in the usual technique may be employed in patch testing to plant oils. These resinous substances are sticky enough to adhere satisfactorily to the skin without tape. Drops of an acetone solution of the plant oils are applied to the skin in rows and allowed to air dry. The rows are marked with a skin pencil, as shown in Figure 12–2. If they tend to rub off, the patient is asked to have someone renew the pencil markings within the 48 hour period. Bathing of the area is prohibited.

Photopatch testing is a technique which has been used as a diagnostic test for photoallergic sensitivity, particularly for certain drug reactions.[5] The test is performed by first applying a conventional patch test with the proper concentration of the suspected drug or chemical allergen, followed by a five minute exposure with ultraviolet light to the site 4 to 24 hours after removal of the patch. The irradiation may be applied with a mercury arc lamp filtered to remove all ultraviolet light below 3100 A, since the short-wave ultraviolet light produces erythema in normal skin. Control tests with the drug alone and with ultraviolet light alone should be performed; and of course the complete photopatch test should be negative in normal individuals.

READING OF PATCH TESTS

When the patient returns in 48 hours the patches are removed. One should wait 10 to 15 minutes before reading the patch test to permit the mechanical irritation to subside. Frequently some reaction to the adhesive tape will be noted; this usually takes the form of redness and perhaps some folliculitis in the area where the adhesive tape was in direct contact with the skin. The mechanism of these reactions to the tape is not understood, but it is probably irritative rather than allergic in most cases. When irritation from the tape is very pronounced, it is well to recheck the patch test reading after a few hours or on the following day. A positive allergic patch reaction usually persists for several days, whereas

---

* Tape with the least pigmented gum is likely to cause less severe reactions on the skin. Dark-brown adhesive material may contain resins which contribute to skin irritation under the tape. A satisfactory tape for this purpose is Micropore Tape No. 530, Minnesota Mining and Manufacturing Co., St. Paul, Minnesota.

† Allergy Patch Test Plasters No. 88, Allergists Supply Co., 90–04 161st St., Jamaica, New York, or Dalmas Patch Test Plasters, Dalgo, Inc., Hackensack, New Jersey.

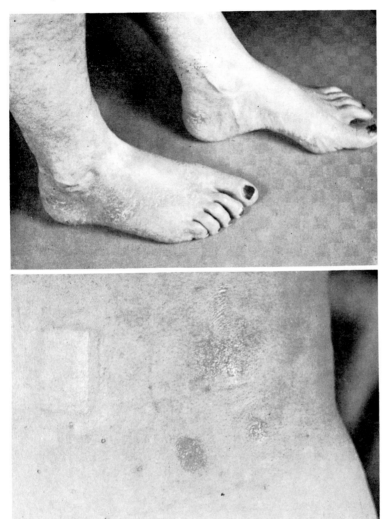

Figure 12–3. (*Top*) Contact dermatitis of the feet. Distribution of these lesions suggests possible allergy to a chemical used in tanning leather, such as a chromate, to a dye in the shoes or socks, to adhesives, or to a foot powder. This case was caused by dichromate. (*Bottom*) Patch test reactions. After 48 hours, this patient has three positive (four plus) reactions on the right side. Although the adhesive tape produces some irritation, note that the vesiculation is primarily in the center of the patch test area.

irritative skin reactions generally subside in a few hours. In those few cases in which the patient really is allergic to adhesive tape, the patches can be held on with Scotch Tape or a gauze flat dipped in collodion. (Sensitivity to collodion is rare.) If the patient reacts to all adhesive preparations, a binder bandage can be used to hold the patches in place.

In reading the patch tests it is important to focus attention only on the center of the patch where the skin was protected from the tape by the square of paper. Various systems are used for grading the intensity of the reactions. We employ the following criteria:

+ Mild erythema

++ Severe erythema, but smooth skin

+++ Erythema and papules

++++ Erythema, papules, and vesiculation

It should be noted that strong 4+ responses may produce coalescense of the vesicles so that the skin may weep when the patch is removed. Some positive patch reactions are shown in Figures 12–2 and 12–3.

After the patch tests have been read, the test area should be thoroughly washed with ether, alcohol, or soap and water, depending upon the solubilities of the substances tested.

Patch test reactions occasionally may be negative in 48 hours and then become positive one or two days after the patch is removed. Reactions of this type are considered significant. In some cases this might indicate photosensitivity if the test site has been exposed to sunlight.

As noted above, the primary skin lesions may flare somewhat during the course of patch testing. Although this is most apt to occur when one or more strongly positive patch reactions are elicited, occasionally this is noted even when all tests are negative. In these cases the patch tests should be repeated later directly on the sensitized skin, if possible.

MATERIALS FOR PATCH TESTING

Patch testing is done after the patient has had a complete history and physical examination and the physician has made a list of the most likely suspected agents. The actual material to be used for patch testing may be obtained either directly from the patient or from a stock supply of some of the common offenders in allergic contact dermatitis.

Material from the Patient's Environment

In most cases the patient himself is the best source of testing materials. Following the list of suspected agents, he may be instructed to bring in all the items which he may have contacted in his household or occupational tasks, all the medications he has applied to his lesions, all the cosmetics and toilet articles he has used, and all the articles of clothing which may have come in contact with the involved skin area. Particularly in cases in which clothing, ointments, cosmetics, or toilet goods are suspected, it is usually best to test the patient with his own articles. Small pieces of cloth or fur for patch testing may be obtained from the seams of clothing without damaging the garments. When testing the patient with his own shoes or slippers, it is advisable to take specimens from the several different portions of the shoe including the tongue, inner lining, inner sole, shoe top, and metallic eyelets. When a large solid object such as a steering wheel is suspected, small patch testing specimens of it may be shaved off with a knife. In cases of suspected plant oil dermatitis, it may be helpful to test with plants obtained from the patients own farm or garden. A crushed moist leaf or stem may be used. If the dermatitis is severe, someone other than the patient should collect the suspected articles, particularly living plants. Otherwise he may induce a serious flare of his dermatitis by handling the offending agent. In addition to testing portions of the plant specimens directly, the species of plant should be identified and the patient should be tested with plant oils from these species, if available (see page 293).

Household and industrial materials which might be primary irritants should be diluted before being used in patch testing in accordance with the principles mentioned above. (Suggested dilutions of various items are given on pages 282 to 284.)

In some cases the offending agent is readily identified; frequently, however, many series of patch tests are required before the specific causative agent is found. In some cases, too, it may be possible for the patient himself to apply the tests after he is instructed about the precautions and the technique to be used. Reading of the patch test results, however, should be done only by the physician or his specially trained assistant.

Physician's Supply of Testing Materials

In addition to relying on his patients for patch testing materials, there are several reasons why the physician who does frequent patch testing should have a supply of the most common contactants on hand in the office. First, it is advisable to establish as precisely as possible the exact chemical substances which cause a contact dermatitis. For example, testing with the patient's own materials may show that he is allergic to his shoes or some article of clothing, but beyond this it is desirable to know whether a certain dye, tanning agent, sizing material, or other compound is the specific substance responsible for the lesions. Identification of the offending chemical by appropriate patch tests not only is of academic interest but also has practical value in enabling the patient to avoid other articles containing the same compound. An available collection of patch testing materials also saves the time required to prepare and dilute the patient's own materials for testing. Finally, there are certain items which patients cannot obtain because of their size or lack of availability, and the physician must be able to furnish satisfactory substitute material in such cases.

A simple, inexpensive method for accumulating a collection of allergens for patch testing is to save samples of various suspected articles which patients bring in. It is surprising to see how rapidly one can develop a fairly extensive library of patch testing materials. In fact, the main problem usually is one of labeling and cataloguing the materials so that a certain item can be located when needed.* It is advisable to store the patch materials in small screw-capped bottles of uniform size. Bottle caps with glass applicators attached are especially convenient.

Although many items for patch testing may be collected in the manner described above, it is well for the physician to purchase certain basic materials. It is especially important to have on hand pure solutions of some of the most important chemical compounds, dyes, and metals which often produce contact lesions. The allergist surely should have all 25 common causative agents of contact dermatitis (see pages 284–285). These may be obtained at low cost from chemical and pharmaceutical supply houses. It is also very desirable to have available the weed oils (listed on page 294) and the cultivated plant oils (listed on page 293.)†

The allergist who has a selection of testing materials on hand can apply patch tests to suspected items at the time of the first office visit, unless there is some contraindication to testing at that time. The patient is given an additional list of articles to bring to the doctor's office from his home or place of work. He can return with these when the first set of tests is read 48 hours later. If the initial procedure has not solved the problem, tests next are applied using the patient's materials together with any others which are suspected.

SELECTION OF ITEMS FOR PATCH TESTING

Identifying the cause of a case of contact dermatitis may be relatively easy or extremely difficult. As pointed out in the previous chapter, there are three considerations which aid in directing one's attention to the offending contactant: the distribution of the dermatitis, the history of the circumstances under which the lesions are present or absent, and a knowledge of substances known to be potent sensitizers. A little further elaboration seems appropriate here.

On pages 280 to 282 are lists of contactants which are suggested by various distributions of the skin lesions. These are helpful check lists in the selection of materials for patch testing. Even more complete lists of this type have been published by Weber.[6] Some of the most common contact patterns merit special mention. In women, lesions on the eyelids and along the sides of the neck should suggest allergy to nail polish even though the fingers are spared. Dermatitis behind the ears, along the neck, and on the forearms may be due to cologne or perfume. If the dorsal surfaces of both feet are involved, some material in the patient's shoes would be the most likely agent (see Figure 12–3). When the hands, face,

---

* We have found it convenient to divide our patch testing materials into the groups listed on pages 284 to 294 at the end of this chapter. It will be seen that this classification is based largely on occupational groupings.

† These may be procured from Hollister-Stier Laboratories, 107 S. Division Street, Spokane, Washington 99202.

and neck are involved a volatile material should be considered if the dermatitis stops abruptly at the collar line in men or forms a "V" pattern over the upper anterior chest in women. An article of clothing should be suspected when the lesions are present only on covered surfaces of the body, especially on areas of intimate contact with clothing such as the axillae, the beltline, and the dorsal thighs. Dermatitis from long-sleeved articles of clothing sometimes appears only in the antecubital fossae, which might mislead the physician into making a diagnosis of atopic dermatitis

In cases of dermatitis involving the axillae, one especially should note whether the apex is involved. Sensitivity to deodorant generally extends to the apex (as does also seborrheic dermatitis, moniliasis, and other fungus infections). See Figure 12–4. On the other hand, the apex is usually spared in contact dermatitis from dress shields or clothing. A finger lesion underneath a ring may be caused by contact sensitivity to a metal in the ring (often nickel), or it may be that the ring has retained in contact with the skin some sensitizing agent or irritant which the patient handles in the course of her daily activities. Contact dermatitis rarely involves the palms of the hands, but when it occurs in this area in a housewife or a butcher, one should suspect allergy to cocobolo wood. A

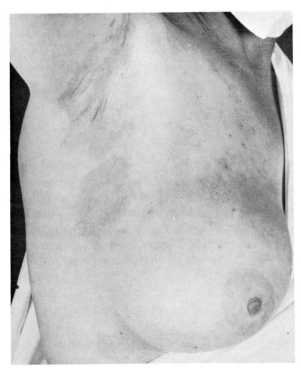

Figure 12–4. Contact dermatitis. This patient used deodorant, with resulting vesicular pruritic dermatitis.

limited area of dermatitis on the upper anterior thigh should suggest sensitivity to someting carried in the patient's pocket. When a person with a localized dermatitis suddenly develops very widespread skin lesions, the doctor should consider a secondary sensitivity to the ointments that have been used on the initial lesion.

The history affords another approach to the problem of selecting from the patient's environment items which might be suspected of causing the dermatitis. As indicated in Chapter 11, contactants generally fall into one of the following categories: household articles, occupational agents, plants, clothing and cosmetics, materials used in hobbies, and ointments or other local applications. Lists of common contactants in each of these categories are given on pages 284 to 294. In utilizing these lists one should determine which articles the patient actually handles, and patch tests should be performed with these and with any other suspected items suggested by the patient's history.

Finally, the allergist should be familiar with the most potent sensitizers and the everyday articles in which they are contained, and he should be especially alert to the patient's possible contact with these agents. Reference already has been made to the list of 25 common contactants (see pages 284, 285.) Chromium compounds are important not only because of their presence in many metal alloys but more importantly because of their use in tanning leathers, in paints, cement, and engine coolants (see Figure 17–3). Many mercury compounds are very potent sensitizers. If the patient has used any ointments or antiseptics containing mercury, these should be strongly suspected. Among the metals, nickel is one of the most potent sensitizers, and dermatitis from jewelry is more likely to be caused by nickel, chromium, or copper than by the precious metals. Local anesthetics or ointments containing them are potent allergens, and such compounds constitute an important occupational hazard among dentists. As discussed on page 181, cross-reactions may occur among many of the local anesthetics, sulfonamides, sunscreens, and azo dyes which have in common the para-aminophenyl group. Phenol, resorcin, and local antibiotics are additional common ointment constituents with a high sensitizing capability. Sodium hypochlorite, commonly found in laundry bleaches, causes many cases of contact dermatitis. Certain dyes and dye precursors produce contact lesions, and no doubt paraphenylenediamine is the most common sensitizer in this group. This compound is a frequent cause of dermatitis from hair dye and occasionally from clothing or fur dye. The para red dyes present in the colored section of many magazines and newspapers also may cause dermatitis.

DERMATITIS FROM PLANT OILS

Although everyone is familiar with the dermatitis resulting from poison ivy, poison sumac, and poison oak, it is not so widely appreciated that many other plants are capable of causing contact dermatitis.* Ragweed, dog fennel (*Anthemis cotula*), feverfew, oriental poppy, geranium, primrose, horsetail (*Equisetum arvense*), and chrysanthemum have been common offenders in our experience, and occasional instances of contact reactions from many other plants have been reported. In tropical areas, the mango tree and its fruit are potent contactants of importance. Many other plant products, such as the oils of orange, lemon, cloves, cinnamon, juniper, rose, bergamot, and lavender (see page 290) may cause contact dermatitis, the contact occurring either from foods or from cosmetics. Lists of oils from a representative group of wild and cultivated plants are given on pages 293 to 294. When indicated, additional tests may be performed with plant specimens which the patient brings in. Although ragweed is a common cause of both hay fever and contact dermatitis, inhalant sensitivity is due to the protein fractions of ragweed pollen, while contact allergy is caused by the oil of the plant or pollen. Clinically, the two conditions may or may not co-exist in the same patient. Most persons with contact dermatitis due to plant oil are farmers, feed handlers, or those who do considerable gardening. Sometimes the sensitivity becomes so intense that even the minute amount of oil in air-borne pollen is sufficient to cause a generalized rash on the face, neck and other exposed skin areas.

DERMATITIS FROM WEARING APPAREL

Articles of clothing are often suspected as causes of allergic contact dermatitis. Sensitization may occur to the fabric itself, chemicals used in processing the fabric, dyes, or metallic or rubber accessories in the article. A list of common fabrics, both natural and synthetic, is given on page 290. In general, the synthetic fibers are relatively free of sensitizing properties.

There are four major ways in which the fabric may be processed. *Sanforizing* involves shrinkage of the material under controlled conditions, and no additives are used. *Mercerizing* is the impregnation of the fabric, usually cotton, with sodium hydroxide in order to improve the strength and luster and to increase the affinity for dyes. *Sizing* is the addition of stiffeners to produce a glaze as in sheeting, mosquito-netting, organdy, and piqué. Stiffeners frequently used include starch, glues, vegetable gums, resins, and shellac. Finally, *anti-wrinkle* finishes are

---

* *Preparation of plant oils.* After obtaining several armloads of the plant in question in a fresh growing condition: (1) Pick off all buds and flowers to remove pollen. (2) Wash leaves and stems while still green with cold water to remove sand and dust. (3) Spread out leaves and stems and allow to dry thoroughly for 14 days. (4) Break up the leaves and stems into small pieces by hand or use a blender. (5) Place in a jar and cover with excess of ether. Put lid on jar. (6) Let stand 48 hours with occasional shaking. (7) Decant solution into evaporating dish and allow ether to evaporate. (8) The remaining substance which does not evaporate contains the plant oil. Dilutions are made from this material by adding olive oil or peanut oil.

achieved by the use of resins, which make the finished products crush-resistant, shrink-resistant, and water repellent. A list of resins used for this purpose is given on page 290. The formaldehyde compounds are probably the most common offenders in this group.

Patch testing for sensitivity to the dyes is best done by using the suspected fabric itself, provided the dye can be eluted from the material. Since axillary sweat is alkaline, the fabric can be soaked in "synthetic sweat" (see page 284). Alternatively, a piece of fabric is soaked in weak acid (a few drops of vinegar in water) for 24 hours, and if the water is discolored by bleeding of the dye, the water extract can be concentrated by vacuum and used in patch testing. Lists of common dyes are given on page 289.

COMMON OFFENDERS IN CONTACT DERMATITIS*

This form is helpful when taking the history of a patient with contact dermatitis and when preparing lists of patch testing materials. It brings to the physician's attention the items which might be important in the investigation. A few of these substances are more likely to act as primary irritants than as allergens.

1. *Head and Neck*

 A. Face. Cosmetics (powder, cream, rouge, lipstick, rubber pads for applying cosmetics), hair tonic, dyes (henna, walnut juice, paraphenylenediamine, mineral dyes), astringent lotions, acne cream, depilatories, nail polish, bleaches, freckle removers, facial masks, perfumes, cologne, vanishing creams, hair lacquer, hair lacquer pads, hair nets, bobby pins, curlers, musical instruments (chin—violin; mouth—flute), bubble gum, wave solutions, soap,† shampoo, insect repellant, suntan lotion, plants, clothing, furs, volatile and fine droplet materials, and all contacts carried through the fingers.

 B. Lips—Perioral. Lipstick, dentifrices, oranges and other citrus fruit, dentures, pipes, mouthwashes, penicillin and other antibiotic drugs, "chap" stick, chewing gum, cigarette holders, musical instruments, rubber dams (dental); pencils, hairpins, and other objects placed in mouth by habit.

 C. Eyelids. Hair dyes, cosmetics (creams, powders, mascara, rubber applicators), soap, shaving lotions, gasoline, cleaning fluids, perfumes, burned coal gas, rims of glasses, penicillin and other antibiotic drugs, paints (new painting), eyelash curlers, artificial eyelash adhesive, hearth and stove polishes, eyewashes, furs, plants (especially primrose), eye drops, orange peels, apple peels, plant pollens, insect sprays, anti-moth preparations, benzine, nasal sprays, nail polishes, nail polish remover, turpentine, carbon paper, hair wave sets, and animal danders.

 D. Nasolabial Area. Nose drops, sprays, paper tissue, antibiotics, "cold" ointments, handkerchief (especially perfumed), and inhalers.

 E. Ears and Retroauricular Area. Nickel (earrings, spectacle frames), bobby pins, goggles, eye shadow, hair lacquer, colognes, perfumes, telephone receivers, hair nets, hearing aids, match heads, scalp lotions, earmuffs, hairpins, hair combs, pencils (behind ear), feathers (pillow), shower caps, and dye from blankets.

 F. Scalp. Hair tonics, hair dyes, lotions, caps (bathing, cloth, fur), wigs, hairpins,

---

* This list was compiled by Stephan Epstein, M.D., Marshfield Clinic, Marshfield, Wisconsin, with modification by the authors.

† Although soaps not uncommonly produce irritant skin reactions, true allergic dermatitis to soaps *per se* is extremely rare, although some additives (e.g., perfumes) may be allergenic.

cold-wave materials, shampoos, rinses, hair nets, olive oil, pomades, hats (lining, band), dandruff removers, curlers, and bobby pins.

G. Neck. Laundry marks (nape), scarves, clothing (fabrics, furs, and dyes), nail polish, penicillin and other antibiotics, jewelry (necklaces, charms), hair nets, cosmetics, collars, permanent-wave solutions, cloth coats, raincoats, shower caps, perfumes, and colognes.

2. *Hands*

A. General. Gasoline, plants (ragweed, primrose, chrysanthemum, tulip, bachelor button, hollyhock, poppy, poison ivy), gloves, instruments, antibiotic solutions, vegetables, utensils, knife handles, hobbies and occupational contacts, nickel (coins, faucets, gadgets), greases, chemicals, bleaches, soaps, polishes (furniture, metal, glass), cleansers (scouring powder), steering wheels, furniture (lacquer, stuffing), scissors, thimbles, sewing needles, knitting needles, yarn, garden equipment (fertilizers, insect sprays), and writing equipment (pen, typewriter ribbon, carbon paper, ink eradicator, ink, pencil, tools).

B. Total Surface of Hands. Gloves, washing powders, lotions and ointments, fruit and vegetable juices, soaps, hand creams, hair tonics, glove powders, insect powders, shampoos, bleaches.

C. Fingers. Thimbles, rings, pencils, scissors, wave setting lotions, rubber (gloves, finger cot), pens, cigarette holders, cigarettes, and pipes.

D. Interdigital Spaces. Golf tees, labels, rubber, yarn, knitting needles, cigarette holders, pens, pencils, and paint and household items such as grease not removed by careful washing.

E. Dorsal Surface. Ragweed, poison ivy, other plants and flowers, and gloves.

F. Finger Tips. Typewriter keys, musical instruments, wave setting lotions, hair tonics, eye ointments, push buttons, starter on car, electric bell buttons, and hair curlers.

G. Finger Grip. Radio dial, safe dial, caps on tubes (toothpaste, cosmetics, paints, and other items), water faucet, lipstick containers, gear-shift lever, hairpins, radishes, peanuts, pills, screw drivers, knitting needles, playing cards, keys, watch stems, radiator valves, electric light switches, light chains, celery, olives, popcorn, pencils and pens, and crochet hooks.

H. Palms and Fingers. Knife handles, rubber hose, dog leash, bridle straps, wires, books, toothbrushes, umbrellas, handbag straps, athlete's bars, steering wheels, tennis racquets, saw handles, electric iron, bicycle grips, handles of pans, golf clubs, powdered food substances, gear shift, soap dispensers, hand mirrors, vacuum cleaner handle, horseradish, carrots, cigarette lighters, lighter fluid, pocket knife, match boxes, key cases, door knobs, electric razors, tin cans, oranges, citrus fruit, cocktail shaker, knob of cane, toothpaste, condiments, tooth powder, and plastics.

3. *Arms and Legs*

A. Arms and Forearms. DDT, plants, greases, chemicals, soaps, bleaches, cleansers, clothing, pins, buttons, metal on chair arms, watch bands (plastic, leather, metal), jewelry, furniture lacquer and polish, antibiotic solutions, oilcloth, nail polishes, colognes, perfumes, handbag straps, menus, magazines, and books.

B. Axillae. Antiperspirant preparations, deodorants, depilatories, dress materials, dress dye, dress shields, rubber, and zippers (unilateral).

C. Thighs. Nickel, rubber (garters), girdles, DDT, matches, keys, other objects in pockets such as money, and lining of pockets.

D. Legs. DDT, laundry marks (lower third), shoes, stockings, garters, socks, ankle bracelets, plants, weeds, trousers, creosote oil used in preserving wood, nail polishes (used to stop runs in nylon stockings), nylon, leather dyes, tanning agents, dyes, finishing materials, plastics, seat covers and furniture coverings, sun tan lotions, and colognes.

E. Feet. DDT, laundry marks (side of feet), shoes, slippers, leather dyes, shoe polishes, socks, foot powders, athlete's foot medications, rubber cement, rubbers, arch support (plantar), and nylon hosiery.

F. Toes. Nail polishes, socks, corn plaster, athlete's foot medications; also certain items listed under *Feet.*

4. *Chest*

    A. Upper Chest. Buttons, identification tags, metal (religious medals), liniments, cold ointments, underwear, "falsies," rubber, and nickel.

    B. Lower Chest. DDT (points of pressure), laundry marks, money belts, leather belts, girdles, shirt tails (dye).

5. *Abdomen*

    Girdles, sanitary belts, nickel, trusses, and rubber.

6. *Upper Back*

    Brassieres (rubber, nickel, nylon), clothing (dyes), and laundry marks.

7. *Trunk*

    Clothing (underwear, night clothes, shirts, sweaters), plants, soap, toilet seat, bath salts, dusting powders, suntan lotions, ointments, and deodorants.

8. *Anogenital Region*

    A. Vaginal-Perineal Region. Antiseptics, contraceptive ointments, foams and jellies, pessaries, deodorants, sanitary pads, safety pins (nickel), sanitary powders, douches, underwear, nylon, silk, rayon, cleansing tissue, toilet tissue, rubber, substances carried on hands (nail polish, perfume, soap, poison ivy).

    B. Perineal Region. Toilet tissue, enema constituents, suppositories, ingested foods, fruits, oils, underwear, rubber, nylon, silk, rayon, nail polishes, toilet seats, perfumes, and colognes.

    C. Penis and Scrotum. Any substances carried on hands, plants (especially poison ivy), clothing, dyes, rubber and elastic supports, underwear, contraceptives; when applicable, all materials listed in 8-A and 8-B above.

*Recommended Concentrations of Substances for Patch Testing**

    This outline indicates accepted concentrations of commonly used testing materials and the manner of testing. The grouping is for convenience in office use; more detailed information is available in other publications.[7, 8]

1. *Acids*

    Moisten gauze with a 1 per cent aqueous solution, except: *Hydrofluoric acid*—moisten gauze with a 0.2 per cent aqueous solution. *Boric acid*—moisten gauze with a pure powder. Some acids may be employed in higher concentrations.

2. *Alkalis*

    Moisten gauze with a 0.5 to 1.0 per cent aqueous solution, except: *Calcium hydrate*—moisten gauze with a 0.1 per cent aqueous solution. Some alkalis may be employed in higher concentrations.

3. *Soaps*

    Moisten gauze with suds in concentrations actually employed in work, except: *Tincture green soap*—moisten gauze with 5 per cent solution in petrolatum or 2.5 per cent alcoholic solution. NOTE: Always perform controls, especially for soaps containing antiseptics and perfume.

4. *Solvents*

    Moisten gauze with a 50 per cent solution in a bland oil (olive oil).

5. *Petroleum Products*

    Moisten gauze with the pure substance, except: *Crude coal tar*—moisten gauze with a 5 to 10 per cent solution in petrolatum. *Petrolatum*—moisten gauze with

---

* Reproduced by courtesy of Dr. M. B. Sulzberger.

a 20 per cent solution. *Benzine, gasoline, kerosene, machine oil*—moisten gauze with a 50 per cent solution in olive oil.

6. *Insecticides*

Moisten gauze with a 25 per cent solution in olive oil, except: *Larvex, creosote*—moisten gauze with a 10 per cent solution in olive oil.

7. *Dyes*

Aniline, cosmetics—moisten gauze with "saline mixture"* and pure substances, powder or paste, except: *Hair, fur*—moisten gauze with a 3 per cent aqueous solution. *Leather*—moisten gauze with a 50 per per cent solution in olive oil of the leather dye; also shoe dye. *Paraphenylenediamine*—moisten gauze with a 2 per cent solution in petrolatum. Use controls.

8. *Dye Intermediates*

Moisten gauze with "saline mixture" and pure powder, except: *Beta naphthol*—moisten gauze with 10 per cent solution in olive oil. *Michler's Hydrol*—moisten gauze with 5 per cent alcoholic solution *P-nitroso-dimethylaniline*—moisten gauze with 1 per cent alcoholic solution. *Dinitro-chlor benzol*—moisten gauze with 0.5 per cent alcoholic solution.

9. *Rubber and Rubber Products*

Latex, balata, gutta sica—moisten gauze with "saline mixture" and pure substance.

10. *Rubber Accelerators*

Moisten gauze with "saline mixture" and pure substance, except: *Para-amido-phenol*—moisten gauze with a 3 per cent solution, or 10 per cent solution of material in olive oil. *Pyrogallol*—moisten gauze with 3 per cent aqueous solution or 10 per cent solution in olive oil. *P-nitroso-dimethylaniline*—moisten gauze with 1 per cent acetone solution.

11. *Rubber Anti-oxidants*

Moisten gauze with "saline mixture" and pure substance.

12. *Paints*

Lacquers, enamels, varnishes, shellac—paint on gauze with 50 per cent solution in olive oil.
Linseed oil, white lead, water and mineral colors, calcimine, plaster, inks, bluing—apply on gauze in full strength. *Note:* Always perform controls with paints or paint ingredients.

13. *Waxes*

Apply on gauze full strength except: *Floor wax*—moisten gauze with 50 per cent solution in olive oil. *Note:* Always perform controls.

14. *Oils*

Almond, barley, codfish, codliver, cottonseed, citronella, cocoanut, glycerine, hempseed, linseed, mineral oil, olive, palm, peanut, pine, poppy seed, walnut, sulfonated lanolin, lard, lubricating—use full strength.

15. *Essential Oils*

Moisten gauze with 5 to 10 per cent solution in olive oil, except: *Oil of orange*—moisten gauze with 1 per cent alcoholic solution. *Perfume oils*—moisten gauze with 1 per cent alcoholic solution. *Flavoring oils*—moisten gauze with 2 per cent alcoholic solution. Always perform controls.

16. *Plants and Woods*

Use pure, in powdered or finely divided form. Use controls.

---

* Formula on page 284.

17. *Photographic Developers*

Moisten gauze with a 5 per cent aqueous solution, except: *Paraphenylenediamine* —moisten gauze with a 2 per cent solution in petrolatum. *Para-amidophenol*— moisten gauze with 2 per cent solution in petrolatum. *Pyrogallol*—moisten gauze with 3 per cent aqueous solution. *Potassium bichromate*—moisten gauze with 0.5 to 1 per cent aqueous solution. *Sodium bichromate*—moisten gauze with 3 per cent aqueous solution.

18. *Clothing and Clothing Materials*

Moisten with "saline mixture" and use as is.

19. *Drugs, Including Antibiotics*

Apply in concentration of suspected exposure; if powder, moisten with "saline mixture." Use controls.

20. *Cosmetics*

If powder, moisten gauze with "saline mixture." Controls. Antihidrotics—if powder, moisten gauze, with "saline mixture."

21. *Foods*

Use full strength except rinds of some fruits, spices, mustards.

22. *Fertilizers*

Full strength; always perform controls.

23. *Polishes*

Apply full strength except: *Shoe*—moisten gauze with 50 per cent solution in petrolatum. *Brass*—moisten gauze with 10 per cent aqueous solution. *Furniture*— moisten gauze with 10 per cent solution in olive oil. Always perform controls.

24. *Antiseptics*

Iodine—tincture, *do not cover.* *Metaphen*—moisten gauze with 0.5 per cent alcoholic solution. *Mercury Bichloride*—moisten gauze with 0.1 per cent aqueous solution. *Lysol, Zonite*—moisten gauze with 1 per cent aqueous solution. *Thymol*— use a 1 per cent solution in petrolatum. *Cresol*—use a 0.5 to 1 per cent aqueous solution. *Creosote*—use a 5 per cent solution in olive oil. *Formaldehyde*—use a 5 per cent aqueous solution. "c-n"—use a 1 to 10 per cent aqueous solution.

25. *Cleaning Fluids*

Noninflammable—full strength. Inflammable—use 60 per cent solution in olive oil. Always perform controls.

26. *Cement and Slaked Lime*

Use as occurs in work exposure. Always perform controls.

27. *Additional Household Articles*

Alum—use in a 10 per cent aqueous solution. Ammonia—use as a 1 to 2 per cent aqueous solution. Camphor—Use as pure powder mixed with "saline mixture." Oil of camphor—use as 10 per cent solution in petrolatum.

Formula for "Saline Mixture" (similar to Perspiration)

Sodium chloride	3	Lactic acid	2
Sodium sulfate	1	Olein	2
Urea	2	Stearin	2
Aq. dist. q.s.	1000		

To make acid, add a drop of acetic acid; to make alkaline, add a drop of ammonia.

Survey Group of Common Contactants

Copper sulfate—1 per cent aqueous solution.
Sodium arsenate—10 per cent solution.
Potassium dichromate—0.5 per cent aqueous solution.

Mercury bichloride—1:1000 aqueous solution.
Nickel chloride—5 per cent aqueous solution.
Procaine—1 per cent aqueous solution.
Metaphen—standard solution.
Mercurochrome—standard solution.
Tincture of pyrethrum—20 per cent tincture.
Butesin picrate—1 per cent in white petrolatum.
Resorcin—10 per cent aqueous solution.
Quinine hydrochloride—1 per cent aqueous solution.
Paraphenylenediamine—2 per cent in white petrolatum.
Sodium hypochlorite—5 per cent aqueous solution.
Potassium iodide—25 per cent in petrolatum.
Formalin—5 per cent aqueous solution.
Iodoform—powder.
DDT—50 per cent solution in olive oil.
Para red (deep) (1)—powder.
Para red (deep) (2)—powder.
Para red (light)—powder.
Methyl orange—5 per cent aqueous solution.
Eosin dye—powder.
Ragweed oil—diluted 1:1000 in olive oil.
Poison ivy oil—diluted 1:5000 in acetone.

Sources of Contact with Mercury*

Medications containing mercury (Mercresin, Mercurochrome, Merthiolate, ammoniated mercury).
Mercurial chemicals in laboratories (bichloride of mercury, mercuric iodide).
Amalgams used by dentists and technicians.
Mercury in industrial processing (printing, artificial silk, paint, lamps, pumps, thermometers).
Curing of furs and pelts.
Photogravure and industrial photography.
Manufacture and repair of storage batteries and electrical equipment, mirror-making, and handling alloys with tin and copper.

Sources of Contact with Nickel

Jewelry—clasps, wrist bands, as hardening agent in soft metals, earrings, buckles.
Coins, nickel chromium steel, armor plating, nickel (German) silver, electrical alloys, stainless steel, Nichrome, case-hardened parts for high-strength casting, bridge steel, forgings, boiler plate, Monel, Permalloy, and Alnico. Nickel alloys are used in some lead wires on electric light bulbs, radio tubes and transformers, telephone equipment, and some gasolines.

Sources of Contact with Paraphenylenediamine

Fur dyes and hair dyes, blue, black, and brown clothing and textile dyes; rubber vulcanization process; materials in chemical laboratories.

Sources of Contact with Chrome

General exposure from handling: detergents and bleaching agents, chrome-tanned leather articles, especially shoes, tattoo (chrome green), match heads, certain yellow and orange paints, olive drab paint (military), wool dyes, and hide glue.

---

* Phenylmercurials are widely employed as antibacterial and antifungal agents in paper manufacturing, protective coatings for leather and canvas, house paints, herbicides and fungicides in agriculture (especially for treating seed), diaper disinfectants, camouflage cosmetics, contraceptives, many medicinals (e.g., eye drops, ointments, biologicals, allergy extracts), air-conditioner filters, toothbrushes, glue, sizing, starch pastes, bentonite gels, and gelatin waving solutions.

Industrial exposure: automobile industry (primer paints with zinc chromate, chromate dip for nuts and bolts), welding (gases and fumes), foundries (cement, sand), cement industry (including cement workers, especially those handling wet cement, masons, tile setters), railroad industry (diesel locomotive radiatior fluid additive), anti-freeze, fur industry, photography and lithography, and ink manufacture.

Household Contact List*

GROUP I
Insect sprays—50% in oil
1. Bugaboo†
2. DDT
3. Flit
4. Fly Ded
5. Gulf Spray
6. Black leaf
7. Bordeaux
8. Moth flakes
9. Pyrethrum (powder)
GROUP II
A. Polishes (wood)—10% in oil
1. Hospital polish
2. Hospital cream
3. Fuller polish
4. Fuller cream
5. Stanley cream
B. Polishes (metal)
1. Metal polish (Stanley)
2. Brass polish (10%)
3. Silver polish (10%)
4. Glass wax (10%)
C. Waxes—10% in oil
1. Floor wax (Aero)
2. Simoniz, self-polish
3. Liquid wax (Fuller)
4. Wax (Stanley EZ Glow)
5. Wax (Johnson's)
GROUP III
A. Cleaners
1. Windex
2. Mystic Foam cleaner
3. Bruce's floor cleaner
4. Cameo cleanser
B. Cleansers, powder—1% aqueous
1. Old Dutch
2. Sunbrite
3. Bab-O
4. Ajax
C. Cleansers, additional
1. Bon Ami
2. Renuzit
3. Carbona (50% in oil)
4. Denatured alcohol (as is)
5. Kerosene (60%)

GROUP III (continued)
6. Brillo soap (1% aqueous)
7. S.O.S
8. Solventol
9. Spic and Span
10. Silver Dust
11. Gold Dust
12. Carbon tetrachloride (50% in oil)
13. Energine
GROUP IV
A. Soda
1. Soda Wyandotte
2. Laundry soda
B. Starch
1. Sizing starch
2. Satina
3. Linit
4. Perma starch
C. Bluing
1. LaFrance
2. Blue-white
D. Borax (10% aqueous)
E. Laundry soap
1. Kirkman's soap (1% aqueous)
2. Fels Naphtha
F. Chlorine compounds—5% aqueous
1. Clorox
2. Roman Cleanser
G. Miscellaneous
1. Ammonia (2%)
2. Lysol (1%)
3. Naphtha (50%)
GROUP V
Miscellaneous
1. Benzine (60% in oil)
2. Flexible plastic (as is)
3. Rubber gloves
4. Cocobolo wood
5. Nickel chloride (5%)
6. Turpentine (50% in oil)
7. Lemon oil (1% alcoholic)
8. Sodium fluoride (2%)
9. Steel wool
10. Ant powder (as is)
11. Shellac (50% in oil)
12. Varnish

* In addition to picking representative materials from each group, the patient is encouraged to submit sample articles from his home to which he is patch-tested.

When no dilution is indicated in this and subsequent lists, refer to p. 282 for recommended concentrations.

† *Note:* The listing of commonly used brand name materials is not meant to imply that these particular brands are especially apt to cause sensitization. They are merely readily available sources of testing material. A number of these items, especially the cleansers and soaps, are much more likely to act as irritants than allergens.

Cosmetic Contact List*

GROUP I
Fitch Shampoo (50% in oil)
Green soap shampoo (2.5% alcohol)
Soapless oil shampoo (50% in oil)
Tar shampoo
Eucalyptus oil shampoo
White henna rinse (50% aqueous)
Wave set (brand)
Permanent-wave oil
Permanent-wave solution
Toni Home Permanent
Bobbi Home Permanent
Rayve Home Permanent
Head and Shoulders Shampoo

GROUP II
Mennen's Antiseptic Oil (50% in oil)
Brilliantine
Fitch's Hair Tonic
Hair lotion (brand)
Scalp oil (brand)
Wildroot oil for hair
Cuticle remover (50% aqueous)
Nail polish undercoat (1% in acetone)
Nail polish remover (10% aqueous)
Nail polish cream (brand) (as is)
Lipstick (as is)

Rouge
Eye shadow
Mascara

GROUP III
Talcum powder
Face powder
Shaving cream (50% aqueous)
Skin bracer
'Lectric Shave
Cold cream
Nivea cream
Propylene glycol
Tooth paste
Tooth powder
Flexible plastic

GROUP IV
Cologne (brand)
Perfume (brand)
Perfumed face powder
Veto
Mum
Pine sachet
Arid
Odorono
Amoline cream
Bath salts (1% aqueous)

* Listing of these materials does not imply that they cause sensitization. Representatives of each group used by patient should be tested.

Anesthetics and Analgesic Ointments*

Novocain (procaine) (1%)
Butesin Picrate (1%)
Picric acid (1%)
Phenol (1%)
Anesthesin (5% aquaphor)
Orthoform
Cocaine, liquid (10%)
Nupercaine Ointment (2%)
Nupercainal
Pontocaine (2%)

Intracaine (2%)
Metycaine
Butyn Sulfate
Surfacaine
Naphthocaine
Benzocaine (10%)
Xylocaine (2%)
Ecogonine
Holocaine
Saligenin (2%)

* This group is of particular help in testing physicians, dentists, and nurses who have dermatitis of the hands. It is also useful when sensitivity from an anesthetic ointment is suspected. The patient should be tested with samples of the ointment he uses.

Artist Contact Group

Badger hair
Sable hair
Camel hair
Chrome yellow oil paint (50% in oil)
Cadmium orange oil paint
Ultramine blue oil paint
Vert Emeralde oil paint
Yellow olive oil paint
Venetian red oil paint
Zinc white oil paint
Lead white oil paint
Red lead oil paint
Shellac (as is)

Fixatif
Lacquer
Turpentine (50% in oil)
Linseed oil (as is)
Poppyseed oil
Paint remover (10% in oil)
Charcoal
Poster paint
Pastelle chalk
Water color paint
Sodium arsenate (10% aqueous)
Canvas sizing compound

Commercial Painter Contact Group*

Acetone (as is)
Aniline
Turpentine (50% in oil)
Benzine (50% in oil)
Denatured alcohol (as is)
Amyl acetate
Tetrachlorethane
Paint thinner (50% in oil)
Paint remover (10% in oil)
Linseed remover
Japanese dryer
Gasoline (60% in oil)
Red lead (50% in oil)
White lead
Zinc white

White enamel (50% in oil)
Flat white
White shellac
Floor varnish (as is)
Chrome yellow (50% in oil)
Gray paint
Black paint
Silver paint
Bronze liquid
Raw sienna
Raw umber
Putty
Plastic putty (as is)
Glue
Roofing tar

* This group and the one preceding are of value in suggesting likely contact agents in commercial and amateur artists. Testing with the worker's own materials is of more help than testing with a prepared group of materials.

Carpenter Contact List

Ash
Balsam fir
Birch
Casein glue
Cedar (red)
Cedar (white)
Oil of cedarwood
Chestnut
Common fir (Douglas)
Creosote (10% in oil)
Elm
Glue (Le Page's)
Hickory
Ironwood
Oil of juniper
Lignum vitae
Mahogany
Maple

Nickel chloride (5% aqueous)
Oak (red)
Oak (white)
Pine (California ponderosa)
Pine (Idaho sugar)
Pine (white)
Pine (yellow)
Poplar (yellow)
Putty
Plastic putty
Plastic wood
Spruce (Englemann)
Spruce (red—Eastern Canada)
Sycamore
Tar (roofing)
Turpentine (50%)
Walnut

Laborer Contact List

White cement (20% aqueous suspension)
Colored cement
Linoleum
Linoleum cement
Rubber cement
Glue (Le Page's)
Oakum
Feldspar

Creosote (10% in oil)
Roofing tar (full strength)
Lime (burnt—10% aqueous)
Lime (slaked)
Plaster (quick-drying)
Gasoline (60% in oil)
Turpentine (50%)
Cutting oil

Baker Contact Group

Allspice (whole)
Ammonium persulfate (2%)
Baking powder
Bay leaves
Bran flour
Cake flour
Cardamon

Carica papaya
Chocolate
Cinnamon
Cloves
Cocobolo wood
Coriander
Corn meal

Ginger
Gluten flour
Lard
Lemon extract (1% alcoholic)
Meat salt
Mustard seed
Nutmeg salt
Papaya
Paprika
Pepper (red)
Pepper (white)

Poppy seed
Pumpernickel flour
Rye flour
Rye oil
Sage
Spices (mixed)
Vanilla (1% in alcohol)
Wheat oil
White cream meal flour
Whole wheat flour

Cleaner Testing Group*

Varnolene (60% in oil)
Acetone (as is)
Alcohol (70% aqueous)
Benzine (50% in oil)
Naphtha
Turpentine (50%)
Carbon tetrachloride

Gasoline (50% in oil)
Kerosene (50% in oil)
Chloroform for silk (as is)
Chloroform for wool
Chloroform for celanese
Ether

* It is important to test the patient with the cleaning preparation which is used in processing his clothes and also with cleaning solutions used in his home.

Dye Contact List*

Sudan III (5%)
Para red deep
Para red light
Methyl orange (5%)
Paraphenylenediamine (2%)
Victoria blue
Chrysoidin brown (20%)
Nile blue
Alizarin red
Bismark brown
Alizarin
Bontamine blue
Soluble blue

Pontachrome blue-black
Sulfogene carbon
Pontacyl black
Nigrosine
Pontamine black
Sulfogene golden brown
Anthraquinone blue
Pontamine diazo black
Naphthol yellow
Tartrazine yellow
Saffranine
Chrome yellow

* When dye contact is suspected, samples should be obtained and the patient tested with them. Control procedures should be carried out.

Basic Aniline Dyes and Dye Precursors

Amido-azotoluol (1% in petrolatum)
Para-aminophenol (10% in petrolatum)
Meta-aminophenol
Paraphenylenediamine (2% in petrolatum)
Aniline
Dimethyl-amino-azobenzene

Additional Dyes*

Midland blue—R. powder
Midland vat blue—5 B
Indigo powder, synthetic
Ciba blue powder 2B
Carbon paper
Ribbon, typewriter
Ink, IBM
Ink, India

Tintex 48 blue
Methyl violet
Malachite green
Eosin
Carbofuchsin
Methylene blue
Sudan III

* Test with substance as is.

Comic-Paper Dyes

Paper ink, blue
Paper ink, red
Paper ink, yellow

Essential Aromatic Oils Group*

Oil of allspice (1% alcoholic)
Oil of anise (25% in oil)
Oil of bergamot (10% in petrolatum)
Oil of bitter almond (as is)
Oil of caraway (1% alcoholic)
Oil of cassia
Oil of cinnamon
Oil of cloves
Oil of coffee
Oil of coriander
Oil of cottonseed
Oil of eucalyptus
Oil of fennel
Oil of juniper
Oil of lavender
Oil of lemon
Oil of lime

Oil of mace (1% alcoholic)
Oil of Melissa (1% alcoholic)
Oil of mustard (1% alcoholic)
Oil of nutmeg (25% alcoholic)
Oil of pepper (black) (1% alcoholic)
Oil of pepper (red)
Oil of peppermint
Oil of pine
Oil of poppy seed
Oil of rose
Oil of rose geranium
Oil of santal
Oil of sassafras
Oil of spearmint
Oil of sweet orange
Oil of wintergreen

* These materials are used in cooking, cosmetics, and as flavorings. They may cause contact dermatitis not only in those who prepare food but also in persons who consume foods containing the oils.

Fabrics Testing Group

GROUP I
Asbestos
Rock wool
Celotex
Red rubber glove
Raw rubber
Rubber band
Rubber finger cot
White rubber glove
Spandex

GROUP II. SYNTHETIC FIBERS
Nylon
Rayon (natural, dyed)
Plastic (flexible)
GROUP III. NATURAL FIBERS
Silk (natural, gummed, glazed)
Hemp
Sheep wool
Cotton
Linen
Mohair

GROUP IV. RESINS USED IN WRINKLE-PROOF FINISHES
Urea-formaldehyde (10% in petrolatum)
Ester gums
Acrylates
Methacrylate
Polystyrene
Vinyl resins
Glycol resins
Alkyd
Melamine formaldehyde (10% in petrolatum)
Ketone resins
Coumarins and indene polymers
Phthalic and maleic anhydride
Rosin

Fur and Furriers' Testing Group

Aniline black (powder or 10% in oil)
Benzine (50% in oil)
Copper sulfate (1%)

Iron sulfate (2%)
Lead chloride
Nutgalls (roasted and ground)

Para-amidophenol (10% in oil)
Paraphenylenediamine (2% in petroleum jelly)
Pontamine black (powder)
Salammoniac (3%)
Sumac leaves (powdered)
Tartar emetic
Tannic acid (3% aqueous)
Logwood (10% aqueous)
Potassium dichromate (1%)
Arsenious trioxide
Bichloride mercury (0.1%)
Badger, chinchilla
Beaver
Caracul

Fox (black, blue, silver)
Hudson seal
Kolinsky (brown)
Lapin (rabbit)
Muskrat (natural)
Muskrat (dyed)
Rabbit (dyed)
Raccoon
Skunk
Squirrel (natural)
Squirrel (dyed)
Weasel (Japanese)
Persian lamb (gray and black)
Mink

Gynecology Contact List*

Sodium borate (powder)
Borax
Potassium alum
Oxyquinoline sulfate (0.02%)
Trioxymethylene (0.04%)
Phenylmercuric acetate (0.05%)
Ricinoleic acid
Chlorothymol
Sodium lauryl sulfate
Cetyl alcohol
Potassium permanganate solution (1%)

Phenol (0.5%)
Hexyl resorcinal
Vinegar (10%)
Cocoa butter
Deodorant powder
Deodorant cream
Rayon
Nylon
Silk
Rubber

* Patients with contact dermatitis of the perineum should be tested with all materials used in contraception and personal hygiene.

Photographer Contact List*

Developer (5% aqueous)
Fixer
Acetic acid (0.05%)
Printing paper
Film
Acetone
Amyl acetate
Aniline (10% in oil)

Butyl alcohol
Bichloride mercury
Benzine
Formalin
Potassium dichromate
Methyl alcohol
Sodium hypochlorite
Silver nitrate (5% aqueous)

* Individuals sensitive to photographic materials must be tested to the particular compounds handled because of wide variation in composition, particularly in developers. See also page 284.

Leather Worker and Shoemaker Testing Group

Leathers*

Alligator skin (white, gray, brown, blue, green, black, red)
Elk skin (white, gray, brown, blue, green, black)
Calf skin (white, gray, brown, blue, green, black, red)
Red lizard skin

Snake skin
Black kid
Black patent leather
Suede (black, brown)
Cowhide
Pigskin
Horse hide

* Patients in whom contact dermatitis from leather is suspected should be tested with selected items from the Leather Worker list and also with samples of leather which they have worn or contacted.

Leather Workers

Ammonia (2% aqueous)
Antimony chloride (2%)
Arsenious trioxide
Amido-azotoluene HCl (1%)
Bichloride of mercury (0.1%)
Copper sulfate (1%)
Carbon tetrachloride (50% in oil)
Ferric chloride (2%)
Formalin (5%)
Glue
Hard rubber

Aniline black
Benzine (60% in oil)
Bismark brown
Paraphenylenediamine (2%)
Nickel sulfate (5%)
Potassium dichromate (1%)
Methyl alcohol
Turpentine (50% in oil)
Shoe polish
Saddle soap (1% aqueous)
Waxed cord lacing

Mechanic Contact List

Gasoline (60% in oil)
Kerosene (60% in oil)
Asphalt
Crude oil
Toluol (50% in oil)
Motor oil (60% in oil)
Ammonium dichromate (0.5%)
Denatured alcohol
Machine oil
Tetra ethyl lead gas (60%)
Lead arsenate (5%)
Lubricating oil (50% in oil)
Auto polish
Auto wax

Weather "undercoat"
Brake fluid
Spring spray
Window spray
Grease solvent
Benzine (60% in oil)
Hard rubber
Chromium chloride (2%)
Copper chloride (1%)
Nickel sulfate (5%)
Antifreeze
Grease-removing soaps (1% in oil)
Plastic, flexible

Metal Worker Contact List

Ferric chloride (2%)
Copper sulfate (1%)
Nickel sulfate (5%)
Antimony chloride (2%)
Cobalt chloride (2%)
Potassium dichromate (0.5%)
Lead chloride
Silver nitrate (5%)
Stannous chloride (10%)
Zinc chloride
German silver scrapings
Aluminum scrapings
Aluminum flux (0.1%)

Cast iron flux
Brass scrapings
Welding brass
Copper scrapings
Tin foil
Osmic acid (osmium) (10%)
Platinum chloride (10%)
Palladium chloride (10%)
Uranium chloride (10%)
Iridium chloride (10%)
Rhodium chloride (10%)
Soldering flux (1%)
Bichloride mercury (0.1%)

Ointments and Medications List

GROUP I
  Zinc oxide ointment
  Cold cream
  Lanolin
  Petrolatum
  Washable base
  Cocoa butter
  Lassar's paste
  Glycerin
  Coconut oil
  Castor oil
GROUP II
  Ichthyol ointment

  Ichthomalis ointment
  Oil of bergamot
  Oil of cade (1%)
  Coal tar (10%)
  Naphthalan (10%)
GROUP III
  Scarlet red ointment (10%)
  Furacin ointment
  Boric acid ointment (2%)
  Desenex
  Ammoniated mercury
  Merthiolate (1%)
  Benzocaine (10%)

GROUP IV
  Sulfur ointment (2%)
  Salicylic acid (5%)
  Methyl salicylate (2%)
  Salvas (3%)
  Whitfield's ointment
  Calamine lotion
  Phenol (1%)
  Balsam of Peru
  Quinine sulfate
GROUP V
  Thymol (1%)
  Resorcin (10%)
  Menthol (1%)
  Butesin Picrate
  Arsenic trioxide (1%)
  Mentholatum
  Noxema

Cuticura
Unguentine
GROUP VI
  Acetic acid (10%)
  Rubbing alcohol
  Burow's solution
  Potassium permanganate
  Vioform
  Phisoderm
  Tincture of iodine
  Copper sulfate (1%)
  Chlorophyll ointment
GROUP VII
  Penicillin
  Neomycin
  Bacitracin
  Tetracycline

Miscellaneous Biologicals and Chemicals

Quince seed
Tragacanth gum
Karaya gum
Bismuth salicylate in oil
Sodium benzoate (20% aqueous)
Acetone

Methyl alcohol
Sodium salicylate
Urethane
Myrrh
Sodium morrhuate (5% aqueous)
Traction glue

Common Domesticated Plants

Group I: Trees
  American elm
  Black walnut
  Hemlock
  Oak
  Red cedar
  Ash
  Box elder
  Hickory
  Osage orange
  Spruce
  Aspen
  Cocobolo

Honey locust
Pine
Sycamore
Basswood
Cottonwood
Maple
Plum
Tree of heaven
Birch
Hackberry
Mulberry
Poplar
Willow

Group II: Flowers
  Bergamot
  Corn flower
  Gaillardia
  Larkspur
  Snapdragon
  Blue myrtle
  Cosmos
  Geranium
  Marigold
  Stock
  Calendula
  Dahlia

Hollyhock
Petunia
Pansy
Chrysanthemum
Feverfew
Iris
Primrose
Verbena
Coreopsis
Four o'clock
Jonquil
Shasta Daisy
Zinnia

Group III: Ornamental Shrubs and Vines
  Amur river privet

Mock orange
Salt cedar

Group III: Ornamental Shrubs and Vines (Cont.)

English ivy	Virginia creeper
Lavender	Clematis
Pyrocantha	Honeysuckle
Spirea	Morning glory
Arbor vitae	Scarlet sage
Forsythia	Wisteria
Lilac	Devil's ivy
Queen's wreath	Lantana
Trumpet vine	Oleander
Bird of paradise	Snowball
Grapevine	Yellow jasmine

Group IV: Fruits, Vegetables, and Farm Products	Oats
	Salsify
Alfalfa	Tomato
Corn	Carrot
Lettuce	Green Bean
Parsnip	Okra
Spinach	Sorghum
Asparagus	Turnip
Flax	Celery
Mustard	Irish Potato
Radish	Orange
Squash	Soybean
Broccoli	Wheat
Grapefruit	

Wild Plants Commonly Encountered in the United States

Group I: Weeds
Yarrow (*Achillea millefolium*)
Smaller burdock (*Arctium minus*)
Sneezeweed (*Helenium autumnale*)
White sweet clover (*Melilotus alba*)
Horse-nettle (*Solanum carolinense*)
Western water hemp (*Acnida tamariscina*)
Common wormwood (*Artemisia vulgaris*)
Sunflower (*Helianthus annuus*)
Evening primrose (*Oenothera biennis*)
Goldenrod (*Solidago serotina*)
Redroot pigweed (*Amaranthus retroflexus*)

Common milkweed (*Asclepias syrica*)
Burweed marsh elder (*Iva xanthifolia*)
Wild feverfew (*Parthenium hysterophorus*)
Dandelion (*Taraxacum officinale*)
Short ragweed (*Ambrosia elatior*)
Lamb's quarters (*Chenopodium album*)
Wild lettuce (*Lactuca scariola*)
Black-eyed Susan (*Rudbeckia hirta*)
Poison ivy (*Rhus radicans*)
Dog fennel (*Anthemis cotula*)
Joe-pye weed (*Eupatorium maculatum*)
Mare's-tail (*Leptilon canadense*)
Russian thistle (*Salsola pestifer*)
Cocklebur (*Xanthium commune*)

Group II: Grasses
Quackgrass (*Agropyron repens*)
Wild oats (*Avena fatua*)
Barnyard grass (*Echinochloa crusgalli*)
Wild barley (*Hordeum jubatum*)
Kentucky bluegrass (*Poa pratensis*)
Red top (*Agrostis alba*)
Sideoats grama; tall grama grass (*Bouteloua curtipendula*)
Yard grass (*Eleusine indica*)
Koeler's grass (*Koeleria cristata*)
Green foxtail grass (*Setaria viridis*)
Little bluestem (*Andropogon scoparius*)
Downy brome grass (*Bromus tectorum*)
Stink grass (*Eragrostis cilianensis*)

Perennial rye (*Lolium perenne*)
Johnson grass (*Sorghum halepense*)
Sweet vernal grass (*Anthoxanthum odoratum*)
Bermuda grass (*Cynodon dactylon*)
Fescue grass (*Festuca elatior*)
Old witch grass (*Panicum capillare*)
Needlegrass; porcupine grass (*Stipa spartea*)
Prairie grass (*Aristida oligantha*)
Orchard grass (*Dactylis glomerata*)
Velvet grass (*Holcus lanatus*)
Timothy (*Phleum pratense*)
Crabgrass (*Syneherisma sanguinalis*)

REFERENCES

1. Becker, S. W., and O'Brien, M. P.: Value of patch tests in dermatology: special study of follicular reactions. Arch. Dermat. & Syph. *79:*569, 1959.
2. Marcussen, P. V.: Eczematous allergy to metals. Acta Allergol. *17:*311, 1962.
3. Raskin, J.: Antigen-antibody reaction site in contact dermatitis. Determination by use of fluorescent antibody technique. Arch. Dermat. *83:*459, 1961.
4. Magnusson, B., and Hersle, K.: Patch test methods: II. Regional variations of patch test responses. Acta Dermato-Venereologica *45:*257, 1965.
5. Epstein, S.: The photopatch test. Ann. Allergy *22:*1, 1964.
6. Weber, L. F.: External causes of dermatitis; a list of irritants. Arch. Dermat. & Syph. *35:*129, 1937.
7. Rostenberg, A., Jr., and Sulzberger, M. B.: Some results of patch tests. Arch. Dermat. & Syph. *35:*433, 1937.
8. Schwartz, L., Tulipan, L., and Peck, S. M.: Occupational Diseases of the Skin. 3rd ed., pp. 41–51, Philadelphia, Lea & Febiger, 1957.

Chapter Thirteen

HEADACHE IN ALLERGY PRACTICE

NEAL A. VANSELOW, M.D.

The allergist may be asked to study the patient whose chief complaint is headache. Unfortunately, the frequency with which allergy can be incriminated as an etiologic factor in headache is still a matter of controversy. For this reason, evaluation of such patients must be performed with thoroughness and caution. Other common causes of headache, such as systemic diseases, intracranial lesions, and psychogenic factors, must be investigated and ruled out. Apparent relationships between the introduction and withdrawal of suspected allergens and precipitation or amelioration of the headache always must be interpreted in the light of two well-established facts: the natural history of headache is often variable, with remissions and exacerbations the rule; and the power of suggestion exerted by an interested physician may itself contribute importantly to relief of symptoms.

The allergist deals most often with three types of headache: migraine and its variants, histamine headaches, and headaches caused by allergic rhinitis.

MIGRAINE HEADACHE

It has been estimated that the incidence of migraine headache in the general population is from 2 to 10 per cent. Women are affected approximately twice as commonly as men. Migraine may begin in childhood, but the onset is most often in early adult life. Frequently there is a family history of migraine, but this disease is not significantly correlated with a family history of atopy.[1]

The typical migraine headache usually is preceded by a prodromal phase. Prodromal symptoms may consist of lethargy, nervousness, irritability, malaise, or, conversely, an unusual sense of well-being. In the period immediately preceding the headache, various visual phenomena may occur including bright flashes of light, blurred vision, or scotomata. These usually disappear in a matter of minutes to an hour and are followed by the headache phase. The pain of migraine typically is described as throbbing or pulsating; it increases in severity for several hours and persists for 12 to 24 hours. On occasion, it may last for several days. In 80 per cent of patients the pain initially is unilateral but shifts from side to side with different attacks. Later in the course of the headache, it may become generalized. The supraorbital, retro-orbital, and temporal areas most commonly are involved. Associated with the typical migraine headache are various other symptoms: nausea, vomiting, photophobia, perspiration, and generalized or localized edema. As the headache subsides, the patient often complains of weakness and residual soreness in the head and neck muscles.

Migraine headaches commonly occur several times per month, but they may occur daily or as infrequently as once in several years. In women they often are temporally related to the menstrual period. In both sexes they have been associated with periods of extreme stress or "let down" periods following stress.

The pathophysiologic mechanisms which produce migraine are well known. Initially there is vasoconstriction of certain extracranial and intracranial arteries, resulting in symptoms associated with the prodrome. Following this phase of vasoconstriction, there is a phase of vasodilation of cranial arteries which produces pain. In time, the dilated arteries become edematous, and the character of the pain changes from a throbbing to a constant type. There is some evidence to suggest that a substance of low molecular weight present in the edematous tissue has the ability to lower the pain threshold in that area.

In contrast with the pathophysiology of migraine, the etiology of this disorder is still uncertain.[2] In the majority of cases there appears to be a hereditary factor involved, although the exact mode of inheritance is unknown. Psychologic disorders, endocrine imbalance, anoxia, electrolyte disturbances, and allergy all have been incriminated as possible precipitating factors, but final proof is lacking. Any vasodilating mechanism such as heat, ingestion of alcohol, sublingual nitroglycerine, hypoglycemia, or an allergic reaction may bring on the characteristic migraine headache. It is possible, therefore, for the etiology of a series of migraine headaches to be variable.

Evidence for a role of allergic factors in the precipitation of migraine headaches is at best circumstantial and is based largely on the results of clinical studies in which remission and exacerbations have been felt to correlate with the withdrawal and re-introduction of suspected allergens. In most cases, the suspected allergens have been foods, particularly wheat, milk, eggs, chocolate, pork, fish, and legumes. It should be noted that most of these studies are poorly controlled, and in only a few has an attempt been made to re-administer a suspected food without the patient's knowledge. The consensus among most allergists seems to be that in the majority of patients migraine headaches are not etiologically related to food sensitivity or to other allergens.[3]

On the other hand, one cannot help but be impressed with an occasional case in which such a relationship does seem to be present. In such instances, the patient often has one of the atopic diseases in addition to migraine headaches, and the suspected allergen is usually a food. Withdrawal of the food in question may be associated with relief of symptoms, while re-introduction of that food on repeated occasions appears to produce a headache. Whether an antigen-antibody reaction is involved in such a situation or whether the patient merely exhibits a nonimmunologic "intolerance" to the food is not known.

Allergic evaluation is not usually a rewarding procedure in the average patient with migraine and, even when indicated, should not be performed without first considering other possible causative factors. Allergy studies seem to be most appropriate under special circumstances: when there is other evidence of atopic disease; when the patient strongly suspects a relationship between exposure to a potential allergen and occurrence of his headache; or when the headaches are particularly severe and frequent and have not responded to the usual therapeutic measures. Although other substances, such as drugs or inhalant agents, have on occasion been incriminated, major attention should be directed toward foods. A detailed discussion of the proper method of evaluating suspected food allergy is given in Chapter 10.

It must be remembered that skin tests are often unreliable in food allergy. A careful history as well as diet manipulation form the basis of the diagnostic approach. If the migraine headaches occur infrequently, it is best to have the patient keep a diet diary. Foods which are ingested in the 24 hour period prior to the headache are particularly suspect. These are then eliminated from the diet and added individually at intervals of several days. The effect of diet manipulation upon occurrence of the headache is noted. If the headaches are occurring frequently, it sometimes is best empirically to place the patient on a more standard elimination diet such as Allergy No. 1 or Allergy No. 2. These diets eliminate the foods which most often have been implicated as etiologic agents in migraine. If the headaches disappear or decrease in frequency, foods are restored to the basic diet at several day intervals and the effect on symptoms noted. It cannot be emphasized too strongly that the association between re-addition of a given food and the occurrence of a headache may merely be one of chance. For this reason, no conclusions can be drawn on the basis of the first re-addition of the food in question, but repeated precipitation of headaches by ingestion of the food must be demonstrated. When the headache can be brought on by ingestion of the food in hidden form, the results are much more significant, for this procedure eliminates the possible effect of suggestion in a worried patient. In addition to considering foods, one also should know that drugs may act as a triggering mechanism. In view of this it may be useful to change to some other compound those medications which the patient has been taking for relief.

The symptomatic treatment of migraine can be divided into two categories: treatment of the acute attack and prevention of subsequent attacks. Aspirin, rest, and cold packs on the head may be of value in controlling acute migraine, but the drug most widely used is ergotamine tartrate. This vasoconstricting agent is helpful in more than 80 per cent of cases, but to be effective, it must be taken early in the attack, preferably at the beginning of the prodrome. Ergotamine tartrate is available in oral 1 mg. tablets. One or two tablets are given at the onset of symptoms. If the headache is not relieved, an additional tablet may be given every 30 to 60 minutes until relief is obtained. No more than six tablets should be used in a 24 hour period. Side effects associated with ergotamine include nausea, vomiting, abdominal pain, and numbness and tingling of the extremities. Because of its effects on uterine smooth muscles and vessel walls, it is contraindicated in pregnant patients and in those with occlusive vascular disease or coronary artery disease.

There are a number of commercial ergotamine preparations. Cafergot combines 1 mg. ergotamine tartrate with 100 mg. caffeine, the latter potentiating the effect of the former. Cafergot P-B contains pentobarbital and Bellafoline in addition to caffeine and ergotamine, the additional drugs counteracting the stimulation caused by caffeine and the nausea induced by ergotamine. Migral combines ergotamine and caffeine with the anti-emetic cyclizine. If a route of administration other than the oral route is preferred, Cafergot rectal suppositories (or Cafergot P-B) containing 2 mg. ergotamine may be used. Ergotamine also may be given by nebulization (Medihaler ergotamine), or it may be administered parenterally.

Several drugs are available for *prevention* of migraine headaches. When given three times daily, Bellergal (ergotamine, Bellafoline, and phenobarbital) has been found to be effective in some cases. There has also been interest in the use of methysergide (Sansert) 2 mg. three times daily for the prevention of migraine. The latter has potential serious side effects because of its vasconstrictive properties, however, and must be used with caution. There also have been reports of retroperitoneal fibrosis in patients receiving methysergide.

HISTAMINE HEADACHES

Histamine headaches (Horton's headaches, cluster headaches, migrainous neuralgia), another type of vascular headache, begin without a prodrome. The pain is unilateral, severe, and pounding. It usually is localized to the eye, forehead, and temple, and it persists for 10 to 60 minutes. The patient typically experiences unilateral lacrimation, nasal stuffiness, rhinorrhea, conjunctival congestion, and facial flushing on the side of the headache. Histamine headaches tend to occur in clusters, with the patient developing several headaches daily for a period of weeks and then experiencing a remission which may last for months or years. Exacerbations have been reported to happen more often in the spring and fall. Unlike migraine headaches, histamine headaches occur more commonly in men. They often start at night and waken the patient from sleep.

Histamine headaches result from dilation of extracranial arteries. The trigger mechanisms which cause the vasodilation usually are unknown. Alcohol can precipitate an attack if given during a period when the patient is subject to headaches. The headaches also can be brought on by the subcutaneous injection of 0.3 to 0.6 mg. of histamine base. Following such an injection normal individuals experience a flush and a transient bilateral pounding headache, but the patient with histamine headaches will in addition experience a typical attack 20 to 40 minutes later. Although the headache may be reproduced by histamine, there is no evidence that spontaneous headaches of this type are due to histamine release. Studies of histamine metabolism in these patients have revealed no abnormality. Likewise, in the vast majority of these patients there is no evidence that allergy causes the headache. Patients may have come to the attention of the allergist mainly for possible testing and desensitization with histamine.

Table 13-1.   *Histamine Desensitization Schedule**

		Dose†	Administration Route
1st day	A.M.	0.25 ml.	subcutaneous
	P.M.	0.30 ml.	subcutaneous
2nd day	A.M.	0.35 ml.	subcutaneous
	P.M.	0.40 ml.	subcutaneous
3rd day	A.M.	0.45 ml.	subcutaneous
	P.M.	0.50 ml.	subcutaneous
4th day	A.M.	0.55 ml.	subcutaneous
	P.M.	0.60 ml.	subcutaneous
5th day	A.M.	0.65 ml.	subcutaneous
	P.M.	0.70 ml.	subcutaneous
6th day	A.M.	0.75 ml.	subcutaneous
	P.M.	0.80 ml.	subcutaneous
7th day	A.M.	0.85 ml.	subcutaneous
	P.M.	0.90 ml.	subcutaneous
8th day	A.M.	0.95 ml.	subcutaneous
	P.M.	1.00 ml.	subcutaneous
9th day	A.M.	1.00 ml.	subcutaneous
	P.M.	1.00 ml.	subcutaneous
10th day	A.M.	1.00 ml.	subcutaneous
	P.M.	1.00 ml.	subcutaneous

Thereafter, 1.0 ml. subcutaneously every day for ten days, or treatment may be modified depending on clinical response (see text).

* The histamine used is 0.275 mg. histamine acid phosphate per ml., which is equivalent to 0.1 mg. of histamine base per ml.

† If the typical headache occurs following an injection, the dosage is decreased by 50 per cent and later raised again if tolerated.

There are two types of treatment for histamine headache: drug therapy and "histamine desensitization." Antihistamines are usually of little benefit, which again suggests that more than histamine is involved in the pathogenesis of the headache. Ergotamine preparations may be useful in the treatment of the acute attack, but because the headaches are short in duration and a rapid drug effect is needed, they should be administered in parenteral, sublingual, rectal, or aerosol form. Oral ergotamine, methysergide (Sansert), and Bellergal have been used prophylactically with some success.

The therapeutic injection of increasing amounts of histamine, so-called "histamine desensitization," has been used for many years. The details of this procedure are outlined in the accompanying table. Following completion of the outlined schedule, histamine injections may be continued one to three times weekly for an indefinite period if the headaches tend to recur.

Since the headaches are likely to appear in clusters, or periodic groups of attacks, it often is hard to decide whether improvement during the course of "histamine desensitization" is spontaneous or due to the injections. Accordingly, many are skeptical about the efficacy of this therapy, though some physicians with much experience with these patients still advocate its use in selected cases. The mechanism of action, if any, of this treatment is unknown but almost certainly does not involve desensitization to histamine in the immunologic sense.

HEADACHE ASSOCIATED WITH ALLERGIC RHINITIS

Patients with allergic rhinitis often experience headache in addition to nasal congestion, rhinorrhea, sneezing, and pruritus of the nose, eyes, and pharynx. The headache usually is described as a dull ache or a pressure sensation and is localized over the face or the frontal or temporal areas. It is seldom as severe as a migraine headache and often is relieved by the administration of vasoconstrictors or antihistamines.

Several mechanisms may account for the pain of this type of headache. Pressure resulting from edema and vascular congestion of nasal mucous membranes or from nasal polyps may produce pain. Edematous closure of the ostia of the frontal and maxillary sinuses may result in pain, since these areas, together with the septum and vestibule, are sensitive to pain. Closure of sinus ostia may also produce pain owing to interference with equalization of pressure in the sinuses or to poor sinus drainage. Purulent sinusitis may accompany allergic rhinitis and may also cause pain. This condition may be distinguished from allergic rhinitis by the presence of pus in the nose or by abnormal sinus x-rays.

The treatment of this type of headache is treatment of the allergic rhinitis. Vasoconstrictors or antihistamines given orally often are effective. If not, *limited* use of vasoconstrictor nose drops may be considered.

Antibiotics as well as vasoconstrictors are indicated when complicating purulent sinusitis is present. Surgical removal of obstructing polyps or submucous resection of hypertrophied turbinates may be indicated. As in all cases of allergic rhinitis, avoidance of offending allergens and hyposensitization are desirable when appropriate.

REFERENCES

1. Schwartz, M.: Migraine an allergic disease? J. Allergy 23:44, 1952.
2. Magee, K. R.: The diagnosis and treatment of headache. I. Vascular headaches. Univ. Michigan Med. Center J. 30:206, 1964.
3. Sherman, W. B., Friedman, A. P., and Merritt, H. H.: Headache: Diagnosis and Treatment. pp. 111–126, Philadelphia, F. A. Davis Co., 1959.

Chapter Fourteen

ALLERGIC
CONDITIONS
OF
THE EYES AND EARS

Like the skin and mucous membranes of the nose, certain tissues of the eye may receive antigenic or chemical insult not only from within but also from direct contact with environmental agents in the atmosphere. Although diagnosis and treatment of allergic conditions of the eye make up a comparatively small part of an allergist's practice, these problems nevertheless are important, and competence in this area will increase the scope of his contribution to medical practice.[1] When there is any question as to diagnosis, an ophthalmologist should be called in for consultation.

CONTACT DERMATITIS OF THE LIDS

Since the skin of the eyelids is very thin, it is easily irritated by chemicals and also is a favorite site for the development of allergic contact dermatitis. The lesions appear on the lids as an erythematous, severely pruritic, often scaly dermatitis which at first may be intermittent, but as time passes and the patient tries to control the condition with various lotions and medications, it may become continuous. When chronic, the skin thickens and feels rough to the examining finger. It often is not possible to get a history of vesicles appearing on the lids, even though this is the usually expected lesion on other skin areas.

Allergic contact dermatitis of the lids is especially common in female patients as a result of sensitivity to nail polish or perfume. Scented powders, cologne, deodorants, mascara, hair sprays, hair dye, laundry chemicals, and eye drops also are common causes of this condition. Eye shadow, especially the perfumed type, and artificial eyelashes which are held on with an adhesive also should be suspected. One should inquire about the use of these articles when taking the history. Any aerosolized agent which can be smelled by the patient is said to be present in sufficient quantity to be a possible offender, either as an allergen or as a primary irritant.

Treatment of erythematous, mildly edematous, and occasionally weeping lids should include a careful attempt to identify and eliminate all possible offending agents. So often a reaction can be initiated by sensitivity to one preparation, only to be aggravated and perpetuated by a second allergen or irritant. For this reason, local applications should be avoided, if at all possible. The patient should be instructed to discontinue use of all cosmetics and should have garments cleaned to be free from all traces of perfume. An "overtreatment cellulitis" is often seen in patients who have applied several ointments and salves in an effort to clear up the condition on the lids. Healing may occur soon after all treatment is stopped. Antihistamines may be given by mouth. If the lesions persist after ten days to two weeks, mild local treatment must be started. Wet saline compresses should be used if there is weeping. Steroids in ointment, lotion, or cream may be applied topically. Antibiotic ointments should be avoided.

All cosmetics, even "nonallergenic" types, and other suspects should be patch tested before allowing resumption of their use (see Chapter 12).

BLEPHARITIS MARGINALIS

A scaling dermatitis along the eyelash borders may be seen in patients who have dandruff. It is likely that the seborrhea is causing the lesions on the lids, the so-called *squamous* type of blepharitis marginalis. Treatment of the seborrhea usually brings about remission of the dermatitis on the lids. There also is an ulcerative type of blepharitis marginalis in which staphylococci can be cultured from the lesions. The sensitivity factor in this condition is questionable. Some ophthalmologists still recommend a course of injections of a staphylococcus vaccine or toxoid and report improvement. Whether or not this is a specific form of therapy is open to conjecture.

DERMATOCONJUNCTIVITIS

A particularly common type of contact dermatitis of the lids and the conjunctivae is that caused by therapeutic agents. Many of the ophthalmic medications are true sensitizers. Eye drops seem more troublesome than ointments. In past years, most ocular allergy was caused by atropine or mercury. More recently, pilocarpine has caused an appreciable incidence of difficulty in glaucoma patients. Penicillin has caused so much trouble topically that it should not be used. Neomycin and Polysporin also are commonly used and may be the causes of a reaction. Bacitracin alone, however, rarely sensitizes. Sulfonamides and many of the local anesthetics, such as Tetracaine, butacaine sulfate, and others of the "caine" or "para" compounds, are major offenders, competing with the antibiotics for the position of being the leading causes for contact dermatitis of the lids. It is worth noting that Holocaine (phenacaine), Metycaine (piperocaine), and Xylocaine (lidocaine) do not cross-react with the other anesthetics and are not related to each other (see also page 182). Contact hypersensitivity to antihistamines has made it inadvisable to employ these compounds in ointments. We have used Antistine ophthalmic drops without difficulty, although reactions to this drug have been observed.

Treatment should be started at once, by giving steroid ophthalmic drops and antihistamines by mouth. A short course of oral or parenteral steroids may be required if the reaction is intense. If there are urgent indications for further treatment of the underlying eye disease, a medication unrelated to the first should be substituted.

Contact reactions to artificial eyes have been reported, the offending substance being methyl methacrylate or polymers of that plastic.[2] In patch testing with this material, which is used for almost all artificial eyes, positive reactions are most likely to be obtained by applying a small piece of the clear plastic to the conjunctival sac. Substitution of a glass or gold prosthesis rarely may be necessary.

ACUTE ALLERGIC CONJUNCTIVITIS

One of the most common ophthalmic syndromes which confronts the allergist is allergic conjunctivitis.* This may be due to pollens, dust, mold spores, foods, and other allergens. The acute, explosive type often is easily recognized, while the chronic, indolent form may be difficult to distinguish from other types of chronic conjunctivitis. The clinical picture of acute allergic conjunctivitis is that of irritation. Intense itching is an extremely common complaint and is made worse when the patient rubs his eyes. There may be moderate redness of the conjunctivae and some thickening or edema of the mucosa which makes it difficult to observe the vascular pattern in the folds of the lower lids. The profuse tearing, at first watery, may later become mucopurulent. There is often a colorless or white, ropy, mucinous secretion which can be strung out from the conjunctiva to a length of several inches as it is collected with an applicator. This secretion should be examined using the Hansel staining technique (page 72) and usually is found to be loaded with eosinophils. Allergic conjunctivitis almost always is bilateral, but unilateral cases are seen occasionally. It is difficult to explain why only one eye reacts when both apparently are exposed to the allergens in the environment.

The diagnosis of acute allergic conjunctivitis is made by following

---

* The term "chronic catarrhal conjunctivitis" is a descriptive one, applying to any etiologic type of chronic conjunctivitis accompanied by a mucinous ophthalmic discharge. The term "allergic conjunctivitis" is preferred for cases in which the cause is extrinsic protein sensitivity. Catarrhal conjunctivitis is reserved for those cases in which the cause is irritation, or in which the cause is unknown but there is no seasonal variation of symptoms.

the usual allergic work-up technique. A careful history followed by examination of the eye and the nasal passages will enable the physician to decide whether the condition is likely to be allergic. Skin testing may be helpful, and examination of the ophthalmic secretions may reveal eosinophils. Since the chemosis of acute allergic conjunctivitis can be confused with the swelling seen also in early epidemic keratoconjunctivitis, a highly infectious virus disease, it is important to differentiate between these two conditions. The virus infection nearly always is associated with definite pre-auricular lymphadenopathy. Also, the mucous discharge will contain mononuclear leukocytes and not eosinophils. The instillation of 1:1000 epinephrine drops will produce blanching of the mucous membranes in acute allergic conjunctivitis. There is very much less blanching if the inflammation is due to infection.

The treatment of allergic conjunctivitis preferably involves removal of the extrinsic protein agent. When this is impossible, hyposensitization to the allergen may be indicated. Often allergic conjunctivitis is associated with hay fever or bronchial asthma, but it also may be the only presenting complaint. Hyposensitization is carried on in the same manner in either instance.

Symptomatic relief by the use of suitable medications usually is possible and extremely gratifying to the patient. An antihistamine drug given by mouth may provide complete relief in mild cases. If several types of these preparations are tried and yet symptoms persist, the use of topical drops is advised. Available ophthalmic drops include 0.5 per cent Antistine, Vasocon A (antazoline), and Preparation A (pyrilamine). All such drops may sting when first applied. Because antihistamine compounds exert a local anesthetic effect, patients should be advised not to rub their eyes while using the drops. Occasionally contact sensitivity to antihistamine drops develops. Further relief can be obtained by irrigation of the conjunctival sacs. A teaspoonful of sodium bicarbonate is added to a pint of water and kept refrigerated. This should be used for lavage of the eyes two or three times daily, especially at night, so the patient doesn't sleep all night with pollen under the eyelids. Epinephrine hydrochloride 1:1000 makes a very good eye drop for relief of severe itching. Because epinephrine oxidizes rather readily, the drops should be made up fresh before being dispensed in brown bottles. In severe cases of acute allergic conjunctivitis, particularly of the seasonal type, some form of corticosteroid ophthalmic drops fortunately will give almost universally good results when other measures have failed. Topical application of the steroids in ophthalmic drops must be carried out with care. Steroid drops are contraindicated in the presence of herpetic lesions or ulceration of the cornea. An important complication that has been seen is mycotic invasion of the cornea. With prolonged use, the steroid drops also may produce glaucoma or posterior subcapsular cataracts in some patients. An ophthalmologist should be consulted when there is a possibility of corneal involvement, and his decision should determine whether steroid drops should be used in the conjunctival sac.

CHRONIC ALLERGIC CONJUNCTIVITIS

In contrast with the severe and impressive inflammatory reaction often seen in the acute form, chronic allergic conjunctivitis shows little inflammation and is characterized by a history of prolonged photophobia, itching, burning, and a feeling of dryness. There is some edema of the conjunctiva, and there may be a watery or mucoid discharge. Eosinophils are found in the mucus or in epithelial scrapings. Diagnosis is difficult, and the patient's appearance may be identical with that of a bacterial (staphylococcal) conjunctivitis or of an irritative reaction. The procedure for diagnosis and treatment is similar to that used in acute allergic conjunctivitis (see above).

VERNAL CONJUNCTIVITIS

This is a relatively uncommon form of conjunctivitis which occurs somewhat more often in children than in adults. Over two-thirds of affected children are males. The sex incidence in adults is about equal. Itching is prominent, especially toward the end of the day. Photophobia, lacrimation, and burning are less common complaints. As described in all ophthalmology texts, vernal conjunctivitis may be subdivided into *palpebral* and *limbal* types. In the former, at first there simply may be hyperemia and thickening of the conjunctivae, but later the characteristic flattened, pale, pink cobblestone-like papillae begin to form on the upper lid (Figure 14–1). The discharge in the eyes is stringy, thick, ropy, and

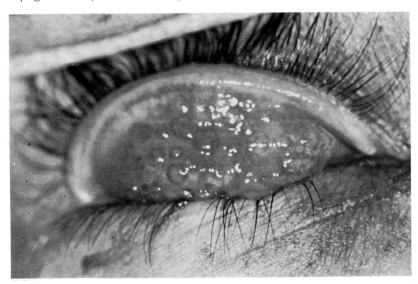

Figure 14–1. Vernal conjunctivitis. The cobblestone-like papules on the upper lid distinguish this condition from allergic conjunctivitis.

remarkably alkaline (pH as high as 9.0). In the limbal form, there are characteristically discrete yellow or gray elevations, which may be capped by white points (Tranta's spots). The limbus is opaque, and there may be an associated superficial punctate keratitis.

As implied by its name, vernal conjunctivitis occurs seasonally in the spring and summer months. This fact, together with the usual occurrence of large numbers of eosinophils in the conjunctival mucus, strongly suggests an allergic cause, with tree and grass pollens being particularly suspect. Nevertheless, careful study of these patients almost invariably fails to reveal any identifiable environmental allergen or allergens as being responsible for the difficulty. In spite of speculation about possible delayed hypersensitivity, physical allergy to warm air, infection, and possible hereditary or endocrine factors, the etiology of vernal conjunctivitis remains unknown. Complete spontaneous remission usually occurs after eight to ten years or more. Meanwhile, corticosteroid ophthalmic drops are helpful in keeping the condition under control. Other methods of treatment are described in standard ophthalmology texts.[1]

PHLYCTENULAR KERATOCONJUNCTIVITIS

This condition, characterized by nodule formation on or near the cornea, is thought to be an allergic response of the ocular tissues to such antigens as tubercle bacilli, staphylococci, or other bacteria. Keratitis may develop and is sometimes quite severe. Although the disease is probably immunologic, it should be handled primarily by an ophthalmologist. Antihistamines may give symptomatic relief while treatment is being started. Under the supervision of the ophthalmologist, steroid therapy is undertaken. A careful search should always be made for active pulmonary tuberculosis.

UVEITIS AND SYSTEMIC DISEASE

The uveal tract, made up of the iris, ciliary body, and choroid, is prone to inflammation. Uveitis has multiple etiologies. This discussion will be confined to endogenous uveitis associated with systemic disease and excludes cases secondary to local diseases or trauma of the eye. Allergy is involved in the pathogenesis of most cases of endogenous uveitis. Because of prolonged disability, pain, and possible secondary glaucoma, cataracts, and blindness, uveitis must be considered the most important form of ocular allergy.

Proper management requires both adequate ophthalmologic care and general medical and immunologic evaluation. With the techniques at his disposal, the ophthalmologist can describe the morphology of the uveal lesion and classify it as granulomatous or nongranulomatous. In some cases, such as those caused by Toxoplasma, Histoplasma, or Toxocara, the funduscopic findings are sufficiently characteristic to permit a tentative etiologic diagnosis on the basis of the appearance of the lesions.[3] Armed with this information, the allergist then subjects the patient to a general evaluation with a complete history, physical examination, chest x-ray examination, urinalysis, test for blood sugar, sedimentation rate, hematocrit, blood count, blood urea nitrogen test, serologic test for syphilis, and stool examination for ova, parasites, and occult blood. Skin tests generally should be done with tuberculin, histoplasmin, coccidioidin and blastomycin antigens. Further studies may be needed depending on the initial findings. Not infrequently these will involve serologic and skin tests for additional infectious diseases.

There are two main types of uveitis based on pathologic appearance: granulomatous and nongranulomatous. In the former, part or all of the uveal tract is involved, particularly the choroid. Actual invasion of the structures by living organisms can take place. Cells may appear in the anterior chamber, keratitic precipitates may form on the posterior cornea, and synechiae can develop between iris and lens. Exudative lesions of choroid and retina may occur, sometimes associated with an outpouring of inflammatory cells into the vitreous body. Unless the disease is checked, eventual destruction of the eye may take place.

Granulomatous uveitis may be seen in toxoplasmosis, histoplasmosis, toxocarosis, sarcoidosis, tuberculosis, syphilis, coccidioidomycosis, blastomycosis, leprosy, leptospirosis, actinomycosis, apergillosis, cryptococcosis, Mucor infection, trypanosomiasis, filariasis, onchocerciasis, echinococcosis, cysticercus infection, and in other types of infection.[3-4] The first two appear to be the most commonly identified etiologic agents in the United States. Treatment of the primary disease is essential. Van Metre's excellent review details the major therapeutic measures, including the possible use of histoplasmin desensitization in appropriate cases.[3]

Nongranulomatous uveitis is found chiefly in the anterior segment of the uveal tract; acute or chronic iritis is a common manifestation of this disease. The eye may be red from injection of the ciliary vessels. Slit lamp examination may show fine keratitic precipitates on the posterior cornea and cells in the aqueous fluid. A fine vitreous haze may occur due to cellular exudation. Subretinal edema, especially near the disk, may be seen. Rapid resolution is not uncommon as the primary condition abates, and visual damage is not expected unless repeated attacks occur. This is the type of uveitis in which a relationship to focal infection (e.g., in the oral cavity, respiratory tract, or genitourinary tract) is suspected, though not unequivocally established. Van Metre has found that about one-third of these cases are associated with a rather distinctive type of arthritis featuring an asymmetrical, nonankylosing, peripheral polyarthritis involving particularly the lower extremities; rheumatoid factor and subcutaneous nodules are absent, and in the male the disease almost invariably is associated with an ankylosing spondylitis.[5] This type of uveitis also may be associated with regional enteritis and ulcerative colitis. Very rarely it occurs in serum sickness. It does not appear to be associated with atopy, though the older literature points to rare instances in which pollens, animal proteins, such as cat dander, and foods and drugs were suspected of bringing on uveitis.[1] Attempts at clearing up symptoms of uveitis by repeated injections of bacterial vaccines continue to be made, with only partial success. There currently is substantial interest in streptococcal desensitization using intravenous injections of multiple Group A β-hemolytic streptococci, which give the largest skin test reactions in 48 hours.[3] Needless to say, suitable symptomatic and local ophthalmic treatment is of the utmost importance.

SYMPATHETIC OPHTHALMIA

It has been known for a long time that injury to the uveal tract of one eye sometimes is followed by an aseptic inflammation of the uveal tract in the opposite eye. It may become so severe as to cause significant loss of vision. It has been suggested that antibodies develop to uveal pigments following the initial injury, and these antibodies may then react with the uveal pigment of the opposite eye, causing sympathetic ophthalmia. Woods reported that many such patients give positive reactions to uveal pigment when skin tested.[6] This has not been universally demonstrated, and there may well be some other factor or factors involved besides the suspected immune reaction.

ENDOPHTHALMITIS PHACO-ANAPHYLACTICA

There is more substantial evidence that patients may become sensitized to lens protein by release of protein from the lens capsule. Subsequent release of lens protein after further trauma or surgery may result in severe intraocular inflammation, called endophthalmitis phaco-anaphylactica. Patients with this disease often exhibit positive reactions to skin tests with lens protein. Attempts at hyposensitization of such patients with lens protein have not been of much help. Corticosteroids are used to try to control this condition. Surgical removal of the lens or cortical substances may be curative. A substantial body of experimental data indicates that lens protein antigens are largely organ-specific.

CATARACTS

One should be aware of the association between atopic eczema and cataracts. It may be that these lesions, usually bilateral, are much more common than is suspected, especially in patients who have had eczema for many years. A slit lamp examination of the dilated pupil is necessary to make this diagnosis in early cases. One should also keep in mind that posterior subcapsular cataracts may develop in patients given long-term steroids for asthma or any medical condition.

The allergist should not hesitate to call upon an ophthalmologist for consultation when there is any question regarding diagnosis and treatment.

ALLERGY OF THE EAR

External Ear

Allergic contact dermatitis not infrequently occurs in this area. Nickel in earrings and bows of glasses, hair dye, cologne or perfume, otic drops, and ointments applied to the ear are the more common offenders (see page 280 for additional items). The lesions involved must be differentiated from seborrhea behind the ear lobes and especially from infectious eczematoid lesions of the external auditory canal and surrounding area. *Atopic dermatitis* also may involve the pinna.

Middle Ear

Prime consideration here should be given to *serous otitis media,* the cause of much of the conductive deafness of childhood.[7]

To understand the mechanism of serous otitis media, one must consider the physiology of the tympanic membrane and its dependence upon air on either side of its surface for normal aural transmission of sound. A normal middle ear space receives air by way of the eustachian tube which usually is in the closed position anatomically. The tube normally opens with swallowing, yawning, or increased intranasal pressure, thus permitting equalization of atmospheric pressure on both sides of the drum. When conditions prevent air from reaching the middle ear by way of the eustachian tube, the air is absorbed and replaced by fluid which dampens and impairs the efficiency of the conductive system. The respiratory type epithelium in the eustachian tube can be affected by pressure changes, by infection, or by allergic reaction. The fluid formed (1) may have a yellow color and low viscosity or (2) may be almost blue in color and very viscous or glue-like. The fluid is not infected, and probably little physical harm is done by its presence. It has been observed to remain for weeks or months without permanent damage to the hearing. However, there is a distressing drop in hearing to the extent of a 20 to 40 decibel loss in all frequencies while it is present.

Since serous otitis media occurs most frequently in small children, especially in the age group of five to ten years, learning in school may be impaired, and social and emotional growth may be delayed. Described almost always by their teachers as "inattentive," the children may have no ear complaints. In fact, the hearing loss may be discovered accidentally in a routine school hearing survey. Parents are astonished to learn that their children miss hearing much of what is said in school, and in fact may have learned to lip read. Some patients state that there is a feeling of fullness in the ears. Pain and vertigo are not associated clinical features. There may be a history of "popping" of the ears, with prompt but

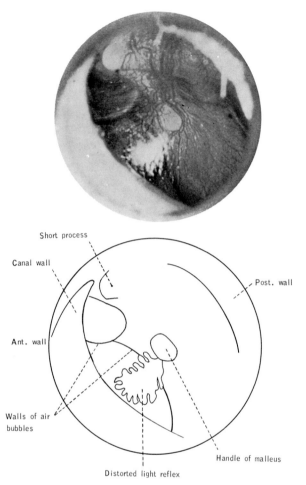

Figure 14-2. Serous otitis media. Drum is amber and retracted, and blood vessels are injected. Note distorted light reflex and large air bubbles.

temporary improvement in hearing. The fluctuating character of the hearing loss is a helpful point in the story.

Careful examination of the ears occasionally (i.e., in 5 to 10 per cent of cases only) shows one, or many, loculated fluid levels behind the eardrum (see Figure 14-2). In order to see a fluid level there must be a small amount of air in the middle ear. It is far more common to see an amber color through the inferior portion of the normally translucent gray eardrum and distortion of the light reflex. There may be an increase in prominence of the short process with retraction of the eardrum, and the malleus will seem to be foreshortened. There may be congestion ("road-mapping") of the vessels of the eardrum.

Attempts to insufflate air to the middle ear through the eustachian tube may confirm the presence of fluid. The Pollitzer method has been useful in children. Using a Pollitzer bag, equipped with an olive tip, air is introduced gently into one nostril while the other is compressed. As air enters the nose, the patient repeats "K-K-K," or swallows. The examiner then looks for bubbles behind the drum, or tests for a change in hearing. One also may look for limitation of excursion of the tympanic membrane after applying pressure with a pneumatic otoscope. If doubt about the presence of fluid still remains, a diagnostic paracentesis is done. As mentioned previously, audiograms may show an acuity loss of 20 to 40 decibels in all frequencies during some phase of the patient's disease. Some children with *allergic rhinitis* are said to show such a reduction even when there is no complaint of hearing loss, presumably due to eustachian tube dysfunction.

   Causes of Serous Otitis Media. Anything which causes obstruction of the eustachian tube may lead to serous otitis media. Possible etiologies include enlarged adenoids, inflammation of the nasopharynx due to infection or allergy, scarring of the eustachian tube orifice from surgical trauma, catheterization or irradiation, neoplasm of the nasopharynx, faulty function of the tensor veli palatini (as in cleft palate), rapid weight gain, hypothyroidism, and possibly congenital stenosis of the eustachian tubes. Incomplete treatment of patients with suppurative otitis media, rapid pressure change, and dental malocclusion with temporomandibular joint dysfunction also may lead to serous otitis media.

   Because patients with serous otitis media, particularly those with thick exudate in the middle ear, often present a difficult problem in management, the possibility of an allergic factor should be thought of in every case. If the child has active, perennial allergic rhinitis, diagnostic studies directed toward finding an allergic reaction contributing to his serous otitis media are warranted after other causes of the disease are excluded. The procedures would be similar to those followed in other types of upper respiratory tract allergy (Chapter 3). A search for eosinophils in secretions aspirated from the middle ear also has been suggested and they may or may not be found.[7]

   Management of Serous Otitis Media. When allergic factors are present, the usual principles of treatment are applicable: avoidance, symptomatic medications, and possible hyposensitization. Rarely, specific food elimination is found to be helpful. In prescribing decongestant drugs in these cases, we use regular, *daily* doses of antihistamines, particularly those combined with ephedrine-like compounds, viz., Actifed, Triaminic, Co-Pyronil, or Dimetapp. It may be necessary to continue antihistamines routinely for as long as several years. Although we cannot support the indiscriminate use of serial injections of dust, mold extract, and bacterial vaccine, we advise hyposensitization when the evidence for presence of allergy in a patient warrants it. When the allergic problem is complicated by infection, antibiotic drugs should be prescribed for a period of at least two weeks. A common error is to stop the antibiotic drugs when the ears are improving but before there is complete control of the infection. Prolonged use of antibiotic drugs, especially in the winter months, should be determined by clinical response. We have not seen these active and otherwise healthy children develop superinfections or unacceptable complications from long-term use of antibiotic drugs. Stained teeth from tetracyclines in children under eight years have been our chief cause for concern.

In general, most patients with serous otitis media should be followed by an otolaryngologist both for a diagnostic evaluation and for treatment of the cases in which allergy is not a factor. Such measures as myringotomy, aspiration, adenoidectomy, eustachian tubal inflation (by the Pollitzer maneuver, the Valsalva maneuver, or by tubal catheterization), the occasional use of irradiation, and the installing of polyethylene tubes through the eardrums are employed. The ultimate prognosis with treatment generally is favorable, but the condition may persist for months or years.

Inner Ear

Vestibular or auditory function may be impaired because of adverse *drug reactions,* but there is no evidence that this type of difficulty is immunologically mediated. In the older literature,[8] there are reports that allergy may be involved in the *Lermoyez syndrome,* which is felt to represent a variation of Ménière's disease.[9] Instead of the sequence of good hearing, sudden vertigo, tinnitus, and deafness, characteristic of Ménière's disease, the patient with Lermoyez syndrome shows a "Ménière's syndrome in reverse," i.e., tinnitus and deafness followed by sudden vertigo and good hearing. The etiology usually is obscure.

In *Cogan's syndrome,* there is interstitial keratitis (nonsyphilitic), sudden nerve deafness, and vertigo. The course is chronic, and deafness may become complete. Mild eosinophilia may be present, and some cases have been associated with vascular lesions of the polyarteritis type.[10]

REFERENCES

1. Theodore, F. H., and Schlossman, A.: Ocular Allergy. Baltimore, Williams and Wilkins Co., 1958.
2. MacIvor, J.: Contact allergy to plastic artificial eyes. Canad. M.A.J. *62:*164, 1950.
3. Van Metre, T. E., Jr.: Role of the allergist in diagnosis and management of patients with uveitis. J.A.M.A. *195:*167, 1966.
4. Woods, A. C.: Endogenous Inflammations of the Uveal Tract. Baltimore, Williams and Wilkins Co., 1961.
5. Van Metre, T., Jr.: The relation between nongranulomatous uveitis and arthritis. J. Allergy. *36:*158, 1965.
6. Woods, A. C.: Allergy and Immunity in Ophthalmology. Baltimore, Johns Hopkins Press, 1933.
7. Fitz-Hugh, G. S., and Stone, R. T.: Serous otitis media in children. Virginia M. Month. *93:*61, 1966.
8. Williams, H. J.: Ménière's Disease. Springfield, Ill., Charles C Thomas, 1952.
9. Eagle, W. W.: Lermoyez's syndrome; allergic disease. Ann. Otol. Rhin. & Laryng. *57:*453, 1948.
10. Oliner, L., Traubenhaus, M., Shapira, R. M., and Leshin, N.: Nonsyphilitic interstitial keratitis and bilateral deafness (Cogan's syndrome) associated with essential polyangiitis (periarteritis nodosa). New England J. Med. *248:*1001, 1953.

Chapter Fifteen

MANAGEMENT OF HYPERSENSITIVITY TO STINGING INSECTS

JAMES A. McLEAN, M.D.

Only in the past few years has the scope of the problem of allergy to Hymenoptera, or stinging insects, been fully realized. More people in the United States die each year from allergic reactions to bee sting alone than from the bite of rattlesnake. Yet, there is a surprising lack of awareness among many physicians of the existence of an effective means of treatment for this hypersensitivity state. Of equal importance is the fact that fatalities occur in the nonatopic population as well as in atopic individuals, even though death from the sting of any one of the Hymenoptera group (bee, wasp, hornet or yellow jacket) is considered to be anaphylactic in type. The following classification has been applied to a group of patients experiencing various types of reactions to sting of the Hymenoptera and it reflects the relative frequency of the types of reactions which have prompted hyposensitization treatment in cases reported to a national registry[1] (see page 322).

I. Immediate
   a. Local, confined to site of sting 13%
   b. Systemic, urticaria, asthma, shock
      mild 16%
      moderate 44%
      severe 24%
II. Delayed 3%

Delayed hypersensitivity reactions result in a serum sickness type of syndrome. There are other less common reactions such as recurrent angioedema, neuritis, cerebral infarction, and possibly nephritis.

The problem of the severe reaction to insect sting is made more intense by at least three factors. *First,* the sensitive individual may be only casually concerned or aware of his allergic state. A previous sting from one of these insects may have evoked only a modest reaction, perhaps generalized urticaria, or a mild but definite systemic response. A subsequent sting may result in sudden and dramatic shock ending in death. About one-half of patients experiencing a severe general reaction report no previous mild reaction which might have warned them of their increasing sensitivity. It is not surprising to find that most stings take place in August, or that young boys with their high incidence of exposure have a higher reaction rate than girls. Adults are likely to suffer increasingly severe reactions after the age of 30.

The clinical picture of insect sting hypersensitivity reveals a progressive degree of severity, especially when there is a lapse of weeks or months between stings. Progression of reactions from local swelling and urticaria to generalized swelling and angioedema is common. This may then progress to dyspnea and wheezing, faintness, collapse in allergic shock and death. The dramatic severity of the reaction to Hymenoptera is one of the most intense in clinical medicine, paralleling that seen from aspirin and penicillin or the severe response to shellfish manifested by certain allergic patients. Autopsy may show pulmonary edema, cerebral intraventricular hemorrhage or cutaneous and cerebral petechiae, but at times anatomical abnormalities are minimal.

As the severity of the clinical reaction progresses, the interval between the sting and the onset of symptoms shortens in an alarming manner. The average time between the sting and death in fatal cases is ten minutes. This is the *second point,* namely, that there is not time for the endangered person to call his physician or run to the drug store for help after being stung. Either he must have his medication for relief with him, or he must be rendered less sensitive by the hyposensitization measures outlined in this section. *Finally,* the problem is complicated because insect stings are likely to occur in an area where the victim is geographically remotely located and where prompt medical aid is not available.

The insects involved in causing severe hypersensitivity are found almost exclusively in the Hymenoptera group, as noted above. The authentic reporting of deaths from *allergic* reactions to sting of mosquito, deer fly, tick or spider is much more difficult to find, although severe local manifestations as well as systemic reactions have been reported.[2] Toxic or neurogenic deaths from spider bite, of course, are familiar in the literature.

IMMUNOLOGY OF HYMENOPTERA SENSITIVITY

It is known that bee venom contains a hemolyzing factor and a neurotoxin as well as a histamine-releasing factor. Another substance, possibly activated by an enzyme, produces a delayed contraction in the guinea pig ileum. Wasp venom also contains large amounts of "H" or histamine-releasing substance which contributes to the pain and edema of the sting as well as an extremely potent, unidentified constituent thought to be a polypeptide which causes a delayed contraction of the guinea pig ileum. This occurs in the presence of atropine and persists after 5-hydroxytryptamine desensitization and thus suggests that it is similar to bradykinin. Wasp venom, in contrast with bee venom, contains 5-hydroxytryptamine as revealed by paper chromatography and challenge of the guinea pig ileum. Foubert and Stier, using sensitized rabbit antisera in gel diffusion studies, have shown that there are two common antigens for the Hymenoptera and two to four antigens which are specific for each species.[3] Yellow jacket was the most potent in anaphylactic sensitization in guinea pig, but it is not known if this is comparable with spontaneous sensitivity in man. It has also been shown that specific venom sac antigens and specific insect body antigens exist, as well as antigens common to both parts.[4] Patients having an allergic reaction to an insect sting may have skin-sensitizing and hemagglutinating antibody against one or several of the Hymenoptera. Immunoelectrophoresis shows that Hymenoptera extracts contain a greater number of antigens than was previously suspected.

Sera from humans having clinical reactions to Hymenoptera insect stings do not react with individual hymenoptera antigens using precipitin-in-gel tests. Human antibodies may produce positive PCA reactions in guinea pigs, but the presence of the antibodies capable of giving a PCA reaction did not correlate with the severity of the clinical insect sting, the skin test reaction or the specificity of the insect identified as causing the reaction.[5] The same may be said of passive hemagglutination tests.

The immunologic mechanism in stinging insect hypersensitivity is probably different from the common human atopic allergies. This sensitivity is induced by irregular, repeated injections of antigen (as stings), and skin-sensitizing antibodies are not as readily demonstrated as they are in human atopy. Many of the features of severe Hymenoptera reactions are typical for human anaphylaxis.[6]

IDENTIFICATION AND HABITAT OF SOME COMMON MEMBERS OF HYMENOPTERA

Thousands of species of North American Hymenoptera are capable of inflicting stings. However, it is primarily the *social* wasps and bees

Figure 15–1. (Left to right) Bumblebee (Bombus), honeybee (*Apis mellifica*), yellow jacket (*Vespula maculifrons*), Southern yellow jacket (*Vespula squamosa*), paper wasp (*Polistes fuscatus*), white-faced hornet (*Vespula maculata*).

which nest in or near places frequented by humans that are of major importance. These include only relatively few species (Figure 15–1).

Terminology

The term "wasp" is very general, and is often used to describe three types of stinging insect, namely, (1) *Polistes* wasps, (2) hornets and (3) yellow jackets. Sometimes it is used in a more restricted sense, when speaking of stinging insects, to refer only to the first of these categories. The term "bee" applies correctly only to the two other major categories of stinging Hymenoptera, namely, (4) honeybees and (5) bumblebees. It should be noted that colloquial use of these terms is erratic and subject to regional variations.

Polistes Wasps. Devoid of hair, they are easily identified by the fusiform abdomen which is gently tapered at both ends and linked with the thorax by a thin waist (Figure 15–2). They are black or dark brown in color, and to a variable extent are marked by yellow, white or red striping. In the South, the general color of these wasps is of a more reddish hue than that in the North. Those with yellow markings are sometimes called yellow jackets, which confuses the situation. *Polistes* wasps tend to build their nests on tree branches or around the shelter of houses, sheds, eaves and porches. They are constructed as small, flat, open combs made of brownish or grayish paper. There are often only a few individuals associated with a nest, and especially in cool weather

Figure 15–2. (Top) The wasp is distinguished by its slender waist. (Bottom) The hornet and yellow jacket have a more oval, blunt body. These two cannot be reliably differentiated without close examination of the face (see text).

they are not very irritable even when the nest is disturbed. They usually sting only if touched or brushed while in flight or on the nest. However, some *Polistes* are aggressive and easily angered.

Hornets (**Dolichovespula**) *and Yellow Jackets* (**Vespula**). These are quite similar, and are differentiated most easily from wasps by their abdomens. The anterior part is almost square, and fits closely to the thorax by a short waist. Both are slightly more hairy than wasps, and coloring may be black and white or black and yellow. It is not possible to differentiate a yellow jacket from a hornet by its color since some hornets have yellow markings. Instead, a detailed examination of the face will show the hornet to have an extra black plate between the lower edge of the eye and the mandible. No such plate is seen in the yellow jacket and the mandible articulates with the margin of the eye.[3] An additional helpful feature in distinguishing hornets from yellow jackets is their habitat. The hornet constructs a large gray or brown paper nest, shaped like a football, on branches, under eaves of houses or against a wall, often five to ten feet above ground. The yellow jacket locates its nest under the ground, often in tall grass, in between the walls of buildings or under stones. They are quite irritable and are likely to sting anyone who approaches the nest. Yellow jackets are seen often in large numbers near rotting fruit, garbage and at picnic grounds. Hornets are particularly aggressive, sometimes attacking without provocation the unwary person who ventures too near the nest.

Figure 15–3. The honeybee sting may leave the stinger in the skin. (1) The bee stings, and the barb on the stinger is implanted. (2–3) As the bee flies away evisceration occurs. The bee will soon die. (4) The throbbing stinger, with venom sac attached must be flicked or scraped out to prevent forcing more venom (protein) into the skin. (Paintings by Hashime Murayama, 1935, National Geographic Society.)

Honeybees (Apis). These are easily recognized with their small stocky bodies, brown or black in color, covered by hair and possessing round abdomens. The large and cumbersome bumblebee (*Bombus*) rarely attacks his tormentor unless the nest is stepped on. Nests are underground, usually in fields. The smaller honeybee is quite different in shape from the wasp and the hornet. Locating either in artificial hives or in natural nests which are found in enclosed areas, under floorboards or in hollow trees, bees are frequently seen at their work on flowers. They may sting if irritated by the gardener or if stepped on by a barefooted child as he plays in clover. Only the female bee stings; only the bee leaves its stinger in the skin (Figure 15–3).

PREVENTION OF HYPERSENSITIVITY REACTIONS

Fortunately, prophylactic treatment of insect hypersensitivity is one of the most successful procedures in the entire field of allergy. More than 90 per cent of patients can be rendered less sensitive following the subcutaneous serial administration of the Hymenoptera protein.[1] In fact, failure of this form of treatment should cause one to wonder whether the procedure was carried out properly.

Usually a mixture of wasp, yellow jacket, honey bee and hornet extracts is employed as antigen. This is justified by the fact that there often is uncertainty regarding the particular insect to which the patient is hypersensitive. Also, there is the aforementioned evidence of common antigens, as well as unique antigens, among different members of the Hymenoptera group.[4] If the offending insect is known and the patient is especially reactive to the corresponding extract by skin test, it may be desirable to augment this extract in the treatment mixture. There is some controversy as to whether the extract may be prepared from the whole body of the insect or merely from the venom. The former is much more practical, older experimental data would justify the use of such material, and most of the extracts used successfully over the years have been prepared from the whole insect bodies.[7] However, the recent data of Schulman et al.,[4] indicating the presence of clinically significant antigens which are present in venom but absent from other parts of the insect, would indicate at least that the venom sacs should be included in the whole bodies extracted in preparation of treatment materials. Hymenoptera extracts are available from a number of commercial sources. These generally are whole body extracts. One should be careful to obtain the extract from a reliable firm.

Selecting the Patient for Treatment

Selection of the patient who should receive treatment is complicated by anxious patients who have been told by friends of the need for prophylactic injections. As usual, a careful history is important. In general, we advise all patients who have had any type of widespread or systemic allergic response following a Hymenoptera sting to undergo treatment. This would include reactions involving any degree of general urticaria, asthma, syncope or shock. Local pain and swelling are normal responses and would not constitute indication for "desensitization" (except possibly for extreme swelling of an entire extremity). The age and the occupation of the patient might influence the decision to give treatment, but the results are so gratifying and a fatality so unfortunate through failure to give treatment that one is justified in advocating a course of injections in borderline cases. It is interesting to note that whereas a few bee-keepers develop sensitivity, many of these persons, who may be stung several hundred times per week, appear to develop such a natural "immunity" that they do not experience even local reactions from stings.

Determination of Starting Dose

Skin tests are not very helpful in reflecting the *degree* of clinical sensitivity of a patient but they may aid in estimating the starting dose.[8] It is best to wait two weeks after the patient has been stung before titration. Tests may be uniformly negative immediately after a sting because of an observed refractory state.

Dilution of the insect mixture into test samples should be carried out so that scratch test extracts in 1:100 million and 1:10 million dilutions are available. Likewise, intradermal dilutions ranging from 1:10 million down to 1:10,000 as well as 1:1000 and 1:100 are needed.[9] We usually place the 1:100 million scratch or prick test first with a saline control, and if the reaction is negative in 15 minutes, we place the 1:10 million next. Extremely sensitive patients are likely to be identified by this procedure. Those who do not show any erythema or whealing reaction to this screening test can safely be subjected to intradermal testing. The intradermal tests should be placed one dilution at a time on the arms, in such a manner that a tourniquet can be placed above the test site if a severe reaction occurs. Also, 15 minute intervals between injections of subsequently stronger dilutions should be observed. At some stage of the testing most patients begin to show erythema and whealing responses. This is regarded as the "end point" of the titration. The patient can be started safely on hyposensitization with injections of mixed stinging insect antigen 10 to 100 times more dilute than the titration end point, depending on the size of the reaction. If all the skin test results are negative, it is important to re-check the history. When one is sure that the patient's experience is authentic, it then is proper to go ahead with the desensitization, starting with the 1:10,000 concentration and building up rapidly through the next stronger dilutions and establishing a maintenance dose at 0.5 cc. of the 1:100 extract.

Injections of the insect antigen are carried out just as they are in the other programs of hyposensitization (Chapter 6). Usually, if the insect season is near at hand and there is pressing need to achieve desensitization rapidly, injections are given twice a week while the dose is being increased. On the other hand, it may be satisfactory to give only one injection weekly while building up the concentration. It is usually possible to progress rapidly through the lower doses, doubling the amount each time. The usual precautions are observed (page 114), and the patient is kept in the office 20 minutes after each injection. A maintenance dose of 0.5 ml. of 1:100 of mixed stinging insects is the final dose we try to reach. The maintenance dose is repeated every one to two weeks during the first treatment season, depending on the severity of the initial reaction to the sting, and then is extended during subsequent years to at least one injection each month. During the winter months or when exposure is unlikely, the interval between injections may be extended to every six weeks. The recommended duration of these injections is still a matter of major uncertainty which is currently under study.[1] Tentatively, three years of treatment are suggested for the average patient, but it may be advisable to maintain the injections indefinitely in patients who have experienced allergic shock.

Experience suggests that patients may be protected after the first few months of "desensitization." After two or three years of injections, the registry of stinging insect reactions maintained by the Insect Allergy Committee of the American Academy of Allergy indicates a highly significant difference in the frequency and severity of reactions to subsequent stings in "desensitized" patients as compared with the reactions in the control group who did not receive these injections.[1] Ninety per cent of treated persons showed less severe reactions to being stung again as compared with 9 per cent of the controls.

IMMEDIATE TREATMENT FOR INSECT STING REACTIONS

By the Patient or His Family. Since, as discussed previously, allergic reactions to insect stings may progress with frightening rapidity and the stings often occur at geographically remote locations, treatment often must be initiated by the patient. A recommended procedure is indicated in the *Instructions for Stinging-Insect-Sensitive Persons* (page 324). Any potent antihistamine can be prescribed, but enteric-coated or prolonged-action dosage forms should be avoided here. Because of their compact size and resistance to being broken, pressurized dispensers containing epinephrine have evident advantages (page 131). Ephedrine could also be made available as a supplementary medication. It would be ideal for the patient to administer epinephrine to himself by subcutaneous injection, but it appears impractical and unrealistic to expect many patients always to have this medication with them and to be prepared to inject it into themselves. In selected cases, however, this appears to be advisable; for example, an intelligent forester who has already experienced allergic shock and has a high risk of further stings while in a remote part of the woods should carry epinephrine for injection. Commercially available disposable syringes containing epinephrine are useful for this purpose (also kits containing epinephrine and other drugs and a tourniquet). Needless to say, considerable instruction in self-injection is required and the patient should be given an opportunity to practice (using saline) under supervision at first. In previous years, patients often were given isoproterenol to be used sublingually in case of a sting. Although this would be effective in preventing or in relieving asthma, it might actually aggravate shock, since it acts only on beta-adrenergic receptors (page 132).

By the Physician. The immediate management of stinging insect reactions is the same as that given for other allergic emergencies on page 118. In addition, in case of stings by worker bees, the stingers should be carefully flicked out without squeezing the attached venom sac (Figure 15–3). Cold applications at the site of the sting also may help to confine the reaction through vasoconstriction and to ease the local pain.

PREVENTION OF STINGS

Prevention of repeated stings is especially important in sensitized patients. It is not a mystery that certain persons seem to be stung frequently. The stinging insects are attracted to bright floral colors and to perfume and cologne. Frequenting the insect's habitat will also increase the chances of being stung. We provide patients with the following instructions in an effort to reduce the probability of further stings.

Figure 15–4. *A*, Bee. *B*, Wasp. *C*, Hornet or yellow jacket. *D*, Hornet (left) with black bar between eye and mandible; yellow jacket (right) with eye and mandible directly articulating.

Instructions for Stinging-Insect-Sensitive Persons

DO:

1. Keep some fast-acting insecticide (Raid or Ortho) as an aerosol bomb spray (a) in the kitchen to be used to spray the trash and garbage can area, (b) in the glove compartment of the automobile (there is more potential danger from an *accident* if a bee or wasp gets loose in the car than from the sting) and (c) nearby when working outdoors for use when an insect approaches you.
2. You have been provided with an antihistamine to swallow and a sprayer of epinephrine. Take the tablet *at once* if stung, as reactions begin to occur very rapidly. Take three to six inhalations from the epinephrine spray. In summer months, always carry your pills and sprayer with you. Boys may use a compartment wrist bracelet or an aspirin tin box which is convenient to carry in the pocket; girls may use a locket and chain around the neck or an aspirin tin box which can be carried in the pocket or purse.
3. If stung, look to see whether the insect (a bee) has left the stinger in the skin. This will look like a black thorn or splinter. Carefully remove it, using a pin or pointed knife to flick it from the skin. Try to get the stinger out without squeezing more venom into the skin.
4. Apply ice or cold compresses to the site of the sting.
5. Even though it may prove unnecessary, it is best for the victim to be taken immediately to the nearest medical facility. In a strange area, the telephone operator can advise you of its location.
6. It is advised that you take a series of injections for "desensitization" so that bee, wasp, yellow jacket or hornet sting will not cause a serious reaction in the future. These injections usually are very effective.

DON'T:

1. Don't use scented preparations if you are going outdoors, e.g., hair tonic, after-shave lotion, hair spray, deodorant, perfume and bath powder. Floral odors especially attract bees and wasps.
2. Avoid wearing dark clothing (brown, black or dark red) and floral prints. White is said to be the least insect-attracting color.
3. Loose-fitting clothing, such as head scarves and billowing skirts, are undesirable because a bee or wasp trapped in these may sting.
4. Never go barefoot or wear sandals outdoors. Bees especially like clover. Yellow jackets burrow in the ground.
5. Activities with particular risk are:
   a. Tampering in any way with wasp nests or yellow jacket burrows. Mowing the lawn, cutting flowers, trimming hedges or shrubs or

painting a house may accidentally do just this. Wasps may also nest on fences or around boat docks.

b. Handling trash or garbage cans (wasps and yellow jackets search for food here). Picnic grounds and clover fields are favorite gathering places for these insects, too.

c. Halting, jerky or fast movements when the insects are near. Sometimes, however, one must run for safety, as when a large nest is disturbed.

REFERENCES

1. Insect Allergy Committee, American Academy of Allergy: Report. J. Allergy *35*:181, 1964; J.A.M.A. *193*:109, 1965.
2. Perlman, F.: Insects as allergen injectants. Severe reactions to bites and stings of arthropods. California Med. *96*:1, 1962.
3. Foubert, E. L., and Stier, R. A.: Antigenic relationships between honeybees, wasps, yellow jackets, yellow hornets, black hornets. J. Allergy *29*:13, 1958.
4. Schulman, S., Langlois, C., and Arbesman, C.: The allergic response to stinging insects. I. Preparation of extracts. J. Allergy *35*:446, 1964.
5. Terr, A. I., and McLean, J. A.: Studies on insect sting hypersensitivity. J. Allergy *35*: 127, 1964.
6. James, L. P., and Austen, K. F.: Systemic anaphylaxis. New England J. Med. *270*:597, 1964.
7. Benson, R. L.: Diagnosis of hypersensitiveness to the bee and to the mosquito. With report on successful specific treatment. Arch. Int. Med. *64*:1306, 1939.
8. Schwartz, H. J.: Skin sensitivity in insect allergy. J.A.M.A. *194*:113, 1965.
9. Mueller, H. L.: Serial intracutaneous testing for bee and wasp sensitivity. J. Allergy *30*:122, 1959.

Chapter Sixteen

AEROALLERGENS

I. Techniques of Air Sampling*

WILLIAM R. SOLOMON, M.D.

The allergist has ample reason for interest in many aspects of air quality. Precise knowledge of pollen and spore concentrations provides an indispensable aid in the diagnosis and treatment of inhalant allergy. Additional factors, including physical properties of ambient air as well as its content of inert particles and irritant gases, may ultimately be shown to affect respiratory responses. Means of measuring the latter air quality variables have been summarized elsewhere.[1-3] This discussion will be confined to suitable methods for sampling particulate aeroallergens which are generally between 2 and 50 microns in size and to the principles which underlie these techniques.

FACTORS THAT INFLUENCE
THE COLLECTION OF AIR-BORNE PARTICLES

At present, all practical sampling procedures require that particles strike and adhere to prepared surfaces where they, or the colonies that they may produce, are counted. Several fundamental physical processes are known to affect this deposition. Even microscopic particles show gravitational settling and, in perfectly still air (a rarity in nature), this process alone fosters deposition. Their interaction with air molecules prevents the falling particles from reaching maximal gravitational acceleration (980 cm./sec.²). Instead, a constant "terminal settling velocity" is reached at which the buoyancy of the particle and the "drag" of the air upon it equal its weight. As expected, particles of greatest

* The author's observations recorded in this chapter have been made through the stimulus of work supported by Grant AP-00001, from the Division of Air Pollution, Bureau of State Services, United States Public Health Service.

size† and density attain the highest settling velocities and are most readily deposited by gravity. It is not surprising that the collecting efficiency of methods based on gravitational settling decreases sharply with diminishing particle size.

In outdoor air, the horizontal movement of particles is of major importance in determining their rate of deposition. Once accelerated, they tend to follow linear paths although they may be variably deflected by interaction with moving molecules of gas. Minute particles, having little linear momentum (which is proportional to mass and to velocity^2), follow closely in speed and direction the air in which they are entrained. As size and linear momentum increase, particles are less disposed to follow deviations in flow of the carrier gas and tend to move across its stream lines. For this reason, heavy particles collide readily with an object in their path (Figure 16–2), whereas smaller particles flow smoothly around the same obstruction. Since they can be made to deviate from their paths easily by changes in air motion, smaller particles (i.e., those less than 10 microns in average diameter) enter suction traps relatively well and can be efficiently recovered from known volumes of aspirated air. Conversely, larger particles tend to become dissociated from air that is rapidly changing in direction and may escape capture by such samplers (see Figure 16–7b.). One can safely conclude that the collection efficiency of any device varies with particle size and density as well as with the speed and direction of local air flow. Average size values for many specific types of wind-disseminated pollen and spores will be found in Chapters 16–II and 16–III.

CHOOSING A SAMPLING STATION

It is well known that particle concentrations rise precipitously as the source of emission is approached. When numerous scattered sources emit in unison, as occurs with the common hay fever plants, turbulent air mixing tends to establish fairly uniform particle concentrations over large areas in the lowermost atmosphere. Such particle "clouds" are conveniently sampled from the flat roof of a building located centrally relative to a patient population. Taller structures should not closely flank the building chosen, and chimneys, elevator housings, and other structures should subtend an angle of elevation, at the sampling device, not greater than 20 degrees (see Figure 16–1). If a parapet is present, the apparatus should be operated at a level at least 30 inches above its top. The roof edge is an especially unsatisfactory site for sampling with gravity slides since maximal wind speeds are encountered here and upward air movement predominates. Porches and window ledges may

---

† For dissimilar particles, the terminal settling velocities vary predictably with particle size (volume) only if the density (mass/volume) of each is the same. If, however, two particles have the same mass but one is twice the size of the other (and, therefore, one half of its density), the larger particle will have more air drag on it and will tend to fall more slowly than the smaller. The term "size" is here used in a general sense and assumes that the density of particles described is constant unless otherwise stated.

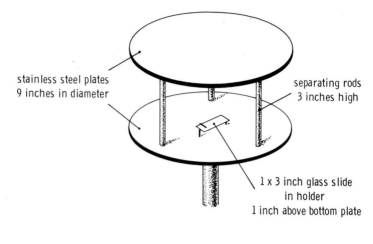

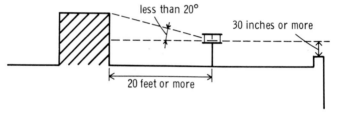

Figure 16-1. The standard Gravity Slide (Durham) Sampler showing its dimensions and spatial considerations when it is used on a rooftop.

share these disadvantages and may, at times, prove unsuitable by acting as stagnation points because of decreased air motion and impaired mixing. By deliberately eliminating the effects of proximate sources, such "central rooftop" air sampling does not detect local particle concentrations that may underlie individual clinical problems. Sampling conducted in and outside a patient's home or place of employment can provide additional useful information. An unobstructed site for equipment should again be sought and careful record made of the place chosen and of its surroundings.

SPECIFIC TYPES OF SAMPLING EQUIPMENT

The Gravity Sampler. The collection of particles, especially pollen grains, on coated glass slides was first undertaken by Blackeley in 1866 and despite numerous limitations this remains a useful technique for atmospheric sampling. A standard device,* described by Durham in 1946, is shown in Figure 16–1.[4] One by three inch microscope slides may

---

* This may be purchased from the Wilkins-Anderson Co., 4525 W. Division St., Chicago 51, Illinois (retail price as of July 1965—$55.00). Alternately, the apparatus may be built at modest cost; a standard working drawing may be obtained from the Chairman of the Pollen and Mold Committee of the American Academy of Allergy, 756 N. Milwaukee St., Milwaukee, Wisconsin 53202.

be prepared for exposure by spreading on them a thin film of glycerin jelly containing Calberla's Solution* or of silicone jelly or soft petrolatum (75 per cent petrolatum and 25 per cent mineral oil). Particles deposited on glycerin jelly with Calberla's Solution imbibe moisture and assume an expanded, stained condition which permits immediate identification of most types of pollen grains. However, this medium has the slight but definite disadvantage of changing its viscosity and adhesivity with variations in atmospheric humidity. Also, the identification of some pollen grains, particularly those of the oaks and grasses, may be facilitated by observing them initially in their unexpanded state, which is preserved on silicone or petrolatum. After preliminary inspection, such preparations should be mounted with Calberla's Solution which, after three to five minutes, expands the pollen grains and stains them a brilliant red. Following the removal of large dirt particles and soot with a needle or fine tweezers, several drops of Calberla's Solution are placed on the slide and a cover glass applied. Only sufficient stain should be used to fill the space beneath the cover slip and any excess should be blotted at the edges. Slides are usually exposed for 24 hours beginning at 8 A.M. Particle counts are best reported as the number of particles of each type observed on 1 square centimeter of slide area.

For microscopic examination, low power is generally used (e.g., a 10× objective with a 10× or a 15× eyepiece) and the width of the slide traversed. High "dry" power (usually a 43× objective) should be employed when necessary. The area covered by each traverse depends on the width of the low or high power field used. This dimension may be closely estimated by observing the calibrated, ruled surface of a hemocytometer.† Alternatively, if a calibrated mechanical stage is used, the change in stage setting produced by shifting a given particle across the full width of the field may be read directly. If a field 1 millimeter in size is used, a full traverse of the width of a standard 25×75 millimeter microscope slide will cover 25 square millimeters, and four such traverses will cover 1 square centimeter. If the microscope field employed differs from 1 millimeter, the particle counts obtained may be divided by the field width in millimeters, to provide "particles/cm²." Especially when particle deposition is small, it is advisable to count several square centimeters and divide the total by the appropriate factor to obtain the count per square centimeter. When particle deposition is heavy, the use

---

* Glycerin jelly may be bought from Fisher Scientific Co., 1458 North Lamon Avenue, Chicago, Illinois. It can be prepared also by combining 5 grams gelatin, 40 milliliters water, and 4 grams phenol with 195 grams (155 milliliters) glycerin and warming the mixture in a water bath. It is advantageous to add 2 milliliters Calberla's Solution to this quantity of glycerin jelly to provide staining properties. Calberla's Solution contains 5 ml. glycerin, 10 milliliters 95 per cent ethanol, 15 milliliters distilled water, and 2 drops of a saturated, aqueous solution of basic fuchsin.

† A stage micrometer will serve the same purpose. When the improved Neubauer chamber hemocytometer is used, it should be recalled that each of the four large corner squares is 1 millimeter on a side whereas each of the 400 smallest squares measures 50 microns on a side.

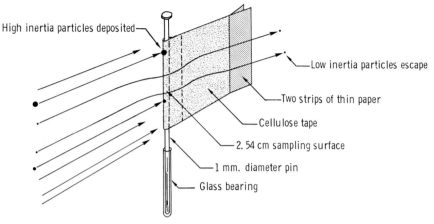

High inertia particles deposited

Low inertia particles escape

Two strips of thin paper

Cellulose tape

2. 54 cm sampling surface

1 mm. diameter pin

Glass bearing

Figure 16–2. The (Pin) Flag Sampler is essentially a wind-oriented vertical cylinder. Its relative capacity to capture large and small particles is in accord with the collection efficiency curves of Fig. 3.

of a Whipple eyepiece disc* is distinctly helpful. This is a glass disc which, when placed in an eyepiece, superimposes a finely etched grid on the microscopic field, effectively dividing it into 100 square sectors. When wind direction during the 24 hours is not entirely random, air flow about the fixed slide often causes particle deposition that is non-uniform. For this reason, the requisite number of traverses should be distributed evenly along the entire length of the sampling surface.

Although designated a "gravity" sampler, most of the particles collected by the greased slide are, in fact, deposited by variable atmospheric turbulence. Since the volume of moving air contributing particles to the slide is always unknown, attempts to obtain volumetric counts by the use of conversion factors which have been empirically derived in still air are entirely unjustified.[5, 6] Occasionally, however, one still finds published pollen counts for ragweed, obtained by counting 3.6 square centimeters of slide area, expressed as "particles/yard³." The allergist must be aware of the fallacy of these derived units and should encourage the local press to relate counts to a unit area (1 cm.²) of slide surface if, indeed, counts *must* be published. The exact dates of sampling to which each reported value refers should also be specified.†

Inertial Samplers. These devices either utilize the natural mo-

_____

* Whipple discs are available from most major manufacturers of microscopes. Since the disc must rest exactly at the focal plane of the eyepiece and since discs from different sources, like ocular micrometers, vary in diameter, purchase from the manufacturer of the microscope *in use* is strongly recommended.

† Patients are often confused by their inability to correlate their symptoms with the pollen counts reported in news media. Besides the basic quantitative limitations of gravity slide counts as an expression of the changing level of atmospheric pollen contamination, several factors contribute additional difficulties. Often there is a substantial delay before counts are reported to the public, and these may reflect the unwarranted use of conversion factors by some reporters. Furthermore, pollen concentrations at the sampler and those in the locale of individual patients often differ markedly. Of additional importance are symptoms due to other allergens, especially fungi, the role of irritant and emotional factors, and, perhaps, individual differences in response to a given pollen exposure.

mentum of particles or artificially accelerate them to induce their deposition on surfaces. These two modes of collection define two classes of apparatus:

1. *Impaction and "Rotating Arm" Collectors.* These samplers were developed following studies of particle deposition from moving air, upon narrow vertical cylinders.[5] The "flag" sampler provides a simple illustration of such collection (Figure 16–2). It consists of a 1 millimeter diameter pin which is free to revolve in a short glass tube, one end of which has been fused by a flame to act as a bearing. By applying a strip of Scotch Tape and joining the trailing ends (as shown), a sampling surface and wind vane are effectively produced. The cylindri-

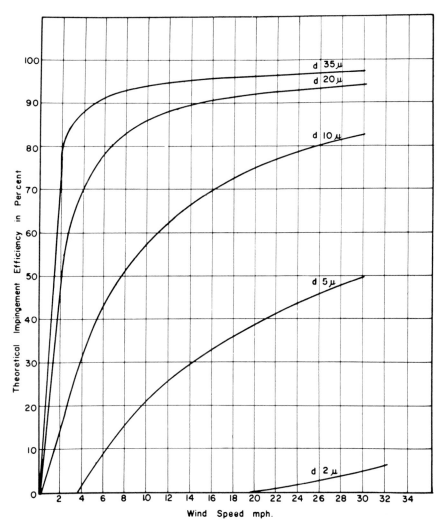

Figure 16–3.   The collection efficiency of a 1 mm. diameter cylinder for particles of unit density having various diameters. Capture of larger particles is seen to be favored at all wind speeds. For particles larger than 10 microns, the efficiency of collection changes markedly with modest changes in wind speed.

cal leading edge of Scotch Tape is coated with silicone grease* and is kept heading into the wind by the wind vane. In contrast with an uncovered gravity slide, the flag sampler theoretically should collect no particles in still air. However, for particles of a given size, collection efficiency rises predictably with increasing wind speed (as shown in Figure 16–3). The flag sampler, therefore, provides precise volumetric data only in special instances in which air speed can be continuously measured.

Most other impaction collectors employ narrow surfaces which are rotated at high speed through the air to be sampled. With each revolution, a volume of air is swept out equal to the product of the sampling area on the leading edge and the circumference of the circle of rotation. Although relatively small particles tend to follow air flow around the leading edge, large, high inertia particles cannot deviate and, therefore, impinge upon it. Understandably, collection efficiency is high for particles larger than 15 microns and diminishes as progressively smaller ones are considered. The high rotational speeds utilized render impingement efficiency essentially independent of wind speed and direction at velocities below 30 m.p.h. Of several such rotating arm samplers developed, only the Rotorod (Figure 16–4) and the Intermittent Rotoslide (Figure 16–5) samplers† have become commercially available. With the latter unit, particles are collected on the leading edges of pairs of glass microscope slides, 75 millimeters long and 1 millimeter thick, which are rotated in metal holders by a 1650 r.p.m. electric motor. A timing device operates the sampler for one out of every twelve minutes; between samples a cylindrical metal shield is raised to protect the slide edges from turbulent particle deposition. Slides are examined on edge in special lucite holders using transmitted light. Identification of particles is facilitated by applying Calberla's Solution and 22 × 50 millimeter cover slips; counts are made of the two 50 square millimeter covered sampling areas.‡ Since the linear travel for each revolution is 0.358 meters, the volume represented by one pair of slide preparations exposed during 24 hours is:

$$120 \text{ minutes} \times 0.0001 \text{ } meters^2 \times 0.358 \frac{\text{meters}}{\text{revolution}} \times 1650 \frac{\text{revolutions}}{\text{minute}}$$

$$= 7 \text{ } meters^3 \text{ or almost } 250 \text{ cubic feet}$$

---

* Dow-Corning high vacuum silicone lubricant is satisfactory for this purpose.

† The Rotoslide sampler is custom-built by the Aquebogue Machine and Repair Shop, Box 205, Main Road, Aquebogue, Long Island, New York, and Charles Thur, P.O. Box 4424, Philadelphia, Pennsylvania 19140. Although blueprints for the Rotoslide sampler are available from the American Academy of Allergy, its construction is a formidable undertaking. The Rotorod sampler is suitable for short periods of sampling. This device can be adapted to either alternating current or battery operation. It is supplied by Metronics Associates Inc., 3201 Porter Drive, Stanford Industrial Park, Palo Alto, California.

‡ By concentrating the particle deposit in a small area, this and similar devices reduce the tedium of counting and encourage study of less common particles as well as of dominant types.

Fig. 16–4

Fig. 16–5

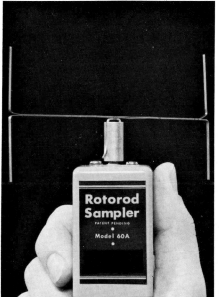

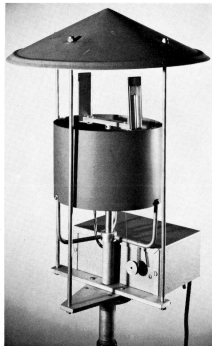

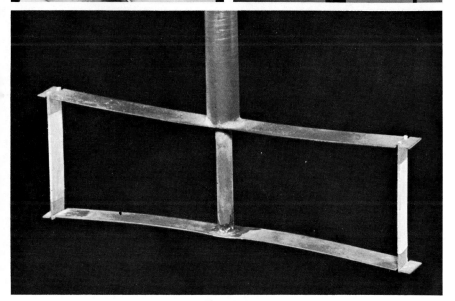

Fig. 16–6

Figure 16–4. The Rotorod Sampler: Particles may be collected directly on the prepared metal surfaces or upon plastic rods which can be examined by transmitted light.

Figure 16–5. The Intermittent Rotoslide Sampler: A pair of slides is shown in place. The cylindrical metal guard has been lowered for purposes of illustration; normally, it is raised automatically to shield the slides between periods of operation. (Courtesy of Brookhaven National Laboratory.)

Figure 16–6. Two rotobars on their supporting strips: The rotobar at the right is wound with transparent tape to create a 1 mm. $\times$ 1 in. sampling surface. The rod at the top is attached to the drive shaft of an electric motor (not shown).

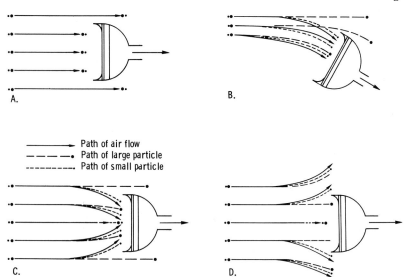

Figure 16–7. Sources of error in the use of suction samplers. A, Isokinetic sampling. Air velocity at sampler intake is identical with that of the air to be sampled. Particles of all sizes are sampled without error. B, Sampler imperfectly wind-oriented. Capture efficiency, particularly for larger particles, is markedly decreased. C, Wind velocity less than that of sampler intake. Particle collection, especially in larger size ranges, is decreased, and factitiously low concentrations will be derived. D, Wind velocity exceeds intake velocity. Particle collection, especially in the larger size ranges, is increased factitiously. Erroneously high particle concentrations will be simulated if wind data are not considered.

Particle concentrations per unit volume of air may be estimated with these instruments, although statements of absolute concentration require also that the collection efficiency for specific particles be known. Samples collected on silicone grease may be kept in dust-proof boxes indefinitely before mounting and examination. However, removal or slipping of the cover glass, once applied, causes a loss of particles and makes storage of samples difficult.

This problem is avoided with the Rotobar sampler (Figure 16–6), used extensively by us.[6] The sampling surface is formed by applying transparent tape, 1 inch in width, to a metal bar 1 millimeter thick. This surface is then coated with Silicone grease or sprayed with rubber cement, diluted 1:10 in thinner. After sampling, the tape may be peeled and applied to a glass slide with the sampling surface up. A cover slip bearing a streak of Calberla's Solution then is placed over the sample, which is examined by transmitted light. Semipermanent preparations made by using a semisolid glycerin jelly (gelatin 45 grams, water 300 milliliters, glycerin 350 milliliters, and phenol 6 grams plus 1 cc. of 2 per cent basic fuchsin aqueous solution) have good optical properties. The melted mounting medium is streaked on a cover glass and this is applied to the 1 inch by 1 millimeter sample strip on which the jelly is permitted to harden.

2. *Inertial Suction Samplers.* These devices draw in measured volumes of air through relatively narrow orifices, and the rapidly moving particles are then deposited by impingement on test surfaces. As previously described, smaller particles, having high drag coefficients and low momentum, are most efficiently collected by these samplers. In any

size range, however, errors are minimal when ambient air movement and flow at the sampler's intake are comparable in rate and direction, a condition referred to as "isokinetic sampling." If the sampler is fitted with a wind vane and mounted on a low friction bearing, it can be aimed continuously into the wind. However, no commercially available device is capable of varying its rate of intake with changes in wind speed. Figure 16–7 c and d shows why true particle concentrations are underestimated when sampler inflow velocity exceeds ambient wind speed and overestimated when the sampler inflow operates at below the free air stream velocity.

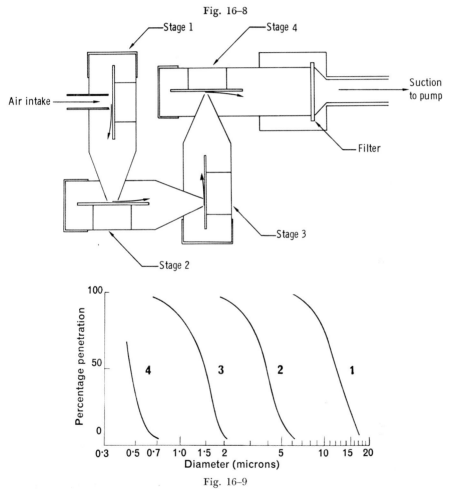

Fig. 16–8

Fig. 16–9

Figure 16–8. The Cascade Impactor: an inertial sampler capable of separating airborne particles into four size classes. The arrows indicate the direction of air flow. Air velocity increases at each succeeding jet orifice.

Figure 16–9. Relative tendency of different sized particles to pass (escape impaction upon) the four stages of the Cascade Impactor (C. F. Casella & Co., Ltd.). Essentially all particles the size of pollen would be collected on the first slide. (Courtesy of C. F. Casella & Co., Ltd.)

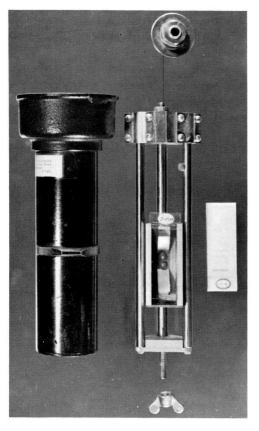

Figure 16–10. T h e H i r s t Spore Trap sampling head disassembled: The black outer cylinder (at the left) has its 2 x 14 mm. intake slit directed forward. The slide carriage with its supporting rods (right of center) fits inside the outer cylinder where it is drawn past the intake slit by a strand of gut or wire attached to a clock mechanism (partly shown at the top). The exposed slide at the right shows definite bands caused by diurnal variations in particle deposition.

Although it is not primarily suited to the needs of allergists, the "cascade impactor" clearly illustrates the principle of inertial collection using suction (Figure 16–8). For its operation, air at 17.5 liters/min. is drawn through four jet orifices of progressively diminishing size. As each jet is traversed, the air is accelerated and forced to accomplish a 90 degree turn; particles which have gained too much linear momentum to remain with the turning air stream impinge on glass discs. This method effectively separates particles, especially those between 1 and 20 microns, into four size ranges (Figure 16–9), the largest being deposited on the first disc.

A dynamic flow arrangement resembling the second stage of the cascade impactor is used in the Hirst Spore Trap,* which samples air drawn through a 2 × 14 millimeter intake slit at a rate of 10 liters per minute (Figure 16–10).[7] Time discrimination in the collection is permitted by a clock mechanism which moves a coated glass slide at 2 milli-

---

* The Hirst Spore Trap is available from C. F. Casella & Co., Ltd., Regent House, Britannia Walk, London, N.1, U.K. The retail price as of February, 1966 is $750.00 without pump. Any of several domestic oil-less pumps capable of generating 10 liters/ min. flow at a pressure difference of 15 centimeters of water, and continuous operation is usable with this device.

meters per hour, along a path located 0.6 millimeter behind the intake orifice. Petrolatum and silicone grease have been used as adhesives. We have obtained semipermanent preparations with good optical properties by coating carefully washed slides with Lubriseal* and, following exposure, mounting them with Permount† and No. 1, 22 × 50 millimeter cover slips. Since the resulting mounts are necessarily rather thick, an oil immersion objective with a working distance greater than 1.8 millimeters is often required for their study.

Particle collection in discrete time-related bands, rather than as a continuous deposit on moving slides, is accomplished by the Kramer-Collins Spore Trap‡ (not illustrated). A flow rate of 1 ft.³/min.(=28.3 liters/min.) is employed. Although this sampler was recently developed for use in relatively quiet air, it might be modified for more general outdoor use by the addition of a wind vane and rain shield.

Filtration Samplers. Samplers employing the filtration of particles from an aspirated air stream easily become overloaded and have not been widely adapted to prolonged use in open air. Molecular membrane filters, however, have been useful in studies of short duration in which a single particle type has been dispersed in an air stream of defined velocity.[8] Removal of all aspirated particles larger than the membrane pore size is complete.§ Because the isokinetic exposure of such filtration samplers provides essentially 100 per cent trapping efficiency for a wide range of particle sizes, they have found use in calibrating other devices. Following exposure, the membrane filters are cleared by mounting them in a fluid medium such as Calberla's Solution and are examined by transmitted light.

Many additional methods of collection including centrifugation, electrostatic precipitation and thermal deposition beside a hot wire, have been exploited in the design of samplers.[2, 5] However, the resulting instruments have not been generally applicable to allergists' purposes.

Cultural Samplers. When sampling involves the growth of living particles, their direct deposition on culture media is advantageous in preserving viability. Media suitable for fungus spore sampling are described on page 432. Open culture plates are simple to use and may be entirely adequate in quiet indoor situations. In outdoor air, however,

---

* More generally used as a stopcock grease and obtainable from Arthur H. Thomas Co., Inc., P.O. Box 779, Philadelphia, Pennsylvania.

† Fisher Scientific Co., 1458 N. Lamon Ave., Chicago, Illinois. Both Permount and Lubriseal are soluble in toluene.

‡ Manufactured and distributed by the GR Electric Mfg. Co., R.F.D. 2, Manhattan, Kansas. Further information concerning use of this sampler may be obtained from C. L. Kramer, Department of Botany and Plant Pathology, Kansas State University, Manhattan, Kansas 66504.

§ Filters having pore sizes of 7 microns and less as well as appropriate holders may be obtained from the Millipore Filter Corp., Boston, Massachusetts. The Gelman Instrument Co., Ann Arbor, Michigan, also supplies filters having pore sizes up to 10 microns.

Figure 16–11. The Andersen Sampler: The unit is partly disassembled to show the intake orifice and six sieve plates (stages) as well as the three retaining hooks which clamp all sections of the sampler rigidly together when they are secured. Tubing (shown at the left) is connected to an exhaust pump. The culture plate on the right has been previously exposed and shows a pattern of depressions in the agar surface, produced by the 400 air jets created by the overlying perforated plate.

the open plate is subject to all the errors inherent in gravitational collection (see page 326). In addition, the vertical sides of the culture plates can effectively shield the agar surface from lateral air motion; plates 10 millimeters in depth are, therefore, preferable to deeper ones. Despite these deficits, the exposure of open plates from 1 to 12 minutes, depending on existing spore concentrations, is well suited to qualitative mold surveys and, when done regularly, reflects general trends in concentration.

The Andersen Sampler (Figure 16–11)* offers a means of exposing media that is volumetric and permits accurate representation of smaller spores.[9] It consists of a series of six sieves or "stages," each containing 400 holes, through which air is drawn by a suction pump at approximately 1 ft.³/min. Particles accelerate progressively as they pass down through holes which decrease in diameter from 0.0465 to 0.0100 inch as the six stages are traversed. By placing special culture plates of medium, poured to a known depth (utilizing 27 ml./plate) beneath any specific sieve plate, inertial deposition of particles above a certain size can be effected. Particles with lesser momentum fail to strike the agar and will pass with the air stream to the next stage. The retention of particles larger than 1 micron that enter this sampler is high, and particle losses

---

* The Andersen 0101 Sampler is supplied by Andersen Samplers & Consulting Service, 1074 Ash St., Provo, Utah. The retail price, as of December 1965, for the sampler complete with a suitable rotary vane pump is approximately $240.00.

by deposition on the walls and plates are reported to be negligible.[9] Although the Andersen Sampler is designed to effect selective deposition by particle size using six culture plates for each exposure, simpler arrangements may be feasible. For example, the authors have used a single culture plate in stage 5 for taking daily mold spore samples, an arrangement which permits the capture of particles larger than 2 microns. The collection efficiency of this sampler in moving air can be increased if it is mounted on a wind vane and exposed on its side, rather than with the intake directed upward. It is worthwhile, also, to check the rate of inflow periodically with a rotameter. When a single plate is used in heavily contaminated air, the duration of exposure may have to be as short as 30 seconds if the resulting colonies are to be discrete.

SUMMARY

Although means are available for monitoring the absolute concentrations of a wide range of air-borne particulates, no single method is sufficient for this purpose. Processes governing deposition of particles on sampling surfaces have been reviewed in a description of the several classes of sampling devices, their relative assets, and their inherent sources of error. The importance of correct sampler orientation and the value of approaching isokinetic conditions have been emphasized.

Its economy and simplicity continue to recommend the gravity slide sampler in situations where grossly semiquantitative data for particles over 10 to 15 microns are sufficient. However, any investigation of absolute particle concentrations requires that the volume of air sampled be known. Accurate information concerning larger particles may be readily obtained by use of a rotating arm inertial sampler. Investigation of very small particles is best undertaken with suction traps that are responsive to wind direction. It is apparent that realistic goals must be set for the operation of any given sampling device if the data resulting from its use are to be valid.

Aeroallergens

II. Pollens
and the Plants That Produce Them

WILLIAM R. SOLOMON, M.D. AND
OREN C. DURHAM*
in collaboration with FLORENCE L. McKAY**

The botanical aspects of clinical allergy constitute some of the most intriguing and important phases of the allergist's work. Through his study of local flowering plants and of pollen aerobiology, the practitioner can increase materially his own diagnostic acumen. In addition, by correlating careful clinical observations with accurate botanical data, he can provide information still needed to fill the gaps in our basic knowledge of inhalant allergy.

The seasonal pattern of symptoms that pollen-sensitive patients present closely reflects their annual exposure to specific offending pollens. Because of this, the dates at which symptoms appear and abate each year must be defined precisely whenever these patients are evaluated. In addition, the physician must be familiar with the seasonal occurrence of tree, grass, and weed pollens in his own locality as well as in other regions.[1] Typical dates for the major pollen seasons are summarized in the pollen calendar (shown on pages 342 and 343), and these describe an "average" season or year accurately. However, unpredictable day-to-day variations in the prevalence of atmospheric pollen and spores often occur. Unless the allergist is alert both to current changes and long-range trends in the air-borne pollen load, he may overlook factors which strongly affect clinical symptoms. Therefore, a survey of air-borne pollen, such as is shown on page 341, and of its botanical sources should be carried on each year.‡

---

* Formerly Chief Botanist, Abbott Laboratories, North Chicago, Illinois.
** Technician, University of Michigan Medical Center.
‡ Valuable data concerning pollen prevalence at many points in the United States and Canada are also published in the annual Statistical Report of the Pollen and Mold Committee of the American Academy of Allergy. The Report may be obtained by writing to the Executive Offices of the Academy, 756 N. Milwaukee St., Milwaukee, Wisconsin 53202.

THE POLLEN SURVEY

Regular air sampling and identification of particles are important features of a pollen survey but not the only activities of value. The allergist must also know his local wind-pollinated plants thoroughly and should remain familiar with their distribution and phase of flower development through regular field observations. No opportunity should be overlooked for spot-testing the productive ability of particular plants or for securing pollen directly from the plants for reference in identification. A continuous field survey complements and increases the value of atmospheric sampling.

The tools for a pollen survey include a textbook of elementary systematic botany, reference manuals of local and regional flora, and one or more books illustrating pollen morphology.[2-5] In addition to an appropriate air-sampling device (see page 328), pollen reference specimens should be available from as many known and suspected local species as possible. At the outset and occasionally thereafter, the allergist makes good use of a set of authentic pollen specimens which may be obtained from the Pollen and Mold Committee of the American Academy of Allergy.* These should, of course, be replaced gradually by a complete set of local reference specimens prepared with the medium upon which pollen is generally collected (usually glycerin jelly or sili-

Monthly Pollen Record for the Season of 1964 *at Ann Arbor, Michigan*

	March	April	May	June	July	Aug.	Sept.	Oct.	Nov.	Total
Elm (*Ulmus* spp.)	24	1888	80							1992
Birch (*Betula* spp.)	3	51	245	4						303
Yew and cedar (*Taxus-Juniperus* spp.)	25	159	17							199
Maple (*Acer* spp.)	5	699	454							1158
Willow (*Salix* spp.)		23	41							64
Hickory (*Carya* spp.)		6	141	13						160
Aspen and Cottonwood (*Populus* spp.)		20	25							45
Ash (*Fraxinus* spp.)		59	458							517
Mulberry (*Morus* spp.)			270	15						285
Oak (*Quercus* spp.)			1526	6						1532
Walnut (*Juglans* spp.)			106	18						124
Grass (Gramineae)			42	273	44	23	15	1	1	399
Sorrel (*Rumex* spp.)			23	79	2					104
Ragweed (*Ambrosia* spp.)					6	2886	1758	11	17	4705
Miscellaneous†			24	40	76	69	64	5	1	279

† Includes the pollens of plantain (*Plantago* spp.), beech (*Fagus* spp.), linden (*Tilia* spp.) goosefoots (Chenopodiaceae) and amaranths (Amaranthaceae), wormwood (*Artemisia* spp.), entomophilous composites (Compositae), and others.

* Write to the Chairman, Pollen and Mold Committee, American Academy of Allergy, 756 N. Milwaukee St., Milwaukee, Wisconsin 53202.

POLLEN CALENDAR

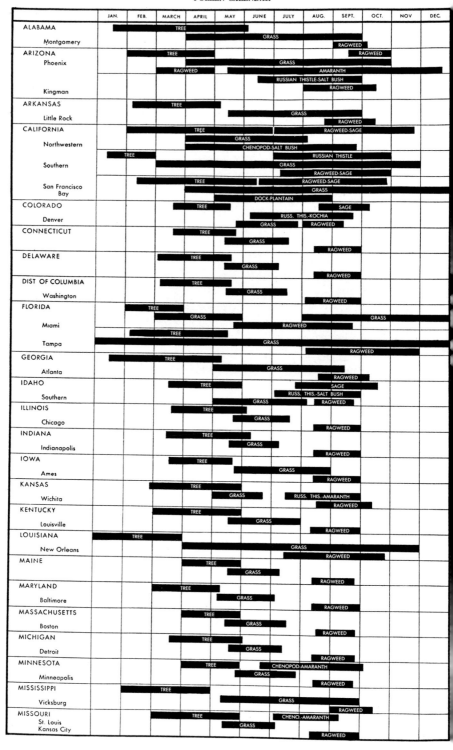

POLLEN CALENDAR (Continued)

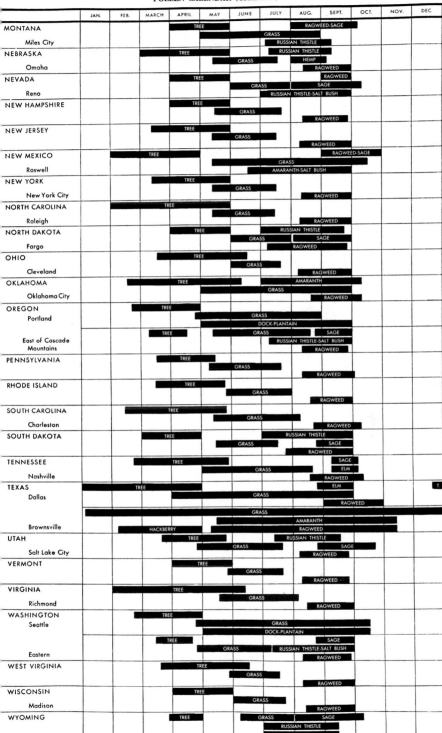

	JAN.	FEB.	MARCH	APRIL	MAY	JUNE	JULY	AUG.	SEPT.	OCT.	NOV.	DEC.
MONTANA				TREE				RAGWEED-SAGE				
						GRASS						
Miles City							RUSSIAN THISTLE					
NEBRASKA				TREE			RUSSIAN THISTLE					
					GRASS		HEMP					
Omaha								RAGWEED				
NEVADA				TREE				RAGWEED				
					GRASS		SAGE					
Reno						RUSSIAN THISTLE-SALT BUSH						
NEW HAMPSHIRE				TREE								
					GRASS							
							RAGWEED					
NEW JERSEY				TREE								
					GRASS							
							RAGWEED					
NEW MEXICO		TREE						RAGWEED-SAGE				
						GRASS						
Roswell					AMARANTH-SALT BUSH							
NEW YORK				TREE								
					GRASS							
New York City							RAGWEED					
NORTH CAROLINA			TREE									
					GRASS							
Raleigh							RAGWEED					
NORTH DAKOTA				TREE			RUSSIAN THISTLE					
						GRASS	SAGE					
Fargo						RAGWEED						
OHIO				TREE								
					GRASS							
Cleveland							RAGWEED					
OKLAHOMA				TREE			AMARANTH					
					GRASS							
Oklahoma City							RAGWEED					
OREGON			TREE									
Portland						GRASS						
					DOCK-PLANTAIN							
East of Cascade Mountains			TREE			GRASS	SAGE					
						RUSSIAN THISTLE-SALT BUSH						
							RAGWEED					
PENNSYLVANIA				TREE								
					GRASS							
							RAGWEED					
RHODE ISLAND				TREE								
					GRASS							
							RAGWEED					
SOUTH CAROLINA			TREE									
					GRASS							
Charleston							RAGWEED					
SOUTH DAKOTA				TREE			RUSSIAN THISTLE					
						GRASS	SAGE					
						RAGWEED						
TENNESSEE				TREE				SAGE				
						GRASS	ELM					
Nashville							RAGWEED					
TEXAS		TREE						ELM				T.
Dallas						GRASS						
							RAGWEED					
						GRASS						
Brownsville							AMARANTH					
			HACKBERRY				RAGWEED					
UTAH				TREE			RUSSIAN THISTLE					
					GRASS		SAGE					
Salt Lake City							RAGWEED					
VERMONT				TREE								
					GRASS							
							RAGWEED					
VIRGINIA			TREE									
					GRASS							
Richmond							RAGWEED					
WASHINGTON			TREE									
Seattle						GRASS						
					DOCK-PLANTAIN							
			TREE			GRASS	SAGE					
Eastern						RUSSIAN THISTLE-SALT BUSH						
							RAGWEED					
WEST VIRGINIA				TREE								
					GRASS							
							RAGWEED					
WISCONSIN				TREE								
					GRASS							
Madison							RAGWEED					
WYOMING				TREE		GRASS	SAGE					
						RUSSIAN THISTLE						
						RAGWEED						

cone grease). A good microscope with a mechanical stage, preferably with graduations, is essential. In general, a 15× eyepiece shows fine details more clearly than a 10× eyepiece, and is preferable. A high-dry objective is frequently needed, but oil immersion is seldom used in routine counting. For measuring pollen grains, an ocular micrometer is necessary (see footnote on page 330. A hand lens with a magnification of 10× or, preferably, 15× is useful for the examination of flowers.

SYSTEMATIC BOTANY

In the study of aeroallergens, particularly pollens, an elementary acquaintance with systematic botany is imperative. This is true not only because of morphologic similarities among pollen grains produced by related plant species but also because of the proved or suspected allergenic relationships of these pollens. The broadest grouping of flowering plants which is useful in the study of allergenic pollens is the order, consisting usually of several families. Each family usually has several to many genera, and each genus in turn has several to many species. For example, the species known as Kentucky bluegrass (*Poa pratensis*) belongs to the genus Poa, of which there are some 60 North American species other than pratensis. (Only the genus and species appear in the Latin name.) The genus Poa is only one of the 159 genera of the grass family Gramineae, or Poaceae. The grass family and the sedge family, Cyperaceae, are grouped by some taxonomists into the order Graminales.

POLLENS AS AEROALLERGENS

Allergenic specificity appears to be seldom, if ever, limited to the pollen of only one of several closely related plant species. For example, certain allergens have been reported as being common to pollens of most members of the grass family but they seem to be absent or inconstant in the related sedge family.[6] However, there is no established rule which permits generalizations concerning all botanical groups. When related species possess common antigenic qualities, one or two members of the genus frequently occur most abundantly or produce especially potent pollen and, accordingly, assume primary clinical significance.

To act as a significant aeroallergen, pollen of a given plant species must become air-borne in large amounts close to human habitation and should possess strong antigens capable of sensitizing and provoking symptoms. Except for pine pollen, most common wind-borne pollens seem to be able to sensitize a greater or lesser portion of exposed atopic persons. On skin testing, these patients often show many strongly positive reactions. The physician, therefore, must rely heavily on his knowledge of the patient's pollen exposure to interpret the history and use it as a basis for specific management. In this regard, the potential importance of limited local sources, especially of specific trees which are located close to the patient's home, deserves emphasis. Many plants individually shed small amounts of pollen but, when grouped in a small area, may produce high but sharply localized pollen concentrations. The wild grape (Vitis), the sumacs (Rhus), tree of heaven (Ailanthus), ornamental plums and cherries (Rosaceae) and many others can exhibit this effect, although they are predominantly insect-pollinated.

Wide day-to-day variations in the levels of air-borne pollen are frequently referable to weather conditions (see page 340). The washout of pollen by falling rain is highly efficient, especially when compared with its lesser scouring effect on the smaller spores of fungi. In common ragweed (*Ambrosia artemisiifolia*), the normal early morning release of pollen is inhibited or delayed by high relative humidity and can be depressed by low overnight temperatures.[7] Moderate degrees of wilting do not appear to diminish anthesis in this species. The effect of climatic factors on pollen release in other plants is largely unstudied. Whether pollen allergenicity varies with growth conditions, such as soil, water, and nutrients, or can be modified by the action of water vapor, sunlight, ozone, and other factors during aerial transport also are matters for speculation.

Symptoms may be rapidly induced in sensitive patients who inhale dry pollen or pollen extracts, a procedure employed in provocative testing which is discussed in Chapter 4. However, the amount of any pollen necessary to provoke symptoms under the more leisurely and continuous challenge of natural exposure is unknown. Although many types of pollen can elicit skin sensitivity and are relatively common in air, their clinical importance, though often assumed, is not easily determined. This limitation should not prompt the clinician to confine his attention to a few pollens of unquestioned allergenicity. It is our impression that symptoms can follow exposure to a combination of allergenic factors while not resulting from any one of them acting alone. In this case, treatment should be directed to each of the factors that may contribute to the allergenic "load" borne by the patient (Chapter 2).

WIND-POLLINATED FLOWERS

A first-hand acquaintance with anemophilous or wind-pollinated flowers is invaluable; attention should be directed not only to their gross appearance, but also to their minute structure and sexual plan. Most wind-pollinated flowers are extremely small and often individually unisexual or "imperfect"; that is, male, or pollen-producing organs, and female, or seed-producing organs, are borne in separate flowers. Furthermore, the colorful petals and the nectaries, so inherent in the popular concept of a "flower," are usually absent or rudimentary. Indeed, these structures are essential features of the functional anatomy of insect-pollinated (entomophilous) flowers. The inconspicuous female flowers are frequently "tucked away" in the axils of leaves (the angle between the leaf stalk and main plant stem), whereas the more numerous male flowers are often borne in crowded clusters at the ends of the branches, where they are most accessible to air currents.

A wind-pollinated male flower consists of several stamens enclosed in a membranous "bract," or scale-like covering, which separates it from other male flowers in the cluster. Each stamen consists of a slender stalk which holds, at its free end, a two-lobed yellow case, or anther. Each lobe is in turn divided into two sacs or pollen-containing cavities. At maturity, with favorable conditions of light, temperature, and relative humidity, the flower covering unfolds or ruptures. The stamens may be actively protruded or exposed passively to the desiccating effects of air and sunlight. After drying, the anthers split open, permitting liberation of the ripe pollen. One of several active mechanisms may aid pollen discharge; in the ragweeds, for example, a piston-like structure, the pistillodium, appears to sweep out the pollen following anther sac dehiscence.[7] Within seconds after the anther wall splits, the pollen grains dry and collapse. This decreases their weight by 30 to 50 per cent, allowing them to reach maximum buoyancy just as they are released. When a pollen grain reaches the receptive stigma of a female flower, it readily reabsorbs moisture and expands. The transfer of pollen from anther to stigma is known as "pollination." The period as well as the process of unfolding of flowers is known as "anthesis." The stigmas of anemophilous plants are often expanded into plume-like lobes, a modification which undoubtedly increases their capture of air-borne pollen.

POLLEN MORPHOLOGY

A typical mature expanded pollen grain is a spherical or oval plant cell, 10 to 100 microns in diameter. It consists of an outer wall, the exine, an inner wall, the intine, and a droplet of contained protoplasm with two nuclei. The exine, which is easily stained by aniline dyes, is usually more or less ornamented. The smooth transparent intine accepts little or no stain; yet, it may sometimes be seen through the thinner portions of the stained exine, mostly because of its refractive properties.

In identifying pollen grains, the surface texture of the exine is an important differential feature; it may be smooth (psilate) or show granularity or reticulations of varying fineness. (Reticulations are regularly interlaced ridges like those on the surface of a peanut shell.) Ridges or spines are commonly present. In addition to these embossed markings, there may be depressions or apertures which take the form of furrows, as well as pits known as "pores" or "germinal pores." During germination of the grain, the pollen tube, an extension of the elastic intine, characteristically emerges through a germinal pore; however, it can make its exit through a furrow which has no visible pore or break through the thin exine of a nonaperturate* grain.

Pores are usually round, or nearly so, with more or less reinforcement about their edges. They are bridged by a transparent membrane which often carries flecks of exine substance on its surface but is otherwise indistinguishable from the intine. A lens-shaped disc of exine, called an "operculum," may be present, as in all grass pollen (see page 357). An additional, fairly common pore accessory is a broad transparent collar termed a "shield" or "aspis" by Wodehouse, which encircles the pore beneath the exine.[3] Although this refractile collar does not accept stain, it is readily seen through the exine, appearing darker or lighter than surrounding areas depending on the focal level used. The prominent air sacs or bladders of pine, fir, spruce, and related conifers are unique structural features.

Some species discharge their pollen only in permanent tetrads (groups of four connected grains), as seen in the broad-leafed cat-tail (Typha), in the rush family (Juncaceae), and heath family (Ericaceae). Multiple tetrads are seen in certain members of the mimosa family.

The color of wind-borne pollen grains, though always some shade of yellow, is of importance in identification. When dry, the nearly colorless grains of grass pollen appear to be almost blue, whereas some weed and tree pollens are deep yellow. The depth of natural color definitely influences the final color of the stained grain. If two neighboring grains in a microscopic field have exactly the same color and tint, they are most likely identical even though the position of one of them hides the typical marks of identification. Occasionally grains collected on petrolatum or silicone grease become so deeply embedded in the collecting medium that they stain slowly or not at all. This difficulty is minimized by applying the adhesive in a thin, even layer. However, one must always be alert for unstained and unexpanded grains while counting.

POINTS OF REFERENCE

A pollen grain with a thin, smooth exine, devoid of markings, can sometimes be identified by the thickness of its intine (e.g., cottonwood, Plate 16–2). The appearance of such a grain is the same in any position, but most pollen grains present a different aspect in each of several positions. Thus, it is necessary for purposes of description to establish standard points of reference.

---

* Pollen grains possessing furrows and/or pores are often referred to as aperturate and distinguished from nonaperturate grains which have none. Those grains which have furrows alone are designated colpate, and may be monocolpate, tricolpate or stephanocolpate, depending on whether one, three, or more than three furrows are present. Pollen grains possessing germinal pores alone are referred to as porate, and may be monoporate, triporate, and so forth. When pores are present within furrows, such grains are spoken of as colporate, the appropriate prefix being used in accord with the specific number of pore-bearing furrows present.

When furrows are present, there are usually three or four arranged like meridional bands, with their ends at the two "polar" areas and their centers furnishing an imaginary equator. Such grains, when dry, have their furrows infolded, causing the polar diameter to be noticeably lengthened and the equatorial diameter shortened. Since the resulting shape resembles a grain of rice or wheat with three longitudinal furrows, the grains invariably lie on their sides until moistened and expanded. The fully expanded grain is essentially spherical but with more or less flattening at the poles. Often, as grains expand they rotate and come to rest on one of these flattened polar areas. This position is called the polar position—one pole pointing toward the observer and the equator just visible around the periphery of the grain. In pollen with three to six pores but without furrows, the pores are usually spaced at equidistant intervals along the equator. Such grains have no meridians. Occasionally the exine or intine is heavier over one polar hemisphere, in which case the more flexible hemisphere is called the "ventral" side and the heavier hemisphere the "dorsal" side. When one wall of a drying grain collapses against the opposite wall, the resulting cup shape is described as "invaginate." Pollen grains are so large that when the proximal surface (that nearest the microscopist) is clearly seen, the periphery and deeper structures are out of focus. With the focus set halfway between the proximal and distal surfaces (an optical cross section), one gains some idea of the thickness of the cell wall and can see clearly, in profile, any continuous surface markings.

A series of drawings and photomicrographs of pollen grains is presented in 15 plates at the end of this section. The scale magnification throughout is approximately 500 diameters. Rather than attempting to illustrate the appearance of each type of pollen grain in every possible position, the pictures and accompanying text call attention to outstanding differential characteristics. No printed picture can possibly duplicate exactly the appearance of actual pollen grains, as seen with transmitted light. The reader, therefore, will best use these illustrations as an aid in examining reference pollen specimens, both dry and in the expanded state, from which details of structure can be verified.

AN INTRODUCTION TO WIND-POLLINATED PLANTS AND THEIR POLLENS

The Conifers (Pinaceae). An immense tonnage of air-borne pollen is produced annually by conifers, especially in sparsely populated areas, but much of it seems to be of little or no clinical importance (Plate 16–1). In general, those evergreens which have cones and needle-like leaves have similar large pollen grains with two bladders. When strict identification of these grains by genus is desirable, difficulty may be encountered in distinguishing those produced by the various species of pine (Pinus), spruce (Picea), and fir (Abies), as well as Deodar cedar

(Cedrus deodara), cedar of Lebanon *(Cedrus libanitica)*, golden larch *(Pseudolarix amabilis)*, or mountain hemlock *(Tsuga mertensiana)*. All have the conspicuous bladders and their sizes range from 45 microns to more than 100 microns, exclusive of bladders. The grains may appear on gravity slides at any time during the spring and early summer even in areas remote from coniferous forests.

In general, the evergreens with scale-like leaves have spherical pollen grains with thick intine and thin exine devoid of pores or furrows—the "mountain cedar" type—varying in size from 20 to 40 microns. These include several species proved to be allergenic and a number whose possible allergenic qualities have not yet been investigated.[8] The list of trees with the spherical pollen grains include mountain cedar *(Juniperus mexicana)* and all of the other junipers (Juniperus), incense cedar *(Libocedrus decurrens)*, Lawson cypress, also called Port Orford cedar, *(Chamaecyparis lawsoniana)*, Monterey cypress *(Cupressus macrocarpa)*, arbor vitae *(Thuja occidentalis)*, tamarack *(Larix laricina)*, Douglas fir *(Pseudotsuga mucronata)*, bald cypress *(Taxodium distichum)*, and both species of redwood (Sequoia). The yews (Taxus), though regarded as members of another family, also have similar pollen grains.

Mountain cedar pollen is noted for its abundance, its strong allergenic quality, and its dissemination from late fall to midwinter, sometimes continuing until early spring. Although the trees are found from central and west Texas to the mountains of central Mexico, most of their allergic victims are in Texas. The closely related Utah juniper *(Juniperus osteosperma)* and one-seeded juniper *(Juniperus monosperma)* of New Mexico, Arizona, and Utah are abundant, but the allergenicity of their pollens has not been determined. Incense cedar, of the Sierra and Cascade ranges, also sheds its very active pollen in midwinter. Cross-reactions have been noted among mountain cedar, Monterey cypress, and Port Orford cedar. Pollens of the other genera and species enumerated above are encountered from late winter to late spring. Although most of them, including bald cypress, are confined to regions of limited population, all of them deserve further evaluation. The distribution of pollens of the yews, cedars, and junipers is shown graphically as "juniper" in Figure 16–12 along with data from other tree pollens. (As discussed in Chapter 16–I, the gravity slide counts on which this and similar diagrams in this chapter are based, are useful for comparative purposes, but do not necessarily reflect actual aerial concentrations.) The increasing use of species of yew and juniper for plantings about homes makes the possible allergenicity of their pollens a matter of particular clinical importance.

Three species of hemlock *(Tsuga canadensis, Tsuga caroliniana* and *Tsuga heterophylla)* furnish a third and very distinct morphologic type of conifer pollen (not illustrated). These grains are large and rough, containing a single bladder-like structure. They are flattened asymmetrically when expanded and become disc-shaped in the dry state.

The Palm Family (Arecaceae).   Members of this family are limited, in general, to tropical and subtropical areas. The form and arrangement of palm flowers, as well as their heavy pollen production, strongly suggest that wind pollination may occur. Although insects are said to play a role in some species, sampling in Florida, Hawaii, and the Near East has confirmed the occurrence of air-borne palm pollen. Rhinitis from date palm pollen *(Phoenix dactylifera)* is reported from Hawaii, whereas pollen of the coco palm *(Cocos nucifera)*, although abundant, is not regarded as an allergen there.[9] Pollen grains of the date palm (not illustrated) are small, deeply invaginate and inrolled when dry, giving the grain the appearance of having a single fold or furrow; when expanded, they are almost spherical with a thin exine. The pollen grains of other species are similar. Pollen of the Ginkgo tree *(Ginkgo biloba)* is also similar and is found in modest amounts in areas where this hardy species is used for street plantings.

The Beefwoods (Casuarinaceae).   These trees are native to Australasia and are sometimes called "Australian pine" because of their "pine-like" leaves and growth habit. They have been widely planted in southern California and southern Florida and have spread readily from cultivation. They shed copious amounts of wind-borne pollen which is known to cause allergy. The grains are triangular in shape when dry and slightly triangular to round when expanded, much like those of bayberry (Plate 16–15, 5 and 6) except for the larger size. The equatorial diameter is 32 microns. The principal season of pollination at Miami is reported to be winter and early spring with another short period in August;[10] at Tampa it is in November.[11]

The Willow-Poplar Family (Salicaceae).   This family consists of only two genera, the willows (Salix) and the poplars (Populus), the latter including the two aspens (Plate 16–2). Native species of these genera are widely scattered and numerous horticultural varieties are planted throughout the temperate parts of North America. One of the aspens, *Populus tremuloides,* is northern in its range though reaching southern California in the Rocky Mountain area. The other, *Populus grandidentata,* is found as far south as Tennessee and North Carolina. The western and southwestern cottonwood poplars may have the most active pollen; that of the eastern cottonwoods and willows is less often incriminated. The poplars shed large amounts of pollen and are all strictly wind-pollinated; the willows are partially adapted to insect pollination. Anthesis in both genera occurs in March, April, and May. The male and female flowers are borne on separate trees, and the seeds are usually equipped with conspicuous "cottony" tufts. These seed hairs have not been shown to be allergenic.

The Walnut-Hickory Family (Juglandaceae).   The walnuts (Juglans), including butternut *(Juglans cineria),* black walnut *(Juglans nigra),* and California black walnut *(Juglans californica),* with numerous cultivated forms and wild hybrids, and the hickories (Carya), including the pecans *(Carya pecan* and *Carya texana)*, shellbark *(Carya ovata)*, pignut *(Carya glabra)*, and a dozen other species, are important sources of allergenic pollen (Plate 16–3). Species of both genera are common in the eastern, southern, and central states but not in the prairie and mountainous areas of the midwestern and western states, except where they are cultivated, as in California. Most species flower in late spring toward the end of the tree pollen season. In the southeast, however, pecan pollen may appear in late February and reach maximal abundance in March when it causes widespread inhalant allergy.

  The Birch Family (Betulaceae). There are five American genera: American hornbeam or blue beech (Carpinus), hop hornbeam or ironwood (Ostrya), the hazelnuts and filberts (Corylus), the birches (Betula) comprising more than a dozen species and varieties, and the alders (Alnus) with six species (Plate 16–4). European alder *(Alnus glutinosa)* has been naturalized in the eastern and central states, and filberts are cultivated in the Pacific Northwest. Birch is the outstanding pollen producer in this family except in the Pacific Northwest where alder leads. Birch pollen is abundant throughout the northeastern states (see Figure 16–12).

  Hazelnuts and filberts flower very early—January in the Gulf states,

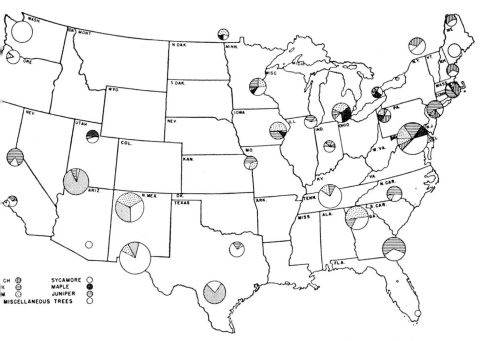

Figure 16–12. Atmospheric incidence of tree pollens as shown by atmospheric surveys in typical areas. The comparative annual totals of pollens of all wind-pollinated species are indicated by the comparative areas of the discs, and for six outstanding genera by the comparative areas of the disc segments. The scale is the same as is used on Figures 16–13, 16–14, and 16–15. (Used by permission of the Journal of the American Medical Association.)

February in the Pacific Northwest, and March in the central and eastern states. Some of the alders follow shortly, but they are much influenced by latitude and altitude; thus, alder pollen may be found in Alberta as late as June. Birch, ironwood, and hornbeam pollens appear in April and May and are often shed concurrently. Birch pollen is known to act as an aeroallergen; however, the relative importance of the various species is uncertain. Alder pollen is regarded as a common cause of early hay fever in western portions of Oregon and Washington but is seldom mentioned elsewhere. The clinical significance of other genera of the birch family remains to be defined.

Alder pollen grains are easily distinguished by their angular aspect and the predominance of four-pored grains. There should be no difficulty in differentiating alder grains from those of other four-pored species, such as ash (Fraxinus) and dock (Rumex). The former are larger than alder and have furrows with ragged openings rather than pores with collars (Plate 16–6, g–i). Dock pollen does not appear until long after the alders have finished pollination; the grains have prominent granules and several slit-like furrows (see Plate 16–14, w–z). All pollens of the birch family, except alder, are predominantly three-pored and are thus similar except for size and surface texture. Any of them could be confused with the pollens of unrelated hackberry (Celtis), sweet fern (Comptonia) and bayberry or wax myrtle (Myrica), all of which appear during about the same season. Hemp pollen could also be confused with any of the above except for its midsummer occurrence, long after the trees and shrubs have finished pollination. Hazelnut pollen grains (not illustrated) are about the size of birch pollen grains (24–26 microns) but occur at an earlier season. Filbert grains are larger (28 microns), and again the early season is helpful. In the polar position the "lips" of the pores of hazelnut pollen are not nearly as prominent as those of birch.[3] Otherwise, there is very little structural difference. Sweet fern, ironwood, and hornbeam pollen grains (not illustrated), which are not often encountered, are decidedly larger than those of birch or hazelnut. For comparisons of birch, bayberry, and hackberry, see Plate 16–15, 5 and 6.

The Bayberry Family (Myricaceae). Wax myrtle *(Myrica cerifera)* is a large shrub found along the Atlantic seaboard from New Jersey to Florida and the coast of Texas (Plate 16–15, 5 and 6). It is locally abundant in wet woods, along seashores, and in sandy swamps. The pollen grains, which resemble those of the birch family, have been recovered regularly at St. Simon's Island, Georgia, and Norfolk, Virginia, but probably occur all along the Atlantic coast in spring. The allergenic qualities of the pollen are not known. Sweet fern *(Comptonia peregrina)* (not illustrated), a small shrub related to wax myrtle, is a native of dry sandy soils of the eastern states and Canada. It is not common, except locally within its range, and the pollen grains, which resemble those of wax myrtle and the birches, are probably rare atmospheric contaminants.

The Beech Family (Fagaceae), Including the Oaks. Interest in this family is directed almost exclusively to the oaks (Quercus) with wide and very abundant distribution and copious pollen production (see Plate 16–5). Most of the states from Kansas and Texas eastward can boast of at least 15 species; many have twice that number.[12] In the western states, oaks are less numerous, being most common in California (see Figure 16–12). Flowering begins in the Gulf states in February and occurs in Canada in May. Because of the slightly different pollinating periods of different species, the total oak pollen season in most areas is long. The pollens of all species are regarded as moderately potent allergens, though generally of less allergenic importance than pollens of the ragweeds and grasses. Specific reactions have not been recognized within the genus, and the pollen grains of all species are very similar in appearance. The dry grains can be confused with those of the maples (though the former appear more angular), or even with those of the ashes, which are more nearly square in outline. Expanded oak grains have coarser textures than most other tree pollen grains, and the three torn furrows are a reliable characteristic. Beech pollen is larger than oak pollen, with a heavier exine. Its furrows are longer and narrower and do not tear in expansion (see Plate 16–15, 9 and 10).

The Elm Family (Ulmaceae). Elms of several species, including American elm *(Ulmus americana)*, slippery elm *(Ulmus rubra)*, the naturalized English elm *(Ulmus glabra)* of New England, and several introduced Chinese species, are almost nationwide in distribution (Plate 16–6, top). In the prairie states as well as the area of the Great Basin, elms are popular trees for ornament and shade. Pollen distribution is shown in Figure 16–12. The pollens of all species appear to be allergenic. They are produced in unusually large quantities for trees with perfect flowers, i.e., male and female parts both in the same flower. The spring-blooming elms are among the earliest flowering trees—January and February in the South, usually March and April elsewhere, except May in Manitoba. September or red elm *(Ulmus serotina)* of Arkansas, Mississippi, and Louisiana and cedar or scrub elm *(Ulmus crassifolia)* of Texas do not reach anthesis until September. Although some Chinese elms also flower in the fall, those in Arizona and New Mexico release their pollen primarily in February and March. The rounded pentagonal grains are almost unmistakable though differing slightly in size for different species.

The Hackberries (Celtis). Trees of this second genus of the elm family are common locally in the eastern half of the United States except along the Atlantic and Gulf coasts (pollen grains shown on Plate 16–15, 5 and 6). Although it is wind-dispersed, usually in April and May, the pollen has been reported as being common in the East only in Nashville, Tennessee. However, hackberry pollen is an abundant air contaminant during February and March in southern Texas, where it is considered to be an important aeroallergen. In Argentina, the species, *Celtis tala,* is reported "to be the chief offender in 44 per cent of patients with hay fever."[13] Antigenic relationships between pollens of the elms and hackberries have not been studied. The three-pored pollen grains are unlike those of elm but do suggest those of the birches, bayberry, Osage orange, hemp, and hop.

The Olive Family (Oleaceae). The ashes (Fraxinus) comprise the only important wind-pollinated genus of the olive family in this country (Plate 16–6). White ash *(Fraxinus americana)* is widely distributed in the central and eastern states and often planted in the prairie states. Sargent describes 16 other species, including Oregon ash *(Fraxinus oregona)* of western Oregon and western Washington, and Arizona ash *(Fraxinus velutina)* of the Southwest.[12] All species produce enormous quantities of pollen per tree. In the East, where ashes are being used increasingly as street trees, the clinical importance of the pollen is being re-evaluated. In Phoenix, Arizona, ash ranks high in production and is one of the chief tree offenders in February and March.[14, 15] Anthesis usually occurs in April or May in other regions. Cultivated olive *(Olea europaea)* (pollen illustrated on Plate 16–15, 7), though not primarily wind-pollinated, is responsible for some cases of inhalant allergy in California and Arizona. Anthesis occurs in April and May. The pollen grains are easily distinguished from four-furrowed ash by their three furrows and triangular outline; also, the reticulations are coarser.

Privet (Ligustrum). This genus comprises several species of cultivated shrubs which are also essentially insect-pollinated (pollen illustrated on Plate 16–15, 7). Nasal symptoms, occurring in close proximity to these bushes, may be due to pollen or to irritant effects of their extremely strong fragrance when in flower. The pollen grains resemble those of olive but are larger with much coarser reticulations.

The Sycamore or Plane Tree Family (Platanaceae). The family has only one genus, Platanus, with five species in North America; all are called sycamore (Plate 16–7). One of these, *Platanus orientalis,* has been introduced sparingly in California; another, *Platanus acerifolia,* is much planted as a street tree in the eastern states and in California.[4] The range of the common native sycamore, *Platanus occidentalis,* is found from western Texas and eastern Nebraska eastward to southern Maine and northern Florida. The tree does not form dense stands, and its pollen is seldom found in large amounts except in cities where it (or some other species) is used for street planting (e.g., Washington, D.C., Philadelphia, and New York). The season of pollination in southern California is March and April; along the Gulf, April and May; in the eastern and central states, May. The pollen is moderately allergenic.

Sweet Gum (Liquidambar styraciflua). This is a tree of moist river-bottom land ranging from east Texas, the Ohio Valley, and New Jersey to Florida (Plate 16–7). The species is planted for shade and ornament as far north as Massachusetts and northern Michigan. Flowering occurs generally in April and May. Pollen production is abundant, but the pollen grains are large and their range of dispersal seems limited. They sometimes appear, however, in appreciable quantity in March and April in the southern states. Whether the pollen is allergenic is yet to be determined.

The Maple Family (Aceraceae). This family is represented in North America by only one genus, Acer. Maples of one or another species are widely distributed in all parts of temperate North America, except in pure coniferous forests and on deserts and prairies. Even in the prairie states, soft or silver maple *(Acer saccharinum)* and box elder *(Acer negundo)* are often planted for shade. Most maples seem better suited to insect pollination than to wind pollination, but all species except the much planted Norway maple *(Acer platanoides)* probably depend partly on the wind. Silver maple *(Acer saccharinum)* and red maple *(Acer rubrum)* produce moderate amounts of rather moist, heavy pollen, but flower early in the spring when relatively few insects are on hand. Probably the only species that is a consistent producer of wind-borne pollen in large amounts is box elder. Pollination of this species occurs late in March and April, a little earlier than the oaks, whose pollen grains are slightly larger than box elder but smaller than those of other maples. The dry grains of oak are more yellow and appear more angular than those of box elder, although box elder pollen has less tendency to bulge at the furrows. With fuchsin stain, box elder pollen exhibits a clear purplish-red color as compared with the dull red of oak—a useful point for differentiation. Four furrowed grains are occasionally found in specimens of both oak and box elder pollen.

American Linden (Tilia americana) (Basswood; Lime). This is the only linden species which is widely distributed in the central, eastern, and northern states, and in Canada (pollen shown on Plate 16–15, 4). Several other species are found locally in the Gulf states. In Germany, linden pollen has been regarded as a cause of allergy, but in this country its role is seriously questioned. The flowers are insect-pollinated, but grains become air-borne in small numbers during the early summer. Their unique furrows serve to distinguish them from all other tree pollens.

The Mimosa Family (Mimosaceae). This family of insect-pollinated plants is mentioned because of occasional reports that various acacias are a minor cause of hay fever in California and that mesquite *(Prosopis juliflora)* causes inhalant allergy in west Texas (pollen grains shown on Plate 16–15, 4,c and 9,a). This same tree, under the local name "algarroba" or "kiawe" is considered an important source of allergenic pollen in the Hawaiian Islands. A related native tree, the koa *(Acacia koa)* is also widely distributed, especially at higher elevations. In restricted areas occasional grains of acacia and mesquite pollen are caught on gravity slides.

Tree-of-Heaven (Ailanthus altissima: synonym, Ailanthus glandulosa). Since its introduction from southeast Asia, this rapidly growing

Figure 16–13. Atmospheric incidence of grass pollens as shown by atmospheric surveys in typical areas. The comparative annual totals of grass pollen counts are indicated by the comparative areas of the discs. The scale is the same as is used on Figures 16–12, 16–14, and 16–15. (Used by permission of the Journal of the American Medical Association.)

tree has established itself from Massachusetts to Ontario, and southward. It thrives in poor soil and limited space and has gained notoriety as an aggressive weed of urban yards. Tall clusters of yellowish-green flowers are formed in April and May; moderate amounts of pollen become air-borne. Although clinical sensitivity to the pollen is described, it appears to be only a rare cause of pollenosis.[16]

The Grass Family (Gramineae). In the grass family the flowers, with few exceptions, are perfect—not unisexual as in most of the wind-pollinated trees and weeds (Plate 16–9 and Figure 16–13). The individual florets are very small, but clusters of significant size known as spikelets are arranged in a great variety of distinct patterns, including dense spikes and open panicles. In tropical and subtropical areas, the grasses are likely to flower at any time of the year, but in temperate latitudes the pollen is shed mostly in late spring and early summer (mid-May to mid-July). In more northern areas and at higher altitudes, anthesis may take place throughout the local growing season. In the eastern, central, and northern states, and in Canada a very large share of air-borne grass pollen, present from late May to July, comes from bluegrass *(Poa pratensis)*, Canada bluegrass *(Poa compressa)*, orchard grass *(Dactylis glomerata)*, redtop *(Agrostis alba)*, and Timothy *(Phleum pratense)*. Velvet grass *(Holcus lanatus)*, most common in the Pacific Northwest and British Columbia, sweet vernal grass *(Anthoxanthum odoratum)* of the eastern seaboard states, and the rye grasses (Lolium) of the west coast are locally important species. Wild native grasses seldom shed pollen in quantities at all comparable with that of the domesticated meadow and lawn grasses mentioned above.

One of the most allergenic of the grass pollens is that of Bermuda grass *(Cynodon dactylon)*, which is the dominant lawn and field grass in the midsouthern and Gulf states. It is common also along the Pacific coast south of British Columbia and in the Southwest. It has been shown that this pollen contains unique antigenic groups as well as antigens in common with the eastern and northern species mentioned above.[17]

Johnson grass *(Sorghum halepense)* is a member of the sorghum group and a troublesome weed in the southern and southwestern states. Its meager pollen output, in late summer and fall, and large pollen grains (40 to 46 microns) suggest that it is not a major factor in inhalant allergy.

The discharge of pollen by a grass species is accomplished rapidly and synchronously by large numbers of florets at a definite time of day. For many species, the flowers open in early morning, but redtop, as well as others have an afternoon schedule. Some grass pollens, especially those of the cereal grains, are too large for extensive wind transport. Although clinical sensitivity to grass pollen in this country is less frequent than that to ragweed pollen, the grasses remain an important source of aeroallergens.

Grass pollen grains can seldom be accurately identified according to species. Of course, the average grain size tends to be different for various genera and species. However, the size ranges overlap widely and, except for pollens of corn and rye, other features are too nearly alike to permit specific identification (see page 382). The operculum, typical of grass pollen pores and shown on Plate 16–9, is a dome-shaped thickening in the otherwise transparent pore membrane. When the grains are expanded and stained, the colorless pore membrane bulges, causing the stained operculum to appear to float unsupported above the germinal pore. When the grain dries, the operculum is drawn into the germinal aperture.

The Sedge Family (Cyperaceae). The pollen of Pennsylvania sedge *(Carex pensylvanica)* is shown on Plate 16–15, 3. Sedges of numerous species are frequently mistaken for grasses or rushes and are widespread in marshes. They are strictly wind-pollinated, and although they shed pollen abundantly in early summer, very few grains reach samplers in centers of population. Convincing evidence of their clinical activity is still lacking.

The Rush Family (Juncaceae). The plants of this family superficially resemble grasses and sedges but have pollen grains, usually united in tetrads, that are distinctive. Wood rushes (Luzula) of many species flower in early spring, but recovery of their pollen away from wooded areas is quite uncommon.

The Cattail Family (Typhaceae). The cattails inhabit wet

meadows, marshes, and roadside ditches and, locally, they produce large amounts of air-borne pollen (shown on Plate 16–15, 8). Two species are frequently encountered: the common cattail *(Typha latifolia)* and the narrow-leafed cattail *(Typha angustifolia)*, the former being more widespread and abundant. Their familiar dark brown spikes bear tiny unisexual flowers—the male grouped above, and the female below. Pollen grains of both species show prominent surface reticulations and single, often indistinct, germinal pores. Those of common cattail are shed in permanent tetrads in contrast with pollen of *Typha angustifolia,* which always is released as single grains. Whether these plants are ever locally important in pollenosis remains undetermined.

The Sunflower or Composite Family (Compositae). This is one of the most diverse and specialized of the families of flowering plants, comprising approximately 15,000 species. Previously, taxonomists have often split the Compositae into several less inclusive families, viz., Ambrosiaceae, Carduaceae, Helianthaceae, and others, but at present the relationships between these subgroups appear too close to permit their segregation at the familial level.[18] Indeed, the entire family may be regarded as a potential source of allergenically similar pollen. Wind-pollinated species are recognized in only three of the subfamilial tribes of the Compositae: the ragweed tribe (Ambrosieae), the tansy tribe (Anthemideae), and the sunflower tribe (Heliantheae). Although the number of anemophilous species is comparatively few, these plants release tremendous amounts of pollen. Pollen of the abundant goldenrods, asters, and other entomophilous composites can also become air-borne at times, but evaluation of their role in any locality requires accurate air sampling data.

The Ragweed Tribe (Ambrosieae). This tribe includes the most important of the hay fever plants—the ragweeds (Ambrosia) (Plates 16–10 and 16–11). Recent work[18] has shown that plants known as "false" ragweeds (Franseria, including Acanthambrosia) should be considered members of the genus Ambrosia, along with the "true" ragweeds, and they are so treated here. The pollens of each of the approximately 41 species are probably antigenically similar, but most of the source plants are restricted in range and abundance. Six of the species, singly or together, are plentiful over large portions of North America, growing as weeds of both waste areas and agricultural land. Throughout most of the northern, eastern, and central states, flowering of the ragweeds begins in the last days of July. Ragweed pollen concentrations are generally high by mid-August and reach maximal levels in late August and early September. Moderate concentrations may continue well into October but pollen production ceases with the occurrence of the first intense killing frost.

In the eastern and central United States and southern Canada, the most important species are annual plants: short ragweed *(Ambrosia artemisiifolia;* synonym, *Ambrosia elatior)* and giant ragweed *(Ambrosia trifida).* Short ragweed is the more abundant of the two, but the larger giant ragweed usually produces more pollen per individual plant and, in certain portions of the Midwest, the latter species may account for the greater share of air-borne ragweed pollen. The species overlap broadly in range. Both are found from the Atlantic coasts of the United States and southern Canada, west through the Appalachian and Ozark regions to the Rocky Mountains. In addition, short ragweed extends west to the Pacific coast in Oregon, Washington, and southern British Columbia (see map, Figure 16–14).

The southern ragweed (*Ambrosia bidentata*) is locally abundant in the Ozark region, extending eastward to southern Illinois and Ohio and southward into Louisiana. It often grows as a weed of heavily pastured areas and may constitute 90 per cent of the summer plant cover on such sites. It undoubtedly contributes greatly to the atmospheric pollen load within its restricted range (Plate 16–10).

To the west, the perennial ragweed (*Ambrosia psilostachya:* synonym, *Ambrosia coronopifolia*), is widely distributed in dry, sandy areas and is most abundant in the Great Plains. Its range is from the Atlantic coast through the northernmost states and adjacent Canada, and it occurs sporadically along the Gulf coast and from southern North Carolina to Florida along the Atlantic. Individuals of this species produce less pollen than the short and giant ragweeds, especially during periods of

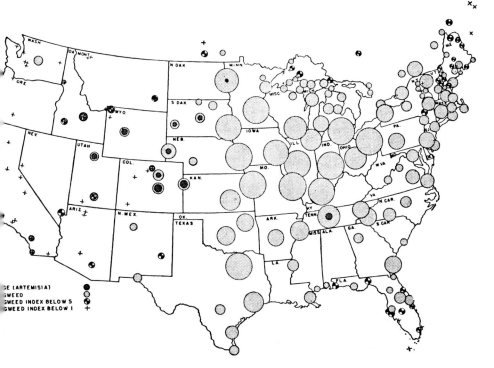

Figure 16–14. Atmospheric incidence of ragweed and sagebrush (*Artemisia*) pollens as shown by atmospheric surveys in typical areas. The comparative annual totals of slide counts of pollens of each type are indicated by the comparative areas of the discs—superimposed in overlapping areas. The scale is the same as is used on Figures 16–12, 16–13, and 16–15. (Used by permission of the Journal of the American Medical Association.)

drought, but it is sufficiently abundant to be an important factor in pollenosis (Plate 16–10).

The perennial slender ragweed (*Ambrosia confertiflora:* syn., *Franseria tenuifolia; Franseria confertiflora* (Plate 16–11) and annual bur ragweed (*Ambrosia acanthicarpa:* synonym, *Franseria acanthicarpa*) occupy dry soils in an area from central and western Mexico, north through the far western and west central United States to southern British Columbia. Within this range, slender ragweed is more abundant in the south and bur ragweed predominates in the north. Both have spiny, bur-like, usually one-seeded fruits and both appear to be extending their ranges and abundance. Several ragweeds of arid southwestern regions are of special interest because they bloom and induce pollenosis in spring; these include rabbit bush (*Ambrosia deltoidea*), burroweed (*Ambrosia dumosa*), and canyon ragweed (*Ambrosia ambrosioides*).

Although the genus Ambrosia is principally American, two Old World species are recognized: the European ragweed (*Ambrosia maritima*), which may be only a form of short ragweed, and the African ragweed (*Ambrosia senegalensis*). Of several American species introduced locally into Mediterranean Europe and eastern Asia, none has become sufficiently well established to cause ragweed pollenosis. Eight species are known from South America, and two or three, including *Ambrosia hispida* and *Ambrosia cumanensis,* are scattered throughout the Caribbean. A number of shrubby species are confined to central and northern Mexico; others contribute to the desert flora of Baja California and of the southwestern states. Lastly, several less common herbaceous species, including *Ambrosia nivea, Ambrosia grayi, Ambrosia tomentosa,* and *Ambrosia linearis,* of negligible importance to allergists occur in the central United States.

Members of the marsh elder genus, Iva (Plate 16–11) produce both staminate and pistillate flowers in the same heads and have fruits which are never burlike. Despite these differences from the true ragweeds, their floral structure, pollen morphology, and antigenicity are similar. Burweed marsh elder (*Iva xanthifolia:* synonym, *Cyclachaena xanthifolia*) and rough marsh elder (*Iva annua:* synonym *Iva ciliata*) are sufficiently abundant to contribute significantly as aeroallergens. The former, also known as prairie ragweed, has spread to occupy much of the area from Quebec to Alberta, south to Arizona, New Mexico, and Texas, and east to Maryland. It is similar in appearance and habitat preference to giant ragweed. The rough marsh elder is a lowland annual plant found from eastern Nebraska, central Illinois, and southern Ohio, south to the Gulf of Mexico. It reaches maximal abundance in the delta area of southern Louisiana, and, in the vicinity of New Orleans, is felt to rival the short and giant ragweeds in pollen productivity. Both marsh elders shed their pollen in late summer and in autumn with the true ragweeds.

Other members of the genus Iva occur in coastal wetlands along the Atlantic and Gulf coasts. *Iva frutescens,* called "high-tide bush," is an especially prominent, tall, shrubby, perennial plant inhabiting brackish marshes. With associated species, *Iva microcephala, Iva angustifolia, Iva texensis,* and others, it appears to shed relatively little pollen. In addition to *Iva xanthifolia,* several marsh elders also occur from British Columbia to California and east to Colorado, New Mexico, and Texas. These include poverty weed *(Iva axillaris),* a low early flowering perennial of rocky and saline soil, *Iva acerosa, Iva nevadensis,* and *Iva ambrosiaefolia.*

Members of the genus Hymenoclea, the winged ragweeds, are prominent in the desert flora of Utah, Arizona, and Texas. Their fruiting involucres are supplied with expanded processes in place of apical spines. Neither they nor the related genus, Dicoria, are of great importance to clinical allergy at present.

Cocklebur (Xanthium). These plants occur in disturbed areas of temperate and tropical regions, being almost worldwide in distribution (Plate 16–11). They are much alike in appearance except for spiny cocklebur *(Xanthium spinosum),* which is distinguished by its laterally lobed leaves, in the axils of which long, sharp, golden, three-pronged spines are borne. This species and other cockleburs are locally abundant in many areas, but the staminate flowers on each plant are few and their pollen output in late summer seems minor.

Except for differences in spine length, pollens of Ambrosia, Xanthium, most of the genus Iva, and other genera of the tribe Ambrosieae are indistinguishable. All are three-pored and have spiny surfaces. The pores are located in furrows, but in most species the furrows so closely surround the pores that they are indistinguishable. Most species have pollen in which layers of the outer wall between the pores have separated to form small bladder-like spaces, most obvious when the grains are dry. Differences in grain size correlate with chromosome numbers; polyploid species tend to have larger grains than diploid species and often produce a few large, four-pored grains.

The Tansy Tribe (Anthemideae). In this tribe (Plate 16–12) major interest is directed to anemophilous members of the genus Artemisia, the sagebrushes, mugworts, and wormwoods. These plants are primarily grayish aromatic shrubs and shrubby perennials of the western prairies and mountains. However, one or more species can be found in almost every part of North America. Generally, they are plants of open places, preferring dry, usually sandy soil, and are absent from damp lowlands and forested areas. As weeds, they are seldom aggressive, and they have largely disappeared from the central and eastern states where cultivation has destroyed their perennial roots. Figure 16–14 shows that although these plants may be locally common, their pollen is recovered in significant quantity at only a few urban stations east of the Rocky Mountains. Heavy exposure to their strongly antigenic pollen in more rural areas can, however, induce allergic symptoms.

The name "sagebrush," if applied strictly, should be used only for woody species such as common sagebrush (*Artemisia tridentata*) of the Rocky Mountain and intermountain states, sand sagebrush (*Artemisia filifolia*) of the western edge of the Great Plains, and coastal sagebrush (*Artemisia californica*) of the coast ranges of California. Herbaceous species should be called "sagewort"; these include prairie sage (*Artemisia ludoviciana*), pasture sage (*Artemisia frigida*) of the northern plains, and tall wormwood (*Artemisia caudata*) which is locally abundant along the shores of the Great Lakes, in addition to many less common species. Annual sage (*Artemisia annua*), introduced from Asia, has become established in Tennessee and surrounding states, where it is recognized as an obtrusive weed and a copious pollen producer. These weedy composites should not be confused with the "sages" which belong to the genus Salvia of the Mint family and are often planted for their showy entomophilous flowers.

Artemisias are found at various latitudes and elevations with anthesis occurring from June through October, although most species shed their pollen in September. The season for coastal sagebrush is especially long. The flowers are typically grouped, yellow-green in color, and contain organs of both sexes. The pollen of the tansy tribe is distinguished by the presence of large and obvious rods (baccula) between the outer walls. In the genus Artemisia, the pollen has extremely short spines and appears essentially smooth.

The Insect-Pollinated Composites. Besides the ragweed and tansy tribes, only the sunflower tribe, or Heliantheae, has some wind-pollinated members. Several of these belong to the genus Parthenium and although their pollens are regarded as significant aeroallergens in central Mexico, they occur only sparsely in the eastern and southern United States. The many thousand remaining composites are insect-pollinated but must still be reckoned with in allergy. A number of these, such as the goldenrods, are abundant and conspicuous in late summer and are readily but erroneously blamed for ragweed pollenosis by the uninformed. The pollen of goldenrods as well as of the cultivated asters, chrysanthemums, dahlias, marigolds, and zinnias can readily cause pollenosis in ragweed-sensitive subjects who are in close contact with the flowers. In addition, rather small quantities of entomophilous composite pollen are recovered from air at many stations. Within their ranges, species of sneezeweed (Helenium) and dog fennel (Eupatorium) seem to be especially frequent sources of such pollen. The grains of most species are remarkably similar, being covered with long, sharp spines and showing three pores and, usually, well-developed furrows (Plate 16–15, 11). Exceptional pollen is found in much of the dandelion tribe, Cichorieae, in which coalescence of the spines has formed patterns of smooth areas separated by palisade-like protrusions.

The Order **Chenopodiales,** *including the* **goosefoot (Chenopodiaceae)** *and* **carelessweed or amaranth (Amaranthaceae)** *families (Plate 16–13 and Figure 16–15).* The close relationship of these two families is reflected in the great similarity of the pollens of all species. Indeed, the round, many-pored, golf-ball-like grains can be identified only as "chenopod-amaranth pollen" in most instances. The identity of the source plants in a specific area must, therefore, be confirmed by careful field study. Pollens produced by several species in each of the two families have been shown to be allergenically similar. Whether all species possess at least some common allergens is still uncertain.

Members of the goosefoot family are abundant and widely distributed, but only a few species are important sources of allergenic pollen. Russian thistle (*Salsola kali* var, *tenuifolia:* synonym, *Salsola pestifer*), a naturalized tumbleweed of farmlands of the Great Plains and intermountain area, produces perhaps the most strongly allergenic pollen of any widely distributed plant in this country, including the ragweeds. Despite its name, it is wholly unrelated to the thistles. A more recently introduced tumbleweed, burning bush (*Kochia scoparia*), has established itself as an aggressive competitor of Russian thistle and the ragweeds for farmland and disturbed habitats of the Great Plains and eastward. Its pollen is heavier than that of Russian thistle and may be somewhat less allergenic.

Figure 16–15. Atmospheric incidence of goosefoot and amaranth pollens as shown by atmospheric surveys in typical areas. The comparative annual totals of slide counts of pollens of all species are indicated by the comparative areas of the discs. The scale is the same as is used on Figures 16–12, 16–13, and 16–14. (Used by permission of the Journal of the American Medical Association.)

Smotherweed (*Bassia hyssopifolia*) is common in arid parts of the southwest, where it is felt to be significant in causing pollenosis. *Bassia hirsuta* is common locally in cultivated ground in Washington, Utah, and California. Both species have pollen grains similar to those of burning bush.

Lamb's quarters (*Chenopodium album*) is an abundant summer weed throughout much of North America. However, its pollen production is meager and it has not been proved to be a significant clinical factor in any portion of its range. Pollens of the above goosefoots usually are shed from early or mid-July until mid-September, their season being somewhat longer than that of the ragweeds.

The saltbush or orache genus, Atriplex, includes one annual species widely distributed over the central and eastern states and several annual species, of which *Atriplex wrightii* is especially important, on saline soils of the West. There are also several shrubby western species called "wingscale" or "shadscale" that are felt to produce significant allergenic pollen beginning in May. Greasewood (*Sarcobatus vermiculatus*), a western shrub, has unique pollen grains since there are fewer pores—only 14 to 16 pores per grain—than in any other of the "golf ball" group. Sugar beet (*Beta vulgaris*) (Plate 16–15, 8), when grown for seeds, sends out vast quantities of very allergenic pollen in April and May (in Arizona, Utah, and western Texas). The grains are much smaller than any of the above species and can thus be recognized.

The carelessweeds (Amaranthaceae) include several members that exceed any of the goosefoot species, and even the ragweeds, in pollen production, plant for plant. Palmer's amaranth (*Amaranthus palmeri*), which somewhat resembles western water hemp (*Acnida tamariscina*) (Plate 16–13), thrives best in tilled areas of the Southwest. Its pollen is very allergenic, evidently more so than that of western water hemp. The latter, with a very similar species, *Amaranthus tuberculata,* produces enormous quantities of pollen but is limited to moist farmland and waste places in the central Mississippi Valley. Torrey's amaranth (*Amaranthus torreyi*), common in the sandy soil of Oklahoma and Kansas, has not been evaluated as a source of aeroallergens. Rough or redroot pigweed (*Amaranthus retroflexus*) (pollen on Plate 16–15, 8) is more widely scattered than any of the above amaranths or goosefoots, except lamb's quarters, with which it is often associated. Both produce so meagerly that neither can be regarded as being of frequent clinical significance. Nevertheless, the pollen of rough pigweed often produces positive reactions in skin testing. Anthesis of Palmer's amaranth in Arizona and southern California occurs from August through October. Western water hemp flowers from late July to early September. Spiny amaranth (*Amaranthus spinosus*) of the middle states seems less important because of its more limited acreage.

The Hemp Family (Cannabinaceae). According to some authors, this family should include only hemp (Cannabis) and hop (Humulus) (pollen grain on Plate 16–15). Others group the mulberries (Morus and

Broussonetia), osage orange (Maclura), the nettles (Urtica), and even the elms (Ulmus) and hackberries (Celtis) with hemp and hop in a family, Urticaceae. Hemp (Plate 16–14) is a source of fiber and the drug marihuana. The drug is not present in the pollen, but the pollen is highly allergenic. The plant, a large annual herb, has become established as a flourishing weed in farmlands and waste places in western Iowa and adjacent areas of the five bounding states. Since anthesis occurs in late summer, the triporate grains need not be mistaken for the very similar pollen of several trees (see page 352). Stinging nettles (Urtica) and common hop (*Humulus lupulus*), as well as Japanese hop (*Humulus japonica*), produce pollen simultaneously with hemp. Nettle pollen is much smaller and is easily recognized if sufficient magnification is used and the pollen samples are stained (Plate 16–15, 5). However, the pollens of nettle and paper mulberry are too similar to separate by microscopy. Because of their small size, nettle pollen concentrations may be significantly underestimated in gravity slide samples (see page 327). Pollen of the nettles has not as yet been shown to contain either allergens or vasoactive substances, although pollen of a closely related genus, Parietaria, is regarded as important in southern Europe.[19] Hemp and hop grains, similar in size and pore characteristics, are difficult to differentiate. Fortunately, hop is scarce in the hemp area and there is probably little hemp in the Pacific Northwest where hops are grown.

The Plantain Family (*Plantaginaceae*). In this family, English plantain (*Plantago lanceolata*) (Plate 16–14) is of interest to allergists. Over a dozen other species are conspicuous weeds of wide distribution. Of these, the common broad-leafed species, *Plantago major* and *Plantago rugelii*, have received almost as much attention as English plantain, although their pollen production is negligible. English plantain, itself, is only a minor contributing factor during and after the grass pollen season in the eastern states and is seldom a specific offender except, perhaps, in the Pacific Northwest where high atmospheric concentrations occur. Pollination occurs in June and July but may begin earlier in the South. On lawns, these weeds continue to flower until early fall. It is impractical to try to separate the pollen of the several species of plantain in atmospheric studies.

The Knotweed Family (*Polygonaceae*). Many of the members of this family are insect-pollinated, but garden rhubarb (*Rheum rhaponicum*) and the docks (*Rumex*) are wind-pollinated. The only dock that sheds appreciable quantities of pollen, however, is sheep sorrel or red sorrel (*Rumex acetosella*) (Plate 16–14), a low, perennial meadow species, pollinating concurrently with the grasses. The male and female plants, bearing reddish-brown or green unisexual flowers, grow in separate, pure stands. They are common in acid soil throughout most of North America and Europe. Pollen production may be quite considerable although, in most areas, it is less than that of the grasses. The allergenic activity of the pollen is probably greater than has been implied in the past.

PLATE 16–1

Scotch Pine (*Pinus sylvestris* L.). Male flowers appearing at the base of the vertical shoots of the current season consist of clusters of simple spikes bearing numerous two-celled anthers. The pollen grains with their two conspicuous bladders are typical of the pollen grains of all true pines, spruces, firs, and some other (but not all) conifers. The average diameter of Scotch pine pollen grains is more than 50 microns, exclusive of bladders. Spruce and fir grains are considerably larger. Note that the elongated bladders dominate the ventral aspect of the grain and can scarcely be concealed in any position.

a–d. Photomicrographs* of dry, unexpanded Scotch pine pollen grains.

a. Ventral view with focus on the coarse reticulations of the surface of the bladders (b). Pine pollens in this position look like "two fried eggs in a pan."

c. This pollen grain is rotated about 90 degrees from the position of a, with its dorsal side at the reader's right and its ventral (furrowed) side at the left. This affords an end view of the bladders.

d. The rotation in this view is only about 45 degrees, with the focus on the necks of the bladders and adjacent ventral surface of the grain.

e–g. Drawings of expanded pine pollen grains.

e. Pollen grain in the same position as in a but with much more of the ventral surface exposed because of expansion of the grain. This takes place mostly on the ventral side, thus pushing the bladders apart.

f. (At lower right of disc.) Dorsal view showing whole of the dorsal cap and only the protruding edges of the two bladders.

g. (Upper drawing.) Grain in approximately the same position as in c but showing the effect of expansion. Note the contrast in texture of the dorsal and ventral surfaces.

Mountain Cedar (*Juniperus mexicana* Spreng., *J. sabinoides* [Nees.]), a common tree of central Texas and the Southwest. Twigs from a male tree show the minute, terminal, male flowers at the time of pollination. The pollen grains possess a thin, easily ruptured exine and a very heavy intine. The latter constitutes a large part of the bulk of the grain. This pollen is typical of all junipers and, except for outer details, is characteristic of those of the redwoods, bald cypress, incense cedar, and several other related genera (see text, page 349). In the dry, shrunken state (not illustrated) the grains are quite colorless and appear as discs with rolled rims and a wide central depression.

h–l. Photomicrographs of stained mountain cedar pollen grains.

h. Optical section with focus at the equatorial plane. Average diameter: 22 microns. The dark, star-shaped central pattern (j) results from the very irregular inner face of the thick intine.

i. Optical section at a higher plane than in h but showing the same irregular central pattern (j).

k. Greatly expanded grain which has slipped out of its ruptured exine (l).

l. Empty and collapsed exine of k.

m–o. Drawings of mountain cedar pollen grains.

m. Stained pollen grains showing surface as well as central figure shown in h and i. The thin exine is almost transparent except for small scattered flecks that readily pick up the stain. Thus, the grains appear much lighter than those of most other pollens. The single germinal pore, if present at all, is said to be extremely difficult to detect.

n. Empty exine from which the overexpanded grain (o) has escaped as in k and l.

---

* These photomicrographs and drawings of Scotch pine pollen are enlarged about 400 times. All other grains on this and the following plates are on the approximate scale of 500 diameters, unless otherwise noted.

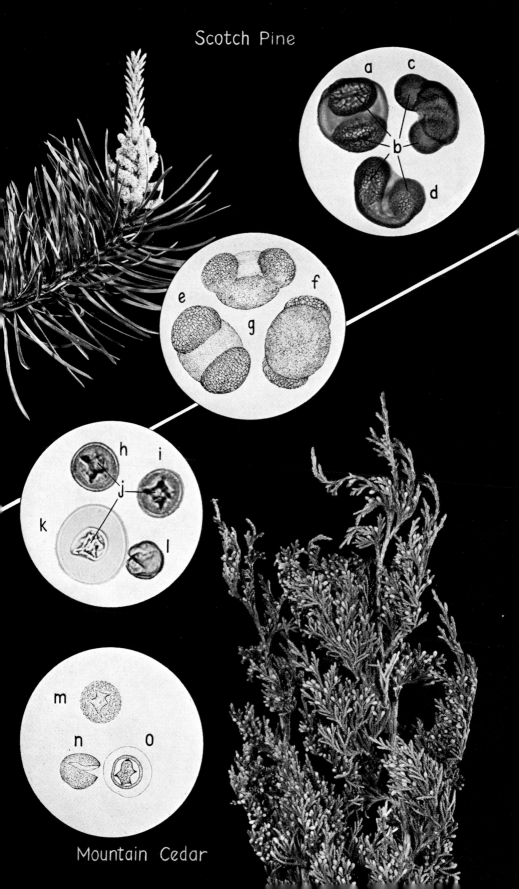

Scotch Pine

Mountain Cedar

PLATE 16–2

COTTONWOOD (*Populus deltoides* Marsh.). A cluster of four catkins of male flowers just reaching anthesis. Leaf buds have not opened. The dry pollen grains (not illustrated) are nondescript, having no distinguishing pattern of shrinkage and no symmetrical surface features. Expansion and staining are absolutely necessary for recognition. The microscopic features here shown are typical of pollens of all poplar species, including the aspens.

h–k. Photomicrographs of two expanded and stained cottonwood pollen grains. Average diameter: 30 microns.

h. Optical section, lightly stained, showing only the heavy intine (*i*). This is the one reliable feature for genus identification.

j. Optical section, heavily stained, at higher focus level than in *h* but with upper surface (*k*) still out of focus.

p–q. Drawings of expanded and stained cottonwood pollen grains.

p. Optical section duplicating photomicrograph *h*.

q. Surface detail showing fragmentary exine. There are no pores or furrows. Some grains show more, some less transparent area than this, but never any consistent design.

BLACK WILLOW (*Salix nigra* Marsh.). The slender and somewhat rigid catkins of male flowers appear at the ends of new leafy branches of male trees. The pollen grains are usually found in clumps rather than singly on atmospheric test slides since they always remain somewhat moist and adherent. The fact that insects are attracted by willow pollen justifies regarding it as only partly wind-pollinated. The small grains are normally three-furrowed and the surface always distinctly reticulate. The microscopic pollen characters shown and discussed here are typical of those of all other willow species.

a–g. Photomicrographs of willow pollen grains.

a–c. Unexpanded willow grains (in mineral oil), measuring about 12 microns by 28 microns.

a. Only one of the furrows is distinct. It shows as a light line reaching almost from pole to pole.

b. Two of the three furrows of the collapsed grain are visible. Note the distinct reticulate surface pattern of the exine, which also gives the optical margins a beady appearance. For a polar view of a typical dry (collapsed) three-furrowed grain, see Red Oak, Plate 16–5, *j*.

c. This is a giant, four-furrowed willow grain seen in polar position. The white cross is caused by refraction and is thus not a true structural feature. Such occasional atypical grains can be recognized as willow by their texture and color.

d–g. Two expanded and stained willow grains.

d. Optical section at the polar plane of an expanded grain in polar position; equatorial diameter about 20 microns. The dry, ellipsoidal grains quickly become spheroidal when moistened, and in changing shape often rotate 90 degrees meridionally in the mounting fluid. Here the three furrows appear as three light wedges (*e*) reaching from the equator halfway to the pole. Note the three heavy ribs of exine as at *f*.

g. Grain in semipolar position, accenting one furrow.

l–o. Drawings of three willow grains.

l. Dry grain with one closed furrow showing.

m. Expanded grain in semipolar position showing contrast between the coarse reticulate mesh on the three rigid ribs of the exine and that of the smooth opened furrows.

n. Surface detail of grain in perfect polar position with all three furrows (*o*) showing as in *d* above.

Tree of heaven (*Ailanthus altissima* Swing.) pollen grains are somewhat similar to those of willow, but the reticulations are coarser and there is a definite pore at the center of each furrow. Diameter: 25 microns (see page 355).

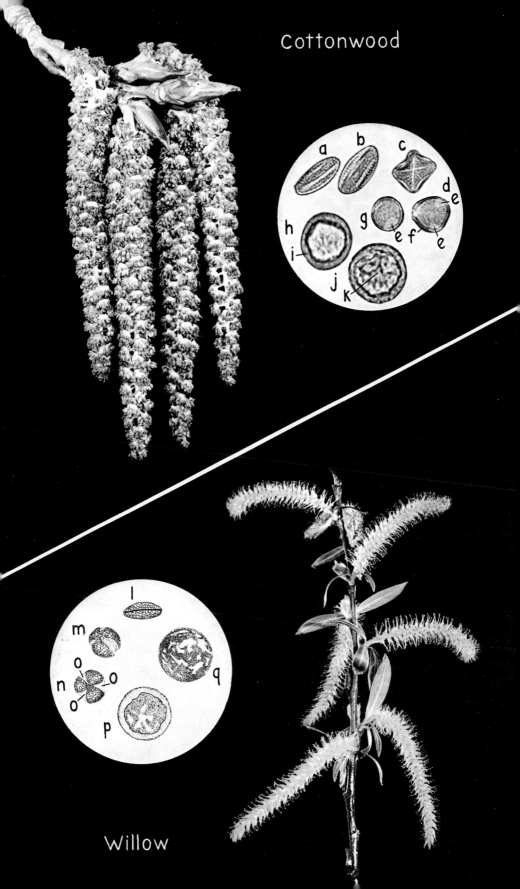

Cottonwood

Willow

PLATE 16–3

In the walnut family (Juglandaceae), consisting of only the walnuts and the hickories, the conspicuous green clusters of male catkins appear in late spring at the same time as the leaves. The inconspicuous female flowers (not shown) are found on the same tree with the male flowers. Pollen grains of the two genera are easily differentiated.

SHELLBARK HICKORY (*Carya ovata* K. Koch.). The catkins of the hickories, including pecan (*Carya pecan* Engl. and Graebn.), are slender and usually hang more loosely than those of the walnuts. Hickory pollen grains are the original "flying saucers." In the dry state (not pictured) with the thin ventral surface collapsed against the rigid dorsal surface, the grain actually is shaped like a saucer with a heavy rim. On atmospheric test slides these invaginate grains are almost invariably seen with the saucer open toward the observer, not in the rim view presented by the similar "dish" of the dry walnut grain, *c*, below. The rim of the dry hickory grain may be rolled slightly toward the center from two opposite sides, or drawn into a triangular pattern.

a. Photomicrograph of an expanded and stained hickory pollen grain in the polar position.

b. Drawing of an expanded hickory grain in the polar position. In views *a* and *b* the three germinal pores are spaced at equal intervals on, or very near, the equator. The shape of the expanded grain is that of a flattened sphere, a typical grain measuring 36 microns from pole to pole and 45 microns in equatorial diameter. Pecan grains' average equatorial diameter: 41 microns; other species: 36 to 52 microns.

BLACK WALNUT (*Juglans nigra* L.). The male flowers of this species are typical of those of all others of the genus, including the cultivated walnuts and butternut. Pollen grains of this genus are on the average smaller, except for butternut, than those of the hickories, and all have decidedly more germinal pores. If dry hickory grains may be compared with saucers, then dry walnut grains are like "cups" or thick bowls, sometimes triangular inside. Instead of a strict equatorial arrangement of pores, there is a fairly even band of seven to ten pores slightly above the equator, and several extra ones on the dorsal hemisphere.

c–h. Photomicrographs of dry, invaginate, collapsed, black walnut pollen grains.

c. Grain showing several of the ring of pores (*d*) around the rim of the cup.

e. Dry grain in the dorsal position (cup upside down) showing three pores, as (*f*), on the dorsal surface. Frequently there are four or five dorsal pores. Those in the peripheral ring of this grain are not in focus.

g. Grain in the ventral position with focus slightly above the equatorial level showing approximately half of each pore area (*h*) in the equatorial band. Average equatorial diameter (expanded) of black walnut pollen grain: 36 microns. [English walnut (*Juglans regia* L.): 41 microns.]

i–o. Drawings of expanded and stained black walnut pollen grains.

i. Equatorial view showing *j*, thin exine of ventral face, and *k*, the heavy pore-studded dorsal hemisphere.

f. Germinal pores as in views *e* and *g*.

l. This projected line suggests the manner in which the ventral surface *j* sinks into the center of the grain, against the thick dorsal surface, when drying takes place.

m. Grain in dorsal position as *e* showing nine equatorial pores, *n*, and three dorsal pores, *h*. Each pore is surrounded by a thick collar (see page 347) which can scarcely be seen at all on unstained specimens.

o. Grain in ventral position, as *g*. This is the usual position of grains found on atmospheric test slides. No rotation takes place on expansion.

j. Note granular texture of ventral surface.

Shellbark Hickory

Walnut

PLATE 16–4

BIRCH FAMILY (Betulaceae). To this family belong not only the birches (Betula) and alders (Alnus) but the hazelnuts and filberts (Corylus), the hornbeams (Carpinus), and the ironwoods (Ostrya). All have unisexual flowers, mostly with both sexes on the same plant. The pollen grains of all species are roughly spherical, more or less flattened at the poles, without furrows but with prominent germinal pores, three or more, spaced at equal intervals along the equator. The broad stiff collars (see page 347) around the pores tend to maintain the angular equatorial outline of the grains both when dry and when expanded.

PAPER BIRCH (*Betula papyrifera* Marsh.). Three male catkins hanging from the tip of a small branch with a small female catkin and a few unfolding leaves showing above. The pollen grains, with comparatively smooth exines and usually with three pores, but occasionally more, are typical of those of all other North American species. The average equatorial diameter of paper birch pollen is 24 microns, but there are occasional giant sized grains—32 microns. See page 352 and Plate 16–15, 5 and 6, for help in differentiation of grains of ironwood, hornbeam, and hazelnut, as well as other unrelated genera having similar three-pored grains.

a–i. Photomicrographs of four expanded and stained birch pollen grains.

a. Grain in polar position showing profile, or "edgewise," views of the three pores and their underlying collars. The focus here is somewhat above the equator.

b. Grain in polar position with focus exactly at the equator showing protruding "lips" (*c*) of germinal pore.

d. Grain in equatorial position, rotated 90 degrees from *b* position, with one pore (*e*) at periphery, one pore (*f*) in full view, and one (*g*) showing through from the distal surface. This grain shows only slight polar flattening.

h. Grain tipped about 45 degrees from the polar position, allowing a full view of one pore (*i*). The polar flattening is apparent but the collar of *i* is not sharp.

s–v. (See third disc.) Drawings of two expanded birch pollen grains.

s. Surface view of grain in polar position with protruding pore *t*, as *c*, and surrounding collar *u*.

v. Grain in equatorial position very much like photomicrograph *d*, but emphasizing the surface appearance.

EUROPEAN ALDER (*Alnus glutinosa* L.). This common introduced species has flowers and fruit typical of the native species. The photograph shows several clusters of long male catkins. Above them are a number of very small female catkins and the much larger woody flower clusters (like small pine cones) of the previous year. The pollen grains, typical of all alder species, are smooth, much flattened (lozenge-shaped), decidedly angular in equatorial outline, and uniform in size. Most of the grains have four pores but threes and fives are not uncommon. The average size varies with different alder species and with different lots of the same species: 21 to 27 microns.

j–n. Photomicrographs of alder pollen grains in polar position.

j–l. Dry, unexpanded grains with six, five, and four pores, respectively. The frequency of five-pored grains is approximately one in ten, of six-pored grains much less.

k. This grain shows the dim, concave curved bands reaching from pore to pore—a marking which, with properly adjusted light and surface focus, shows best in stained grains. This is a distinctive characteristic of alder pollen grains.

m–n. Photomicrographs of expanded and stained alder pollen grains.

m. Typical grain with four pores.

n. Grain with five pores. Only one of the five curved bands shows distinctly, between 10 and 12 o'clock on the grain. Compare with the dim bands on unexpanded grain *k*.

o–r. Drawings of expanded alder pollen grains.

o. Typical four-pored grain in polar position showing surface view of collars (*p*).

q. Five-pored grain in polar position.

r. Grain in equatorial position (on edge) showing only two of its four pores. Note the short polar diameter as compared with the equatorial diameter.

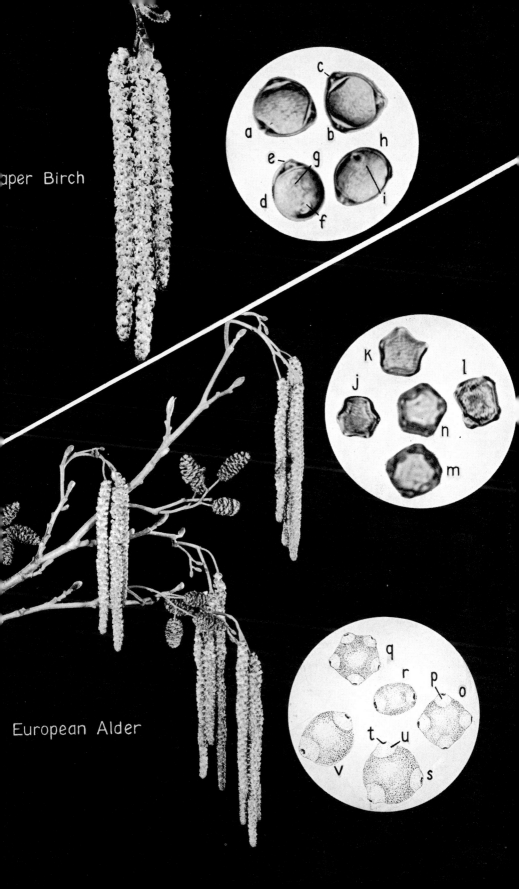

Paper Birch

European Alder

PLATE 16–5

THE OAKS (Quercus). The conspicuous clusters of green male catkins with green or brown anthers reach anthesis when the leaves are still small.

Flowers of MOSSY CUP or BUR OAK (*Quercus macrocarpa* Michx.), of the white oak group, and of RED OAK (*Quercus rubra* L.), of the black oak group, are shown. The pollen grains of all species are too similar in microscopic detail to permit specific differentiation of oak grains found on atmospheric test slides.

a–b. Photomicrographs of dry, unexpanded, oak pollen grains. Note the angular elliptical outline. The shrinkage pattern here shown is the usual but not invariable pattern.

a, a. Grains with two of the three normal furrows showing. Four-furrowed grains are infrequent.

b. Grain with only one of its three furrows showing. Dimensions of a typical dry grain: equatorial diameter (width) 21 microns; polar diameter (length) 37 microns.

h–j. (See third disc.) Drawings of dry, unexpanded oak grains.

h. Grain showing one of its furrows, corresponding to photomicrograph *b*.

i. Grain showing two of its furrows, corresponding to photomicrograph *a*.

j. Polar view of a dry grain—actually standing on end. Note depth of furrows.

c–g. Photomicrographs of three expanded and stained oak grains, two in polar position and one "on edge" (equatorial position). Dimensions of expanded grain: equatorial diameter, exclusive of the bulging intine, 32 microns; polar diameter 24 microns. These measurements are from the same identical grain as the dry measurements given above (*b*). Thus, on moistening, the equatorial diameter expanded from 21 to 32 microns, and the polar dimension shortened from 37 to 24 microns.

e. Optical section at equatorial plane. In spite of its coarse granulations, the exine is evidently thin.

c. Open furrow with exine torn by pressure of the cell contents.

d. The bladder-like intine usually protrudes an equal distance through each of the three torn furrows, giving the grain a symmetrical semitriangular outline when in the polar position.

k–m. Drawings of two expanded oak grains, one in polar position showing rough granulated exine (*k*) and one in equatorial position showing: *m,* a complete expanded furrow crossing the equator as in *g* above, and *l,* glimpses of the pore membrane bulging from the other two furrows. These drawings and photomicrographs emphasize the shape of the expanded oak grain as being that of a triangular lens or a much flattened sphere with three equatorial bulges.

Oak pollens may be confused with those of maple unless careful attention is given to the longer furrows, smoother surface, and larger size of the latter (see Plate 16–8 and page 355. Also compare dry oak grains with dry ash grains (Plate 16–6).

The dry pollen grains of beech (*Fagus grandifolia* Ehrh.), a genus in the same family as the oaks, are very similar to dry oak grains, except for their much greater size and heavier exine. Expanded grains are not alike. See comparison, Plate 16–15, 10.

Bur Oak

Red Oak

PLATE 16–6

The two species on this plate are *not* related botanically.

AMERICAN ELM (*Ulmus americana* L.). The perfect flowers of this common elm open in very early spring, long before its leaves appear. Pollen production is abundant. The grains are typical of those of the other five North American elm species as well as of water elm (*Planera aquatica* Gmel.), except as noted below. Elm pollen grains normally have five pores at approximately equal intervals along the equator; occasionally four; very rarely three or six. In some lots of slippery or red elm (*Ulmus rubra* Muhl.: synonym, *Ulmus fulva* Michx.), four-pored grains are frequent; in others no more so than in American elm. Average equatorial diameter of American elm: 33 microns; slippery elm: 30 microns; scrub elm (*Ulmus crassifolia* Nutt.): 24 microns.

Dry elm grains (not illustrated) have no consistent shrinkage pattern, though a large proportion of them are invaginate or partially so. The equatorial outline is often pentagonal, but the pores are not readily visible.

a–b. Photomicrographs of expanded and stained American elm pollen grains in the polar position.

a. Optical section at the equatorial plane showing characteristic pentagonal outline and typically circular inner face of the cell wall.

b. Section taken near the polar surface showing irregular corrugations of the exine —a helpful diagnostic character.

c–d. Drawings of American elm pollen grains, expanded and stained.

c. Grain in the equatorial position showing three germinal pores, one in full view, and two others as notches at the ends of the equator. Compare the equatorial diameter with the considerably shorter polar diameter.

d. Grain in the polar position showing pentagonal shape and the irregular surface of the exine.

Elm grains should not be confused with the five-pored grains of alder, being larger, much coarser, and without visible collars. Dry elm grains might be confused with dry walnut grains, since both are often similarly invaginate, but walnut pollen is larger than elm and is never angular in outline. Moreover, the seasons are mostly distinct.

Although the hackberries (Celtis) are members of the elm family (Ulmaceae), their pollen grains do not resemble those of the elms (see Plate 16–15, 5, 6).

WHITE ASH (*Fraxinus americana* L.). Branch from a male tree with dense clusters of reddish purple flowers—mostly a mass of bare anthers. Pollination is completed before the leaves appear. The pollen grains of this species are typical of those of all ash species except for minor differences in the texture of the reticulate exine.

e–f. Drawing of ash pollen grains.

e. Expanded grain in the polar position showing the four opened furrows and the reticulate surface. Grains with three or five furrows are occasionally found. Average equatorial diameter, expanded: 25 microns; polar diameter: 19 microns (not illustrated).

f. Dry, unexpanded grain in the position usually observed on atmospheric slides, showing only one of its four infolded furrows. Note the rectangular shape, nearly twice as long as the width. Dry measurements, equatorial diameter: 17 microns; polar diameter: 32 microns. An end view (not shown) resembles a small Greek cross, similar to dry red sorrel, Plate 16–14, *q*.

g, *h*, and *i*. Photomicrographs of ash pollen grains in polar position, expanded and stained.

g and *h*. Optical sections at the equatorial plane allowing a cross-sectional view of reticulations on the exine, also of the smooth outline of the inner face of the complete cell wall.

i. Polar view showing surface detail at the periphery. Reticulations of the exine are best seen using very light staining. The furrows, apparently torn open, still show tiny flecks of stained exine, particularly at the four corners, regardless of focal level.

Ash pollen should not be confused with the four-pored alder grains since they are larger and have furrows rather than collared pores.

The insect-pollinated privets (Ligustrum) and the olives (Olea) are members of the same family (Oleaceae) as the ashes. These pollens are similar in texture but have only three furrows (see Plate 16–15, 7).

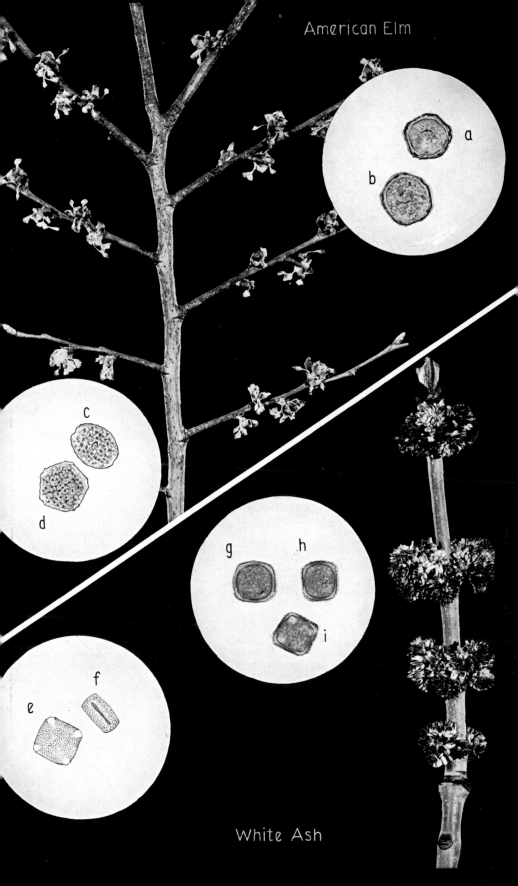

American Elm

White Ash

PLATE 16–7

Although the flowers of the two trees on this plate are somewhat similar, the trees are not related, and the contrast in their pollen grains is extreme.

Sʏᴄᴀᴍᴏʀᴇ (*Platanus occidentalis* L.) (plane tree). The berry-like heads beside each leaf cluster in the photograph are densely packed, minute male flowers, green or light brown in color. Similar female flower heads (not shown) are borne on the same tree. The small, three-furrowed (occasionally four) pollen grains of this species are typical of those of the several other native and introduced species. Average equatorial diameter of expanded pollen grain: 22 microns. These pollens could be confused with those of willow because of their similar small size (willow 20 microns) and surface markings (see Plate 16–2). In the dry state sycamore grains might even be mistaken for small oak grains except that the size is much too small for any species of oak.

a–j. Photomicrographs of sycamore pollen grains.

a–e. Dry grains, unexpanded, mounted in oil.

a and *b.* Two grains of different size from the same specimen, each in meridional position and each showing two of its three deep furrows (*c*).

d and *e.* Dry sycamore grains in polar position—standing on end—showing depth of the furrows. One, *d,* has three furrows and the other, *e,* has four.

f–j. Photomicrographs of three expanded and stained sycamore grains.

f. Grain in approximate meridional position allowing a distinct view of one broad expanded furrow. *j* and *j* indicate the polar points.

g. Grain in a semipolar position allowing light to penetrate through two of the three expanded furrows (*h*).

i. Equatorial section of grain in polar position showing thin exine (very dark) and thicker intine. The three blunt furrows, when compared with those of willow, are shorter.

k and *l.* Drawings of sycamore pollen grains.

k. Dry, unexpanded grain lying in same position as *a* and *b* above.

l. Expanded and stained grain, as *i* above, showing reticulate surface of exine and flecking of the exine of the furrows. The reticulations are much finer than those of willow and the size of the grain slightly larger.

Sᴡᴇᴇᴛ Gᴜᴍ (*Liquidambar styraciflua* L.). The heads of male flowers are clustered on erect stalks, the female flowers solitary and pendant, the leaves star-shaped. There are no other species in this genus, at least in the United States. The large pollen grains are so characteristic and unlike those of any other wind-pollinated species that identification offers no difficulty.

m. Drawing of expanded and stained sweet gum pollen grain showing seven bulging pore membranes (*n*) on the visible hemisphere. The exine is pitted and the pore membranes strongly flecked. Average diameter of expanded sweet gum grains: 38 microns.

o. Photomicrograph of dry sweet gum grain showing countersunk pore membranes (*p*) at the periphery.

q and *t.* Photomicrographs of expanded and stained grains with several bulging pore membranes (*r*) showing on the periphery and an indistinct face view of one rather elongated pore, *s.*

t. Note the difference in sizes of the pores. Their number varies from 12 to 20.[3]

Sycamore

Sweet Gum

PLATE 16–8

In the maple genus (Acer), the flowers of the different species vary somewhat in general appearance and in the degree to which they are wind- or insect-pollinated, but the pollen grains are similar—normally with three furrows. Frequently they are found in clumps on atmospheric test slides.

SOFT MAPLE (*Acer saccharinum* L.). A twig of greenish-yellow male flower clusters at anthesis. Note exserted anthers and the entire absence of leaves on the twig. Male and female flowers may be found on the same tree, or on separate trees.

a–d. Two grains of dry, unexpanded, soft maple pollen. Equatorial diameter (width): 30 microns; polar diameter (length): 50 microns. The surface actually is finely granular, although it appears rough in the photograph.

a. Grain showing only one furrow (*c*). Two are hidden beneath the grain. Note the tapering elliptical outline.

b. Grain in position to show two of its three furrows running almost from pole (*d*) to pole (*d*).

e–h. Photomicrographs of three grains of maple pollen expanded and heavily stained. Equatorial diameter about 38 microns; polar diameter 34 microns.

e and *f*. Two grains in approximately polar position—*f* more nearly so than *e*—each showing three expanded furrows (*g*). Occasionally there are four.

e. Optical section focused slightly above the plane of the equator. The intine may protrude very little or not at all beyond the spherical surface of the grain.

f. Here the focus is nearer the polar surface than in *e*. Note that the wide triangular halves of the furrows when in perfect alignment above and below the equator allow maximum transmission of light from below (compare *e*).

h. Refers to polar point of *f*, and of the grain below it (not lettered) which is in meridional position, affording a full length view of one expanded furrow. The slight flattening at the poles is evident.

SUGAR MAPLE (*Acer saccharum* Marsh.). Clusters of flowers which appear at the same time as the leaves and are hung on long slender, slightly hairy stalks. There are distinct male and female flowers, but the sexes may be encountered both in the same cluster, or in separate clusters appearing on the same tree or on separate trees.

o. Drawing of expanded and stained grain of sugar maple pollen in the polar position showing the three furrows and the granular surface of the exine. Diameter: 39 microns. The tendency toward a striated arrangement of the granulations, somewhat resembling fingerprints, is characteristic of all maples except box elder but difficult to see except under high power and with careful staining. The common species other than box elder can hardly be separated either by size, shape, or surface features.

BOX ELDER (*Acer negundo* L.). Clusters of male flowers appear just as the leaf buds open. The flowers are distinguished by their long pendant green filaments and their green or reddish-brown anthers. Flower sexes are borne on separate trees. The dry pollen grains, smaller than those of other maples, are more variable in shrinkage pattern, and more coarsely and more irregularly granulated.

i–n. Photomicrographs of expanded and stained box elder pollen grains.

i. Optical section at equatorial plane showing furrows between crescents of heavy exine. Note also the turgid intine *j* protruding through tears in the thin exine of the furrows, giving the grains a triangular equatorial outline.

k. Optical section at higher plane than *i*.

l. The shrunken and discarded exine from grain *m*.

n. Grain in equatorial position with one visible furrow similar to soft maple *g*.

p. Drawing of expanded box elder pollen grain. The coarser granulations and shorter furrows, as well as the smaller size, serve to differentiate box elder pollen from that of the other maples. Its earlier season of dispersal will help to lessen confusion with oak pollen grains.

Soft Maple

Sugar Maple

Box Elder

PLATE 16–9

GRASSES (Gramineae). The allergist's interest in this large and important family revolves around the common meadow and lawn grasses since they produce the bulk of this type of air-borne pollen. Nevertheless, all the hundreds of species of wild and cultivated North American grasses, including some of the cereals, are potential sources of allergenic pollen. The arrangements of florets and flower clusters of the various grasses differ widely, but the pollen grains of all species are so similar that they are practically indistinguishable on gravity test slides. There is little chance of mistaking grass pollen grains, with their thin, smooth exines and single germinal pores, for those of any other plant family. However, the germinal pore is not visible on every grass pollen grain. Size range, except for corn: 25 to 55 microns, mostly 30 to 40 microns.

TIMOTHY (*Phleum pratense* L.). Fresh pollen grains (in the anther) are approximately spherical in shape. Upon their discharge they immediately lose about 50 per cent of their weight by evaporation and assume one of several typical shrinkage patterns shown in the photomicrographs,

a–d. Photomicrographs of four timothy pollen grains. Only *d* is expanded.

a. Dry, unexpanded and unstained timothy pollen grain showing invaginate shrinkage pattern, similar to that of a partially deflated rubber ball. The germinal pore is barely visible at a point near the letter *a*. The exine is essentially smooth, intine rather heavy and the color a very light yellow. Dry grains are comparatively transparent and may be overlooked if too much light is used while examining gravity slides.

b. This stained but *unexpanded* grain is mounted in oil. It shows another typical shrinkage pattern with two or more smooth indentations. On such dry, pear-shaped grains the germinal pore, if visible, will be found on the large end of the grain.

c. Germinal pore on an unexpanded grain with shrinkage pattern somewhat similar to *b*. The apparent granulations to the right of the pore are not on the smooth exine but represent light diffusion patterns caused by the cell contents.

d. Expanded and stained grain with focus on the germinal pore. The coarse granular starch content of the pollen grain appears only faintly but would show plainly at a lower focus level. Average diameter expanded: 34 microns.

e–g. Drawings of grass pollen grains showing detail of the germinal pore.

e. Under high magnification the exine shows a very fine meshwork of lace-like markings, but with low or high dry powers they are not visible. Nor are they necessary for recognition.

f. The germinal pore (extra enlarged) is roughly circular with a raised, crater-like edge and distinct central "operculum" of exine substance. (See page 357).

g. The germinal pore (extra enlarged) on the periphery affording a cross-sectional view of pore and operculum.

BLUEGRASS (*Poa pratensis* L.) (also known as Kentucky bluegrass and in some areas as June grass). Anthesis in this species occurs two or three weeks earlier than timothy. Pollen grains are similar to those of timothy but average smaller: 30 microns.

ORCHARD GRASS (*Dactylis glomerata* L.). Anthesis almost simultaneous with bluegrass. Pollen grains are similar to those of timothy and about the same size: 34 microns.

BERMUDA GRASS (*Cynodon dactylon* L., Pers.). A west coast and southern grass, shedding small amounts of pollen over a long period. Pollen grains vary greatly in size with different lots: 38 to 42 microns.

RYE (*Secale cereale* L.) pollen grains are decidedly ellipsoidal in shape, even when expanded, averaging 42 by 63 microns (not illustrated).

CORN (*Zea mays* L.) pollen is typical in shape, but far larger than that of any other grass: 90 to 100 microns (not illustrated).

hy

Bluegrass

ard Grass

Bermuda Grass

PLATE 16–10

The classification employed here for the ragweed tribe (Ambrosieae) differs from that of Rydberg,[20] who assigned it familial status, in that the genus Franseria is here considered to be co-generic with Ambrosia.[18] Plates 16–10 and 16–11 illustrate only eight of the allergenically important species in three genera of the Ambrosieae. All members of the ragweed tribe have pollen with common morphologic features and antigenic groups shared among themselves and with other species of the Compositae. Pollen grains of the genera illustrated are so much alike that all are often identified as "ragweed" and, at best, are separable as "ragweed," "cocklebur," and "burweed marsh elder."

THE RAGWEEDS (Ambrosia L.). All four species of "true ragweed" shown on this plate, and some 35 other North American Ambrosias, have similar long terminal spikes of clustered male flowers and similar arrangements of female flowers usually solitary, in the axils of the upper leaves. The expanded pollen grains of the Ambrosias are approximately spherical, usually measuring between 18 and 24 microns. The surface is evenly covered with short conical spines, or spicules. There are three (occasionally four) germinal pores, usually inconspicuous, spaced at equal intervals along the equator.

a–c. Photomicrographs of three dry, unexpanded and unstained ragweed pollen grains mounted in oil. Collapse is local and slight, never approaching invagination.

a. Grain in meridional position showing a slight difference in the polar and equatorial diameters.

b. One of the several curved lines caused by slight collapse of limited areas of the cell wall. These lines are always visible on unexpanded pollen grains, particularly when in the polar position or approximately so.

c. Three slight indentations in the equatorial periphery indicate the location of the three germinal pores. The obscure pores are very difficult to see without expansion and staining.

d and e. Expanded and stained ragweed pollen grains of slightly different size. Usually one of the three small pores is plainly visible on each grain if stain has been allowed to penetrate thoroughly.

f–h. Drawings of three dry grains with accent on the typical lines caused by shrinkage of the cell wall, as in a–c.

h. On this grain in polar position the locations of the three pores are indicated as in c above. The triangular center pattern will disappear completely if the grain is expanded.

i and j. Drawings of expanded and stained pollen grains, neither one in polar position.

j. Germinal pore just inside the periphery.

SHORT OR COMMON RAGWEED (Ambrosia artemisiifolia L.). This is an annual species with finely divided leaves slightly resembling those of ferns. Under average soil and weather conditions the plants grow to a height of two and a half feet, but at the extreme northern edge of their range may blossom when only two or three inches high. In Florida, with its long growing season, the weeds sometimes reach a maximum height of ten feet. The spicules on the pollen grains are a little more closely set than on the pollens of southern ragweed and giant ragweed. Average diameter: 20 microns (Wodehouse[3] gives 17.6 to 18.2 microns).

SOUTHERN RAGWEED (Ambrosia bidentata Michx.). An annual weed averaging smaller than short ragweed with small lance-shaped leaves without leaf stalks. The entire plant is hairy and resinous. The spines on the pollen grains are farther apart than on other Ambrosias, and the grains themselves are larger than those of short ragweed. Average diameter: 22.5 microns.

WESTERN RAGWEED (Ambrosia psilostachya DC.). A coarse perennial species somewhat resembling short ragweed but with creeping rootstocks. The leaves are not only coarse and leathery but have no leaf stalks. The pollen grains are definitely larger than those of short ragweed or giant ragweed, averaging 23 microns. There are occasional four-pored grains.

GIANT RAGWEED (Ambrosia trifida L.). This annual ragweed is the tallest of the Ambrosias (up to 15 feet) and has much the largest leaves. The individual leaves are typically three-lobed although many plants show upper leaves that are two-lobed or that lack lobulations. The pollen grains average slightly smaller than short ragweed, 19 microns, but with spines a little farther apart.

Other Ambrosia species and their pollens are discussed on pages 358–360.

See Plate 16–11 for related ragweed genera.

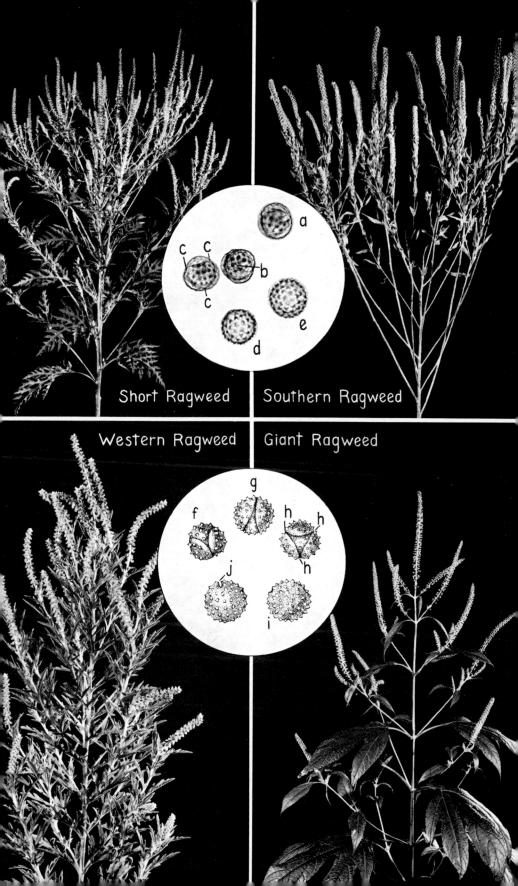

Short Ragweed   Southern Ragweed

Western Ragweed   Giant Ragweed

PLATE 16–11

RAGWEED TRIBE (Ambrosieae) continued. Burweed Marsh Elder (*Iva xanthifolia* Nutt.; synonym, *Cyclachaena xanthifolia* [Fresen]; prairie ragweed). This plant, which is almost as large as giant ragweed, has broad silky leaves more like those of cocklebur than of the common ragweeds. The pollen grains have short spicules quite like those of short and giant ragweed, but the exine is heavier and the three pores are centered in three long meridional furrows which afford a collapse mechanism like that of most other three-furrowed pollen grains. Identification is thus not too difficult.

a–c. Photomicrographs of three dry, unexpanded, burweed marsh elder pollen grains.

a and *b.* Grains in the meridional position showing one long furrow on the right side of *a* and two on *b.*

c. Grain in polar position (on end) but with focus too far above the equator to show the deep furrows.

d–f. Photomicrographs of three expanded burweed marsh elder grains. Equatorial diameter: 18.5 microns.

d, d, d. Grain in polar position with the focus slightly above the equator, showing three deep notches in the periphery, and the tapering furrows.

e. Germinal pore in the center of one of the three long furrows, surface focus.

f. Grain in semipolar position with focus near the surface.

k–n. Drawings of four burweed marsh elder pollen grains.

k. Dry shrunken grain with only one of the three furrows showing.

l–n. Drawings of expanded and stained grains.

l. Grain about 45 degrees off polar position showing one peripheral notch and one furrow.

m, m, m. Pore openings and furrows of grain in exact polar position.

COCKLEBUR (*Xanthium commune* [*Britton*]). The large coarse leaves and burs of the cockleburs are unmistakable, but at the time of pollination the burs are mostly undeveloped. In the photograph one cluster of spherical male flower heads may be seen at the lower left and another cluster against the edge of the top leaf. The pollen grains of all North American cockleburs, except spiny cocklebur (see text), are distinguished from those of all other ragweeds by their larger size and much shorter spicules. But the spicules are so small that in examining atmospheric test slides it is usually necessary to switch frequently to high dry power to identify suspected cocklebur grains.

g. and *h.* Photomicrographs of expanded cocklebur pollen grains, 25 microns in diameter. Compare the minute spicules with those of burweed marsh elder (*b*) and note difference in size. Average equatorial diameter: 28 microns.

g. Grain showing one of its three germinal pores. In any given position, except polar, it is usually difficult to see more than one pore.

h. Grain with focus near periphery to show spicules in profile.

i and *j.* Drawings of cocklebur pollen grains.

i. One pore showing on expanded grain.

j. Dry, unexpanded cocklebur grain showing typical shrinkage lines as in other ragweeds (Plate 16–10, *f*, *g*, *h*). In this drawing the spicules are overly accented.

ROUGH MARSH ELDER (*Iva ciliata* Willd.). This annual species from the lower Mississippi Valley is scarcely typical in gross characters of the ten other marsh elders, including poverty weed, some of which are annuals and some perennial shrubs. In this genus, as in Cyclachaena, the separate male and female flowers are found together in the same flower heads. The pollen grains of all species of marsh elder are so similar to those of Ambrosia (Plate 16–10) and Franseria as to prohibit certain identification of individual marsh elder grains found on atmospheric test slides. Average equatorial diameter: 23.5 microns.

SLENDER FALSE RAGWEED (*Ambrosia confertiflora:* synonym *Franseria tenuifolia*). This perennial species, like the numerous other American "false ragweeds," resembles the "true ragweeds" in appearance, as well as in pollen size (average 22 microns) and morphology. The flower arrangement is like that of the other Ambrosias, but the fruits are bur-like with several or numerous spines.

Burweed Marsh Elder

Rough
Marsh Elder

Cocklebur

False
Ragweed

PLATE 16–12

The Sagebrushes (Artemisia) (mugworts; wormwoods). Of the numerous American species of this wind-pollinated genus, there is room to picture only four. The foliage of the perennial species is usually gray and strongly aromatic. Flower heads are small and pollen production is far below that of most ragweeds. The pollen grains of the various species differ somewhat in size (19 to 25 microns) and surface characters but not enough to allow specific identification. However, as a genus, they are easily differentiated from the pollens of ragweeds by their heavier exine and from those of all other composites by their almost total lack of spines.

Sagebrush (*Artemisia tridentata* Nutt.) (common sagebrush; mountain sage). This is a common shrub of the Rocky Mountain and intermountain area with shredded bark and silver gray foliage, two to twelve feet high. The expanded pollen grains are nearly spherical, with heavy exine and three furrows with germinal pores (occasional giants with four furrows). The fine pebbly surface markings are even less prominent than are the tiny spicules on cocklebur grains.

a–c. Photomicrographs of three dry, unexpanded sagebrush pollen grains, one (*a*) in polar position (on end), and two in meridional position.

b, b. Two of the three furrows.

c. Grain showing only one of its three furrows.

d and e. Optical sections at the equatorial plane of expanded and stained sagebrush grains in polar position. Diameter: 25 microns. The surface markings can barely be seen on the periphery, but the three crescent-shaped cross-sections of heavy exine and the bulging pores are sufficient for identification.

f and g. Drawing of sage pollen grains.

f. Unexpanded grain, in meridional position, showing one furrow with elongated pore at its center. Note the pebbled surface of the grain.

g. Polar view of expanded sage pollen, showing typical crescent appearance of the thick exine and bulging of the intine at the three pores. (Similar to *d* and *e* above.) The rod-like baccula in the outer walls of the grain are indicated.

Pasture Sage (*Artemisia frigida* Willd.) (carpet sage). A small 8 to 20 inch, woolly perennial of the high plains and foothills of the Rockies. The pollen grains average a little smaller than those of *Artemisia tridentata*.

Sand Sagebrush (*Artemisia filifolia* Torr.) A silky, feathery shrub of the plains from Wyoming and western Nebraska to northern Mexico, one to three feet high. Its pollen production is probably light. The grains conform to the generic type.

Annual Sage (*Artemisia annua* L.) (sweet Annie). A tall, fern-like, green, fragrant annual weed growing abundantly in larger cities from Louisville, Kentucky, and Nashville, Tennessee, southward. The pollen production is appreciable and in Nashville, Tennessee, actually is a complicating factor in ragweed allergy. Expanded pollen grains average about 20 microns.

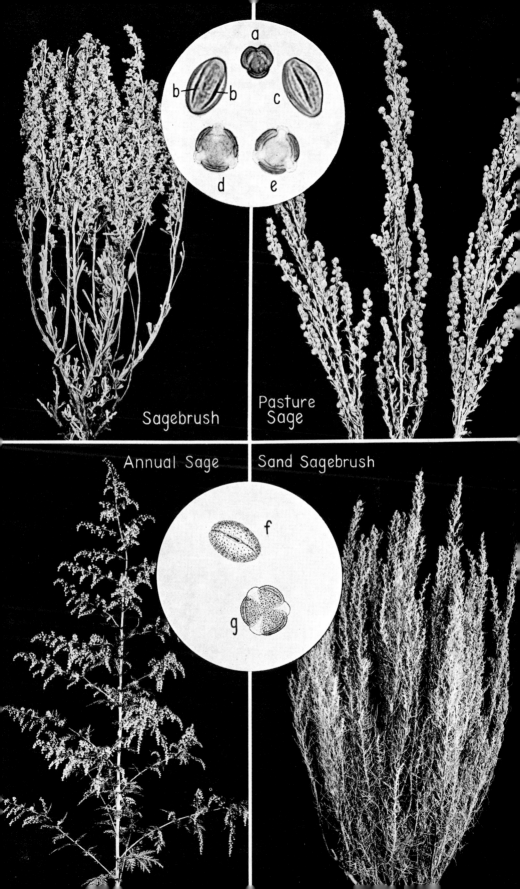

Sagebrush

Pasture
Sage

Annual Sage

Sand Sagebrush

PLATE 16–13

The Carelessweed or Amaranth (Amaranthaceae) and Goosefoot (Chenopodiaceae) Families. The close botanical relationship of these two families is reflected in the marked similarity of their "golf ball-like" pollen grains.

Western Water Hemp (*Acnida tamariscina* [Nutt.] Wood). A tall, spindly "pigweed" of the amaranth family closely resembling Palmer's amaranth (*Amaranthus palmeri* S. Wats.) and Torrey's amaranth [*Amaranthus torreyi* (A. Gray) Benth.]. All three bear male and female flowers on separate plants. In the photograph the larger specimen is the male, pollen-producing plant. Productivity in this species is extremely heavy. The pollen grains are spherical when expanded and usually invaginate when dry. The pores are round, larger than the pores on lamb's quarters pollen (*Chenopodium album* L.), smaller and more numerous than those on common pigweed pollen (*Amaranthus retroflexus* L.), and closer together than those on any other of the Amaranthaceae. On close examination small dark flecks will be seen in the center of each pore. The grains vary considerably in size: 20 to 29 microns in diameter, expanded.

    a. Photomicrograph of three pollen grains of western water hemp expanded and stained. The pores, as *b*, show clearly near the periphery (note those of the grain at 5 o'clock on this field, or on the surface, depending on the level of focus.

    g–j. (Fourth disc.) Drawings of three western water hemp pollen grains.

    g–i. Dry, invaginate grains. The cell wall at *h* in each grain has collapsed against the opposite wall giving *g* a "doughnut" appearance and *i* that of a bowl standing on edge.

    j. Grain expanded and stained. Note the group of stained flecks in the center of the pore membranes.

The two remaining species on this plate belong to the goosefoot family.

Burning Bush (*Kochia scoparia* L. Schrad.) (Mexican fireweed, firebush, summer cypress). This rapidly spreading tumbleweed of the plains, now invading vacant lots of cities as far east as Detroit, is the wild relative of a finer and more symmetrical garden ornamental. The plant resembles Russian thistle in shape and often in its fall coloration, and is a member of the same family. Pollen production is abundant, the grains being spherical when expanded. They are often invaginate—as western water hemp—when dry, and larger than the pollen grains of any other common member of the goosefoot family. Also, they are larger than any of those of the amaranth family. The size, when expanded, is from 20 to 32 microns—mostly 29 microns. The pores are comparatively small, usually far apart and flecked at the center. The exine is coarse.

    c. Photomicrograph of two expanded and stained pollen grains of burning bush with surface focus showing round pores, as at *d*.

    k. Drawing of expanded and stained burning bush pollen grain showing central flecking of the pore membranes.

Russian Thistle (*Salsola kali* var *tenuifolia*). This is the ubiquitous tumbleweed of the dry farmlands of the "dust bowl" and intermountain states. The flowers are perfect, small, and very inconspicuous (invisible on the photograph). The pollen grains are spherical when expanded, partially and irregularly collapsed when dry, but not usually invaginate. The exine is coarse and the pores fewer and larger than on any other common member of the goosefoot family. Flecking of pore membranes is pronounced.

    e. Photomicrograph of four expanded and stained Russian thistle pollen grains showing heavy exine and large, well separated pores, as *f*.

    l. Drawing of Russian thistle pollen grain showing pores and granular surface of exine. Compare the number and spacing of pores in *j*, *k*, and *l*.

Pollens of other goosefoots and amaranths, except for that of sugar beet, which is very small, are not as easily separated as are the three above species (see text). See Plate 16–15, 8, for illustrations of other members of these families.

Western Water Hemp

ning Bush

sian Thistle

a
b

c
d

e
f

g
h
i
j
K
l

PLATE 16–14

MISCELLANEOUS WIND-POLLINATED PLANTS. The three weeds portrayed here belong to entirely different plant families.

HEMP (*Cannabis sativa* L.) (marihuana). The photograph shows the male plant only. Hemp is closely related botanically to cultivated hop (*Humulus lupulus*) and to wild Japanese hop (*Humulus japonica*) whose pollens are very similar to each other and to those of hemp. Hemp also is closely related to the mulberries (Morus), paper mulberry (*Broussonetia papyrifera*), Osage orange (*Maclura pomifera*), and the hackberries (Celtis), as well as to the nettles (Urtica). All these, as well as the unrelated birches, have pollens with common characters (see text, page 352, and pollen grain illustrations, Plate 16–15, 5 and 6; also Plate 16–4). Hemp pollen production is abundant. The pollen grains are spherical and flattened when expanded, with three pores with collars. The exine is smooth and the cell wall very weak. There is no typical shrinkage pattern, but the dry transparent grains collapse as though made of paper, with creases at various angles. The expanded grains are of uniform size: 25 microns.

a–e. Photomicrographs of three hemp pollen grains.

a. Dry, unexpanded grain, not necessarily typical in shape.

b and *e*. Grains expanded and stained. The mottled appearance of these grains is due to the cell content, not to surface marks.

b. Grain in the polar position, equatorial section, with three prominent pores, *c*, and dim profiles of collars, as at *d*.

e. Grain in equatorial position. The third pore, on the distal side of the grain and out of focus, shows through dimly at the center of the equator.

j. Drawing of expanded hemp pollen grain in the polar position showing germinal pore *k* and collar *l*.

ENGLISH PLANTAIN (*Plantago lanceolata* L.). A small (one and one-half feet or less), widely distributed weed of lawns and waste places. Pollen production is moderate but far more than that of other plantain species. The grains are approximately spherical, variable in size—19 to 34 microns—with variable numbers of pores. Four to seven pores (with opercula) are usually visible on the proximal hemisphere, including the periphery. The exine is thin with inconspicuous granulations, the whole cell wall having about the same thickness and density as that of grass pollens. This causes the collapse to be either partially or completely invaginate, like that frequently seen in grass pollen grains. In fact, plantain pollen must be expanded and stained to be sure of its identity.

f–i. Photomicrographs of three expanded English plantain pollen grains, high focus, showing surface and only the uppermost pores.

m and *n*. Drawings of two expanded plantain pollen grains. Note operculum on the pore of *m*, on its periphery at 11 o'clock (see page 347).

RED SORREL (*Rumex acetosella* L.) (sheep sorrel; red sorrel). Only male plants are portrayed here. The pollen grains are uniform in size with four long, narrow furrows (occasionally three or six) with small germinal pores. The furrows are difficult to see except with high power and good staining. The exine is thin and its surface characters obscured by the coarse granular cell contents. The grains of this species are generally typical of those of all other docks.

o–v. Photomicrographs of red sorrel pollen grains.

o–r. Three dry, unexpanded grains showing usual shrinkage pattern.

o and *r*. Grains in meridional position showing furrowed cell wall (*p*).

q. Grain in polar position (on end) showing the four folds as *p, p*.

s–v. Three grains expanded and stained, one (*s*) inclined from the polar position, and two in polar position.

s. One or two furrows (*t*) show very dimly.

u. The coarse appearance of this grain is due to the expanded starch grains of the cell content—as in grass pollens—and not to surface markings.

v, v, v. Of the four pores on each of these grains only two or three each are plainly visible. The squarish equatorial outline is not always apparent (see drawings below).

w–z. Drawings of four red sorrel pollen grains, one (*w*) dry, as *o* and *r* above, and three expanded and stained, lying in different positions.

x. Grain in meridional position showing one complete furrow and centrally located pore.

y and *z*. Grains in approximately polar position. The furrows are not always strictly meridional at their ends. Note circular equatorial outline of *y* as compared with squarish outline of *z*.

English Plantain

Hemp

Red Sorrel

PLATE 16–15

Miscellaneous spores and pollen grains.*

1. Drawings of fungus spores frequently recovered in air sampling   (Chapter 16–III)
a, a. Conidiophores of Cladosporium (Hormodendrum) showing typical branching. Conidia are 4 to 18 microns long.

b, b, b. Conidia of Helminthosporium showing multiple septa. Spore length varies from 40 to 130 microns.

c, c, c. Conidia of Alternaria. The length varies from 12 to 90 microns.

2. Photomicrographs of bracken fern spores [*Pteridium aquilinum* (L.) Kuhn.], and urediospores of stem rust *(Puccinia graminis)*.

a. A single spore of bracken fern, expanded and stained.

b. Two urediospores of stem rust, dry, mounted in oil, showing pores *c, c, c*. Surface slightly warted. The size of stem rust spores is extremely variable, averaging 25 to 35 microns.

d, d. Urediospores of stem rust, expanded and stained, showing profiles of two of the four pores (*c, c*) on one specimen. A third pore appears dimly on the surface of the grain directly between these two.

3. Photomicrographs of sedge (*Carex pensylvanica* Lam.) and grass pollen grains.

a, a. Sedge grains, expanded and stained, showing the single indistinct, ragged pore always at the large end (b). These specimens, about 30 microns by 40 microns.

c. Timothy pollen grain, dry, mounted in oil.

4. Photomicrographs of linden or basswood (*Tilia americana* L.), and of *Acacia baileyana* pollens.

a. Linden pollen grains, dry, mounted in oil, polar position, equatorial section. Diameter: 40 microns. Note the deep countersunk pores. The exine is decidedly reticulate.

b. Expanded and stained linden pollen grain in the polar position, equatorial section, showing the expanded pores. The grains typically come to rest in the polar position.

c. A compound unit of acacia pollens (16 grains in four tetrads). Total diameter of unit: 50 microns. This pollen is mostly insect-borne. For another mimosa type, see mesquite grain on field 9 of this plate.

5. HACKBERRY (*Celtis laevigata* Willd.) with related and similar species having two or three germinal pores (occasionally more) with collars. For similar pollen grains, see also Plates 16–4 and 16–14. Drawings of expanded and stained grains.

a–c. Hackberry grains, *a* in polar position, *c* in equatorial position. Note the coarse texture and that the pores do not protrude beyond the nearly circular equatorial outline of the grain, except for the tiny caps, *b*. Equatorial diameter: 28 microns. See also photomicrographs, 6, *e* and *f*, below.

d. STINGING NETTLE (*Urtica gracilis* Ait.) grain in polar position, 14 microns in diameter. This very small pollen grain is so nearly the same size as the grains of paper mulberry that it is difficult to distinguish, except by the season of dispersal. Usually it has three pores but occasionally only two.

e. PAPER MULBERRY (*Broussonetia papyrifera* Vent.) pollen grain showing typical arrangement of its two pores—usually not opposite. 14 microns in diameter.

f. OSAGE ORANGE (*Maclura pomifera*). Grain in the polar position showing three (capped) pores, with collars. Grains with four pores are common. Average diameter of three-pored grains: 22 microns; four-pored: 25 microns. Staining is necessary.

g. BAYBERRY (*Myrica cerifera* L.) or wax myrtle. Grain in the polar position showing three large pores and surrounding collars. The grains are uniform (except for occasional four-pored giants), about 25 microns. Pollen of this species is morphologically similar,

(Legend continued on page 396.)

---

* Some of the species are shown for comparative purposes, supplementing the illustrations on other plates. Others are of little or no importance in allergy but puzzling when encountered in routine atmospheric studies.

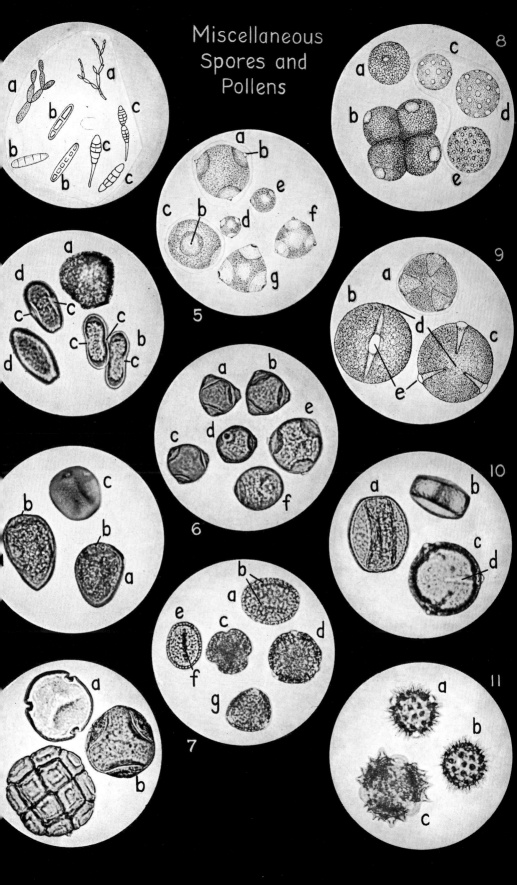

Miscellaneous
Spores and
Pollens

PLATE 16–15 *(Continued)*

but unrelated botanically, to the above pollens. It is also very much like the pollen of beefwood, or Australian pine (Casuarina), except that the latter is much larger—32 microns. Note the triangular equatorial outline as compared with that of hackberry pollen. The grains collapse in very irregular fashion. See also 6, *a, b,* below.

6. Photomicrographs of unrelated pollens having three pores with collars.

a and *b.* Two grains of bayberry pollen showing the same characteristic triangular equatorial outline and protruding pores as in 5, *g,* above. Compare these with the slightly smaller birch grains, *c* and *d,* which have a more circular equatorial outline and less prominent pores.

c. Note that in profile the collars of birch pollen appear more curved than those of bayberry. See also Plate 16–4.

d. Birch grain in a semipolar position allowing face view of one pore.

e and *f.* Grains of hackberry pollen (28 microns), larger than birch or bayberry and with cell contents decidedly more granular. See drawings 5, *a–c,* above.

7. Insect-borne pollens of the olive family (Oleaceae), of which ash (Plate 16–6) is also a member.

a–d. Photomicrographs of privet (*Ligustrum vulgare* L.) pollen grains.

a. Dry, unexpanded grain, mounted in oil, in meridional position, showing two of its three folded furrows (*b*) and coarsely reticulate texture of the exine. The perimeter appears as if "beaded."

c. Dry privet grain in the polar position showing shrinkage by infolding at the furrows. Compare with an expanded grain, *d.*

d. Expanded grain in polar position, equatorial section showing three small germ pores (occasionally four are seen). Equatorial diameter: 32 microns.

e–g. Photomicrographs of olive (*Olea europaea* L.) pollen grains.

e. Dry, unexpanded grain, mounted in oil, in meridional position, showing one of the three furrows (*f*) and reticulate exine with beaded edge as in privet above.

g. Grain expanded, polar position, equatorial section, showing the thin exine of the furrows. Equatorial diameter: 25 microns.

8. Drawings of pollens of cattails (Typha), and Chenopodiales. These two groups are entirely unrelated.

a. Expanded and stained grains of narrow-leaved cattails (*Typha angustifolia* L.). The size is variable, 19 to 27 microns in longest diameter, mostly 20. Collapsed grains are irregular in shape. The single pore is difficult to see even on a stained grain except on the proximal surface. In this species the grains are single, not in tetrads.

b. Tetrad of common cattail (*Typha latifolia* L.). Note the reticulate texture of the exine and the single germ pore as in the above species. The arrangement of the four grains shown here is the one most frequently encountered, but often they appear in other regular or irregular arrangements, even side by side in a row. The pores may be obscured on one or more grains in each tetrad.

c–e. Pollens of goosefoots and amaranths, supplementing Plate 16–13.

c. Sugar Beet (*Beta vulgaris* L.) pollen grain, expanded and stained, for comparison with pigweed and lamb's quarters (*d* and *e*). This is one of the very smallest of this type pollen grain—12 to 22 microns, average 20.

d. Pigweed (*Amaranthus retroflexus* L.). These rather uniform grains, averaging 27 microns, are fairly easy to identify.

e. Lamb's quarters (*Chenopodium album* L.); 18 to 32 microns, average 29 microns. The great variation in size makes rapid recognition of lamb's quarters very difficult. The small pores are not helpful since a number of the amaranths have small pores. See text, page 363, for a further discussion of pollens of these families.

9. Drawings of mesquite (*Prosopis glandulosa* Torr.) and beech (*Fagus grandifolia* Ehrh.) pollens. These species are not related.

a. Mesquite grain, expanded and stained. Although this plant is also a member of the mimosa family, the pollen grain is far different from that of Acacia. Both are insect-borne; they occasionally cause allergy.

b–e. Two grains of beech pollen, *b* in meridional position, and *c* in polar position.

PLATE 16-15 *(Continued)*

Average diameter: 32 microns, *d* indicating pole in each position, respectively.

e. Germ pore in the center of the long furrow and thus on the equator.

For dry pollen grains of beech, see field 10 below.

10. Comparison of pollen grains of beech family Fagaceae. Photomicrographs.

a. Typical dry, unexpanded beech grain, mounted in oil, meridional position, showing two of its three furrows.

b. Oak grain, dry, in oil. Note the similarity of the shrinkage pattern and contrast in size and surface texture of these two grains of the same family.

c. Beech grain, expanded and stained, polar position as in 9, *c*, above, but in equatorial section showing furrows only dimly. Note the heavy cell wall.

11. Photomicrographs of composite (Compositae) pollens.

a. Cosmos pollen grain in polar position showing the three pores and long sharp spines, focus on the periphery. Diameter, not including spines: 26 microns.

b. Cosmos grain, not in polar position. The focus is at the periphery, no pores visible.

c. Chrysanthemum grain in the polar position, equatorial section. Note the large, comparatively blunt spines. Diameter not including spines: 35 microns.

These two composite pollens with spines much more prominent than the spicules of the ragweeds are typical of the grains of other wild and cultivated insect-pollinated composite species.

The preceding plates of pollen producing plants were prepared by Oren C. Durham.

Aeroallergens

III. Fungi

WILLIAM R. SOLOMON, M.D.

Clinical sensitivity from inhaled fungal spores is now widely recognized and should be seriously considered in evaluating persons with allergy. Of the many thousands of individual types of terrestrial fungi, only a few dozen have been implicated in allergy. However, these common species alone are such prolific spore producers that their emanations usually outnumber the air-borne pollens. Fungi that produce allergenic spores are, in general, distinct from agents of the deep human mycoses. Thus, although knowledge of these fungi and their local patterns of occurrence is essential for the allergist, he frequently approaches them without prior training. This chapter introduces the allergenic fungi and provides help in the identification of air-borne spores and of the colonies developed on laboratory media.

FUNCTIONAL ANATOMY OF FUNGI

The basic structural units of all fungi, except unicellular forms, are branching threads called *hyphae*. These filaments have distinct nuclei and walls fortified with cellulose or chitin. Many fungi show cross-walls or septa at intervals along the hyphal filaments, each septum having a minute central pore. Other fungi have few or no septa, their hyphae being referred to as *coenocytic*. Hyphae in aggregate are termed *mycelium*. The vegetative portion of the mycelium often invades and enzymatically digests the substrate on which the fungus grows.* In some fungi such as the mushrooms and puffballs, another portion of the mycelium forms conspicuous leathery, woody, or fleshy reproductive structures or *fruiting bodies*. The term *mold* generally denotes fungi with reproductive parts of microscopic size. Occasionally, however, the inconspicuous vegetative mycelium of fungi with macroscopic reproductive structures is also designated "mold." All fungi lack chlorophyll, but many enjoy its benefits by living (as *lichens*) in fixed association with specific algae.

In contrast with the filamentous fungi, yeasts demonstrate predomi-

---

* The word *thallus* is sometimes used to designate the vegetative portions of fungi as distinguished from primarily reproductive structures. This term is also widely used in referring to algae and denotes any plant body which lacks a defined vascular system.

nantly unicellular growth. Many yeasts occur only as discrete rounded cells that multiply by budding or binary fission, the daughter cells separating completely. Other yeasts can bud successively in one dimension without separation of the daughter cells, which then form a chain, termed a *pseudomycelium.* Some fungi grow as yeasts under certain conditions and form hyphae at other times. It is clear that yeasts, such as we may culture from air, form a very heterogenous group. Since more than one of the classes of higher fungi has evolved such unicellular members, antigenic uniformity among yeasts, as a group, would not be expected.

The structure of the spore-bearing parts provides the basic features for classifying fungi. Asexual spores are of two basic types: *sporangiospores,* which are formed within closed, sac-like structures termed *sporangia,* and *conidia,* which are not. Some conidia are borne on hyphae specialized for their production as *conidiophores.* Certain fungi form conidia by simple segmentation of hyphae (*arthrospores* or *oïdia),* by the rounding of intercalary hyphal cells which then develop thick walls (*chlamydospores*), or by direct budding from hyphal filaments or yeast cells (*blastospores*). The spores of the more familiar allergenic molds are produced asexually. However, many air-borne fungal spores are sexual spores produced by two large and distinct groups, the Ascomycetes and the Basidiomycetes. It is well known that a single fungal organism may produce, either concurrently or at different times, both sexual and asexual spores. The reproductive structures that form these two spore types differ in form and are often referred to as "perfect" and "imperfect" stages, respectively. Often, however, these "stages" have been separately described in the past as different organisms and have been named as such. For example, the "red bread mold," *Monilia sitophila,* is known to be the imperfect (asexual) stage of the ascomycete, *Neurospora sitophila.* Similarly, the familiar *Aspergillus glaucus* has been shown to be the imperfect stage of another ascomycete, *Eurotium herbariorum.*

In addition, organisms which have morphologically different sexual stages and are considered to represent different genera may have imperfect stages which are morphologically similar. For example, several genera besides Eurotium have species of Aspergillus as imperfect stages. Obviously, the present classification of imperfect fungi, based on structure alone, does not necessarily reflect actual genetic relationships. Because of this, species of imperfect fungi with similar asexual reproductive structures are often grouped as "form genera." These, in turn, may be grouped into "form families," "form orders," and so forth, which are helpful categories, but lack some of the usual significance of natural taxonomic groupings.

CLASSIFICATION OF FUNGI

Four major groups among the fungi are of particular interest to allergists: the classes Zygomycetes, Ascomycetes, Basidiomycetes, and the "form class" Fungi Imperfecti or Deuteromycetes. Several excellent texts present in detail the structural bases for subgroups within these classes.[1-4]

Zygomycetes*

This class, which includes the bread molds and fly fungi, comprises mostly terrestrial forms. The production of a sexual resting cell, or *zygospore*, is a typical feature of this class. More readily observed are the asexual spores, which are sporangiospores or conidia. Several members of this class show especially broad hyphae and, in some, the hyphal septa are infrequent or absent; some zygomycetes show neither of these features, however. Mucor and Rhizopus, representing the order Mucorales of this class, are familiar to allergists.

Ascomycetes

In this class, sexual spores (ascospores) are formed within a sac-like cell or *ascus*. Frequently, eight spores develop in each ascus, and these may be shot out at maturity or extruded from the fruiting body (*ascocarp*) in a viscous fluid. Spores of the genus Chaetomium have been shown to elicit positive immediate skin test reactions. Ascospore formation is prominent in the cells of Brewer's yeast (*Saccharomyces cerevisiae*).

Basidiomycetes

Sexual spores (*basidiospores*) are produced, often in groups of four, upon specialized structures (*basidia*). Many of these fungi discharge their spores explosively. Such spores that are actively shot into the air are often termed *ballistospores*. Basidiospores usually show a short projection or *apiculus* marking their original point of attachment to the basidium. Two subclasses are distinguished: Heterobasidiomycetidae, which includes the rusts, smuts, and jelly fungi, and Homobasidiomycetidae, typified by mushrooms and puffballs. Clinical sensitivity to spores of rusts and smuts has been reported. Inhalant allergy has also been ascribed to spores of the dry-rot fungus, *Merulius lacrymans*.[5] The possibility that other basidiomycete spores may act as aeroallergens merits investigation.[6] Spores of rusts and smuts are shown in Figure 16–50 while Figure 16–51 shows several common types of spores produced by fleshy basidiomycetes.

---

* The present class Zygomycetes was previously one subclass of a large and heterogeneous class Phycomycetes. Although the term "phycomycetes" is still used, the originally defined class Phycomycetes has been largely discarded as a taxonomic unit. The class Oömycetes is another former subclass of Phycomycetes. Within this class, the downy mildews (family Peronosporaceae) and the potato late blight organism (*Phytophthora infestans*) are important plant pathogens. Since their wind-dispersed spores are often locally abundant, these fungi deserve further study.

Fungi Imperfecti

As previously described, this "form class" contains imperfect stages of other fungi, although many of its members have no known perfect stage. By definition, none of the imperfect fungi produces sexual spores. Four distinctive form orders are defined.

1. Sphaeropsidales (Phomales). Conidia originate on short hyphae within fruiting structures, termed *pycnidia,* that are usually globular or flask-shaped. The genus Phoma is most familiar to allergists.

2. Melanconiales. Conidia are borne on cushion-like masses of hyphae (*acervuli*), which burst up through the surface of the substrate. Although members of this order are widespread as plant pathogens and saprophytes, none is, as yet, implicated in inhalant allergy.

3. Moniliales. This form order is the largest in the Fungi Imperfecti and contains most of the fungi which are known to be allergenic. Its members produce conidia that are not associated with pycnidia or acervuli.

4. Mycelia Sterilia. This small form order comprises about 20 form genera in which no specialized reproductive structures or spores are known. A few of these fungi are known to be infertile forms of ascomycetes or basidiomycetes; others are known only from the sterile forms considered here. Many additional fungi are unable to sporulate on various culture media although abundant hyphal growth occurs. **Note:** It is quite erroneous to regard such sterile colonies as "Mycelia Sterilia" without additional evidence.

GROWTH HABITS AND SPORE DISSEMINATION

Although fungi have colonized almost every possible habitat, the growth requirements of individual types are often remarkably specialized. All fungi, unlike some bacteria and actinomycetes, require elemental oxygen for growth; usually preformed carbohydrate is also essential. The vegetative parts of most fungi grow optimally between 65° and 90° F. At subfreezing temperatures, most types of fungi become dormant, but a few grow and sporulate well between 20° and 32° F. Extremely low temperatures are often well tolerated, but exposure to heat exceeding 160° F. is, usually, rapidly lethal. Most terrestrial fungi can survive prolonged drying; however, optimal growth generally requires a relative humidity exceeding 65 per cent. Even though the surrounding air is relatively dry, fungi may enjoy localized conditions of high humidity in deep shade, with condensation at cool surfaces and also in places where water seepage occurs. In addition, the metabolic processes of fungi and bacteria liberate free water.

Apart from effects upon spore formation, atmospheric processes profoundly affect the spore load of air. One of the most dramatic effects is the washout of particles, especially those larger than 10 microns, during rainfall. Simultaneously, however, many tiny ascospores and basidiospores may be shot into the air by processes requiring high humidity or free water. Other fungi produce spores in mucoid masses which are dispersed primarily by rain splash and dew. Numerous genera of fungi including Trichoderma, Fusarium, Pullularia, and Phoma produce these "slime spores." Spores of many fungi are merely blown from their naked attachments by air currents. Such "dry spore" liberation is typical of species of Rhizopus, Penicillium, Cladosporium, (Hormodendrum) and Alternaria as well as of the asexual spores of rusts and smuts. Commonly, the aerial concentrations of "dry spore" types rises with increasing wind speed. Many remarkable mechanisms of spore liberation among the fungi have been lucidly described by Ingold.[7]

Once a spore has become air-borne, its travel is largely determined by atmospheric motion, since small particles settle quite slowly. Air turbulence can disperse particles widely in the lower atmosphere. On sunny days, spores are carried aloft on rising masses of heated air, and Stakman has found "dry" spore types to be both numerous and viable at 11,000 feet.[8] After sunset this spore-laden air cools and descends toward the ground. The layer in which air mixing occurs and the height to which heated air rises are often limited, above, by *temperature inversions* (where warm air overlies cold).

Differences between the day and night spore populations at one point are well recognized. "Dry spores" of Cladosporium and Alternaria, as well as smut and rust spores, show peak levels in daylight when the solar heating is maximal and relative humidity lowest. During hours of darkness, ballistospores, especially those of Sporobolomyces and the agaric mushrooms, may be abundant, their concentrations dropping just before sunrise. Similar low temperature and high humidity are required for the discharge of many ascospores and help to explain their abundance in night air.

MOLD EXPOSURES—SEASONAL AND SITUATIONAL

The air is never free from fungus spores, but their numbers are fewest when the ground is snow-covered. In midwestern and eastern North America, sensitivity to the spores of Cladosporium (Hormodendrum) and Alternaria is especially common. These and some other "dry" spore types occur maximally between June and September, especially when hot, dry, windy weather follows periods of high humidity. Many mold-sensitive patients have especially significant symptoms during these months, the annual peak of severity often occurring in July. This typical seasonal pattern is a valuable point in the history and differs from that of pollinosis patients in that the most major difficulty occurs *between* the grass and weed pollen seasons in northeastern North America. Warm periods in early spring and those which follow a killing frost often sharply increase the atmospheric spore load. Therefore, highly mold-sensitive individuals can experience symptoms from fungus spore exposure at any time after the snow melts in the spring until substantial snow falls the following autumn. Persistence until well after frost has appeared is another point which helps to differentiate symptoms in these cases from pollinosis, although dust allergy and infection also can cause a continuation of symptoms in the fall. Also highly suggestive of mold allergy is the occurrence of symptoms with exposures to high local concentrations of spores (page 404). Of course, some patients are allergic both to pollens and to fungus spores, and it is more difficult to evaluate the etiologic possibilities by history alone in these cases. Furthermore, in frost-free areas, high air-borne spore concentrations can occur at any season without a distinct midsummer peak. Even in northern states spore concentrations of certain fungi, such as Aspergillus, Penicillium, Rhizopus, Mucor, and Pullularia, may show little annual variation or actually increase slightly during the winter.

Persons allergic to inhaled fungus spores also may have respiratory, or less commonly, gastrointestinal symptoms when they ingest foods containing fungi or their products. Cheeses, spiced meats, and fermented drinks are common offenders. Symptoms following modest amounts of beer or wine may be associated with mold allergy in some cases, but apparently not in others.* Occasionally fermented beverages that may be tolerated during the winter months cause acute symptoms when they are ingested in midsummer or during major pollen seasons. When ingestant sensitivity to fungus products is known or suspected, dietary elimination of potential food offenders may be beneficial. In general, patients are instructed to avoid the following foods:

All cheeses including cottage cheese,
   sour cream, sour milk, and buttermilk
Beer and wine
Cider and home-made root beer

Mushrooms
Soy sauce
Canned tomatoes
   unless home-made

Pickled and smoked meats and fish including sausages, hot dogs, corned beef, pastrami, and pickled tongue
Vinegar and vinegar-containing foods such as mayonnaise, salad dressings, catsup, chili, and shrimp sauce, pickles, pickled vegetables, relishes, green olives, and sauerkraut
Soured breads (e.g., pumpernickle), fresh rolls, coffee cakes, and other foods made with large amounts of yeast
All dried and candied fruits including raisins, apricots, dates, prunes, and figs
Melons, especially cantaloupe

Dietary mold elimination can be made more complete by eating only freshly opened canned foods. Leftovers, particularly meat and fish more than 24 hours old, should be avoided, and if hamburger is eaten, it should be made from freshly ground meat. Canned and frozen juices are also generally restricted. It is often worthwhile to follow such a restricted diet for five to nine days and then to challenge the patient with large amounts of previously restricted foods (see Chapter 10) to see whether symptoms are precipitated. When ingestant mold symptoms

---

* Many such patients lack positive skin test reactions to brewer's yeast although most commercial beer and wine is made using this organism alone, with elaborate precautions to exclude other fungi. Saké, a notable exception, is produced from rice by *Aspergillus oryzae.*

occur, there is merit in prolonged dietary elimination of those mold-containing foods which have been demonstrated to precipitate symptoms.

The spores of fungi growing indoors can cause perennial symptoms in mold-sensitive subjects. Sampling conducted in homes and factories has yielded especially Penicillium, Aspergillus, Rhizopus, and Mucor.[9] Favored sites for domestic mold growth include vegetable containers, refrigerator drip trays, garbage pails, house plants, and planters, as well as sinks and laundry areas. Most organic substrates, such as wool carpeting and food-stained upholstery, are readily colonized. Cellulose-splitting organisms (e.g., Chaetomium) grow well on wallpaper, kapok, and cotton fibers. Foam rubber in bedding and furniture may be heavily contaminated after several years of use, showing that high humidity and moisture condensation can foster growth where nutrients are limited. Wood-rotting fungi found in damp, older frame buildings may rarely be important.[5]

Food storage and processing areas, farms, grain elevators, breweries, and dairies provide important industrial exposures to saprophytic fungi. Severe symptoms can occur while one is cutting grass, working with hay and ensilage, or being exposed to fallen leaves, mulch piles, and organic fertilizers. Symptoms associated with these exposures strongly suggest allergy to fungi. Spores of parasitic fungi—the rusts, smuts, and mildews—are encountered in especially high concentrations by agricultural workers. These spores are also abundant, along with those of Alternaria, Cladosporium and Helminthosporium, plant debris, and arthropod remnants, in grain mill dust.[10] Farmers and grain handlers often report that symptoms follow exposure to this material, and extracts of grain mill dust often elicit positive skin reactions in these patients.*

Mold avoidance procedures often are imperative for sensitive subjects. When activities known to entail mold spore exposure must be performed, wearing a double layer of surgical masks or a commercial dust mask can lower the number of particles inhaled. Where indoor mold growth is suspected, the type and extent of contamination often can be estimated by exposing open culture plates for 10 or 20 minutes. (Suitable media are discussed on page 432.) To eradicate indoor fungi, known sources and favored substrates must first be eliminated. Moisture condensation may be prevented by use of an electric dehumidifier which must be emptied frequently. When less refined means can be used, a cloth sack containing two or three pounds of calcium chloride may be suspended above a pail to collect drippings from the sack. Several of these bags can help to dry a damp basement. To decontaminate walls and ceilings, Zephiran is especially useful. Four ounces of commercial Zephiran (available as "Roccal") are added to four gallons of water.

---

* Skin tests to some grain mill dusts may show false-positive reactions caused by irritating substances contained in the extracts. The results of control tests, made on normal subjects, should be carefully observed.

After careful mixing, the solution is applied to the surface to be treated with a large brush or forced air sprayer, until it is thoroughly wet. Heavily contaminated areas should be re-treated in one week. If it is applied in this way, Zephiran usually prevents mold regrowth for two or three months. Small rooms and closets may also be decontaminated if wide-mouthed jars containing two ounces of paraformaldehyde crystals are left open inside of them for several days. Areas so treated must be thoroughly ventilated prior to re-use.

STUDY OF FUNGI IN AIR

The spore content of air is studied by identifying colonies produced on exposed laboratory media and by microscopic examination of deposited particles. Many ascospores and basidiospores may be identified as such although they fail to produce distinctive growth on artificial media. In general, the common fungi which are *now* known to produce allergenic spores form identifiable colonies in culture, permitting standard mold surveys to utilize this method. Sterile 100 millimeter Petri dishes containing suitable media are opened and exposed for periods up to 15 minutes, then covered, inverted, and kept at room temperature and at high humidity. After four to seven days, colonies are identified, and the number of each type is recorded. When many small colonies occur, counting is facilitated if the plate is placed upon a background divided into small squares.

Colonies often can be classified according to genera by their gross appearance alone. Finer details may be observed, when this is necessary for identification, by microscopic examination with a low power objective and transmitted light. Characteristic spore-bearing structures generally appear first in the older, central portions of colonies and may be difficult to observe. When primary growth cannot be directly identified, examination of slide cultures is helpful.* Many fungi produce crystalline

---

* Squares of sterile nutrient agar are cut from a Petri dish, poured to a depth of 1 to 2 millimeters. The agar square is placed on a sterile microscope slide, inoculated from the unknown colony using a bacteriologic loop, and covered with a sterile 18 to 22 millimeter square cover slip. The slide culture is incubated in a clean container at high relative humidity. Hyphae growing out from the agar onto adjacent glass surfaces are then observed microscopically. Identification may be facilitated by mounting and staining the culture using lactophenol-cotton blue. Lactophenol is a mounting fluid with good optical properties for microscopic fungi. To prepare it, combine 20 milliliters of 85 per cent lactic acid solution, 40 milliliters glycerol, and 20 milliliters distilled water. Twenty grams of phenol crystals are dissolved in this mixture with gentle heating. Staining of the mounted molds is effected by prior addition of 50 milligrams of cotton blue (aniline blue) to the lactophenol mixture. However, for dark hyphae and spores, a mounting fluid without cotton blue is preferred. Mounts must be made with caution to prevent disruption of fragile spore-bearing parts. The slide and cover slip are gently separated and each mounted individually so that two preparations result from each slide culture. To eliminate air bubbles, a drop of propanol is applied to the culture and allowed to evaporate partially before the lactophenol is added. The useful life of such mounts is lengthened if they are shielded from light and the cover slip edges are sealed with colorless nail polish.

metabolic products that may be mistaken for spores, and growing hyphae can carry these crystals, as well as agar fragments, for several millimeters. Care is also needed, when examining mounted cultures, to avoid mistaking air bubbles for spores. Dry cultures offer an additional source of error since droplets of water, which form on the hyphae, may be misinterpreted as spore clusters.

The processes governing deposition of air-borne particles, discussed in Chapter 16-I, must be considered in evaluating fungus spore and colony counts. As with pollens, the heavier particles are preferentially deposited upon open culture plates and gravity slides. Lighter spores are far more efficiently sampled by volumetric suction devices (see page 334). Gravity slide data for fungus spores are best reported as "spores/ cm.^{2} of slide surface" collected during a known period of time. Relatively few genera comprise the great majority of colonies obtained by air sampling in regions with temperate climate. Most surveys suggest that spores of Cladosporium and Alternaria are most numerous, but beyond this point regional differences have been prominent.[11]

FUNGI IDENTIFIED IN CULTURE

Although few allergists conduct continuous daily surveys by means of cultures, many take samples at regular intervals to monitor changes in the local fungus flora. Sampling in and around the homes of patients who present problems in diagnosis may help to define their level of exposure to specific air-borne spores. The exposure of culture plates also provides an objective test of the success of mold eradication measures. As an aid in identifying the fungi recovered during these studies, this section includes a "key" to the more commonly grown fungi as well as illustrations and verbal descriptions of most of these.

A Key to Air-borne Fungi Commonly Recovered in Culture

For those unfamiliar with the use of keys, a short explanation is necessary. This key consists of 45 numbered pairs of statements, each pair dealing with one or more structural characteristics of fungi. The members of each pair, designated "a" and "b," always contrast sharply with each other, and, in considering the two alternatives, one statement will be found to apply to the fungus to be identified, if it is included in the key, whereas the other will not. To the right of each statement is either the generic name of the fungus in question or the number of the next pair of statements between which a decision is required. It is always necessary to begin with 1 (a and b), which in effect separates (a) fungi consisting of single cells from (b) fungi with well developed hyphae. The choice between these two alternatives leads the user to pair No. 2 or to pair No. 4, respectively. Comparison of the appearance of the unknown fungus with the illustration of the genus derived from the key provides a useful check on the correctness of the identification.

1a. True hyphae not formed; single cells reproducing by budding or binary fission _____ 2
1b. True hyphae formed _____ 4
2a. Colonies red or pink _____ 3
2b. Colonies not red or pink _____ *Yeasts including Torulopsis,
Cryptococcus, and Saccharo-
myces (Figure 16–16 A and B)

3a. Colonies producing white "mirror deposits" on
covers of inverted Petri dishes _____ Sporobolomyces (Figure 16–16C)
3b. Colonies producing no "mirror deposits" as
described _____ Rhodotorula
4a. Hyphae 1 to 2 microns wide_____ Actinomycetes (Figure 16–16D)
4b. Hyphae more than 1 to 2 microns wide _____ 5
5a. Spores arising in sporangia (see Figures 16–17,
18, 19, 20) borne on elongated stalks _____ 6
5b. Spores not arising in stalked sporangia _____ 9
6a. Sporangia tubular, radiating from a swelling at
the stalk tip, enclosing lines of squared
spores _____ Syncephalastrum (Figure 16–19)
6b. Sporangia globular or pear-shaped_____ 7
7a. Tufts of root-like hyphae (rhizoids) (see Figures
16–18 and 16–20) present at or near the origin
of the stalks; stalks usually unbranched _____ 8
7b. Tufts of root-like hyphae (rhizoids) absent;
stalks frequently branched _____ Mucor (Figure 16–17)
8a. Sporangia globular; rhizoids arise directly opposite origin of stalks_____ Rhizopus (Figure 16–18)
8b. Sporangia pear-shaped; rhizoids arise between
points of origin of stalks_____ Absidia (Figure 16–20)
9a. Spores produced in fruiting bodies _____ 10
9b. Spores produced on hyphae not enclosed in
fruiting bodies_____ 13
10a. Fruiting body beset with numerous straight or
curled hairs; spores one-celled and brown_____ Chaetomium (Figure 16–22)
10b. Fruiting body without hairs; spores other than
one-celled and brown_____ 11
11a. Spores many-celled _____ Pleospora (Figure 16–52B)
11b. Spores one- or two-celled_____ 12
12a. Spores one-celled, colorless _____ Phoma (Figure 16–23)
12b. Spores two-celled, brown or tan_____ Diplodia (not illustrated)
13a. Spores borne singly _____ 14
13b. Spores borne in groups, chains, or clumps_____ 16
14a. Spores one-celled, borne above inflated colorless
cells _____ 15
14b. Spores two- or three-celled, the upper cells dark
and warted_____ Trichocladium (Figure 16–24)
15a. Spores jet black, oval, smooth _____ Nigrospora (Figure 16–25)
15b. Spores light in color, round, warted _____ Mycogone (not illustrated)
16a. Spores borne in distinct chains _____ 17
16b. Spores borne in clusters or slimy masses but not
in distinct chains _____ 26
17a. Spores many-celled _____ Alternaria (Figure 16–27)
17b. Spores one- or two-celled _____ 18
18a. Spores inconstantly divided by septa into two
cells _____ Cladosporium (Hormodendrum)
(Figure 16–28)
18b. Spores always one-celled_____ 19
19a. Spore-producing structures arising from swollen
hyphal tip _____ 20

* Smut spores also germinate to form sterile yeast-like colonies on some artificial media.

19b. Spore-producing structures not arising from swollen hyphal tip _____ 21

20a. Spore chains encased in delicate tubular membranes _____ Syncephalastrum (Figure 16–19)

20b. Spore chains free _____ Aspergillus (Figure 16–29)

21a. Spores budding to form branched chains _____ 22

21b. Spores not budding; chains unbranched _____ 23

22a. Colonies dark green to gray green, appearing black from below _____ Cladosporium (Hormodendrum) (Figure 16–28)

22b. Colonies light salmon pink, appearing light-colored from below _____ Monilia sitophila (Figure 16–30)

23a. Spore chains produced from phialides* always arranged in broom-like clusters; colonies usually green _____ 24

23b. Spore chains from phialides or similar structures borne singly and in pairs as well as in broom-like clusters; colonies not green _____ 25

24a. Colonies always dry and powdery; spore chains discrete _____ Penicillium (Figure 16–31)

24b. Colonies becoming mucoid with maturity; spore chains blending into mucinous masses _____ Gliocladium (Figure 16–32)

25a. Spores without thickened basal ring, produced from long, tapering phialides _____ Paecilomyces (Figure 16–33)

25b. Spores, each with thickened basal ring, produced by long or short truncated structures (annelophores) _____ Scopulariopsis (Figure 16–34)

26a. Spores one-celled _____ 27

26b. Spores two-celled or more _____ 39

27a. Spores produced by budding at many points along hyphae _____ 28

27b. Spores borne terminally on conidiophores only _____ 29

28a. Colonies white or cream-colored; hyphal cells colorless and thin-walled _____ Candida (Figure 16–35)

28b. Colonies blackening early or with age; hyphal cells becoming dark and thick-walled _____ Pullularia (Figure 16–36)

29a. Spores (arthrospores) produced by terminal segmentation of hyphae _____ Geotrichum (Figure 16–37)

29b. Spores produced other than by terminal segmentation of hyphae _____ 30

30a. Conidiophores unbranched _____ 31

30b. Conidiophores branched _____ 34

31a. Spores dark, produced by whorls of rounded phialides _____ Stachybotrys (Figure 16–39)

31b. Spores colorless; phialides single or absent _____ 32

32a. Spores borne in rows and rosettes, on short projections (sterigmata) of the conidiophore _____ Sporotrichum (Figure 16–38)

32b. Spores borne in masses, not separately in rows and rosettes _____ 33

33a. Spores borne in round mucoid masses; colonies low _____ Cephalosporium (Figure 16–40)

33b. Spores borne in loose nonspherical masses; colonies with much aerial growth _____ Fusarium (microspores) (Figure 16–45)

34a. Spores dark brown, disc-shaped; mycelium with prominent aerial growth _____ Papularia (Figure 16–26)

34b. Spores colorless or light-colored, globular or ovoid; mycelium low, spreading _____ 35

---

* Phialides (singular = phialide) are small peg-like or bottle-shaped structures from which spores are extruded or abstricted.

35a. Terminal branches of conidiophores swollen___ 36
35b. Terminal branches of conidiophores not swollen _____ 37
36a. Spores over 10 microns long, smooth, in clusters on swollen conidiophore branches _____ Botrytis (Figure 16–42)
36b. Spores less than 8 microns long, spiny, arranged radially about tip of conidiophore and its subterminal branches _____ Cunninghamella (Figure 16–21)
37a. Conidiophores with broom-like branching at tips; spores in mucoid masses formed from confluent chains _____ Gliocladium (Figure 16–32)
37b. Conidiophores branched subterminally; spores in mucoid balls from the first _____ 38
38a. Conidiophore branches distinctly whorled ___ Verticillium (Figure 16–41)
38b. Conidiophores branching irregularly _____ Trichoderma (Figure 16–44)
39a. Spores two-celled _____ Trichothecium (Cephalothecium) (Figure 16–43)
39b. Spores more than two-celled _____ 40
40a. Spores colorless, banana-shaped _____ Fusarium (Figure 16–45)
40b. Spores dark; round or elliptical _____ 41
41a. Spores round, warted _____ Epicoccum (Figure 16–46)
41b. Spores elliptical or fusiform, warted or smooth _____ 42
42a. Spores in whorls terminally and at septa of conidiophores _____ Spondylocladium (not illustrated; see page 426)
42b. Spores single or in irregular groups, not whorled _____ 43
43a. Spores prominently curved, with one central cell darker than the others _____ Curvularia (Figure 16–48)
43b. Spores straight or slightly curved with all cells of comparable color _____ 44
44a. Conidia with transverse and longitudinal septa _____ Stemphylium (Figure 16–47)
44b. Conidia with transverse septa only _____ 45
45a. Conidia arising directly from successive growing tips or branches of conidiophore; conidia over 40 microns long _____ Helminthosporium (Figure 16–49)
45b. Conidia attached to terminal conidiophore cell by short narrow cells; conidia less than 30 microns long _____ Brachysporium (not illustrated) (see page 425)

The following descriptions and line drawings treat the common fungi as they are recovered from air on nutrient agar media. Growth produced by these organisms in liquid cultures or on nutritionally deficient solid media may differ from that described in this section. The genera are arranged in the approximate order of their appearance in the preceding key; the sequence does not imply an order of prevalence in air or necessarily reflect taxonomic affiliation. Several well illustrated references are available to the physician seeking additional help in identifying these fungi.[12–15]

Yeasts and Yeast-like Organisms

Fungi with a unicellular growth form are recovered commonly from air and abound in orchards, dairies, and breweries. Figure 16–16 (a–c) shows representatives of three important families. Their growth

YEASTS

A   SACCHAROMYCES   C   SPOROBOLOMYCES

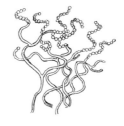

B   CRYPTOCOCCUS   D   ACTINOMYCETES

Figure 16–16

on agar is paste-like or mucoid and must be differentiated from growth of bacteria.* With media of neutral or alkaline pH, the drier, often wrinkled, colonies of actinomycetes (Figure 16–16, d) may be seen. These, unlike yeasts, exude a characteristic "earthy" odor and show, on microscopic examination, minute hyphae (1 to 2 microns wide) and terminal, often coiled, spore chains. It is worth noting that hyphae of all fungi and actinomycetes take on a basophilic appearance with Gram's stain. Most yeasts defy identification on purely morphologic grounds. Even the determination of those that form ascospores (family Endomycetaceae) (Figure 16–16, a) is exacting, and requires special media and stains. Among the white yeasts, species of Cryptococcus, Torulopsis, and Saccharomyces have been commonly recovered from the air. In the case of the common red and pink yeasts which synthesize carotenoid pigments, some further identification is possible. Those isolates which reproduce by budding only, in general, belong to the genus Rhodotorula. Other colonies may be grown, especially from night air, which forcefully discharge spores approximately 2.5 × 8 microns in size. When culture dishes are left inverted, these ballistospores form "mirror" deposits on the inner surface of the covers. Such colonies are assumed to belong to the genus Sporobolomyces if they are red or pink. Bullera, a close relative, forms yellow or cream-colored colonies which discharge their spores similarly. Both genera are leaf parasites and, when locally abundant in late summer, may play a role in certain cases of inhalant allergy.[16]

---

  * Inspection of the edge of a yeast colony with reduced illumination and 100 × magnification usually allows visualization of individual cells, each having two dimensions. Conversely, bacterial cells are not seen as discrete two-dimensional units on such examination.

Mucor, Rhizopus, Syncephalastrum, Cunninghamella, and Absidia

These are members of the order Mucorales which seem to abound in nature, but are recovered most frequently from air samples taken indoors. They rapidly overgrow and obscure other colonies and, microscopically, display rather broad hyphae. Hyphal septa are rare or absent in most species of Mucor (Figure 16–17) and Rhizopus (Figure 16–18), and this is a useful point in identification. Both Mucor and Rhizopus develop off-white hyphae that bear stalked black sporangia. In Rhizopus the stalks (*sporangiophores*) are unbranched and arise opposite a tangle of root-like hyphae (*rhizoids*) which penetrate the agar. The individual dark sporangia are just visible to the naked eye. Rhizoids are not present in members of the genus Mucor. Furthermore, the sporangiophores branch and terminate in black sporangia which are less conspicuous than those

Figure 16–17   Figure 16–18

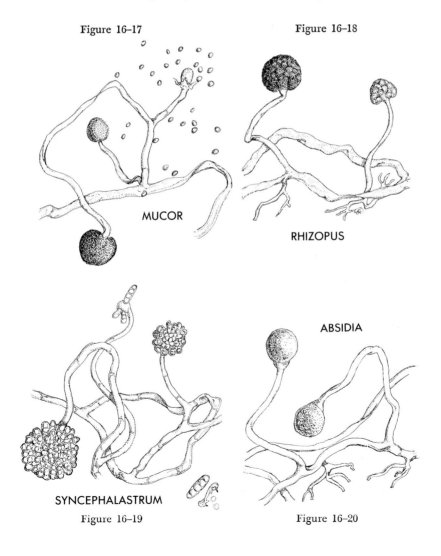

MUCOR

RHIZOPUS

ABSIDIA

SYNCEPHALASTRUM

Figure 16–19   Figure 16–20

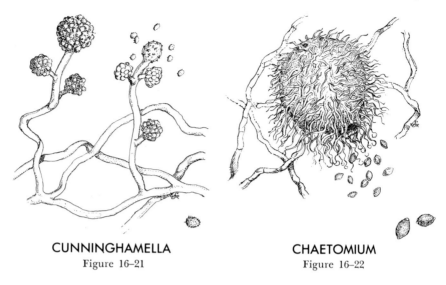

CUNNINGHAMELLA
Figure 16–21

CHAETOMIUM
Figure 16–22

of Rhizopus. In both genera, a bulbous extension of the sporangiophore, called a *columella,* projects into the sporangium. When the latter ruptures, as often occurs in mounted specimens, the columella remains intact (see Figure 16–17 upper right).

Syncephalastrum species produce light bluish-gray colonies which, as in Mucor, have branched stalks and no rhizoids (Figure 16–19). Uniquely, the tip of each stalk is swollen and bears many tubular sporangia, each containing a single row of gray, squared spores, 2 to 4 microns broad. In appearance, these clustered sporangia may closely resemble the heads of species of Aspergillus. The hyphae and sporangiophores of Syncephalastrum are prominently septate. Cunninghamella species form white to silvery colonies with abundant hyphae which develop at least some septa with age (Figure 16–21). Tenuous rhizoids occur and there are conidiophores which may have side branches, each of which is terminally swollen into a spherical head or vesicle. Round or oval, often spiny, conidia are attached to tiny projections from the periphery of each enlarged portion. Colonies formed by species of Absidia are obtained especially from the air about barns and silos (Figure 16–20). Typical growth is white or pale gray and a dense mycelium is formed. Small sporangia occur, each with a funnel-shaped base or *apophysis* at which it joins the sporangiophore. There are small rhizoids, but these develop at points which are not exactly opposite the sporangiophores.* The spores of species of Rhizopus, Mucor, and Absidia are round or oval, 3 to 6 microns in average diameter, and spiny or smooth.

---

* Unfortunately, some species of Rhizopus also show a small apophysis, and rhizoids in Absidia may be difficult to observe. Therefore, although Absidia is clearly defined by its zygospore morphology, the secondary characteristics cited above are not always adequate for identification of specific isolates.

Chaetomium

Certain members of this genus of the Ascomycetes grow rapidly on artificial media, forming green to brown or olive-gray colonies (Figure 16–22). Hyphal growth is particularly well developed about the oval fruiting bodies (*perithecia*), which are often just visible macroscopically. Characteristically, the perithecia show openings (*ostioles*) densely surrounded by bristles or coiled hairs. The lemon-shaped ascospores are usually some shade of brown and approximately 8 × 11 microns in size; a tiny clear area or a short protrusion may be seen at either end. Unlike most other ascomycetes, the asci of species of Chaetomium lyse as the ascospores mature, and the spores are extruded from the perithecia in a viscid fluid.

Phoma and Diplodia

Although the colonies of their members may be light-colored or dark, these genera of imperfect fungi produce round brown *pycnidia* which require differentiation from the dark perithecia of Chaetomium and Pleospora. Characteristically, pycnidia of Phoma (Figure 16–23) lack coiled hairs, and the oval or oblong conidia are hyaline, rather than dark. The conidia do not exceed 4 × 12 microns, and are exuded in slimy adherent masses which appear grossly as opaque droplets atop the pycnidia. Species of Phoma are of especially frequent occurrence in soil and as leaf parasites. Rarely other members of the Sphaeropsidales (see page 401) with long-necked pycnidia or with dark or two-celled spores are obtained in culture. Of these, Diplodia is perhaps most frequently encountered; here dark two-celled spores are exuded from pycnidia that are like those of Phoma.

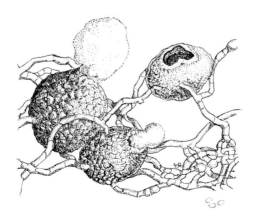

PHOMA

Figure 16–23

Figure 16–24

TRICHOCLADIUM

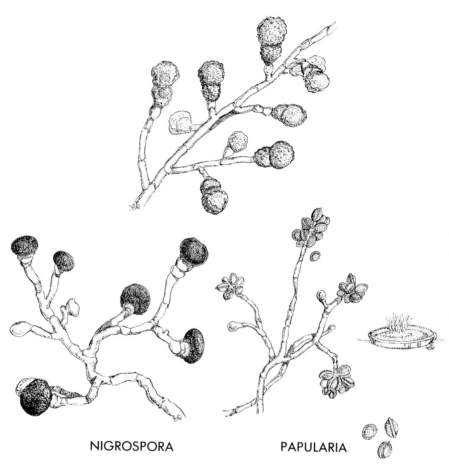

NIGROSPORA   PAPULARIA

Figure 16–25   Figure 16–26

Pleospora

This, like Chaetomium, is a genus of the Ascomycetes, but one whose members only occasionally produce perithecia from a dark mycelium in culture. In species of Pleospora (not illustrated), the perithecia are beaked and are free from hairs. In addition, the mature ascospores are forcefully discharged. Individual spores are brown, rounded at both ends and multicellular (see Figure 16–52, b), somewhat resembling small conidia of Alternaria or Stemphylium (Figures 16–27, 47). Interestingly, several form species of Stemphylium are known to be imperfect states of species of Pleospora.

Trichocladium and Mycogone

Trichocladium species form two-celled spores which arise singly, on short branches, from yellowish-brown hyphae (Figure 16–24). The terminal or upper cell of each spore is deep brown and coarsely warted whereas the lower is often smaller, smoother, and lighter in color. These conidia average 21 × 12 microns in overall size. Mycogone may appear similar to Trichocladium since the former shows warty, colored, unicellular spores (average size, 12 to 20 microns). These are borne on short hyphae above smooth, hyaline, inflated cells. Species of Mycogone also produce conidiophores with whorled branches (compare Verticillium, Figure 16–41), each branch bearing solitary one-celled hyaline conidia. The off-white colonies, tinged with yellow or gray, are a further point of distinction from the darker colonies of Trichocladium species. Grossly and microscopically similar to Mycogone are species of Sepedonium (not illustrated); members of both genera are parasitic on fleshy fungi.

Nigrospora and Papularia

Both of these genera produce dense white colonies, having aerial hyphae with considerable vertical development (note Figure 16–26) and tending to darken with age. The 11 × 15 micron black subspherical spores of Nigrospora, borne upon swollen basal cells, are striking and unmistakable (Figure 16–25). By contrast, Papularia produces clumps of brown lenticular spores, each 3 to 4 microns thick and 7 to 9 microns in diameter (Figure 16–26). The typical spore has a hyaline rim which, in side view, appears as a distinctive light band.

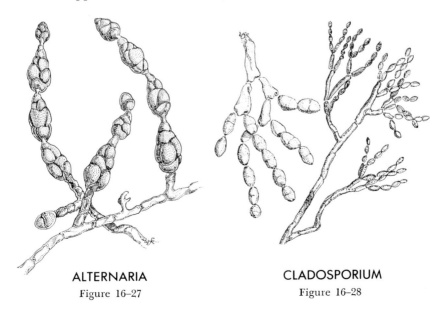

ALTERNARIA
Figure 16–27

CLADOSPORIUM
Figure 16–28

Alternaria

This is a ubiquitous genus; its members are common throughout the United States except for the Pacific Northwest. These fungi are chiefly plant parasites in nature, and maximal local concentrations usually follow the cutting of infected grain. Many species of Alternaria, however, grow rapidly in culture, forming light greenish-gray to greenish-black raised colonies which appear bluish-black from below. Young colonies often show concentric rings of light and dark growth; with age, their surfaces tend to become covered with white sterile hyphae. Occasionally an initially sterile colony may be induced to form spores by scratching its surface. Large, brown, tadpole-shaped spores are formed in definite chains which may branch (Figure 16–27). The spores have both transverse and longitudinal septa and one or both ends are narrowly tapered. Most mycologists now do not recognize Macrosporium, in which similar spores are borne singly, as a genus distinct from Alternaria. Colonies fitting this latter description are occasionally found and are generally slow to produce spores.

Cladosporium (Hormodendrum)

Members of this genus grow readily on most synthetic media (Figure 16–28). Colonies are olive or grayish-green to black and somewhat powdery except at the margins. From below, growth appears to be bluish-black. Intricately branched chains of smooth or finely warted, oval or fusiform spores are borne on upright branched conidiophores. Depending upon the species, the conidia may have average lengths of 4 to 18 microns. Individual spores often show thickening at the terminal points of attachment and a thin transverse septum may be present, especially in spores of older cultures. Species lacking septate spores were formerly assigned to the genus Hormodendrum but, at present, most mycologists (but not allergists) have abandoned this generic name. Cladosporium species often form the dominant growth on dead vegetation by overgrowing the pioneer saprophytes which typically are species of the genera Rhizopus and Aspergillus.

Aspergillus

Species of Aspergillus are ubiquitous, especially in indoor air. Various strains are utilized in the production of saké and soy sauce as well as in the manufacture of commercial citric acid. In culture, the mycelium may be variously colored, but it is never black or dark brown. In *Aspergillus niger,* the spores *alone* are dark, and the black spore-bearing heads on conidiophores, two-tenths to several millimeters in length, are easily seen against the white mycelium. The fertile branches of most other aspergilli are microscopic, and those of all species, when young, show terminal swellings which are covered completely or in part, by short phialides. These give rise to unbranched chains of round spores each 2 to 9 microns, which create a striking sunburst appearance (Figure 16–29). As the heads mature, this pattern is obscured, and the spore chains form tangled masses. The derivation of the generic name then becomes quite appropriate (Latin, *aspergillum*—a mop.) Many aspergilli can form perithecia in culture, and these perfect forms are assigned to the ascomycete genus Eurotium and to several closely releated genera.

Monilia Sitophila

This "red bread mold," is a prominent organism in bakeries and flour mills, but is not usually common in outdoor air which is free from industrial contamination (Figure 16–30). An especially rapid grower.

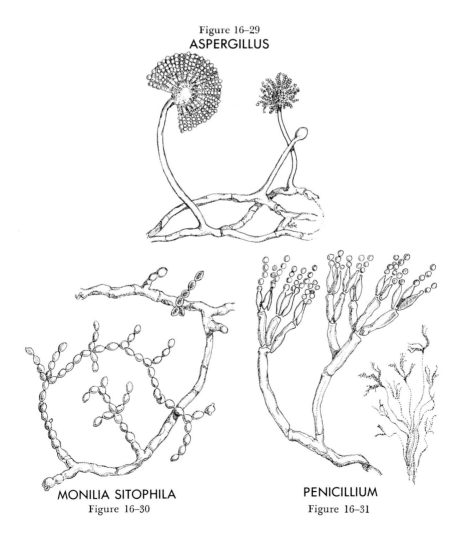

Figure 16–29
ASPERGILLUS

MONILIA SITOPHILA
Figure 16–30

PENICILLIUM
Figure 16–31

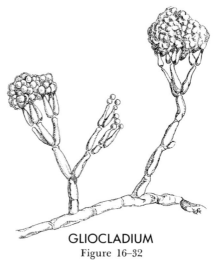

GLIOCLADIUM
Figure 16–32

this fungus can fill a Petri dish with its powdery light salmon-pink hyphae in 48 hours. Dry conidia occur, characteristically, in complexly branched chains which tend to aggregate and form irregular clumps. Other species of Monilia, forming light gray or tan colonies, may be encountered; some of these produce "brown rot" of fruits.

Penicillium

This extremely large genus of imperfect fungi is especially encountered in indoor air (Figure 16–31). Many of its members are utilized commercially to produce antibiotic drugs, organic chemicals, and cheeses, particularly Gorgonzola, Roquefort, and Camembert. It should be noted that inhalant sensitivity to the spores of Penicillium species and allergy to the antibiotic drug, penicillin (commerically produced by *Penicillium chrysogenum* and *Penicillium notatum*) are not related conditions. In culture, colonies are low, granular, and usually of a green color, the hue often changing with time. Short conidiophores bear one or more series of branches ending in *phialides* (see page 408); terminally, each phialide gives rise to an unbranched chain of 2 to 3.5 micron spores. The resemblance to a brush (Latin, *penicillus*) is often striking. Dense tufts or bundles of conidiophores (*coremia*) occur in some species as depicted in Figure 16–31. Certain form species of Penicillium produce *cleistothecia,** a feature which indicates their genetic link with specific genera of ascomycetes.

---

* Cleistothecia are ascocarps which resemble perithecia but have no opening. Spore release occurs only after disintegration of the fruiting body.

Gliocladium, Paecilomyces, and Spicaria

These genera have characteristics which often cause them to be confused with Penicillium. Gliocladium is frequent in soil and is said to be common on damp canvas (Figure 16–32). Ovoid spores (2.5 to 4 $\times$ 3 to 7 microns) are produced in chains which rapidly fuse and form adherent masses embedded in a slimy matrix. Grossly, young colonies are white or pink, and these may later acquire a dark green surface with droplets of "mucus." Colonies of the various species of Paecilomyces are white, pink, tan, or, quite commonly, khaki-colored, and are flat and dry (Figure 16–33). Unlike many species of Penicillium, frankly green colonies are not encountered. Microscopically, chains of round or ovoid spores, each 2 to 4 $\times$ 3 to 6 microns, originate from long tapering structures (phialides, often 10 to 18 microns). Two or three of the latter are often borne on a single hyphal branch, an arrangement superficially suggesting Penicillium. Some species of Paecilomyces also produce large solitary oval spores on short stalks. A related genus, Spicaria* (not illustrated), resembles Penicillium closely but its phialides are less compactly grouped and its spore chains more spreading.

Scopulariopsis

Members of this genus help to decompose many types of organic matter and often appear on cheeses and meat (Figure 16–34). They can

---

* The identification of fungi as Spicaria requires considerable specialized knowledge, the experts frequently disagreeing over the generic affinity of specific organisms.

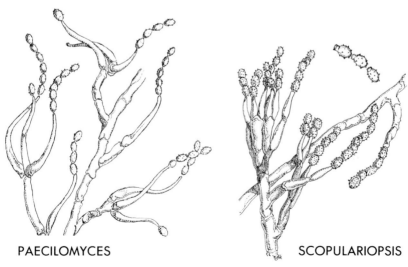

PAECILOMYCES   SCOPULARIOPSIS

Figure 16–33   Figure 16–34

be easily mistaken for species of Penicillium on microscopic examination. In culture, Scopulariopsis species are never green; the colonies usually appear to be white at first and become yellow, yellowish-brown, or grayish-brown with maturity. The ovate or lemon-shaped conidia are produced in intertwining chains by elongated cells (called *annelophores*) which arise both singly and in brush-like groups. Close examination of the conidia shows each to have a broad thickened ring at one end, marking its area of previous contact with the annelophore. Depending upon the species, the spores may be spiny or smooth and are 4 to 6 × 5 to 11 microns in size.

Candida

Besides being widespread on plants, members of this genus readily colonize the human skin, bronchi, and gut, and occasionally produce overt serious disease, termed *Candidiasis* (Figure 16–35). Extracts of *Candida albicans* have been shown to cause positive bronchial provocative tests in some asthmatic subjects; both immediate and delayed skin test reactions are also commonly seen.[17] The generic names Torula and Monilia, previously applied to this genus, are used properly now to designate entirely different fungi. On most solid media, species of Candida form white or cream-colored mucoid colonies. Both pseudomycelium (page 399) and true septate hyphae may occur, and both forms typically produce very large clusters of hyaline oval blastospores by lateral budding at many points. Typically, the hyphae are closely applied to the agar surface and mycelial growth often forms rays which originate from a central mass. On some substrates, single budding cells alone may be formed.

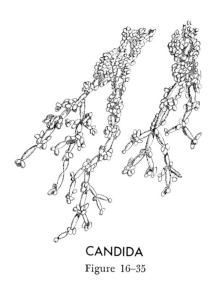

CANDIDA

Figure 16–35

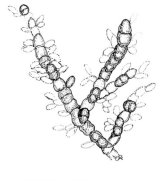

PULLULARIA

Figure 16–36

Pullularia (Dematium)

This genus is very common in soil and on vegetation and causes deterioration of painted and plastic surfaces under subtropical conditions. Young colonies resemble colorless yeasts or members of the genus Candida and are composed of slender pale hyphae (Figure 16–36). After several days, many of the hyphae darken and are transformed into chains of thick-walled cells so that colonies assume a dull black appearance. Both hyaline and dark hyphae bud off huge numbers of colorless or gray blastospores. In addition, the mature hyphae divide into pairs of dark rounded cells which may separate from the hyphae and become air-borne. Occasional isolates of Pullularia produce only masses of single and paired dark cells, without forming hyphae.

Figure 16–37
GEOTRICHUM

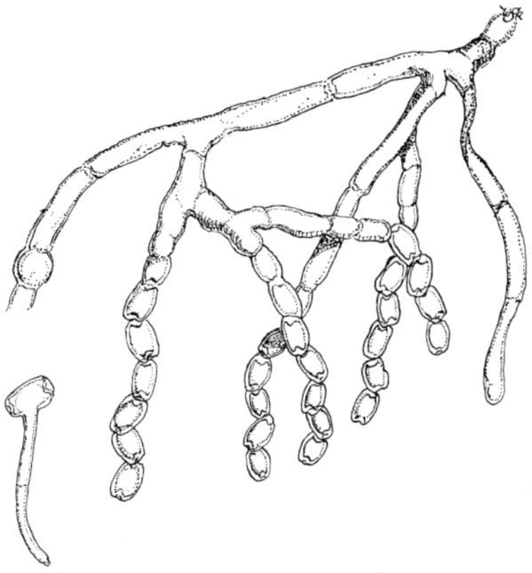

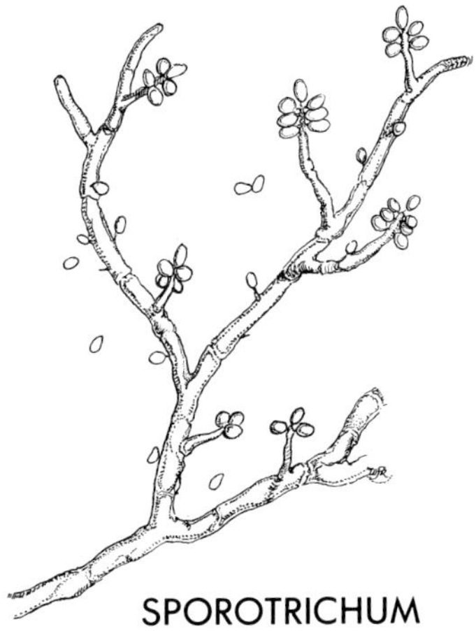

SPOROTRICHUM
Figure 16–38

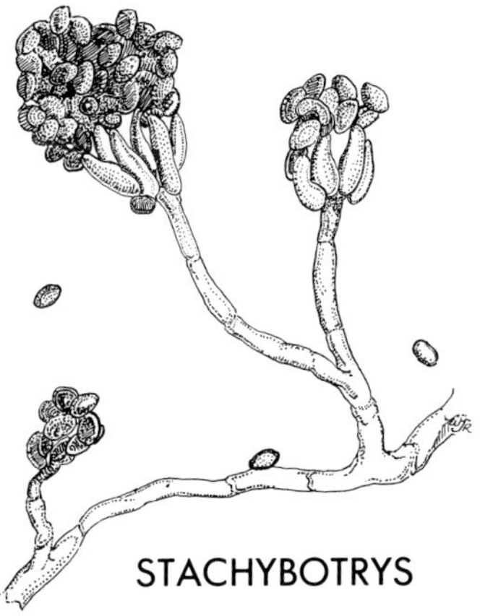

STACHYBOTRYS
Figure 16–39

Geotrichum

Hyphae which break up extensively into arthrospores are characteristic of this genus (Figure 16–37). The species most commonly encountered is *Geotrichum candidum* (synonym, *Oöspora lactis*), which is widely distributed in soil and frequently contaminates dairy products. On agar, this species forms low, white, spreading colonies that acquire a coarse powdery or floccular appearance with age. The individual arthrospores are cylindrical or barrel-shaped and measure 5 to 10 × 4 to 5 microns.

Sporotrichum

Although one species, *Sporotrichum schenckii*, causes human disease, most members of this genus are innocuous saprophytes on soil and plant materials (Figure 16–38). The mycelium generally spreads slowly in culture and is light in color; gray, white, or reddish colonies are common. Conidia are borne laterally and terminally on short conidiophores to which they are attached either directly or by short projections (*sterigmata*). Individual conidia are round or elliptical and are often less than 5 microns in greatest dimension.

Stachybotrys

Of the few recognized species, *Stachybotrys atra* seems to be especially common and is often found on rotting canvas, paper, and decaying wood (Figure 16–39). Young colonies of this species are white and very low-growing, but they darken rapidly with age. Microscopically, each conidiophore is erect and terminally branched with a whorl of plump phialides at the apex. Masses of dark brown or black slimy spores are produced by the phialides; the spores are 4.5 to 7 × 7 to 12 microns, smooth or rough, and often slightly curved.

Cephalosporium and Verticillium

White or pinkish colonies, which are at first flat and mucinous, typically are produced; these later acquire some short, dense aerial growth. Species of Cephalosporium (Figure 16–40) produce wedge-shaped spores at the ends of short conidiophores, where they adhere in globular clusters. Such a group of spores within its mucinous matrix may be mistaken for a single large spore on casual examination. Superficially similar in gross and microscopic appearance is Verticillium, the species of which show whorls of stalked spore masses, particularly where septa occur along the fertile hyphae (Figure 16–41).

Botrytis and Trichothecium (Cephalothecium)

Wooly spreading colonies are typical of both genera; those of Botrytis are gray or off-white, and those of Trichothecium usually are white, becoming pink with age. The unmarked spores of Botrytis are ovoid, often 10 to 12 microns long and borne on the short swollen branches of erect conidiophores (Figure 16–42). Colonies often produce black hard masses of hyphae (*sclerotia*). In Trichothecium, the conidia are pear-shaped, roughly 8 × 16 microns, and unequally two-celled (Figure 16–43). Although formed in sequence, they often remain grouped in situ and form rosettes or irregular clusters at the ends of the straight, unbranched conidiophores.

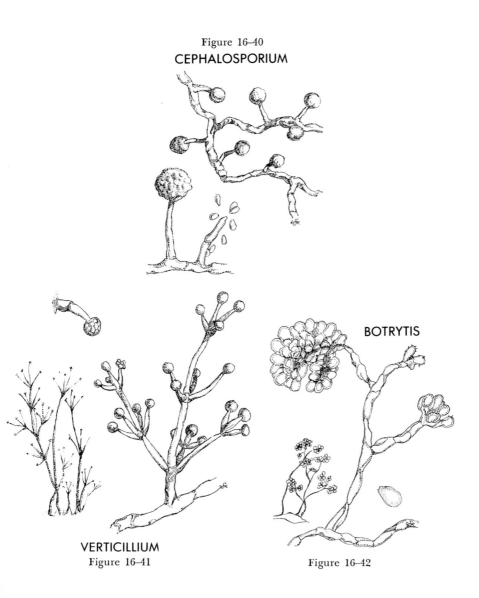

Figure 16–40
CEPHALOSPORIUM

BOTRYTIS

VERTICILLIUM
Figure 16–41

Figure 16–42

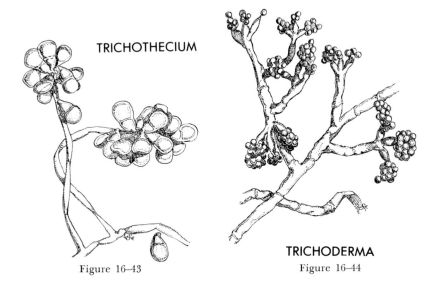

TRICHOTHECIUM

TRICHODERMA

Figure 16–43   Figure 16–44

Trichoderma

This genus comprises a single (or, at the most, two) extremely wide-spread and variable species, which may be found commonly in damp soil and on decaying timber (Figure 16–44). On most media, low, white, rapidly spreading colonies are formed, which in time develop irregular velvety patches of green, the color of the spore mass. The underside of the colonies and the surrounding media may appear yellow or tan. The conidiophores are complexly branched and each final branchlet terminates in a pair or triad of fusiform structures which give rise to globular masses of adherent spores. In the common species, *Trichoderma viride*, the conidia are round or oval and 2.5 to 3 microns in average diameter.

Fusarium

Hyphae that form masses of septate, hyaline, or faintly-colored, banana-shaped macroconidia are readily identified as belonging to this genus (Figure 16–45). The appearance of the spores is similar to that of many fusiform ascospores (see Figure 16–52, d). Colonies are often white or buff-colored and may secrete lavender or wine-colored pigments into the agar. However, many isolates of Fusarium species do not sporulate readily or form, unlike the more typical spores, masses of ovate or comma-shaped (2 to 4 $\times$ 3 to 6 microns) conidia, which are not distinctive. Many species also form round chlamydospores and, in some, dark sclerotia are produced. It is probable that conventional open-plate sampling has underestimated the actual prevalence of small-spored types of Fusarium. In the related genus, Cylindrocarpon, multiseptate spores are also produced, but these are more cylindrical and have more rounded ends than the spores of Fusarium species.

Epicoccum

Rapidly developing colonies with much white aerial growth are typical of this genus; brownish pigments often color the mycelium and diffuse into the agar (Figure 16–46). Round spores, 20 to 25 microns in diameter, which are typically brown, warted, and multicellular, are borne singly on extremely short conidiophores. The latter are clustered along rope-like hyphal strands forming masses termed *sporodochia,* and these appear grossly as black dots, often best seen at the margins of colonies. As with Fusarium, the production of spores by colonies of Epicoccum often is delayed and may require drying or a medium low in sugars.

Stemphylium, Brachysporium, Curvularia, Helminthosporium, and Spondylocladium

Although encountered less often than Alternaria, members of these genera are widely distributed and their spores may show distinct seasonal patterns of incidence. Species of Curvularia and Helminthosporium are especially abundant in subtropical regions. Greenish-brown to grayish-black velvety colonies are typical of the five genera, and viewed from below, all appear black. Spores of Stemphylium species have septa like those in Alternaria, but they are more definitely rounded without the elongated "beaked" ends seen in Alternaria, and they are borne singly (Figure 16–47). Species of Brachysporium (not illustrated) produce single, dark, oval spores, but these possess transverse septa only, forming three or more unequal cells. The spores of Curvularia also show two to four transverse septa, but unlike Brachysporium, these spores are distinctly curved or angled and frequently have a central cell which is larger and darker than the end cells (Figure 16–48). Among the largest spores encountered are the elongated grayish-brown conidia of Hel-

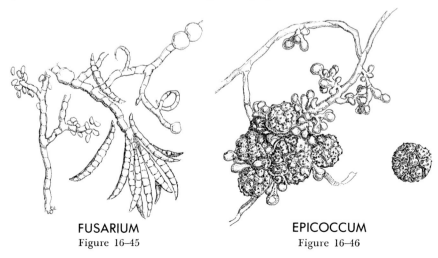

FUSARIUM
Figure 16–45

EPICOCCUM
Figure 16–46

Figure 16–47

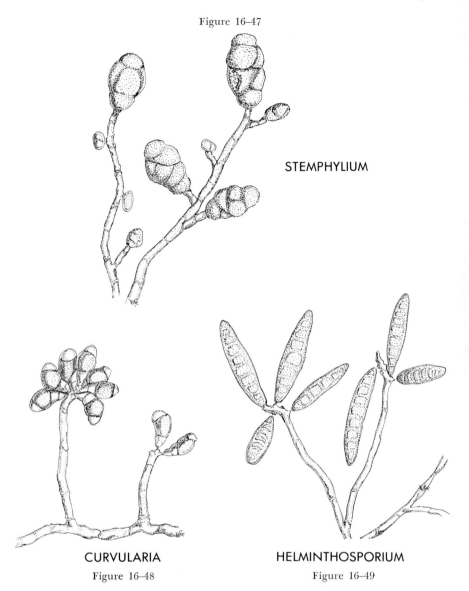

STEMPHYLIUM

CURVULARIA   HELMINTHOSPORIUM
Figure 16–48   Figure 16–49

minthosporium species (12 to 20 × 60 to 130 microns), usually with 6 to 14 transverse septa and tapering slightly at both ends (Figure 16–49). In some species, true septa are absent and the spores show a row of central structures (*protoplasts*) which have no connection with the outer spore wall. In some members of this genus, the conidia suggest those in Curvularia, being slightly curved and having pale terminal cells, but they are readily distinguished by their huge size. Spores in Helminthosporium and Curvularia are both clustered about the ends of the conidiophores. The dark erect multiseptate conidiophores of species of Spondylocladium (not illustrated), by contrast, produce conidia terminally and in lateral whorls, or rosettes, at the septa. Individual conidia are spindle-shaped, roughly 12×32 microns in size, and show two or more prominent septa. Members of this genus do not seem to appear frequently in northern states.

FUNGI IDENTIFIED AS ISOLATED SPORES

The microscopic appearance of many common spores is sufficiently distinctive to permit determination of the genus or, at least, the class of the fungus that has produced them. In the case of species of Alternaria, Cladosporium, Helminthosporium, Epicoccum, and others, the characteristic spores are formed in culture and have been treated earlier in this chapter. However, many other air-borne spores fail to grow on artificial media, and knowledge of their occurrence is gained only through identifying them by direct examination. Certain of these particles, including spores of the parasitic smuts and rusts, have been recognized as aeroallergens. The possible clinical importance of other spores which are often abundant in air, but do not grow in culture, merits further evaluation. Only a few of the most common types are described.

Rusts, Smuts, and Mildews (Figure 16–50)

Rusts (order Uredinales) are parasitic basidiomycetes with complex life cycles which may involve several different plant species as hosts and the production of several different types of spores. The rusts are of universal economic importance because they attack many major crop and ornamental plants. Basidiospores of the rusts are not distinctive, but *teleutospores** of the several genera are identifiable. Indeed, teleutospore morphology is the basis for the formal classification of these fungi. In the genus Puccinia, these spores are brown, roughly 18×40 microns in size, two-celled and often carry a short stalk (Figure 16–50, a). Teleutospores of Uromyces species (Figure 16–50, b) are brown, thick-walled, and unicellular. Distinctive spores of other rust genera that may be locally abundant have been illustrated by Cummins.[18] Rust fungi also produce *urediospores* in large numbers, but those of the different genera are similar (Figure 16–50, c). Generally, these spores are unicellular and are either diffusely pale orange in color or contain yellow or reddish-orange granules which impart a rusty color to the spore masses. Most urediospores are ovoid, and from 25 to 35 microns in length, and many have a narrow-waisted appearance. Minute spines on the spore surface are not always obvious; one or more pores may be apparent.

Smuts (order Ustilaginales) are parasitic fungi which form black dusty spore masses on their plant hosts, especially the cereal grains. That

---

* Teleutospores are thick-walled resting spores. They germinate to form structures which produce basidiospores.

RUSTS, SMUTS AND MILDEWS

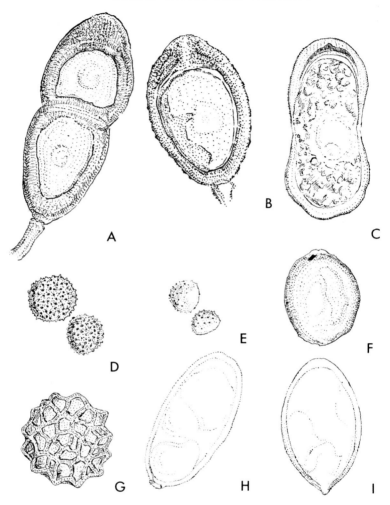

Figure 16–50

Figure 16–50. *A,* Teleutospore typical of the genus *Puccinia* which includes the black stem wheat rust. *B,* Teleutospore of the rust genus *Uromyces. C,* Urediospore typical of many common rust genera. *D,* Spore (teleutospore) of corn smut (*Ustilago maydis*). *E,* Spores of oat smut (*U. avenae*). *F, Tilletia foetida* and *G, Tilletia caries* spores are associated with stinking smut (bunt) of grains. *H,* Hyaline conidium of a powdery mildew, *Erysiphe graminis. I,* Spore of powdery mildew (family Peronosporaceae).

inhalant allergy to smut spores does occur, particularly in farm workers, has been strongly suggested.[19] More often, the dense spore clouds that form when smutted grain is cut seem to act as respiratory irritants. Where corn is raised, it is common to find the brown, round, spiny spores of corn smut (*Ustilago maydis*), each 5 to 9 microns in diameter (Figure 16–50, d). The slightly smaller spores of *Ustilago avenae,* which produces loose smut of oats and barley, show half their surface to be brown and spiny whereas the other half is paler, relatively flattened, and almost free from spines (Figure 16–50, e). (Spores of these and other species of Ustilago can be confused with the violet-brown spiny spores of true slime molds [Myxomycetes] that may be locally common in summer and fall.) Members of the genus Tilletia, which are the cause of stinking smut or "bunt" of grains, usually have spores that exceed 14 microns in diameter. Smooth, gray or olive, thick-walled spores are characteristic of *Tilletia foetida* (Figure 16–50, f), but in *Tilletia caries* the outer wall is beautifully reticulated and bears projecting spicules (Figure 16–50, g). These spores are teleutospores and are quite distinctive also in many other genera of the smuts; some are cemented together as specialized, brown "spore balls" (e.g., those of Urocystis). Excellent photographs of smut spores have been published by Fischer.[20]

Both powdery and downy mildews comprise important obligate plant parasites that produce no growth on artificial media. Powdery mildews (family Erysiphaceae) are ascomycetes, whose imperfect stages form dense layers of conidia upon their hosts. Each spore is approximately 10×30 microns in size and without distinctive markings (Figure 16–50, h). Black cleistothecia, which are often unapparent, are formed in fall and winter. The downy mildews are often locally abundant owing to extensive parasitism of grasses and cultivated plants, especially the grape and onion. The organisms are oömycetes of the family Peronosporaceae. The round or oval, smooth, hyaline conidia, each of which measures 14 to 18×20 to 24 microns, may show numerous vacuoles and granules that stain faintly with fuchsin (Figure 16–50, i). Skin sensitivity to the conidial stage of a powdery mildew, *Microsphaera alni*, has been reported, and both groups deserve further study.

Basidiospores

Hyaline and colored basidiospores, of which a few common types are shown in Figure 16–51, are widely distributed and are produced by the mushrooms, puffballs, and shelf fungi as well as by the rusts and smuts. Most of these spores are ovoid or elliptical particles without surface markings and show a projection or "apiculus" at one end; most can be recognized only as "basidiospores," although a few permit a more specific identification. Members of the genus Coprinus, including the common "inky-cap" mushrooms, have tan to dark brown, oval or barrel-shaped spores measuring 6 to 16 microns in length (Figure 16–51, A). Similarly shaped spores produced by shelf fungi of the genus Ganoderma are usually 6 to 7×10 microns in size (Figure 16–51, b). These spores, however, have a dull orange inner wall bearing many short spines that project into a thick hyaline outer wall. This distinctive appearance is completed by a funnel-shaped depression at the end opposite the apiculus. Spores, typical of the genus Amanita and of the genus Boletus, are shown respectively in Figure 51 c and d. However, similar spores are

BASIDIOSPORES

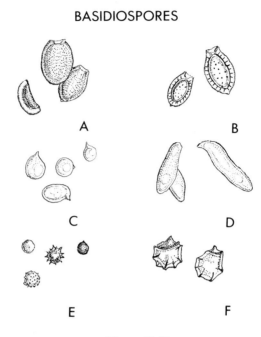

A   B

C   D

E   F

Figure 16–51

Figure 16–51. *A,* Dark spores of Coprinus sp. *B,* Distinctive spores of the shelf fungus, Ganoderma. *C,* Hyaline spores typical of Amanita sp. and several other genera. *D,* Elongate spores of Boletus sp. *E,* Spores of several of the puffballs *F,* Spores characteristic of Russula and Lactarius sp.

produced by representatives of many other basidiomycete genera. The puffballs generally elaborate round, more or less spiny spores that are 3.5 to 6.0 microns in diameter and lack a prominent apiculus (Figure 16–51, E). An additional type of basidiomycete spore that may be locally common is associated with Russula, Lactarius, and several other genera (Figure 16–51, f).

Ascospores

Despite the relative abundance of these spores, their clinical importance is still not clear. Only a few of the great variety of morphologic types are shown in Figure 16–52. Dark brown, smooth, oval spores (Figure 16–52, a) are formed by species of Sordaria, Xylaria, Daldinia, and others; similar spores that are covered with delicate gyrate markings are typical of Neurospora. Dark, many-celled spores (Figure 16–52, b) with transverse and longitudinal septa, are usually associated with species of Pleospora (see page 414). Unequally two-celled spores are seen in members of the genus Venturia, which includes pathogens causing apple scab, but occur also in other genera (Figure 16–52, c). Many ascomycetes produce "fusiform" ascospores (Figure 16–52, d) which recall the banana-shaped macroconidia of Fusarium (compare Figure 16–45).

ASCOSPORES

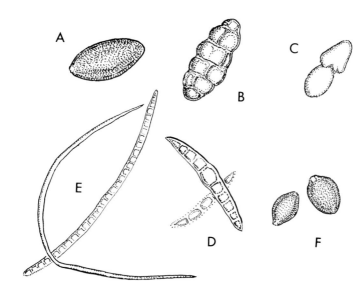

Figure 16–52

Figure 16–52. *A,* Dark unicellular spore of Sordaria. *B,* Multicellular Pleospora ascospore. *C.* Unequally 2-celled spore of Venturia sp. *D,* Fusiform spores typical of Leptosphaeria sp. *E,* Filiform ascospores. *F,* Brown lemon-shaped spores of Chaetomium sp.

A large proportion of these spores are thought to originate from species of Leptosphaeria; the presence of an enlarged central cell is especially common in ascospores of this genus. Extremely long and slender ascospores (e.g., 2 to 3 $\times$ 120 microns), termed "filiform," are often encountered (Figure 16–52, e); these may be septate, as in Ophiobolus which causes "take-all" disease of wheat, or they may lack septa as in Claviceps, the ergot organism. Brown lemon-shaped ascospores, which are typical of species of Chaetomium, may also be common in air (Figure 16–52, f). In color and size, they are similar to basidiospores of Coprinus, with which they may be confused.

FUNGI USED FOR TESTING AND TREATMENT

Present knowledge of the antigenic relationships among fungal spores of different genera is severely limited. In one group (the so-called Dematiaceae) including Alternaria, Cladosporium, Helminthosporium, Spondylocladium, and several other genera with dark hyphae and spores, skin test reactivity to the several individual members is said to be closely correlated. Many allergists have voiced the clinical impression that, within this group, the spores of species of Alternaria are the most potent aeroallergens. Within specific genera, the skin reactivity to spores of several individual species has often been similar, but this is not a constant finding.[21]* Therefore, it appears that a wide variety of fungi should be employed for testing mold-sensitive patients and considered for use in treatment. The fungi chosen should be those that are most common in the patient's locality. Practical considerations usually force the allergist to make the hopeful assumption that reactions to many or all members of a genus may be inferred from those elicited by one or two species.

In the Midwest and the Northeast, the most important genera appear to be Cladosporium and Alternaria, with Helminthosporium, Aspergillus, Penicillium, Fusarium, and Rhizopus of secondary importance. Species of additional genera, including Stemphylium, Phoma, and Candida, are common locally and frequently produce positive skin test reactions. The preparation of fungus extracts is discussed on page 522. Fungus extracts are apt to produce small irritant reactions, especially when used for intracutaneous testing.

Hyposensitization (see Chapter 6) is usually carried out with extracts of species representing several of the most common genera (Chap. 16). Extracts of additional fungi may be added if the results of air sampling and skin or mucosal testing implicate them in specific cases. Therapeutic "mixed mold" extract also may be made by empirically extracting the heterogeneous growth developing on large numbers of culture dishes exposed to the open air (see page 522). Agricultural workers frequently manifest clinical allergy to many types of fungi. Skin testing with extracts of smut fungi should not be omitted in these patients, and smut or grain mill dust extract often should be included in their treatment materials.

MEDIA FOR CULTURING FUNGI

A large number of media are available for culturing fungi. Not one of the preparations used approaches the ideal of a "universal medium," and each differs slightly from the others in the spectrum of microbial growth that it can support. Therefore, the interested allergist may wish to explore the potential advantages of several types. It is equally important that he be entirely familiar with one or two media that he uses consistently to study air-borne spores. Probably the two most favored media are potato (decoction)-dextrose agar (PDA) and malt extract agar.† Several useful modifications of these, as well as additional media, will be described.

---

* Although limited experience suggests that related species do often react in a similar way, no rule can be stated. Feinberg has suggested that *Aspergillus niger* is one specific exception and that reactions to it and to the other Aspergilli often differ.

† Potato-dextrose agar and malt agar are supplied in dehydrated form by the Difco Co., P.O. Box 1058A, Detroit, Michigan.

Potato-Dextrose Agar

This medium may be purchased as a dry powder. It is extremely hygroscopic and should be protected from moisture during storage. Approximately 10 grams of potato-dextrose agar is added to 250 milliliters of water and the mixture autoclaved in a cotton-plugged, flat-bottomed flask at 15 pounds of pressure for 15 minutes. Following sterilization, 15 milliliter portions of the melted medium may be decanted into sterile Petri dishes which are then re-covered and allowed to cool. When the agar has solidified, the culture plates are inverted and stored at 4° C. This medium has a pH of 5.6 and is useful both for general air sampling and for maintenance of fungus cultures.

Acid Potato-Dextrose Agar

Especially for indoor mold studies, in which Mucor, Rhizopus, and other genera rapidly overgrow conventional media, acid potato-dextrose agar (PDA) is useful. Potato-dextrose agar is dissolved in water and autoclaved at 15 pounds for 15 minutes as described. After partial cooling 0.8 milliliter of 10 per cent tartaric acid is added per 100 milliliters of the melted medium. (Addition of acid *before* sterilization will hydrolyze the agar.) The resulting pH of 3.5 restricts the size of all mold colonies and prevents growth of most bacteria and actinomycetes. A medium with similar selective properties may be readily prepared by adding 10 milligrams of the dye, rose bengal, to each 250 milliliters of nonacidified potato-dextrose agar. Since rose bengal is activated to a fungistatic form by ultraviolet radiation, media containing it should be protected from direct sunlight.

Malt Extract Agar

Malt extract is obtained from grain that has been allowed to germinate in water and contains many growth-promoting factors. This medium may be obtained in dehydrated form and is excellent for many fungi, although for some it is too rich to permit optimal spore production. Usually 12 grams of the powdered medium is added to 250 milliliters of distilled water; after sterilization, the mixture has a pH of 5.5. The addition of rock salt to malt extract agar produces a medium that has been proved to be especially useful for isolating species of Aspergillus from damp basements, barns, and grain bins. Malt-salt agar is quite simple to make up and is composed of:

Malt extract	20 grams
Agar	20 grams
Sodium chloride	80 grams
(technical grade)	
Water to 1 liter	

These components are combined and the mixture sterilized by auto-claving.

Modified Mehrlich's Medium

This medium has been used widely in surveys of air-borne fungal spores. Primary growth of many fungi is good, and since the colonies remain relatively small, identification of them is facilitated. Somewhat higher colony counts are said to be obtained with other media, however.[22] Modified Mehrlich's medium contains:

Malt extract	5 gm.
KH_2PO_4	1 gm.
Peptone	1 gm.
Dextrose	15 gm.
Sodium chloride	75 gm.
Agar	15 gm.
Water to 1 liter	

Protein Hydrolysate Media

These media are not recommended for differential fungal spore counts but have been quite useful for growing fungi that are to be used in making allergenic extracts (page 522). At present, however, the authors are not aware of any commercial source for such material.*

Particularly when work with fungi must be carried out with limited space and equipment, the disposal of cultures may produce heavy environmental contamination. This can be minimized if cultures are first killed by storing them for 12 hours in a closed container (e.g., a large wide-mouthed, fruit jar with a screw cap) with several milliliters of propylene oxide. The contamination of sterile dishes of medium during storage can also be prevented if these are kept in a container with propylene oxide. Before exposing such culture plates, they should be removed from the storage receptacle for at least one to two hours to permit the rather volatile chemical to escape.

---

* A dehydrated medium, designated "product No. 211" was previously marketed by the Mead Johnson Co., Evansville 21, Indiana. A very similar mixture that we have used comprises:

Protein hydrolysate powder, obtainable from the Mead Johnson Co.,			189.9 gm.
Dextrose	778.6 gm.	$FeSO_4 \cdot 7H_2O$	0.145 gm.
Citric acid (anhydrous)	5.6 gm.	Thiamine hydrochloride	0.0057 gm.
Sodium chloride	11.4 gm.	Riboflavin	0.0057 gm.
Calcium carbonate	3.8 gm.	Niacinamide	0.0380 gm.
Dibasic calcium phosphate	1.9 gm.	Ascorbic acid	0.1900 gm.
K_2HCO_3	8.5 gm.		

Fifteen grams of this mixture and 6 grams of agar are dissolved in 300 milliliters of water to prepare the final growth medium for sterilization and subsequent use.

REFERENCES

I

Techniques of Air Sampling

1. Magill, P. H., Holden, F. R., and Ackley, C.: Air Pollution Handbook. New York, McGraw-Hill Book Co., 1956.
2. Air Sampling Instruments. Ed. 2, 1962. Prepared by and obtainable from the American Conference of Governmental Industrial Hygienists, 1014 Broadway, Cincinnati 2, Ohio.
3. Field, F.: Measurement of weather in Medical Climatology. New Haven, Conn., Elizabeth Licht, Publisher, 1964.
4. Durham, O. C.: The volumetric incidence of atmospheric allergens. J. Allergy 17:79, 1946.
5. Gregory, P. H.: The Microbiology of the Atmosphere. New York, Interscience Publishers, Inc., 1961.
6. Harrington, J. B., Gill, G. C., and Warr, B. R.: High efficiency pollen samplers for use in clinical allergy. J. Allergy 30:357, 1959.
7. Hirst, J. J.: An automatic volumetric spore trap. Ann. Appl. Biol. 39:257, 1952.
8. Cryst, S., Gurney, C. W., and Hansen, E.: A method for determining aeroallergen concentrations with the molecular filter membrane. J. Lab. & Clin. Med. 46:471, 1955.
9. Andersen, A. A.: A new sampler for the collection, sizing, and enumeration of viable airborne bacteria. J. Bact. 76:471, 1958.

II

Pollens

1. Samter, M., and Durham, O. C.: Regional Allergy of the United States, Canada, Mexico and Cuba. Springfield, Ill., Charles C Thomas, 1955.
2. Hyde, H. A., and Adams, K. F.: An Atlas of Air-borne Pollen Grains. New York, St. Martin's Press, 1958.
3. Wodehouse, R. P.: Pollen Grains. New York, Hafner Co., 1959.
4. Wodehouse, R. P.: Hay Fever Plants. Waltham, Mass., Chronica Botanica Co., 1945.
5. Wodehouse, R. P.: in Am. Assoc. Advancement Science Publ. No. 17, 1942. (Both 4 and 5 are out of print but may be available in libraries.)
6. Coca, A. F., Walzer, M., and Thommen, A. A.: Asthma and Hay Fever in Theory and Practice. Springfield, Ill., Charles C Thomas, 1931.
7. Bianchi, D. E., Schwemmin, D. J., and Wagner, W. H.: Pollen release in common ragweed (Ambrosia artemisiifolia). Botanical Gaz. 4:235, 1959.
8. Tas, J.: Hay fever due to the pollen of Cupressus sempervirens. Acta Allergol. 20:405, 1965.
9. Roth, A., and Shira, J.: Allergy in Hawaii. Ann. Allergy 24:73, 1966.
10. Fly, L. B.: A preliminary pollen analysis of the Miami, Florida area. J. Allergy 23:48, 1952.
11. Metzger, F. C.: The climatic treatment of hay fever and asthma. J.A.M.A. 112:29, 1939.
12. Sargent, G. S.: Manual of the Trees of North America. Boston, Houghton Mifflin Co., 1933.
13. Walker, H., and Carron, R. F.: A contribution to the study of pollinosis in the Argentine Republic. A new plant allergen. Celtis tala. Dia. Med. 6:140, 1940.
14. Randolph, H., and McNeil, M.: Pollen studies of the Phoenix area. J. Allergy 15:125, 1944.
15. Walkington, D. L.: A survey of the hay fever plants and important atmospheric allergens in the Phoenix, Arizona metropolitan area. J. Allergy 31:25, 1960.
16. Tas, J.: Ailanthus glandulosa pollen as a cause of hay fever. Ann. Allergy 14:47, 1956.
17. Wodehouse, R. P.: Antigenic analysis by gel diffusion. 2. Grass pollen. Int. Arch. Allergy 6:65, 1955.

18. Payne, W. W.: A re-evaluation of the genus Ambrosia (Compositae). J. Arnold Arboretum *45*:401, 1964.
19. Serafini, U.: Studies on hay fever—with special regard to pollinosis due to *Parietaria officinalis*. Acta Allergol. *11*:3, 1957.
20. Rydberg, P. A.: North American flora (Carduales). Vol. 33, Part I, New York Botanical Garden, New York, 1922.

III

Fungi

1. Ainsworth, G. C., and Bisby, G. R.: A Dictionary of the Fungi. Ed. 5. The Commonwealth Mycological Institute, Kew, Surrey, U.K., 1961.
2. Alexopoulos, C. J.: Introductory Mycology. Ed. 2. New York, John Wiley & Sons, Inc., 1962.
3. Wolf, F. A., and Wolf, F. T.: The Fungi. Vol. 1. New York, John Wiley & Sons, Inc., 1949.
4. Bessey, E. A.: Morphology and Taxonomy of Fungi. Philadelphia, P. Blakiston Son & Co., 1950.
5. Frankland, A. W., and Hay, M. J.: Dry rot as a cause of allergic complaints. Acta Allergol. *4*:186, 1951.
6. Gregory, P. H., and Hirst, J. M.: Possible role of basidiospores as air-borne allergens. Nature *170*:414, 1952.
7. Ingold, C. T.: Dispersal in Fungi. Oxford, Clarendon Press, 1953.
8. Stakman, E. C., and Christiansen, C. M.: Aerobiology in relation to plant disease. Botanical Rev. *12*:205, 1946.
9. Van der Werff, P. J.: Mould Fungi and Bronchial Asthma, Vol. 1. Springfield, Ill., Charles C Thomas, 1958.
10. Harris, L. H.: Allergy to grain dusts and smuts. J. Allergy *10*:327, 1939.
11. Morrow, M. B., Meyer, G. H., and Prince, H. E.: A summary of air-borne mold surveys. Ann. Allergy *22*:575, 1964.
12. Funder, S.: Practical Mycology—Manual for Identification of Fungi. Ed. 2. New York, Hafner Publishing Co., 1962.
13. Smith, G.: An Introduction to Industrial Mycology. Ed. 5. London, Edward Arnold, Ltd., 1960.
14. Gilman, J. C.: A Manual of Soil Fungi. Ed. 2. Ames, Iowa, Iowa State College Press, 1957.
15. Barnett, H. L.: Illustrated Genera of Imperfect Fungi. Ed. 2. Minneapolis, Minn., Burgess Publishing Co., 1960.
16. Gwyn Evans, R.: Sporobolomyces as a cause of respiratory allergy. Acta Allergol. *20*:197, 1965.
17. Itkin, I. H., and Dennis, M.: Bronchial hypersensitivity to extract of *Candida albicans*. J. Allergy *37*:187, 1966.
18. Cummins, G. B.: Illustrated Genera of Rust Fungi. Minneapolis, Minn., Burgess Publishing Co., 1959.
19. Waldbott, G. L., and Ascher, M. S.: Rust and smut, major causes of respiratory allergy. Ann. Int. Med. *14*:215, 1940.
20. Fischer, G. W.: Manual of the North American Smut Fungi. New York, The Ronald Press Co., 1953.
21. Feinberg, S.: Allergy in Practice. Chicago. The Yearbook Publishers, Inc., 1946.
22. Rogerson, C. T.: Kansas aeromycology. 1. Comparison of media. Tr. Kansas Acad. Sc. *61*:155, 1958.

Chapter Seventeen

HOUSE DUST
AND
MISCELLANEOUS
ALLERGENS

HOUSE DUST

Allergy to house dust is regarded by many physicians as the most common cause of *perennial* allergic rhinitis. The symptoms of dust allergy vary considerably in intensity. A typical patient, perhaps a housewife, may present a history of sneezing, rhinorrhea, lacrimation, and mild asthma every time she cleans the house, beats rugs, or makes beds. She notices that she is somewhat better out of doors during the summer months and usually is troubled at night throughout the year. Often she awakens in the morning with nasal congestion even before getting out of bed—a symptom that distinguishes perennial allergic rhinitis from other forms of vasomotor rhinitis which usually bother a patient only after he stands up and his feet touch the cold floor. Such a dust-sensitive person hardly needs skin tests to confirm the presence of house dust sensitivity. Best patient cooperation, however, sometimes is obtained by demonstrating a positive skin test reaction to dust from his *own* home. On the other hand, there are also dust-sensitive persons whose histories are not nearly so obvious as that just cited. In addition, dust is a potential etiologic factor in any of the atopic diseases.

The House Dust Antigen

The house dust allergen probably is a specific antigen or group of antigens. It produces positive skin test reactions in sensitive persons and positive passive transfer test reactions, and when injected repeatedly into sensitive individuals in small amounts it appears to provide protection from further symptoms at a time when the patient is exposed to more house dust.

The dust antigen is believed by many workers to consist of degenerated cellulose. It is known that extracts of fresh cotton linters will not give positive skin test reactions in dust-sensitive patients. But as the cotton stuffing gets older and is broken down through the mechanical and chemical trauma of use, apparently a change takes place in the cellulose which converts it to the dust antigen. Immunochemical studies of house dust extracts have shown active fractions to be rich in carbohydrate but also to contain nitrogen.[1-2] It has been suggested that fungus growth products or even microscopic acarids (mites) are important sources of house dust antigens,* but this appears to be the case only in special circumstances.[3] After use and aging, bedding and furniture stuffing are potent sources of the dust antigen. Feathers used in pillow stuffing also would appear to be rich in the dust antigen, because dust-sensitive patients almost invariably react also to the extract made from old feathers.

Autogenous Dust

In some cases in which the history is suggestive of dust sensitivity but reactions to the skin test for dust are negative by both the scratch and the intradermal techniques, the allergist may direct the patient to obtain some "autogenous dust" from his own home. This can be procured by means of an ordinary vacuum cleaner and its attachments. A piece of clean, porous cloth (a scrap of sheet or pillowcase linen) is inserted at the point where the attachment joins the cleaner, or the cloth may be tied over the open end of the attachment. The machine should be run along the patient's mattress until the square of the cloth shows a collection of dust on it. Then the square is folded and placed in an envelope and labeled. Using another piece of cloth, the machine next is run over the stuffed furniture in the living room. Separate samples are obtained in this manner from the patient's kitchen, bedroom, and living room, and from all the stuffed furniture. In addition, a sample of the vacuum cleaner bag contents should be submitted as an overall sample of dust from the home. By testing the patient with dust from his own environment (page 64), it is possible sometimes to demonstrate positive reactions even when those reactions to tests with the stock dusts are negative. When an allergist utilizes *autogenous* dust, he is working with a conglomerate mixture with multiple possible antigens including animal danders, molds, and other antigens, so that he is not necessarily testing with a specific dust antigen.

An interesting example is that of an interior decorator who had his own studio containing many samples of cloth and fabric. This man gave a typical story for dust sensitivity, yet his reactions to skin tests with the usual house dust extracts were negative. However, when he obtained autogenous samples from his studio, a strong reaction was seen when he

---

* The mite *Dermatophagoides scheremetewski* is found in some house dust samples with as many as 500 mites per gram of dust. They have been found in specimens from Dutch, Swiss, English, and German homes.

was tested to the dust which he had collected from the floor. Upon further study it was found that this material contained mohair, which is prepared from hair of the Angora goat. Treatment with the usual house dust antigen probably would not have helped.

Even when positive reactions are obtained with stock dusts, additional testing with autogenous specimens sometimes is worthwhile; for example, it may aid in determining which specific pieces of furniture should be removed from the patient's environment. Furthermore, some persons are more impressed by positive reactions to their own dust than to stock extracts and thus are likely to follow the treatment program more carefully. Instructions for preparation of autogenous dust extracts are given on page 64. Material for scratch testing is easy to prepare, whereas the preparation of intracutaneous test extracts is sufficiently time-consuming that few allergists employ such tests liberally. It is also necessary to test a normal control group with autogenous dust extracts, particularly when the intracutaneous technique is used. Inhalational challenge tests also may be useful when there is uncertainty about the clinical importance of dust allergy (page 68).

Anti-Dust Program and Hyposensitization

If the allergist suspects house dust sensitivity in his patient and if skin tests confirm his suspicions, it often is worthwhile before starting hyposensitization to try an anti-dust program to see whether there is any change in symptoms. It is usually tried for a period of four to six weeks. By having the patient avoid exposure to heavy concentrations of dust, one sometimes is able to see remarkable improvement, thus confirming the fact that dust sensitivity actually is present. In a few cases there is complete and dramatic disappearance of symptoms. Such individuals need only to stay on a modified anti-dust program, and as long as they remain free from symptoms, hyposensitization is not indicated. Patients may, however, notice at best only partial improvement from the anti-dust regimen. This may be due to the fact that they have not gone far enough in carrying out an effective regimen; for example, the dust-sensitive asthmatic sufferer who spends an evening lying on an overstuffed, dusty sofa reading a book and then retires to a bed which is protected with anti-dust covers certainly is lucky if he does not experience asthma during the night. However, many patients react to such small amounts of dust that adequate avoidance is impossible. Nevertheless, it is felt that an adequate anti-dust program contributes significantly to treatment, since hyposensitization is less likely to be successful if the patient is unnecessarily exposed to large amounts of house dust. This implies that the dust avoidance measures should be continued beyond the trial diagnostic period, and in fact patients should be encouraged to maintain at least a modified program as long as they are having difficulty

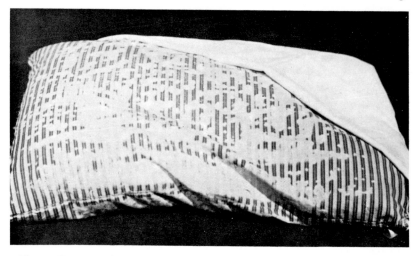

Figure 17–1. Feather dust. This pillow was covered for two years with an effective anti-dust cover. The patient was protected from significant exposure to the dust that he otherwise would have inhaled. A cover on the mattress is equally useful.

from dust. For the patient who reports that he has not improved after having tried an anti-dust program, it is a matter of judgment as to whether hyposensitization should be started. If reactions to his skin tests with dust were strongly positive and the history is at least suggestive, it usually is proper to undertake hyposensitization.

One of the quickest means for detemining whether or not a factor peculiar to the home environment is important in causing the patient's symptoms is to ask him to remain away from home over a weekend. Sometimes prompt clearing of symptoms is observed.

Instructing the Patient in an Effective Anti-Dust Program

A good anti-dust program is best attained if the patient is carefully instructed regarding all sources of house dust and placed on a program which can be modified after its effect is observed. The suggested regimen, though inconvenient, may provide relief whereas a less vigorous effort may bring no result. Once established, the program is not so difficult to maintain if it appears to be necessary.

If the patient has a room in his house which is almost dust-free and especially if he spends his sleeping time in that room, he may be able to prevent severe allergic symptoms. Also, it is helpful to point out the possibility that adequate rest, uninterrupted by asthma or a stuffy nose, may keep the patient's threshold of reactivity so high that he may be able to get by with fewer symptoms throughout the day even though exposed to normal amounts of dust.

It is best if the patient is spared the task of cleaning his own dust-free room, since the person who first cleans the room must usually experience a heavy dust exposure. If the patient has no relatives or friends who can prepare the room, he should cover his nose and mouth with several layers of cloth while working, such as a double layer surgical mask or a Martindale mask.* A handkerchief with strings tied to the corners may be used until a better type of mask is obtained. If necessity demands that he maintain his room, the patient should wear the mask during the daily cleaning activity. He ought not to use a broom or carpet sweeper and preferably should be out of the house for at least an hour after the room is cleaned.

A copy of "Instructions for the Avoidance of House and Feather Dust" (page 442) should be given to the patient. It is essential to personally review these instructions with the patient in detail, emphasizing points which are especially important in his particular home (as brought out in the environmental survey, page 36).

Questions often are asked about the pillow and mattress. Plastic covers are readily available in department stores, are relatively inex-

---

* Martindale masks and filters may be obtained from the Martindale Electric Company, Box 617, Edgewater Branch, Cleveland, Ohio 44107. (Price, 1965—Mask $1.00, extra filters 30 cents each. Minimum order: $2.50)

Figure 17-2. An effective room-level filter can be applied to a hot air heating system by placing a thin layer of fiberglas over the grating. Layer should be thick enough to catch the dust and thin enough to permit heat to come through.

pensive, and are impervious to dust. On the other hand, as compared with the heavier but more flexible covers provided by suppliers specializing in this field, the plastic covers are more apt to be uncomfortable (warm in summer, stiff in winter, and always slippery) and are more liable to tear. Alternatively, the patient could obtain a Dacron or foam rubber pillow (Figure 17–1). The latter is less satisfactory, since it has been shown that fungi may start to grow within the pores of the sponge rubber after a period of usage. This limitation also applies to foam rubber mattresses. It is important not to neglect encasing the box springs. The physician may prefer to test the effect of dust avoidance by having his patient sleep on an army cot for a few nights, thus removing mattress dust in a different way from the patient's environment. Instead of a pillow, a rolled cotton blanket in a pillowcase is used. Frequently laundered cotton blankets are also permitted. A fiberglas register covering may be held in place by the metal grill (Figure 17–2). Certain expensive bedroom carpeting may be covered over by tightly fitting sheets of thin plastic, and the patient should be advised to avoid permanent types of bedroom floor covering in the future. If patients are about to move, they should avoid old, hot air-heated houses, especially those without adequate filters on the furnace. The new house should be kept relatively bare. Padding under rugs, when necessary, should be made of rubber. When obliged to use a double-deck bed, the dust-sensitive patient should sleep on the top deck. Children's toys should be stuffed with sponge rubber or, preferably, materials such as Dacron.

The following printed form summarizes in one page the important points of dust avoidance:

Instructions for the Avoidance of House and Feather Dust

If you will carefully follow these instructions, you can eliminate much of the troublesome dust in your home. House dust comes from mattresses, pillows, box springs, overstuffed furniture, and such stuffed articles as toys and comforters which cannot be washed.

1. Avoid rooms which are being cleaned. If *you* must do the cleaning, wear a mask to cover your mouth and nose.
2. To prepare and maintain a dust-free room, follow these instructions:
   a. Take everything from the room, including (if possible) floor coverings, curtains, and drapes. Take everything out of the closets.
   b. Clean the room thoroughly—walls, woodwork, ceiling, and floor. Clean the closet. Wax the floor.
   c. Scrub the bed (or beds) and the metal springs, if any. (This must be done outside the room.) Set up the beds in the cleaned room.
   d. Encase the mattresses, box springs and pillows with air-tight, dustproof covers.* Bring them into the room and place them on the cleaned beds.
   e. This room should contain a minimal amount of furniture. Bare floors and windows are preferable, though washable rugs and curtains may be used. Avoid bed pads, comforters, heavy rugs, drapes, upholstered furniture, chenille spreads, toys, and knick-knacks.

---

    f. The room must be dusted daily and cleaned thoroughly at least once a week, using a vacuum cleaner, damp cloth, and oil mop. Do not use a broom or duster.

3. Keep the windows and doors of this dust-free room closed as much as possible. If you have hot air heat, keep the register in this room (and preferably in all other rooms throughout the house) covered with glass fabric, Styrofoam, or cloth.† The air filter in your furnace should be replaced at least twice a year.

4. Throughout the house clean all overstuffed furniture and rugs every day at first with a vacuum cleaner. Do not sit on overstuffed furniture or use feather pillows.

5. Avoid damp and dusty places. Stay away from attics, basements, closets, and storerooms. Avoid the living room whenever possible.

6. Dust-sensitive children should not have ordinary stuffed dolls or teddy bears. The major portion of their play should be in their own clean room with clean toys.

7. In summary, keep your entire home as dust-free as possible, especially the bedroom. Wear a mask when dusting or cleaning. Try to spend most of your time in the cleanest, barest rooms—bedroom and kitchen.

   * Zippered air-tight encasings are recommended for covering your mattresses, box springs, and pillows. Plastic covers of this sort are available at department stores, or more comfortable and sturdy covers may be obtained from suppliers such as: Allergen-Proof Encasings, Inc., 4046 Superior Ave., Cleveland, Ohio, or in Canada at 325 Devenshire St., Windsor, Ontario; Allergy-Free Products, 1431 N. Broadway, Springfield 1, Missouri; or Expert Bedding Co., 2454 N. Halstead St., Chicago 24, Illinois, or 17 East 46th St., New York 17, New York.

   † Because of the fire hazard, flammable materials such as cloth should not be used in places where metal becomes hot.

Oil Emulsions in Dust Control

The use of emulsified oil compounds, such as Dustseal‡ and Allergex §, has been advocated to help reduce the dissemination of dust from fabrics and blankets. Spraying this material on furniture and fabrics may reduce the amount of dust released into a room, but there may be some alteration of the fabrics in valuable furniture treated with oil emulsions. This form of dust control should be regarded as an ancillary measure and should not be relied upon as the chief means of treatment. Simply tacking oilcloth over the bottom of upholstered chairs and sofas also may help to prevent emission of dust.

Nonallergic Bedclothes

Cotton sheets are generally not allergenic. A starch filler or irritating agent is removed by frequent laundering. Cotton blankets with no

---

‡ L. S. Green Associates, 160 W. 59th St., New York, New York.
§ Hollister-Stier, Los Angeles, California.
Also, see list of dust avoidance equipment suppliers above.

combined wool are available.* Most allergists feel that there is no objection to the use of wool blankets provided that they are washed frequently and do not come in contact with the skin of patients with dermatitis (see page 450). We advise a wide fold of the cotton sheet over the top of a wool blanket so that it does not touch the face of the patient. Electrically heated blankets are useful in areas where cold weather is common if they are cleaned regularly.

VEGETABLE GUMS

Vegetable gums, especially karaya, tragacanth, and acacia, are important causes of allergic disease. The symptoms produced are usually respiratory when the gums are inhaled by a sensitive person, but any type of allergic manifestation may be brought on by the ingestion of gums. Routine testing to the vegetable gums may uncover sensitivity which might otherwise be overlooked, as sometimes it is difficult to suspect these ubiquitous substances from the history. Since there is not much cross-reactivity among the various gums, skin tests should be undertaken for each of them separately. The most widely used and clinically important gum is karaya. It also is sometimes called Indian tragacanth, since it is obtained from the gummy exudate of a tree which grows largely in India. It is used in a number of popular wave-setting lotions, and is very inexpensive. When the wave-setting lotion dries and the hair is combed, there is dispersal into the air of flakes of the dry gum. Inhalation of these flakes can cause symptoms. Gum tragacanth, quince, or flaxseed also may be used as the wave-setting agent in some hair preparations, but the usual spray lacquers are composed of inert ingredients and polyvinylpyrrolidone. Reactions to these chemicals are more likely to be due to primary irritation.

Because the vegetable gums are inexpensive, they are used as fillers to provide bulk weight in many commercially prepared foods. A home-made cherry pie is runny and difficult to serve. However, a restaurant pie which has had a gum added to the filling cuts evenly, and the contents do not run out easily. Vegetable gums also are used in commercial preparations of dairy products such as ice cream and ice cream substitutes in order to retard melting. Gums are used as fillers in some medications and as the active principle in many laxatives (see list). They also are employed in printing and in making adhesives. A complete list of ingestants containing vegetable gums is almost impossible to obtain, but some of the common foods and preparations likely to have gum in them are listed below. Knox gelatin and Jello brands do not contain vegetable gums. Adding to the problem is the common practice

---

* Beacon Mfg. Co., 300 West Adams St., Chicago, Illinois, or Pacific Mills, 214 Church St., New York, New York. Also, see list of dust avoidance equipment suppliers, page 443.

*Materials Which May Contain Vegetable Gums**
(Karaya or Indian gum, Tragacanth, Arabic or Gum Acacia) [4, 5]

Foods	Other Sources
Gelatin preparations (some brands)	Adhesives
Jelly beans, gum drops	Cigar wrappers
Lozenges	Laxatives—at least a dozen including
Chewing gums	the following:
Candy with soft centers	Karaba
Marshmallows	Karabim
Junket	Saraka
Ice cream (many commercial brands)	Muscara
Borden's and Fairmont's cream cheese	Imbicoll
Cheddar cheese (commercial)	Bassoran
Swiss cheese (commercial)	Kaba
Whipped cream (commercial)	Karajel
Frozen custard (commercial)	Baravit
Lemon custard (commercial)	Granaya
Ices and flavoring (commercial)	Toxelem
Pie fillings (commercial)	Fillers in pills, including Pyribenza-
Pie crust (commercial—some "ready	mine
mix")	Wave-setting preparations (contain
Cake icing (commercial)	flaxseed, karaya, and/or quince seed)
Charlotte russe	Emulsified mineral oils
Potato salad (commercial)	Tooth paste (several brands)
Gravies (commercial)	Mouthwash (including Listerine)
White sauce (commercial)	Dr. Wernet's powder
Shrimp sauce (commercial)	Dr. Lyon's tooth powder
Salad dressings (some commercial)	Denture adhesive powders, e.g., Dent-a-
Mustard (commercial)	firm
Diabetic foods (soybeans and almond	Stix
wafers)	Nyko
Wheat cakes, griddle cake flours (com-	Adherent powder
mercial)	Rouge
	Face powders
	Hand and face lotions

of a manufacturer using different types of gum in making a particular product, depending on which is most readily obtainable at certain times.

Tragacanth is a water insoluble gum obtained in southeast Europe, including Greece and Turkey. It is used in printing, sizing, paper-making, and candy manufacture, and as a filler in medicine. Urticaria, angioneurotic edema, and asthma have been caused by tragacanth.

Carobseed gum (locust bean gum) is found in seeds of pods from the carob tree. It belongs to the tragacanth gum group. It is used, like tragacanth, in sizing, paper-making, and calico printing. It also is encountered in foods and pharmaceutical products including antidiarrheal medications.

---

* Adapted from Gelfand, H. H.: The vegetable gums by ingestion in the etiology of allergic disorders. J. Allergy *20:*311, 1949; and Nilsson, D. C.: Sources of allergenic gums. Ann. Allergy *18:*518, 1960.

Acacia gum,* or gum arabic, is obtained from trees growing in the Sudan. The viscous property of this gum when combined with water is used commercially in sizing, as a drying powder in printing, and in hair dressings and pharmaceutical products. Sensitivity to acacia is due particularly to inhalation of the dried powder.

Quince seed gum is used in hair preparations, hand lotions, and as an excipient (filler) in medicines. Another gum, chicle, is included in many chewing gums; thus, patients who chew gum and have symptoms should be tested for sensitivity to chicle.

COTTONSEED

After cotton is harvested, it is processed by a cotton gin, which removes the long fibers from the small seeds in the cotton. Adherent to the seeds are short fibers, the "linters," which provide a source of allergenic material in mattress and upholstery stuffing, pads, and cushions. The seed of the cotton plant likewise is important to the allergist. The *water-soluble* fraction of the cottonseed may act as a potent antigen and cause severe reactions, particularly of the respiratory tract. Besides the occasional contamination of cheap upholstery and mattresses with this antigen, cottonseed meal has been used as fertilizer and also as feed for cattle, hogs, and poultry. It may be a constituent of dog food. Cottonseed flour is used in the baking industry as an ingredient in pan-greasing compounds. Some brown cookies, fried cakes, and fig bars may contain cottonseed meal or flour.

In recent years clinical sensitivity to cottonseed is seen less often since the rather expensive meal is used less now for fertilizer. We skin test to cottonseed only by the scratch technique. Careless injection of this potent protein substance could cause death. Purified allergens from cottonseed have been studied extensively by Coulson et al.[6] Cottonseed oil is not an allergenic hazard. In the processing of the oil, it is washed, bleached, and distilled at a temperature of over 400° C. When this process is completed, it is extremely unlikely that any undenatured water-soluble fraction would remain in the oil as an allergen.

FLAXSEED

This material, also known as linseed, is a potent allergen, too. Workers involved in grinding flaxseed into meal are especially at risk of becoming sensitized. The more common sources of flaxseed are listed below. Again, we perform skin tests with flaxseed by scratch technique only. There is cross-sensitivity between mustard and flaxseed so that one almost always sees a positive skin test reaction to both when there is hypersensitivity to either one.

---

* Gum Acacia and a pneumococcal capsular polysaccharide share a common antigen, as do tomato and a pneumococcal antigen.

Possible Sources of Flaxseed

Flaxseed or linseed is the seed of the flax plant. This potent allergen may cause allergic symptoms by inhalation, contact, or ingestion.

Flaxseed may be inhaled or contacted in:
  Cattle and poultry feed
  Dog foods
  Wave setting preparations, shampoos, and hair tonics
  Flaxseed poultices
  Depilatories (some brands)
  Patent leather
  Insulating materials
  Rugs and some cloth using flax fiber
Flaxseed may be ingested in:
  Roman Meal
  Uncle Sam's Breakfast Food, Malt-O-Meal
  Flaxseed tea
  Milk obtained from cows which were fed flaxseed meal
  Cough remedies
  Muffins
  Laxatives
Sources of flaxseed oil or linseed oil (of importance only in contact dermatitis) are:
  Furniture polishes
  Linseed oil
  Paints, varnishes, putty
  Linoleum (particularly dust from old linoleum)
  Bird lime
  Carron oil
  Printers' and lithographers' ink
  Soft soaps

CASTOR BEAN

Castor bean plants are raised as ornamentals in some warmer parts of the United States. The large pollen rarely is a source of allergic symptoms among agricultural workers. However, the seeds of the castor plant are used in industry. They are potently allergenic. The beans are pressed to obtain the oil which is used in laxatives and linoleum manufacture, and as a lubricating oil. The pulp and the hulls, which remain after the oil is squeezed from the bean, are called *castor pomace* and are used in fertilizer. If this powdered meal is blown in the air it can sensitize and cause respiratory symptoms in a significant number of exposed persons, often accompanied by urticaria. A colony of sensitized patients was found in the vicinity of a castor bean processing factory which contaminated the atmosphere with castor bean pomace.[7] Subsequently it was noted that workers sensitive to castor bean developed symptoms upon handling burlap sacks, which had previously been used to transport crude coffee.[8] Presumably, this was due to contamination of these bags with castor antigens, since both coffee and castor beans may be shipped from South America in the holds of the same ships. Another possibility is that castor and coffee beans contain a common antigen.

Chlorogenic acid appears to be an important allergen in green coffee bean dust[9] and in orange. It is said to cross-react partially with skin-sensitizing antibodies to castor antigen. However, the allergenicity of chlorogenic acid has not as yet been substantiated.[10]

Since castor bean pomace contains a toxin (ricin) as well as an extremely potent antigen, one should be careful to test only with detoxified materials such as can be obtained from a licensed allergy extract supplier. Because many of these patients are extremely sensitive, we perform only scratch tests.

SOYBEAN

Soybean belongs to the legume family (e.g., pea, bean, and peanut). The meal obtained after expressing the oil is used in foods for livestock and also for humans. Allergic symptoms of any type may be encountered in patients sensitive to soybean flour or meal. Soybean oil apparently causes no trouble. We test by the scratch method only. A list of sources of soybean follows:

Foods Containing Soybean Flour or Meal

Bakery Goods
    Soybean flour containing only 1 per cent oil is now used by many bakers in their dough mixtures for breads, rolls, cakes, and pastries. This keeps them moist and salable several days longer. K-Biscuits and several crisp crackers have soybean flour in them.
Sauces
    LaChoy Sauce
    Heinz Worcestershire Sauce
Cereals
    Sunlets—American Dietaids Co., Yonkers, New York
    Cellu Soy Flakes—Chicago Dietetic Supply House, Chicago, Illinois
Meats
    Pork link sausage, frankfurters, and lunch meats may contain soybean flour as a filler
Candies
    Soy flour is used in hard candies, nut candies, and caramels.
    Lecithin frequently is derived from soybean, and it is used in candies to prevent drying out and to emulsify the fats.
Milk substitutes
    Sobee—Mead Johnson & Co.
    Mull-Soy—Borden Co.
    Some bakeries use soy milk instead of cow's milk.
Ice cream
Joy Anna—American Dietaids Co.
Soups
Vegetables
    Fresh soy sprouts are served as a vegetable especially in Chinese dishes
Soy nuts
    Roasted and salted, these may be used instead of peanuts.

ANIMAL DANDERS

Allergy to animal emanations, especially those of cats, dogs, and horses, is well known by the public. Exposure to household pets is commonplace in American families. Of all the domesticated animals, the cat is probably the worst offender in causing animal inhalant sensitivity. A short-haired pet does not eliminate the hazard since, in addition to particles from the fur and skin, the animal's dried saliva can act as a potent allergen. Even though a patient fails to react to skin tests with animal dander extract, this does not absolve his own pet dog or cat. Many persons are sensitive to only one breed of dog, such as a collie or a scotch terrier, and they may not react to any other breed.[11] The same is true of reactions to cats. Thus, when animal dander allergy is suspected but the patient does not react to stock extracts, it is worthwhile to obtain some dander from the suspected animal for testing. This can be done by placing the animal on a newspaper, brushing him vigorously, and collecting the dander and hair which is deposited on the paper. The dander is particularly desirable for testing, and crude extracts can easily be prepared by the same procedure used for autogenous house dust (page 64).

Of particular interest in this area is the story passed among some patients that possession of a Mexican chihuahua dog would alleviate asthmatic symptoms. Investigation of several of our patients who purchased such dogs showed that skillful promotion had prompted the sale, and as suspected no effect could be shown by exposure to the small dogs.

It is best when evaluating the possible presence of sensitivity to animal danders to insist that the patient "farm out" his pet for two or three months while he is undergoing study. The house should be thoroughly cleaned after the pet has departed. This later may become a permanent "break" in which the pet is finally eliminated from the patient's home. In general, atopic persons should be encouraged not to have pets and certainly not to acquire new ones. An "outdoor" dog is less likely to cause trouble and may be permitted for cooperative patients not sensitive to dogs. A patient with inhalant allergy may at any time develop sensitivity to his pet, and if this occurs while he is receiving hyposensitization, the physician is likely to interpret these symptoms as resulting from the hyposensitization program. He then may begin to juggle the dose of antigen given the patient, and in this way the whole program is upset.

Occasionally horsehair is encountered in stuffed chairs, couches, and orthopedic mattresses. The dander contaminating these articles may share antigen(s) with horse serum. A course of tetanus toxoid should be recommended for persons sensitive to horses or horse serum, with a booster dose given at regular intervals. Patients allergic to horses also should be urged to discontinue horseback riding as a hobby.

Besides cats, dogs, and horses, a number of other pets and farm animals may cause difficulty, e.g., hamsters, rabbits, parakeets, cattle, hogs, and others. Urban dwellers may be exposed to the latter two allergens from the padding used under rugs or carpets. These pads may contain cattle or hog hair, a by-product of the meat-packing industry. Although the hair may have been treated with ozone, it still may be allergenic. Goat hair, either as mohair (Angora goat), cashmere (from Cashmere goat) or alpaca (from a Peruvian goat), can occasionally cause difficulty in clothing or furniture workers. Not infrequently animal dander allergy is occupational. Laboratory workers, veterinarians, ranchers, farmers, and furriers have experienced allergic reactions from a wide variety of danders. Scratch testing materials for unusual animal danders may be prepared as described above, with emphasis on collecting dander rather than hair. Allergy to human hair has been reported in wigmakers and barbers, but we have never seen an authenticated case.

Treatment of allergy to animal danders usually is carried out by avoidance and occasional symptomatic medications. Hyposensitization generally is restricted to occupationally related cases. Even in these cases, however, it should be employed only when necessary, since these potent allergens are prone to cause severe reactions. Accordingly, low initial doses are recommended (page 108). Although the patient's tolerance for the allergen usually increases, often he still may experience symptoms upon moderate or heavy exposures to the offending substance.

GLUE

Several kinds of glue are made from animals or fish. These glues may cause considerable trouble, particularly respiratory symptoms in sensitized persons. LePage's glue, a common household glue, is made mainly from fish, and fish-sensitive patients may experience symptoms either from inhalation of dried particles or possibly from ingestion of even small amounts of the material. In addition to the obvious uses for glue in woodworking, furniture joints, and book-binding, it also is found in sandpaper, in sizing for fabrics and paper, as a stiffener for wicker and straw items, and as sizing for carpets. Gummed labels and stickers may contain animal glue, but these glues are more likely to be prepared with vegetable gum. United States postage stamps do not contain fish or animal glues.

We use only scratch testing with glue, since deaths have occurred from the intradermal injection of glue extracts.

Most adhesives used in recent years are not derived from animal sources. These may cause contact dermatitis (for example, the rubber cement in footwear).

WOOL

Although some allergists feel that allergic reactions to wool are not uncommon, it is our impression that in the vast majority of cases intolerance to wool is on an irritant basis (both in respect to skin and respiratory tract symptoms). Microscopic inspection of wool fabrics reveals sharp, barbed fibers which would be expected to produce irritation. Regardless of whether it is acting as an allergen or irritant, however, patients who experience difficulty from wool should avoid exposure to it.

FIBERS AND PLANTS

Jute, which comes from a plant fiber grown in India, may be a source of allergy. It is used to make certain kinds of rope, burlap bags, carpet pads, and the underside of some carpets. Jute may contribute to the material which comprises the house dust antigen.

Kapok, which is also a fiber derived from tropical plants, is used for stuffing in sleeping bags, pillows, and cushions used in boats (because of its resistance to water absorption and resultant extreme buoyancy). As it ages and is subjected to the deterioration brought on by use and by fungal and bacterial growth, it becomes increasingly allergenic. Skin tests may show significant reactions. The practice of substituting kapok pillows for feather pillows was abandoned many years ago.

Pyrethrum is derived from a plant belonging to the composite family of which ragweed also is a member. Pyrethrum is used in insecticide dusts and sprays, which may cause inhalant symptoms. Although much of this difficulty may be due to irritation, some patients who commonly are ragweed-sensitive may have true allergic reactions to pyrethrum. Reading labels carefully will aid such persons to avoid this exposure.

Orris root is derived from plants which belong to the iris family. When dried and ground up, the powder exudes a delicate fragrance. It also has exceptional capacity for holding a scent; thus, it is used as a mordant in cosmetic powders. It would make an ideal base for powder and cosmetics were it not for the fact that it causes inhalant allergy in many of the persons who use it.[12] At present cosmetic manufacturers are aware of this, and the use of orris root has become much less common than it was 30 years ago. Orris root also may be found in tooth powders and pastes, shaving creams, bath powders, facial creams, rouges, perfumes, scented soaps, toilet waters, hair tonics, shampoos, lotions, lipsticks, and sachets. Brands of cosmetics which are advertised as being "nonallergic" or "hypoallergic" are generally free from orris root. No cosmetics are truly completely nonallergic, however, for rare cases of hypersensitivity might develop to almost any substance used in cosmetics. An allergy to orris root usually is manifested by asthma or rhinitis.

TOBACCO

Tobacco smoking per se rarely if ever causes clinical allergy. When one encounters tobacco intolerance, it usually is caused by chemical or mechanical irritation of the respiratory tract. Occasionally a certain type of cigarette causes allergic symptoms which are relieved when a different brand is used. The explanation for this lies in the fact that each kind of cigarette may contain a different type of compound to provide the aroma and flavor which is singular to that particular brand. Instances of apparent allergy to smoking tobacco may occur, however.

Most of the alleged cases of allergy to tobacco have been of an asthmatic nature. Handling of the leaves by workers in the tobacco industry has caused dermatitis. The possibility that tobacco allergy may play an important part in the pathogenesis of thromboangiitis obliterans is still a matter of dispute (page 480). The indictment of tobacco smoking as a contributing cause of other diseases grows stronger, but allergy has not been advanced as the mechanism. Because of respiratory tract irritation, we feel that it is undesirable for asthmatic persons to smoke. Skin test reactions occasionally are obtained with tobacco or tobacco smoke extracts, but the significance of these usually is too obscure to encourage this type of testing.

ALGAE

The universal distribution in nature of algae, especially of the green and blue-green types, and the finding that some patients have positive skin test reactions to algae extracts has prompted research into the possibility that clinical sensitivity to this group of plants exists. Bronchial mucosal tests with extracts of algae have resulted in wheezing in some individuals with positive skin test reactions. Further study in this area is awaited.[13-14]

INHALANT INSECT ALLERGENS*

The lower part of the atmosphere is substantially contaminated with insect debris in many parts of the earth, though it is difficult to identify the specific insect source of most of this material. Furthermore, routine skin testing of allergic patients with a variety of insect allergens has been found to yield large numbers of positive reactions.[15-18] One has to be on guard against irritant insect extracts, especially for intracutaneous testing, but even nonirritant materials give many positive skin reactions, which can be passively transferred. The significance of most of these reactions is uncertain at present, since it is difficult to make correlations with the clinical history when so little is known about aerobiological aspects of the subject. In certain cases, however, the clinical importance of inhalant insect allergens seems unquestionable. Table 17-1 summarizes the types and classifications of arthropods which have produced allergic symptoms by inhalation. An unexpected source of daphnia antigen is found in canary feed. Gel diffusion and passive hemagglutination tests show that different orders of insects share common

---

* Hymenoptera (stinging insect) hypersensitivity is discussed in Chapter 15.

Table 17-1. *Arthropods Reported to Have Caused Allergic Rhinitis and Asthma* †*

Class: Arachnida	Class: Hexapoda (*Continued*)
Araneae (spiders)	Order: Coleoptera
Acarina (mites, ticks)	Beetles
Class: Crustacea	Bean weevil
Sowbugs	Order: Neuroptera
Daphnia (water flea)	Lacewing flies
Shrimp (plankton)	Order: Trichoptera
Shrimp (edible)	Caddis flies
Crab	Order: Lepidoptera
Class: Hexapoda (Insecta)	Moths, butterflies
Order: Orthoptera	Order: Diptera
Locusts	Houseflies
Grasshoppers	Mushroom flies
Cockroaches	Sewer flies
Crickets	Midges
Order: Isoptera	Deer flies
Termites	Black flies
Order: Dermaptera	Order: Siphonaptera
Earwigs	Rat fleas
Order: Ephemeroptera	Order: Hymenoptera
May flies	Honeybees
Order: Hemiptera	Bumblebees
Bedbugs	Hornets
Order: Homoptera	Wasps
Aphids	Parasitic wasps
	Yellow jackets
	Ants

* From Perlman, F.: Insects as inhalant allergens. J. Allergy *29:*302, 1958.
† Nonrespiratory reactions to biting and stinging insects are excluded.

antigens.[19] However, these common antigens are not necessarily those which give rise to skin-sensitizing antibodies.[20]

May Fly

There are almost 100 varieties of May fly (Ephemerida) found in the United States, with Brown Drake being the chief type found in the Great Lakes region. In past years, May fly caused allergic symptoms primarily at the western end of Lake Erie. These insects also swarm in some areas along the Mississippi River in vast numbers from June through July.[21] After two or three years of underwater life in larval form, the nymphs come to the surface and split open. There emerges a winged insect which lives only a few hours, during which it flies to land and sheds its friable outer skin or pellicle. In past years, the air of the southwestern Lake Erie (Toledo, Ohio) region was showered with pellicle fragments and debris from dead insects. Sensitized patients showed symptoms in June and July and exhibited positive skin test reactions to extract of May fly. Lake Erie has become so contaminated by industrial chemical waste that May flies no longer swarm as they did prior to 1962. Simultaneously, patients with inhalant symptoms from May fly have almost vanished.[22]

Caddis Fly (Sand Fly, Trichoptera)

The Caddis fly is widely distributed but has been described as an important factor in inhalant sensitivity mainly in the area of Buffalo, New York. The nymph of the Caddis fly prefers clear, cool, moving water, as in the Niagara River. Under the microscope, the adult Caddis fly is seen to be covered with innumerable hairs which may contaminate the air, since these flies do not shed a pellicle. The season in Buffalo extends from June to late August, with peak exposure in mid-August. The contamination of Lake Erie has not influenced these insects much. They continue to swarm in large numbers during the season in the Buffalo area.[23] Sensitized patients react by skin testing with the Caddis fly antigens and may merit treatment by hyposensitization. A purified fraction of Caddis fly extract has been found to contain two peptides or glycopeptides having sedimentation coefficients of 0.72 S.[24]

SILK

Although allergy to silk is encountered less frequently at present than in past years, it must be kept in mind as a possibility. Silk usually acts as an inhalant allergen capable of provoking eczema, asthma, or urticaria. It also has caused allergic reactions by injection of vaccines and toxoids which had been passed through silk bacteriologic filters. Contact reactions from silk fabrics usually are due to added substances, such as dyes, or "weighting" chemicals (tin, lead, or iron).

The silk cocoon is made up of small fibers composed of fibroin, which is insoluble in water. These fibers are held together by a glue material, sericin, which is water-soluble and allergenic. In processing most silk, the sericin is removed by soaking, but in certain types the glue is left in the fibers. Inhalation of dried sericin may produce allergic symptoms among workers who handle the untreated silk or among ladies who wear the unwashed silk fabric. A significant exposure also may be incurred by electrical workers who handle silk wrapping used on certain kinds of indoor electric wiring. Paterson, New Jersey, is the center for manufacture of silk goods in the United States.

Skin testing should be done using extract prepared from silk material containing sericin. Patients with inhalant insect allergy quite frequently react to silk as well as those clinically sensitive to silk itself. Therapeutically, it is relatively easy to avoid exposure to silk in the United States.

ADDITIONAL INHALANT ALLERGENS

The list of materials which may at some time cause allergic symptoms is vast. Almost any vegetable matter or animal protein conceivably might be allergenic if inhaled in fine particles or ingested in quantity by a potentially sensitive person. Also, in rare instances, simple reactive chemical substances appear to act as allergens in addition to being irritants. Some of these, such as toluene diisocyanate (T.D.I.), are important in industry.[25] Fortunately for the allergist, the majority of patients whom he sees are allergic to a few common substances. It is the unusual patient, who has become sensitized to some obscure allergen or to a common allergen acting in a peculiar disguise, who challenges the acumen of the allergist. Therefore, the solutions to such interesting problems provide great satisfaction to the allergist.

REFERENCES

1. Vannier, W. E., and Campbell, D. H.: A starch block electrophoresis study of aqueous house dust extracts. J. Allergy *32:*36, 1961.
2. Rimington, C., Stillwell, D. E., and Maunsell, K.: The allergen(s) of house dust: purification and chemical nature of active constituents. Brit. J. Exper. Path. *28:*309, 1947.
3. Voorhorst, R.: University Hospital, Leiden, Netherlands, Proc. Vth Interasma Congress, May, 1966.
4. Gelfand, H. H.: The vegetable gums by ingestion in the etiology of allergic disorders. J. Allergy *20:*311, 1949.
5. Nilsson, D. C.: Sources of allergenic gums. Ann. Allergy *18:*518, 1960.
6. Spies, J. R., Chambers, D. C., and Coulson, E. J.: The chemistry of allergens. XIII. Ion exchange fractionation of the cottonseed allergen and immunological properties of the products. Arch. Biochem. *84:*286, 1959.
7. Figley, K. D., and Elrod, R. J.: Endemic asthma due to castor bean dust. J.A.M.A. *90:*79, 1928.
8. Figley, K. D., and Rawling, F. F. A.: Castor bean: an industrial hazard as a contaminant of green coffee dust and used burlap bags. J. Allergy *21:*245, 1950.
9. Freedman, S. O., Drupey, J., and Sehon, A. H.: Chlorogenic acid: an allergen in green coffee bean. Nature *192:*241, 1961; Am. J. M. Sc. *244:*548, 1962.
10. Layton, L. L., Greene, F. C., Panzani, R., and Corse, J. W.: Allergy to green coffee. J. Allergy *36:*84, 1965.
11. Hooker, S. B.: Quantitative differences among canine danders. Ann. Allergy *2:*281, 1944.
12. Prickman, L. E.: Common allergens. I. Orris root. Proc. Staff Meet. Mayo Clin. *9:*291, 1934.
13. McElhenney, T. R., et al.: Algae: a cause of inhalant allergy in children. Ann. Allergy. *20:*739, 1962.
14. Bernstein, L. I., and Safferman, R. S.: Sensitivity of skin and bronchial mucosae to green algae. J. Allergy (Abstr.) *37:*106, 1966.
15. Feinberg, A., Feinberg, S., and Benairn-Pinto, C.: Asthma and rhinitis from insect allergens. I. Clinical importance. J. Allergy *27:*437, 1956.
16. Wiseman, R. D., Wooden, W. G., Miller, H. C., and Myers, M. A.: Insect allergy as a possible cause of inhalant sensitivity. J. Allergy *30:*191, 1959.
17. Perlman, F.: Insects as inhalant allergens. J. Allergy *29:*302, 1958.
18. Perlman, F.: Insect allergens: their interrelationship and differences. J. Allergy *32:*93, 1961.
19. Langlois, C., Shulman, S., and Arbesman, C. E.: Immunologic studies of Caddis fly. V. Cross-reaction with other insects. J. Allergy *34:*385, 1963.
20. Parlato, S. J.: Emanations of flies as exciting causes of allergic coryza and asthma. V. A study of the reagins of the Caddis fly, butterfly, and moth. J. Allergy *3:*459, 1932.
21. Figley, K. D.: Asthma due to May fly. Am. J. M. Sc. *178:*338, 1929.
22. Figley, K. D., and Rawling, F. F. A., Toledo, Ohio, personal communication, 1966.
23. Arbesman, C.: Buffalo, New York, personal communication, 1966.
24. Shulman, S., Bronson, P., and Arbesman, C. E.: Immunologic studies of Caddis fly. III. Physical and chemical characterization of the major antigen. J. Allergy *34:*1, 1963.
25. Silver, H. M.: Toluene diisocyanate asthma. Arch. Int. Med. *112:*401, 1963.

Chapter Eighteen

SERUM SICKNESS, VASCULAR ALLERGY AND CONNECTIVE TISSUE DISEASES

Serum sickness was relatively more common in the pre-antibiotic and chemotherapeutic era in which many patients were given large volumes of foreign sera in treatment for several infectious diseases. Though it is less common now, patients still have this type of adverse reaction not only from equine tetanus antitoxin but also from several other foreign sera still in clinical usage: snake antivenins, black widow spider antivenin, rabies antiserum and antitoxins for botulism, diphtheria and gas gangrene. In addition, reactions to several drugs, particularly penicillin, may simulate serum sickness reactions very closely in regard to their clinical manifestations and probably in respect to pathogenesis.

Although serum sickness presents a problem of only moderate clinical importance, investigations of the mechanism of this disease have been of crucial importance in providing information relevant to a variety of hypersensitivity reactions. Unlike the atopic diseases, serum sickness can be induced at will in laboratory animals, and this experimental model has been very fruitfully exploited by a number of investigators (page 12). Furthermore, several immunologic techniques can be utilized profitably to evaluate this disease in humans, and this experience may usefully serve to familiarize clinicians with immunologic procedures which are becoming increasingly important in clinical medicine.

EXPERIMENTAL SERUM SICKNESS

Relatively definitive work in this area became possible with the availability of substantial quantities of highly purified serum proteins;

tagging these proteins with radioactive isotopes facilitated the observations. Figure 18–1 depicts events following the intravenous injection of bovine serum albumin (BSA) into rabbits[1] (similar results have been observed in man). The solid line on the left shows the serum level of bovine serum albumin after varying periods of time. It may be noted that there are three phases in the clearance of antigen from the blood stream: first is an equilibration phase during which serum levels of bovine serum albumin fall rapidly; in the second phase there is gradual clearance of antigen from the serum; the rate of bovine serum albumin clearance is accelerated during the third or immune elimination phase. This third phase would be absent if there were no immunologic response. It occurs much sooner in a secondary or hyperimmune response. Not until the antigen is completely eliminated does one find *free* antibody in the serum (solid line on the right-hand side of Figure 18–1). However, there is good evidence that antibody formation has already commenced before the beginning of immune elimination of antigen, but the antibody at first is present in serum in the form of soluble antigen-antibody complexes. When isotopically tagged albumin antigen is used, these complexes can be demonstrated by the Farr technique (precipitation of radioactivity at half-saturation with ammonium sulfate). It is evident that soluble complexes can be formed only to antigens which persist in the blood stream until antibody formation is established. When these complexes are present, serum complement activity often is diminished.

Figure 18–1 also illustrates that microscopic lesions of serum sickness

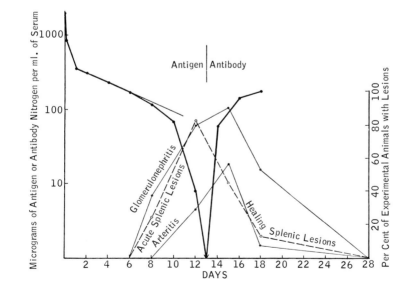

Figure 18–1. Relation of the time of occurrence of tissue lesions of serum sickness to clearance of antigen from the blood and subsequent appearance of free antibody in the serum. (From Germuth, F. G.: A comparative histologic and immunologic study in rabbits of induced hypersensitivity of the serum sickness type. J. Exper. Med. *97*:257, 1953.

first appear at the beginning of immune elimination of antigen. If sections of vessels are stained with fluorescein-tagged antiserum to bovine serum albumin, specific fluorescence can be demonstrated within the lesions, indicating deposition of antigen there. Likewise, staining thoroughly washed sections with fluorescein-tagged antiserum to autologous gamma globulin shows this material to be fixed in the tissue in the same region as the bovine serum albumin. Complement components can be demonstrated by similar methods. There is a striking correlation between areas of localization of antigen, gamma globulin and complement and the distribution of inflammatory lesions. In addition to this spatial relationship, it is noteworthy that temporally inflammatory changes do not begin until there is localization of antigen and gamma globulin in vessels. Furthermore, antigen, gamma globulin and complement appear to be deposited in tissues simultaneously and following the appearance of soluble antigen-antibody complexes in serum. The lesions resolve after antigen is cleared from the blood and free antibody appears. All these facts strongly support the hypothesis that soluble antigen-antibody complexes play a pathogenetic role in the production of the lesions of serum sickness. However, additional factors probably are involved, and those which determine the focal localization of antigen-antibody complexes in certain areas are not well understood in spite of a number of investigations of this question.

Examination of tissues from animals with experimental serum sickness shows lesions especially in the heart, arteries, kidneys and joints.[2] The former may exhibit inflammatory changes in the endocardium, myocardium and pericardium. Verrucous valvular vegetations may be present. All layers of artery walls may be involved in focal inflammatory lesions, which may show fibrinoid necrosis or a mononuclear reaction. The coronary arteries are most frequently affected. The kidneys often are involved in a glomerulonephritis manifested by endothelial proliferation of the glomerular capillaries and slight basement membrane thickening. Focal mononuclear infiltrates, edema and fibrinoid formation may be seen in the synovial tissues. In past years, Klinge and Rich have pointed out the similarity of many of these lesions to those of the human collagen diseases.

The concept of biological activity of soluble antigen-antibody complexes, arising from the study of experimental serum sickness, has importantly influenced studies on the mechanism of many forms of hypersensitivity reactions. Of particular interest has been the capacity of soluble antigen-antibody complexes formed in vitro to elicit various biological effects. These can be prepared either by precipitating antibody in antigen excess (recovering the supernatant) or by dissolving antigen-antibody precipitates in excess antigen. Germuth and McKinnon showed that these preparations could elicit fatal anaphylactic shock in *unsensitized* guinea pigs.[3] Subsequently, it has been demonstrated that antigen-antibody complexes can activate complement, fibrinolysin, anaphylatoxin and kinins.[2] They can fix to tissues and produce smooth muscle contraction, histamine release, increased capillary permeability in skin, chemotaxis of leukocytes, endothelial proliferation and serum-sickness-like disease.

Antigen-antibody complexes in moderate antigen excess are most active, whereas complexes produced in far antigen excess (consisting of two molecules of antigen and one molecule of antibody per complex) are inactive. The active differ from the inactive complexes since they contain antigen molecules to which two or more molecules of antibody are bound. Since antibody molecules are much larger than most antigens, the possibility arises that in the active complexes there is interaction among antibody molecules being brought into close proximity to each other since they are bound to the same molecule of antigen. This finding was supported by the observation that, unlike biologically inactive complexes formed in far antigen excess, active complexes have optical rotatory properties suggesting a biophysical alteration in the antibody molecules.[4] Ishizaka provided strong support for the concept that antibody-antibody interaction may account for the biological activity of soluble antigen-antibody complexes by demonstrating that gamma globulin which has been aggregated by nonspecific means, such as heat or bisdiazotization, can exhibit some of the biological activities of soluble antigen-antibody complexes.[5] Among the reported activities of aggregated gamma globulin are increased capillary permeability of skin, complement fixation, Arthus-like reactions, histamine release, fixation to skin, wheal and erythema type skin reactions and immune adherence.[6] The F_c portion of the gamma globulin molecule apparently is responsible for these activities.

IMMUNOLOGY OF HUMAN SERUM SICKNESS

As mentioned previously, antibodies to foreign sera can be demonstrated in patients recovering from serum sickness by a variety of techniques. These include complement fixation, precipitation, gel diffusion, immunoelectrophoresis, passive anaphylaxis, accelerated immune disappearance, smooth muscle sensitization, passive hemagglutination, skin tests, passive transfer, passive cutaneous anaphylaxis, Farr technique and antiglobulin methods. In general, however, there is not a good correlation between the titer of these test responses and the clinical severity of the serum sickness.[7] Within weeks to months many of these tests no longer give demonstrable reactions. The direct skin tests, however, usually become positive early in the course of serum sickness and often remain so for a long time; passive transfer test responses may be more transient. Arbesman and his colleagues have shown not only that hemagglutinating antibodies to horse serum proteins, as measured by the tanned cell technique, increase more in patients developing serum sickness than in those who do not, but that the former patients usually have significant titers of hemagglutinating antibodies to horse serum proteins *before* receiving tetanus antitoxin.[8] Since these patients presumably had not been injected with foreign sera previously, the origin of these antibodies is obscure, but the observations were so consistent that their presence indicated that a serum reaction could be anticipated. Hemagglutination reactions can be obtained with red cells sensitized with a variety of mammalian sera, and the test usually remains positive for a prolonged period of time.

It should be noted that in contrast with sera of patients with serum sickness, sera of patients with atopic disease fail to react in many of the aforementioned immunologic tests (e.g., precipitation, passive anaphylaxis and passive cutaneous anaphylaxis in *guinea pigs*). Serum sickness also differs from atopy in that the hereditary factor seems less important and the disease is more transient. The specificity of skin-sensitizing antibody in serum sickness seems more marked; that is, a variety of mammalian sera and epidermal extracts elicits passive transfer reactions with sera from patients with atopic hypersensitivity (asthma and rhinitis) to horses, whereas reagin from a serum sickness patient reacts only to horse serum.[9] Terr and Bentz[10] have shown that unlike the usual atopic reagins these skin-sensitizing antibodies may be associated with the I_gG and/or I_gM fractions of the human serum as well as with I_gA. The I_gG reagins were relatively heat-stable. Several investigators have studied the components of horse serum which stimulate antibody formation in man, particularly by immunoelectrophoresis and gel diffusion. There is a variable pattern of response, but many patients react to multiple horse serum proteins, particularly the alpha macroglobulin. When unmodified horse serum is administered, some of the antibodies may be of the heterophil type. It is noteworthy that most of these human antibodies are directed toward fractions of horse serum which have no therapeutic antitoxic or antibacterial activity. This suggests the possibility of reducing the incidence of serum sickness by further purification of foreign antisera.

INCIDENCE AND PREVENTION OF SERUM SICKNESS

The quantity of foreign serum administered is the most important factor determining the incidence of serum sickness. Years ago, it was observed that as many as 90 per cent of patients developed this disease when given over 100 milliliters of foreign serum, whereas about 10 per cent reacted from 10 milliliters of serum. The incidence of serum sickness is reduced by use of partially purified and "despeciated" serum globulin, which has been subjected to peptic digestion; essentially all equine tetanus antitoxin in use today is of this type.

Universal, active immunization of the populace with tetanus and diphtheria toxoids would largely eliminate the need for foreign serum administration and hence markedly reduce the incidence of serum sickness. Persons whose occupation predisposes them to a risk of tetanus following injury, as well as those who are sensitive to horse dander and horse serum, should be especially admonished to maintain active immunization for tetanus. As has been so well documented by military experience, booster injections of tetanus toxoid suffice very well to protect an adequately immunized person following injury; no tetanus antitoxin is necessary.[11] Accumulating experience reveals that there is an adequate rise in tetanus antitoxin titers following toxoid booster injections for more than ten years following primary immunization. Of course, it is necessary to give some nonimmunized persons tetanus antitoxin for legal as well as for medical reasons, but judgment should be exercised concerning the need for administering this foreign serum based on the time, type and circumstance of the injury and the adequacy of surgical débridement. It has been pointed out that if there is a real risk of tetanus, it is advisable to give 3000 to 10,000 units of antitoxin rather than the usual prophylactic dose of 1500 units.[11]

PREVENTION OF IMMEDIATE SERUM REACTIONS OR SERUM ACCIDENTS

Persons already sensitive to foreign serum proteins by virtue of atopic allergy to horses or previous administration of horse serum are in danger of developing immediate reactions from serum injections. Whether or not different mechanisms are involved in these two types of reaction—which some would consider to be atopic and anaphylactic, respectively—both clearly differ from serum sickness. In either case these constitute another important hazard of foreign serum administration which merits consideration here. Several procedures have been suggested for trying to identify individuals who are likely to experience this type of reaction. The first step is to obtain a history of the patient's symptoms on exposure to horses, previous foreign serum injections and any reactions experienced from previous injections. The latter is a matter for special concern if the reaction occurred within the previous few months. Since deaths have resulted from diagnostic intracutaneous tests with horse serum, in the rare instances in which the history is suggestive of allergy to this substance, it appears advisable when possible to abandon the use of equine serum on the basis of the history alone or else to do a prick test with serum on an extremity before attempting intracutaneous or conjunctival testing. If the history is not suggestive of horse or horse serum allergy, it is usual to proceed directly to intracutaneous and/or conjunctival tests.

Some surgeons have become rather disenchanted with the value of intracutaneous tests, since they felt that many patients reacted nonspecifically. Very likely this has resulted in part from injecting an excessive volume of too concentrated serum. As with intracutaneous testing in general (page 60), 0.02 milliliter of serum more than suffices to produce a definite response in sensitized persons; 0.05 milliliter is less desirable but perhaps acceptable in situations in which syringes are not available for measuring 0.02 milliliter quantities; 0.1 milliliter is excessive for tests of this type. In the absence of a history suggestive of sensitivity, the most usual serum concentrations are 1:10 and 1:1 for intracutaneous and conjunctival tests, respectively. If the conjunctival test is positive, a drop of epinephrine can be applied to the eye. The inexperienced physician generally finds intracutaneous tests easier to interpret, and this is facilitated by simultaneously performing a control skin test with sterile saline.

If the history or tests indicate a significant possibility of horse serum allergy, antiserum prepared in another species should be used, if possible. Bovine tetanus antitoxin is available, but it should be noted that a substantial number of horse-serum-sensitive patients appear to be allergic also to bovine serum. It is important, therefore, to test the patient with the bovine serum in a manner similar to that suggested with horse serum. Alternatively, one may turn to employing human tetanus anti-toxin, and this would be definitely called for in patients who react to skin or conjunctival tests with bovine serum as well as with horse serum. When antisera from these other species are available, they should be used in preference to attempted "desensitization" to horse serum. There is no alternative to the latter procedure, however, when one wishes to give types of antisera or antivenins which are available only in equine form. The package directions should be consulted, but we suggest a more conservative initial dose than commonly is recommended in the package directions when there are indications of marked hypersensitivity. One should be especially concerned about the atopic, horse-sensitive patient who reacts by prick test to the antiserum. If it is absolutely essential to administer equine serum to such an individual, we suggest an initial dose of 0.05 milliliter of a 1:100 serum dilution given subcutaneously in an extremity, with drugs and equipment on hand to treat a possible reaction. If this is tolerated, the dose could be doubled every 30 minutes until the therapeutic dose has been given or there are signs of a reaction. If large doses are required, one may try switching from subcutaneous administration to a smaller dose of diluted serum given intravenously after a 1:1 concentration of serum has been tolerated by the former route. A slow intravenous infusion may prove satisfactory after the patient's tolerance of intravenous serum has been established.

There is more likely to be a difficulty in "desensitizing" patients with atopic horse allergy than those sensitized by previous serum administration. In this instance it may be necessary to repeat small doses of serum at frequent intervals over a long period of time. Even though one succeeds in giving the serum to a sensitive patient, the question might be raised concerning whether this is therapeutically useful, since there might be concern that the antitoxin would be removed from the circulation at a very accelerated rate (page 457). Theoretically, this depends on whether the patient is sensitive to the antitoxin globulin or to other components of the foreign serum. In agreement with this expectation, actual measurements of the persistence of antitoxin titers in sensitive patients have shown variable results.

CLINICAL FEATURES OF SERUM SICKNESS

Symptoms of serum sickness begin 6 to 21 days following the serum injection, most typically after 7 to 12 days. If the patient has received the same type of foreign serum previously, he may experience an *accelerated serum reaction* after 1 to 5 days. These lie between serum sickness and immediate or anaphylactic reactions in their latent period and acuteness of onset. Their clinical features usually resemble serum sickness, and the reaction not uncommonly is relatively severe. The onset of serum sickness may be heralded or accompanied by local itching, swelling and redness at the injection site, a point of some diagnostic value. Sometimes there seem to be two or more "waves" of serum sickness, probably due to successive reactions to different components of horse serum.

There has been little new information in recent years to add to the classic clinical description of serum sickness found in all medical, pediatric and allergy texts. Briefly, there are four cardinal manifestations of this disease: *skin lesions, fever, joint symptoms* and *lymphadenopathy.* Cutaneous manifestations occur in over 90 per cent of cases and usually are the first sign of serum sickness. Most often there is urticaria or angioedema or both, but erythematous maculopapular rashes, erythema multiforme, purpura or other types of skin lesions may be present. Pruritus is common. Temperature elevation usually is slight to moderate but can be considerable in association with severe reactions in young persons. It may be associated with malaise and headache. Joint symptoms occur in about 50 per cent of cases. Most often there simply is arthralgia, but actual arthropathy, with inflammatory joint effusion, is not rare. Usually multiple joints are affected. Involvement of the temporomandibular joint may be confused with the development of tetanus. Lymphadenopathy usually occurs first in the regional nodes near the site of the serum injection. They may be slightly tender. Generalized edema, weight gain, nausea, vomiting and abdominal pain also may occur.

Occasionally there are other manifestations which may be of more serious consequence. The *nervous system* may be involved, most often in the form of a peripheral neuropathy which is apt to affect the brachial plexus. Guillain-Barré syndrome associated with serum sickness also has been well documented. Central nervous system involvement with transient hemiplegia, optic neuritis and stupor or coma also may develop. The *coronary arteries* can also become involved with subsequent clinical and electrocardiographic evidence of myocardial ischemia. Transient *renal* disease also may occur. Indeed, any vascular bed may be involved.

The total white blood cell count may be low, normal or, most commonly, slightly elevated. Occasionally there is eosinophilia late in the course of the disease. Atypical lymphocytes have been reported,[12] and occasionally there is plasmocytosis, which rarely may be of substantial degree. Our experience has been that the sedimentation rate frequently is slightly elevated. Albuminuria and a few hyaline casts may be present. Immunologic tests for antibodies to foreign serum proteins were discussed on page 459.

The clinical features of serum sickness are so characteristic that the diagnosis usually presents no problem. There are superficial resemblances between this condition and rheumatic fever, but the character of the skin lesions, pulse rate, signs of carditis, sedimentation rate and anti-streptolysin titer usually leave no doubt about the correct diagnosis. Occasionally infectious mononucleosis needs to be considered in the differential diagnosis. A more common difficulty lies in deciding whether a foreign serum or penicillin is responsible for the reaction in patients who have received both agents. The tests described on pages 193 and 459 may help to resolve this problem.

COURSE AND PROGNOSIS OF SERUM SICKNESS

Serum sickness may run a highly variable course ranging from a few days of a trivial urticaria to a week or slightly more of disabling illness (longer in serum-sickness-like reactions from some drugs). Intense itching and arthralgia are the most distressing symptoms. The greatest threat to life is laryngeal edema. Although neurologic involvement may be severe, complete recovery usually occurs eventually. Necrotizing arteritis and focal periarteritis together with perivascular granulomas and fragmentation of collagen have been observed in the rare autopsies of patients dying with serum sickness. Prominent inflammatory changes in the endothelium and intima of the major vessels and in the interstitial tissues of the myocardium, liver, kidneys and adrenal glands also were noted.[13]

TREATMENT OF SERUM SICKNESS

Treatment is symptomatic; the objective is to tide the patient over the time until the antigen is cleared and spontaneous recovery may be expected. The patient may be unduly apprehensive because of the striking skin lesions. Reassurance about the self-limited nature of the process is helpful, but at the same time he should be advised to seek emergency medical care if he feels any swelling in the throat. Choice of medications depends upon the patient's most distressing complaints. Usually these relate to his urticaria and angioedema and, therefore, antihistamines, epinephrine, ephedrine, hydroxyzine, cyproheptadine, sedatives or tranquilizers may be very helpful, as discussed on page 249 and in Chapter 7. Salicylates may be prescribed for fever and joint symptoms, though they are not uniformly effective in relieving the latter. The use of corticosteroids or ACTH is a matter of judgment based on circumstances in the individual patient; they are clearly indicated for severe disease, such as that with neurologic involvement. Usually a brief course of five to seven days suffices. The patient should be informed of the diagnosis and of the possible hazard from subsequent administration of foreign serum. He should carry a card bearing this information (signed by his physician) in his wallet or purse, or preferably a metal tag may be worn for the same purpose. Adequate active immunization for tetanus should be strongly urged.

The treatment for accelerated serum reactions is the same as the above. Immediate or anaphylactic type serum reactions are managed by the procedure described on page 118.

ARTHUS REACTIONS

Although extensively studied in experimental animals, true Arthus reactions from foreign serum are rarely encountered in clinical medicine, since substantial titers of precipitating antibody are required. Precipitating antibodies, complement components and leukocytes are involved in this process which is manifested grossly by swelling and necrosis at the injection site (see page 13).

OTHER VASCULAR DISEASES OF POSSIBLE ALLERGIC ETIOLOGY

Many years ago it was shown that the injection of foreign serum proteins into rabbits not only produced serum sickness, but many animals developed lesions closely simulating human periarteritis nodosa[14] and rheumatic carditis.[15] These and other observations have led to the concept that serum sickness may be regarded as a prototype reaction at one end of a spectrum of vascular diseases. Whereas it is clear that serum sickness is produced through the effects of antigen-antibody complexes, the pathogenetic role of immunologic mechanisms becomes increasingly uncertain as one moves across this spectrum. Morphologic similarities do not necessarily bespeak a common pathogenesis, particularly in tissues as limited as blood vessels in the ways that they can react. Thus, one must be cautious about making unwarranted inferences concerning etiology from morphologic findings alone. Unfortunately, however, there are few experimental data concerning the mechanism of many of the diseases to be considered here. Investigative work in many instances is hampered by a lack of suitable models in experimental animals. Consequently, inadequate as they may be, detailed morphologic studies provide the main basis for current understanding of many forms of vasculitis.

In an attempt to make some order out of a confusing subject, Zeek

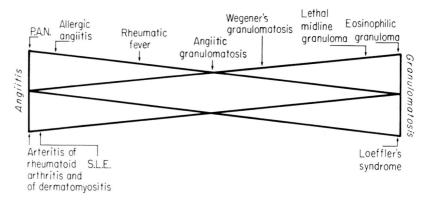

Figure 18–2. Graphic representation of the spectrum of relationships of granuloma and angiitis in the necrotizing angiitides. (From Alarcón-Segovia, D., and Brown, A. L., Jr.: Classification and etiologic aspects of necrotizing angiitides: an analytical approach to a confused subject with a critical review of the evidence for hypersensitivity in polyarteritis nodosa. Mayo Clin. Proc. *39*:205, 1964.)

has offered a classification of diseases exhibiting necrotizing angiitis.[16] The main features of this classification are in Table 18–1 (page 469). Not all pathologists agree with the details of this analysis, particularly the points of differentiation between hypersensitivity angiitis and periarteritis nodosa, but it has served at the least to stimulate more critical scrutiny of these diseases. Since blood vessels are a component of mesenchymal and connective tissue, perhaps it should not be surprising to find that some forms of vasculitis merge into diseases usually thought of as connective tissue diseases, which also will be considered here in this context. It also is noteworthy that granuloma formation is a prominent feature of many of these conditions. As shown in Figure 18–2, Alarcón-Segovia and Brown have depicted this relationship as two overlapping triangles, the one on the left representing angiitis and the one on the right indicating granulomatosis.[17] The basis for this relationship is obscure; possibly the granulomas may be secondary to damaged vessel walls in some instances. From the relatively little information available concerning the immunologic aspects of granuloma formation, one might be more inclined to associate this process with delayed than with humoral hypersensitivity (see page 265). There also is a variable and sometimes prominent participation of the eosinophil in these vascular diseases. It is evident that complex processes are involved in the production of many of these lesions, and much remains to be learned regarding their pathogenesis.

As mentioned previously, there is uncertainty about the role of hypersensitivity in producing many of the diseases to be considered. Lesions similar to some of these can be induced by alternative means, such as by experimental hypertension. Even if one accepts an immunologic basis for some of these conditions, the question arises concerning how such diverse manifestations of disease can arise from immunologic reactions. A substantial amount of experimental data indicates that antigen-antibody reactions, antigen-antibody complexes or delayed hypersensitivity can result in quite varied effects on the host depending upon the *conditions* which prevail; that is, the relative quantities of antigen and antibody, cellular fixation of antibody, type of antibody, location of antigen, participation of complement and many other factors importantly affect the nature of hypersensitivity reactions. In addition, nonimmunologic factors may condition the development of these lesions; for example, anatomic or physiologic factors may be important in determining the localization of antigen-antibody complexes. It also might be noted that although experimental serum sickness following a single injection of foreign protein is an acute, transient process, *chronic* vascular lesions can be produced under other circumstances. For example, Dixon and his colleagues have produced chronic renal lesions closely simulating human glomerulonephritis by repeatedly injecting small amounts of antigen over a long period of time under conditions in which soluble antigen-antibody complexes in moderate antigen excess would repeatedly be formed in vivo.[18]

In spite of the production of a variety of lesions in experimental animals by immunologic means, it is difficult to prove that these mechanisms pertain to human diseases. A major problem is that in most instances the antigen is unknown. Indirect evidence sometimes cited in support of an immunologic mechanism includes similarity to some animal experimental model in respect to morphologic features, presence of gamma globulin in the lesions as shown by immunofluorescent staining techniques, demonstration of electron-dense deposits suggestive of antigen-antibody complexes in electron micrographs of the lesions, decreased serum complement activity during the disease, hypergammaglobulinemia, demonstration of specific circulating antibodies or delayed hypersensitivity and the finding of rapidly sedimenting molecular aggregates suggesting antigen-antibody complexes on ultracentrifugation of the serum. Other suggestive features include the presence of plasma cells or lymphocytes in the lesions, multisystemic disease and therapeutic response to corticosteroids.

Because of the large number of diseases to be considered, the following review must be limited to a brief summary of immunologic aspects of these conditions and other features of special interest to allergists. A major objective is to cite a limited number of "classic" and also more recent references with which allergists should be familiar. Further references are given in the standard texts listed in Appendix II.

Serum Sickness Type Reactions from other Foreign Proteins and Drugs

Foreign proteins such as bacterial vaccines rarely cause vascular reactions resembling serum sickness. Probably a major reason why this does not occur more frequently is that potential antigens of this type generally are cleared rapidly from the circulation. It is of interest that a group of laboratory workers who had been immunized with an extraordinarily large quantity and variety of vaccines for years has shown no morphologic abnormalities attributable to immunization.[19] However, a fatal reaction beginning with features of serum sickness has recently been reported following pertussis vaccine.[20] Serum sickness occurs occasionally after stinging insect bites. Similar reactions are not unusual manifestations of drug allergy, especially to penicillin. It is assumed that the mechanism is analogous to serum sickness, though at present there is little direct evidence to substantiate this supposition.

Hypersensitivity Angiitis

Major features of this condition are summarized in Table 18–1, page 469. These lesions were seen with special frequency during the years in which sulfonamide drugs were most abundantly used. French and Weller noted lesions of this type in the myocardium in about half of 283 autopsied patients who had received sulfonamides within a few weeks before death.[21] Sulfonamide administration produced similar changes in experimental animals. Clinically, fever is usual.[22] Renal involvement is suggested by microscopic or macroscopic hematuria with or without azotemia. Cutaneous manifestations include maculopapular rashes and purpura. Pneumonitis may be present, and occasionally there is arthropathy, wheezing or evidence of carditis. Hypertension and eosinophilia are infrequent. The disease tends to run a much shorter course than periarteritis nodosa, and the history relatively frequently suggests a possible relationship to the administration of some drug, particularly a sulfonamide. Fatal cases often terminate in uremia. Typical patients show a number of clinical and pathologic differences from classic periarteritis nodosa, but there are many overlapping features which may make it difficult to categorize individual cases and which also lead some students to question whether this should be regarded as an entity separate from periarteritis nodosa.

Anaphylactoid or Schönlein-Henoch Purpura

There is little recent information to add to the classic descriptions of this syndrome, which is seen most often in children and adolescents. The *skin lesions* differ somewhat from most other types of purpura in that they may be maculopapular or urticarial early in their evolution;[23] pruritus or a prickling sensation commonly is present at this time. After 24 hours the skin lesions evolve into dusky, red macules of variable size, which do not blanch on pressure. These spots are most prominent over the lower extremities and buttocks. In contrast with many other forms of purpura, biopsy specimens of fresh lesions show the small vessels in the

Table 18-1. Classification of the Necrotizing Angiitides

Types of Lesions	Associated Clinical Conditions	Duration of Terminal Illness Related to Vascular Lesions	Caliber of Vessels Involved	Sites of Predilection and Distribution	Special Features of Lesions	Other Frequently Associated Lesions	Healed Stage
Hypersensitivity angiitis	Hypersensitiveness to serum, sulfonamides, drugs, etc.	Few days to few weeks. Usually less than one month.	Arterioles, venules, capillaries and small arteries	Kidneys and heart. Usually widespread. Often in pulmonary vessels and splenic follicular arterioles. Uncommon in pancreas and gastroenteric tract.	All of about same age. Exudative reaction.	Interstitial inflammation in viscera. Necrotizing glomerular nephritis.	Uncertain
Allergic granulomatous angiitis	Asthma and other allergic states, with bouts of fever and eosinophilia	Several months to several years	Probably any sized vessel, especially small arteries and veins	Heart. Widespread. Often in pulmonary vessels and splenic follicular arterioles.	Various ages. Necrosis of eosinophilic exudate. Multinucleated giant cells. Granulomas.	Granulomas in extravascular connective tissues and serous membranes. Loeffler's pneumonia. Sequelae of vascular obstruction.	Nonspecific scarring
Rheumatic arteritis	Fulminating rheumatic fever	Masked by rheumatic carditis	Small arteries and occasionally veins	Heart and lungs. Occasionally widespread. Uncommon in pancreas and gastroenteric tract.	Associated with Aschoff bodies. Otherwise simulates hypersensitivity angiitis.	Rheumatic carditis, pneumonitis and aortitis	Nonspecific scarring
Periarteritis nodosa	Polyneuritis, fever and "multiple systems disease," usually with hypertension	Several months to a year or more	Small and medium-sized muscular-type arteries near hilums of viscera, in striated muscles, and near peripheral nerves	Bifurcations and branchings. Common in wall of gastroenteric tract, near mesenteric attachment, in pancreas and kidneys. Often widespread. Usually absent in pulmonary vessels and splenic follicular arterioles.	Various ages. Proliferation precedes exudation in adventitia. Forms granulation tissue. Prone to form small aneurysms.	Sequelae of hypertension and vascular obstruction	Marked distortion of vessels. Scars sweeping through segments of wall with focal rupture of media. Aneurysms.
Temporal arteritis	Pain over involved vessels, malaise, fever, anorexia	Nonfatal	Temporal and other cranial arteries	Temporal arteries	Multinucleated giant cells. No tubercles. No aneurysms.	Cellulitis of contiguous tissues	Spontaneous regression or nonspecific scarring

* From Zeek, P. M.: Periarteritis nodosa: a critical review. Am. J. Clin. Path. 22:777, 1952.

corium to be surrounded by a cuff of white blood cells. Leukocyte-platelet thrombi may be present in some minute vessels,[24] and occasionally necrosis may be observed in the walls of inflamed vessels. There also may be considerable edema in the subcutaneous tissues.

Gastrointestinal symptoms include abdominal pain and vomiting; bleeding from the gastrointestinal tract may be slight or severe, with varying degrees of melana or hematemesis. Intussusception may occur.[25] *Joint* manifestations usually consist of arthralgia or periarticular joint swelling. Multiple joints generally are afflicted, but the involvement is not migratory, and hemarthrosis does not occur. Fever and leukocytosis are common. The incidence of an associated *glomerulonephritis* varies widely in different reported series of cases, averaging about 30 to 50 per cent. Gross or microscopic hematuria and albuminuria are the usual signs of renal involvement; hypertension and azotemia occur in the more severe cases. Renal biopsy shows focal involvement of glomeruli with endothelial proliferation, deposition of fibrinoid material and capillary thrombosis.[24] The lesions somewhat resemble lupus nephritis. After several years about three-fourths of these children show no evidence of renal disease, and many of the remainder have abnormal Addis counts with no evidence of impaired renal function;[25] only a few experience progressive renal impairment. Without nephritis, anaphylactoid purpura usually subsides in two to four weeks. Recurrence occurs in about 40 per cent of cases, generally within six weeks. Renal involvement and a more prolonged course are more common in older children than in those under two years of age.

Although anaphylactoid purpura appears to represent a hypersensitivity reaction, in our experience the responsible antigen cannot be identified in the majority of cases. Frequently, there is a history of an antecedent respiratory infection, but it is difficult to prove an etiologic relationship to this. In view of past reports stressing the importance of streptococcal infections, antistreptolysin antibody titers and throat cultures should be obtained, but these have been found to indicate the recent presence of streptococcal infection scarcely more often than in control groups of children.[24] Likewise, anaphylactoid purpura only very rarely is a sequel to scarlet fever. Miescher has reported purpuric reactions to intracutaneous tests with bacteria-free filtrates of organisms cultured from patients with anaphylactoid purpura, and this reactivity could be passively transferred with viable leukocytes. Food allergy has been reported to be responsible for some cases. It is difficult to evaluate the effects of an elimination diet, because the disease usually subsides spontaneously after a relatively short period of time. Repeatedly reproducing the purpura by food additions would provide the most convincing evidence for food allergy. However, we have never found dietary manipulation to influence the disease in those cases associated with nephritis. Many drugs have been reported to produce anaphylactoid purpura. Although proof of the relationship frequently is inadequate, it nevertheless is important to take a careful drug history and, if possible, to stop all drugs. Treatment with corticosteroids is not particularly rewarding. The renal disease usually is not benefited, and the other manifestations generally subside soon without steroid treatment. Paradoxically, substantial or persistent gastrointestinal bleeding probably is the best indication for corticosteroid therapy in these patients; marked joint symptoms or edema also are likely to improve.

Rheumatic Fever and Rheumatic Arteritis

A large body of data strongly implicates infection with group A beta hemolytic streptococci as the initiating event in the development of rheumatic fever. The latent period, averaging 19 days, between the acute infection and the onset of rheumatic symptoms and the fact that viable organisms usually cannot be recovered from rheumatic lesions have suggested that some form of hypersensitivity may be involved. However, much remains to be learned about the exact nature of the antigen or antigens involved and the variable response of the host to these substances.

Infection with any of the more than 50 types of group A streptococci appears capable of initiating rheumatic fever. Since resistance to re-infection is largely type-specific, these patients are at risk to further infection with other types of group A streptococci and subsequent recurrence of rheumatic fever. The organisms contain or elaborate many potentially antigenic substances. The best known surface antigens are the M proteins, which determine type specificity and are important in respect to virulence, and the A polysaccharide, which provides group specificity. The more extensively studied extracellular antigens include the erythrogenic toxin (which produces the rash in scarlet fever), streptolysin O, streptokinase, DNase, hyaluronidase and DPNase. Antibodies may be detected to any or all of these antigens following infection, but these antibodies do not appear to protect the patient against re-infection. Antibodies against the specific M proteins probably are protective and tend to persist for a long time. Since antistreptolysin (ASO) titers remain elevated for only a few weeks after active infection, this abnormality, when present, suggests recent infection. A negative Dick test indicates antibodies to the erythrogenic toxin. Group A streptococci may or may not be recovered from throat cultures obtained after the onset of rheumatic fever. Of uncertain significance is the development of delayed hypersensitivity to M protein and some of the extracellular antigens.[26] In addition to these specific immunologic responses, patients with acute rheumatic fever also usually demonstrate several other abnormalities which, in a nonspecific manner, are suggestive of an immunologic and/ or connective tissue response. These include elevations of the serum gamma and alpha-2 globulins, complement activity, glycoproteins and C-reactive protein (CRP). The latter is of special interest[27] both because of its quite constant occurrence in acute rheumatic fever and because of the evidence suggesting that it might be derived from injured myocardial fibers.[28] However, other studies suggest that C-reactive protein is formed in the liver.[29]

Several studies have indicated that about 3 per cent of persons with untreated acute group A streptococcal infections of the respiratory tract will subsequently develop rheumatic fever; as many as 30 to 50 per cent of rheumatic subjects will have a recurrence following such infections. This can be remarkably reduced by suitable prophylactic therapy.[30] The host factors responsible for the selective response have not been clearly identified. Some data suggest that a genetic factor may be involved. Although rheumatic subjects have been found to produce normal amounts of circulating antibodies to most antigens, these patients generally exhibit higher titers of several streptococcal antibodies following infection than nonrheumatic individuals. Recurrence of rheumatic fever has been found to correlate with the rise in antistreptolysin titers,[31] though this does not necessarily imply a direct cause and effect relationship. Whatever streptococcal antigen or antigens may be involved, they might lead to the vascular lesions of rheumatic fever by the formation of soluble antigen-antibody complexes, by fixation to suitable tissues with subsequent reaction with antibodies, by delayed hypersensitivity and/or by autoimmune mechanisms, including cross-reactions between streptococcal cell wall and myocardial antigens (see page 491).

Some pathologic features of rheumatic arteritis are outlined in Table 18–1.

Glomerulonephritis

Four major lines of immunologic investigation have been pursued in studies of glomerulonephritis.

1. Epidemiologic data and clinical observation of individual patients firmly establish that acute glomerulonephritis is anteceded by group A *streptococcal infections* in a substantial portion of cases. However, this relationship differs from that just discussed in regard to rheumatic fever in several important respects.[26] The latent period between infection and nephritis tends to be relatively short, averaging ten days. Only a few types of group A streptococcal infection are associated with glomerulonephritis, type 12 being the most prominent of these. Following infection with these particular types of streptococci, the incidence of nephritis may be as high as 60 per cent. Thus, epidemics can occur. Since, as discussed previously, the type-specific antigen is related to virulence and immunity, patients who have completely recovered from glomerulonephritis rarely have a recurrence of the disease. Serum complement activity is reduced during the acute disease (and in some instances of lipoid nephrosis).

Although many data support the concept that certain types of strep-tococci initiate acute glomerulonephritis, much remains to be learned concerning the mechanisms by which this occurs and the reasons for chronicity of the disease in some cases. The following lines of inquiry have sought to elucidate these problems.

2. Soluble *antigen-antibody complexes* prepared in vitro localize particularly in the glomeruli when injected intravascularly in normal animals. Complexes formed in vivo during a prolonged course of intra-venous antigen injections also localize in the glomerular capillaries (see page 467). Antigen, autologous gamma globulin and complement com-ponents can be demonstrated scattered along the basement membrane by immunofluorescent staining techniques. Some investigators believe that this localization of immune complexes may relate simply to the rich blood supply and filtration function of the basement membrane rather than to some specific immunologic affinity.[18] Electron microscopy of these experimental lesions shows dense deposits on the external sur-face of the basement membrane which are remarkably similar to electron micrographs of various stages of human glomerulonephritis and lupus nephritis.[2] Light microscopy also shows major resemblances between these lesions. Immunofluorescent staining of the human material also shows deposits of autologous gamma globulin and complement com-ponents along glomerular basement membranes. In addition, streptococ-cal antigens have been identified by this technique, but this finding is not specific because other bacterial antigens may be found, too.[32]

3. An alternative approach is to produce antibodies which react specifically with kidney components (*nephrotoxic or Masugi nephritis*). Extensive studies, dating from 1901, have shown that nephritis can be produced in experimental animals by heterologous "nephrotoxic" sera prepared by immunizing animals of another species with kidney anti-gens.[33] The glomerular lesions appear to be initiated by the uptake of antibodies from the nephrotoxic serum by glomerular basement mem-brane antigens. Secondarily, there is a further immunologic reaction to the presence of this foreign gamma globulin in the glomeruli. These lesions differ somewhat in their morphology from the "serum sickness nephritis" type lesions discussed in the previous paragraph. Immuno-fluorescent stains show a smooth deposit of gamma globulin and com-plement components along the basement membrane. On electron micro-scopy the dense deposits are found on the *inside* of the basement mem-brane.[34] Thus, these lesions differ in detail from most forms of clinical nephritis, and how nephrotoxic antibodies would develop in humans is not known. Past reports of their presence in serum during human glomerulonephritis are yet to be confirmed. It is noteworthy that anti-lung antibodies may cross-react with glomerular basement membrane. This has stimulated speculation that antibodies of this type might play a role in *Goodpasture's syndrome* (pulmonary alveolar hemorrhage and

glomerulonephritis).[35] Immunofluorescent stains also have indicated the presence of gamma globulin and complement components in the glomeruli in this disease.[36]

4. Autoimmune type renal disease can be induced in experimental animals by injecting emulsions of kidney antigens in immunologic adjuvants in a manner analogous to that for the production of other experimental autoimmune diseases discussed in the next chapter.[37] The clinical relevance of these experiments is uncertain at present. Although delayed hypersensitivity is thought to play a role in these experimental diseases, skin tests with normal kidney extract have been negative in nephritic patients.[32]

Polyarteritis Nodosa
(Periarteritis Nodosa)

This term will be used here in a restricted sense, according to Zeek's classification.[16] As indicated in Table 18–1, involvement of medium sized arteries, lesions of varying ages, the presence of healed lesions and the usual sparing of the lungs have been used to differentiate this from other forms of necrotizing angiitis. Other students of this subject have also included under polyarteritis nodosa cases which will be discussed here as hypersensitivity angiitis or allergic granulomatous angiitis.[38] Since the vascular lesions are focal but disseminated in a variable pattern, the clinical and pathologic manifestations of this disease are unusually diverse.[39] Many of the lesions are caused by local interference with the blood supply to the affected organs. Granulomas usually are absent unless the respiratory tract is involved.

A number of facts suggest the possibility that polyarteritis nodosa may be, in some instances, a hypersensitivity disease: the disseminated focal nature of the lesions, fluctuating clinical course, response to corticosteroids and hypergammaglobulinemia in some cases. Gamma globulin has been demonstrated in the lesions by immunofluorescent staining techniques, but fibrinogen also has been found by this method. Some of the renal lesions are similar to those of glomerulonephritis, and polyarteritis nodosa sometimes is associated with other diseases of possible immunologic etiology, such as rheumatic fever or rheumatoid arthritis. Rheumatoid factor is present in some cases. The hypersensitivity hypothesis was supported by the production of lesions simulating polyarteritis nodosa in experimental animals by foreign sera and drugs.[14] However, there is at present no firm evidence that immunologic mechanisms are responsible for most or all cases of this disease in man, and similar lesions can be produced by nonimmunologic methods.

If hypersensitivity is involved in some cases, the responsible antigen usually is not apparent. Whereas drugs, especially sulfonamides, are rather frequently suspected of provoking hypersensitivity angiitis, only rarely can an association be made with polyarteritis nodosa. Rose and

Spencer noted that the incidence of this disease is not diminishing in spite of decreased use of sulfonamides.[38] Twenty-four of their patients received a sulfonamide during the course of polyarteritis nodosa without any exacerbation of the disease, and the course is much more prolonged following cessation of drug therapy than would be expected on the basis of hypersensitivity. Thiourea drugs have been implicated in some of the rare instances in which classic polyarteritis nodosa seemed to be related to therapeutic agents. On the other hand, an immune response to some infectious agent, including beta hemolytic streptococci, has been repeatedly mentioned as a possible pathogenetic mechanism. Some similarities between polyarteritis nodosa and certain viral diseases of horses and mink lend some support to this possibility, but much more evidence is required to establish this type of association.[40]

Allergic Granulomatous Angiitis

As indicated in Table 18–1, asthma, fever and eosinophilia are the prominent clinical characteristics of this disease.[41] The patients also have many other manifestations of polyarteritis nodosa. Cutaneous involvement is relatively common, especially in the form of purpura or cutaneous nodules. Biopsy of the latter may be helpful in establishing the diagnosis during life. Recurrent episodes of pneumonitis may be of the type seen with Loeffler's syndrome. Asthmatic symptoms usually precede the other manifestations by months to years. Pathologically, widespread vascular lesions of the type seen in polyarteritis nodosa are present, including frequent involvement of the pulmonary arteries. In addition, there characteristically are eosinophilic infiltrates and extravascular, granulomatous nodules in connective tissue. These appear to form around necrotic cells or altered collagen fibers; epithelioid and giant cells often are present. Granulomatous lesions also occur in vessel walls throughout the body. The lungs frequently show a pneumonic process. Granulomas are very common in the heart.

There is a major degree of overlapping between allergic granulomatous angiitis and polyarteritis nodosa with lung involvement.[38] The former has also been combined with Wegener's granulomatosis under the term "pathergic granulomatosis."[42]

Allergic granulomas of the prostate are a rare disease which also may be related to allergic granulomatous angiitis.[43] Symptoms of vesical neck irritation or obstruction, occurring exclusively in asthmatic patients, are apt to appear following a recent exacerbation of chronic asthma. The hard and/or nodular consistency of the prostate on palpation is suggestive of neoplasm. Blood eosinophilia is common, and the urine sediment generally shows no pus in spite of symptoms suggestive of lower urinary tract infection. Microscopic examination of the prostate reveals fibrinoid, necrotizing granulomas with an intense eosinophilic infiltration. Although there usually is no clinical evidence of systemic disease, it is noteworthy that in three cases autopsy showed systemic angiitis and eosinophilic infiltration of many organs, particularly the lungs.

Wegener's Granulomatosis

This syndrome is characterized by the following three features: (1) necrotizing, granulomatous lesions of the upper or lower respiratory tract; (2) generalized, focal, necrotizing arteritis, which usually involves the lungs as well as the other organs, and (3) focal glomerulitis.[44] The upper respiratory tract giant cell granulomas are often very aggressive, destructive processes involving the nose, sinuses or orbit. These lesions usually precede the vascular and renal disease and serve to distinguish this syndrome from other forms of necrotizing angiitis. When the necrotizing process is located in the lung, the clinical features are hemoptysis and unresolved pneumonia rather than asthma. Eosinophilia often is lacking, and the disease cannot be associated with drugs or any other known etiologic agent. Corticosteroid therapy generally is helpful since it at least temporarily slows the rate of progression of the disease.[45] Recently, antimetabolites also have been used with some success.[46, 47] Antibiotic drugs or chemotherapy are valuable for secondary bacterial infection, and ionizing irradiation may help in treatment of the inflammatory response.

Lethal Midline Granuloma

This may be regarded as a localized form of the same process just described as Wegener's granulomatosis. However, careful study of these patients usually reveals evidence of dissemination of the disease, at least by the time of autopsy, and thus these conditions may be considered as essentially synonymous. Initial symptoms commonly are nasal obstruction, epistaxis, persistent nasal discharge, headache, facial pain and swelling, dysphagia, persistent sore throat or hoarseness, loose teeth or ulcers in the mouth. The cervical lymph nodes usually are not enlarged.[45] With early involvement of the orbit, patients may present pseudotumors of the orbit.

Pulmonary Infiltration with Eosinophilia (PIE Syndrome)

Clinically, patients with some of the aforementioned diseases may first be seen with pulmonary infiltrates and eosinophilia. Since other types of allergic reactions also can produce this syndrome, brief consideration of the differential diagnosis seems appropriate here. Frequently, this heterogeneous group is divided into five major categories, as proposed by Crofton et al.:[48] (1) simple pulmonary eosinophilia (Loeffler's syndrome), (2) prolonged pulmonary eosinophilia, (3) pulmonary eosinophilia with asthma, (4) tropical eosinophilia[49] and (5) polyarteritis nodosa. Groups 3, 4 and 5 will not be discussed further here, except to note that many asthmatic patients have transient pulmonary infiltrates in addition to those rare patients with allergic granulomatous angiitis. Symptoms of group 2 patients resemble Loeffler's syndrome, except that the course of the disease is prolonged to over a month and symptoms may be somewhat more severe. There is a major degree of overlapping in respect to etiologic agents implicated in these two groups.[50, 51] Some of these are summarized in Table 18–2. Opportunities for microscopic examination of tissues of these two groups have been infrequent. Biopsies in some cases showed only eosinophilic infiltration of lobular septa and of perivascular adventitia, whereas autopsy of another case also revealed focal pulmonary granulomatous and necrotizing arteritis and arteriolitis.

The assumption has been made that pulmonary infiltration with eosinophilia usually reflects a special form of hypersensitivity reaction to a variety of agents, but there is little immunologic data concerning the nature of this response. Of considerable theoretical interest is the observation that Loeffler's syndrome occurred after inhalation of nickel carbonyl fumes in a patient with eczematous dermatitis and a positive patch test reaction to nickel.[52]

Farmer's lung, bagassosis and pigeon breeder's lung also manifest pulmonary granulomas in their acute stages, but they usually are not accompanied by eosinophilia and are not generally classified under the PIE syndrome. It is of interest to note, however, that precipitating antibodies have been demonstrated to *Thermopolyspora polyspora* antigen in cases of farmer's lung, to crude bagasse extracts in bagassosis and to pigeon antigens in pigeon breeder's lung, but the relationship of these antibodies to their respective diseases is uncertain.[53]

Rheumatoid Arteritis

When diligently searched for, arteritis has been found in striated muscle of up to 30 per cent of autopsied patients with rheumatoid arthritis. A minority of these cases shows necrotizing lesions associated with clinically evident abnormalities, such as neuropathy or skin lesions. This more prominent type of vascular disease, which resembles peri-

Table 18–2. *Possible Etiologies of PIE Syndrome, Groups 1 and 2*

Parasites	Fungi	Bacteria	Neoplasm,	Drugs	Other Inhalants	Others
Ascaris, Strongyloides, Hookworm, Toxicara, Schistosomes, *Paragonimus westermani*, *Wuchereria bancrofti*, Endamoeba, Trichuris, Fasciola, Trichina, *Ancylostoma braziliense*	Coccidioides, Sporotrichum, Histoplasma	Brucella, Staphylococci	Lymphoma, carcinoma	Sulfonamides, PAS, Prontosil, Penicillin, Mephenesin, Chlorpropamide, Aurothioglucose, Nitrofurantoin, Hydralazine, Mecamylamine	Nickel and zinc fumes, smoke	Postpartum, viruses, unknown

arteritis nodosa in many respects, is most apt to occur in patients who have been on relatively high doses of corticosteroids for a substantial period of time (e.g., those with so-called "malignant rheumatoid arthritis"). These individuals also usually have subcutaneous nodules and relatively high titers of rheumatoid factor. The most common and benign form of rheumatoid vascular disease is an obliterative endarteritis which is especially apt to affect the digital and visceral (but not renal) vessels. There often is no clinical evidence of this condition, but it may be associated with symptoms related to ischemia; angiograms may demonstrate its presence. Arteritis in early subcutaneous nodules has led some observers to postulate that the vascular disease plays a role in the development of these characteristic lesions of rheumatoid arthritis.[54]

Among the many manifestations of rheumatoid disease, some investigators have felt that rheumatoid factor is especially likely to be responsible for the development of arteritic lesions. In particular, a reaction between antigen-antibody complexes and rheumatoid factor on vascular endothelium has been postulated. However, rheumatoid factor was not found by immunofluorescent staining techniques in digital vessels of rheumatoid patients with the obliterative endarteritic type of vascular disease.[55] More general aspects of the immunology of rheumatoid arthritis have been reviewed elsewhere[56, 57] and will be discussed briefly in the next chapter.

Systemic Lupus Erythematosus

Vasculitis may constitute the primary pathologic lesion in this connective tissue disease. Besides the characteristic "wire loop" lesions often found in the glomeruli and periarteriolar fibrosis in spleen, there also may be generalized lesions which involve veins as well as arterioles. Increasing evidence indicates a genetically determined predisposition to this and other connective tissue diseases. The initiating event, however, is usually not clinically evident in the large majority of cases. Unlike some of the previously discussed diseases, systemic lupus erythematosus (SLE) does not appear to be precipitated *initially* by a specific infection. Exposure to sunlight or various drugs sometimes has been incriminated. There is no doubt that certain medicaments, particularly hydralazine, can produce a systemic lupus erythematosus-like disease accompanied by the development of antinuclear factors.* Usually these are self-limited processes which abate when the drug is discontinued. However, further observations have raised the question concerning whether these patients have an underlying lupus diathesis, which is uncovered by the drug.[58]

Immunopathologic techniques for studying the vascular lesions of systemic lupus erythematosus are similar to those employed in glomerulo-

---

* Other drugs implicated relatively frequently in precipitating systemic lupus erythematosus-like disease include mephenytoin, diphenylhydantoin, trimethadione, procainamide, aminosalicylic acid and penicillin.

nephritis (page 472). Immunofluorescent staining shows that the glomerular basement membrane contains I_gG, I_gM, B_{1c} globulin (C'3) and fibrinogen, whereas I_gA, albumin and alpha-2 macroglobulin are largely absent.[59, 60] Similar results are obtained on staining the arteriolar lesions of spleen, heart and liver, whereas normal tissues fail to fluoresce. Some material eluted from the glomeruli has antibody activity toward nuclear antigens in the presence of fresh normal serum.[61] Relatively little nuclear fluorescence is observed in studies of this type, in keeping with the concept that antinuclear antibodies cannot react with the nuclei of viable cells. Other evidences of an immunologic abnormality in systemic lupus erythematosus include hypergammaglobulinemia, decreased serum complement activity (especially with renal involvement) and delayed skin test reactions to autologous leukocytes, leukocyte homogenates or DNA.† On the other hand, these patients usually respond normally to exogenous antigens. Much attention has been paid to the common occurrence of auto-antibodies to erythrocytes, platelets, leukocytes, thromboplastin, thrombin and several components of cell nuclei and cytoplasm; Wassermann reagins and rheumatoid factor also may be present. The immunology of systemic lupus erythematosus is complex, partly because antinuclear and anticytoplasmic antibodies may be of either the I_gG, I_gM or I_gA type,[64] and they may be directed against a variety of nuclear and cytoplasmic antigens. Several reviews of the clinical[65] and immunologic[56, 66] aspects of this important subject should be very helpful to the uninitiated. Autoimmune aspects of systemic lupus erythematosus are discussed briefly in the next chapter. It should be noted that as far as the vascular lesions of systemic lupus erythematosus are concerned, the data cited above are compatible with the concept that they are associated with the localization of antigen-antibody complexes and complement components in the affected vessels. It is particularly noteworthy that antinuclear antibodies apparently are deposited in the glomerular basement membrane, which lacks nuclear antigen.[61] This suggests, as discussed previously, that anatomic and physiologic factors rather than autoimmunity may account for the localization of these immunologic reactants under some circumstances.

Other Possibly Related Diseases

Dermatomyositis and *polymyositis* are additional connective tissue diseases which may have some clinical features similar to systemic lupus erythematosus. The inflammatory infiltrate in muscle sometimes is more conspicuous about blood vessels, especially in the childhood type. About half these patients have hypergammaglobulinemia and, more occasionally, rheumatoid factors may be present. In rare instances the disease

---

†DNA hypersensitivity also appears to be present in hemorrhagic cutaneous anaphylaxis.[62] This should not be confused with the Gardner-Diamond syndrome, which also features ecchymoses in the skin, but auto-erythrocyte sensitization has been postulated as the cause for this latter condition.[63]

appears to have been precipitated by drug reactions. The most intriguing immunologic observations are that adult patients with dermatomyositis associated with neoplasm may show immediate type skin test reactions to extracts of their own tumors.[67, 68] In *scleroderma* or *progressive systemic sclerosis* there likewise may be clinical features overlapping some of the other collagen diseases, vasculitis (especially early in the disease), hypergammaglobulinemia in about half the cases, antinuclear factors in a high percentage of patients and less frequently latex agglutination and lupus erythematosus cell reactions. In *Sjögren's syndrome* there typically is the triad of one of the aforementioned connective tissue diseases with keratoconjunctivitis sicca and xerostomia; rheumatoid factors also are so consistently present that there is a growing tendency to consider these to be part of the syndrome. Thyroid enlargement, often resembling Hashimoto's thyroiditis, malignancies of the lymphoreticular system and necrotizing arteritis may occur. Serologic abnormalities are rife: hypergammaglobulinemia, rheumatoid factors and antinuclear factors are observed in a majority of cases; antithyroglobulin antibodies also are commonly demonstrated, and more infrequently the lupus erythematosus cell phenomenon, positive Coombs tests and biological false-positive reactions for syphilis are encountered. Sera from these patients sometimes give complement fixation or precipitin reactions with human salivary or lacrimal gland extracts, but these antibodies also react with extracts of other human tissues.[69] In regard to the occurrence of lymphoreticular malignancies in those patients with connective tissue disorders associated with immunologic abnormalities, it is of interest to note that Schwartz and Beldotti have reported that long-term survivor F_1 hybrid mice injected with parental spleen cells developed lymphoid neoplasms of host origin.[70] Some observers have felt that hypersensitivity may play a role in the pathogenesis of *thromboangiitis obliterans*.[71] Some of the features of *temporal arteritis* or *giant cell arteritis* were outlined in Table 18–1, though it should be noted that widespread arterial involvement can occur in this disease. Little immunologic information is available. Hypersensitivity has been considered as a possible etiologic factor in the *Takayasu's arteritis* form of the aortic arch syndrome, but there is little to support this conjecture beyond the occurrence of hypergammaglobulinemia in some cases.[72] Vascular lesions are prominent in *thrombotic thrombocytopenic purpura,* but immunofluorescent staining of the lesions shows fibrinogen to be prominent. It has been suggested that this may represent a form of Shwartzman's phenomenon. Additional forms of possible hypersensitivity reactions are considered in the next chapter.

REFERENCES

1. Germuth, F. G.: A comparative histologic and immunologic study in rabbits of induced hypersensitivity of the serum sickness type. J. Exper. Med. *97:*257, 1953.
2. Dixon, F. J.: Experimental serum sickness. *In* Samter, M. (ed.): Immunological Diseases. p. 162, Boston, Little, Brown and Co., 1965.

3. Germuth, F. G., and McKinnon, G. E.: Studies on the biological properties of antigen-antibody complexes: I. Anaphylactic shock induced by soluble antigen-antibody complexes in unsensitized normal guinea pigs. Bull. Johns Hopkins Hosp. *101*:13, 1957.
4. Ishizaka, K., and Campbell, D. H.: Biologic activity of soluble antigen-antibody complexes. V. Change of optical rotation by the formation of skin reactive complexes. J. Immunol. *83*:318, 1959.
5. Ishizaka, T., and Ishizaka, K.: Biological activities of aggregated gamma globulin. J. Immunol. *85*:163, 1960.
6. Ishizaka, K.: Gamma globulin and molecular mechanisms in hypersensitivity reactions. Progr. Allergy *7*:32, 1963.
7. Arbesman, C. E.: Clinical anaphylaxis and serum sickness. *In* Samter, M. (ed.): Immunological Diseases. p. 655, Boston, Little, Brown and Co., 1965.
8. Reisman, R. E., Rose, N. R., Witebsky, E., and Arbesman, C. E.: Serum sickness. II. Demonstration and characteristics of antibodies. J. Allergy *32*:531, 1961.
9. Cooke, R. A., Menzel, A., Meyers, P., Skaggs, J., and Zeman, H.: Spontaneous and induced allergies of the immediate type in man. J. Allergy *27*:324, 1956.
10. Terr, A. I., and Bentz, J. D.: Skin-sensitizing antibodies in serum sickness. J. Allergy *36*:433, 1965.
11. Edsall, G.: Specific prophylaxis of tetanus. J.A.M.A. *171*:417, 1959.
12. Ley, D. C. H., and Fitzgerald, J. D. L.: Changes in white blood cell and bone marrow morphology and serum protein fractions in induced and spontaneous hypersensitivity states. J. Allergy *28*:220, 1957.
13. Clark, E., and Kaplan, B. I.: Endocardial, arterial and other mesenchymal alterations associated with serum sickness in man. Arch. Path. *24*:458, 1937.
14. Rich, A. R., and Gregory, J. E.: The experimental demonstration that periarteritis nodosa is a manifestation of hypersensitivity. Bull. Johns Hopkins Hosp. *72*:65, 1943.
15. Rich, A. R., and Gregory, J. E.: Further experimental cardiac lesions of the rheumatic type produced by anaphylactic hypersensitivity. Bull. Johns Hopkins Hosp. *75*:115, 1944.
16. Zeek, P. M.: Periarteritis nodosa: a critical review. Am. J. Clin. Path. *22*:777, 1952.
17. Alarcón-Segovia, D., and Brown, A. L., Jr.: Classification and etiologic aspects of necrotizing angiitides: an analytical approach to a confused subject with a critical review of the evidence for hypersensitivity in polyarteritis nodosa. Mayo Clin. Proc. *39*:205, 1964.
18. Dixon, F. J., Feldman, J. D., and Vasquez, J. J.: Experimental glomerulonephritis, the pathogenesis of a laboratory model resembling the spectrum of human glomerulonephritis. J. Exper. Med. *113*:899, 1961.
19. Peeler, R. N., Kadull, P. J., and Cluff, L. E.: Intensive immunization of man. Evaluation of possible adverse consequences. Ann. Int. Med. *63*:44, 1965.
20. Bishop, W. B., Carlton, R. G., and Sanders, L. L.: Diffuse vasculitis and death after hyperimmunization with pertussis vaccine. New England J. Med. *274*:616, 1966.
21. French, A. J., and Weller, C. V.: Interstitial myocarditis following the clinical and experimental use of sulfonamide drugs. Am. J. Path. *18*:109, 1942.
22. Knowles, H. C., Zeek, P. M., and Blankenhorn, M. A.: Studies on necrotizing angiitis. IV. Periarteritis nodosa and hypersensitivity angiitis. Arch. Int. Med. *92*:789, 1953.
23. Gairdner, D.: The Schönlein-Henoch syndrome (anaphylactoid purpura). Quart. J. Med. *17*:95, 1948.
24. Vernier, R. L., Worthen, H. G., Peterson, R. D., Colle, E., and Good, R. A.: Anaphylactoid purpura. I. Pathology of the skin and kidney and frequency of streptococcal infection. Pediatrics *27*:181, 1961.
25. Allen, D. M., Diamond, L. K., and Howell, D. A.: Anaphylactoid purpura in children (Schönlein-Henoch syndrome). A.M.A. J. Dis. Child. *99*:833, 1960.
26. Cluff, L. E., and Johnson, J. E., III: Poststreptococcal disease *in* Samter, M. (ed.): Immunological Diseases. p. 418, Boston, Little, Brown and Co., 1965.
27. Hedlund, P.: Clinical and experimental studies on C-reactive protein (acute phase protein). Acta Med. Scand. (Suppl. 361) *169*:1, 1961.
28. Kushner, J., Rakita, L., and Kaplan, M. H.: Studies of acute-phase protein: II Localization of C x-reactive protein in heart in induced myocardial infarction in rabbits. J. Clin. Invest. *42*:286, 1963.

29. Hurlimann, J., Thorbecke, G. J., and Hochwald, G. M.: The liver as the site of C-reactive protein formation. J. Exper. Med. *123*:365, 1966.

30. Rheumatic fever in children and adolescents. Ann. Int. Med. (Suppl. 5) *60:* 1964.

31. Taranta, A.: Factors associated with the rheumatic fever attack rate following streptococcal infections. Arthritis Rheum. *4:*303, 1961.

32. Cruickshank, B.: Nephritis, nephrosis, rheumatic fever, and myocardial infarction *in* Gell, P. G. H., and Coombs, R. R. A. (eds.): Clinical Aspects of Immunology. p. 583, Philadelphia, F. A. Davis, 1963.

33. Smadel, J. E.: Experimental nephritis in rats induced by injection of anti-kidney serum. I. Preparation and immunological studies of nephrotoxin. J. Exper Med. *64:*921, 1936.

34. Feldman, J. D., Hammer, D., and Dixon, F. J.: Experimental glomerulonephritis. III. Pathogenesis of glomerular ultrastructural lesions in nephrotoxic serum nephritis. Lab. Invest. *12:*748, 1963.

35. Benoit, F. L., Rulon, D. B., Theil, G. B., Doolan, P. D., and Whatten, R. H.: Goodpasture's syndrome. A clinicopathologic entity. Am. J. Med. *37:*424, 1964.

36. Duncan, D. A., Drummond, K. N., Michael, A. F., and Vernier, R. L.: Pulmonary hemorrhage and glomerulonephritis. Ann. Int. Med. *62:*920, 1965.

37. Heymann, W., Haekel, D. B., Harwood, S., Wilson, S. G. F., and Hunter, J. L. P.: Production of nephrotic syndrome in rats by Freund's adjuvants and rat kidney suspensions. Proc. Soc. Exper. Biol. Med. *100:*660, 1959.

38. Rose, G. A., and Spencer, H.: Polyarteritis nodosa. Quart. J. Med. *26:*43, 1957.

39. O'Duffy, J. D., Scherbel, A. L., Reidbord, H. E., and McCormack, L. J.: Necrotizing angiitis: I. A clinical review of twenty-seven autopsied cases. Cleveland Clin. Quart. *32:*87, 1965.

40. Henson, J. B., Gorham, J. R., Leader, R. W., and Wagner, B. M.: Experimental hypergammaglobulinemia in mink. J. Exper. Med. *116:*357, 1962.

41. Churg. J., and Strauss, L.: Allergic granulomatosis, allergic angiitis, and periarteritis nodosa. Am. J. Path. *27:*273, 1951.

42. Feinberg, R.: Pathergic granulomatosis (editorial). Am. J. Med. *29:*829, 1955.

43. Kelalis, P. P., Harrison, E. G., and Greene, L. F.: Allergic granulomas of the prostate in asthmatics. J.A.M.A. *188:*963, 1964.

44. Fahey, J. L., Leonard, E., Churg, J., and Godman, G.: Wegener's granulomatosis. Am. J. Med. *17:*168, 1954.

45. Blatt, I. M., Seltzer, H. S., Rubin, P., Furstenburg, A. C., Maxwell, J. H., and Schull, W. J.: Fatal granulomatosis of the respiratory tract (lethal midline granuloma— Wegener's granulomatosis). Arch. Otolaryng. *70:*707, 1959.

46. Von Leden, H., and Schiff, M.: Antimetabolite therapy in midline lethal granuloma. Arch. Otolaryng. *80:*460, 1964.

47. Greenspan, E. M.: Cyclophosphamide–Prednisone therapy of lethal midline granuloma. J.A.M.A. *193:*74, 1965.

48. Crofton, J. W., Livingstone, J. L., Oswald, N. C., and Roberts, A. T. M.: Pulmonary eosinophilia. Thorax *7:*1, 1952.

49. Coutinho, A.: Tropical eosinophilia: clinical, therapeutic and etiologic considerations. Experimental work. Ann. Int. Med. *44:*88, 1956.

50. Lindesmith, L.: Prolonged pulmonary infiltration with eosinophilia. N. Carolina M. J. *25:*466, 1964.

51. Reeder, W. H., and Goodrich, B. E.: Pulmonary infiltration with eosinophilia (P. I. E. syndrome). Ann. Int. Med. *36:*1217, 1952.

52. Sunderman, F. W., and Sunderman, F. W., Jr.: Loeffler's syndrome associated with nickel sensitivity. Arch. Int. Med. *107:*405, 1961.

53. Pepys, J.: Pulmonary hypersensitivity disease due to inhaled organic antigens (editorial). Ann. Int. Med. *64:*943, 1966.

54. Sokoloff, L., McCluskey, R. T., and Bunim, J. J.: Vascularity of the early subcutaneous nodule of rheumatoid arthritis. Arch. Path. *55:*475, 1953.

55. Douglas, W.: The digital artery lesions of rheumatoid arthritis. An immunofluorescent study. Ann. Rheum. Dis. *24:*40, 1965.

56. Symposium on immunologic aspects of rheumatoid arthritis and systemic lupus erythematosus. Arthritis Rheum. *6:*402, 1965.

57. Rheumatism and arthritis review of American and English literature for the years 1963 and 1964. Arthritis Rheum. *9:*93, 1966.

58. Alarcón-Segovia, D., Worthington, J. W., Ward, E., and Wakim, K. G.: Lupus diathesis and the hydralazine syndrome. New England J. Med. *272:*462, 1965.
59. Mellors, R. C., Ortega, L. G., and Holman, H. R.: Role of gamma globulins in pathogenesis of renal lesions in systemic lupus erythematosus and chronic membranous glomerulonephritis, with an observation on the lupus erythematosus cell reaction. J. Exper. Med. *106:*191, 1957.
60. Paronetto, F., and Koccler, P.: Immunofluorescent localization of immunoglobulins, complement, and fibrinogen in human diseases. I. Systemic lupus erythematosus. J. Clin. Invest. *44:*1657, 1965.
61. Freedman, P., and Markowitz, A. S.: Isolation of antibodylike gamma globulin from lupus glomeruli. Brit. M. J. *1:*1175, 1962.
62. Levin, M. B., and Pinkus, H.: Autosensitivity to Deoxyribonucleic Acid (DNA). Report of case with inflammatory skin lesions controlled by Chloroquine. New England J. Med. *264:*533, 1961.
63. Gardner, F. H., and Diamond, L. K.: Autoerythrocyte sensitization. Blood *10:*675, 1955.
64. Barnett, E. V., North, D. F., Jr., Condemi, J. J., Jacox, R. F., and Vaughan, J. H.: Antinuclear factors in systemic lupus erythematosus and rheumatoid arthritis. Ann. Int. Med. *63:*100, 1965.
65. Harvey, A. M., Shulman, L. E., Tumulty, P. A., Conley, C. L., and Schoenrich, E. H.: Systemic lupus erythematosus: review of the literature and clinical analysis of 138 cases. Medicine *33:*291, 1954.
66. Holman, H. R.: Systemic lupus erythematosus *in* Samter, M. (ed.): Immunological Diseases. p. 737, Boston, Little, Brown and Co., 1965.
67. Grace, J. T., and Dao, T. L.: Dermatomyositis in cancer: a possible etiological mechanism. Cancer *12:*648, 1959.
68. Curtis, A. C., Heckaman, J. H., and Wheeler, A. H.: Study of the autoimmune reaction in dermatomyositis. J.A.M.A. *178:*571, 1961.
69. Block, K. J., Buchanan, W. W., Wohl, M. J., and Bunim, J. J.: Sjögren's syndrome. A clinical, pathological and serological study of sixty-two cases. Medicine *44:*187, 1965.
70. Schwartz, R. S., and Beldotti, L.: Malignant lymphomas following allogenic disease: transition from an immunological to a neoplastic disorder. Science *149:*1511, 1965.
71. Harkavy, J.: Vascular Allergy and Its Systemic Manifestations. p. 121, Washington, D.C., Butterworth, Inc., 1963.
72. Judge, R. A., Currier, R. D., Gracie, W. A., and Figley, M. M.: Takayasu's arteritis and the aortic arch syndrome. Am. J. Med. *32:*379, 1962.

Chapter Nineteen

IMMUNOLOGIC ASPECTS OF SOME OTHER NONATOPIC DISEASES

NEAL A. VANSELOW, M.D.

In recent years many allergists have assumed an increasingly greater role in the treatment of patients with nonatopic disorders. The knowledge of basic immunology which the allergist must possess in order to understand the rationale for diagnosis and treatment of atopic disease has aided in his understanding of other diseases which involve immunologic processes or in which immunologic responsiveness may be altered. Some allergists have prepared themselves to serve as clinical immunologists who participate on transplantation teams or assist in the diagnosis and treatment of patients with infectious disease, immunologic deficiency disorders, or diseases with proven or postulated autoimmune features. These nonatopic disorders will be discussed in this chapter. A comprehensive review of the subject is not intended and is impossible in the space allotted; rather, it is hoped that the discussion will serve to pinpoint those areas of potential concern to the allergist with a broad interest in clinical immunology and to provide references by which each particular topic may be explored in more detail. Some connective tissue and vascular diseases were treated in a similar manner in the previous chapter.

INFECTIOUS DISEASE

Within one to several weeks following exposure to an infectious agent, circulating antibodies and the development of delayed hypersensitivity to the invading organism often can be demonstrated in the host. Infectious agents are a mosaic of complex chemical substances, many of which are potential antigens. Rather than being directed against a single substance, the hypersensitivity response is aimed at a variety of these antigens. Circulating antibodies can often be demonstrated against both protein and polysaccharide antigens of the responsible organism, whereas in most cases the delayed hypersensitivity response is directed against protein fractions.[1] The clinical significance of immunologic phenomena in infectious disease can be considered in three phases: (1) the role which measurement of the immunologic response plays in the diagnosis of infectious disease; (2) the beneficial effect which the immune response might have for the host by modifying the course of the disease or by preventing re-infection; and (3) the potential adverse effects which might be associated with the development of hypersensitivity to infectious agents.

Delayed hypersensitivity to infectious agents is most commonly measured by the intradermal skin test. The test site is read for induration and erythema 24 and 48 hours after the antigen is injected. In the absence of nonspecific irritants in the test material, a positive response indicates infection with the organism in question or with a cross-reacting organism. Because delayed hypersensitivity may persist for many years following the initial infection, the delayed skin test reaction can seldom separate old from recent infection or active disease from a healed or inactive form. Known conversion of a skin test reaction from negative to positive, however, obviously is of major clinical importance in diseases such as tuberculosis. Conversely, a definite lessening of the skin test reaction may be an ominous sign in some infectious diseases such as the deep mycoses.

Tests to detect the presence of circulating humoral antibody directed against the organisms are also widely used in the diagnosis of infectious disease. Techniques commonly used include complement fixation, agglutination, hemagglutination inhibition, precipitation, fluorescent antibody studies, protection tests, and skin tests to detect immediate wheal and flare reactivity. As with delayed hypersensitivity, circulating antibody may persist for years following acute infection. For this reason, acute and convalescent sera are often obtained and their specific antibody titers determined simultaneously. A rising titer of antibody in the absence of recent immunization is strong evidence for recent active infection. In interpreting the results of tests for both circulating antibody or delayed hypersensitivity, it must be remembered that false-negative and false-positive reactions can occur. An example of a false-negative reaction is the anergy to tuberculin associated with disorders such as Hodgkin's disease, sarcoidosis, and measles. Because of antigenic cross-reactivity, patients with active histoplasmosis, for example, may give false-positive delayed skin test reactions when tested with blastomycin. Biologic false-positive reactions in those serologic tests measuring syphilitic reagin may occur in patients with a wide variety of diseases including malaria, leprosy, systemic lupus erythematosus, and infectious mononucleosis.

The ability to resist infection with a pathogenic micro-organism is derived from both *native* and *acquired* defense mechanisms. *Native immunity* is usually relatively nonspecific and includes *active* mechanisms such as phagocytosis, bactericidal enzymes, and inflammation, as well as *passive* mechanisms as illustrated by change in body temperature in response to infection.[2] In contrast with native immunity, the development of delayed or immediate hypersensitivity may be regarded as *acquired immunity.* Acquired defense mechanisms tend to be more specific and may be classified as *active* or *passive; natural* or *artificial. Natural active immunity* is exemplified by the immunity to reinfection seen after infection with measles, whereas *artificial active immunity* is illustrated by the immunity resulting from immunization with measles vaccine. *Passive acquired immunity* may result from *natural* transfer of antibodies via the placenta or from *artificial* transfer of antibodies with materials such as gamma globulin.

It is difficult to generalize regarding the protective role played by the development of delayed or immediate hypersensitivity. Regarding circulating antibody it has been shown to exert a major protective effect in some diseases (e.g., diphtheria antitoxin; anticapsular antibody in pneumococcal disease), to be of little protective significance in other diseases (e.g., tuberculosis), and to have unknown significance in a third group of diseases. The role which the development of delayed hypersensitivity might play in protection against infectious disease is even more variable. In certain instances (e.g., pneumococcal infection), its development can be regarded as having little effect on the immune status of the host; in other instances, as in histoplasmosis in which a good prognosis is associated with the presence of delayed hypersensitivity and negative serologic tests, it may be related to clinical immunity.

The immune response to an infectious agent could be harmful to the host if the reaction elicited resulted in significant tissue damage but did little to halt the multiplication and spread of the invading organisms. In this respect, Raffel has emphasized that in pneumococcal infection, for example, circulating antibody to the capsular polysaccharide provides protection.[3] The delayed hypersensitivity response, which is directed against a nucleoprotein antigen, results in inflammation and tissue damage but does not appear to be associated with resistance to the organism. Similarly, the delayed hypersensitivity response to tuberculoprotein results in inflammation but does not seem to be a basic feature of acquired resistance in tuberculosis.[3] There is also evidence which suggests that in some cases the heightened inflammatory response associated with the development of delayed hypersensitivity to an organism may actually increase the spread of the organism through the tissue rather than retard it.[4]

The immune response to an infectious agent could also be harmful to the host if, as a result of it, an immune reaction occurred against the host's own tissue. This might occur if a microbial substance combined with or altered host tissue and thus rendered it autoantigenic, or if there were antigenic cross-reactivity between a microbial fraction and a tissue component of the host. These mechanisms are discussed in more detail on page 491.

IMMUNOLOGIC DEFICIENCY STATES

Decreased immunologic responsiveness in humans may be either *physiologic* or *pathologic*. An example of a physiologic state is the hypogammaglobulinemia found in the normal two- to three-month-old infant. This results from the combined effects of catabolism of maternal 7S gamma globulin transferred via the placenta and the relative inability of the normal infant to manufacture his own immunoglobulins. Pathologic states of decreased immunologic responsiveness are of three types: primary, secondary, and iatrogenic.

The major primary pathologic states involving immunologic deficiency are the agammaglobulinemias and hypogammaglobulinemias.[5] The *congenital sex-linked recessive* form of agammaglobulinemia is characterized by low levels of all three major immunoglobulins, hypoplastic lymphoid tissue, and the complete absence of plasma cells. Clinically, patients with this disease have recurrent bacterial infections such as pneumonia, conjunctivitis, otitis media, sinusitis, and meningitis. The organisms most commonly involved are extracellular pyogenic pathogens such as pneumococcus, hemophilus influenzae and beta hemolytic streptococci. With the exception of hepatitis, viral infections are handled satisfactorily. Delayed hypersensitivity is normal. A high incidence of connective tissue disease, atopic eczema, sprue-like syndromes, and hematologic disorders such as neutropenia and aplastic anemia have been found in patients with this disorder. The diagnosis of agammaglobulinemia may be made by serum protein electrophoresis, although unavoidable errors in this technique may produce misleading results. For this reason, immunodiffusion and immunoelectrophoresis should be used to confirm the diagnosis in suspected cases. The former procedure provides quantitative data concerning the level of each of the three major immunoglobulins and can be carried out easily in a clinical laboratory utilizing commercially available reagents.* The *congenital sporadic* form of agammaglobulinemia is similar to the sex-linked form except for its sporadic occurrence, somewhat higher immunoglobulin levels, and the fact that enlargement of lymphoid tissue and hepatosplenomegaly may be present. A particularly interesting variant of this group of diseases is Swiss type agammaglobulinemia.[6] This is congenital and is usually transmitted as an autosomal recessive. It is characterized by lymphopenia and the failure of both immunoglobulin production and delayed hypersensitivity. Afflicted infants show marked susceptibility to fungal, viral, and bacterial pathogens, diarrhea, and a hypoplastic thymus. Death usually occurs before age two years.

Acquired agammaglobulinemia usually is manifested in adult life and may also be associated with hyperplasia of lymphoid tissue and hepatosplenomegaly. Benign thymomas have been reported in some adults with this disorder.

---

* Available from Hyland Laboratories, Los Angeles, California.

In patients with *dysgammaglobulinemia* there is a selective deficiency of just one or two immunoglobulins. These patients also may be susceptible to pyogenic infections. Since IgM may be markedly increased in patients with IgG deficiency, the total serum gamma globulin value may be near the lower limits of normal. This underscores the importance of the previously mentioned advice that paper electrophoresis be supplemented by immunodiffusion and/or immunoelectrophoretic studies before an immunoglobulin abnormality is excluded. Other types of immunoglobulin deficiency states are indicated in the classification given in the following outline.

*Classification of the Hypogammaglobulinemias**

I. Defects in gamma globulin synthesis
   A. Agammaglobulinemia—deficiency of IgG, IgA, and IgM
      1. Congenital agammaglobulinemia
         a. Sex-linked recessive
         b. Sporadic
         c. Swiss type
      2. Acquired agammaglobulinemia
         a. Idiopathic
         b. Secondary to granulomatous or neoplastic involvement of lymphoid system
      3. Transient or physiologic hypogammaglobulinemia
   B. Dysgammaglobulinemias—deficiency of specific immunoglobulins in presence of normal or increased concentrations of other immunoglobulins.
      1. Deficiency of IgA and IgG with increase in concentration of IgM
      2. Deficiency in IgA and IgM with normal concentration IgG
II. Increased catabolism or loss or both
   A. Nephrotic syndrome
   B. Exudative gastroenteropathies
   C. Idiopathic hypercatabolic hypoproteinemia

* This classification represents a slight modification of that proposed by Gitlin, D.: The hypogammaglobulinemias. Disease-a-Month. Chicago, Year Book Publishers, May, 1962.

The therapy of primary agammaglobulinemia involves the use of intramuscular gamma globulin, 0.6 ml./kg. of body weight every three weeks. This is usually only partially successful. Bacterial infections continue to occur and should be promptly treated with appropriate antibiotic drugs. Good and co-workers have also recommended the prophylactic use of broad-spectrum antibiotic drugs.[5]

Secondary deficiencies in immunologic responsiveness have been noted to occur in association with a number of diseases. Patients with Hodgkin's disease have an increased susceptibility to tuberculosis and fungus diseases. Immunologically, Hodgkin's disease is usually characterized by normal ability to form circulating antibodies but by impairment of delayed hypersensitivity and decreased ability to reject skin allografts.[5] Impairment of delayed hypersensitivity occurs early in the course of the disease. Kelly et al. have shown that if a patient with Hodgkin's disease is sensitized to dinitrophenol (DNP), his lymphocytes transfer delayed hypersensitivity against dinitrophenol to a normal recipient in spite of the fact that the donor himself does not react when challenged with dinitrophenol.[8] It has also been shown that patients with Hodgkin's disease cannot be passively sensitized by the injection of lymphocytes from reactive donors.[5] These observations suggest that immunologic sensitization can take place in Hodgkin's disease but that the evolution of the cutaneous reaction is inhibited.

In contrast with Hodgkin's disease, inhibition of delayed hypersensitivity occurs only as a late manifestion of leukemia, other lymphomas, or carcinoma. An increased incidence of bacterial and fungal infections has been noted in leukemia and in lymphomas other than Hodgkin's disease. The reasons for this are undoubtedly complex but may be due at least in part to defects in antibody synthesis which have been reported in some cases.

Patients with sarcoidosis are similar to those with Hodgkin's disease since they have relatively normal ability for circulating antibody formation but have impairment of delayed hypersensitivity. Patients with co-existent sarcoidosis and tuberculosis, for example, commonly exhibit cutaneous anergy to tuberculin. Unlike patients with Hodgkin's disease, however, persons with sarcoidosis can be passively sensitized for delayed hypersensitivity by transfer of peripheral blood leukocytes from sensitive donors.[9]

The deficiency in immunologic responsiveness associated with uremia has been emphasized by Wilson and co-workers.[10] Uremic patients show impaired allograft rejection, decreased delayed hypersensitivity responses to antigens such as tuberculin and histoplasmin, impaired antibody production involving all three major classes of immunoglobulins, and relative suppression of reagin-mediated immune responsiveness. The evidence suggests that the immunologic defect in uremia involves the early inductive phase of the immune response rather than its visible expression, as appears to be the case in Hodgkin's disease. The immunologic defects associated with chronic uremia may be important factors in the success of renal transplantation in man.

Iatrogenic decreases in immunologic responsiveness may occur in patients receiving total body irradiation, corticosteroids, or immuno-suppressive drugs.[11–14] Total body irradiation has been shown to have a suppressive effect upon several types of immunologic responsiveness including antibody formation, delayed hypersensitivity, and allograft rejection. In therapeutic doses corticosteroids have little effect on antibody formation in man,[14] but their ability to suppress inflammation and thereby minimize the tissue response associated with hypersensitivity reactions is well known. Other drugs with immunosuppressive properties include alkylating agents such as nitrogen mustard, purine analogues such as azathioprine (Imuran) and 6-mercaptopurine, halogenated pyrimidines such as 5-fluorouracil, folic acid antagonists such as methotrexate, and certain antibiotic drugs such as chloramphenicol and the actinomycins. When given in adequate dosage and under the proper conditions, these agents have been shown to suppress the primary and secondary antibody response, delayed hypersensitivity, and allograft rejection. In some cases their administration has led to drug-induced immunologic tolerance. It must be remembered that patients receiving immunosuppressive agents are particularly prone to infection and that organisms which are nonpathogenic under usual circumstances may be involved. Adequate measures must therefore be taken to prevent infection in these patients and to treat it promptly when it occurs.

AUTOIMMUNE DISEASE

For many years, Ehrlich's concept of "horror autoxicus" was regarded as an inviolable principle of immunology. This basic tenet stated in effect that an organism was immunologically tolerant of its own body constituents. The immune response was considered largely in terms of its protective effect against infectious disease, and little interest was shown in the possibility that antibody formation or delayed hypersensitivity reactions might at times cause disease rather than prevent it. In recent years, these concepts have undergone considerable revision. The inability of an organism to react immunologically to its own body antigens still may be regarded as fundamental under most circumstances, but it has clearly been shown that in some situations both circulating antibody and delayed hypersensitivity may be demonstrated against autoantigens in the host. The possibility that these reactions might be responsible for the production of disease has intrigued investigators and has led to considerable interest in the concept of autoimmune disease.

Several mechanisms have been postulated to explain the development of immunologic reactivity to autoantigens.[15, 16] It has been suggested that an organism never develops immunologic tolerance to autoantigens which normally are isolated from contact with immunologically competent cells. Under such circumstances, an antigen which was released from its isolated site would not be recognized as "self" and would elicit an immunologic response. Thyroglobulin, myelin, and the lens of the eye are examples of such isolated antigens. It has been suggested that stimuli such as viral infections or trauma might cause their release and trigger an immunologic response which resulted in autoimmune disease. The development of experimental immune thyroiditis in rabbits following the injection of homologous thyroglobulin in complete Freund's adjuvant has been regarded as one possible experimental model for this form of autoimmunization.[17] However, it is notable that thyroglobulin or other tissues generally must be incorporated into immunologic adjuvants in order to produce autoimmune disease.

Another possible mechanism of autoimmunization involves the alteration of normal body antigens by exogenous stimuli such as burns, infectious agents, or irradiation to produce a new antigen which is no longer recognized as "self" by immunologically competent cells. Antibodies would then be formed against the altered autoantigen and might cross-react with unaltered body constituents. Weigle has demonstrated in rabbits that acquired immunologic tolerance to bovine serum albumin (BSA) or to bovine gamma globulin (BGG) can be lost following the injection of BSA or BGG which has been structurally altered by the addition of certain organic radicals.[18] If one accepts the fact that acquired tolerance to heterologous proteins is similar to tolerance to normal body constituents, these experiments provide an experimental model for another method of producing autoimmune reactions.

A third possible mechanism for producing autoimmunity involves initial immunization of the host by an exogenous antigen such as a drug or infectious agent. If the exogenous antigen were similar to a normal body antigen yet sufficiently different from it to evoke an immune response, the result might be antibodies and/or delayed hypersensitivity directed primarily against the exogenous antigen but also cross-reacting with normal body constituents. An example of this mechanism of autoimmunization has been provided by Kaplan, who demonstrated cross-reactivity between an antigen found in the cell walls of certain group A streptococci and an antigen present in human cardiac myofibers.[19] It has been postulated that this cross-reactivity might explain the association between group A beta hemolytic streptococcal infection and rheumatic fever.

The possible mechanisms of autoimmunization listed above presume that the abnormality is in the antigenic stimulus and that the immunologic reactivity of the host is normal. A fourth theory postulates that the abnormality leading to autoimmunity is in the immunologically competent cells themselves. This theory suggests that "forbidden clones" of immunologically competent cells might develop under genetic influence or because of spontaneous mutation. Such cells would be capable of reacting against normal unaltered body constituents to produce autoimmune disease. Attention has been directed to runt disease in rodents as a possible experimental model of such a mechanism (see page 19).[20] A further example of autoimmunity occurring as a result of an alteration in immunologically competent cells might be found in a spontaneous disease occurring in the NZB/Bl strain of mice.[21] This disorder is under genetic influence, and there is serologic and pathologic evidence which suggests that it is autoimmune in origin.

A variety of autoimmune diseases can be produced in experimental animals by the injection of appropriate antigens.[22] *Experimental allergic encephalomyelitis* has been produced by the injection of homologous or heterologous brain or spinal cord in complete Freund's adjuvant. Paralysis and other neurologic signs develop two to three weeks after immunization and may lead to death of the animal. This particular model has proved attractive to investigators because the disease can be produced by microgram quantities of a highly purified basic protein derived from myelin. Circulating antibodies to myelin antigen have

Table 19–1.   *Auto Allergic Diseases Produced in Experimental Animals**

Name of Experimental Disease	Parenchymal Elements Affected	Histologically Similar Human Diseases	
		Acute Monocyclic	Chronic Relapsing
Allergic encephalomyelitis	Myelin	Post-infectious encephalomyelitis	Multiple sclerosis
Allergic neuritis	Myelin	Guillain-Barré-polyneuritis	—
Phako-anaphylactic endophthalmitis	Lens	—	Phako-anaphylactic endophthalmitis
Allergic uveitis	Uvea	Post-infectious iridocyclitis	Sympathetic ophthalmia
Allergic orchitis	Germinal epithelium	Mumps orchitis	Non-endocrine chronic infertility
Allergic thyroiditis	Thyroglobulin	Mumps thyroiditis	Subacute and chronic thyroiditis
Allergic adrenalitis	Cortical cells	—	Cytotoxic contraction of the adrenal

* From Waksman, B.: Experimental allergic encephalomyelitis and the "auto-allergic" diseases. Internat. Arch. Allergy & Appl. Immunol. (Suppl.) *14:*2, 1959.

been detected by complement fixation in afflicted animals, but there is little correlation between the clinical course of the disease and the titer of this antibody. Indeed, humoral antibodies have been shown to have a protective function against the development of the experimental disease. The creation of delayed hypersensitivity to brain tissue may be of more pathogenic significance, since it has been found that there is a correlation between dermal sensitivity and the manifestations of the disease. Experimental allergic encephalomyelitis may be passively transferred with lymph node cells but not with serum, again suggesting that the delayed hypersensitivity response is important. *Experimental autoimmune thyroiditis* develops in rabbits or in rats following immunization with heterologous, homologous, or autologous thyroid extracts emulsified in complete Freund's adjuvant. The disease is characterized histologically by infiltration of the thyroid with lymphoid cells and eosinophils. Both circulating antibodies and delayed hypersensitivity to thyroid antigens can be demonstrated. As in the case of experimental allergic encephalomyelitis, the clinical course of the disease correlates best with the delayed hypersensitivity response. Other examples of laboratory-induced autoimmune disease in animals include *experimental uveitis, experimental allergic adrenalitis,* and *experimental orchitis.*

The production of autoimmune disease in experimental animals has fostered interest in the concept that certain human diseases of unknown etiology might be caused by autoimmune phenomena.[15, 16, 23–25] In interpreting the evidence accumulated in this regard, it must be remembered that the presence of circulating antibodies or delayed hypersensitivity directed against normal body antigens does not necessarily prove that the disease in question is autoimmune in etiology, since the immunologic response observed might be the result rather than the cause of the disease. It is also necessary to identify the antigen against which the immune response is directed before a disease can be termed autoimmune. Shulman has presented evidence which suggests that an immune response directed against an exogenous antigen, such as a drug, can secondarily involve red blood cells, white blood cells, or platelets with resultant anemia, leukopenia, or thrombocytopenia. The affected cell or platelet acts merely as an "innocent bystander" which is damaged by adsorption of the drug-antibody complex to its surface. If the antigen against which the antibody response was directed were not discovered, such a disease might easily be misinterpreted as being of autoimmune etiology.

Circulating autoantibodies have been thought to play an important role in certain human diseases involving tissue accessible to the blood stream. These include acquired hemolytic anemia, idiopathic thrombocytopenic purpura, and certain hemorrhagic disorders. The evidence for autoimmune factors is best substantiated in acquired hemolytic anemia. Both 7S ("warm") hemolytic antibodies and 19S ("cold") antibodies inactive above 32°C. have been demonstrated in patients with this disease. The "warm" antibodies are usually directed against unknown red blood cell antigens but at times may be active against Rh antigens such as "e." Since the chemical nature of the antigen is unknown in many cases, however, the possibility must be considered that the antibodies involved are not true autoantibodies but rather are directed against an exogenous antigen such as a drug or a virus which is attached to the red blood cell surface. Similar considerations apply to thrombocytopenic purpura. The evidence is strong that in immunologic thrombocytopenic purpuras related to drug administration the platelet is involved secondarily as an "innocent bystander" (see above). However, the fact that plasma from patients with *idiopathic* thrombocytopenic purpura can produce a profound thrombocytopenia when transfused into normal individuals supports, but does not prove, the concept that antibodies in these plasmas are directed toward components of platelets themselves. On the other hand, the large majority of cases of immunoneutropenia in man appears to be due to isoantibodies or antibodies to drugs rather than to autoantibodies.

An autoimmune etiology has been postulated for many human diseases of unknown cause involving solid parenchymal organs and tissues. Circulating antibodies reactive with extracts of the organ or tissue in question have been found in many of these disorders, but the antibody titer seldom correlates with the clinical course of the disease. For this and other reasons, it has been suggested that a delayed hypersensitivity response might be responsible for these diseases.[16]

The role of autoimmune factors in human thyroid disease has been of considerable interest. Four types of antibodies have been found in the sera of many patients with chronic thyroiditis: precipitating or hemagglutinating antibodies which react with thyroglobulin, antibodies which react with a second colloid antigen, complement-fixing antibodies directed against a microsomal antigen, and antibodies which are cytotoxic for human thyroid cells in tissue culture.[23] Delayed hypersensitivity to thyroglobulin or crude thyroid extract can also be demonstrated in some patients with chronic thyroiditis. These findings together with the histologic appearance of the thyroid gland have led some investigators to propose that chronic thyroiditis in humans is analogous to experimental autoimmune thyroiditis in experimental animals. The evidence is still inconclusive, however, and the mechanism that initiates the process of autoimmunization in the first place is still unknown. An autoimmune mechanism has also been considered in certain cases of hypothyroidism. Circulating antibodies reactive with thyroid antigens have been found in some apparently normal individuals as well as in some patients with other thyroid diseases including hyperthyroidism and thyroid carcinoma.

The histologic similarity between the lesions of experimental allergic encephalomyelitis and the encephalomyelitis that sometimes occurs in man following injection of Pasteur type rabies vaccine, which contains rabbit nervous tissue, has led to the proposition that the latter is an autoimmune disease. Other neurologic disorders in which autoimmune factors have been postulated but not proved include multiple sclerosis, myasthenia gravis,[23] and the Guillain-Barré syndrome. The work of Kaplan suggests that autoimmune factors might be important in the pathogenesis of rheumatic carditis.[19] Diseases of the gastrointestinal tract with possible autoimmune features include pernicious anemia,[23] chronic gastritis, some types of cirrhosis, aphthous ulcer, and chronic pancreatitis. The demonstration that lymphocytes taken from patients with ulcerative colitis are cytotoxic for human fetal colonic mucosal cells in tissue culture has led to interest in the role of autoimmunity in this disorder.[27] A delayed hypersensitivity reaction may be involved. Other diseases in which autoimmune factors have been considered include idiopathic forms of Addison's disease, glomerulonephritis, the postmyocardial infarction and postcardiotomy syndromes, sympathetic ophthalmia, endophthalmitis phacoanaphylactica, and certain types of infertility. In most of these the evidence is still controversial, however, and final proof of the autoimmune nature of the process is lacking.

Autoimmune factors may also play a part in the pathogenesis of certain diseases involving multiple organs and systems. These disorders include systemic lupus erythematosus (SLE), rheumatoid arthritis, and Sjögren's syndrome. They are characterized by the appearance of antibodies which react with antigens found in most body tissues. The lupus erythematosus cell factor found in systemic lupus erythematosus and sometimes in other disorders is a circulating 7S gamma globulin which reacts with nucleoprotein found in cell nuclei. Other antinuclear factors reacting with DNA or with histone may also be present. In addition, non-organ-specific complement-fixing antibodies are present which react with a complex variety of antigens present in mitochondrial, microsomal, and soluble subcellular fractions of organ extracts. Rheumatoid arthritis is characterized in the majority of cases by the presence of circulating 19S rheumatoid factors which are felt to be antibodies directed against denatured or altered gamma globulin. Patients with Sjögren's syndrome have a high incidence of circulating rheumatoid factors, antinuclear factors, and non-organ-specific complement-fixing or precipitating antibodies. All three disorders may be associated with hypergammaglobulinemia, cryoglobulinemia, and antibodies producing biologic false-positive Wassermann reactions. The diversity of autoantibodies found in this group of diseases, their not uncommon familial occurrence, and their frequent association with other disorders of postulated autoimmune etiology (acquired hemolytic anemia, thrombocytopenic purpura, chronic thyroiditis) have led to the suggestion that they are human counterparts of runt disease and NZB disease seen in experimental animals. As with most other disorders of proposed autoimmune etiology, however, final proof is lacking. The possibility still exists that the immunologic phenomena present are the *results* of tissue damage caused by an exogenous agent, such as an infectious organism or a drug, and are not the cause of the disease.

TISSUE TRANSPLANTATION

An *autograft* may be defined as an organ or tissue graft in which the donor is also the recipient. Grafts between genetically identical individuals are referred to as *isografts,* whereas the term *allograft* or *homograft* is used to describe grafts between genetically dissimilar members of the same species. A *xenograft* or *heterograft* is a graft between members of different species.

It has been recognized for many years that tissue autografts or isografts survive in the recipient when transplantation is performed with proper technical skill, whereas allografts and xenografts are rejected under normal circumstances. In the case of skin autografts in humans, for example, vascularization occurs rapidly and the graft is indistinguishable from surrounding normal skin by the twelfth day. Initial vascularization also occurs in human skin allografts, but shortly thereafter the graft becomes inflamed and edematous and is completely destroyed within two weeks. Histologically, the rejection of skin allografts is characterized by infiltration of the dermis with mononuclear cells and by vascular thrombosis with infarction.[28]

It has been clearly established that graft rejection is an immunologic phenomenon.[29] As discussed on page 18, the antigens initiating the immunologic response are called *histocompatibility antigens* and are determined by co-dominant *histocompatibility genes* which have chromosomal locations known as *histocompatibility loci.* There are a number of strong and weak histocompatibility loci in each animal species in which studies have been performed. Although antigenic specificity determined by the strong H-2 histocompatibility locus in mice probably resides in a lipoprotein complex, the chemical nature of histocompatibility antigens in man is still unknown.

The immunologic mechanisms involved in allograft rejection have been studied extensively. Circulating antibodies directed against histocompatibility isoantigens present in the donor but not in the recipient can be demonstrated in the latter's serum by a number of immunologic techniques. These antibodies may be important in the rejection of grafts composed of dissociated cells but are probably not of much significance in the rejection of solid tissue allografts. It appears likely that the rejection of solid tissue allografts is a cell-mediated phenomenon involving cells of the lymphoid series.[30, 31] An important piece of evidence supporting this theory is the observation that sensitivity to solid tissue allografts can be passively transferred from one individual to another with lymphoid cells but not with serum. The mechanism by which "sensitized" lymphocytes might cause actual graft destruction is unknown.

Graft survival can be prolonged in experimental animals by a variety of techniques which suppress the immune response.[30] These include neonatal thymectomy, removal of circulating lymphocytes via a thoracic duct fistula or with heterologous antilymphocyte serum, blockade of the reticuloendothelial system by injection of colloidal or particulate matter such as trypan blue, whole-body irradiation, and the use of various immunosuppressive drugs. These techniques are nonspecific since they tend to block a variety of immunologic responses in the recipient rather than merely suppress the rejection of a particular allograft. The specific suppression of graft rejection without concomitant alteration of the host's ability to respond to other antigens is obviously more desirable but also more difficult to obtain. The production of immunologic tolerance to the graft is one specific method which is promising.[32] A second method involves the phenomenon of *immunologic enhancement*.[30] This term refers to the ability of circulating antigraft antibody to delay graft rejection. The mechanism underlying this seemingly paradoxical effect is still unknown.

Allografts have been performed in humans with a variety of tissues and organs[30, 33] but have been most successful in the case of the kidney. A large number of renal allografts have been performed in patients with chronic renal insufficiency resulting from diseases such as chronic glomerulonephritis or chronic pyelonephritis.[34] The need for histocompatibility typing of donor and recipient prior to transplantation is apparent, but few satisfactory techniques are available as yet.[35] Most clinicians performing renal transplants have matched the donor and recipient only on the basis of major blood group antigens. Kidneys have been transplanted between unrelated donor-recipient pairs, but there is good evidence indicating that the graft has a better chance of survival when the donor and recipient are related.[34] More sophisticated techniques for donor selection are still in the process of development. Methods which have been tried include skin testing prospective donors with the recipient's leukocytes, grafting recipient and prospective donor skin into a "third man," tissue culture of lymphocyte mixtures from recipient and prospective donors, and comparison of the capacity of the donor and recipient's leukocytes to be agglutinated or injured by a battery of antisera. Further basic information about human histocompatibility antigens and the development of specific typing sera should help greatly in solving these problems.

Immunosuppressive therapy is begun prior to or at the time of transplantation. The immunosuppressive agent most widely used is azathioprine (Imuran), a purine antimetabolite. Corticosteroids also have been useful in suppressing graft rejection. Numerous other procedures have been tried including local irradiation, whole-body irradiation, splenectomy, thymectomy, and use of many other immunosuppressive drugs.

Although the surgical techniques involved have been perfected, renal transplantation in humans still presents a number of problems. Infection with a variety of organisms, hepatitis as a result of multiple blood transfusions, hypercortisonism, and bone marrow depression caused by immunosuppressive agents have all occurred frequently in the recipient. In spite of treatment with immunosuppressive drugs, rejection crises commonly occur. These usually present themselves with fever, pain in the graft area, and a decrease in renal function. Fortunately, rejection crises can often be aborted by treatment with corticosteroids, Actinomycin C, or local graft irradiation. Another encouraging aspect of the problem is the observation that graft rejection need not be an all-or-none phenomenon and that renal allografts can continue to function for prolonged periods in the presence of histologic evidence of rejection. In spite of the difficulties encountered, the overall results of renal transplantation have been encouraging enough to stimulate investigative work with other types of allografts.

IMMUNIZATION BY PREGNANCY AND TRANSFUSIONS

In a sense, pregnancy constitutes the most common type of allograft. The question concerning why the fetus is not rejected by its mother has only recently received serious attention from immunologists.[36] Information about this subject may have clinical relevance in regard to some cases of infertility or habitual abortion. Aside from these points, immunization of the mother to fetal antigens which reach the maternal circulation is not infrequent. This event is potentially hazardous to the fetus if the mother forms IgG antibodies which can cross the placenta; it also may predispose the mother to reactions to subsequent transfusions of blood containing antigens in common with the fetus.

Transfusions constitute the next most common type of "allograft," and again there is the potentiality of isoimmunization of the recipient.

A discussion of the several neonatal and post-transfusion disorders which result from isoimmunization to erythrocyte, leukocyte, or platelet antigens is beyond the scope of this text, but the clinical immunologist will find that these topics are thoroughly reviewed elsewhere.[37, 38] Interest in this area of immunohematology has been heightened recently by active efforts to prevent and treat Rh isoimmunization.[39–41]

REFERENCES

1. Raffel, S.: Immunity. Ed. 2. p. 333, New York, Appleton-Century-Crofts, 1961.
2. *Ibid.*, pp. 3–31.
3. *Ibid.*, p. 357.
4. *Ibid.*, p. 358.
5. Good, R., Kelly, W., Rotstein, J., and Varco, R.: Immunological deficiency diseases. Progr. Allergy 6:187, 1962.
6. Peterson, R., Cooper, M., and Good, R.: The pathogenesis of immunologic deficiency diseases. Am. J. Med. 38:579, 1965.
7. Gitlin, D.: The hypogammaglobulinemias. Disease-a-Month, Chicago, The Year Book Publishers, May, 1962.
8. Kelly, W., Lamb, D., Varco, R., and Good, R.: On investigation of Hodgkin's disease with respect to the problem of homotransplantation. Ann. New York Acad. Sc. 87:187, 1960.
9. Urbach, F., Sones, M., and Israel, H.: Passive transfer of tuberculin sensitivity to patients with sarcoidosis. New England J. Med. 247:794, 1952.
10. Wilson, W., Kirkpatrick, C., and Talmage, D.: Suppression of immunologic responsiveness in uremia. Ann. Int. Med. 62:1, 1965.
11. Taliaferro, W.: Modification of the immune response by radiation and cortisone. Ann. New York Acad. Sc. 69:745, 1957.
12. Hitchings, G., and Elion, G.: Chemical suppression of the immune response. Pharmacol. Rev. 15:365, 1963.
13. Schwartz, R.: Immunosuppressive drugs. Progr. Allergy 9:246, 1965.
14. Mirick, G.: The effects of ACTH and cortisone on antibodies in human beings. Bull. Johns Hopkins Hosp. 88:332, 1951.
15. Dameshek, W.: Autoimmunity: theoretical aspects. Ann. New York Acad. Sc. 124:6, 1965.
16. Waksman, B.: Autoimmunization and the lesions of autoimmunity. Medicine 41:93, 1962.
17. Rose, N., and Witebsky, E.: Studies on organ specificity. V. Changes in thyroid gland of rabbit following active immunization with rabbit thyroid extracts. J. Immunol. 76:417, 1956.
18. Weigle, W.: Termination of acquired immunologic tolerance to protein antigens following immunization with altered protein antigens. J. Exper. Med. 116:913, 1962.
19. Kaplan, M., and Svec, K.: Immunologic relation of streptococcal and tissue antigens. III. J. Exper. Med. 119:651, 1964.
20. Oliner, H., Schwartz, R., and Dameshek, W.: Studies in experimental autoimmune disorders. I. Clinical and laboratory features of autoimmunization (runt disease) in the mouse. Blood 17:20, 1961.
21. Holmes, M., and Burnet, F.: The natural history of autoimmune disease in NZB mice: a comparison with the pattern of human autoimmune manifestations. Ann. Int. Med. 59:265, 1963.
22. Waksman, B.: Experimental allergic encephalomyelitis and the "auto-allergic" diseases. Internat. Arch. Allergy (Suppl.) 14:2, 1959.
23. Rose, N., and Taylor, K.: The autoimmune diseases. Med. Clin. North America 49:1675, 1965.
24. Doniach, D., and Roitt, I.: Autoantibodies in disease. Ann. Rev. Med. 13:213, 1962.
25. Kunkel, H., and Tan, E.: Autoantibodies and disease. Advances Immunol. 4:351, 1964.

26. Shulman, N.: A mechanism of cell destruction in individuals sensitized to foreign antigens and its implication in autoimmunity. Ann. Int. Med. *60:*506, 1964.

27. Perlmann, P., and Broberger, O.: *In vitro* studies of ulcerative colitis. II. Cytotoxic action of white blood cells from patients on human fetal colon cells. J. Exper. Med. *117:*717, 1963.

28. Henry, L., Marshall, D., Friedman, E., Dammin, G., and Merrill, J.: The rejection of skin homografts in the normal human subject. III. Histological findings. J. Clin. Invest. *41:*420, 1962.

29. Billingham, R., and Silvers, W., *in* Samter, M.: (ed.) Immunological Diseases. pp. 172–187, Boston, Little, Brown & Co., 1965.

30. Russell, P., and Monaco, A.: The biology of tissue transplantation. New England J. Med. *271:*502–510; 553–562; 610–615; 664–671; 718–725; 776–783, 1964.

31. Gowans, J.: The role of lymphocytes in destruction of homografts. Brit. Med. Bull. *21:*106, 1965.

32. Shapiro, F., Martinez, D., Smith, J., and Good, R.: Tolerance of skin homografts induced in adult mice by multiple injections of homologous spleen cells. Proc. Soc. Exper. Biol. & Med. *106:*472, 1961.

33. Woodruff, M.: Biological and clinical aspects of organ transplantation. Brit. Med. Bull. *21:*176, 1965.

34. Murray, J., Gleason, R., and Bartholomay, A.: Fourth report of the human kidney transplant registry: 16 September 1964 to 15 March 1965. Transplantation *3:*684, 1965.

35. Goldsmith, K.: Donor selection and compatibility typing. Brit. Med. Bull. *21:*162, 1965.

36. Billingham, R.: Transplantation immunity and the maternal-fetal relation. N. England J. Med. *270:*667, 720, 1964.

37. Mollison, P. L.: Blood Transfusion in Clinical Medicine. Oxford, Blackwell Scientific Publications, 1961.

38. Ackroyd, J. F. (ed.): Immunological Methods. Philadelphia, F. A. Davis Co., 1964.

39. Wheeler, W., and Ambuel, J.: Use of exchange transfusion in the treatment of erythroblastosis. Pediat. Clin. North America *4:*383, 1957.

40. Liley, A.: The use of amniocentesis and fetal transfusion in erythroblastosis fetalis. Pediatrics *35:*836, 1965.

41. Finn, R., Clarke, C., Donahoe, W., McConnell, R., Sheppard, P., Lehane, D., and Kulke, W.: Experimental studies on the prevention of Rh haemolytic disease. British Med. J. *1:*1486, 1961.

Chapter Twenty

PSYCHOLOGICAL ASPECTS OF ALLERGY

JAMES A. McLEAN, M.D.

RELATIONSHIP BETWEEN PSYCHIC ILLNESS AND IMMUNOLOGIC DISEASE

Every person who presents himself to a physician with a complaint must be evaluated not only from an organic standpoint but also on a psychological basis. A great deal of misinformation has been published concerning psychiatric factors in allergic disease. In allergic patients the importance of functional elements varies considerably; it may be the major factor in one patient, of no demonstrable part in another, and of intermediate significance in still others. When symptoms both of allergy and of nervous tension are present, there are four major theoretical possibilities: (1) allergy may cause the behavioral symptoms; (2) psychic illness associated with the state of nervous irritability may accentuate the allergic symptoms; (3) the two conditions may have nothing other than a coincidental relationship; (4) both may be due to some third factor or combination of factors.

There is no doubt that the first of these possibilities actually does occur. It is common experience for patients and particularly their families to note that during the hay fever season they may be nervous, tired, and irritable. Children with hay fever may misbehave and be resistant to normal discipline. Improvement of this psychological symptom is an important benefit of the management of allergy. The dyspnea of severe bronchial asthma is a frightening experience for anyone. Even the most stable individual is apt to become frightened when he is unable to breathe. The relief of this anxiety is most gratifying as the asthma is brought under control. In addition to these relatively mild nervous reactions, more severe psychological disturbances at times have been attributed to allergy.

The next possibility—that psychic illness may influence allergic symptoms—also merits careful consideration. The general assumption is that psychic factors as well as weather changes, infections, and endocrine disturbances act as aggravating, secondary or precipitating factors in the production of allergic symptoms (see Chapter 2). It is common experience to observe flare-ups in atopic dermatitis, urticaria, asthma, and other allergic diseases following periods of emotional stress; although this sequence of events does not necessarily prove a cause-and-effect relationship, the frequency with which it occurs strongly implies that such is the case. It is of interest in this connection that Wolf and his associates have reported producing, by means of pain and psychic stimuli, changes in the eosinophil content of the nasal secretions and in the appearance of the nasal mucosa which are essentially identical with those produced by exposure to a known allergen.[1] In asthma, also, there is nothing in the physical examination of the chest to distinguish asthma attacks which have been precipitated by emotional or allergenic stimuli.

The concept that psychogenic disturbances act as trigger mechanisms or precipitating factors implies that there is some underlying abnormality upon which the psychic elements act. This raises the question whether emotional disturbances can be completely responsible for allergic symptoms in some individuals. From clinical observations, there seem to be cases in which the patient's symptoms appear to be accounted for entirely by emotional upsets, and no immunologic disturbance can be demonstrated. However, other nonspecific factors are often important in these patients. Damp or rainy weather, "cooling" temperature drop in late afternoon and early evening, exercise, exertion (physical or emotional), minor upper respiratory infections, yawning or laughing, and other factors also seem to trigger symptoms or aggravate or prolong existing ones. Furthermore, the importance of emotional elements seems to vary not only from one patient to another but also within the same patient from time to time.

It should be emphasized that although there seems to be a definite relationship between the patient's symptoms and certain emotional stresses, evaluation of the case from an immunologic standpoint should not be neglected. The physician who overlooks the allergic investigation may miss a further opportunity for helping many of his patients and also may cause considerable justifiable resentment on the part of those who sought his help. The response of a patient to psychotherapy will be disappointing unless he is under good immunologic management, and, likewise, immunologic and pharmacologic management alone will fail unless the psychological aspects are considered. Treatment, therefore, depends upon individual evaluation of both factors in each case.

The third possible relationship between psychic and immunologic factors in allergic patients, i.e., that the two are present only by coincidence, is frequently the case. This, of course, can be observed, and the preoccupation with which the neurotic patient regards the symptoms of his seasonal hay fever or lists in great detail his gastrointestinal complaints to the allergist are behavior patterns well known to all who care for the sick. There is no reason why the patient may not have both psychoneurosis and ragweed hay fever, but it is not necessary to be emotionally unstable in order to have hay fever. The substantial prevalence of both types of illness makes it inevitable that their coincidental occurrence will not be infrequent.

An additional, hypothetical possibility is that both psychic and immunologic disturbances might be caused by some third factor or combination of factors. A genetic predisposition to both types of disease merits consideration, but there appears to be no data to support this possibility.

Conversely, several observers have been impressed by the low incidence of asthma in mental hospitals, which is suggestive of an inverse relationship between *psychoses* and asthma. There has not been uniform agreement on this point, however, and a more precise definition of the types of both asthma and psychoses is necessary in order to clarify possible relationships with more certainty.[2]

PSYCHOLOGICAL VARIABLES

The role of psychological characteristics in allergic disorders has been investigated from a description of the personalities of allergic and nonallergic individuals. This engenders much controversy in the literature, and many reports describe the typical asthmatic personality profile without adequate specification concerning the patients and control group studied. One study, in which allergic patients were classified by skin testing and inhalation challenges, reported no differences between the neurosis scores of "allergic" and "nonallergic" adult female asthmatic groups, although the asthma patients had a higher score than a control group of normal adult females.[3] Another investigator studied children with asthma and children with chronic cardiac disease along with their well siblings and matched control children by personality test interpretations.[4] No distinctive personality pattern emerged between the chronically ill children (asthmatic or cardiac) and their siblings, although all three groups were more neurotic and dependent than the control group.

Dependence on the mother with fear of separation, the "suppressed cry," and family interaction are examples of conflict which have also been hypothesized as being etiologic in respiratory allergies. While Miller and Baruch found maternal rejection etiologically important in the development of allergic symptoms, their control group of children also had behavioral problems.[5] Studies by Fitzell, Cutter, and Margolis have shown no differences between mothers of asthmatic children and those of children with other medical problems.[6-8] Fitzell also found no differences between mothers of children with mild or severe asthma. Dubo and associates discerned no relationship between either asthmatic severity or response to medical treatment and the emotional tone of the family; also, no asthmatic personality was found.[9] An interesting alternate hypothesis to the suppressed cry symbolism in asthma is that since both crying and laughing provoke asthma in some children, crying is avoided as is laughter because of the fear of precipitating an attack.[10]

The assumption that a particular psychosomatic illness evolves out of the psychological accompaniments to a particular psychological stress, that is, psychosomatic specificity, has not been substantiated in allergic disorders. However, recent work has suggested that psychological differences may exist in a population of allergic patients. Purcell studied asthmatic children in a residential treatment center and found two groups: a rapidly remitting group characterized by more neurotic symptoms and later onset of asthma and a steroid-dependent group of asthmatic children.[11] The mothers of the former scored higher in authoritarian control and hostility rejection and the fathers showed a higher "psychologically unhealthy" score than the latter group. These findings suggest that the allergic population is both immunologically and psychologically heterogenous, and this could explain many of the discrepancies between various conflicting reports in the literature.

The concept of "conditioned asthma" has been investigated in the laboratory utilizing the responses of sensitized animals to aerosol inhalation challenge and auditory stimuli and later re-challenge with only auditory stimuli. Dekker was able to obtain a learned "asthma response" in some human subjects.[12] Whether this is an operating force in the development and maintenance of asthma is speculative at present. In recent literature a reawakened interest in the role of hypnosis as a tool for research (suppression of immediate skin tests[13]) and possible therapy has been brought out. However, it still remains to be seen whether a sound basis of insight can be developed and whether control therapeutic studies will be forthcoming.

Leigh,[14] and Freeman and his colleagues,[2] in an excellent review in 1964, concluded that methodological problems, lack of standardization of techniques of allergic and psychiatric treatment, and insufficient follow-up have hampered the meaningful interpretation of research results in this important field. However, as newer studies develop, the theoretical possibilities enumerated earlier in this chapter can be more clearly delineated. With this fuller understanding of the basic allergic and psychological factors involved will come better methods of diagnosing and treating this group of diseases.

TREATMENT OF THE NEUROTIC PATIENT

It is difficult to care for the individual who presents himself with symptoms of allergy in whom, after exhaustive study, the etiologic basis appears to be largely psychological disturbance. When the patient is a wage earner or a mother, not only does the afflicted person suffer, but also those in the family feel the effect of the patient's illness. A large percentage of these persons do not need very specialized attention. The interested physician who not only is familiar with the organic features of his patient's illness, but also knows the home environment may often be able to help significantly by manner, suggestion, and reassurance, or simply by listening.

It is not within the scope of this manual to outline extensively the manner in which psychotherapy should be conducted. A number of excellent books on the subject are available.[14, 15] Often if the physician takes time to ask, problems of employment, family life, or marital adjustment may be unburdened to a sympathetic and accepting listener. Perhaps little more is needed in many cases than the sharing of a problem with friendly reassurance. Interviews in which the patient is permitted to discuss his feelings may lead to a better living adjustment. From such interviews the physician may be able to help his patient to recognize tensional features in his illness. There may be some conditions in the patient's life about which nothing can be done. An adjustment of attitude toward such situations, once they are identified, may be effected so that the patient can come to accept them without an excessive degree of reaction. The physician eases problems by talking frankly about them with his patient, without passing judgment.

Tensional factors in the life of the patient will come to light in the interview as being less profound, and perhaps here the physician can gradually point out that it is the attitude of the individual which exaggerates the situation. In such situations the patient may be brought to see that changes may be made which will resolve the problem. If the physician can help his patient to see minor irritations in their proper perspective, he can improve that person's outlook on life. Many patients are unaware of the possibility that manifestations of organic illness may be caused by psychogenic factors. When it seems to be propitious, the physician can explain how sometimes such symptoms as headaches or gastrointestinal upsets can be based on tensional problems.

Thus, through guided interviews the allergist can carry on superficial psychotherapy in which the patient is helped to study the problems confronting him and is trained to recognize and differentiate between those problems which are perhaps unchangeable and those which are present only because of the patient's attitude toward them. If it can be pointed out that it is the reaction to a situation which causes a patient's illness rather than the situation itself, the person can be directed into a more healthy type of reaction to the many factors which make up his life.

When the psychogenic disturbance is deep and this superficial approach seems inadequate, the patient should be referred to a psychiatrist.

ALLERGIC TREATMENT FOR THE NEUROTIC PATIENT

There still remains the problem of treating patients in whom an immunologic basis for their symptoms remains uncertain by current techniques, and perhaps some of these symptoms may well be on a psychological basis. To conduct a course of hyposensitization in such people may indeed provide transient or protracted improvement, but this is poor medical practice. It brands the patient's condition as unalterably "allergic," for he has been to the allergist, gone through the evaluation, and come out of this experience receiving "allergy treatment" for his condition. In a situation in which the physician is uncertain of the diagnosis and must undertake a therapeutic trial for a short period, for example an elimination diet or perhaps a dust avoidance program, it is essential that he inform the patient that he is entering a trial—a diagnostic experience and nothing more—so that patient and doctor know that the question of allergy is not settled. Suggestion to the patient that he has nonexistent allergies makes future psychotherapy much more difficult.

In patients whose psychoneurotic features are significant, there should be definite pharmacologic indications for any drug given. Administration of a drug is justified only in order to modify some definite physiologic or immunologic disturbance. The simple program usually works best.

Meanwhile, the patient should be encouraged to try to adjust to his problems under the guidance of the physician. Psychiatrists point out the dangers of untrained persons delving too deeply into the causes of psychological illnesses. Probing, in such instances, may bring forth material which the physician cannot handle, and the patient may quickly misinterpret the physician's ineptitude in dealing with such material as rejection. Each patient fears this rejection, and such an episode will make the problem even worse. The more a patient is accepted by his physician and regarded as a fellow human being, the more he will benefit from his treatment.

REFERENCES

1. Wolf, S., Holmes, T. H., Trenting, T., Goodell, H., and Wolff, H. G.: An experimental approach to psychosomatic phenomena and rhinitis and asthma. J. Allergy 21:1, 1950.
2. Freeman, E. H., Feingold, B. F., Schlesinger, K., and Gorman, F. J.: Psychological variables in allergic disorders: a review. Psychosom. Med. 26:543, 1964.
3. Dekker, E., Babendregt, J. T., and deVries, K.: Allergy and neurosis in asthma. J. Psychosom. Res. 5:83, 1961.
4. Neuhaus, E. C.: A personality study of asthmatic and cardiac children. Psychosom. Med. 20:181, 1958.
5. Miller, H., and Baruch, D. W.: Psychosomatic studies of children with allergic manifestations. I. Maternal rejection: a study of 63 cases. Psychosom. Med. 10:275, 1948.
6. Fitzell, G. T.: Personality factors in certain attitudes toward child rearing among parents of asthmatic children. Psychosom. Med. 21:208, 1959.
7. Cutter, F.: Maternal Behavior and Childhood Allergy. Washington, Catholic University of America Press, 1955.
8. Margolis, M.: The mother-child relationship in bronchial asthma. J. Abnorm. & Soc. Psychol. 63:360, 1961.
9. Dubo, S., McLean, J. A., Ching, A. Y. T., Wright, H. L., Kauffman, P. E., and Sheldon, John M.: A study of relationships between family situations, bronchial asthma, and personal adjustment in children. J. Pediat. 59:402, 1961.
10. Purcell, K.: Distinctions between subgroups of asthmatic children's perception of events associated with asthma. Pediatrics 31:486, 1963.
11. Purcell, K., Bernstein, L., and Bukantz, S. C.: A preliminary comparison of rapidly remitting and persistently "steroid dependent" asthmatic children. Psychosom. Med. 23:305, 1961.
12. Dekker, E., Pelser, H. E., and Groen, J.: Conditioning as a cause of asthmatic attacks. J. Psychosom. Res. 2:97, 1957.
13. Black, S.: Shift in dose-response curve of Prausnitz-Küstner reaction by direct suggestion under hypnosis. Brit. J. Med. 1:990, 1963.
14. Hollender, M. H.: The Psychology of Medical Practice. Philadelphia, W. B. Saunders Co., 1958.
15. Masserman, T. H.: The Practice of Dynamic Psychiatry. Ed. 2, Philadelphia, W. B. Saunders Co., 1955.

Appendix I

PREPARATION OF ALLERGENIC EXTRACTS FOR TESTING AND TREATMENT

GEORGE L. PHILLIPS, B.S., M.S.*

The physician who does considerable work in the field of allergy may find it advantageous to prepare his own testing and treatment materials. By so doing, he need not rely upon the assurance of others regarding the quality and potency of extracts he uses. There also is considerable monetary benefit from making one's own allergenic materials if relatively large quantities are used. The preparation of extracts preferably should be carried out in a separate room used for no other purpose (Figure A–1). It should be as free from dust as possible and well lighted, and should have an air-conditioning unit which will keep the air relatively pollen-free and clean.

A sink with a suction apparatus attachment is useful. Suction for filtering extracts can also be secured by means of a pump obtained from a laboratory equipment source for less than 100 dollars. Shelves, cupboards, and storage space are needed. A table for allergen preparation is required. A fume hood with a ventilator is used in disposing of fumes and other vapors during evaporation and in performing nitrogen determinations. A Bunsen burner or an alcohol lamp is of value in preparing seals and in flaming vials before filling.

GENERAL PROCEDURES

In the preparation of extracts the original material should be altered as little as possible. It would theoretically be desirable to use purified allergens from which extraneous materials have been removed, and a start has been made on the development of suitable (but complex) techniques for obtaining purified fractions from ragweed under mild conditions. Unfortunately, however, present knowledge is too limited to

---

* Chief Pharmacist, University Hospital, University of Michigan Medical Center.

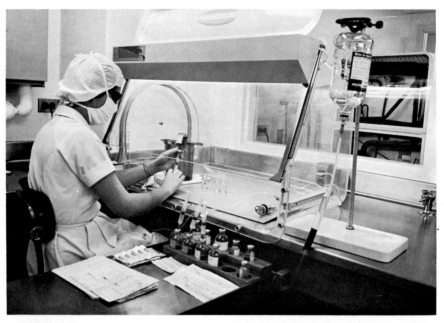

Figure A–1. Allergy treatment sets are prepared from stock bottles in a clean, well lighted area.

permit routine purification of allergenic extracts. Since multiple allergens may be present in some extracts, it is not wise to make premature attempts at extract purification until the immunochemistry of each allergenic substance is adequately worked out. At present the guiding principle is that the more crude a preparation is, the more likely it is to contain all the allergenic portions. If stored in a refrigerator in a glycerin mixture, the materials stay potent for at least one year. Therefore, large quantities, or one year's supply, can be made at one time.

The following general procedures are usually applicable to the preparation of all extracts.[1, 6] (In certain cases, some of the steps may be omitted, and in others, portions of the procedures must be modified.)

1. Grinding
2. Defatting
3. Extraction
4. Clarification
5. Dialysis
6. Concentration
7. Sterilization
8. Sterility tests
9. Standardization

Grinding

The pharmaceutical term for grinding is comminution. Its purpose is to increase the surface area of material to be extracted and to break up the cell membranes, since efficient extraction depends upon the state of subdivision.

Methods

*Blender.** The blender is useful for grinding materials which contain small amounts of moisture. It produces a shearing action, with six rotating blades or knives (two curving up, two down, and two straight) and rotates at 10,000 to 12,000 revolutions per minute. It can be used on dry materials only; if moisture is present, emulsions will form. All foods in group 1 except avocado and mushrooms are ground in the blender. Other items which are ground in this machine are: tobacco, tragacanth, quince seed, and caddis and May flies. Pollens are not ground.

*Juicer.** This is useful for breaking up and extracting materials containing a large amount of moisture, e.g., carrots, apples, pears, tomatoes (all foods in group 2) (Figure A–2). It consists of a high-speed revolving basin with shearing ridges on the bottom and perforated sides through which the extracted juice is hurled by centrifugal force into a collecting chamber. This in turn feeds out of a spout on the side of the machine. Fitting snugly over the whole unit is a metal cover that has an opening directly over the shearing surfaces, and through this opening the washed foods are fed. Fruits with an outer rind are peeled to remove

---

* Available from most appliance stores.

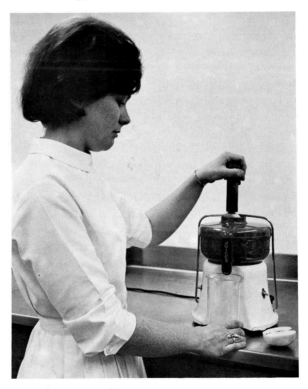

Figure A–2. Food is ground in juice squeezer to provide first stage in preparation of food testing material.

the rind. An ordinary food grinder might serve as a substitute for a Juicer.

Scissors or Shears. The third method of comminution is that of cutting by means of scissors. This is about the only way certain types of material can be put into a state of fine subdivision. The substances cut by scissors include: hair from camel, cat, cattle, dog, goat, hog, horse, and rabbit; feathers; kapok; and silk. (See note on animal dander, page 517.)

Defatting

Defatting is done to obtain clear solutions. Foods with a large amount of moisture usually do not require defatting. Ether (diethyl ether) is employed most commonly for defatting. The procedure is carried out effectively by shaking the material to be defatted at room temperature with successive portions of ether (enough to cover the material) and then decanting the oily ether extract before adding a fresh portion of ether. Finally it is filtered through fluted paper.

All pollens are defatted. It is advisable to save the oily ether extract and concentrate it by evaporation. The oil is stored for use as patch testing material. The pollen oil usually is diluted with peanut oil or olive oil before use.

It is more efficient and convenient to defat a large amount of pollen at once. Therefore, when a new supply of pollen is received, the whole quantity should be defatted at once by adding ether directly to the bottle (if there is room), allowing the pollen to settle, and then decanting, saving the ether as well as the pollen. More thorough defatting can be achieved in a Soxhlet apparatus, but this is not necessary for routine clinical purposes. The pollen then is dried completely over calcium chloride, sealed in a dry jar, and labeled "defatted." When completely dry and defatted, the pollen stays potent indefinitely. Alternatively, the physician may request that the pollen be defatted at the commercial source when purchased. This can be done at moderate extra cost.

Some materials contain large amounts of irritating oils, resins, and waxes. Examples are coffee, tea, cocoa, cottonseed, pepper, mustard, and ginger. In defatting these materials, it is advisable to use three different solvents, such as toluene, alcohol, and ether, and to wash or extract with three portions of each. The volatile solvents (ether, and others) may be removed merely by allowing them to evaporate in air at room temperature or by using a hair dryer or fan to hasten the process. One should be sure to remove all the ether because a flame must be used to sterilize the neck of the bottles, and an explosion may result if residual ether is present.

Extraction

The purpose of extraction is to remove the active allergenic substances from the material and to put them into solution. Slightly alkaline buffer solutions commonly are used for extractions, since the pH tends to fall as extraction progresses. We employ a buffered saline mixture at pH 8. Usually extraction is carried out in a wide-mouthed bottle, which can be capped tightly and agitated, preferably on a shaking machine. For extraction, bottles should lie on their sides, exposing more surface. Extracting menstruums include:

1. Buffered saline (used at University of Michigan Hospital):

Sodium chloride, A.R.*	5.0 gm.
Monobasic potassium phosphate, A.R.	0.36 gm.
Dibasic sodium phosphate, A.R. (anhydrous)	7.0 gm.
Phenol crystals	4.0 gm.
Water for injection, to make	1000.0 ml.

2. Coca's solution (protein extractive solution):

Sodium chloride, A.R.	20.0 gm.
Phenol crystals	16.0 gm.
Sodium bicarbonate, A.R.	10.0 gm.
Water for injection, to make	4000.0 ml.

3. Glycerinated Coca's solution:

Sodium chloride, A.R.	2.5 gm.
Phenol, A.R.	2.0 gm.
Sodium bicarbonate, A.R.	1.25 gm.
Glycerin	500.00 ml.
Water for injection, to make	1000.00 ml.

In the preparation of the above solutions adjust pH to approximately 8.0, using sodium hydroxide or hydrochloric acid as indicated.

4. Physiological saline
5. Tenth normal sodium hydroxide
6. Sodium bicarbonate solution
7. Glycerin saline solution
8. Alcohol saline solution
9. Dextrose solution
10. Dextrose saline solution

All these require addition of preservative such as 0.5 per cent phenol.

All these solutions may be sterilized by filtration through a sterile microporous cellulose membrane filter (see page 514 for details,) † and transferred aseptically into previously sterilized containers.

Extraction is carried out by soaking (macerating) the material in question in extracting fluid for 24 to 72 hours at room temperature with occasional shaking. Extraction is improved by shaking on a machine for 30 minute periods at least eight times during the maceration period. Bacterial fermentation is arrested by adding 2 milliliters toluene.

In the case of scratch test materials, only enough saline is used to make the final volume isotonic.

Clarification

After the material has been extracted, the solvent containing the active ingredient must be separated from the residual material. Clarifica-

---

* A.R. (analytical reagent) specifies the grade of the material to be used.
† Millipore Filter Corp., Bedford, Massachusetts 01730; Gelman Instrument Co., Ann Arbor, Michigan 48104.

tion, or preliminary filtration, is done to remove excess suspended materials which might clog the bacteriologic filters used later to sterilize the solution.

Any of the following procedures may be used either singly or in combination to achieve the desired result. Materials, especially foods, may vary from one batch to the next. Therefore, the number of steps required may vary.

Methods used are:

1. Coarse filter paper
2. Cotton pledget in filter
3. Buchner suction funnel and coarse filter paper
4. Centrifugation and decanting of supernatant fluid
5. Allowing to stand overnight in refrigerator
6. Freezing in ice tray compartment followed by thawing

In the case of foods containing a large amount of moisture, the freshly extracted juice is filtered through coarse filter paper. Because this process is slow, it often is better, with a slowly filtering substance, to use two 6 inch funnels with fluted coarse paper or a Buchner funnel with suction. Most other items can simply be filtered through coarse paper. House dust can best be separated by placing it first in a Juicex and centrifuging off the solvent and then filtering through paper.

Dialysis

The purpose of dialysis is to dispose of irritating substances and coloring material which might stain the skin of the patient. Theoretically, the active ingredients are not removed by dialysis, but with the assumption that the less manipulation the materials are subjected to the more potent the extract will be, the technician uses dialysis usually for five substances, namely, house dust, mustard, potato, spinach, and beet. For some reason these seem to give universally positive reactions to scratch tests unless dialyzed.

Suspend the liquid to be dialyzed in a cellophane tube* about three feet long, and immerse the tube in buffered saline. Dialyze against the buffered saline for 24 hours or more as required. However, if one subsequently is going to concentrate the material ten times in preparation of concentrated, glycerinated scratch test extracts, the dialyzing fluid should consist of 85 per cent water, 10 per cent buffered saline, and 5 per cent glycerin. Change the dialyzing fluid every four hours. If the vol-

---

*Visking Tubing. Tubing is available in a number of sizes and weights from the Visking Corporation, 6733 West 65th Street, Chicago 38, Illinois.

We have found the 24/32-inch diameter (100 foot rolls) "NoJax" casing to be best suited for dialyzing small batches and also best for concentrating, as will follow in the next section.

For best results, the smaller the diameter of the tubing, the faster the material will be concentrated. If 24/32 inch tubing is used, 7 inches equals 50 milliliters.

ume tends to increase, the extract may be concentrated by suspending the tube in air and allowing it to reconcentrate after dialysis is finished.

Concentration

The purpose of concentration is to obtain a large amount of active ingredients in a small volume. Most materials are concentrated to one-tenth the original volume (500 to 50 milliliters). This process takes two to three days.

We use the same $2\frac{4}{32}$-inch Visking Tubing described under "Dialysis." A length of 7 inches of this tubing holds 50 milliliters of extract. Thus, we can tell at a glance when the process is completed. A 3 to 4 inch length of $\frac{1}{2}$ inch diameter glass tubing, with the ends slightly flared, is tied to the open end of the cellophane tube and this serves as a funnel for pouring into the tube (Figure A–3). It also serves as a means for clamping the tube onto a ring stand or other support neces-

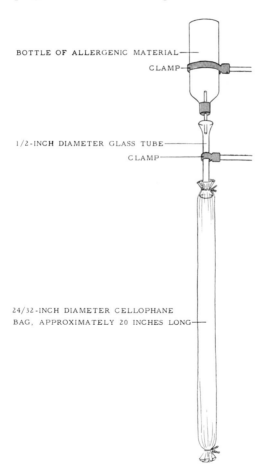

BOTTLE OF ALLERGENIC MATERIAL

CLAMP

1/2-INCH DIAMETER GLASS TUBE

CLAMP

24/32-INCH DIAMETER CELLOPHANE BAG, APPROXIMATELY 20 INCHES LONG

Figure A–3. Concentration apparatus.

sary to suspend it in air for drying. A fan blowing air onto the bag hastens evaporation or concentration. In order to keep the cellophane bag full, a bottle of the proper size containing extract is inverted above the bag so that a glass tube inserted into a cork in the neck of the bottle runs directly into the glass tube, holding the cellophane bag. In this way constant filling of the cellophane tube is provided.

Sterilization

Allergenic extracts are thermolabile and are sterilized by bacterial filtration. The following equipment is required (Figure A–4):

1. Vacuum pump, either water or electric
2. Collection flask with stopper and sidearm
3. Storage vials and stoppers
4. Filters

Seitz filters (SF-4, open type, three wing-bolts for vacuum filtration). Capacity of 100 milliliters with S-1 pads have been initially used in the past and are easily cleaned. However, the Millipore filter is very efficient and does not absorb protein from the material as does the Seitz filter. With Millipore equipment one needs first to filter glycerinated material through an xx40–047–00 stainless pressure filter using a series of increasingly fine mesh to prevent plugging.

a. An AP20–047–00 Microfiber glass prefilter
b. An RAWP–047–00 Millipore filter
c. An AAWP 047–AO Millipore filter
d. An HAWP 047–AO Millipore filter

Finally, a GSWP–047–AO Millipore filter is used with a superimposed AP20–042–00 (42 mm.) Microfilter glass prefilter. Complete instructions come with the equipment. Other types of microporous cellulose membrane filters also are available, such as the Gelman filters.

Figure A–4. STERILIZATION WITH BACTERIAL FILTRATION. A millipore filter is attached to suction (note circular air filter) and extract is drawn into flask. Sterile material can be removed by aseptic technique through tube at bottom of flask.

A sterile filter is employed and the substance is filtered into a sterile filling flask fitted with a cotton or Millipore air filter on the sidearm. It is important to standardize the extract *after* filtration. To decrease the amount of absorption, use the smallest filter that is convenient, as the amount absorbed is directly proportionate to the size of the filter.

After filtration, the substances are aseptically transferred to sterile allergy vials, capped with a sterile stopper, and labeled.

Extracts for scratch testing containing 50 per cent glycerine are not sterilized.

Sterility Tests

Sterility tests for both aerobic and anaerobic organisms should be run on the final product. Brain-heart infusion with 0.1 per cent agar and Thioglycollate medium with 0.1 per cent agar* make suitable media for testing for both aerobes and anaerobes. The transfer sample should be shaken well down into the medium in the test tube. The lower portion of the tube simulates anaerobic conditions.

Standardization

There are no accurate chemical methods for determination of allergenic potency. Several different systems have evolved for giving an approximate expression of the potency of allergenic extracts. The relative merits of these different methods of labeling allergens has been discussed on page 105. Tables A–1 and A–2 provide information which is helpful in converting from one type of unit to another, but it should be emphasized that most of these relationships are empirically derived and thus are not necessarily universally applicable owing to variations in materials and techniques. If one wishes to standardize extracts on the basis of "protein" nitrogen content, it is customary to determine the amount of nitrogen precipitated by phosphotungstic acid under the conditions described by Cooke.[3] Nitrogen generally is determined by the micro-Kjeldahl method. If a fume hood is not available or if one is not experienced with this method, the physician may have the determinations performed in a commercial laboratory.

PREPARATION OF ALLERGENS

The following specific directions serve to illustrate how the general procedures are combined in actual preparation of extracts.

Since a given volume of extracting solution takes up only a certain amount of the active ingredient of a substance, it is necessary to extract with a fairly large volume and then concentrate the resulting solution to a smaller volume. In order not to have too much salt and phenol

---

* These media are available in capped tubes ready to use from Difco Laboratories, Inc., Detroit, Michigan. Simply add 0.1 milliliter of material to be tested. Shake well and let stand preferably at 37° C. for seven days.

Table A–1. *Equivalents of 1:50 Dilution Extract**

1.00 ml. of a 1:50 Dilution Extract (Pollen Weight by Volume) Is Equivalent to:

1. 20,000 pollen units
2. 20,000 Noon units
3. 10,000 P.N. (protein nitrogen) units (Cooke)
4. 0.26 mg. total nitrogen (N)
5. 26,000 total nitrogen units

* Cooke, R. A.: Allergy in Theory and Practice. Philadelphia, W. B. Saunders Co., 1947.

Table A–2. *Equivalents of 0.001 mg. of Extracted Pollen**

0.001 mg. of Extracted Pollen Is Contained in:

1. 1 ml. of a 1:1,000,000 dilution extract (W/V)
2. 1 Noon unit
3. 1 pollen unit
4. 0.5 P.N. units (Cooke)
5. 0.000,013 mg. total nitrogen
6. 1.3 total nitrogen units

* Cooke, R. A.: Allergy in Theory and Practice. Philadelphia, W. B. Saunders Co., 1947.

in the final concentrated extract, only that amount which should be in the final volume of the concentrated extract is used. The final volume of scratch material contains 50 per cent glycerin as a preservative. For example:

Camel dander	10.0 gm.
Glycerin	25.0 ml.
Buffered saline	50.0 ml.
Distilled water	175.0 ml.
The 250 ml. is concentrated to	50.0 ml.

Allergens for Group 1

This group consists of:

Camel	Dog	Feathers	Orris root
Cat	Hog	Kapok	Caddis fly
Cattle	Horse	Silk	May fly
Goat	Rabbit	Tobacco	Brewer's yeast
			Pyrethrum

Preparation of Scratch Material (Final Concentration 1:5)

1. Cut hairs, feathers, kapok, and silk into fine pieces with scissors. Powder tobacco, orris root, and others in grinder.

2. Defat three times with ether. Cover material contained in a beaker with ether, stir well, and allow to stand for five minutes; then decant ether and dry with air.

3. Weigh 14 grams of the material.

4. To a sterile 32 ounce screw-capped, wide-mouth bottle add:

Material	14.0 gm.
Glycerin	35.0 ml.
Buffered saline	70.0 ml.
Freshly distilled water	244.0 ml.
Toluene	1.0 ml.
Total	350.0 ml.

Notice that 350 milliliters is made to ensure collection of 250 milliliters when filtered.

5. Extract at room temperature for 72 hours. Shake on machine four hours, preferably on second day of extraction.

6. Filter through coarse paper and collect 250 milliliters.

7. Concentrate to 50 ml. in cellophane tube $2\frac{4}{32}$-inch in diameter.

Preparation of Intracutaneous and Treatment Material (Final Concentration 1:50). It is important to remember that the final concentrations given here are stock dilutions, convenient for storage, but *further dilution* must be made prior to using these extracts for intradermal testing or treatment.

Material, defatted	4.0 gm.
Sterile buffered saline	196.0 ml.
Toluene	1.0 ml.

1. Cut hair, feathers, kapok, and silk into fine pieces with scissors. Powder the orris root, pyrethrum, and all others that are not powdered.

2. Defat the material and dry in the air.

3. Add 4 grams defatted material and 1 milliliter toluene to sterile buffered saline.

4. Extract at room temperature 72 hours. Shake in machine four hours, preferably on the second day of extraction.

5. Filter through a coarse paper. Obtain a 200 milliliter yield.

6. Sterilize by filtration.

7. Transfer aseptically to sterile 50 milliliter bottles.

8. Test for sterility. Label.

Notes on Collecting Material for Group 1

Hair. Cut hair is not a good source of the allergen to which the patient is sensitive. Rather, it is the epithelial debris (dandruff) which is the important factor. Combing and brushing the animal over a paper gives a yield of epithelial material which contains a large quantity of the allergen required to make good testing and treatment material.

Feathers. Freshly plucked feathers are not allergenic. Something related to the aging process or some external factor which is introduced through time and usage causes the feathers to become allergenic. The effective material is closely related to the house dust allergen.

The best source of feather dust is stuffing from used pillows and down comforters obtained from a renovating company. In our experience, there is not a specific allergen for duck, chicken, goose, or turkey feathers. Therefore, a mixture of old used feathers provides excellent testing material.

Kapok. Kapok allergen is obtained from kapok seed fibers (see page 451).

Silk. Two factors should be considered when making testing material of silk. The silk sericin acts as the glue which sticks the fibers together. This is water-soluble and is felt to be the cause of trouble in silk-sensitive patients. It can be removed from silk cloth by serial washing with soap and water. The other part of silk, the fibroin, is insoluble and unlikely to cause allergic symptoms. Therefore, to obtain silk extract for testing, unwashed sericin-containing silk should be obtained from a silk hose company, or unbleached silk cocoons may be purchased through silk processing firms.

Allergens for Group 2

Vegetable Gums. These may be obtained from any moderately large pharmaceutical supply house (see page 530).

This group consists of:

Karaya (Indian gum)	Acacia (gum arabic)
Tragacanth	Quince (cydonium)*

Preparation of Scratch Material

1. Assemble the following ingredients:

Gum	0.5 gm.
Glycerin	50.0 ml.
Toluene	1.0 ml.
Sterile buffered saline	50.0 ml.
Sterile distilled water	890.0 ml.

2. Mix all ingredients thoroughly.

3. Extract for 72 hours at room temperature under 1 milliliter toluene. Shake four hours.

4. Filter through coarse filter paper. Use 6 inch funnel. Keep adding enough of the following mixture—85 per cent distilled water, 10 per cent isotonic saline, and 5 per cent glycerin—to the residue on the filter paper to obtain 500 milliliters of filtrate.

5. If material becomes too viscous during preparation, stop and add sufficient glycerin to yield a 50 per cent concentration. Extract is now ready for use.

Preparation of Intracutaneous and Treatment Material

1. Assemble the following:

Gum	1.0 gm.
Toluene	1.0 ml.
Sterile buffered saline	490.0 ml.

2. Add the gum plus 1 milliliter toluene to the saline.

---

* The mucilage derived from quince seed is the allergenic substance used.

3. Extract at room temperature for 72 hours. Shake for four hours.
4. Filter through coarse filter paper.
5. Sterilize by filtration.
6. Test for sterility. Label.

Allergens for Group 3 (Dusts)

This group includes:

House floor dust	Thresher dust
Mattress dust	Autogenous dust
Mill dust	

In preparing house dust a more representative preparation is obtained if dusts from several sources are pooled and the extract made from this material. Dust should be obtained from houses containing no dogs, cats, or other animals. Old cotton linters, employed as stuffing from used mattresses, contain the best and most potent of house-dust allergen. This material may be obtained from a bedding renovating company.

Preparation of Scratch Material

1. Assemble the following:

Dust	100.0 gm.
Glycerin	25.0 ml.
Toluene	2.9 ml.
Buffered saline	50.0 ml.
Distilled water	325.0 ml.

2. Defat the dust three times with ether; dry in air.
3. Mix the ingredients plus 2 milliliters of toluene and extract at room temperature for 72 hours.
4. Filter all but house dust through paper. Note quantity of solvent obtained. Place house dust in Juicex and centrifuge off solvent. Note amount obtained.
5. Place in cellophane tube and dialyze 24 hours against a mixture containing 5.0 per cent glycerin, 10 per cent buffered saline, and 85 per cent distilled water. Change dialysate three times. Mark original volume on tube.
6. Concentrate to one-tenth original volume as obtained in step 4.

Endo House Dust. Because of its usual potency, Endo House Dust* extract is recommended as an additional testing material.

Preparation of Intracutaneous and Treatment Material

1. Assemble the following:

Dust	100.0 gm.
Toluene	2.0 ml.
Sterile buffered saline	400.0 ml.

2. Defat dust three times with ether.

---

* Made by Endo Products, Inc., Richmond Hill, New York. Order 1:40 concentration and dilute to 1:400 to 1:4000 for clinical use.

3. Dry with air. Add buffered saline plus 2 milliliters of toluene.

4. Extract 72 hours at room temperature.

5. All dusts but house dust filter through paper. For house dust, place in Juicex and centrifuge off solvent. Note quantity of solvent obtained. Filter through filter paper.

6. Place in cellophane tube and dialyze 24 hours against buffered saline, changing the dialysate three times during the course of dialysis. Measure column of fluid at point of original volume.

7. Concentrate to original volume by allowing cellophane tube to hang in air. The toluene also will evaporate during this time.

8. Take pH and if below 5.5 or above 8.5 adjust to that range with sodium hydroxide or hydrochloric acid.

9. Sterilize by filtration. Transfer to 50 milliliter bottles. Test for sterility. Label.

Allergens for Group 4 (Horse Serum)

Obtain nondespeciated horse serum from state biologic laboratories.

For scratch material use:

Horse serum	50 per cent
Glycerin	50 per cent

For intracutaneous material (1:50) use:

Horse serum	4.0 ml.
Sterile buffered saline	196.0 ml.

Add the horse serum to the sterile buffered saline. Filter through sterilizing filter and transfer aseptically to sterile 50 milliliter bottles. Test for sterility. Label. (Be sure to dilute to 1:500 or 1:5000 before using for intradermal testing.)

Allergens for Group 5 (Pollens)

This group consists of:

Alder (tag)	Bermuda grass	Sagebrush (common)
Birch (paper)	Kentucky bluegrass	Kochia
Box elder	Orchard grass	Russian thistle
Maple (mixed)	Redtop	Western waterhemp
Mountain cedar	Timothy	Wormwood (tall)
Cottonwood poplar	Plantain (English)	Shadscale
Elm (American)	Burweed marsh elder	Lamb's quarters
Hickory (shellbark)	Cocklebur	Pigweed
Oak (mixed)	Ragweed (giant)	Mesquite
Sycamore	Ragweed (short)	Mulberry (paper)
Walnut (black)	Ragweed (western)	Other pollens for
Willow (black)	Sagebrush (biennial)	special cases

Source and Collection of Pollen. The source of testing material is very important. Pollen has been collected on paper placed underneath pollinating plants, but there has been increasing use of techniques whereby pollen is aspirated directly from the flower into various trapping devices attached to a vacuum pump. The most important factor at the time of collection is immediate dehydration. Moisture is likely to cause loss of allergenic activity, whereas dehydrated pollen may be stored almost indefinitely in a stoppered bottle. We have some dry ragweed pollen which is potent after more than 20 years' storage. There is variation in the allergenicity of pollen collected from one year to the next. The only way to compensate for this is to assay potency biologically, such as by comparative skin tests with different lots of pollens.

One can purchase pollen from large collectors more inexpensively than one can collect the material oneself, but it should be inspected microscopically to make certain that there has not been an error in labeling and that there is no contamination by extraneous pollen, insect material, and other debris. Different types of pollen prepared by commercial houses vary substantially in cost depending particularly upon ease of collection. Competitive bids from reliable supply houses are suggested when purchasing large quantities of pollen.

Preparation of Scratch Material*
1. Assemble the following:

Pollen, defatted	10.0 gm.
Glycerin	25.0 ml.
Toluene	1.0 ml.
Buffered saline	50.0 ml.
Sterile distilled water	415.0 ml.

2. Defat pollen three times with ether (see section on defatting, page 510). One may wish to save the pollen oils. Label.
3. Pour out all but 415 milliliters from a liter bottle of sterile water. Add pollen, buffered saline, glycerin, and 1 milliliter toluene.
4. Extract for 72 hours at room temperature. Shake four hours.
5. Filter through fluted paper. Wash with a mixture of 85 per cent water, 10 per cent isotonic saline, and 5 per cent glycerin, and bring volume to 500 milliliters. If pollens filter slowly, filter material before adding glycerin.
6. Concentrate to 50 milliliters in cellophane tube $^{24}/_{32}$ inch in diameter.

An easy alternative method of making scratch testing material is as follows: Equal volumes of glycerin and saline are placed in a testing bottle and then an excess of dried pollen (e.g., 25 per cent of the weight of the glycerosaline) is poured into the bottle and the mixture shaken. To maintain the potency of the testing material, it may be wise to add more pollen to the bottle about once each month.

* One year's supply of pollen extract should be made at one time. It is confusing to change extracts after treatment has begun.

Even for a busy allergy practice not more than 5 milliliters of scratch testing material is needed for a one to two month period. Bottles of 5 to 10 milliliter capacity with dropper or glass applicators attached to the caps are inexpensive and satisfactory.

Preparation of Intracutaneous and Treatment Material (1:50)

1. Assemble the following:

Pollen	8.0 gm.
Toluene	1.0 ml.
Sterile buffered saline	392.0 ml.

2. Defat pollen three times with ether. Add to saline (see section on defatting).

3. Extract for 72 hours at room temperature under 1 milliliter toluene. Shake four hours.

4. Filter through coarse paper. Evaporate toluene.

5. Sterilize by filtration through sterilizing filter.

6. Transfer aseptically to sterile 50 milliliter bottles.

7. Test for sterility. Label.

Alternatively, 1:33 treatment material sometimes is used instead of the above-described 1:50. Dilute the concentrated extract with buffered saline for intracutaneous testing (1:500) and make additional dilutions for treatment.

Allergens for Group 6 (Fungi)

It is more difficult to prepare satisfactory mold extracts for testing or treatment purposes than pollen extracts. Most commercial extracts employ fungi grown in liquid media, whereas the following procedure permits extraction of allergens from fungi grown on a solid medium.

Preparation of Allergenic Mixed Fungus Extract from Culture Plates

1. Expose a protein hydrolysate medium in Petri dishes for approximately 12 minutes (seven minutes on a windy day) from the top of a high building. Use different Petri dishes each day. Collect plates on many different days so that a representative group of prevalent air-borne fungi will be harvested.

2. Cover plates, and let stand at room temperature for 21 days or until the growth of fungi covers the entire plate.*

3. Cover the entire plate with diethyl ether for 24 hours.

---

* It is important to obtain the spore fraction, and growth is watched until spores are observed. By using solid media, one gets maximal spore production. Scratching across the surface of the culture with a sterile wire loop stimulates sporulation. When spores are seen to be present on the cultures, the lids are removed from the Petri dishes and ether is poured on. Large quantities of mold extract should be made. If small quantities are to be run through, use a Swinney filter (for 5 to 10 milliliter quantities). Ordinarily, 50 to 100 milliliters of filtrate should be obtained for a satisfactory yield.

4. Remove cover and let stand to allow the ether to evaporate.

5. When plate is completely dry, add 10 milliliters Coca's solution to each plate. Let stand for 48 hours in refrigerator at 35 to 40° F., with frequent shaking.

6. Pour off the supernatant fluid into a large beaker and filter through a sterilizing filter. Pour into sterile bottle and label.

7. Test for sterility. Label. Scratch materials are prepared by adding an equal volume of glycerin to fungus extract.

Preparation of Intracutaneous and Treatment Material (1:50)

1. Assemble the following: defatted mold spores, to total 10 grams. In Michigan, we use:

Alternaria	2 gm.	Mucor	1 gm.
Hormodendrum	2 gm.	Penicillium (sp.)	1 gm.
Helminthosporium	1 gm.	Phoma	1 gm.
Aspergillus (sp.)	1 gm.	Toluene	1.0 ml.
Monilia (sp.)	1 gm.	Sterile buffered saline	500.0 ml.

2. Extract for 72 hours under toluene at room temperature. Shake frequently.

3. Filter through coarse paper. Evaporate toluene.

4. If Seitz filtration is to be used, first place material in centrifuge bottle, and spin at 2000 r.p.m. for four hours to separate the thick plug that may clog the Seitz filter. (Millipore series of filters do not become plugged and then centrifuging is not required.)

5. Filter to sterilize.

6. Transfer aseptically to sterile 50 milliliter bottles.

7. Test for sterility. Label.

Extracts of Single Fungi, Smuts, and Rusts. This group consists of:

Alternaria	Hormodendrum	Mucor
Aspergillus	Monilia	Penicillium
Fusarium	Representative smut	Yeast
Helminthosporium	Representative rust	Other fungi for special cases

Extracts of these types can be obtained from commercial sources (see page 531). Dilutions with buffered saline may be necessary for intracutaneous test and treatment material.

Allergens for Food Group 7

Since these foods contain only a small amount of moisture—usually about 5 per cent—it is safe to ignore their moisture content. Therefore, 20 grams of dried material are used to 80 grams of buffered saline. This preparation equals a concentrate analogous to the freshly extracted juice of the foods of group 2 which contain about 80 per cent moisture. For scratch test material the extract is concentrated to one-tenth its original volume.

Foods in group 1 consist of:

Oats	Corn (meal)	Avocado
Rice	Navy bean	Peanut
Rye	Coconut (dry)	Almond
Wheat	Buckwheat	Pecan
Barley	Mushroom*	Walnut

Preparation of Scratch Material

1. Assemble the following:

Food material	150.0 gm.
Sterile buffered saline	75.0 ml.
Glycerin	25.0 ml.
Butoben (10 per cent alcoholic solution)†	0.5 ml.
Sterile distilled water	500.0 ml.

2. Grind the pure grain well with a blender or run it through a hash grinder and then pound on a smooth surface until powdered.

3. Defat this powder. This is done with ether or toluene. Ether is more expensive, and toluene has the advantage of removing the water from the grain also.

4. Weigh the material.

5. Add buffered saline, glycerin, Butoben (10 per cent alcoholic solution), and water.

6. Extract for 72 hours at room temperature. Shake in shaking machine for four hours. Wheat or rye may become pigmented. If so, it should be dialyzed against 85 per cent water, 10 per cent isotonic saline and 5 per cent glycerin until clear. Other grains probably do not discolor and need not be dialyzed.

7. Filter through coarse filter paper.

8. Collect 500 milliliters. If necessary, wash material with water to obtain 500 milliliters.

9. Concentrate to 50 milliliters in cellophane tube $24/_{32}$ inch in diameter.

For coconut scratch material, use the shredded product (unsweetened). After defatting with ether, weigh out 150 grams and follow the same procedure as that described for other foods of group 1. For mushroom scratch material, cut up or chop the mushrooms (two 14 ounce packages) in pieces, defat with ether, and dry on paper until just moist. Weigh out 150 grams and follow the same procedure as that described for other foods in group 1.

Preparation of Intracutaneous Material. Instead of using a 20 per cent solution of the material and diluting it, the dilutions are in reality made prior to extraction, a 2 per cent extract being used.

---

* Fresh mushroom contains considerable moisture and may be easier to prepare following procedure for foods of group 8.

† Butoben (butyl parahydroxybenzoate) may be obtained from Goldschmidt Chemical Corp., 153 Waverly Place, New York, New York 10014.

1. Assemble the following:

Food material*	5.0 gm.
Toluene	1.0 ml.
Sterile buffered saline	245.0 ml.

2. Grind dry materials in blender, if necessary.

3. Defat with ether.

4. Weigh material.

5. Add the saline and 1 milliliter toluene.

6. Extract for 72 hours at room temperature. Shake in machine for four hours.

7. Filter through paper.

8. Sterilize by filtration through small sterilizing filter.

9. Transfer aseptically to sterile 50 milliliter bottles.

10. Run sterility test. Label. Use in this concentration for intracutaneous testing.

Allergens for Food Group 8

This group consists of:

Grapefruit†	Carrot	Cantaloupe
Orange†	Celery	Squash
Lemon†	Apple	Onion
Lettuce	Apricot	Asparagus
Pineapple	Peach	Cabbage
Sweet potato	Pear	Broccoli
Potato	Strawberry	Cauliflower
Tomato	Beet	Spinach
String bean		
Pea		

Remove the outer peel from grapefruit, orange, and lemon. Dialyze mustard, beet, potato, and spinach before concentrating.

Preparation of Scratch Material

1. Extract juice using Juicex.

2. Filter 500 milliliters through paper.

3. Add 25 milliliters glycerin and mix.

4. Add 0.5 milliliter alcoholic Butoben (10 per cent)

5. Shake in order to mix.

6. Concentrate to 50 milliliters in a cellophane tube $2\frac{4}{32}$ inch in diameter.

---

* Use the following formula to prepare the intracutaneous extracts of oats, rice, wheat, rye, and barley.

Material	2.5 gm.
Ascorbic acid	0.3 gm.
Sterile buffered saline	122.5 ml.

† Frozen foods are a source of allergen when fresh foods are not available. Fresh foods are preferred to avoid possible foreign substances such as sugar or preservatives.

Preparation of Intracutaneous Material

1. Dilute the freshly extracted juice 1:10 with sterile buffered saline.
2. Filter through paper.
3. Sterilize by filtration.
4. Transfer to sterile 50 milliliter bottles and allow to stand in refrigerator for one month.
5. Re-filter through sterile filter if necessary to clarify.
6. Transfer to sterile 50 milliliter bottles.
7. Test sterility. Label.

Allergens for Food Group 9 (Animal Protein)

This group consists of:

Beef	Lamb
Chicken	Pork

Preparation of Scratch Material. Fresh whole blood is obtained at minimal cost by contacting a local slaughter house. Do not allow it to remain longer than 48 hours or it may hemolyze. Add 25 milliliters glycerin to 25 milliliters undiluted bacteriologically filtered serum.

Preparation of Intracutaneous Material. The serum as above is diluted 1:10 with sterile buffered saline and is sterilized by filtration.

Serum	18.0 ml.
Sterile buffered saline	162.0 ml.

Allergens for Food Group 10 (Seafoods)

This group consists of:

Clam	Shrimp	Smelt
Oyster	Salmon	Perch
Lobster	Whitefish	

Protein from the specific fish may be used as a source of allergen. These may be obtained from commercial sources. Scratch material only is prepared from this group.

Preparation of Scratch Material

1. Assemble the following:

Fish protein	1.0 gm.
Sodium hydroxide (N/10)	20.0 ml.
Sterile buffered saline	5.0 ml.
Glycerin	25.0 ml.

2. Weigh the fish protein.
3. Add the sodium hydroxide to a sterile, stoppered, wide-mouthed bottle.
4. Add the fish protein.

5. Allow to stand with occasional shaking for 72 hours.

6. Add the buffered saline and glycerin. Shake. Label.

Allergens for Food Group 11 (Egg)

Put the whole fresh egg in 70 per cent alcohol for several hours. Then insert a large sterile needle through the shell and aspirate egg white with a syringe. Put it directly into a sterile container.

Preparation of Scratch Material. To 32 milliliters of fresh egg white (white of one large egg) add 32 milliliters of 50 per cent glycerin.

Preparation of Intracutaneous Material. Dilute the fresh egg white 1:1000 with sterile buffered saline. Sterilize by filtration. Test for sterility; label.

Egg white	0.2 ml.
Sterile buffered saline	199.8 ml.

Allergen for Food Group 12 (Milk)

To obtain lactalbumin fraction:

1. Defat fresh skim milk twice with ether, using a separatory funnel.

2. To 600 milliliters of the milk, add 1 rennin (junket) tablet and incubate at 37° C. for one and one-half hours. This produces a casein curd.

3. Filter.

Preparation of Scratch Material. To 500 milliliters of the filtrate obtained in step 3, add 25 milliliters glycerin and dialyze overnight. Concentrate to 50 milliliters in cellophane tubing $2\frac{4}{32}$ inch in diameter.

Preparation of Intracutaneous Material

1. Dilute the filtrate in step 3 to 1:10 with sterile buffered saline.

2. Sterilize by filtration.

3. Transfer to sterile 50 milliliter bottles.

4. Test for sterility. Label.

Allergens for Food Group 13

This group consists of:

Coffee*	Cottonseed	Mustard
Tea	Pepper	Ginger
Cocoa		

This group is made up of substances which contain a large amount of resins, volatile oils, and other irritating substances. In order to remove these substances, the material is washed three times with the following: toluene, 95 per cent alcohol, and ether, in the order given. Then scratch and intracutaneous material extracts are prepared exactly as for foods in

---

* Use roasted coffee beans.

group 7 except that they should be dialyzed after extraction (page 512, step 6).

Allergens for Food Group 14 (Banana)

Preparation of Scratch Material

1. Assemble the following:

Banana	800.0 gm.
Glycerin	25.0 ml.
Buffered saline	64.0 ml.
Butoben (10 per cent alcoholic solution)	0.8 ml.
Distilled water	711.0 ml.

2. Slice the banana into thin slices.
3. Defat with ether. Then weigh.
4. Add the glycerin, buffered saline, Butoben, and water, and extract for 72 hours at room temperature under toluene. Shake for four hours.
5. Filter through coarse paper.
6. Concentrate 500 milliliters to 50 milliliters in cellophane tube.
7. Place in bottle and label.

Preparation of Intracutaneous Material

1. Assemble the following:

Banana	40.0 gm.
Toluene	1.0 ml.
Sterile buffered saline	360.0 ml.

2. Slice banana into thin slices.
3. Defat with ether, then weigh.
4. Add the buffered saline and 1 ml. of toluene and extract for 72 hours at room temperature. Shake for four hours.
5. Filter through coarse paper; collect 200 milliliters.
6. Sterilize by filtration.
7. Transfer to sterile 50 milliliter bottles.
8. Test for sterility and label.

Allergen for Food Group 15 (Flaxseed)

Preparation of Scratch Material. Scratch material only is prepared from flaxseed.

1. Assemble the following:

Flaxseed	50.0 gm.
Glycerin	25.0 ml.
Toluene	2.0 ml.
Buffered saline	64.0 ml.
Butoben (10 per cent alcoholic solution)	0.8 ml.
Distilled water	711.0 ml.

2. Grind flaxseed in blender.

3. Defat three times each with toluene, 95 per cent alcohol, and ether. Then weigh.

4. Add the remainder of the ingredients.

5. Extract for 72 hours under toluene at room temperature. Shake for four hours. Concentrate to thickest usable consistency. Add glycerin q.s. 50 per cent.

PRESCRIPTION PREPARATION

The allergy prescription should be filled under a semisterile hood or shield taking all the precautions required for aseptic technique (Figure A–1).* The rubber diaphragms of the extract storage vials should be disinfected with a cotton swab saturated with isopropanol 50 per cent or ethanol 70 per cent. Sterile 5 milliliter syringes are used for withdrawing the extracts from the stock bottles and then for making the dilutions. The most concentrated solution is prepared as follows:

Allergenic Extract 1:50

Mixed fungus,	1:50	30 per cent	3.0 ml.
Ragweeds,	1:50	20 per cent	2.0 ml.
House dust,	1:50	50 per cent	5.0 ml.

---

* A convenient vial for dispensing the allergy prescription is the Type I glass vial similar to that manufactured by the Wheaton Glass Co., of Millville, New Jersey, under the trade name of "Twentieth Century Line." These vials may be obtained in two neck finishes and several different capacities. A good grade of rubber stopper for allergens is essential. We have used the 124 stock manufactured by the West Co. of Phoenixville, Pennsylvania. These stoppers are available in pink, white, yellow, and green. Some clinicians prefer to color code the various dilutions of the allergenic extracts and the colored stopper serves this purpose. Aluminum foil closures as well as the Fermpress closing tool (crimper) may also be obtained from the West Co. (Figure A–5).

Figure A–5. PLACING CAPS ON VIALS. With closing tool, sterile rubber stoppers are held snugly in place with aluminum collars.

This mixture constitutes the 1:50 extract. Serial dilutions are prepared from this initial bottle as follows:

Initial extract mixture (percentages indicated by the physician)	1.0 ml.
Sterile buffered saline	9.0 ml.

Thus, the 1:500 extract is prepared, and the 1:5000 extract is made in a similar fashion using the 1:500 extract as starting material.

Labels should be written carefully, giving the patient's name, components of extract, and date of preparation. Since the allergy prescription must be stored under refrigeration, label varnish or Scotch Tape over the label helps maintain legibility for identification.

Federal Licensure

The manufacturing or compounding of allergenic products intended for *interstate* sale, export, or import must be carried out in laboratories that have been licensed as required by Section 351 of the Public Health Service Act.* The provisions of this act do not prohibit the compounding of allergenic materials which would be dispensed by prescription or by a physician when dispensing and administration is intended for use within the state of origin.

Use of Pollen Mixtures

Since a patient allergic to a given pollen often is also sensitive to other pollens from botanically closely allied plants, it is common to treat such individuals with mixtures of the related pollens (page 103). In anticipation of this need, it is our practice to stock pollen mixtures for hyposensitization, such as "mixed trees" and "mixed weeds." The composition of these mixtures should, of course, be varied in accordance with the pollens prevalent and allergenically potent in the part of the country in which the patient lives. Mixtures which we have found useful in the Great Lakes region are shown on page 531.

SOURCES OF ALLERGY SUPPLIES

Powdered allergens (for preparing testing and treatment extracts):
  Abbott Laboratories, North Chicago, Illinois.
  C. G. Blatt & Co., 10930 E. 25th St., Independence, Missouri 44231.
  Greer Drug Co., Lenoir, North Carolina.
  Hollister-Stier, Downer's Grove, Illinois; Los Angeles, California; Spokane, Washington; and Wilkinsburg, Pennsylvania.
  Lederle Laboratories, 30 Rockefeller Plaza, New York, New York.
  Sharp & Sharp, P. O. Box 8, Everett, Washington 98201.

---

* For a complete discussion of the federal licensing requirements the reader should refer to Public Health Service Publications No. 437 and No. 50, which are available from the Division of Biologic Standards, National Institutes of Health, Bethesda 14, Maryland.

Mixed Weeds: 1:50		Pollen to make 1000 ml. use:	Early Trees: 1:50		Pollen to make 1000 ml. use:
Short ragweed	64%	12.8 gm.	Maple	20%	4.0 gm.
Giant ragweed	16%	3.2 gm.	Box elder	20%	4.0 gm.
Mugwort	10%	2.0 gm.	Elm	20%	4.0 gm.
Russian thistle	5%	1.0 gm.	Willow	20%	4.0 gm.
Pigweed	5%	1.0 gm.	Poplar	20%	4.0 gm.
Ragweeds: 1:50			Late Trees: 1:50		
Short ragweed	80%	16.0 gm.	Oak	40%	8.0 gm.
Giant ragweed	20%	4.0 gm.	Ash	20%	4.0 gm.
			Birch	20%	4.0 gm.
			Hickory	10%	2.0 gm.
			Walnut	10%	2.0 gm.
Mixed Grasses: 1:50			Mixed Trees: 1:50		
June Grass	25%	5.0 gm.	Early Trees	50%	
Orchard Grass	25%	5.0 gm.	Late Trees	50%	
Redtop	25%	5.0 gm.			
Timothy	25%	5.0 gm.			

Southwest Mold and Antigen Laboratories, 1009 N. E. 17th St., Oklahoma City, Oklahoma.

Stemen Laboratories, 1205 N. E. 18th St., Oklahoma City, Oklahoma.

As mentioned previously, large savings can often be made by obtaining bids from several reliable sources prior to actual purchase. Geographic location and other factors influence the cost of pollen collection to the various suppliers.

Allergenic extracts (prepared allergens ready for conducting skin testing and hyposensitization):

Abbott Laboratories, North Chicago, Illinois.
Center Laboratories, Inc., Port Washington, New York.
Cutter Laboratories, 4th and Parker Sts., Berkeley, California.
Endo Products, Inc., Richmond Hill 18, New York (Endo House Dust).
Hollister-Stier (see page 530).
Lederle Laboratories, 30 Rockefeller Plaza, New York, New York.
Purex Laboratories, 346 Broadway, Staten Island, New York.
Wyeth Incorporated, 1600 Arch St., Philadelphia, Pennsylvania.

Allergy clinic equipment may be obtained from:

Allergists Supply Co., 458 Broadway, New York, New York.
Bernard Medicals Co., 246 5th Ave., New York, New York.
Center Laboratories Inc., Port Washington, New York.
International Medical Products, 183 Beaumont St., Brooklyn, New York.
Purex Laboratories, 346 Broadway, Staten Island, New York.

REFERENCES

1. Durham, O. C.: The pollen harvest. Economic Bot. 5:211, 1951.
2. Cooke, R. A.: Allergy in Theory and Practice. p. 529, Philadelphia, W. B. Saunders Co., 1947.
3. Ibid, p. 530.
4. Kabat, E. A., and Mayer, N. M.: Experimental Immunochemistry. p. 476, Springfield, Ill., Charles C Thomas, 1961.
5. Lowe, R. W., and Worrell, L. F.: Preparation, assay and standardization of allergens. Am. J. Hosp. Pharm. 18:1, 1961.
6. Remington's Practice of Pharmacy. Ed. 12. pp. 1395–1402, Easton, Pa., Mack Publishing Co., 1961.

Appendix II

SUGGESTED READING

The following journals carry articles dealing exclusively with recent clinical and experimental developments in the field of allergy. Papers of interest to the allergist also may be found in many of the journals of internal medicine, pediatrics, pulmonary disease, dermatology, otolaryngology, and immunology.

1. The *Journal of Allergy,* official organ of the American Academy of Allergy, published monthly by C. V. Mosby Co., 3207 Washington Blvd., St. Louis, Missouri 63103.
2. *Annals of Allergy,* official journal of the American College of Allergists, published monthly at 2642 University Ave., St. Paul, Minnesota 55114.
3. *International Archives of Allergy and Applied Immunology,* published monthly by S. Karger, Basel, Switzerland, and New York, New York.
4. *Review of Allergy,* containing abstracts and bibliography of current literature of allergy and allied fields, published monthly at 2642 University Ave., St. Paul, Minnesota 55114.
5. *Acta Allergologica,* official organ of the Northern Society of Allergology and of the European Academy of Allergology published at irregular intervals (generally 6 or more issues per year) by Munksgaard, Prags Boulevard 47, Copenhagen S, Denmark.

Comprehensive review articles of various topics in allergy and immunology may be found in these two review series:

1. *Progress in Allergy,* published at irregular intervals by S. Karger, Basel, Switzerland, and New York, New York.
2. *Advances in Immunology,* published annually by Academic Press, Inc., 111 Fifth Ave., New York, New York.

Of the many texts and reference works in the field of allergy and clinical immunology, the following volumes are among the best currently for the student and practitioner:

1. Samter, M. (chief editor): Immunological Diseases. Boston, Little, Brown, 1965.
2. Humphrey, J. H., and White, G.: Immunology for Students of Medicine. Ed. 2. Philadelphia, F. A. Davis Co., 1964.
3. Raffel, S. (editor): Basic and clinical immunology. Med. Clin. North America, *49:*1487, W. B. Saunders Co., 1965.
4. Lawrence, H. S. (editor): Cellular and Humoral Aspects of the Hypersensitive States. New York, Hoeber, 1959.
5. Shaffer, J. H., LoGrippo, G. A., and Chase, M. W.: Henry Ford Hospital International Symposium; Mechanisms of Hypersensitivity. Boston, Little, Brown, 1959.
6. Bates, D. V., and Christie, R. V.: Respiratory Function in Disease. Philadelphia, W. B. Saunders Co., 1964.
7. Comroe, J. H., Jr.: The Lung. Clinical Physiology and Pulmonary Function Tests. Ed. 2. Chicago, Year Book Medical Publishers, 1962.
8. DeWeese, D. D., and Saunders, W. H.: Textbook of Otolaryngology. St. Louis, C. V. Mosby Co., 1960.

9. Pillsbury, D. M., Shelley, W. B., and Kligman, A. M.: A Manual of Cutaneous Medicine. Philadelphia, W. B. Saunders Co., 1961.

10. Schwartz, L., Tulipan, L., and Birmingham, D. J.: Occupational Diseases of the Skin. Ed. 3. Philadelphia, Lea & Febiger, 1957.

11. Samter, M., and Durham, O. C. (editors): Regional Allergy of the United States, Canada, Mexico, and Cuba. Springfield, Ill., Charles C Thomas, 1955.

12. Wodehouse, R. P.: Pollen Grains: Their Structure, Identification, and Significance in Science and Medicine. New York, Hafner, 1959.

13. Hyde, H. A., and Adams, K. F.: An Atlas of Airborne Pollen Grains. London, Macmillan, 1958.

14. Sherman, W. B., and Kessler, W. R.: Allergy in Pediatric Practice. St. Louis, C. V. Mosby Co., 1957.

15. Gregory, P. H.: The Microbiology of the Atmosphere. New York, Interscience, 1961.

16. Gell, P. G. H., and Coombs, R. R. A.: Clinical Aspects of Immunology. Philadelphia, F. A. Davis, 1963.

INDEX

The letter f following a page number refers to the footnote on that page.